Contents

Managing Editor: Ed Mulhall/Cillian de Paor Editor: Deirdre McCarthy Associate Editor: Conor McMorrow Statistics: Sean Donnelly
Design: Brendan McCarthy Design Consultant Editor: Aoife Byrne Chief Sub-editor: Deirdre Sheeran Production Manager: Mary Keating
Cover and Contributors Photographs: John Cooney, RTÉ Publishing Prepress: Niamh Hogan and David Mahon Executive Director RTÉ Publishing:
Muirne Laffan Photographs: Getty Images, Photocall, Mick Quinn Photography, The Roscommon People, MacMonagle Photography (Killarney), John D
Kelly Photography (Clonmel), Maxwell Photography, Glen Mulcahy, Provision, Johnny Brambury, Press Association, Merrionstreet.ie and the Oireachtas
Press Office. Printer: Boylan Print Group ISBN No: 978-0-9568945-0-2 © RTÉ 2011

Acknowledgments

Deirdre McCarthy,
Editor, 'The Week in Politics'

First and foremost thank you to all those politicians elected to the 31st Dáil for their co-operation in supplying their biographical details for this election book. In particular, a special thanks to their parliamentary assistants and constituency office staff, who were unfailing in their efforts to assist us in our research.

We are most grateful to Daniel English and Ciaran Brennan from the Oireachtas Press Office for their assistance.

A special thanks to the political party press officers and advisers including Feargal Purcell, Deborah Sweeney, Yvonne Hyland, Joanne Lonnergan and Sarah Meade from Fine Gael. In Sinn Féin, thanks to Kaniah Cusack, Seán Mac Brádaigh, Shaun Tracey and Richard McAuley. To Elaine O'Meara, Adam Ledwith, Jimmy Healy, Suzanne Collins and Pat McParland from Fianna Fáil. In the Labour Party, thanks to Tony Heffernan, Deirdre Ward, Shauneen Armstrong and Dermot O'Gara. Also thanks to Michael O'Brien from the Socialist Party/United Left Alliance.

This book would not have been possible without the co-operation of Aoife Byrne and Mary Keating from RTÉ Publishing, who gave so willingly of their expertise and time, as well as Niamh Hogan, David Mahon and John Cooney from the *RTÉ Publishing*.

A special thanks also to Carolyn Fisher from RTÉ, Brendan McCarthy of McCarthy Design and Sub-Editor Deirdre Sheeran.

Great appreciation is also due to all on the editorial team and in particular to Conor McMorrow and Sean Donnelly.

What really makes *The Week in Politics* so worthwhile is our loyal Sunday night viewers; those who join us on RTÉ One and those watching on RTÉ.ie. The programme is also indebted to all of our contributors who, over many years, have given up their valuable time on a Sunday to discuss the political events that shape all our lives.

Deirdre McCarthy

Foreword

Ed Mulhall, Director of News and Current Affairs, RTÉ

Cillian de Paor, Managing Editor Television News, RTÉ

We have just come through one of the most significant elections since the foundation of the State. All the certainties that underlay Irish politics have been challenged and in many cases overturned. Throughout this campaign, *The Week in Politics* was at the heart of the national debate. From Dermot Ahern's now famous "fiction" response to Seán O'Rourke when asked if the IMF was about to come knocking at our door, to Enda Kenny's first campaign interview and the dramatic interviews with Brian Cowen and Micheál Martin as Fianna Fáil first didn't and then did change its leader, it was all there on the programme. In the end, you could almost see the government coalition forming before your eyes as Phil Hogan and Pat Rabbitte exchanged nuanced messages across the studio floor.

Because of the slow collapse of the Fianna Fáil/Green coalition last autumn, it was a very long election campaign. RTÉ News and Current Affairs covered all the chapters of this story up to the opening of the boxes and the late-night drama of the election count. It is a truism that the Irish love elections and Election 2011 was never going to disappoint lovers of drama. From early morning on count day, beginning with the RTÉ/Millward Brown/Lansdowne exit poll, then with the special election programmes on radio and television that ran all day and into the night, an Irish audience and a worldwide audience online watched and listened and participated through social media. It all added up to an exceptional event as, once again, political change was achieved through the ballot box. The huge amount of information generated for the election coverage by our reporters, correspondents and presenters has been augmented with additional articles and analysis and distilled to form the basis of this book.

In producing *The Week in Politics* book of Election 2011 we were always mindful of our colleague and friend Gerald Barry, who died just as this story reached its climax. Gerry was on the original pilot of *The Week in Politics* many years ago and through his long and distinguished career was a rock of common sense and ethical enquiring journalism both for RTÉ and from time to time for other media outlets.

"I always ask questions," was one of the last things Gerry said to us. He always did. We hope that will continue to be the role of his successors in our newsroom and in others in years to come. In that spirit we dedicate this book to him.

Ed Mulhall and Cillian de Paor

Election 2011: The Story

Irish politics has changed dramatically. Sean O'Rourke, presenter of 'The Week In Politics', looks back on a tumultuous four-year period in Irish political life

From there to here

Leabharlanna Fhine Gall

When the 30th Dáil was dissolved, the new lexicon of Irish politics included words like bailout, bondholders, regulator, recapitalisation, IMF, liquidity, negative equity, ghost estate, zombie, toxic, Nama, sustainable and – especially – guarantee.

Meanwhile, words from the 1970s and '80s had returned: recession, liquidation, unemployment, cutbacks, emigration, borrowing, and deficit.

For over two years, appalled citizens had endured the colossal failure of the institutions supposedly looking after their interests – in government, civil service, financial regulation and banking. Its sovereignty lost, Ireland was on financial life-support provided by unsentimental outsiders.

It was a world away from the election fought in 2007, when 4% growth, light-touch regulation, further personal tax cuts and a 'soft landing' for the roaring property market were the working assumptions of most parties.

Then, Fianna Fáil held onto office by persuading voters that it would preserve the gains of the boom years. Now, in early 2011, having long towered over all others, the party was fighting for survival as the political and economic horror show continued.

For the first time, a Fianna Fáil Taoiseach would not lead his troops into battle, as Brian Cowen made way for Micheál Martin. At best, it might avoid the ignominy of finishing third, behind Labour, through a vigorous campaign and the muscle memory of voters when pencils were poised over ballot papers.

How had it come to this?

Brian Cowen's period as Taoiseach had been a rollercoaster ride through hell, something nobody would have predicted on the spring morning he was unanimously chosen to succeed Bertie Ahern, Fianna Fáil's longest-serving leader since its founder Eamon de Valera. Immediately after his third election as Taoiseach, in coalition with six Greens and two Progressive Democrats, Ahern had designated his Finance Minister and Tánaiste as his eventual successor. Embarrassed by awkward revelations and implausible explanations about his personal finances at the Mahon Tribunal, the Taoiseach abruptly resigned at Easter 2008, over a year ahead of his intended departure. Finally, government could operate beyond the lengthening Tribunal shadow.

"Brian Cowen's period as Taoiseach had been a rollercoaster ride through hell"

Brian Cowen was widely regarded as the best choice to lead Fianna Fáil. Shrewd, popular, untainted, and experienced in senior ministries, he was probably the sharpest brain in Irish politics since Charles Haughey. However, almost immediately after becoming Taoiseach, his journey downhill began, as the global economic uncertainty and market volatility that he'd warned about as Finance Minister deepened dramatically.

It was hard for the new government to break old habits formed over a decade when day-to-day spending trebled, fuelled by taxes generated by a property boom built on cheap credit. Unnerved, perhaps, by the defeat of the Lisbon Treaty Referendum, Cowen conceded pay increases (later abandoned) for public servants. Finance Minister Brian Lenihan raised spending by 3.4% in a budget delivered two months prematurely to demonstrate strong economic management. These resources were about to dry up dramatically.

The Cowen government's fire-fighting included momentous decisions, like cuts in state pay and welfare rates. Most fateful of all was a late-night 'incorporeal' cabinet decision that gave a blanket guarantee for all deposits and liabilities in Irish banks.

Along with a National Asset Management Agency, set up to deal with huge toxic loans held by once-swaggering developers, the guarantee was intended to fix the banks and revive economic activity. It did neither, and within two years the bill was €46bn and counting, with Anglo Irish Bank, Irish Nationwide and AIB falling into state control.

By 2010, as unemployment rocketed, tax receipts were down 35% on 2007, and a €20bn gulf between government income and spending had opened up. The state needed a bailout for itself and its banks from the EU, ECB and IMF.

The economic crisis provided a target-rich environment for an opposition which tirelessly highlighted Fianna Fáil's connections with the building industry, along with government's failure to curtail the banks' excesses. Fine Gael referred back to the warnings of its finance spokesman Richard Bruton about the huge growth of government spending and easy pay rises for public servants, unaccompanied by productivity improvements.

As the cost of the banking crisis rose, and details emerged of bankers' malpractices, Labour's opposition to the guarantee was vigorously recycled by Finance spokesperson Joan Burton, who had also challenged continuing tax shelters for construction.

In Dáil Éireann, Labour leader Eamon Gilmore articulated public anger more effectively than Fine Gael's Enda Kenny, and when Labour briefly overtook Fine Gael in poll ratings in mid-2010, Labour Youth's 'Gilmore For Taoiseach' posters began to seem plausible. Gilmore's decision, on becoming leader in 2007, to shun pre-election pacts was certainly paying off. Labour's claim that the next election would be a three-way contest, with Gilmore entitled to equal status in broadcast debates involving potential Taoisigh, was gaining ground.

The Labour surge panicked Kenny's frontbench colleagues, most of whom despaired of his ability to "connect" with voters. But a challenge fronted by the deputy leader Bruton had long been anticipated by the leader's minders, and Kenny saw off the plotters.

Having rebuilt Fine Gael after an election disaster in 2002, Enda Kenny had now shown strength in a crisis. The failed coup led to the return as Finance spokesman of the wily veteran, Michael Noonan, who outperformed Lenihan at budget time, while leaving few hostages to fortune.

The Green Party's first experience of government had proven much more daunting than it expected. Like Cabinet colleagues, its two ministers could only assent as Cowen and Lenihan, with senior officials, drove the economic agenda.

Publicly, the senior pair concealed their differences, and Lenihan heroically battled serious illness while contending with an unprecedented crisis. But all too frequently his predictions of better times didn't materialise.

Former PD leader Mary Harney, a key advocate of the Ahern-McCreevy policies that ended in catastrophe, concentrated on her health ministry after her party's dissolution. The most influential woman minister of any era, she failed to end hospital overcrowding but reorganised cancer services and eased care costs for elderly citizens.

While the bailout ultimately sank the Greens, they had achievements in planning, energy, taxation, civil rights and animal protection. But the savaging they suffered in the 2009 local elections suggested that opportunities would arise for left-wing rivals like Sinn Féin and the Socialist Party.

Brian Cowen's final act was to push through another austerity budget, to the scarcely concealed relief of the opposition. In the end, however, the bedraggled state of his government was reflected in his inability, in chaotic circumstances, to replace the many ministers who opted for retirement rather than face the voters. The quintessential Fianna Fáil man, whose star had once shone brightly, Brian Cowen also chose to retire, aged 51. Occasional flashes aside, he had failed to inspire his party or the Irish people. But given the immense weight that high office piled upon his shoulders, who would have done better?

Taoiseach Enda Kenny and Tánaiste and Labour leader Eamon Gilmore with President Mary McAleese at Áras an Uachtaráin after receiving their seals of office

The end of the affair

It was, one Fianna Fáil insider conceded bitterly afterwards, "an appropriately chaotic end to a dysfunctional administration". Brian Cowen had been mulling over a reshuffle during the Christmas break. Two ministers had said they weren't running again and it was clear others were going to follow suit, and the pressure was on to introduce new blood into the cabinet. Others had counselled the Taoiseach against such a move, arguing that the time for a reshuffle had been before Christmas when Dermot Ahern and Noel Dempsey announced their plans; it was too late now and would look appalling, they argued.

As TDs gathered for the new Dáil term on Wednesday 12 January, it was clear the reverberations from the weekend newspaper disclosure of Cowen's golf game with disgraced Anglo boss Sean FitzPatrick were serious; nonetheless, up to late that night he persisted in his reshuffle plans, phoning two ministers to say he intended to press ahead the following day.

But Thursday brought chaos as the FitzPatrick row deepened. Ministers met in Batt O'Keeffe's office as the clouds gathered over the Taoiseach's head. The bluff Corkman was personally friendly with Brian Cowen, but told his colleagues someone would have to go to him to outline the political facts of life, that he should step down but stay on as caretaker Taoiseach. Others demurred, arguing that Cowen had repeatedly said he wouldn't serve on probation.

At one o'clock, they met in Brian Cowen's office. Noel Dempsey and Batt O'Keeffe spoke bluntly, insisting as friends that it was time to go. Present too were Mary Coughlan, Dermot Ahern, Tony Killeen and John Curran. All were in sombre mood. The Taoiseach asked for a tally of backbenchers. Phone calls were made. Forty to 41 would support him. "Not great, is it?" he said, shrugging his shoulders.

However, he then nonplussed even his closest supporters by putting down a confidence motion. For Fianna Fáil, the following week was a blur, but ultimately it decided it was just too late to change leader.

All this was just the scene-setter for the real drama to come.

The Green Party had picked up the reshuffle talk over the Christmas break and had signalled its unhappiness. The party's programme manager Donall

"You can bully Fianna Fáil but you won't bully the President of Ireland"

Geoghegan warned his Fianna Fáil counterpart Joe Lennon that if there was to be a wholesale shake-up "my lads won't wear it".

However, the public signals weren't strong – the Greens didn't want to throw down the gauntlet and have the same fate as the PDs under Michael McDowell.

John Gormley now concedes that if his party made one mistake it was in not communicating this more brutally to Fianna Fáil.

On Wednesday 19 January, the Leinster House tom-toms were beating out the reshuffle rhythm as the Greens met with the Taoiseach; already he had put in an ebullient performance in the Dáil and was visibly buoyed by victory in the confidence debate the previous day.

Accounts of that meeting differ wildly. Suffice to say that the Greens insist that they sent up unmistakable flares, while Fianna Fáil claims no warnings were sounded.

At 5.30pm, Brian Cowen texted Mary Harney to say the reshuffle was on; it was a heads-up to the Health Minister to get her resignation statement ready. She went one step further. As RTÉ's David McCullagh was preparing his report for the *Nine o'clock News,* he was delighted to get a call from Harney's spokesman Mark Costigan to see if he could get a camera crew to interview the minister. The doomed reshuffle was underway.

But no one had told John Gormley. The Green Party leader had been on the *Six One News*, where he gave equivocal responses when quizzed about the reshuffle. The party would have to be consulted, but there might be a case for, say, Dermot Ahern to be shifted as he was in hospital. Cue a phone call from a furious Justice Minister who insisted that whatever happened he remained fully capable of discharging his official duties. Later, Gormley bumped into the Health Minister who asked about the *Six One* interview but she gave no inkling of her own intentions.

As it happened, Dermot Ahern had been talking to Mary Harney on the phone from his hospital bed when the Gormley interview came on, and broke off the conversation to watch. He too was trying to piece together what was up. He didn't have long to wait.

At 7.30pm, the Taoiseach phoned to call in a resignation that had been discussed since November

Taoiseach Brian Cowen (centre) with Tánaiste Mary Coughlan (left) and Chief Whip John Curran (right) at a press conference to announce his resignation as Taoiseach

when the Louth TD indicated he wouldn't be standing again.

Mary Harney announced her resignation on the *Nine o'clock News*. To those outside the Merrion Street beltway, it came out of the blue and was the first indication that something big was happening.

It was certainly a shock for the Green Party leader, who was told the news by his wife. Little did he know that the resignations of Ahern, Killeen and Dempsey would shortly follow. Later in the evening, Batt O'Keeffe's name would be added to the roll call of ministers resigning. The Taoiseach forced the pace by sending their names to the president before midnight. The news broke at 11pm that evening.

The next morning, Paul Gogarty made it plain on *Morning Ireland* that there were real problems. For the Green Party, a reference in the *Irish Times* to the resignations being rushed through to "thwart" their ministers' opposition to a reshuffle was proof positive they'd been stitched up. Shortly afterwards, John Gormley texted Brian Cowen with a similar message. The response read: "John, it is the convention within coalitions that it is a matter for the party concerned to determine who represents it in government."

A series of increasingly frantic meetings followed as Tánaiste Mary Coughlan gamely held the fort in the Dáil. The Green Party leader was told the resignations had gone to President McAleese and the first phase of the reshuffle was a fait accompli.

But has she accepted them, he asked, urging the Taoiseach to call the Áras.

At one stage, an increasingly agitated Brian Lenihan tracked Gormley over to his party rooms,

demanding to speak to him. "Ring the Áras," the Green Party leader said again to the Finance Minister who exploded: "You can bully Fianna Fáil but you won't bully the President of Ireland," in an outburst audible to all in an adjoining meeting room.

But the game was up. John Gormley went to one final meeting in the ante room off the Taoiseach's office to be greeted by the remnants of the Fianna Fáil cabinet.

More in sorrow than in anger Brian Cowen told him: "This is all that's left, thanks to you."

All was made plain when the Taoiseach led his depleted team into the Dáil chamber an hour later. The gasps from government backbenchers told their own story. They didn't conceal their despair and anger as they filed out minutes later. Within 48 hours Brian Cowen was gone as party leader.

His behaviour in pushing through the reshuffle was, in the words of his friend and constituency colleague Johnny Moloney, "unfathomable", but in the end merely hastened the end of a government that had been on life support since the previous November when the Greens first signalled their pull-out.

When he left office, I cited the judgement of Tacitus on the emperor Galba – *capax imperii nisi imperasset* – "regarded by all as capable of ruling until he had to rule".

There was no doubting his intelligence and capacity but there were always question marks over his appetite for office, begging the question, 'can a reluctant leader ever rule?'.

The Government (Appointed 9 March 2011)

Taoiseach
Enda Kenny
Tánaiste and Minister for Foreign Affairs and Trade
Eamon Gilmore
Minister for Finance
Michael Noonan
Minister for Education and Skills
Ruairí Quinn
Minister for Public Expenditure and Reform
Brendan Howlin
Minister for Enterprise, Jobs and Innovation
Richard Bruton
Minister for Social Protection
Joan Burton
Minister for Arts, Heritage and Gaeltacht Affairs
Jimmy Deenihan
Minister for Communications, Energy and Natural Resources
Pat Rabbitte
Minister for the Environment, Community and Local Government
Phil Hogan

Minister for Justice, Equality and Defence
Alan Shatter
Minister for Agriculture, Marine and Food
Simon Coveney
Minister for Children
Frances Fitzgerald
Minister for Health
Dr James Reilly
Minister for Transport, Tourism and Sport
Dr Leo Varadkar
Attorney General
Márie Whelan SC

Ministers of State (Appointed 9 March 2011)

Government Chief Whip and Defence (Department of Taoiseach and Department of Defence) Paul Kehoe

Housing and Planning (Department of Environment, Community and Local Government) Willie Penrose

Gaeltacht Affairs (Department of Arts, Heritage and Gaeltacht Affairs) Dinny McGinley

Primary Care (Department of Health) Roisin Shortall

Small Business (Department of Enterprise, Jobs and Innovation) John Perry

Tourism and Sport (Department of Transport, Tourism and Sport) Michael Ring

Trade and Development (Department of Foreign Affairs and Trade) Jan O'Sullivan

Disability, Equality and Mental Health (Department of Health and Department of Justice, Equality and Defence) Kathleen Lynch

Public Service Reform and OPW (Department of Public Expenditure and Reform and Department of Finance) Brian Hayes

New Era Project (Department of Communications, Energy and Natural Resources and Department of Environment, Community and Local Government) Fergus O'Dowd

Food, Horticulture and Food Safety (Department of Agriculture, Marine and Food) Shane McEntee

European Affairs (Department of the Taoiseach and Department of Foreign Affairs and Trade) Lucinda Creighton

Research and Innovation (Department of Enterprise, Jobs and Innovation and Department of Education and Skills) Sean Sherlock

Training and Skills (Department of Education and Skills) Ciaran Cannon

Public and Commuter Transport (Department of Transport, Tourism and Sport) Alan Kelly

Back row (L-R): Alan Kelly, Fergus O'Dowd, Sean Sherlock, Brian Hayes, Ciaran Cannon, Lucinda Creighton, Michael Ring, Shane McEntee, Willie Penrose.
Front row (L-R): Jan O'Sullivan, John Perry, Paul Kehoe, An Taoiseach Enda Kenny, Tánaiste Eamon Gilmore, Kathleen Lynch, Roisin Shortall, Dinny McGinley

Pollster **Sean Donnelly** does the sums and analyses how each vote was cast in the most groundbreaking election in decades

How the nation voted

Electorate

3,209,249 people were registered to vote in the 2011 general election, an increase of 98,328 on 2007. Munster had the largest electorate at 911,486 with Leinster next at 869,916. Dublin had an electorate of 806,936 with Connacht/Ulster the smallest region with 620,911. But these figures come with a health warning as the register of electors has been proven in the past to be substantially inaccurate despite the efforts to update it for the 2007 election.

Turnout

2,243,176 voters actually turned out, 69.9%, up from 67.03% in 2007. Munster had the largest regional turnout at 71.34%, marginally ahead of Connacht-Ulster at 71.32% with Roscommon-South Leitrim having the best constituency turnout at 78.75%. Dublin had the lowest regional turnout – 68.20%. Dublin South-East had the lowest constituency turnout – 53.78% in 2007 and held the same position in 2011 with 60.54%.

Seats Won (Change since 2007)		
FF	20	(-58)
FG	76	(+25)
Lab	37	(+17)
SF	14	(+10)
Soc	2	(+2)
PBP	2	(+2)
Others	15	(+9)
Total	166	

Denis Murphy and Noel Murphy from Listowel listen to the radio at the South Kerry count centre in the Killarney Sports Arena

Spoiled votes

There were 22,817 spoiled votes, 1.02%, up marginally on 2007 (0.93%). Dublin South-Central had the highest percentage of spoiled votes – 1.58% as it had in 2007 (1.63%). Kildare North had the lowest at 0.75%, as it had in 2007 (0.51%).

Valid Poll

The overall valid poll was 69.19%, up three points from 2007 (66.41%) and the highest since 1987 (72.67%). Roscommon-South Leitrim had the largest valid poll at 77.88% with Tipperary North next at 76.34%, a reversal of their 2007 positions. With the lowest turnout, it was inevitable that Dublin South-East would have the lowest valid poll – 59.98%, and was the only constituency below 60%.

Quota

The quota is calculated by dividing the valid poll by the number of seats plus one and adding one, ignoring any decimal points, e.g. Carlow-Kilkenny (5 Dáil seats): Quota = 73,743 ÷ 6 (5 seats + 1) = 12,290.5 + 1 = 12,291 Because of the automatic return of Ceann Comhairle Séamus Kirk, Louth was reduced to four seats and thus had by far the highest quota at 13,864. Wexford was next at 12,590. Laois-Offaly and Mayo had the same quota – 12,360. Dublin Central had the lowest quota at 6,923 and was one of only two below 7,000, with Dublin South East on 6,984.

Candidates

There was a record 566 candidates for the 165 seats in this election, 96 more than in 2007. Fine Gael ran 104, up 13 on last time and Labour increased its number from 50 in 2007 to 68 in 2011. Fianna Fáil recognised its changed political position and reduced its candidates from 106 in 2007 to just 75. Sinn Féin ran 41, the same as 2007 and the Greens ran 43, one less than last time but lost all their seats. The number of small-party and independent candidates was up from just 138 in 2007 to a record 235. Wicklow had the highest number of candidates, 24, with Laois-Offaly next at 21. Kildare South and the two Tipperarys had the smallest number – eight.

Counts

It took 361 counts to fill the 165 seats in this election. This was up from 290 in 2007, 304 in 2002, 320 in 1997 and down from 377 in 1992. Wicklow had the highest number of counts, 19, and in contrast it took only three counts to complete Tipperary.

Photo: ©McMonagle.com

Constituency turnouts 2011

Constituency	Seats	Electorate	Total Votes Cast	% Turnout	Invalid Votes	% Invalid	Total Valid Poll	% Valid	Quota	Candidates 2007	2011	No. of Counts
Carlow-Kilkenny	5	105,449	74,564	70.71%	821	1.10%	73,743	69.93%	12,291	11	19	13
Cavan-Monaghan	5	99,178	72,142	72.74%	867	1.20%	71,275	71.87%	11,880	9	14	9
Clare	4	82,745	58,495	68.68%	579	0.99%	57,916	69.99%	11,584	12	16	12
Cork East	4	83,658	57,459	68.68%	526	0.92%	56,933	68.05%	11,387	10	13	7
Cork North Central	4	75,302	52,709	70.00%	572	1.09%	52,137	69.24%	10,428	13	15	11
Cork North West	3	62,870	46,194	73.48%	454	0.98%	45,740	72.75%	11,436	7	9	6
Cork South Central	5	91,619	64,664	70.58%	624	0.96%	64,040	69.90%	10,674	14	17	12
Cork South West	3	62,967	46,048	73.13%	390	0.85%	45,658	72.51%	11,415	7	13	6
Donegal North East	3	59,084	38,324	64.86%	406	1.06%	37,918	64.18%	9,480	11	11	9
Donegal South West	3	64,568	43,595	67.52%	332	0.76%	43,263	67.00%	10,816	7	9	5
Dublin Central	4	56,892	35,069	61.64%	457	1.30%	34,612	60.84%	6,923	13	16	8
Dublin Mid West	4	64,880	43,193	66.57%	471	1.09%	42,722	65.85%	8,545	11	14	9
Dublin North	4	70,413	49,799	70.72%	452	0.91%	49,347	70.08%	9,870	13	9	7
Dublin North Central	3	52,992	39,187	73.95%	413	1.05%	38,774	73.17%	9,694	7	9	7
Dublin North East	3	58,542	42,287	72.23%	448	1.06%	41,839	71.47%	10,460	8	11	9
Dublin North West	3	49,269	33,262	67.51%	451	1.36%	32,811	66.60%	8,203	8	12	7
Dublin South	5	102,387	73,105	71.40%	459	0.63%	72,646	70.95%	12,108	13	16	8
Dublin South Central	5	80,268	51,744	64.46%	817	1.58%	50,927	63.45%	8,488	16	18	13
Dublin South East	4	58,217	35,246	60.54%	327	0.93%	34,919	59.98%	6,984	13	16	10
Dublin South West	4	70,613	47,475	67.23%	511	1.08%	46,964	66.51%	9,393	8	10	8
Dublin West	4	62,348	42,799	68.65%	327	0.76%	42,472	68.12%	8,495	8	10	5
Dun Laoghaire	4	80,115	57,157	71.34%	481	0.84%	56,676	70.74%	11,336	11	14	11
Galway East	4	83,651	59,836	71.53%	560	0.94%	59,276	70.86%	11,856	14	13	9
Galway West	5	88,840	61,268	68.96%	643	1.05%	60,625	68.24%	10,105	15	17	13
Kerry North-West Limer	3	63,614	46,027	72.35%	413	0.90%	45,614	71.70%	11,404	10	11	7
Kerry South	3	59,629	44,679	74.93%	299	0.67%	44,380	74.43%	11,096	8	10	6
Kildare North	4	77,959	51,610	66.20%	388	0.75%	51,222	65.70%	10,245	11	12	5
Kildare South	3	58,867	38,623	65.61%	353	0.91%	38,270	65.01%	9,568	8	8	7
Laoighis Offaly	5	108,142	75,213	69.55%	1,055	1.40%	74,158	68.57%	12,360	16	21	13
Limerick	3	65,083	45,512	69.93%	471	1.03%	45,041	69.21%	11,261	14	10	4
Limerick City	4	64,909	43,617	67.20%	429	0.98%	43,188	66.54%	8,638	7	13	7
Longford-Westmeath	4	85,918	58,186	67.72%	661	1.14%	57,525	66.95%	11,506	13	15	8
Louth	5	99,530	70,190	70.52%	871	1.24%	69,319	69.65%	13,864	12	16	13
Mayo	5	101,160	74,795	73.94%	641	0.86%	74,154	73.30%	12,360	13	15	8
Meath East	3	64,873	43,098	66.43%	346	0.80%	42,752	65.90%	10,689	11	9	4
Meath West	3	62,776	40,591	64.66%	413	1.02%	40,178	64.00%	10,045	10	13	5
Roscommon-South -Lei	3	60,998	48,035	78.75%	531	1.11%	47,504	77.88%	11,877	9	10	6
Sligo-North Leitrim	3	63,432	44,837	70.69%	409	0.91%	44,428	70.04%	11,108	10	13	9
Tipperary North	3	63,235	48,789	77.16%	516	1.06%	48,273	76.34%	12,069	9	8	3
Tipperary South	3	57,420	41,793	72.78%	432	1.03%	41,361	72.03%	10,341	11	8	5
Waterford	4	78,435	54,298	69.23%	578	1.06%	53,720	68.49%	10,745	13	15	11
Wexford	5	111,063	76,351	68.75%	812	1.06%	75,539	68.01%	12,590	11	14	7
Wicklow	5	95,339	71,311	74.80%	811	1.14%	70,500	73.95%	11,751	15	24	19
2011 43	166	3,209,249	2,243,176	69.90%	22,817	1.02%	2,220,359	69.19%	10,636	470	566	361
2007 43	166	3,110,914	2,085,245	67.03%	19,435	0.93%	2,065,810	66.41%			470	290
2011-2007		+98,335	+157,931	+2.87%	+3,382	+0.09%	+154,549	+2.78%			+96	+71
Dublin	47	806,936	550,323	68.20%	5,614	1.02%	544,709	67.50%		129	155	102
Leinster	42	869,916	599,737	68.94%	6,531	1.09%	593,206	68.19%		118	151	94
Munster	46	911,486	650,284	71.34%	6,283	0.97%	644,001	70.65%		135	158	97
Connaught/Ulster	31	620,911	442,832	71.32%	4,389	0.99%	438,443	70.61%		88	102	68

Red: **Maximum** Blue: **Minimum**

Election Facts

"At 566, there was a record number of candidates in Election 2011. The previous record was 484 in 1997"
Professor Michael Gallagher, TCD

Party vote per constituency 2011

Constituency	Fine Gael Votes	%	Labour Votes	%	Fianna Fail Votes	%	Sinn Fein Votes	%	Socialist Pty Votes	%	PBPA Votes	%	Greens Votes	%	WP Votes	%	CS Votes	%	Non Party Votes	%	Total Votes	ULA Votes	%
Carlow-Kilkenny	28,924	39.22	11,980	16.25	20,721	28.10	7,033	9.54	1,135	1.54			2,072	2.81					1,878		73,743	1,135	1.54
Cavan-Monaghan	28,199	39.56	4,011	5.63	14,360	20.15	18,452	25.89					530	0.74					5,723	8.03	71,275	0	0.00
Clare	24,524	42.34	8,572	14.80	12,804	22.11							1,154	1.99					10,862	18.75	57,916	0	0.00
Cork East	20,847	36.62	17,563	30.85	9,642	16.94	6,292	11.05					635	1.12					1,954	3.43	56,933	0	0.00
Cork North Central	13,669	26.22	13,801	26.47	7,896	15.14	7,923	15.20	4,803	9.21			524	1.01	681	1.31	324	0.62	2,516	4.83	52,137	4,803	9.21
Cork North West	22,321	48.80	6,421	14.04	11,390	24.90	3,405	7.44			1,552	3.39	651	1.42							45,740	1,552	3.39
Cork South Central	22,225	34.70	11,869	18.53	17,936	28.01	5,250	8.20					1,640	2.56					5,120	8.00	64,040	0	0.00
Cork South West	22,162	48.54	6,533	14.31	10,787	23.63	3,346	7.33					765	1.68					2,065	4.52	45,658	0	0.00
Donegal North East	11,987	31.61	4,090	10.79	6,613	17.44	9,278	24.47					206	0.54					5,744	15.15	37,918	0	0.00
Donegal South West	8,589	19.85	2,209	5.11	9,745	22.53	14,242	32.97					527	1.22					7,931	18.33	43,263	0	0.00
Dublin Central	6,903	19.94	9,787	28.28	5,141	14.85	4,526	13.08					683	1.97	274	0.79	235	0.68	7,063	20.41	34,612	0	0.00
Dublin Mid West	13,214	30.93	13,138	30.75	5,043	11.80	5,060	11.84	622	1.46	2,471	5.78	1,484	3.47	694	1.62			996	2.33	42,722	3,093	7.24
Dublin North	15,488	31.39	13,014	26.37	7,634	15.47			7,513	15.22			4,186	8.48					1,512	3.06	49,347	7,513	15.22
Dublin North Central	14,644	37.77	8,731	22.52	5,017	12.94	2,140	5.52			1,424	3.67	501	1.29					6,317	16.29	38,774	1,424	3.67
Dublin North East	12,332	29.47	14,371	34.35	4,794	11.46	5,032	12.03	869	2.08			792	1.89					3,649	8.72	41,839	869	2.08
Dublin North West	5,496	16.75	14,158	43.15	3,869	11.79	7,115	21.68			677	2.06	328	1.00	345	1.05	173	0.53	650	1.98	32,811	677	2.06
Dublin South	26,404	36.35	13,059	17.98	6,844	9.42	1,915	2.64			1,277	1.76	4,929	6.78			277	0.38	17,941	24.70	72,646	1,277	1.76
Dublin South Central	11,956	23.48	18,032	35.41	4,837	9.50	6,804	13.36			6,574	12.91	1,015	1.99			239	0.47	1,470	2.89	50,927	6,574	12.91
Dublin South East	12,402	35.52	8,857	25.36	3,922	11.23	1,272	3.64			629	1.80	2,370	6.79					5,467	15.66	34,919	629	1.80
Dublin South West	13,044	27.77	17,032	36.27	5,059	10.77	8,064	17.17	2,462	5.24			480	1.02					823	1.75	46,964	2,462	5.24
Dublin West	11,549	27.19	12,313	28.99	7,044	16.59	2,597	6.11	8,084	19.03			605	1.42					280	0.66	42,472	8,084	19.03
Dun Laoghaire	19,591	34.57	17,217	30.38	8,632	15.23					6,206	10.95	2,156	3.80			434	0.77	2,440	4.31	56,676	6,206	10.95
Galway East	25,409	42.87	7,831	13.21	10,694	18.04	3,635	6.13					402	0.68					11,305	19.07	59,276	0	0.00
Galway West	18,627	30.72	7,489	12.35	12,703	20.95	3,808	6.28					1,120	1.85					16,878	27.84	60,625	0	0.00
Kerry North	18,599	40.77	9,159	20.08	5,230	11.47	9,282	20.35					239	0.52					3,105	6.81	45,614	0	0.00
Kerry South	14,482	32.63	4,926	11.10	5,917	13.33							401	0.90					18,654	42.03	44,380	0	0.00
Kildare North	17,050	33.29	14,979	29.24	7,436	14.52	2,896	5.65					905	1.77					7,956	15.53	51,222	0	0.00
Kildare South	12,755	33.33	10,645	27.82	8,307	21.71	2,308						523	1.37					3,732	9.75	38,270	0	0.00
Laoighis Offaly	25,032	33.75	5,802	7.82	19,860	26.78	8,032	10.83	561	0.76			306	0.41					14,565	19.64	74,158	561	0.76
Limerick	21,925	48.68	7,910	17.56	9,361	20.78							354	0.79					5,491	12.19	45,041	0	0.00
Limerick City	18,696	43.29	8,764	20.29	9,259	21.44	3,711	8.59	721	1.67			490	1.13			186	0.43	1,361	3.15	43,188	721	1.67
Longford-Westmeath	21,887	38.05	15,366	26.71	11,197	19.46	4,339	7.54					309	0.54					4,427	7.70	57,525	0	0.00
Louth	21,825	31.48	13,264	19.13	10,858	15.66	15,072	21.74					3,244	4.68					5,056	7.29	69,319	0	0.00
Mayo	48,170	64.96	3,644	4.91	11,920	16.07	4,802	6.48					266	0.36					5,352	7.22	74,154	0	0.00
Meath East	17,471	40.87	8,994	21.04	8,384	19.61	3,795	8.88					461	1.08					3,647	8.53	42,752	0	0.00
Meath West	18,450	45.92	5,432	13.52	7,285	18.13	6,989	17.40					479	1.19	189	0.47	234	0.58	1,120	2.79	40,178	0	0.00
Roscommon-South Leit	18,303	38.53	4,455	9.38	7,103	14.95	4,637	9.76					220	0.46					12,786	26.92	47,504	0	0.00
Sligo-North Leitrim	16,378	36.86	4,553	10.25	9,708	21.85	5,911	13.30					432	0.97					7,446	16.76	44,428	2,284	5.14
Tipperary North	11,425	23.67	9,559	19.80	7,978	16.53	3,034	6.29					409	0.85					15,868	32.87	48,273	0	0.00
Tipperary South	14,298	34.57	4,525	10.94	5,419	13.10	1,860	4.50					367	0.89					14,892	36.00	41,361	8,818	21.32
Waterford	20,416	38.00	10,192	18.97	7,515	13.99	5,342	9.94					462	0.86	873	1.63			8,920	16.60	53,720	0	0.00
Wexford	26,034	34.46	15,462	20.47	14,027	18.57	4,353	5.76					391	0.52					14,531	19.24	75,539	0	0.00
Wicklow	27,926	39.61	12,087	17.14	7,467	10.59	7,089	10.06			741		1,026	1.46					14,905	21.14	70,500	741	0.98
Total 43	801,628	36.10	431,796	19.45	387,358	17.45	220,661	9.94	26,770	1.21	21,551	0.97	41,033	1.85	3,056	0.14	2,102	0.09	284,398	12.81	2,220,359	59,423	2.68
Dublin	163,023	29.93	159,709	29.32	67,836	12.45	44,525	8.17	19,550	3.59	19,258	3.54	19,529	3.59	1,313	0.24	1,358	0.25	48,608	8.92	544,709	38,808	7.12
Leinster	217,354	36.64	114,011	19.22	115,542	19.48	61,906	10.44	1,696	0.29	741	0.12	9,716	1.64	189	0.03	234	0.04	71,817	12.11	593,206	2,437	0.41
Munster	245,589	38.13	121,794	18.60	121,134	18.90	49,445	7.68	5,524	0.86	1,552	0.24	8,091	1.26	1,554	0.24	510	0.08	90,808	14.10	644,001	15,894	2.47
Connaught/Ulster	175,662	40.06	38,282	8.73	82,846	18.90	64,785	14.78					3,703	0.84					73,165	16.69	438,443	2,284	0.52
Ulster	48,775	31.99	10,310	6.76	30,718	20.15	41,992	27.54					1,263	0.83					19,398	12.72	152,456		

Red: Maximum Blue: Minimum

Dublin summary 2011 Party vote

Party	Cand	1st	%	Quota	Seats	Cand	1st	%	Quota	Seats	%	Seats
		2011					**2007**				**Change**	
FG	24	163,023	29.93%	14.36	17	18	94,788	18.74%	8.99	10	+11.19%	+7
LB	24	159,709	29.32%	14.07	18	15	73,490	14.53%	6.97	9	+14.79%	+9
FF	17	67,836	12.45%	5.98	1	27	196,029	38.75%	18.60	19	-26.30%	-18
SF	10	44,525	8.17%	3.92	4	13	35,256	6.97%	3.35	1	+1.20%	+3
SP	5	19,550	3.59%	1.72	2	3	11,518	2.28%	1.09		+1.31%	+2
PBPA	7	19,258	3.54%	1.70	2						+3.54%	+2
GP	12	19,529	3.59%	1.72		13	41,813	8.27%	3.97	5	-4.68%	-5
WP	3	1,313	0.24%	0.12		3	862	0.17%	0.08		+0.07%	
CS	5	1,358	0.25%	0.12		3	625	0.12%	0.06		+0.13%	
PD						10	20,919	4.14%	1.98	1	-4.14%	-1
Others	48	48,608	8.92%	4.28	3	24	30,552	6.04%	2.90	2	+2.88%	+1
Total	**155**	**544,709**	**100.0%**	**11,349**	**47**	**129**	**505,852**	**100.0%**	**10,540**	**47**	**0.00%**	**0**
Electorate		**806,936**	**67.50%**				**812,181**	**62.28%**			**+5.22%**	
Spoiled		**5,614**	**1.02%**				**4,800**	**0.94%**			**+0.08%**	
Turnout		**550,323**	**68.20%**				**510,652**	**62.87%**			**+5.32%**	

Leinster summary 2011 Party vote

Party	Cand	1st	%	Quota	Seats	Cand	1st	%	Quota	Seats	%	Seats
		2011					**2007**				**Change**	
FG	26	217,354	36.64%	15.75	21	26	147,843	27.08%	11.37	12	+9.56%	+9
LB	17	114,011	19.22%	8.26	8	13	62,317	11.42%	4.79	5	+7.80%	+3
FF	23	115,542	19.48%	8.37	7	27	246,899	45.23%	19.00	22	-25.75%	-15
SF	11	61,906	10.44%	4.49	3	9	32,301	5.92%	2.49	1	+4.52%	+2
SP	2	1,696	0.29%	0.12							+0.29%	
PBPA	1	741	0.12%	0.05							+0.12%	
GP	10	9,716	1.64%	0.70		10	23,614	4.33%	1.82	1	-2.69%	-1
WP	1	189	0.03%	0.01		1	193	0.04%	0.01		-0.00%	
CS	1	234	0.04%	0.02		2	280	0.05%	0.02		-0.01%	
PD						8	14,122	2.59%	1.09		-2.59%	
Others	59	71,817	12.11%	5.21	3	22	18,300	3.35%	1.41		+8.75%	+3
Total	**151**	**593,206**	**100.0%**	**13,796**	**42**	**118**	**545,869**	**100.0%**	**12,998**	**41**	**0.00%**	**1**
Electorate		**869,916**	**68.19%**				**822,421**	**66.37%**			**+1.82%**	
Spoiled		**6,531**	**1.09%**				**5,279**	**0.96%**			**+0.13%**	
Turnout		**599,737**	**68.94%**				**551,148**	**67.02%**			**+1.93%**	

Munster summary 2011 Party vote

Party	Cand	1st	%	Quota	Seats	Cand	1st	%	Quota	Seats	%	Seats
		2011					**2007**				**Change**	
FG	31	245,589	38.13%	17.92	21	27	178,183	29.62%	14.22	17	+8.52%	+4
LB	18	119,794	18.60%	8.74	9	14	59,707	9.92%	4.76	5	+8.68%	+4
FF	19	121,134	18.81%	8.84	7	32	256,955	42.71%	20.50	22	-23.90%	-15
SF	10	49,445	7.68%	3.61	3	11	31,910	5.30%	2.55	1	+2.37%	+2
SP	2	5,524	0.86%	0.40		1	1,700	0.28%	0.14		+0.58%	
PBPA	1	1,552	0.24%	0.11							+0.24%	
GP	13	8,091	1.26%	0.59		13	21,310	3.54%	1.70		-2.29%	+0
WP	2	1,554	0.24%	0.11		2	1,971	0.33%	0.16		-0.09%	
CS	2	510	0.08%	0.04		1	171	0.03%	0.01		+0.05%	
PD						7	8,870	1.47%	0.71		-1.47%	
Others	60	90,808	14.10%	6.63	6	27	40,840	6.79%	3.26	2	+7.31%	+4
Total	**158**	**644,001**	**100.0%**	**13,703**	**46**	**135**	**601,617**	**100.0%**	**12,536**	**47**	**0.00%**	**-1**
Electorate		**911,479**	**70.65%**				**879,055**	**68.44%**			**+2.22%**	
Spoiled		**6,283**	**0.97%**				**5,287**	**0.87%**			**+0.10%**	
Turnout		**650,286**	**71.34%**				**606,904**	**69.04%**			**+2.30%**	

How the nation voted

Connacht/Ulster summary 2011 Party vote

Party	Cand	1st	%	Quota	Seats	Cand	1st	%	Quota	Seats	%	Seats
		2011					**2007**				**Change**	
FG	23	175,662	40.06%	12.82	17	20	143,614	34.82%	11.14	12	+5.25%	+5
LB	9	38,282	8.73%	2.79	2	8	13,661	3.31%	1.06	1	+5.42%	+1
FF	16	82,846	18.90%	6.05	5	20	158,682	38.47%	12.31	15	-19.58%	-10
SF	10	64,785	14.78%	4.73	4	8	43,943	10.65%	3.41	1	+4.12%	+3
SP											+0.00%	+0
PBPA											+0.00%	+0
GP	8	3,703	0.84%	0.27		8	10,199	2.47%	0.79		-1.63%	+0
WP											+0.00%	+0
CS						2	629	0.15%	0.05		-0.15%	+0
PD						5	12,485	3.03%	0.97	1	-3.03%	-1
Others	36	73,165	16.69%	5.34	3	17	29,259	7.09%	2.27	1	+9.59%	+2
Total	102	438,443	100.0%	13,702	31	88	412,472	100.0%	12,891	31	0.00%	0
Electorate		620,911	70.61%				597,257	69.06%			+1.55%	
Spoiled		4,389	0.99%				4,069	0.98%			+0.01%	
Turnout		442,832	71.32%				416,541	69.74%			+1.58%	

FF seats include outgoing Ceann Comhairle Seamus Kirk

National summary 2011 Party vote

Party	Cand	1st	%	Quota	Seats	Cand	1st	%	Quota	Seats	%	Seats
		2011					**2007**				**Change**	
FG	104	801,628	36.10%	60.29	76	91	564,428	27.32%	45.62	51	+8.78%	+25
LB	68	431,796	19.45%	32.47	37	50	209,175	10.13%	16.91	20	+9.32%	+17
FF	75	387,358	17.45%	29.13	20	106	858,565	41.56%	69.40	78	-24.11%	-58
SF	41	220,661	9.94%	16.60	14	41	143,410	6.94%	11.59	4	+3.00%	+10
SP	9	26,770	1.21%	2.01	2	4	13,218	0.64%	1.07		+0.57%	+2
PBPA	9	21,551	0.97%	1.62	2	0					+0.97%	+2
GP	43	41,039	1.85%	3.09		44	96,936	4.69%	7.84	6	-2.84%	-6
WP	6	3,056	0.14%	0.23		6	3,026	0.15%	0.24		-0.01%	+0
CS	8	2,102	0.09%	0.16		8	1,705	0.08%	0.14		+0.01%	+0
PD						30	56,396	2.73%	4.56	2	-2.73%	-2
Others	203	284,398	12.81%	21.39	15	90	118,951	5.76%	9.62	5	+7.05%	+10
Total	566	2,220,359	100.0%	13,297	166	470	2,065,810	100.0%	12,371	166	0.00%	0
Electorate		3,209,249	69.19%				3,110,914	66.41%			+2.78%	
Spoiled		22,817	1.02%				19,435	0.93%			+0.09%	
Turnout		2,243,176	69.90%				2,085,245	67.03%			+2.87%	

Dublin South East Fine Gael TD Lucinda Creighton celebrates her election with her husband, Senator Paul Bradford, in the RDS count centre

Seats summary 2011

#	Constituency	Seats	FG	LB	FF	SF	ULA	GP	Others
1	Carlow-Kilkenny	5	3	1	1			0	
2	Cavan-Monaghan	5	3		1	1			
3	Clare	4	2	1	1				
4	Cork East	4	2	1	0	1			
5	Cork North Central	4	1	1	1	1			
6	Cork North West	3	2		1				
7	Cork South Central	5	2	1	2				
8	Cork South West	3	2	1	0				
9	Donegal North East	3	1		1	1			
10	Donegal South West	3	1		0	1			1
11	Dublin Central	4	1	1	0	1			1
12	Dublin Mid West	4	2	2	0			0	
13	Dublin North	4	2	1	0		1	0	
14	Dublin North Central	3	1	1	0				1
15	Dublin North East	3	1	2	0				
16	Dublin North West	3		2	0	1			
17	Dublin South	5	3	1	0			0	1
18	Dublin South Central	5	1	2	0	1	1		
19	Dublin South East	4	2	2	0			0	
20	Dublin South West	4	1	2	0	1			
21	Dublin West	4	1	1	1		1		
22	Dun Laoghaire	4	2	1	0		1	0	
23	Galway East	4	2	1	1				
24	Galway West	5	2	1	1				1
25	Kerry North-West Limerick	3	1	1	0	1			
26	Kerry South	3	1		0				2
27	Kildare North	4	2	1	0				1
28	Kildare South	3	1	1	1				
29	Laoighis Offaly	5	2		2	1			
30	Limerick	3	2		1				
31	Limerick City	4	2	1	1				
32	Longford-Westmeath	4	2	1	1				
33	Louth	5	2	1	1	1			
34	Mayo	5	4		1				
35	Meath East	3	2	1	0				
36	Meath West	3	2		0	1			
37	Roscommon-Sth Leitrim	3	2		0				1
38	Sligo-North Leitrim	3	2		0	1			
39	Tipperary North	3	1	1	0				1
40	Tipperary South	3	1		0		1		1
41	Waterford	4	2	1	0				1
42	Wexford	5	2	1	1				1
43	Wicklow	5	3	1	0				1
	2011	**166**	**76**	**37**	**20**	**14**	**5**	**0**	**14**
	2007	**166**	**51**	**20**	**78**	**4**	**0**	**6**	**7**
	Change 2011-2007	**+/-**	**+25**	**+17**	**-58**	**+10**	**+5**	**-6**	**+7**
12	Dublin	47	17	18	1	4	4	0	3
10	Leinster	42	21	8	7	3	0	0	3
13	Munster	46	21	9	7	3	1	0	5
8	Connaught-Ulster	31	17	2	5	4	0	0	3

Gain — Loss
Double Gain — Double Loss

Election Facts

"With a 28.52% of the vote Róisín Shortall in Dublin North West was the female TD who received the highest percentage share of the vote in the country."
Sean Donnelly

RTÉ Political Correspondent **David McCullagh** looks at how this election compares with other historical contests

Watershed?

W hen we talk about watershed elections, we tend to look at 1918, when Sinn Féin destroyed the old Home Rule Party; or 1948, when coalition was first introduced into Irish politics; alternatively, we could mention Jack Lynch's sweeping victory in 1977 or the Spring Tide of 1992. But in terms of lasting changes to the balance of power between the political parties, two elections stand out – 1932, and, it would seem, 2011.

On 9 March 1932, the seventh Dáil met for the first time, after a hard-fought election which saw a decisive shift in Irish politics.

Power was transferred peacefully for the first time in the history of the State. Éamon de Valera of Fianna Fáil was elected President of the Executive Council, succeeding William T Cosgrave of Cumann na nGaedheal, who had held the office since the foundation of the state a decade before.

Colourful stories abound about the transfer of power. Fianna Fáil deputies were said to have revolvers in their pockets in case the outgoing government resorted to violence to overturn the decision of the voters. James Dillon later claimed he saw an elderly gentleman assembling a machine gun in a telephone box inside Leinster House!

The machine gun was most likely a figment of Dillon's imagination. The coup never materialised either. While some elements in the army and the gardaí may have considered it, the politicians didn't. Cosgrave, according to his Attorney General, John A Costello, was playing cards with a few cronies in the upper reaches of Leinster House as TDs assembled, rather than plotting a counter-revolution.

But the tension was real enough, as the losers of the Civil War took power through the ballot box, putting in place a new political order in the process.

In the 79 years since 9 March 1932, Fianna Fáil was always the largest party in the Dáil; it held power most of the time (for 61 years to be exact); and it never spent two consecutive terms in opposition. It was the natural party of power, the natural party of government.

Another way to look at it is to think of the party

> "For the first time, Fine Gael was the largest party; Labour the second largest; Fianna Fáil reduced to a rump, barely in third place"

leadership: Fianna Fáil has never changed leader in opposition; Fine Gael has never done so in government. The reason is simple – Fianna Fáil never spent long enough on the opposition benches and Fine Gael never spent long enough in government for a leader's time to run out there.

When the 31st Dáil convened on 9 March 2011 – after another hard-fought election which saw another decisive shift in Irish politics – it was exactly 79 years to the day after that seventh Dáil transformed the Irish political landscape. There were no guns this time, real or imagined. The only dangers to public health were disappointed office seekers throwing tantrums, boisterous supporters of the new government celebrating, and freshly elected TDs driving on the plinth. For the first time, Fine Gael was the largest party; Labour the second largest; Fianna Fáil reduced to a rump, barely in third place.

The indications of a Fianna Fáil collapse had been there for a long time, as opinion polls showed the party falling into second place in the autumn of 2008, and then, disastrously, into third place the following year. The appalling figures became so consistent that they started to lose their impact.

There was a reminder of how much Irish politics had changed with the close of nominations for the general election, when it became clear that, for the

Left: Garda Ronan McNamara, accompanied by electoral officer Hugh O'Donnell, carries the ballot box away from a local resident's house that was used as a polling station on Inishfree Island

Above: An election official sorts ballots in Castlebar

first time since its foundation in 1926, Fianna Fáil wasn't running enough candidates to form a government even if all were elected.

Now, a single party Fianna Fáil government hasn't seemed likely (with the exception of 2002) for many years, and clearly was out of the question in 2011. The reduction in candidates was a smart move by a party trying to minimise its losses through concentration of the vote – the perils of running too many candidates became all too clear in constituencies like Dún Laoghaire. But here's the point – for the first time, Fianna Fáil was admitting to itself that it had no prospect of ruling alone, admitting it was no longer the natural party of power or of government.

Of course, the party hopes that this is just a temporary little arrangement. But with only 20 TDs, and struggling to make itself heard over Sinn Féin, ULA and independent voices in the Dáil, it has a mountain to climb if it is ever to lead a government again. The party's reputation for invincibility has been shattered.

It wasn't just the eclipse of Fianna Fáil which made 9 March 2011 notable in historic terms. It was also the size of Enda Kenny's majority in the vote nominating him as Taoiseach – the largest in the history of the state. He had a majority of 90, made up of 75 Fine Gael TDs (Ceann Comhairle Seán Barrett did not, of course, vote), 37 Labour and five independents (Stephen Donnelly, Noel Grealish, Michael Healy-Rae, Michael Lowry and Mattie

McGrath), giving a total of 117. Only 27 – Sinn Féin, the United Left Alliance and independent TDs voted against him.

There were no other nominations for the office, which is not unprecedented after a sweeping election victory – the opposition didn't put up an alternative to de Valera in 1957 or Jack Lynch in 1977 (nor did they nominate anyone to oppose the successor who followed each man after two years – Seán Lemass in 1959 and Charlie Haughey in 1979).

What was unprecedented was Fianna Fáil's abstention in the vote. It was the first time the main opposition party hasn't taken part in a vote for the head of government since June 1927 – and the reason for Fianna Fáil not voting then was that the party was at the time refusing to take its seats in the Dáil.

On the face of it, then, this election has been a watershed. Fianna Fáil seems certain to be confined to the opposition benches for a number of Dáil terms, and the coalition partners can feel secure in office – they could lose up to 30 seats in the next election before losing their majority.

But there's one final analogy from history Fine Gael and Labour should bear in mind. The only comparable victory for a Taoiseach was the 42-vote margin enjoyed by Albert Reynolds in January 1993. His Fianna Fáil/Labour coalition also seemed unassailable – and yet it collapsed within two years. We can't know what lies in store for any of the parties – and until we find out, we won't know if Election 2011 was simply an aberration, or a true watershed in Irish politics.

Election 2011 saw Fine Gael and Labour, two parties who had shared government on six previous occasions, once again in coalition. RTÉ's Political Reporter **Brian Dowling** examines how they got back together

Together again

I n the hours after Fine Gael delivered its most successful ever election result, the party leader Enda Kenny declared on RTÉ that the country had witnessed "a democratic revolution at the ballot box". Indeed it had. Fine Gael was the largest party in Ireland for the first time and the Labour Party was the second largest. Between them, they had secured an astonishing 113 seats in the 31st Dáil, the largest majority in the history of the State. Fine Gael's 76 seats was six more than its best previous performance in 1982 under Dr Garret FitzGerald, while Labour's 37 seats was again four more than the 'Spring Tide' of 1992.

On 9 March when the Dáil assembled, Enda Kenny, just a month short of his 60th birthday, was elected Taoiseach by a margin of 117 votes to 27, again the largest victory margin in the history of the State. The Fine Gael and Labour Party members were joined in the vote by four independents who also voted for Kenny.

No other Taoiseach had ever received such a massive endorsement. But it could have all been so different.

From September 2008, as the banking and economic collapse unfolded, Fine Gael and Labour were locked in competition with each other to win the public's backing to lead the next government. Given their respective sizes historically, that should never have been an issue. In the old political order, Fine Gael was always the senior partner. The reason there was a doubt was simple: Enda Kenny. In spite of electoral successes since taking over the reins in 2002, doubts continued, inside and outside his party, about Kenny's leadership. In the Dáil and in media performances, Gilmore was proving a consistently more formidable critic of Taoiseach Brian Cowen and his government. It was paying political dividends for Labour and it began to gradually build support over successive opinion polls. At its 2009 conference in Mullingar, Labour began rallying behind the slogan 'Gilmore for Taoiseach'. The gap between Fine Gael

and Labour, in polling terms, was beginning to narrow.

On 10 June 2010, the *Irish Times* ran an Ipsos/MRBI poll. It caused turmoil within Fine Gael. Fianna Fáil had fallen to a historic low of 17% support, but Fine Gael had also fallen by 4% to 28% and the Labour Party jumped by 8% to a record 32%. The poll spooked most of the Fine Gael front-bench, including deputy leader, Richard Bruton. A hastily organised leadership challenge to Kenny ensued. It proved a game changer: for Enda Kenny. He sacked Bruton, dissolved his entire front-bench and saw off his critics. In the aftermath, he brought back former leader Michael Noonan as Finance spokesman and reappointed leaders of the putative coup like Bruton, Simon Coveney, Fergus O'Dowd and Leo Varadkar to a new front-bench.

Noonan proved an inspired choice. He was steely but calm. His political style was incisive from the off. It began to show in the autumn as the country began sliding into the EU-IMF rescue package. Increasingly, Noonan struck a chord with the deepest worries of middle Ireland. With the EU-IMF team knocking on the door in November, the government announced it would publish a four-year plan and challenged opposition parties to do likewise.

Fine Gael produced a four-year plan, endorsing the objective of a €15bn budgetary adjustment by 2014 to ensure a 3% deficit. But it differed on how to achieve this outcome. Labour, in contrast, published a one-year programme and rejected the scale of the proposed adjustment as too harsh, arguing it would do more damage to the economy. This raised doubts about Labour's readiness to confront the scale of the national crisis. By the time the Greens fired the starting gun for Election 2011 on 22 November, Fine Gael had already recovered most of the ground it had lost in the previous year.

Something else was happening. Fine Gael's core backroom team – Mark Mortell, Frank Flannery,

"From the off it was clear that Labour had no prospect of becoming the largest party in the Dáil. A Fine Gael-Labour Party coalition looked the inevitable outcome"

Terry Murphy, Ciaran Conlon and general secretary Tom Curran – working with Kenny and director of elections Phil Hogan, were seeing trends in their own private polls that seemed too good to be true.

Several polls in individual constituencies were showing Fine Gael stronger than national polls. Focus group research had also helped them sharpen previous policy initiatives into what was to become 'The Five Point Plan', a simple but effective message on key issues: jobs, budgetary strategy, the health system, public sector and political reform. A target of 70-plus seats was now a realistic objective. Research also showed that brand 'Fine Gael' was working. Kenny's leadership was less of an issue than might have been feared.

Labour too planned Election 2011 like never before. The party rented modern offices with a media centre and glass walls emblazoned with the legend 'Gilmore for Taoiseach'. Even though support had fallen back, the party was still at a historically high point in the polls. Party strategists still hoped that once the campaign commenced, Gilmore's standing as the most popular party leader would help 'pull' Labour ahead. It didn't.

From the start it was clear that Labour had no prospect of becoming the largest party in the Dáil. A Fine Gael/Labour coalition looked the inevitable outcome, the only issues being the respective sizes of the two parties and the extent of their majority.

The early part of the campaign was lacklustre. Several polls showed Fine Gael edging from the mid-to the high-30s with Labour dipping from the mid-to low-20s.

However, on 13 February the *Sunday Business Post/* Red C poll showed Fianna Fáil languishing at 15%. Labour at 20% but Fine Gael had moved to 38%. Four days later, an OI Research poll showed Labour and Fine Gael at 18% and 39% respectively. Fine Gael was showing double the support of Labour. With the momentum moving to Fine Gael, people began to think the previously unthinkable – Fine Gael in government on its own or with backing from a few independents.

Labour was jolted into a fight back. It protested that Fine Gael, especially Michael Noonan, had unfairly tainted it a 'high-tax' party. It accused Fine Gael of planning stealth taxes and even worse cuts than outlined in its manifesto. The focus of the campaign shifted to the battle between Fine Gael and Labour, leaving the other parties on the margins.

In the final days, Fine Gael hit 40% support in one poll. However, the Labour political counter-attack worked. Come polling day Fine Gael secured just over 36%. While less than the 39% won in 1982, there was a much better seat bonus, giving it a record 76 Dáil seats. Labour won 19.4% of the popular vote to take 37 seats.

Where the harmony of the 'Mullingar Accord' failed to deliver in 2007, the battle between the two parties delivered huge dividends in 2011. Having shared government, in various forms, on six occasions before, they were once again in coalition.

Above: Taoiseach Enda Kenny looks back at Tánaiste Eamon Gilmore as they leave after a group photograph with newly-elected ministers at Áras an Uachtaráin

Opposite: Enda Kenny and Eamon Gilmore shake hands in Herbert Park, Dublin, after announcing they will form the next Government following six days of negotiations

RTÉ's Political Reporter **Brian Dowling** explores the implosion of Fianna Fáil and the Greens and how voters got their revenge

Payback time

lection 2011 drew to a close on the night of 25 February. Ballot boxes were sealed and transported to count centres around the country. But the political fate of Fianna Fáil and the Greens had been sealed well before then.

From September 2010, their coalition increasingly resembled a slow-motion political car crash, eventually imploding in January 2011.

If one moment marked a tipping point it was the morning of Monday 22 November. The Greens issued a terse media alert signalling the party intended to make an important announcement.

It was a critical juncture in Irish politics. The country had endured a week of chaos following the arrival of the IMF and the Greens' alert triggered feverish rumours of their imminent departure from government.

In the event, the Greens stopped short of collapsing the government there and then. But party leader John Gormley started the countdown to Election 2011, demanding an election in the second half of January.

The Greens, he pledged, would remain in government to see through the budget in December and the Finance Bill.

The previous evening, Taoiseach Brian Cowen had publicly confirmed his government had formally requested financial aid from the EU and the IMF.

But for days before this, the Taoiseach and his ministers dismissed stories in the national and international media that Ireland was preparing for an EU-IMF rescue. A state of utter denial prevailed.

On Sunday 15 November on *The Week in Politics*, the Minister for Justice Dermot Ahern was asked if the media reports were "fiction". He insisted they were indeed "fiction".

The next day an increasingly astonished, and at times frightened public, watched in disbelief as Ahern, accompanied by the Transport Minister Noel Dempsey, again denied talks were underway on a bailout plan.

Along with other ministers, they were sticking to the line they had been given. There had been no Cabinet discussions up to then, let alone a decision on a bailout application.

But from the standpoint of the public it was an appalling vista – either senior Cabinet ministers were genuinely ignorant of an impending momentous

> "They didn't have to speak a word. The images were stark evidence that the government had lost control of the national finances. Its credibility was fatally damaged"

development in our history or they were misleading the public.

On the morning after the Ahern and Dempsey interview, Brian Lenihan informed his Fianna Fáil Cabinet colleagues that events were moving quickly. Some were stunned, others angry.

The mood in Fianna Fáil descended into despair and near panic. That Wednesday, the Kildare South TD Seán Power told the Dáil the government could not treat the public "like fools". Still, the frenzied state of denial continued for another 24 hours.

Then something extraordinary happened. On Thursday morning the Governor of the Central Bank, Prof Patrick Honohan, who was in Frankfurt for a meeting of the ECB, phoned RTÉ to ask to go on *Morning Ireland*.

In the midst of confusion, denial and misinformation, he offered clarity: Ireland was in discussions for a loan facility from the EU and the IMF. The game was up.

The following week, in the full glare of national and international media, the head of the IMF delegation to Ireland, Ajai Chopra and his colleagues from the European Central Bank, walked into the Department of Finance and the Central Bank.

They didn't have to say a word. The images of neatly tailored suits, briefcases and polite smiles spoke for them. The government's credibility was in tatters. Seldom has such a humiliation been delivered with such grace.

Even more telling was that Chopra, dubbed 'Chopper' by the tabloids, was greeted warmly by passers-by. For a weary public, it seemed someone was going to take charge.

It was hard to imagine that it could get any worse politically, even with a dire budget in December. The coalition was at rock bottom, it seemed. But it got worse, much worse.

Throughout the months of financial and political uncertainty, rumours of challenges to Brian Cowen's leadership would surface, only to disappear as quickly. With no challenge before or after the budget, he seemed destined to lead his party into the election.

That was about to change. January began with another shocking poll for the party, quickly followed by the publication of *The FitzPatrick Tapes* in the *Sunday Times*.

The disclosure of previously unknown contacts between the Taoiseach and Sean FitzPatrick was about as toxic as it could get. Coming on top of the poll, it plunged Fianna Fáil into political paroxysms.

With huge pressure mounting on him, the Taoiseach, urged on by his supporters, turned the tables on his critics. On Sunday 16 January, he announced he was tabling a motion of confidence in himself for a parliamentary party meeting the following Tuesday.

Micheál Martin broke ranks, in a fashion. He confirmed he would oppose the confidence motion. It was, he said, a battle for the survival of Fianna Fáil. But at Cowen's request he remained as Foreign Affairs Minister until the contest was settled. When the Taoiseach prevailed, Martin resigned.

Within hours of winning, the Taoiseach sought the resignations of four ministers – Noel Dempsey, Dermot Ahern, Tony Killeen and Mary Harney.

In spite of warnings from some insiders, the Taoiseach seemed determined to go for a 'game changer'. Four Cabinet vacancies would allow him bring forward new faces and re-position his party.

Instead, he ended up with a political shambles that plunged his party and the country into further turmoil.

Up to this point the Greens held the line on government business, albeit under increasing pressure to bring about a speedy end to the 30th Dáil.

Cowen's botched reshuffle changed everything. The Taoiseach was forced to announce an election on 11 March. And he was forced to reassign portfolios to existing ministers.

Most of his parliamentary colleagues watched in horror as events unfolded on an almost hourly basis. The party was reeling and facing electoral annihilation. Faced with the prospect of another leadership contest, a party in free fall, his government in chaos and a public growing ever more angry and bewildered, Cowen announced on 22 January he would step down. He pledged to remain as Taoiseach until the Finance Bill was completed.

The next day the Greens walked from government, their patience with Fianna Fáil had finally snapped.

Now left with a seven-member Cabinet, the bare constitutional minimum, Cowen had little option but to concede an election on 25 February in the teeth of no-confidence motions from the opposition.

Martin succeeded him as leader. He started the election with 21 TDs retiring, including Cowen and several of his ministers. Their handsome pensions and severance payments fuelled public anger further.

It was a battle for survival and its one-time partners faced a similar do-or-die struggle.

Voters blamed Fianna Fáil for getting the country into the mess; the Greens for contributing to it. Both parties also took the hit for implementing harsh measures to correct the public finances; for the fall in living standards and for not being seen to be tougher with bankers.

Ireland does not do civil unrest or street riots. The public waits in the long grass and strikes when the opportunity arises. The depth of its pent-up hostility became evident once the ballot boxes were opened on the weekend of 26-27 February.

Returning to the 31st Dáil with 20 TDs, Fianna Fáil just about survived, albeit with an uncertain future ahead. The Greens lost their six seats.

Justice Minister Dermot Ahern and Transport Minister Noel Dempsey at a press conference on 15 November 2010 where they famously refuted rumours of an EU/IMF bailout

Gerry Adams took his seat on the opposition benches on the first day of the 31st Dáil with a record number of Sinn Féin TDs. It marked a milestone in Sinn Féin's electoral history. *'The Week In Politics'* Editor Deirdre McCarthy examines the party's long road to success

Towards 2016

T he walk from the lobby down to the seats in the Dáil chamber is just a few steps. When he took his seat in the 31st Dáil, Gerry Adams had completed a long, difficult and controversial journey that began in the Mansion House in 1986.

Twenty-five years earlier at the Sinn Féin Ard Fheis, Gerry Adams advocated a strategic move away from the party's abstentionist policy in Leinster House. Changing political conditions required a change in Republican strategy, he said, and the only feasible way to win support for the party and its policies in the Republic was by gaining public support at electoral level.

Gerry Adams entered the Dáil and walked towards the opposition benches accompanied by a line of Sinn Féin deputies. He took his place in the same front row as Fianna Fáil's Micheál Martin but the leaders sat at opposite ends. The 14 Sinn Féin and 20 Fianna Fáil deputies sat side by side, each party with its own distinct but separate republican tradition, each party with a very different election story to tell but closer now than ever on the opposition benches.

Before polling day, the Sinn Féin leadership had predicted gains of three or maybe four seats in addition to the five sitting deputies, but the election results far exceeded expectations. The party had been buoyed up by the victory of Pearse Doherty in the Donegal South-West by-election three months earlier and his series of strong and passionate Dáil and media contributions set the tone for Sinn Féin ahead of the general election.

The events of November 2010 and, in particular, the by-election victory, signalled a dramatic change in the political fortunes of all the parties – none more so than Sinn Féin. Not since 1923 had the party held a seat in Donegal. Pearse Doherty's capture of the seat vacated by Pat 'the Cope' Gallagher pushed Fianna Fáil into third place behind Sinn Féin and Fine Gael in the county. Three months later, Sinn Féin was threatening to overtake Fianna Fáil on the national stage as the third largest party in Dáil Éireann.

In the general election, Sinn Féin ran 41 candidates in 38 constituencies and secured 9.9% of the national vote. In many constituencies it was in with a fighting chance for the last seat. It won the

party an unexpected 14 seats. The party made significant and in some cases historic gains in constituencies such as Laois-Offaly with the election of Brian Stanley and Meath West with the election of Peadar Tóibín. Sinn Féin had not held a seat in either constituency since 1923.

However, the last seat proved to be elusive in constituencies like Wicklow with John Brady narrowly edged out for the fifth seat by the independent Stephen Donnelly. There was another disappointment in Dublin North-East when five-time Sinn Féin election candidate Larry O'Toole was beaten by the second Labour candidate John Lyons for the third and final seat in that constituency.

Election 2011 saw the party vote increase by 3% on the previous election of 2007. That result had been a disappointment and Seán Crowe lost his seat in Dublin South-West, reducing Sinn Féin seats in the Dáil from five to four. The party had hoped to do better with a bounce from events in the peace process.

Prior to 2007, the party was making steady inroads. The breakthrough for the party in the Republic had happened in 1997 when Caoimhghín Ó Caoláin became the first Sinn Féin deputy to take his seat in Dáil Éireann. In the general election of 2002, four new deputies, including Arthur Morgan, Aengus Ó Snodaigh, Seán Crowe and Martin Ferris were elected to join him.

The mixed fortunes of the party at national level were also reflected at local level. In the local elections of 2009, Sinn Féin managed to hold its 54 seats on the back of just 6.9% of the vote and in the European elections Mary Lou McDonald lost her seat.

Within months of the party's lacklustre local election campaign in June 2009, four high-profile councillors resigned from the party, adding to speculation that Sinn Féin had reached its ceiling in the Republic. There was unhappiness with the internal decision-making process and disagreement over the party's future direction. The resignations of New Ross councillor John Dwyer and Christy Burke in Dublin were a serious blow to the party. Christy Burke had been the party's longest-serving councillor in the country and resigned within days of the local elections, claiming a lack of support in his Dublin

"Short of a united Ireland, Adams and the Sinn Féin leadership want to see the party sharing government in Northern Ireland and the Republic in 2016"

The 14 Sinn Féin deputies in the current Dáil

Central by-election campaign. Sinn Féin lost two more of its seven members on Dublin City Council when Ballyfermot/Drimnagh-based councillor Louise Minihan resigned, after accusing the party of lacking commitment to its socialist and republican values. This was followed early last year by the resignation of councillor Killian Forde, who claimed the party had become increasingly staid, unresponsive and directionless in the South.

There was, however, another issue. Gerry Adams' own leadership was becoming a focal point. The political debate was increasingly centred on the economic crisis the country faced. The Sinn Féin leader was widely seen as weak and uncomfortable with the details of policy on this front. In the face of all the criticisms of his leadership on economic matters, Adams took a bold political step. It caught the political establishment by surprise when he announced he would seek a nomination to contest the Louth constituency. It was, nonetheless, the logical end-game of the strategy adopted in 1986.

Securing the party nomination in Louth was a formality and there was a sizeable and comfortable core republican vote in the constituency. Arthur Morgan had held the seat since 2002 and was retiring. In both 2002 and 2007, he won the fourth

and final seat with around 15% of the first-preference vote. In the end, Gerry Adams topped the poll and took the first seat with 21.7% of the first-preference votes. It was a ringing endorsement of the party leadership and its strategy.

The victory in Dublin Central for deputy leader Mary Lou McDonald, after a number of failed attempts in the constituency took the fourth and final seat, was the achievement of a further objective. She had been appointed to the position in 2009 as part of the party strategy to widen its appeal in the Republic and to bring fresh faces to the ageing profile of the party leadership.

Adams and the Sinn Féin leadership view their strength in the 31st Dáil as vindication of the political strategy adopted in the Mansion House. Back then it was characterised as coming to power "with a ballot paper in one hand and an armalite in the other". The armalite is gone. The party has completed the transition. It is now accepted as a partner in government in Northern Ireland, even by the DUP.

The next challenge is to enter government in the Republic. Short of a united Ireland, Adams and the Sinn Féin leadership want to see the party sharing government in Northern Ireland and in the Republic in 2016.

The Week In Politics reporter **Mícheál Lehane** explores the success of some of the independent and 'smaller party' candidates in Election 2011

Independents' Day

I f one result typifies the uniqueness of this election, it is surely the poll-topping performance of builder and developer Mick Wallace in Wexford. Owing the banks more than €40m and vowing never to fix a pothole proved no obstacle to success as he got more than 13,000 first-preference votes.

In many ways, the emergence of the pink-shirted TD, replete with an earring and flowing blonde hair, neatly captures the altered landscape. Voters did not care that the man who wanted to represent them had seen his property portfolio fall in value by €60m. Even his pledge never to "help people dodge hospital or housing queues", was welcomed.

Today, most of the 19 successful independent candidates sit together in the 31st Dáil in a loosely aligned group. But there are many strands to this new force in Irish politics. It is made up of TDs from the Socialist Party, the People Before Profit Alliance and some who can trace their political origins back to the main parties.

TDs like Mattie McGrath and Tom Fleming are former Fianna Fáil elected members. They became acceptable to the electorate after they had renounced Fianna Fáil, albeit very close to polling day. Skewing the new radical trend somewhat was Michael Lowry. The former Fine Gael minister saw his vote in Tipperary North actually increase by more than 1,200 votes, even though he had supported a deeply unpopular government.

Ditto the Healy-Raes in Kerry South, where Michael succeeded his father Jackie. Tom Fleming's success here too made this the first constituency to return two independent candidates in more than 60 years. Fianna Fáil strategists must have wondered how two men from their 'gene pool' had prospered while the party lost both its seats in Kerry.

Mattie McGrath also took a seat after throwing off the Fianna Fáil colours in Tipperary South. He had lost the party whip when he voted against the bill to ban stag hunting in June 2010. Then in January 2011 he left the party entirely to run as an independent. He secured 6,074 votes and vowed never to return to Fianna Fáil.

In the same constituency, Seamus Healy of the Workers and Unemployed Action Group won back the seat he had lost narrowly in 2007. This time, Healy was running under the umbrella of the United Left Alliance. The group was formed in November

2010 and was committed to scrapping the four-year recovery plan. It brought together the People Before Profit Alliance and the Socialist Party.

Other groupings formed in the lead-up to the election. Democracy Now, the brainchild of prominent media figures like Fintan O'Toole, David McWilliams and Eamon Dunphy, was looking like a radical alternative. But the group did not contest the election, saying it was called too early for them.

New Vision had promised to "change the way we do politics". It ran 19 candidates but only Luke 'Ming' Flanagan in Roscommon South-Leitrim got elected. The long-time campaigner for the legalisation of cannabis capitalised on a strong support base built during his time as Mayor of Roscommon.

Another group that did well were the enterprise candidates. Their policies focused on tackling cronyism and radically overhauling the government's banking policy. Management consultant Stephen Donnelly had gained much prominence as the holder of an all too relevant PhD in the interaction between the IMF and small countries and he won the last seat in Wicklow. In Dublin South, Shane Ross's win was emphatic. He got 17,075 first-preference votes and was elected after the first count.

The core views of the People Before Profit Alliance and the enterprise candidates were fundamentally opposed. But both were adamant that the government's banking policy was wrong. That struck a chord with voters in Dublin South-Central, where the alliance's Joan Collins trebled her 2007 vote and took the fourth seat. Weeks earlier, she made the news after a spat with former Taoiseach Bertie Ahern on his final day in the Dáil. Collins had confronted Ahern, who was doing a TV interview, and told him that he should be ashamed of himself.

Her party inflicted more damage on Fianna Fáil in Dún Laoghaire, where Richard Boyd Barrett won the last seat. His nearest challenger was the new deputy leader of Fianna Fáil, Mary Hanafin. Having narrowly missed out on winning a seat in 2007, this time after 11 counts he was still standing.

The other party running under the United Left Alliance banner also had a good day. Socialist Party leader Joe Higgins regained the seat he had lost in Dublin West almost four years earlier. He got 8,084 first-preference votes to comfortably take the third seat. If Higgins' re-election was expected, there was

> "Owing the banks more than €40m and vowing never to fix a pothole proved no obstacle to success as he got more than 13,000 first preference votes"

less certainty about Councillor Clare Daly's prospects in Dublin North. She had failed to get elected in the three previous elections. But on this occasion she got her highest-ever share of the vote, 15.2%, and was elected after the sixth of seven counts.

Another left-wing independent candidate won against the odds in Waterford. John Halligan described himself as "a pro-business socialist". It was a combination that appealed to the public in troubled times. Twice previously he had run unsuccessfully for the Workers' Party in general elections. The changed economic climate saw him more than treble his vote in this election and he won the last of the four seats.

Other independent TDs who held their seats included: former Progressive Democrat Noel Grealish in Galway West, Finian McGrath in Dublin North-Central, and Maureen O'Sullivan in Dublin Central. Catherine Murphy won back the seat she had lost in Kildare North in 2007.

In Donegal South-West, Thomas Pringle, who had once been a Sinn Féin councillor, benefitted from his solid showing in the by-election there just months earlier. Pringle had spoken repeatedly about renewable energy as an optimum way to create jobs in Donegal.

Pringle's victory comments reflected the changed political landscape in Donegal South-West, where the Tánaiste failed to hold her seat. "We would have seen elections over the years when Donegal wasn't even talked about on the TV because it was seen as Fianna Fáil country," he said.

In the new Dáil, 16 of the 19 TDs elected from outside the big parties have formed a technical group. Only Michael Lowry, Noel Grealish and Michael Healy-Rae did not join. This unlikely alliance gives TDs more speaking time and it will allow some of them to become part of Oireachtas committees. It ensures that they will have a strong voice and a significant presence in Leinster House.

Independent TDs Mattie McGrath, Mick Wallace, Shane Ross and Finian McGrath speak to the media on the plinth at Leinster House

After voters savagely rejected TDs from political dynasties, *The Week In Politics* reporter **Mícheál Lehane** looks at the wipe-out of some of the biggest names in Irish politics

Bonfire of the dynasties

"At one time he knew that the party had promised something that was close to political certainty, almost an eternal life of electoral loyalties." Thomas McCarthy, *'Without Power'*

"Names like Haughey, Lenihan, Andrews, Blaney, Coughlan, McEllistrim, Hanafin, Flynn. Now only traces remain of these dynasties after the voters savagely rejected them"

They were the families that were at different times and in varying ways central to the growth of Fianna Fáil. Names like Haughey, Lenihan, Andrews, Blaney, Coughlan, McEllistrim, Hanafin, Flynn. Now only traces remain of these dynasties after the voters savagely rejected them. Loyalty cultivated over generations counted for nothing in this changed world. Not that any politician with a famous lineage would ever see it that way. They would always point to their own record as the reason they held their seats for so long.

Brian Lenihan forcefully vented this view on another difficult day for his party after the 2009 local and European elections: "I don't come from a Fianna Fáil family. I'm an elected member of Dáil Éireann. I decided to go into politics myself. I'm a bit sick of this shite now to be quite honest with you. I'm in the party because I believe in it, not because I come from a Fianna Fáil family," he said. He added that the repeated use by the media of the words "Fianna Fáil dynasty" somehow implied that the people from these families did not have a legitimate place in the Dáil. Whatever the implications of the description, the voters would this time say farewell to many of those clans steeped in the party's history.

Early on count day it was clear that Seán Haughey would be a big-name victim of the new political climate. Twice he ran for election when his father, former Taoiseach Charles J Haughey was in the Dáil. He failed both times – in 1987 and 1989. Then, with the retirement of his father, came a Dáil seat in 1992 in Dublin North-Central. Throughout his time as a TD and later a Minster of State, he would have looked at the portraits of his father and grandfather on the circular walls at the top of the stairs before entering the Dáil chamber: Seán Lemass to his left, wearing an inscrutable look and behind him, his father sitting down, debonair and regal. But the results of 25 February meant that for the first time in 54 years there would be no Haughey elected on the northside of Dublin City. Seán's aunt Eileen Lemass and his uncle Noel Lemass had also been TDs.

The scale of Seán Haughey's defeat was dramatic,

with the Fianna Fáil vote down 31 points leaving him with just half a quota after the first count. Asked what his forefathers would have made of a doomsday like this one, he concluded that Seán Lemass would have given little away and got on with it. His father was more likely to say: "Fight, fight and fight back."

Brian Lenihan held his seat and is now his party's sole TD in Dublin. He is also deputy leader of the party, a position his father Brian held when he was appointed Tánaiste in 1987. His brother and aunt fared less well. Both were comprehensively defeated. Conor Lenihan spoke about the "tide going out" on Fianna Fáil. In his four-seat Dublin South-West constituency, both he and his party colleague, Charlie O'Connor, lost their seats. Mary O'Rourke saw her first-preference vote fall by more than 5,000 votes in Longford-Westmeath. Such was the resounding nature of this result that she was eliminated after just the second count. She concluded though that it was better to have faced the electorate rather than in her words "taking her pot of money and running away".

Mary Coughlan could be forgiven if she had considered retiring after she watched six of her cabinet colleagues wave goodbye before the election. In the Dáil since she was 21, she succeed her late father Cathal. Three years before that, he had retained his brother Clement's seat in a by-election. The former Tánaiste must have worried when she saw the results of the Donegal South-West by-election in late 2010. Nonetheless, with her party winning 21% of the vote that day, taking one of the three seats in a general election must have seemed feasible. Again, against all the advice of the strategy gurus, the party selected two candidates. Brian Ó Domhnaill, who had performed well in the by-election, was added to the ticket. The plan failed miserably and even with 0.9 of a quota there would be no seat for the party. But in a sign of the dwindling power of the Coughlan name, the Tánaiste was eliminated from the count before her running mate.

The two-candidate approach was equally baffling in

the four-seat Dún Laoghaire constituency. Here, Fianna Fáil did try to persuade Mary Hanafin and Barry Andrews that one of them should move to Dublin South, where the chances of taking one of the five seats were more favourable. Neither Hanafin nor Andrews blinked.

Children's Minister Barry Andrews, the son of former Foreign Affairs Minister David, himself a TD from 1965, had impeccable Fianna Fáil credentials. Mary Hanafin, a full cabinet minister of almost seven years and a TD since 1997, had built a strong political base in Dún Laoghaire. Her father Des from Thurles, Co Tipperary, had been a long-serving senator and a former treasurer of the party. Her brother John was a senator too. Two political heavyweight families going head to head, at a time when support for their party had tumbled, was always going to be dramatic.

So it proved when Hanafin got 5,090 first-preference votes to 3,542 for Barry Andrews. In the end the Tourism Minister would stay in contention right until the last count when People Before Profit's Richard Boyd Barrett won the final seat. Even though she did remain in the contest to the end, it was widely accepted in the count centre that the seat was out of her reach for several hours before the result was announced. It meant another once glittering Fianna Fáil star had fallen.

For the Andrews family there was disappointment also in Dublin South-East where Chris Andrews, Barry's first cousin, lost his seat. The son of the late TD and MEP Niall Andrews saw his first preference support fall by almost 6,000 votes.

Others with famous names like Niall Blaney and Beverley Flynn decided not to run. Neil T Blaney's sons, Dara and Eamonn, did endeavour to maintain the family tradition in the Dáil. Dara was an unsuccessful independent candidate in Donegal North-East and Eamonn was unsuccessful New Vision candidate in Dublin North-East. Áine Brady's loss in Kildare North means there is now only one Kitt in Leinster House. It came with Michael Kitt's success in Galway East, the constituency where his father was first elected in 1948. Their brother Tom

A glum-looking Seán Haughey, Fianna Fáil candidate for Dublin North-Central, prepares for an interview with RTÉ at the count centre at the RDS in Dublin

did not contest the election in Dublin South.

There were lesser-known names too who did not get re-elected. Tom McEllistrim, the quiet Kerry North TD first elected in 2002, always spoke about the "ground war". He never talked to the media but was a serial canvasser. His grandfather and father had both been TDs. Never shy about using their names, he had hoped the people who had known them, especially in the new Limerick West part of the constituency, would help him buck the national trend. However, it was another well-known dynasty that prevailed: Arthur Spring, Dick's nephew, took McEllistrim's seat for the Labour Party. Once again the people had spoken with clarity.

There were dramatic changes in voting patterns in Election 2011. Professor Michael Marsh analyses the pre-election opinion polls

Poll position

S ince its election victory in 2007, opinion polls have not been kind to Fianna Fáil, with surveys over the five years suggesting the party would lose more than half of the support gained in 2007 (see Table 1). The sharp fall between 2008 and 2009 can be attributed to the bank guarantee, while further losses last year can be blamed on the continuing downward spiral of the economy, culminating in the government decision to withdraw from the bond markets. The arrival of the ECB/IMF in November 2010 only confirmed what had been clear to international investors for some time: government policy was not working. In electoral terms, the question was not whether Fianna Fáil would suffer a heavy defeat, but simply how heavy that defeat would be and who would benefit most. The goose was cooked, but who would feed off the carcass?

Fine Gael and Labour both made gains in late 2008, and Labour briefly seemed to be winning the popularity contest in 2010, but its peak arrived too early and by January 2011 Fine Gael was reasserting its position.

At the same time, Sinn Féin, boosted by its by-

"Well before the election it was evident the electorate was volatile. Fianna Fáil's collapse left much more room for uncertainty"

election victory in Donegal South-West in late November 2010, was threatening to push Fianna Fáil into fourth place, and 'Others' were also making their best showing for many years.

The campaign polls indicated some clear trends. Table 2 shows averages for each week, as well as the election result and the differences between the election result and polls in the last week and the polls overall. Fine Gael's support went up and Labour's declined throughout the campaign, although these trends owed much to early changes. Sinn Féin's surge in December 2010 and January 2011 looked short-lived, but 'Others' showed steady progress, while

Table 1: Poll averages 2007-January 2011

	FF	FG	Labour	Green	SF	Others
Election 2007	41.6	27.3	10.1	4.7	6.9	9.3
2007	37.0	28.6	11.8	6.8	7.0	9.2
2008	35.6	29.6	11.9	6.1	8.4	8.5
2009	23.0	33.4	19.9	4.8	8.7	10.1
2010	21.6	31.7	24.5	3.4	9.6	9.2
Jan 2011	15.3	34.0	22.0	2.3	12.3	12.0

Table 2: Poll averages during the campaign

		FF	FG	Labour	Green	SF	Others
Jan 28-Feb 3	(6 polls)	16.3	33.7	22.3	1.7	12.7	13.7
Feb 4-10	(1 poll)	15.0	38.0	20.0	3.0	10.0	14.0
Feb 11-Feb 17	(4 polls)	15.3	38.3	19.5	1.5	11.0	14.5
Feb 18-Feb 24	(3 polls)	15.0	38.3	19.0	2.0	10.7	15.0
Election		17.4	36.1	19.4	1.8	9.9	15.4
Difference		-2.4	+2.2	-0.4	-0.2	+0.6	-0.4
Campaign average		15.6	36.3	20.6	1.8	11.6	14.2
Difference		-1.8	+0.2	+1.2	-0.2	+1.7	-1.0

Presiding electoral officer
Hugh O'Donnell prepares
ballots for the seven
residents on Inishfree
Island, off the Donegal
coast

Fianna Fáil was anchored around 15%.

Overall, the polls gave a fairly accurate picture of what happened, but expectations of Fine Gael winning its best ever vote were misplaced, while Fianna Fáil's collapse was not quite as great as suggested by the polls.

Common explanations for these 'errors' are firstly, that some voters deserted Fine Gael as the possibility of a single-party government became more real, and secondly, that some voters were too embarrassed to admit they would support Fianna Fáil.

Labour's campaign in the last week certainly tried very hard to alert voters to the fact that one party could find itself with an overall majority, just as Michael McDowell had done in 2002. We can explore this later with the aid of the RTÉ/Lansdowne exit poll, but campaign polls showed that not all Fine Gael voters favoured a single-party government, any more than many Fianna Fáil voters did in recent years. As for the so-called 'shy Fianna Fáil' syndrome, this is also a real possibility, but, significantly, those same polls had no difficulty finding people who admitted voting Fianna Fáil in 2007.

An internal analysis of its last poll by RED C's Richard Colwell after the election gave some support to both of these theories, but it also raised other possibilities. There were net shifts from Fine Gael to Labour and independents in the last few days, and concerns about single-party government were linked to this. A second factor was delayed awareness of local candidates, with independents gaining here, while Fianna Fáil was also helped. This analysis also indicated evidence to support the 'shy Fianna Fáil' explanation, as indeed RED C analysis had done throughout the campaign. The 'don't knows' were more likely to have voted Fianna Fáil in 2007, and were slightly more likely to vote for Fianna Fáil in 2011 than typical treatments of 'don't knows' would assume. Perhaps significantly though, the RTÉ/Lansdowne exit poll also underestimated the Fianna Fáil vote, an error that cannot be explained by the fact that people said they were undecided rather than admit a Fianna Fáil preference.

Well before the election it was evident the electorate was volatile. Fianna Fáil provided much of the stability in electoral decision-making for several generations and its collapse left much more room for uncertainty. According to the exit poll, people made their mind up much later in Election 2011, with 62% deciding during the campaign, an increase of 12 percentage points over the 1997-2007 average. Late deciders were also more likely to have voted

Labour and independent – this was particularly so when they decided in the last week.

Not only did people leave it late to decide, most changed their voting preference from 2007. In all, one in every two voters altered their behaviour from the previous election, an increase of almost 30 percentage points from the 1997-2007 average. This increase can be attributed to the exodus from Fianna Fáil. Thirty of the 48 in every 100 people who voted in both elections and who changed their preference deserted that party. Of those who changed, 17 moved to Fine Gael, 12 to Labour and 11 to independents.

The motivation for much of the movement, at least the movement from Fianna Fáil, needs little explanation. Asked what lay behind their decision on what way to vote, the exit poll's respondents were clear that it was motivated by the economy or banking crisis (30%) or anger directed against the political system or the government and politicians (36%).

There is little difference between the parties in terms of the importance of the economy, but Fianna Fáil voters were much less likely than those of other parties to emphasise anger or disappointment with politicians. We see much the same picture in responses to a question asking about people's emotional response to the "way things are going nowadays". On a four-point scale from 'not at all' to 'very', voters were most typically angry (3.3), outraged (3.1), worried (3.0 and afraid (2.8), with hopeful (2.5) edging out confident (2.1). Fianna Fáil voters were least angry (2.9) and afraid (2.5), and

most hopeful (2.7) and confident (2.3); Sinn Féin voters were most angry (3.6) and least confident (1.8).

There was some expectation that this election would be different to previous elections, with more emphasis on policy and less on personality, and more concern with the national and less with the local. The evidence suggests that such change was generally muted. Asked to choose between several factors in terms of what was most important in their decision, voters chose between the policies set out by the parties (41%) and "choosing a candidate to look after the needs of the constituency" (37%) over choosing the set of ministers who would form the government (12%) and choosing who would be Taoiseach (3%). This is in marked contrast to previous exit poll findings in some respects. Typically, the choice of Taoiseach is more important (22% in 2007) and policies less so (24% in 2007), suggesting that issues were more important this time. However, the percentage picking "candidate" is almost unchanged from the 39% in 2007.

It is striking that Fianna Fáil voters, who were more inclined to stress national factors in the past, were this time much more likely (with voters for independents and other parties) to stress the importance of the local candidate. This adds weight to the possibility that Fianna Fáil's incumbents did serve to mitigate the anti-Fianna Fáil swing.

This election seemed to offer clear policy differences between many of the parties on major issues, for instance in the balance of spending cuts

"Not only did people leave it late to decide but most changed their voting preference from 2007"

and tax increases in addressing the deficit. Fine Gael was strongest on its emphasis on spending cuts while Labour and Sinn Féin emphasised increases in taxes. Fianna Fáil fell between Labour and Fine Gael. However, these policy choices were not clearly reflected in comparisons between voters for different parties, a result that undermines a conclusion that policy really did motivate vote choice for most people. While Fine Gael voters clearly favoured public spending cuts over tax increases (by +16), Fianna Fáil (-17), Labour (-15) Independents/Others (-9) and, perhaps surprisingly, Sinn Féin voters (-1) all favoured tax increases.

People may vote for candidates or parties but at least since 1989 governments have been coalitions. This raises the question of whether people got what they voted for. In 2007, when the Greens entered government, and in 1989 when the PDs came to power, and most notoriously when Labour joined a Fianna Fáil government in 1992, many claimed that it was not what they voted for. It is hard to make that assertion this time. Firstly, we might conclude that people voted to get rid of the Fianna Fáil/Green government and this was achieved. Secondly, a Fine Gael/Labour coalition was the option most popular with voters, with 41% opting for this as against Fine Gael alone (18%) and Fine Gael with independents (12%). Thirdly, this was clearly not unexpected. Labour campaigned in the last few days for precisely this outcome. Finally, both Fine Gael and Labour voters indicated support for this option by giving their lower preferences to the other party. According

The stack of ballots for Fine Gael's Enda Kenny as ballots are sorted in Castlebar

to the exit poll, Fine Gael voters who voted for a second party were more inclined to transfer to Labour than anyone else, with 31% opting for Labour as their next preference and 21% for an independent candidate. Labour voters were not quite as enthusiastic, but while 32% chose an independent, 31% picked a Fine Gael candidate as their next preference.

Indeed, it was partly the support extended across these two parties that helped them to achieve many more seats than might have been expected simply on the basis of first-preference votes.

Fianna Fáil, on the other hand, struggled in this respect, winning few transfers from other parties – only 8% of voters gave that party a second preference after supporting another party or an independent.

With just 20 seats, Fianna Fáil finds itself the largest opposition party in the new Dáil, but for the first time provides only a minority of opposition deputies. Voters in 2011 were fairly pessimistic about the party's chances of returning to major party status anytime soon, with 56% believing Fianna Fáil will not lead a government in the next 10 years, as against 37% who believe it will. Most of the optimists are current Fianna Fáil voters, but a majority of those who voted for the party in 2007 and deserted this time do not expect such a resurgence anytime soon, if at all.

Michael Marsh is Professor of Comparative Political Behaviour and pro Vice-Provost/Chief Academic Officer at TCD

Campaign Diary 2011

Day 1 – Tuesday, February 1

14.35

In his final address, Brian Cowen tells the chamber his time as Taoiseach has been a period of great "trial and test" before leaving the Dáil for Áras an Uachtaráin to advise President Mary McAleese to dissolve the house and to summon the 31st session to meet at 12pm on Wednesday 9 March.

14.49

Fine Gael leader Enda Kenny begins his speech to the Dáil, saying his party would "make Ireland the best small country in the world in which to do business".

15.00

In his address to the Dáil, Labour leader Eamon Gilmore says the election is all about "change".

16.05

The government confirms the election will be held on Friday 25 February.

19.00

Campaigning gets underway with Fine Gael leader Enda Kenny outlining his party's election strategy containing "five simple points".

19.18

Fianna Fáil leader Micheál Martin tells the media there are three pillars to the party's election campaign – reduction in public spending, job creation and political and parliamentary reform.

19.38

Labour Party leader Eamon Gilmore says that for the first time in the state's 90-year history there is an opportunity to have a Labour-led government.

Fianna Fáil launches its election campaign

Day 2 – Wednesday, February 2

09.20

The Labour Party launches its election campaign at the Guinness Storehouse in Dublin, with a promise not to increase income taxes on people earning less than €100,000 a year if elected to government. Gilmore says: "For the first time ever in the 90-year history of this state, we can elect a government which is led by neither Fianna Fáil nor Fine Gael. For the first time people have a choice – to elect a government led by Labour."

10.00

At the launch of Fianna Fáil's election campaign, party leader Micheál Martin claims: "The fundamental problem with the plans that Fine Gael proposed yesterday is that Labour, their prospective partner, is opposed to so many of them. Ireland cannot afford a tug-of-war government."

10.15

Sinn Féin leader Gerry Adams on Labour's electoral ambition: "It doesn't make sense to me how any party which is progressive could have a vision which is as narrow and as stunted as that which is about putting Fine Gael into power."

13.15

United Left Alliance candidate Joe Higgins claims the reduction in the minimum wage marks the start of an "employers' offensive" on workers' rights and people on social welfare.

18.00

Fine Gael Finance spokesperson Michael Noonan confirms the party's proposals for balancing the budget by 2016 was for a ratio of cuts to taxes of a little over 2:1. He says: "To claim we are moving towards Labour is not true. Labour has said it wants 50% cuts and 50% taxes. There remains a big difference between the approaches of the two parties."

Day 3 – Thursday, February 3

10.20

At the Fianna Fáil news conference, Brian Lenihan says Fine Gael and Labour accepted the universal social charge and it will not be withdrawn by both parties if they are in government.

10.41

The Green Party launches its campaign at the Sugar Club. John Gormley tells reporters the party hopes to contest every constituency – 39 candidates have already been nominated. "Realistically we will be targeting the last seat in nine constituencies," Gormley says.

11.43

Fine Gael launches its Five-Year Plan to get Ireland working. Not to be outdone, Sinn Féin reveals a 10-point plan on job creation.

WHAT? THEY ASKED FOR CUTS!

Graffiti in Cork

11.53

twitter Bryan Dobson: "Standing room only at the Labour news conference – the prospect of power is a media magnet."

12.02

Eamon Gilmore says the first choice Irish voters have to make in this election is whether our budgets are decided in Frankfurt or by the democratically elected government of the Irish people. "It's Frankfurt's way or Labour's way."

17.00

In Limerick, Eamon Gilmore says achieving a 3% deficit by 2015 is "not reasonable" as there has to be time to allow the economy to grow.

17.57

Paschal Sheehy reports that an opinion poll published in today's *Kerry's Eye* indicates Fianna Fáil could be without a seat in Kerry after the election for the first time in the party's history.

Day 4 – Friday, February 4

08.17

A draft of the Fine Gael policy on the Irish language says it is committed to overhauling the way Irish is taught and it would not be compulsory after Junior Cert level under Fine Gael plans.

10.46

Asked why a political donation from Owen O'Callaghan of IR£5,000 ended up in his wife's bank account – Micheál Martin says there is no issue and the funds were spent on the election campaign within weeks.

11.11

Fine Gael proposes a mortgage interest relief scheme which would cost €120m.

11.34

Michael Noonan says: "Nama is not working, but it is so complicated, dealing with it is like unscrambling an egg."

11.52

On the renegotiation of the EU/IMF deal, Ruairí Quinn says: "Labour is not saying it will go back and unilaterally tear up the deal... some aspects of the deal are not negotiable."

12.50

People Before Profit says the overall United Left Alliance is looking at "eight or nine seats on a good day".

15.15

Commenting on forthcoming leaders' debates Enda Kenny says: "I will not participate in any programme that Vincent Browne has anything to do with."

16.26

Further to Kenny's remarks, the Broadcasting Authority of Ireland says a complaint about a comment made by Vincent Browne has not been upheld.

16.26

Gerry Adams says Sinn Féin will support a Labour minority government if they can agree a programme for reform.

Eamon Gilmore canvasses in The Square Shopping Centre in Tallaght, Dublin.

Sinn Féin president Gerry Adams and Sinn Féin candidate Cllr Peadar Tóibín with Liam Bowland and Janet Oyetoro at the Navan Travellers Workshop in Navan, Co Meath

Day 5 – Saturday, February 5

11.20

Fine Gael's Richard Bruton announces the party would introduce a ministerial car pool system, which he says would cut costs by half.

11.58

Fine Gael leader Enda Kenny dismisses any attempt by European leaders to get changes to Ireland's corporate tax rate onto the reform agenda.

13.02

Green Party candidate for Dún Laoghaire Ciaran Cuffe calls for all Irish citizens who have emigrated to retain the right to vote in national and local elections and in referenda for up to five years.

13.08

Fianna Fáil leader Micheál Martin says: "Fine Gael's plan to give mortgage interest relief to those experiencing negative equity must be properly costed."

14.05

TV3 presenter Vincent Browne says he will step aside as moderator of a three-way leaders' debate if Enda Kenny agrees to take part.

18.00

The *Sunday Business Post*/Red C poll shows Fine Gael on 35%, up two points from a week ago. Labour is on 22%, up one. Fianna Fáil is up one to 17%, Sinn Féin unchanged on 13%, the Greens are also unchanged on 2%, while independents and others drop four to 11%.

Green Party leader John Gormley canvasses in Donnybrook, Dublin 4

Day 6 – Sunday, February 6

12.03

Labour releases its plan for a strategic investment bank. Finance spokesperson Joan Burton says: "It is part of our vision for an economy driven by trade and innovation, rather than the casino economy created by Fianna Fáil."

12.12

At Sinn Féin's campaign launch, it announces it will run 41 candidates in 38 constituencies.

13.10

Speaking on RTÉ's *This Week*, Labour leader Eamon Gilmore says the EU-IMF deal is crippling the Irish economy and putting the entire burden on the Irish taxpayer. He says he wants a mandate to walk into the European Council to demand the rescue deal be renegotiated.

13.50

Green Party leader John Gormley tells RTÉ's *This Week* there was more reform in the last government than in any other.

15.25

Fine Gael health spokesperson Dr James Reilly says there will be 8,000 redundancies under his party's plan to abolish the HSE.

16.00

Enda Kenny says his schedule means he cannot take part in TV3's proposed three-way leaders' debate.

Fine Gael's Richard Bruton speaking at a press conference during his party's election campaign

Day 7 - Monday, February 7

07.41

Fine Gael leader Enda Kenny confirms that proposals will be included in the party's election manifesto to provide for the abolition of Irish as a compulsory subject in the Leaving Certificate examination.

09.12

The Green Party outlines policies aimed at helping small business owners.

10.28

twitter Shane Ross: "Eamon Ryan drops in to my office to say that our posters are covering his name on his. Sorry Eamon, will investigate. Good guy."

11.13

Fine Gael says it will abolish severance pay for ministers leaving office and ban corporate donations if elected. Enda Kenny also says his party will reduce the Taoiseach's salary to €200,000.

11.31

Labour publishes political reform proposals including a convention to draw up a new constitution and a whistleblower's law.

11.37

Speaking about the following night's leaders' debate, Enda Kenny says: "Fianna Fáil should spend their time not in TV studios but out and about meeting people and seeing the scale of destruction that has befallen the country."

11.41

Fianna Fáil publishes its election manifesto.

14.48

Labour says it intends to replace tribunals with investigative committees.

Independent candidate for Dublin South East Dylan Haskins takes a break

Day 8 - Tuesday, February 8

09.44

Today is the last day for people not yet registered to vote to get their names on the supplementary register.

10.17

The Green Party launches its jobs plan at the IFSC.

11.08

twitter Bryan Dobson: "Someone in a chicken suit has just arrived at the FG news conference – one of the hazards of holding it outside."

11.10

Fine Gael says it will increase the number of schoolteachers by 2,500.

11.42

Labour proposes universal primary care insurance for every citizen.

13.38

On a lunchtime walkabout in Dundrum Town Centre, Fianna Fáil leader Micheál Martin faces criticism from a number of people over the government's record.

19.49

Speaking at a town-hall style meeting at a hotel in Carrick-on-Shannon, Fine Gael Leader Enda Kenny says a lot of time has been wasted talking about leadership debates during the past week.

20.00

The TV3 leaders' debate gets underway between Micheál Martin and Eamon Gilmore.

20.10

The debate ends after covering topics from job creation to ministerial "golden handshakes".

21.16

Sinn Féin leader Gerry Adams says the debate was lamentably short on solutions.

21.58

In Carrick-on-Shannon, a heckler called 'Bobby' prompts an angry reaction from the crowd after continually shouting and repeatedly refusing to sit down. It later turns out to be a prank.

People Before Profit candidate for Dún Laoghaire Richard Boyd Barrett talks with Clare Callaghan

Day 9 - Wednesday, February 9

10.40

Green Party spokesperson Dan Boyle criticises Fine Gael and Labour for a "dishonest and cavalier" attitude to Irish voters. He says their numbers simply do not add up.

11.21

Leo Varadkar starts a Fine Gael news conference by admitting he probably shouldn't be in politics as he's "not really a people person".

12.00

Nominations for Election 2011 close. Initial indications show more than 470 candidates will contest the election. For the first time since its foundation, Fianna Fáil is not fielding enough candidates to allow it to have a majority. There are at least 170 independents/other candidates in this election.

12.03

Commenting on last night's debate, Labour's Roisin Shortall says: "What was remarkable about Micheál Martin's performance on last night's debate was his attempt to reinvent himself."

12.54

Labour's Eamon Gilmore says he will not be changing tactics or adopting a more aggressive approach for the next leaders' debate.

13.51

Enda Kenny reiterates that Fine Gael will not give any more money to Anglo Irish Bank.

18.10

The total number of people on the electoral register is 3,161,854. This compares to 3,066,517 on the register in 2007 – a rise of 95,337. This does not include additions to the supplementary register.

Day 10 – Thursday, February 10

08.13

A deputy leaders' debate takes place on RTÉ's *Morning Ireland* featuring Mary Hanafin, James Reilly and Joan Burton.

9.50

A commercial plane with 12 people on board crashes while trying to land at Cork Airport. Six people die in the crash, another six are injured.

10.00

It is confirmed that a record number of 564 candidates have declared in the general election. This year's election also sees a record number of independent and other party candidates at 233.

11.10

Fianna Fáil leader Micheál Martin and Labour leader Eamon Gilmore offer their sympathies to the families of those killed in the plane crash at Cork Airport.

11.25

Fine Gael leader Enda Kenny says his prayers are with those who lost their lives in Cork.

Leo Varadkar, Richard Bruton and Fine Gael leader Enda Kenny at the launch of the party's fiscal plan

11.41

Fine Gael launches its fiscal plan. It proposes cutting the 13.5% rate of VAT for two years by at least 1.5% for a range of labour-intensive industries.

11.51

Sinn Féin launches its manifesto and promises more frontline healthcare workers, fewer bureaucrats and an end to the "two-tier" health system.

12.37

The Socialist Party launches its general election manifesto, putting job creation and a rejection of the IMF/EU deal at the centre of its policies.

12.45

A number of candidates standing in Cork South-Central, the constituency in which Cork Airport is located, have cancelled their canvassing for the day.

16.09

The United Left Alliance launches its manifesto.

Day 11 – Friday, February 11

09.15

"Brian Lenihan has shown once again that he cannot be trusted on the banks," says Fine Gael Finance spokesperson Michael Noonan. He makes the comments in response to Lenihan's decision to delay the recapitalisation of the banks.

10.15

Fine Gael leader Enda Kenny declares his intention is "to keep Fianna Fáil out of government for 10 years".

11.44

Fine Gael proposes setting up a €100m fund for new start-up companies if in government.

11.46

Labour Party publishes its election manifesto at the Aviva Stadium, promising economic, political and social reform.

13.20

"This election is a three-way contest and Labour's objective is to lead the next government," Eamon Gilmore tells RTÉ's *News At One*.

14.15

The Green Party says it will reduce the number of TDs from 166 to 120.

14.57

The Green Party launches its manifesto, promising that if returned to government, it will hold a referendum on creating a new constitution.

17.52

Fine Gael says it is not prepared to guarantee a 100% reversal of the threatened student nurses' pay cut in the course of an election.

Labour Party leader Eamon Gilmore launches the party's manifesto at the Aviva Stadium, Dublin

Independent candidate Cllr Mannix Flynn canvassing in Ranelagh

Day 12 – Saturday, February 12

11.36

Fine Gael outlines its plans to abolish or rationalise 145 state agencies, boards, committees, taskforces and public bodies. Leo Varadkar says the plans would "help us hit the deficit reduction target without affecting frontline services".

11.48

Fianna Fáil leader Micheál Martin claims promises being made by other parties undermine their commitment to tackling the deficit. He says proposals Fine Gael has made on health will never materialise as they are "massively expensive".

12.27

Speaking on the campaign trail in Swords, Eamon Gilmore says Fine Gael's criticism of the Labour Party's economic proposals was a case of "Fine Gael siding with the bankers again rather than siding with the taxpayers".

16.35

Sinn Féin president Gerry Adams says the current row between Fianna Fáil, Fine Gael and Labour is a phoney debate.

17.26

The latest Red C Poll in tomorrow's *Sunday Business Post* indicates that Fine Gael could be on course to form a government on its own.

Day 13 – Sunday, February 13

11.00

Fine Gael leader Enda Kenny outlines his party's political reform plans, including a referendum to be held within the first year of government.

11.15

Bookmaker Paddy Power halves the odds on Fine Gael getting an overall majority.

11.35

Launching its education manifesto, Sinn Féin's Aengus Ó Snodaigh says the party is committed to a "proper and free" education system.

12.12

The Workers' Party launches its manifesto, saying it will "completely change the political system which it believes has allowed corruption, cronyism and economic ruin to flourish".

13.30

Enda Kenny tells RTÉ's *This Week* he will not go past the planned €9bn in adjustments over the next four years, as that was "absolutely more than enough austerity" for Ireland.

16.10

Following the announcement that Enda Kenny will meet with German Chancellor Angela Merkel tomorrow, Micheál Martin says it's a photo opportunity to make the Fine Gael leader "look prime ministerial".

17.28

Labour's Joan Burton says Fine Gael's Fiscal Strategy, published last week, contains no economic forecasts. She says Enda Kenny on *This Week* "once again ran away from questions about the blank pages in his economic strategy".

17.46

The Fianna Fáil leader says he does not agree with the Fine Gael plan to make Irish optional for the Leaving Cert. Micheál Martin says it would have a very negative impact on the Gaeltacht.

Enda Kenny and Michael Noonan at the launch of Fine Gael's manifesto

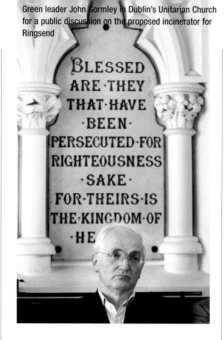

Green leader John Gormley in Dublin's Unitarian Church for a public discussion on the proposed incinerator for Ringsend

BLESSED ARE THEY THAT HAVE BEEN PERSECUTED FOR RIGHTEOUSNESS SAKE FOR THEIRS IS THE KINGDOM OF HE

Day 14 – Monday, February 14

11.09

At its policy launch for small and medium enterprise Fianna Fáil promises it will appoint a Minister of State for Small Business.

11.44

Launching the Labour Party's Jobseeker proposals, Ruairí Quinn says his party would establish a national service to replace FÁS.

12.53

Enda Kenny's 40-minute meeting with German Chancellor Angela Merkel in Berlin ends. He raised the issue of Ireland's corporate tax rate, the interest rates on the Irish bailout and burden sharing among senior bond holders.

15.10

Over 500 students protest outside Leinster House against proposals to end compulsory Irish in the Leaving Certificate.

The five main party leaders at RTÉ's leaders' debate, which is chaired by Pat Kenny

15.45

Finance Minister Brian Lenihan says there is "no lee-way"' to renegotiate the EU-IMF deal and to suggest it is possible is "very misleading".

15.53

Olli Rehn rejects suggestions of a unilateral Irish renegotiation of the EU/IMF deal, but indicates the interest rate could be changed. The EU Commissioner for Economic and Monetary Affairs says he is watching the Irish election "very closely".

Day 15 – Tuesday, February 15

10.31

Figures for RTÉ's five-way leaders' debate are released revealing it attracted an average audience of 961,000, an overall audience share of 59.85%.

10.38

At Fianna Fáil's news conference, Micheál Martin says: "Gerry Adams should come clean and admit his membership of the IRA".

11.14

Fine Gael publishes its election manifesto, which Enda Kenny says is about transforming Ireland.

11.20

An *Evening Herald* opinion poll in Dublin shows Labour in the lead in the capital, followed by Fine Gael, with Fianna Fáil in fourth place behind Sinn Féin.

11.37

Labour launches its plan for the rural economy.

11.47

Fine Gael Finance spokesperson Michael Noonan says "AIB should be put on the market and sold off".

14.15

John Gormley says there is potential for agreement between his party and Fine Gael to form a government after the election.

14.52

twitter David McCullagh: "Reading the Fine Gael manifesto. Page 43: 'FG will tackle leaking septic tanks'. Now you know who to call!"

14.58

Fine Gael says it is going to use the National Pension Reserve Fund to pay for a job stimulus, which will cost €7bn.

21.05

Fine Gael retains the lead in the latest opinion poll, due to be published in tomorrow's *Irish Independent*. Fine Gael is up eight points to 28%, Labour drops one to 23%, Fianna Fáil is down four to 12%, Sinn Féin is down three, Greens unchanged on 1% and independents and others up one to 16%

Day 16 – Wednesday, February 16

10.13

Enda Kenny, Eamon Gilmore and Micheál Martin arrive to pre-record the TG4 leaders' debate.

11.25

Asked again about IRA membership, Gerry Adams says: "I wish you wouldn't ask me a question to which you know the answer. The answer is no."

11.32

Outlining of job plans continue. Fergus O'Dowd says Fine Gael will create 15,000 places to allow people to upskill, while the Greens say they want to employ 20,000 people to retro-fit one million houses.

12.11

Leaving the TG4 studios after the pre-recording of the leaders' debate, Fianna Fáil leader Micheál Martin says it went very well, that there were good exchanges and he is delighted with it.

12.16

Labour says if it were in government it would be committed to abolishing upward-only rent reviews.

12.16

twitter▶ David McCullagh: "Just bumped into a group of retiring FF TDs in the corridor of Leinster House. They looked relaxed and happy. Unlike their colleagues."

15.35

Micheál Martin says: "A Fine Gael/Labour government would have no mandate from the Irish public."

15.45

The Greens launch proposals for the reform of the Irish political system.

16.34

Enda Kenny says advertisements placed by the Labour Party in the national newspapers, which are similar to supermarket advertisements, "smacks of panic" on the part of Labour.

18.00

A Red C poll for the *Irish Farmers' Journal* suggests 60% of farmers support Fine Gael.

Day 17 – Thursday, February 17

8.50

On RTÉ's *Morning Ireland*, Eamon Gilmore defends his comments on "Frankfurt's way or Labour's way" and describing Jean Claude Trichet as a civil servant.

10.30

Speaking on *Today with Pat Kenny* about going into government with Fianna Fáil, John Gormley says "coalition was simply the best way of implementing policies".

11.16

Fine Gael publishes plans to deal with mortgage holders in difficulty, saying there's no property market just a lot of "fire sales".

12.10

Tánaiste Mary Coughlan rejects accusations she is being hidden away during this campaign. Asked if she was the "Dick Roche" of this election, she says she certainly doesn't look like him.

12.12

Joe Higgins says ordinary homes bought at the height of the property bubble should be re-valued and mortgages then based on that new figure.

12.39

"Leo Varadkar is beginning to sound like the Maggie Thatcher of Irish politics," says Labour's Róisín Shortall.

12.41

Figures show last night's three-way leaders' debate attracted TG4's highest audience so far this year. The debate was viewed on average by 132,000 people.

14.20

A single-party Fine Gael government would be worse than the previous coalition, Gerry Adams claims.

Pat Rabbitte and Brendan Howlin at the Labour Party's launch of its plan for a new constitution

Day 18 – Friday, February 18

08.34

Fine Gael leader Enda Kenny tells RTÉ's *Morning Ireland* the jobs Fine Gael plans to cut from the public sector will be "voluntary".

10.38

Asked on *Today with Pat Kenny* if Ireland is ready for an atheist Taoiseach, Labour leader Eamon Gilmore says it should not be an issue as it is a private matter.

10.44

Minister for Finance Brian Lenihan says: "Fianna Fáil's national recovery plan is the key to economic growth."

11.02

Green Party leader John Gormley calls on people not to vote for independents in the general election but to use their vote to elect a stable government.

11.15

Fine Gael unveils its 'New Era' stimulus plan "to create thousands of jobs".

12.50

Asked at a news conference where it all went wrong for Labour in relation to its 'Gilmore for Taoiseach' campaign, Pat Rabbitte says Eamon Gilmore's leadership of the party has been unrivalled.

17.51

Sinn Féin's Gerry Adams says if the Labour Party is genuinely concerned about Fine Gael's policies then it should not be willing to go into government with it.

Green Party supporters pose as independent TD Jackie Healy-Rae and Fine Gael Leader Enda Kenny after the party's press conference in Dublin

Day 19 – Saturday, February 19

10.48
Sinn Féin President Gerry Adams describes a statement by Eamon Gilmore that he would not cut TDs' salaries as "unbelievable" when TDs have more security and are better paid than most.

14.02
Campaigning in West Cork, Fianna Fáil leader Micheál Martin says he is picking up renewed energy within the party.

14.39
Members of Jean McConville's family say the decision by Gerry Adams to stand in Louth is "a slap in the face".

17.46
Gerry Adams responds to the statement saying: "Let me reject as forcefully as I can any suggestion that I played any part in the death of Jean McConville. I did not."

18.00
Sunday Independent/Millward Brown poll suggests Fine Gael is down one point to 37%, Labour is down three points to 20%, Fianna Fáil is up four to 16%, Sinn Féin is up two points to 12%, the Greens stay unchanged at 1%, while independents and others are down two points to 14%.

18.05
Sunday Business Post/Red C poll indicates Fine Gael is up one to 39%, Labour is down three to 17%, Fianna Fáil is up one to 16%, Sinn Féin is up two to 12%, the Greens are down one to 2% and independents and others have stayed the same at 14%.

Fine Gael Leader Enda Kenny is congratulated by supporters after the party's final public rally at the Aviva Stadium in Dublin

Fine Gael Leader Enda Kenny and election candidate Lucinda Creighton at the party's press conference on high-tech jobs

Day 20 – Sunday, February 20

12.35
Responding to the opinion polls over the weekend, Eamon Gilmore says around 25% of voters are undecided or say they will change their minds. He claims that will decide the outcome of the election.

13.32
Sinn Féin's Gerry Adams says a referendum should be held on the EU/IMF loans to Ireland.

15.09
Micheál Martin says it's wrong the country found out today that Enda Kenny is entitled to a teacher's pension – a lump sum of €100,000 in April and €30,000 a year – even though he only worked as a teacher for four years.

16.09
Fine Gael leader Enda Kenny addresses a crowd of more than 1,000 supporters at the Aviva stadium saying "there are five more days to this crucial election, and with one mark on the ballot paper, you decide".

16.25
Enda Kenny says he will not draw any money from his teacher's pension and challenges Micheál Martin to resign from his own teaching position in the morning.

18.47
Fine Gael's Leo Varadkar says his party is not ruling out going into coalition with the Labour Party.

20.42
In a keynote address to supporters in Navan, Co Meath, Micheál Martin says his party will be the vehicle for social and economic development. He says he is proud of Fianna Fáil's past. He says his party will fight for every vote.

21.00
Ipsos/MRBI poll conducted for the *Irish Times* shows support for Fianna Fáil is up one since its last poll to 16%; Fine Gael is up four to 37%, while Labour drops five to 19%. The Green Party is up one to 2%; Sinn Féin is down one to 11%, and independents and others are unchanged at 15%.

Day 21 – Monday, February 21

10.29
Fine Gael vehemently denies suggestions it tried to censor an interview with party leader Enda Kenny on Newstalk.

10.39
Fianna Fáil says party leader Micheál Martin "agreed to answer questions on all topics" on this morning's *Newstalk Breakfast*.

11.50
Asked about whether he told Newstalk he would not speak about his teacher's pension, Enda Kenny says he spoke to the station's Chris Donoghue on Saturday and said he would like an opportunity to speak about the campaign the party had had the week before in the west. So, he says, when they spoke, the interview was in that context.

Labour leader Eamon Gilmore campaigns in Dún Laoghaire

11.57
Enda Kenny says people have known since 1970 that he entered the teaching profession. He says he has never drawn a red cent from teaching.

14.42
Socialist MEP Joe Higgins attacks the Labour Party, claiming it has been running a dishonest campaign.

14.50
Newstalk chief executive Frank Cronin says there is no reason that Enda Kenny could not have been asked questions about his pension entitlements as a former school teacher during an interview on the radio station.

15.31
In a statement, Newstalk confirms Fine Gael set no preconditions ahead of its interview with Enda Kenny which was broadcast today.

18.50
"A monopoly of power is not desirable for the country," says Labour leader Eamon Gilmore on the *Six One News*.

Day 22 – Tuesday, February 22

10.51
Sinn Féin launches its billboard campaign on the 'consensus for cuts', saying: "Fianna Fáil, Fine Gael and Labour are one and the same."

11.15
Fine Gael says it wants to pass its proposed 'Jobs Creation Bill' by 1 July, if in government. Enda Kenny tells a news conference the young generation is the one taking punishment.

11.37
At its news conference, Labour leader Eamon Gilmore says his "abiding memory" of this campaign is that people want to vote in the way that is best for their children.

14.35
Jean McConville's daughter asks Louth voters to pose questions to canvassers acting on behalf of Sinn Féin candidate Gerry Adams.

14.38
Green party leader John Gormley acknowledges his party is facing a difficult fight in Friday's election.

18.47
On RTÉ's *Six One,* Joe Higgins says the United Left Alliance will have six TDs in the next Dáil.

20.01
The Millward Brown/Lansdowne poll for the *Irish Independent* shows Fianna Fáil down two to 14%, Fine Gael up one to 38%, Labour unchanged at 20%, Green Party unchanged at 1%, Sinn Féin down one to 11% and independents and others up two to 16%.

20.55
The three leaders arrive at RTÉ studios ahead of the debate.

21.30
The *Prime Time* debate gets underway.

23.11
The debate is dominated by banking and the economy.

Day 23 – Wednesday, February 23

08.18
A vote for Fianna Fáil is a vote for policies and the party will be a vital force in the next Dáil, claims Micheál Martin on RTÉ's *Morning Ireland.*

09.21
Eamon Gilmore says a vote for independents may produce a single-party Fine Gael government and to avoid this people should vote Labour. He says it is inevitable that parties will dispute policies.

A tourist photographs Gerry Adams while he addresses the media on O'Connell Street

10.25
On *Today with Pat Kenny*, Enda Kenny says Fine Gael wants to get as many people as possible off social welfare and into jobs. He says Fine Gael will offer retraining opportunities.

11.00
Today with Pat Kenny hears there could be as many as 80 new TDs in the next Dáil.

11.45
Micheál Martin attacks Fine Gael's Five-Point Plan, saying it is "full of blackholes".

'Primetime' presenter Miriam O'Callaghan with the three party leaders before leaders' debate

13.24
Figures show overall increase of approximately 50,000 in the supplementary register.

15.01
John Gormley says last night's debate between the leaders of the three main parties was "leadránach".

17.54
It's revealed that an average of 800,000 people watched the final leaders' debate on RTÉ's *Prime Time* last night.

19.20
Voting ends on the four smallest Donegal islands. There was a turnout of around 50% on Tory Island, but only 15 people out of 67 registered on Inishbofin cast a vote.

Day 24 – Thursday, February 24

07.30
Sinn Féin's Caoimhghín Ó Caoláin tells RTÉ's *Morning Ireland* that Sinn Féin will be "transfer-friendly" in this election.

08.27
Barry Andrews says Fianna Fáil's campaign is "very upbeat" and polls underestimate the performance of individual candidates.

09.05
In an interview on RTÉ's Raidió na Gaeltachta, Enda Kenny says Fine Gael will not be changing the status of Irish as a compulsory subject for the Leaving Cert until a full review of the curriculum has been completed.

10.25
Fianna Fáil leader Micheál Martin says the high number of retirements from the party makes this election more difficult.

10.43
On *Today with Pat Kenny*, Fine Gael's Michael Noonan says Joan Burton is dealing in "magic beans economics" is "spoofing" and "has no clue about anything". Burton replies: "You sound like you're shouting from Limerick." Noonan answers back: "Well, you're very far away."

10.54
Also on *Today with Pat Kenny*, Minister for Finance Brian Lenihan says: "I cry in my department when I see the number of contracts leaving the state… to countries with a cheaper minimum wage."

Preparing for Election 2011 at St Audeen polling station, Dublin

Prime Time reporter **Katie Hannon** looks at the role the four TV debates played in this election campaign

Word wars

W hile the novelty of televised leaders' debates got the British media into a lather of excitement in the run-up to their most recent general election, Irish voters have enjoyed these gladiatorial displays before every general election since the early 1980s.

But this year was different. Having broadcast just seven such debates in the 29 years since the practice began, Election 2011 would see four debates broadcast over just 15 days. In a turbulent political climate, all four broadcasts attracted big audiences and over 1.4 million viewers tuned into each of the two RTÉ debates at some point.

The format also got a shake-up. The previous seven contests had pitted the outgoing Taoiseach against the man who wanted his job. The Election 2011 debates reflected the utterly changed political landscape. To begin with, the outgoing Taoiseach was not actually contesting the election. The opinion polls strongly indicated that Ireland was no longer a two-and-a-half party state and consequently these debates would be more crowded affairs.

However, by the time the election campaign was underway, those same opinion pollsters were suggesting that the so-called 'Gilmore Gale' had dropped to a soft breeze and the 'Gilmore for Taoiseach' posters were looking more than a little previous. Nevertheless, the first of the four debates, broadcast by TV3 on 8 February, was to feature the leaders of the three largest parties for the first time.

In the event, the debate went ahead without the Fine Gael leader after Enda Kenny refused to take part in a debate hosted by the journalist and broadcaster Vincent Browne. The debate went ahead as a two-header, featuring the bullish newly-minted Fianna Fáil leader Micheál Martin and a more subdued Labour leader Eamon Gilmore.

The two Dáil veterans clashed on a wide range of issues ranging from the economy to the health service and political reform, but there were no major errors and no knock-out blows. The audience averaged 354,000 and peaked at 450,000. The programme was a hit with tweeters, who made it one of the top five trending topics in the world that evening.

The second debate was another first. A live studio audience of undecided voters, chosen by Millward Brown/Lansdowne, posed the questions through

"The Election 2011 debates reflected the utterly changed political landscape. To begin with, the outgoing Taoiseach was not actually contesting the election"

moderator Pat Kenny in the RTÉ *Frontline* studio. Five party leaders battled to make an impression from behind a semi-circle of podiums in a format where party handlers had insisted on strict time limits and no spontaneous applause.

All eyes were on Enda Kenny. After a number of poor media performances as opposition leader, and much scathing criticism of his decision not to take part in the initial debate, the Fine Gael leader had a great deal to prove.

He got off to a good start, winning the lottery for the prime centre position. It quickly became clear that the man who would be Taoiseach had done his homework and delivered his carefully crafted script with some panache. While he stumbled somewhat when pressed on his policy detail, he delivered a competent, polished performance which did much to maintain his party's gathering momentum.

Eamon Gilmore was dogged and strong on substance but the consensus opinion was that he failed to sparkle. Micheál Martin, an assured debater who had clearly decided that attack was the best form of defence, went after his party's main rivals for third place, Sinn Féin, with a series of barbs.

Sinn Féin's Gerry Adams struck a populist note, promising not to inflict cuts on low- and middle-income earners, while John Gormley was dignified and conciliatory but had the air of a beaten docket.

The 90-minute broadcast had an average audience of 961,000, with 1.5 million people tuning in at some point. There were also indications that interest was high among young Irish emigrants who could watch the debate live on RTÉ.ie. Tweets were followed across the world, with new peaks in countries such as Australia and Canada.

Next up was yet another first – a three-way leaders' debate as Gaeilge chaired by TG4's Eimear Ní Chonaola on 16 February. This debate, which was pre-recorded in order to be broadcast later that evening with English subtitles, attracted a big audience to the Irish language channel, with 408,000 viewers tuning in for at least some portion of the programme.

Ní Chonaola challenged the party leaders on their plans for the economy and the banks, while also pressing them on a number of issues of special interest to the station's core audience in Gaeltacht areas, such as the parties' policies on the future of the Irish language, and European policies on

Party leaders John Gormley (Green Party), Eamon Gilmore (Labour), Enda Kenny (Fine Gael), Micheál Martin (Fianna Fáil) and Gerry Adams (Sinn Féin) before the five-way RTÉ leaders debate

agriculture and fishing.

All three leaders impressed with their Irish language skills in a debate that won praise for its passionate exchanges and genuine policy engagement. Again, while Kenny may not have won on points, neither did he make any damaging mistakes.

Nothing could stop him now, bar a major meltdown in the final showdown – the debate between the three main party leaders was hosted by Miriam O'Callaghan in the *Prime Time* studio on 22 February. Despite a relatively dull election campaign, interest in these clashes remained steady. This final contest had an average audience of 800,000, with 1.4 million viewers tuning in for some portion of the programme.

After a bruising campaign it appeared that peace had broken out between Enda Kenny and Eamon Gilmore. With the outcome of the election now looking clear, the erstwhile rivals patched up their differences in a debate again dominated by banking and the economy. The Fianna Fáil leader's attempts to highlight inconsistencies in their policies were batted away by both leaders in what appeared to be a joint strategy. Kenny and Gilmore, meanwhile, combined forces to highlight Fianna Fáil's failed economic legacy.

In general, all four debates reflected the campaign in that the parties were careful not to offer up too many hostages to fortune, insisting that much would depend on the true state of the banking and public finances.

But with just days to go to Election 2011, Enda Kenny, by now a racing certainty to become Taoiseach, could dare to dream.

Asked by Miriam O'Callaghan why he believed he was the leader for these challenging times, he said he had a deep sense of conviction that he knew "how to fix what's been wrong in Ireland for so long" and give people a sense of comfort and security.

By the centenary of 1916, he concluded, he wanted to be able to say "that we've sent the IMF home, that we are borrowing only for investment and job creation, that we have the best small country in which to do business, and the best small country in which to raise a family, and finally, the best small country in which to grow old with a sense of dignity and respect".

The Tweet and other forms of social media played a prominent role in Election 2011 coverage. RTÉ online journalist **Blathnaid Healy** monitored the online traffic

Defeat by Tweet

"Ten per cent of tallies counted. All in my strong area. Loads of 2, 3, 4, which is comforting, but not enough No. 1s. I concede, with good grace," Paul Gogarty said shortly after counting got underway in his constituency of Dublin Mid-West on that sunny Saturday morning of 26 February.

But the former Green TD didn't say these words in a live television interview or across the radio airwaves; instead he tweeted the news directly to hundreds of his followers. Within minutes, the tweet was re-tweeted dozens of times, and radio stations, TV programmes, newspapers and news websites had all been informed that Gogarty had thrown in the towel.

If 2007 was the web election, 2011 was most certainly the social media election.

Long-time tweeter Gogarty wasn't the only political candidate who found a voice on the social media platform. Dr Ciarán McMahon of candidate.ie, a website that measured the number of candidates on Twitter and Facebook, said that by voting day, 326 of the 566 general election candidates had a presence on Twitter – 148,000 accounts were following the candidates, waiting for the latest dispatches of 140 characters or less.

While we heard a lot about Twitter throughout the campaign, there were actually more candidates with Facebook profiles and fan pages. Candidate.ie found that 455 candidates had Facebook accounts, which were 'friended' or 'liked' by more than 282,500 accounts.

Facebook's popularity over Twitter is hardly surprising considering that it is Ireland's favourite social media platform, with some 1.8 million individual accounts registered.

Some parties were better than others when it came to canvassing their constituents via social media. The Greens were very active on Twitter, while Sinn Féin put its time into Facebook. Bigger parties like Fine Gael and Labour invested their resources in both, while Fianna Fáil didn't pursue either to the same extent.

Of the candidates who won, few were without a social media presence, according to Dr McMahon, who added that it was a very competitive environment.

Twitter was used by candidates to speak directly to potential voters, but the candidates weren't the only ones tweeting. Ireland's 180,000 tweeters were busy talking amongst themselves about the election – or #ge11 as it was more commonly referred to. Between Tuesday 22 February, and Sunday 26 February, 85,000 tweets were sent containing the #ge11 hashtag, according to analysis from knexsy.com.

"It was incredible to see the amount of political engagement between people on social media", Stephen O'Leary of O'Leary Analytics said. On the first day of the count, O'Leary said 22,000 individual tweets were sent containing #ge11. "It's a staggering number of conversations... I didn't anticipate the sheer volume," he said.

Even before the main event, Twitter was busy with #ge11 chatter. There was a strong 'social viewing' element to each of the four leaders' debates – with tweeters commenting on Twitter using unique debate hashtags while simultaneously watching the debate live on television and online.

During the TV3 two-way leaders' debate between Eamon Gilmore and Micheál Martin, some 2,500 individual tweets were sent containing the debate's hashtag – #tv3ld. This grew for the first of the RTÉ televised debates when 3,300 tweets were sent with the #rtedeb hashtag. Interest peaked for the final leaders' debate between Enda Kenny, Gilmore and Martin – some 6,000 individual tweets contained the #rtedeb hashtag.

The level of interest in these three debates and, more importantly, the volume of tweets, meant all three trended worldwide on Twitter. Most of the Twitter traffic for these debates came from within Ireland, but there was also a large amount of activity from the US, Canada, New Zealand and Australia – probably because the debates were streamed live on the internet.

The growing size of the audience on Twitter and Facebook in Ireland, combined with the appetite for election news on social media platforms, led most news organisations to increase their social media offerings for the campaign and the count.

RTÉ established a dedicated election social media desk, which was staffed 24 hours a day, seven days a week. It re-launched the RTÉ_Elections Twitter

> "If 2007 was the web election, 2011 was most certainly the social media election"

10% of tallies counted. All in my strong area. Loads of 2, 3, 4, which is comforting, but not enough No. 1s. I concede, with good grace.

about 1 month ago from Twittelator

Gogsyi

Green TD Paul Gogarty's count day tweet

account – initially set-up for the local and European elections in 2009 – and created a dedicated Facebook elections page. YouTube, Audioboo, Wordle and other platforms were also used.

RTÉ's election Twitter account, with more than 12,000 followers, was the most re-tweeted account when it came to #ge11, and RTÉ's content was the most linked to on Twitter.

For the count weekend, RTÉ created 43 Twitter accounts – one for each constituency. These accounts were updated by RTÉ journalists on their phones and laptops from count centres throughout the country. In total, around 10,000 people followed these accounts, which gave a detailed, constituency-level view of the election.

RTÉ was not alone. The *Irish Times* set up an elections Twitter feed and used Audioboo extensively in the lead-up to voting day, while thejournal.ie used Twitter to track how much individual parties were discussed and which candidates were trending. It also set up a dedicated Facebook elections page.

While social media certainly found its footing during the election, people had an even greater number of websites to choose from than they did in previous elections. Supply of web content increased – but so did demand.

Top Five on Facebook
Michael Lowry
Mary Lou McDonald
Pearse Doherty
Willie O'Dea
Micheál Martin

Top Five on Twitter
Dan Boyle
Eamon Ryan
Enda Kenny
Joan Burton
Joe Higgins

Almost four years on from the previous election, traffic to the RTÉ website more than doubled over the count weekend – 18.95 million page impressions were served to 1.1 million browsers, while 670,000 streams were watched via the website.

Predictably, perhaps, the National Summary of Results page was the most popular page on the RTÉ website over the weekend as people browsed the overall picture before drilling down to constituency level.

Established organisations such as RTÉ thrived on the web during Election 2011, but interestingly, the gap between media outlets and blogs reduced even further. Political bloggers like Maman Poulet (Suzy Byrne) and Cian O'Flaherty (of Irishelection.com) more than held their own as mainstream election commentators – participating in radio and television coverage – while Slugger O'Toole (Mick Fealty) linked up with RTÉ to create unique web coverage.

For social media and Irish politics, #ge11 marked the end of the beginning. Social media may not have influenced the outcome in any particular constituency this time out but, according to Dr McMahon, one thing is almost certain: this was the last Irish election where politicians could chose whether or not they wanted to engage with social media.

Bryan Dobson takes readers behind the scenes at the RTÉ studios on count day

Show Time

"In this business, winners take precedence over losers"

'Still waiting" – the text message is from RTÉ's Political Correspondent David McCullagh. It is 7.30am on Saturday 26 February, election count day 2011. I had set the alarm for 7am to hear the first main radio news bulletin of the morning and, in particular, the results of the RTÉ/Millward Brown/Lansdowne exit poll conducted at polling stations across the country the previous day. The poll would give the first indication of how the people had voted. But the 7 o'clock news had no news of the exit poll.

During election campaigns, opinion polls are an addiction for political junkies; they provide little real nourishment, the effect is short-lived and quickly replaced by hunger for the next 'fix'. But the exit poll is different. It sets out to record what a voter has done rather than what they say they'll do and in the 2007 election it had proved highly accurate.

So, what was the poll saying about Election 2011? Surely David McCullagh, the political correspondent on duty in RTÉ that morning, would have the details. "Do u have the poll?" I text him. A swift reply comes back and so I just have be patient like everyone else.

Of course, the exit poll is also a bit of a 'spoiler'. Why follow the actual election results when you can get a preview over breakfast? In 2007, we knew Bertie Ahern would be Taoiseach before a single ballot box had been opened, the only question was would Fianna Fáil govern alone?

On this count morning, we can already be certain that Enda Kenny will be Taoiseach but could Fine Gael be on target to form a single-party government? The answer, delivered by the exit poll when it finally comes at 8 o'clock, is no. Fine Gael will be forming a coalition with Labour.

By mid-morning we are on the floor of Studio 4 for a final programme rehearsal before the RTÉ television coverage of Election 2011 gets underway. As Director Pat Cowap checks shots and camera angles, Pat Kenny practises with a large touch-screen monitor which will be used to illustrate some of the information from the exit poll and later to analyse the actual results.

As votes tumble out of ballot boxes in count centres across the country, in studio the countdown

begins to the start of one of the marathons of Irish broadcasting. We will be on the air from 11am until at least the early hours of tomorrow morning. Miriam O'Callaghan, Pat Kenny and I take our places, the floor manager Dara Ó Broin counts off the seconds, the opening music blasts out from speakers high above us and we are away.

After weeks of election campaigning and political spin, the day has finally arrived when we hear the verdict of the voters. Politicians, wary of speaking frankly at the best of times, can demonstrate surprising candour when it comes to discussing the election result. Perhaps weariness has kicked in (holding the party line must be an exhausting exercise) or maybe they recognise that on this day the voters have spoken and what they say must be acknowledged and respected. And, of course, you cannot argue with the figures.

And for Fianna Fáil, even at this early stage, the figures are pointing to a huge number of seat losses. On the basis of the exit polls and the tallies, former minister Noel Dempsey concedes: "It's looking pretty grim. To get a result in the low 20s would be good."

The initial trickle of tally reports is swelling. For the first time there are RTÉ television cameras and reporters at every count centre in the country, with live satellite or other links to all but a few. So the opening hours of the results programme are spent hearing from our reporters, with occasional comments from the studio guests. Sitting opposite me in the studio, former Fianna Fáil TD Seán

Ardagh says Fianna Fáil might be doing better than the exit poll suggests. Fine Gael's Deputy Director of Elections Frank Flannery doesn't disagree but also has the confident glow of someone who sees a carefully thought-through plan coming to fruition.

As the sorting and counting of votes continues, it looks likely that big political names will be tumbling before the day is over. Tánaiste Mary Coughlan, ministers Mary Hanafin and Barry Andrews, former minister John O'Donoghue and Green Party leader John Gormley are among those struggling to hold their seats.

It becomes clear that across the country Fine Gael, Labour and Sinn Féin are feasting on the carcass of Fianna Fáil. But it is also turning into Independents' Day. According to the tallies, Shane Ross has topped the poll in Dublin South but more surprisingly Mick Wallace has achieved the same in Wexford, although both will have to wait some time before those results are declared.

The distinction of being the first TD elected to the 31st Dáil goes to Joan Burton of Labour. Her result in Dublin West is announced just after 2.45pm, opening the next and most significant stage in the count process – the filling of seats.

Results are now coming in rapidly and they bring victory and defeat. Re-elected or newly elected TDs speak to us from their count centres; outgoing TDs who have lost their seats explain how they knew all along that things were not looking good.

Fianna Fáil's Mary O'Rourke comes on the satellite link from Longford-Westmeath to concede defeat but we have to cut the interview short because there is a result due from Louth, where Gerry Adams of Sinn Féin and Fine Gael's Fergus O'Dowd are both elected on the first count. In this business, winners take precedence over losers.

As the evening advances, the discussion shifts towards how the new government will be formed. Michael Noonan has already said he favours a stable government that would not have to rely on independents, which rules out a minority Fine Gael administration. Ruairí Quinn of Labour also talks of the need for stable government.

By the time the programme takes a break for the *Nine o'clock News*, fewer than a third of the Dáil seats have been filled so there are still hours (days as it turns out) more counting to come. But the overall shape of the 31st Dáil is now clear.

The lights go down on the studio floor and the opening music plays once again. The programme resumes and from behind the studio set strides a familiar figure. Settling into his seat across from Richard Crowley, Enda Kenny prepares to give his first interview as Taoiseach-elect. He promises the Irish people there will be no delay in forming the next government. "We don't have any time to lose, we don't have an hour to waste."

As the interview concludes I check my watch. It can't be that time already. A camera swings in my direction and through my earpiece I hear Pat Cowap call out: "Bryan, we've another result coming in."

RTÉ's Nuacht political editor **Ronán Ó Domhnaill** explores how Election 2011 was the election where the Irish language became a headline issue

The Irish question

O ne of the more surprising features of Election 2011 was the prominence of the Irish language, not least for those in the Irish language media who are used to ploughing a lonely furrow.

This election was different – partly because the leaders of the three main parties spoke good Irish and partly because the historic first three-way leaders' debate took place in Irish. This placed the language centre-stage in a way that hadn't happened since 1961.

Throughout the campaign, Fianna Fáil and Fine Gael were engaged in a war of words about Enda Kenny's proposal to give students the choice of opting out of studying Irish after the Junior Certificate, while the Labour Party, which eventually came out against Fine Gael's proposal, largely stayed above the fray.

Fianna Fáil was on the offensive from the start, with Micheál Martin claiming that Enda Kenny's proposal would lead "to the gradual extinction of the language". In a series of tough press releases from senior figures, the government party accused Enda Kenny of pressing an agenda that would kill the thing he professed to love.

Fianna Fáil argued that this policy would lead to a catastrophic decline in the number of students taking Irish for the Leaving Cert, as happened in the UK when the study of languages was made optional there.

The Fianna Fáil assault culminated in a press conference devoted to the issue on the Sunday before polling at which the party's deputy leader Mary Hanafin accused Enda Kenny of seeking to perpetuate an act of "cultural vandalism".

Fine Gael countered by accusing Fianna Fáil of engaging in "scaremongering and political attacks" to disguise the fact that it had no real plan for the Irish language.

One press release, from Fine Gael's Simon Harris, now the youngest member of the 31st Dáil, was directed at Tánaiste Mary Coughlan and began by tweaking the lyrics to a well-known song to read: "Oh Mary, why don't you have some sense? Don't blame teachers, for your incompetence."

But in an election where Enda Kenny often appeared immune to the brickbats of his opponents,

> "The issue dogged Enda Kenny, and it was raised with him almost on a daily basis as he stopped at different towns around the country"

his party was on the back-foot on the Irish language issue. *Nuacht* reporter Tomás Ó Mainnín, who followed Enda Kenny for the campaign's duration, said: "The issue dogged Enda Kenny, and it was raised with him almost on a daily basis as he stopped at different towns around the country."

Fine Gael claimed the party wasn't taken by surprise by the amount of coverage given to the issue, both in the media and on the campaign trail. A party spokesman said: "The status quo has failed the language and when you take up a position that offers a radical alternative that is motivated by attempting to increase the number of people speaking Irish, it is going to meet with some objections."

However, some Fine Gael candidates in Gaeltacht areas, where there were fears that moves to change the status of Irish would threaten the viability of Irish language summer colleges, felt uneasy with the proposal. Worrying about losing votes on the issue, some candidates publically expressed their dissatisfaction with the official policy of their party.

So, for the first time since 1961, when a similar proposal from Fine Gael regarding the teaching of Irish added some spark to a lacklustre campaign, the language became, to borrow from American political parlance, a 'hot-button' issue.

The question of compulsory Irish was the subject of news reports and opinion pieces and of television, radio and online debate. Several commentators, some of whom regularly seem affronted by the very existence of Irish, found it unfathomable that the issue of the teaching of Irish was given any degree of prominence at a time when the IMF had entered the country and the very future of the Irish economy was at stake.

But it was probably the extremity of the economic situation and the consequent lack of room for manoeuvre in the formulation of policy that left a vacuum filled by other issues – issues like the teaching of Irish – giving them coverage they would not normally enjoy.

So what exactly did the prominence of the Irish language in General Election 2011 mean? Did the TG4 debate help redefine attitudes to Irish and challenge lazy stereotyping and prejudice that may have hobbled the development of the language in the

past, or was it a one-off, the result of a happy coincidence where all leaders of the three major parties were fluent in the 'first official'?

What implications if any will the Irish language's brief moment in the sun during Election 2011 have for a language that is still in a very vulnerable position?

Given the seismic shift in the Irish political landscape that followed Election 2011, it is probably fanciful to imagine that the TG4 debate and the ruckus surrounding 'compulsory Irish' will be anything more than a footnote when the political history of this period is written.

There is a possibility, however, that Election 2011 will come to be seen as an important event when future histories of the Irish language are written. Head of RTÉ's *Nuacht* Michael Lally

TG4 presenter Eimear Ní Chonaola with party leaders Eamon Gilmore, Enda Kenny and Micheál Martin ahead of the first ever Irish language leaders' debate

said: "General Election 2011 will be remembered as the election where Irish language broadcasting came of age. The historic leaders' debate where the language itself became an issue was one of the highlights."

Those who care about the future of Irish will hope that this election marked a turning point in the normalisation of Irish in public discourse.

In one respect, the prominence given to the Irish language during the election had a very tangible effect. Fine Gael and Labour's Programme for Government sees a retreat from Fine Gael's position on 'compulsory Irish'.

This was one argument that Enda Kenny lost but over the course of the next Dáil, we will see if the Irish language, like Kenny, was one of the real winners of the 2011 general election.

The scale of the economic crisis and its devastating effects led to some poignant exchanges between the voter and the politician on the doorstep. Political columnist **Olivia O'Leary** was on the campaign trail to assess the public mood

The saddest election

"At the doors, the people wanted to talk, to confess how they had been taken in"

It was like a delayed funeral. The government had died a long time ago, but it still had to be buried. And it was, under an avalanche of hurt and disillusionment. People wanted to show their wounds. Candidates were clung to like therapists, held on the doorsteps for ages. People felt cheated and betrayed but what hurt even more was that many of them felt they'd been foolish.

Time and again, they broke down and cried, like the woman in Tallaght who had trusted her financial adviser and, with her husband, had remortgaged the house. Now her husband was out of work. Her daughter was ill. Her sons were emigrating. She was 61. He was 63. Their savings were gone, she said. "My son-in-law is bringing us down food. That is what we have come to." It was all there: the realisation that you had made a foolish decision; the humiliation of having to depend on the in-laws; the fear of facing into old age with most of your children gone away; the dread of losing the house and losing your status as an owner-occupier.

The dream that Fianna Fáil sold so successfully for 14 years was one of upward social mobility. Indeed, it is the dream that Fianna Fáil has always sold, and its appeal to people's proper and legitimate aspiration to better themselves has seen it almost permanently in power. Fine Gael was never too interested in shattering the existing social hierarchy and Labour sometimes forgot that the working classes don't always want to stay working class.

Fianna Fáil, instead, goes for quick growth, at almost any cost, and the builders and developers and irresponsible public spending it relied on to fuel the shameful second half of the boom brought a wave of new entrants into the middle class; people who maybe for the first time owned their own houses, went on two and three holidays a year, and had an investment property here or abroad. Never mind that the holiday flat was in Bulgaria or that the Irish home was in Cavan or Carlow and involved hours of commuting. They were properties – and property brought status.

Now all the dreams were shattered. At the doors, people wanted to talk, to confess how they had been taken in. An ordinary soldier in Dublin, on an ordinary soldier's pay, had managed to amass eight apartments in recent years, all now worth a fraction of what his mortgage implied. At door after door, it was all about the mortgage. In older estates, parents talked about three children or four children all in negative equity and you knew that these parents had probably stumped up for the deposits from savings or remortgaging of their own houses. In new estates, younger couples sagged under the weight of a mortgage twice as big as the present value of their house. Sometimes the women were working but the men were not. Formerly self-employed in the construction sector, they now couldn't claim welfare. Time and again, nicely dressed women would come to the door and whisper: "I've never been on welfare in my life before."

Saddest of all, maybe, were the parents who told how their children had emigrated last week, last month, to Australia, the US, London. The youngsters, you guessed, would be okay. It was the parents who would grieve.

Out on the canvass with Fianna Fáil politicians, you found that the day divided in two. In the afternoons, they got a fairly polite reception from older people who would point out that the party always looked after pensioners and Charlie Haughey gave them free travel. In the evening, they were meeting young people, just home from working – or not working. Some were mocking, like the two former supporters who greeted Minister Pat Carey in Finglas. "You're very cute bringing a lady with you. I heard on the radio that it's so bad some Fianna Fáil candidates are bringing babies with them." Others were white hot angry, and Minister Barry Andrews got it in the neck in Devitt Villas in Glasthule: "We got robbed. None of the banks got robbed," said a man in a neat, well-kept house. "Why should we vote for you? The highest paid didn't get hit." When Barry argued this point with him, the man listed all the cuts and increased charges his family had to face. "We put yez in. What did we get? Nothing. You shouldn't have touched social welfare. All yez want is your big money. You'll get no vote off me."

Fine Gael fought a flawless election, sticking to the focus group advice that told it to stress its simple five-point plan and also the management competence of the Fine Gael team. Following Dr James Reilly's triumphant march around Swords in the first week was like following a senior consultant on his rounds, one determined to deal with the serious outbreak of collywobbles about the Fine Gael leader.

Gillian at the Pavilions Shopping Centre in Swords told James: "I'm going to vote for you. But what about Enda?" James gave the focus-group answer, talked about Enda being a hard worker, the head of a team. "But I don't think he comes across strong enough, he doesn't tell me everything is going to be all right!" James leans over to take her hand: "Everything IS going to be all right. We are going to fix the health service, the banks and the economy." Another voter isn't sure about Enda's management skills. " We have lots of good managers," says James. "Michael Noonan, Brian Hayes, Leo Varadkar, and may I mention... myself."

A week or so later, Enda was no longer a factor, no longer mentioned on the doorsteps. People had decided to vote the Fine Gael package anyway, and support was slipping away from Labour. Ruairí Quinn, canvassing in Donnybrook, knew the truth. Labour's exuberant poll ratings in the months before the election overestimated their actual vote. Middle-class supporters who like to think of themselves as lefties pull back when it comes to their pockets, and Fine Gael had done a good job at labelling Labour as a high-tax party. "This is a conservative country," shrugged Quinn. In Donnybrook Manor, one man didn't put a tooth in it. "I wouldn't be voting for Labour," he told Quinn. "I am a property owner and you want to tax me out of existence!"

Ultimately though, most people just wanted the government out. The cold certainty with which they delivered that verdict was breathtaking. As ever, it's only when you see the election result laid out physically in the Dáil chamber that you grasp it fully: Fine Gael and Labour deputies overflowing two thirds of the seats. Then, overwhelmed by Sinn Féiners to their right, and above and on their left by a colourful and restless band of independents, there is what remains of the once proud Fianna Fáil party. You have to search now to pick them out.

They still look shocked, bewildered. But if they ever have to ask themselves why it happened, they can consult a set of election notebooks I have sitting on my desk at home, corrugated from the rainy nights of canvassing, ink running miserably off the pages, a sodden record of broken dreams.

I have never covered a sadder election.

Sligo-North Leitrim Labour Party candidate Susan O'Keeffe pictured canvassing a local woman with Knocknarea and Queen Maeve's grave in the backround

Irish elections traditionally focused on local issues. Professor David M Farrell (UCD) and Dr Jane Suiter (UCC) show how in Election 2011, party manifestos mattered

It's the policy, stupid

'Elections turn most upon local feeling and local bribery than upon great public questions, except in moments of extraordinary crisis.' Lord Palmerston (1845)[1]

In a political system renowned for its emphasis on localism, Irish elections are usually dominated by a focus on constituency campaigns and local candidates.

The common refrain throughout this book is the extraordinary nature of this election, and no more so than with regard to the unprecedented emphasis on the policy proposals of the parties – clearly demonstrating the accuracy of Palmerston's adage.

This campaign was unusual in three regards: the emphasis by the parties on their policies, as shown particularly by the launch of additional (and in some cases very detailed and closely argued) policy documents throughout the campaign[2]; the close scrutiny of the parties' policies by both the media and a range of independent experts (not least through social media outlets[3]); and (as we shall see below) the unusual degree of attention paid by voters when making up their minds on who to vote for.

Policy 'matters' for the parties

The classic understanding of a manifesto is that it represents the policy package a party offers to voters. International studies suggest that the attention manifestos devote to policy areas predicts much of the focus of subsequent government spending.

We were invited by RTÉ to come up with a way of comparing the main political parties' election manifestos in a number of key policy areas. The policy areas included in the project were chosen using an extensive RTÉ audience survey into the issues that had the greatest daily impact on the electorate[4]. After selecting 10 specific areas, we examined the party manifestos of the five parties that had representation in the 30th Dáil – Fianna Fáil, Fine Gael, Labour, the Greens, and Sinn Féin. We looked at the parties' position in each area and how each party's manifesto dealt with these policy areas. Where the party's manifesto did not deal with the policy in a particular area, other party documents were used.

The comparison of the main manifesto commitments revealed a remarkable degree of consensus. For example, all five parties agreed on

some sort of jobs stimulus, with Fine Gael largely targeting measures such as tax incentives and Vat restructuring. Labour, on the other hand, focused on a €500m Jobs Fund, which also made it to the Programme for Government.

What was most remarkable was the degree of overlap in the manifestos of the main policies of Fine Gael and Labour. Both parties also agreed on renegotiating the rate paid to the ESF, on renegotiating with some bank bondholders as well as reversing the minimum-wage cut. Both parties also largely agreed with the necessity for a deal for those in negative equity. Fine Gael put forward a deferred interest scheme which would allow borrowers who could pay two-thirds of their mortgage interest defer the remaining interest payments for up to five years. Labour proposed the introduction of a two-year moratorium on housing repossessions and also planned a personal debt management agency.

In fact, of the top 10 areas coded by the project in only three were there significant differences between Fine Gael and Labour. Firstly, Fine Gael called for the abolition of the HSE and splitting it into two separate bodies. Labour had a different emphasis, although not planing to abolish the HSE, it proposed to split the functions along similar lines to Fine Gael.

Secondly, the parties differed on the reintroduction of third-level fees. Labour was firmly opposed to the re-introduction of fees which it had abolished in a previous coalition. Fine Gael, on the other hand, was in favour of increasing student contributions so they would cover one-third of the cost of third-level education. The plan was to do this with the introduction of a graduate tax with the eventual phasing out of registration fees.

The third area in which the parties differed was perhaps the best-known and the one which Fianna Fáil vainly tried to highlight during the campaign – the balance between tax and spending in the budget. Of all the parties, Fine Gael put the least emphasis of on taxation in its deficit-reduction strategy. It proposed that tax increases would only constitute 27% of the budget-adjustment measures to reduce

"The comparison of the main manifesto commitments revealed a remarkable degree of consensus on the majority of the issues"

the deficit. Other revenue-raising measures such as the sale of state assets and spending cuts would make up the rest of the budgetary adjustment. Labour, on the other hand, planned to close the gap in the public finances on the basis of 50:50 ratio of tax to spending cuts, and its manifesto argued: "Labour believes the composition of the adjustment should be fairer and more balanced, including fairer taxation and ongoing investments in education and other vital services.'"

Policy 'matters' for Government

Another strand of research shows that fairly large shares of manifesto pledges are implemented.[5] Checking the fulfilment of socio-economic pledges from Irish manifestos issued between 1977 and 2002, political scientist Lucy E Mansergh found that 50% of government and 45% of opposition policies were actually implemented. In a follow-up study, political scientists Costello and Thomson[6] show that implementation rates were higher following the 2002 elections, when 70% of government and 44% of opposition pledges in the socio-economic realm were (at least partially) fulfilled. Even if parties are not able (or not willing) to keep all their promises, manifestos thus guide post-electoral policy-making.

In order to ascertain the provenance of the Programme for Government, we ran it through Turnitin, a software package designed to catch plagiarism. This revealed that some 51% of the

Programme for Government was cut and pasted from the relevant manifestos with small sections emanating from the parties' websites and a few other sources. The section on the economy consisted of much new material but where it came from a manifesto it was primarily Fine Gael's. Exceptions to this pattern included Labour proposals for a pool of credit to be made available to fund small and medium businesses, to dispose of the public stakes in the banks, to introduce a bank levy, undergo a review of state support to banks and to establish a Strategic Investment Bank.

On the other hand, the vast bulk of labour market policy came directly from the Labour manifesto, as did most of the proposals on increasing exports. The section on innovation and commercialisation was more mixed, with Fine Gael's 'digital island' and innovation fund and IP protocol making an appearance, while Fine Gael proposal provided the bulk of the text for supporting SMEs. Green jobs, tourism, international education and social enterprise were covered equally by both parties. 'New Era', unsurprisingly, was a Fine Gael only section, while fiscal policy was largely new material, no doubt decided during the negotiations. The section on political reform was again predominately Fine Gael's, with Labour proposals on Freedom of Information, the Official Secrets Act and post public sector employment all making an appearance along with the party's proposal for an Investigations, Oversight and Petitions Committee. The section on more effective

Labour candidate for Dublin South East Kevin Humphreys (right) celebrates his election with Ruairí Quinn at the RDS count centre

financial scrutiny was also reasonably evenly divided, while the section on the EU came from Labour documents.

Public-sector reform was almost completely Fine Gael policy, with the exception of a few details on performance management and development. Interestingly, health was largely new text, with the exception of the sections on mental health and bio ethics which reflected the manifestos of both parties. On education, text from both parties featured prominently with Labour having a slight edge with its policies on third-level reform, patronage, literacy and outcomes all featuring. On the other hand, playing to its traditional concerns, justice and law reform was predominately Fine Gael text, while equality and social protection was largely Labour. All other areas including planning, housing, the environment, communications and children were all more or less evenly divided.

Policy 'matters' to voters, too

Despite the increasing prominence of manifestos, there is a view that most voters do not, in fact, read them and that traditionally just over 20% report voting on the basis of policy. However, during the 2011 campaign there was much debate about whether policy was featuring to a larger extent than previously.

The RTÉ/Lansdowne Exit Poll asked: "What is the main factor influencing your vote – choosing the set of ministers who will form the government; choosing who will be Taoiseach; choosing between the policies as set out by the parties; or choosing a candidate to look after the needs of the constituency." The answers revealed that in 2011 the number of people who professed to be choosing between the policies as set out by the parties almost doubled, up from just 24% in 2007 to 42%, while those choosing a candidate to look after the constituency dropped to 37% from 39% in 2007. Just 12% were choosing a set of ministers and 7%

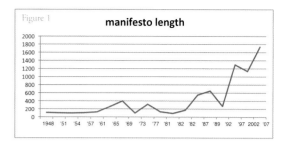

Figure 1

manifesto length

the Taoiseach, compared with 12% and 22% in 2007. It thus appears that many who had previously voted on the basis of who would be Taoiseach in 2007 had now changed their stated view to choosing between policies[7] (See Figure 2).

The patterns revealed here among different party's voters are illuminating. Some 50% of Fianna Fáil voters said they would choose a local candidate to look after their constituency with only 27% deciding on policy. This pattern was reversed for Fine Gael

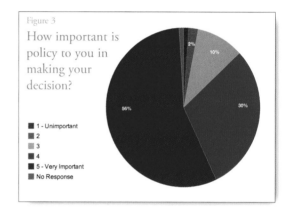

Figure 3

How important is policy to you in making your decision?

- 1 - Unimportant
- 2
- 3
- 4
- 5 - Very Important
- No Response

voters, with 29% voting on the basis of a local candidate and 45% choosing between policies. Labour party voters were similar, with 32% voting for a local candidate and 48% on policy and despite the 'Gilmore for Taoiseach' campaign message, only 5% said they would vote on the basis of who would be Taoiseach. Sinn Féin and independent voters remained more persuaded by local factors than policy.

Similar patterns were found in a poll run by the authors on the RTÉ website underneath the comparison of the party manifesto positions. Some 86% of the respondents to this survey said that policy was either important or very important to them in making their decision while some 74% (See Figure 3) said party was more important than the candidate in making their decision on who to vote for.

In terms of specific policies, unsurprisingly it was the economy which concerned most voters, with 49% reporting in the exit poll that this was the prime factor influencing their vote. This compared with just 35% who felt angry or let down and just 2% who said they voted for tactical reasons. The largest part of this was on managing the economy at 17% followed by the banking crisis at 13%,

Figure 2

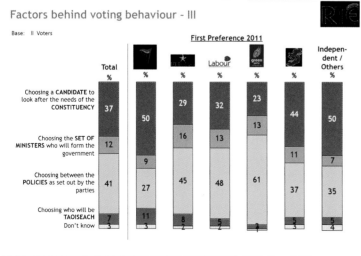

Factors behind voting behaviour - III

Base: ll Voters

First Preference 2011

unemployment at 6%, pay cuts at 5% and higher taxes at 2% and emigration at just 1%. Indeed, the economy was the prime consideration of a plurality of Fianna Fáil, Fine Gael and Labour voters.

In short, policy 'mattered' in Election 2011

This was the most unusual of elections in a number of respects, and certainly with regard to the prominence given to the policies of the competing parties. Ireland famously stands out from its European neighbours in having elections focused on local candidates and local concerns. But not on this occasion. Election 2011 saw great effort by all the parties to put out their policy stalls in detailed manifestos and other supporting policy documents. These policies were pored over by all the media – including a detailed analysis on the RTÉ website. And, as we have seen, the policies played an especially significant role in determining voter choice.

Notes
1. From *Palmerston: A Biography* by David Brown, Yale University Press, 2011. The quote was picked out by former Fianna Fáil minister of state Martin Mansergh in a book review published in the *Irish Times* on 15 January 2011.
2. See for example Fine Gael's *New Politics, Reinventing Government, FairCare* and *NewEra* documents as well as Labour's *Plan for Open Government* and *Plan for Children*
3. One example was the www.reformcard.com initiative with which we were involved to score the parties' manifestos on their political reform proposals.
4. The RTÉ audience survey was carried out from 28 January to 1 February inclusive and a total of 1,207 people completed the survey. The effective sample size was 611. The margin of error was +/- 4%. We are grateful to Stephen Quinlan and Mark Canavan for helping us to code the parties' manifestos.
5. See Lucy E Mansergh and Robert Thomson. 'Election Pledges, Party Competition and Policymaking.' *Comparative Politics* 39 (2007): 311-29.
6. See Rory Costello and Robert Thomson, 'Election Pledges and their Enactment in Coalition Governments: A Comparative Analysis of Ireland', *Journal of Elections, Public Opinion and Parties* 18 (2008): 239-56.
7. From the RTÉ Landsdowne 2011 Exit Poll.

Presiding electoral officer Hugh O'Donnell and Garda Ronan McNamara carry the ballot box from the ferry on Inishfree Island

Number Cruncher:
Sean Donnelly's Results Analysis

Candidates 2011 - 1989

Party	2011 Cands	2011 % Total	2007 Cands	2007 % Total	2002 Cands	2002 % Total	1997 Cands	1997 % Total	1992 Cands	1992 % Total	1989 Cands	1989 % Total
FG	104	18.34%	91	19.32%	85	18.36%	90	18.60%	91	18.88%	86	23.18%
LB	68	11.99%	50	10.62%	46	9.94%	44	9.09%	42	8.71%	33	8.89%
FF	76	13.40%	107	22.72%	106	22.89%	112	23.14%	122	25.31%	115	31.00%
SF	41	7.23%	41	8.70%	37	7.99%	15	3.10%	41	8.51%	14	3.77%
ULA	20	3.53%										
SP			4	0.85%	5	1.08%	5	1.03%				
GP	43	7.58%	44	9.34%	31	6.70%	26	5.37%	19	3.94%	11	2.96%
WP	6	1.06%	6	1.27%	8	1.73%	7	1.45%	18	3.73%	23	6.20%
CS	8	1.41%	8	1.70%	23	4.97%	8	1.65%				
PD			30	6.37%	20	4.32%	30	6.20%	20	4.15%	35	9.43%
SW					7	1.51%	4	0.83%				
DL							13	2.69%	20	4.15%		
Others	201	35.45%	90	19.11%	95	20.52%	130	26.86%	109	22.61%	54	14.56%
Total	567	100.00%	471	100.00%	463	100.00%	484	100.00%	482	100.00%	371	100.00%

Candidates include outgoing Ceann Comhairle when returned automatically

2011 Number of seats won per party per constituency

Party	4 Seats	3 Seats	2 Seats	1 Seat	0 Seats	Total	Seats
FG	1	4	23	14	1	43	76
LB			6	25	12	43	37
FF			2	16	25	43	20
SF				14	29	43	14
Others			2	15	26	43	19
Total	1	4	33	84	93		166

Parties highest and lowest % vote 2011

Party	Highest	Constituency	Lowest	Constituency
FG	64.96%	Mayo	16.75%	Dublin North West
LB	43.15%	Dublin North West	4.91%	Mayo
FF	28.01%	Cork South Central	9.42%	Dublin South
SF	32.97%	Donegal South West	3.64%	Dublin South East
ULA	21.32%	Tipperary South	0.76%	Laois-Offaly
GP	8.48%	Dublin North	0.36%	Mayo
Others	42.03%	Kerry South	0.66%	Dublin West

Largest change in % vote 2011

Party	Gain	Constituency	Loss	Constituency
FG	+18.93%	Dublin Mid-West	-3.15%	Donegal South West
LB	+22.85%	Dublin North West	-2.38%	Kerry South
FF			-37.10%	Dublin North West
SF	+11.73%	Donegal South West	-3.52%	Kerry South*
GP			-8.18%	Dublin North
Others	+26.68%	Kerry South	-10.11%	Dublin South Central

*Did not contest in 2011

Election 2011

Fine Gael's top constituencies

	Constituency	Seats	1st Prefs	%	Quotas	FG Seats
1	Mayo	5	48,170	64.96%	3.90	4
2	Wicklow	5	27,926	39.61%	2.38	3
3	Cavan-Monaghan	5	28,199	39.56%	2.37	3
4	Carlow-Kilkenny	5	28,924	39.22%	2.35	3
5	Dublin South	5	26,404	36.35%	2.18	3
6	Limerick City	4	18,696	43.29%	2.16	2
7	Galway East	4	25,409	42.87%	2.14	2
8	Clare	4	24,524	42.34%	2.12	2
9	Cork South Central	5	22,225	34.70%	2.08	2
10	Wexford	5	26,034	34.46%	2.07	2
11	Laois-Offaly	5	25,032	33.75%	2.03	2
12	Cork North West	3	22,321	48.80%	1.95	2
13	Limerick	3	21,925	48.68%	1.95	2
14	Cork South West	3	22,162	48.54%	1.94	2
15	Longford-Westmeath	4	21,887	38.05%	1.90	2
16	Waterford	4	20,416	38.00%	1.90	2
17	Meath West	3	18,450	45.92%	1.84	2
18	Galway West	5	18,627	30.72%	1.84	2
19	Cork East	4	20,847	36.62%	1.83	2
20	Dublin South East	4	12,402	35.52%	1.78	2

Fine Gael's top 10 increased support

	Constituency	Seats	2011	2007	Gain	FG Seats
1	Dublin Mid-West	4	30.93%	12.00%	+18.93%	2
2	Limerick City	4	43.29%	25.52%	+17.77%	2
3	Dublin North	4	31.39%	14.03%	+17.36%	2
4	Meath West	3	45.92%	29.03%	+16.89%	2
5	Dublin South East	4	35.52%	18.65%	+16.87%	1
6	Wicklow	5	39.61%	23.15%	+16.46%	2
7	Kildare South	3	33.33%	17.17%	+16.16%	1
8	Meath East	3	40.87%	25.88%	+14.99%	2
9	Tipperary South	3	34.57%	21.14%	+13.43%	1
10	Cork South West	3	48.54%	36.00%	+12.54%	2

Enda Kenny casts his vote, accompanied by his daughter Aoibhinn and wife Fionnuala at St Patrick's national school in Castlebar

Labour's top constituencies

	Constituency	Seats	1st Prefs	%	Quotas	LB Seats
1	Dublin South Central	5	18,032	35.41%	2.12	2
2	Dublin South West	4	17,032	36.27%	1.81	2
3	Dublin North West	3	14,158	43.15%	1.73	2
4	Dublin Mid-West	4	13,138	30.75%	1.54	2
5	Cork East	4	17,563	30.85%	1.54	1
6	Dun Laoghaire	4	17,217	30.38%	1.52	1
7	Kildare North	4	14,979	29.24%	1.46	1
8	Dublin West	4	12,313	28.99%	1.45	1
9	Dublin Central	4	9,787	28.28%	1.41	1
10	Dublin North East	3	14,371	34.35%	1.37	2
11	Longford-Westmeath	4	15,366	26.71%	1.34	1
12	Cork North Central	4	13,801	26.47%	1.32	1
13	Dublin North	4	13,014	26.37%	1.32	1
14	Dublin South East	4	8,857	25.36%	1.27	2
15	Wexford	5	15,462	20.47%	1.23	1
16	Kildare South	3	10,645	27.82%	1.11	1
17	Cork South Central	5	11,869	18.53%	1.11	1
18	Dublin South	5	13,059	17.98%	1.08	1
19	Wicklow	5	12,087	17.14%	1.03	1
20	Limerick City	4	8,764	20.29%	1.01	1

Labour's top 10 increased support

	Constituency	Seats	2011	2007	Gain	LB Seats
1	Dublin North West	3	43.15%	20.30%	+22.85%	2
2	Dublin Mid-West	4	30.75%	10.91%	+19.84%	2
3	Dublin North East	3	34.35%	15.16%	+19.19%	2
4	Dublin North	4	26.37%	9.62%	+16.75%	1
5	Dublin South West	4	36.27%	19.99%	+16.28%	2
6	Dublin Central	4	28.28%	12.57%	+15.71%	1
7	Dublin North Central	3	22.52%	7.27%	+15.25%	1
8	Dun Laoghaire	4	30.38%	16.00%	+14.38%	1
9	Dublin South Central	5	35.41%	21.13%	+14.28%	2
10	Louth	4	19.13%	4.98%	+14.15%	1

The late Michael Bell (right), who was a Labour party TD for Louth from 1982 to 2002, celebrates the election of Labour candidate Gerald 'Jed' Nash in Dundalk

Election 2011

Fianna Fáil's top constituencies

	Constituency	Seats	1st Prefs	%	Quotas	FF Seats
1	Carlow-Kilkenny	5	20,721	28.10%	1.69	1
2	Cork South Central	5	17,936	28.01%	1.68	2
3	Laois-Offaly	5	19,860	26.78%	1.61	2
4	Galway West	5	12,703	20.95%	1.26	1
5	Cavan-Monaghan	5	14,360	20.15%	1.21	1
6	Clare	4	12,804	22.11%	1.11	1
7	Wexford	5	14,027	18.57%	1.11	1
8	Limerick City	4	9,259	21.44%	1.07	1
9	Cork North West	3	11,390	24.90%	1.00	1
10	Longford-Westmeath	4	11,197	19.46%	0.97	1

Fianna Fáil's top 10 lost support

	Constituency	Seats	2011	2007	Loss	FF Seats
1	Dublin North West	3	11.79%	48.84%	-37.05%	0
2	Meath West	3	18.13%	51.59%	-33.46%	0
3	Tipperary South	3	13.10%	46.42%	-33.32%	0
4	Donegal North East	3	17.44%	50.26%	-32.82%	1
5	Waterford	4	13.99%	46.49%	-32.50%	0
6	Dublin South	5	9.42%	41.33%	-31.91%	0
7	Dublin North Central	3	12.94%	44.02%	-31.08%	0
8	Laois-Offaly	5	26.78%	56.38%	-29.60%	2
9	Dublin Central	4	14.85%	44.45%	-29.60%	0
10	Kildare South	3	21.71%	50.37%	-28.66%	1

Sinn Féin's top constituencies

	Constituency	Seats	1st Prefs	%	Quotas	SF Seats
1	Cavan-Monaghan	5	18,452	25.89%	1.55	1
2	Donegal South West	3	14,262	32.97%	1.32	1
3	Louth	4	15,072	21.74%	1.09	1
4	Donegal North East	3	9,278	24.47%	0.98	1
5	Dublin North West	3	7,115	21.68%	0.87	1
6	Dublin South West	4	8,064	17.17%	0.86	1
7	Kerry North-West Limerick	3	9,282	20.35%	0.81	1
8	Dublin South Central	5	6,804	13.36%	0.80	1
9	Cork North Central	4	7,923	15.20%	0.76	1
10	Meath West	3	6,989	17.40%	0.70	1

Sinn Féin's top 10 increased support

	Constituency	Seats	2011	2007	Gain	SF Seats
1	Donegal South West	3	32.97%	21.23%	+11.74%	1
2	Cork North West	3	7.44%		+7.44%	1
3	Cork North Central	4	15.20%	8.16%	+7.04%	1
4	Donegal North East	3	24.47%	17.47%	+7.00%	1
5	Louth	4	21.74%	15.04%	+6.70%	1
6	Meath West	3	17.40%	11.29%	+6.11%	1
7	Dublin North West	3	21.68%	15.74%	+5.94%	1
8	Cavan-Monaghan	5	25.89%	20.01%	+5.88%	1
9	Carlow-Kilkenny	5	9.54%	3.80%	+5.74%	1
10	Laois-Offaly	5	10.83%	5.11%	+5.72%	1

Election Facts

"Fine Gael ran 104 candidates, which was the party's highest number since 1982 but well short of its highest ever, 126 in 1981"
Professor Michael Gallagher, TCD

TURNOVER OF SEATS 2011

This election delivered the highest number of retirements from any Dáil. Thirty-nine deputies retired, which was well above the previous high of 29 in June 1927. This number included the three deputies who had retired earlier but for whom the by-elections had not been held: George Lee, Fine Gael Dublin South; Martin Cullen, Fianna Fáil, Waterford; and Dr James McDaid, Fianna Fáil, Donegal North East.

Most of those retiring were from Fianna Fáil (23) with nine from Fine Gael, four from Labour, one from Sinn Féin and two independents. There was a high rate of attrition in this election with 45 outgoing deputies losing their seats, up 15 on 2007. Thus, there were 84 new TDs (49 in 2007), eight of whom were former deputies.

Fine Gael had the highest number of new members (34), with two former deputies also returned. The Labour Party gained 19 new faces, along with two former deputies. Fianna Fáil, despite its sharp decline, returned three new faces. Sinn Féin returned nine new TDs and one former deputy. The ULA got three new deputies elected along with two former members. There were eight new independent deputies returned along with former independent Catherine Murphy.

It was all change in Cork South-West and Kerry South as all three TDs returned in both three-seaters were new members. There were also three new deputies in Carlow-Kilkenny, Cavan-Monaghan, Dublin Mid-West, Dublin North, Dublin South, Dublin South-Central, Galway West, Laois-Offaly, Louth, Waterford and Wicklow. In Galway East, three of its four sitting deputies retired and it returned three new TDs. With all this change it came as no surprise that not a single constituency returned the same deputies as 2007.

Election 2011

Turnover of seats 2011

	Constituency	Seats	Outgoing TD's who did not run	Party	Outgoing TD's who lost	Party	New TD's	Party
1	Carlow-Kilkenny	5	M.J. Nolan	FF	Bobby Aylward	FF	Ann Phelan	LB
					Mary White	GP	John Paul Phelan	FG
							Pat Deering	FG
2	Cavan-Monaghan	5	Rory O'Hanlon	FF	Margaret Conlon	FF	Joe O'Reilly	FG
			Seymour Crawford	FG			Sean Conlan	FG
							Heather Humphreys	FG
3	Clare	4	Tony Killeen	FF			Michael McNamara	LB
4	Cork East	4	Ned O'Keeffe	FF	Michael Ahern	FF	Tom Barry	FG
							Sandra McLellan	SF
5	Cork North Central	4	Bernard Allen	FG			Jonathan O'Brien	SF
			Noel O'Flynn	FF			Dara Murphy	FG
6	Cork North West	3	Batt O'Keeffe	FF			Aine Collins	FG
7	Cork South Central	5			Deidre Clune	FG	Jerry Buttimer	FG
8	Cork South West	3	Jim O'Keeffe	FG	Christy O'Sullivan	FF	Jim Daly	FG
			P.J. Sheehan	FG			Noel Harrington	FG
							Michael McCarthy	LB
9	Donegal North East	3	James McDaid	FF			Padraig MacLochlainn	SF
			Niall Blaney	FF			Charlie McConalogue	FF
10	Donegal South West	3			Mary Coughlan	FF	Thomas Pringle	NP
11	Dublin Central	4	Bertie Ahern	FF	Cyprian Brady	FF	Paschal Donohoe	FG
							Mary Lou McDonald	SF
12	Dublin Mid West	4	Mary Harney	NP	John Curran	FF	Frances Fitzgerald	FG
					Paul Gogarty	GP	Derek Keating	FG
							Robert Dowds	LB
13	Dublin North	4			Trevor Sargent	GP	Brendan Ryan	LB
					Darragh O'Brien	FF	Clare Daly	SP
					Michael Kennedy	FF	Alan Farrell	FG
14	Dublin North Central	3			Sean Haughey	FF	Aodhan O Riordain	LB
15	Dublin North East	3	Michael Woods	FF			Sean Kenny	LB
16	Dublin North West	3	Noel Ahern	FF	Pat Carey	FF	Dessie Ellis	SF
							John Lyons	LB
17	Dublin South	5	Tom Kitt	FF	Eamon Ryan	GP	Shane Ross	NP
			George Lee	FG			Alex White	LB
							Peter Mathews	FG
18	Dublin South Central	5	Mary Upton	LB	Michael Mulcahy	FF	Eric Byrne	LB
			Sean Ardagh	FF			Michael Conaghan	LB
							Joan Collins	
19	Dublin South East	4			Chris Andrews	FF	Eoghan Murphy	FG
					John Gormley	GP	Kevin Humphreys	LB
20	Dublin South West	4			Charlie O'Connor	FF	Sean Crowe	SF
					Conor Lenihan	FF	Eamonn Maloney	LB
21	Dublin West*	4					Joe Higgins	SP
22	Dun Laoghaire*	4			Mary Hanafin	FF	Mary Mitchell O'Connor	FG
					Barry Andrews	FF	Richard Boyd Barrett	PBPA
					Ciaran Cuffe	GP		
23	Galway East	4	Paul Connaughton	FG			Paul Connaughton	FG
			Ulick Burke	FG			Ciaran Cannon	FG
			Noel Treacy	FF			Colm Keaveney	LB
24	Galway West	5	Michael D. Higgins	LB	Frank Fahey	FF	Derek Nolan	LB
			Pauric McCormack	FG			Brian Walsh	FG
							Sean Kyne	FG
25	Kerry North-West Limerick	3			Thomas McEllistrim	FF	Arthur Spring	LB
26	Kerry South	3	Jackie Healy-Rae	NP	John O'Donoghue	FF	Michael Healy Rae	NP
					John Sheahan	FG	Brendan Griffin	FG
							Tom Fleming	NP
27	Kildare North	4			Aine Brady	FF	Anthony Lawlor	FG
					Michael Fitzpatrick	FF	Catherine Murphy	NP
28	Kildare South	3			Sean Power	FF	Martin Heydon	FG
29	Laoighis-Offaly	5	Olwyn Enright	FG	John Moloney	FF	Barry Cowen	FF
			Brian Cowen	FF			Brian Stanley	SF
							Marcella Corcoran-Kenned	FG
30	Limerick	3	John Cregan	FF			Patrick O'Donovan	FG
31	Limerick City*	4			Peter Power	FF		
32	Longford-Westmeath	4			Mary O'Rourke	FF	Nicky McFadden	FG
					Peter Kelly	FF	Robert Troy	FF
33	Louth*	5	Arthur Morgan	SF			Gerry Adams	SF
			Dermot Ahern	FF			Gerald Nash	LB
							Peter Fitzpatrick	FG
34	Mayo	5	Beverley Flynn	FF			Michelle Mulherin	FG
35	Meath East	3	Mary Wallace	FF	Thomas Byrne	FF	Regina Doherty	FG
							Dominic Hannigan	LB
36	Meath West	3	Noel Dempsey	FF	Johnny Brady	FF	Peadar Toibin	SF
							Ray Butler	FG
37	Roscommon-South Leitrim	3	Michael Finneran	FF			Luke "Ming" Flanagan	NP
38	Sligo-North Leitrim	3	Jimmy Devins	FF	Eamon Scanlon	FF	Tony McLoughlin	FG
							Michael Colreavy	SF
39	Tipperary North	3			Maire Hoctor	FF	Alan Kelly	LB
40	Tipperary South	3			Martin Mansergh	FF	Seamus Healy	ULA
41	Waterford	4	Martin Cullen	FF	Brendan Keneally	FF	Paudie Coffey	FG
			Brian O'Shea	LB			Ciara Conway	LB
							John Halligan	NP
42	Wexford	5			Sean Connick	FF	Mick Wallace	NP
					Michael D'Arcy	FG	Liam Twomey	FG
43	Wicklow	5	Liz McManus	LB	Dick Roche	FF	Simon Harris	FG
					Joe Behan	NP	Anne Ferris	LB
							Stephen Donnelly	NP
43	Total	166						

Red: Former TD *Change in number of seats since 2007

TRANSFERS 2011

Fine Gael got the largest share of transfers in 2011 – at 28.99% down slightly on 2007 (31.29%). Labour was next with 17.73% (14.24% in 2007) of all transfers, just ahead of Fianna Fáil on 17.13%, which was down nine points on 2007 (25.78%). Sinn Féin was in fourth place with 6.95% of all transfers (3.46%). The Fine Gael internal transfer rate of 56.44% was up on 2007 (54.92%) and above 2002 (46.33%), 1997 (52.45%) and 1992 (54.42%). After internal transfers, Labour was the main recipient of Fine Gael transfers winning 12.77% with Fianna Fáil gaining 10.26%. The majority of Labour transfers (28.57%) went to Fine Gael with an internal rate of 24.71%. Fianna Fáil's internal transfer rate was 37.78%, with 18.19% going to Fine Gael, up slightly on 2007 (16.30%). The majority of Sinn Féin's transfers were non-transferrable at 26.54% (16.91%) with Labour the main beneficiary with 23.71%.

In the 2011 general election, 812,424 votes (665,516 in 2007, 589,948 in 2002 and 590,816 in 1997) or 36.59% of all votes cast were transferred while 15% were non-transferable (11% in 2007, 12% in 2002 and 1997). This level of transfers was up four percentage points on 2007 and was a reflection of the large increase in the number of independent candidates contesting this election, most of whom polled poorly and were eliminated. The net total of transfers was 688,214, or just 31% of the valid vote, which was up two percentage points on previous elections.

Parties usually get a similar share of the transfers as of the first preferences. Fine Gael got 36.10% of the first preferences (27.32% in 2007) and got 28.99% (31.29%) of all transfers and won 45.78% (30.72%) of the seats. Labour got 17.73% (14.24% in 2007) of the transfers and converted its 19.45% (10.13% in 2007) share of the first preference vote into 22.29% (12.05%) of the seats. Fianna Fail got 17.45% (41.56% in 2007) of the first preferences and 17.13% (25.78%) of the transfers and just 12% (47%) of the seats. Sinn Féin got 9.94% of the first-preference vote and 6.95% of the transfers and ended up with 8.43% of the seats.

Fine Gael did well on transfers and increased its vote by 4.59% (3.89% in 2007) to 40.69% (31.21%). All other parties and independents ended up with fewer votes at the conclusion of the counts, with independents the biggest losers with a net loss of 4.21%.

Election 2011

From	To	FG	LB	FF	SF	SP	PBPA	GP	WP	Others	Non Trans
FG	25,482	9,477	6,183	3,279	787	82	1,700	164		401	3,409
		37.19%	24.26%	12.87%	3.09%	0.32%	6.67%	0.64%		1.57%	13.38%
LB	34,815	7,685	10,080	2,899	1,538	1,607	3,110	1,980	10	2,609	3,297
		22.07%	28.95%	8.33%	4.42%	4.62%	8.93%	5.69%	0.03%	7.49%	9.47%
FF	38,415	6,683	7,009	7,494	2,319	546	281	441		3,077	10,565
		17.40%	18.25%	19.51%	6.04%	1.42%	0.73%	1.15%		8.01%	27.50%
SF	10,313	985	4,418	782				434		1,444	2,250
		9.55%	42.84%	7.58%				4.21%		14.00%	21.82%
SP	5,861	966	1,300	460	1,686		217	95		247	890
		16.48%	22.18%	7.85%	28.77%		3.70%	1.62%		4.21%	15.19%
PBPA	7,688	975	2,539	421	1,960			208		777	808
		12.68%	33.03%	5.48%	25.49%			2.71%		10.11%	10.51%
GP	24,692	8,591	4,114	3,580	924	1,924	613			936	4,010
		34.79%	16.66%	14.50%	3.74%	7.79%	2.48%			3.79%	16.24%
WP	1,391	124	384	92	268		245	38		118	122
		8.91%	27.61%	6.61%	19.27%		17.61%	2.73%		8.48%	8.77%
Others	33,841	6,807	7,944	3,608	3,052	625	1,517	1,803	68	4,322	4,095
		20.11%	23.47%	10.66%	9.02%	1.85%	4.48%	5.33%	0.20%	12.77%	12.10%
Total	182,498	42,293	43,971	22,615	12,534	4,784	7,683	5,163	78	13,931	29,446
		23.17%	24.09%	12.39%	6.87%	2.62%	4.21%	2.83%	0.04%	7.63%	16.13%

From	To	FG	LB	FF	SF	SP	PBPA	GP	Others	Non Trans
FG	20,668	10,526	1,819	2,708	1,470			425	2,509	1,211
		50.93%	8.80%	13.10%	7.11%			2.06%	12.14%	5.86%
LB	41,444	11,583	13,867	4,056	1,934			101	4,242	5,661
		27.95%	33.46%	9.79%	4.67%			0.24%	10.24%	13.66%
FF	65,335	11,530	4,485	30,252	3,719				3,400	11,949
		17.65%	6.86%	46.30%	5.69%			0.00%	5.20%	18.29%
SF	29,645	6,373	3,878	3,753	1,885			114	3,094	10,548
		21.50%	13.08%	12.66%	6.36%			0.38%	10.44%	35.58%
SP	1,821	361	353	222	398			85	189	213
		19.82%	19.38%	12.19%	21.86%			4.67%	10.38%	11.70%
PBPA	778	151	237	110	152					128
		19.41%	30.46%	14.14%	19.54%					16.45%
GP	11,236	2,601	3,343	1,817	748	22			1,292	1,413
		23.15%	29.75%	16.17%	6.66%	0.20%			11.50%	12.58%
WP	189	60	39	21	40					29
		31.75%	20.63%	11.11%	21.16%					15.34%
Others	57,069	13,908	9,825	8,519	6,023	103	37	795	8,172	9,687
		24.37%	17.22%	14.93%	10.55%	0.18%	0.06%	1.39%	14.32%	16.97%
Total	228,185	57,093	37,846	51,458	16,369	125	37	1,520	22,898	40,839
		25.02%	16.59%	22.55%	7.17%	0.05%	0.02%	0.67%	10.03%	17.90%

Munster 2011 transfer analysis

From	To	FG	LB	FF	SF	SP	GP	WP	Others	Non Trans
FG	51,744	32,841	6,255	4,620	1,578	19	38		1,958	4,435
		63.47%	12.09%	8.93%	3.05%	0.04%	0.07%		3.78%	8.57%
LB	39,754	11,589	9,781	2,975	3,487		5		5,978	5,939
		29.15%	24.60%	7.48%	8.77%		0.01%		15.04%	14.94%
FF	40,300	7,611	4,382	12,537	1,955		1		7,402	6,412
		18.89%	10.87%	31.11%	4.85%		0.00%		18.37%	15.91%
SF	19,836	2,635	7,142	2,301					3,064	4,694
		13.28%	36.01%	11.60%					15.45%	23.66%
SP	6,118	513	2,003	311	2,801					490
		8.39%	32.74%	5.08%	45.78%					8.01%
PBPA	1,552	448	454	178	360					112
		28.87%	29.25%	11.47%	23.20%					7.22%
GP	8,594	2,405	2,736	848	607	67		36	1,049	846
		27.98%	31.84%	9.87%	7.06%	0.78%		0.42%	12.21%	9.84%
WP	1,678	120	414	98	379	191			382	94
		7.15%	24.67%	5.84%	22.59%	11.38%			22.77%	5.60%
Others	46,781	12,840	9,454	5,058	3,798	317	459	88	8,379	6,388
		27.45%	20.21%	10.81%	8.12%	0.68%	0.98%	0.19%	17.91%	13.66%
Total	216,357	71,002	42,621	28,926	14,965	594	503	124	28,212	29,410
		32.82%	19.70%	13.37%	6.92%	0.27%	0.23%	0.06%	13.04%	13.59%

Connacht 2011 transfer analysis

From	To	FG	LB	FF	SF	GP	Others	Non Trans
FG	35,815	22,628	2,820	3,116	921	16	3,952	2,362
		63.18%	7.87%	8.70%	2.57%	0.04%	11.03%	6.60%
LB	30,417	10,979	2,451	3,185	3,296		4,745	5,761
		36.09%	8.06%	10.47%	10.84%		15.60%	18.94%
FF	38,233	7,330	2,015	18,581	2,182		3,928	4,197
		19.17%	5.27%	48.60%	5.71%		10.27%	10.98%
SF	25,030	5,833	4,086	2,488	1,428	141	5,774	5,280
		23.30%	16.32%	9.94%		0.56%	23.07%	21.09%
GP	3,893	869	865	483	356		1,094	226
		22.32%	22.22%	12.41%	9.14%		28.10%	5.81%
Others	51,996	17,510	7,348	8,341	4,382	33	7,693	6,689
		33.68%	14.13%	16.04%	8.43%	0.06%	14.80%	12.86%
Total	185,384	65,149	19,585	36,194	12,565	190	27,186	24,515
		35.14%	10.56%	19.52%	6.78%	0.10%	14.66%	13.22%

Election Facts

"Election 2011 was only the second time since 1927, the other being 1969, that Fine Gael ran more candidates than any other party"
Professor Michael Gallagher, TCD

Election 2011

National 2011 transfer analysis

From	To	FG	LB	FF	SF	SP	PBPA	GP	WP	Others	Non Trans
FG	133,709	75,472	17,077	13,723	4,756	101	1,700	643		8,820	11,417
		56.44%	12.77%	10.26%	3.56%	0.08%	1.27%	0.48%		6.60%	8.54%
LB	146,430	41,836	36,179	13,115	10,255	1,607	3,110	2,086	10	17,574	20,658
		28.57%	24.71%	8.96%	7.00%	1.10%	2.12%	1.42%	0.01%	12.00%	14.11%
FF	182,283	33,154	17,891	68,864	10,175	546	281	442		17,807	33,123
		18.19%	9.81%	37.78%	5.58%	0.30%	0.15%	0.24%		9.77%	18.17%
SF	88,849	17,041	21,062	9,789	3,313			689		13,376	23,579
		19.18%	23.71%	11.02%	3.73%			0.78%		15.05%	26.54%
SP	13,800	1,840	3,656	993	4,885		217	180		436	1,593
		13.33%	26.49%	7.20%	35.40%		1.57%	1.30%		3.16%	11.54%
PBPA	10,018	1,574	3,230	709	2,472			208		777	1,048
		15.71%	32.24%	7.08%	24.68%			2.08%		7.76%	10.46%
GP	48,415	14,466	11,058	6,728	2,635	2,013	613		36	4,371	6,495
		29.88%	22.84%	13.90%	5.44%	4.16%	1.27%		0.07%	9.03%	13.42%
WP	3,258	304	837	211	687	191	245	38		500	245
		9.33%	25.69%	6.48%	21.09%	5.86%	7.52%	1.17%		15.35%	7.52%
Others	185,662	49,850	33,033	25,061	17,255	1,045	1,554	3,090	156	28,566	26,052
		26.85%	17.79%	13.50%	9.29%	0.56%	0.84%	1.66%	0.08%	15.39%	14.03%
Total	812,424	235,537	144,023	139,193	56,433	5,503	7,720	7,376	202	92,227	124,210
		28.99%	17.73%	17.13%	6.95%	0.68%	0.95%	0.91%	0.02%	11.35%	15.29%

Share of transfers 1992-2011

Election	FG	LB	FF	SF	SP	PBPA	GP	WP	PD	Others	Non Trans	Total	Net Trans	Valid
2011	235,537	144,023	139,193	56,433	5,503	7,720	7,376	202		92,227	124,210	812,424	688,214	2,220,359
	28.99%	17.73%	17.13%	6.95%	0.68%	0.95%	0.91%	0.02%		11.35%	15.29%	36.59%	31.00%	
2007	208,239	94,742	171,575	23,059	3,791		39,044	402	14,288	38,736	71,640	665,516	593,876	2,065,810
	31.29%	14.24%	25.78%	3.46%	0.57%		5.87%	0.06%	2.15%	5.82%	10.76%	32.22%	28.75%	
2002	162,991	78,244	154,380	19,329	3,673		29,201	383	20,037	51,298	70,412	519,948	519,536	1,857,902
	27.63%	13.26%	26.17%	3.28%	0.62%		4.95%	0.06%	3.40%	8.70%	11.94%	31.75%	27.96%	
1997	148,776	77,619	188,531	7,175	2,270		16,306	1,979	23,661	52,874	71,625	590,816	519,191	1,788,985
	25.18%	13.14%	31.91%	1.21%	0.38%		2.76%	0.33%	4.00%	8.95%	12.12%	33.03%	29.02%	
1992	166,618	32,881	168,496	3,190			15,598	32,891	31,496	31,319	82,538	565,027	482,489	1,724,853
	29.49%	5.82%	29.82%	0.56%			2.76%	5.82%	5.57%	5.54%	14.61%	32.76%	27.97%	

Share of transfer v share of votes and seats 2011

Party	1st	%	Gained	%	Lost	Net	Total	%	Change	Seats	% Seats	S/V
FG	801,628	36.10%	235,537	28.99%	133,709	+101,828	903,456	40.69%	+4.59%	76	45.78%	126.81%
LB	431,796	19.45%	144,023	17.73%	146,430	-2,407	429,389	19.34%	-0.11%	37	22.29%	114.61%
FF	387,358	17.45%	139,193	17.13%	182,283	-43,090	344,268	15.51%	-1.94%	20	12.05%	69.06%
SF	220,661	9.94%	56,433	6.95%	88,849	-32,416	188,245	8.48%	-1.46%	14	8.43%	84.86%
SP	26,770	1.21%	5,503	0.68%	13,800	-8,297	18,473	0.83%	-0.37%	2	1.20%	99.93%
PBPA	21,551	0.97%	7,720	0.95%	10,018	-2,298	19,253	0.87%	-0.10%	2	1.20%	124.13%
GP	41,039	1.85%	7,376	0.91%	48,415	-41,039	0	0.00%	-1.85%			
WP	3,056	0.14%	202	0.02%	3,258	-3,056	0	0.00%	-0.14%			
Others	286,500	12.90%	92,227	11.35%	185,662	-93,435	193,065	8.70%	-4.21%	15	9.04%	70.03%
Non-trans			124,210	15.29%		+124,210	124,210	5.59%	+5.59%			
Total	2,220,359	100.0%	812,424	100.0%	812,424	0	2,220,359	100.0%	0.0%	166	100.0%	

Sean Donnelly's Election Count Rules

1. Candidates have to be in the frame after the first count

For a candidate to have a good chance of getting elected they have to be in the frame on the first count. This means that as a general rule in a five-seat constituency the candidate has to come in the first five on the first count. In a three-seat constituency the candidate has to be in the first three places and in the first four in a four-seat constituency. In the 2011 general election there were only 11 candidates who came from outside the frame to get elected. In other words, 93% of those elected were within the frame on the first count.

An example of one of those 11 occurred in the four-seat Clare constituency in 2011 where Fine Gael's Tony Mulcahy was in fourth place on the first count. Fianna Fail's Timmy Dooley was in fifth place but managed to overtake Mulcahy and went on to take the fourth and final seat. Thus Dooley came from just outside the frame to claim a seat. The idea of a 'Lazarus' type recovery rarely happens and when this rule is broken it is usually from a position just outside the frame as in Dooley's case. Transfers are important but they don't always have the influence that we often think they do.

2. Candidates must have at least half a quota after the first count

A candidate must have at least half a quota on the first count to have any chance of getting elected. Only four of those elected in 2011 got below half a quota on the first count with only two in 2007 and three in 1997. In other words, 98% of those elected had at least half a quota on the first count. It is important to note that half a quota will not guarantee a seat but less than that level will leave a candidate with very little chance of getting elected.

These two election rules are usually broken by political parties running too many candidates. A good example of this in 2011 was in the constituency of Donegal South-West where Fianna Fáil ran two candidates, Mary Coughlan and Brían Ó Domhnaill. Both candidates were outside the frame on the first count and both were below the half quota level and independent Thomas Pringle slipped through for the final seat. Thus Fianna Fáil with 0.9 of a quota on the first count was beaten by Pringle who had just 0.5 of a quota. The Fianna Fáil Donegal South-West performance contrasted sharply with its neighbouring constituency of Donegal North-East, where it won just 17.44% of the first-preference vote as against 22.53% in South-West but won a seat by running just a single candidate. It is not so much the number of votes you have but rather how you manage these votes.

The Donnelly Rules and Election 2011: Seats Changed By Transfers

Our voting system is based on proportional representation using the single transferable vote (PR-STV). The general view is that the distribution of transfers substantially affects the final outcome in most constituencies. But on closer examination, this is not quite the case. Of the 165 seats filled in the 2011 election, in only 11 cases (14 in 2007) was the first-count result changed after the transfers were completed. In other words, if the election had been declared after the first count, it would have differed by only 11 seats from the eventual result or by just 7% of the total seats. This figure was 8% in 2007, 11% in 2002 and 1997 and 10% in both 1992 and 1987 and only 8% in 1989. In 2011, two of these were battles between two candidates of the same party, thus the transfers only changed the overall party seats by nine, or just 5% of the total.

Of course, if we were operating a first-past-the-post system, parties would run fewer candidates and the result would be different, but the point remains that the transfers do not significantly change the first-count result. Thus, the first count is extremely important and what the figures clearly indicate is that if a candidate is not 'in the frame' on the first count, he or she has less than a 10% chance of eventually winning a seat. This illustrates the advantage of running the minimum number of candidates as once the vote is divided the chances are that the candidates end up outside the frame on the first count.

Furthermore, as can be seen from the table of first -count bases from which candidates were elected, it is obvious that to have a reasonable chance of a seat, a candidate must attain at least half a quota on the first count as all but four of the candidates elected in 2011 (two in 2007 and 2002 and three in 1997 and 1987) had at least that level of support. Only two of the members elected in 1992 had less than 0.5 quotas. Cyprian Brady really pushed the boat out in 2007 as he went on to win a seat from a first count of 939, just 0.1 of a quota or a mere 2.71% of the first-preference vote.

Election 2011

Seats changed by transfers

	Constituency	Seats	Winner	Party	1st Count Position	Loser	Party	1st Count Position
1	Clare	4	Dooley, Timmy	FF	5	Mulcahy, Tony	FG	4
2	Cork North Central	4	Murphy, Dara	FG	5	Burton, Pat	FG	4
3	Dublin North East	3	Kenny, Sean	LB	5	O'Toole, Larry	SF	3
4	Dublin South East	4	Humphreys, Kevin	LB	5	Andrews, Chris	FF	4
5	Galway East	4	Keaveney, Colm	LB	8	McHugh, Tom	FG	4
6	Galway West	5	Kyne, Sean	FG	7	Healy-Eames, Fidelma	FG	5
7	Longford-Westmeath	4	Troy, Robert	FF	6	Burke, Peter	FG	3
8	Meath West	3	Butler, Ray	FG	4	McHugh, Jenny	LB	3
9	Waterford	4	Halligan, John	NP	5	Kenneally, Brendan	FF	3
10	Wexford	5	Browne, John	FF	6	D'Arcy, Michael	FG	3
11	Wicklow	5	Ferris, Anne	LB	6	Brady, John	SF	4

Seats changed by transfers – General Elections

	2011	2007	2002	1997	1992	1989	1987	2011-1987
Total Seats	166	166	166	166	166	166	166	166
Seats Changed by Transfers	11	14	18	18	16	14	16	15
% Seats Changed by Transfers	7%	8%	11%	11%	10%	8%	10%	9%

Seats changed by transfers – Local Elections

	2009	2004	1999	1991	2009-1987
Total Seats	883	883	883	883	883
Seats Changed by Transfers	66	86	70	79	75
% Seats Changed by Transfers	7%	10%	8%	9%	9%

First count base from which candidates were elected

	2011		2007		2002		1997		1992		1989	
Quotas	Elected	%	Elected	%	Elected	%	Elected	%	Elected	%	Elected	%
2.3			1	0.60%								
2.0											1	0.60%
1.8			1	0.60%								
1.7							1	0.60%	2	1.20%		
1.6			1	0.60%	3	1.81%			1	0.60%	1	0.60%
1.5	1	0.60%					2	1.20%	3	1.81%	1	0.60%
1.4	3	1.81%					1	0.60%	5	3.01%	1	0.60%
1.3	2	1.20%	3	1.81%	0	0.00%	2	1.20%	5	3.01%	2	1.20%
1.2	2	1.20%	8	4.82%	4	2.41%	5	3.01%	5	3.01%	6	3.61%
1.1	7	4.22%	5	3.01%	8	4.82%	7	4.22%	12	7.23%	25	15.06%
1.0	19	11.45%	22	13.25%	20	12.05%	16	9.64%	16	9.64%	24	14.46%
>1.0	34	20.48%	41	24.70%	35	21.08%	34	20.48%	49	29.52%	61	36.75%
0.9	22	13.25%	23	13.86%	26	15.66%	27	16.27%	19	11.45%	28	16.87%
0.8	35	21.08%	25	15.06%	39	23.49%	34	20.48%	35	21.08%	35	21.08%
0.7	31	18.67%	33	19.88%	31	18.67%	29	17.47%	23	13.86%	19	11.45%
0.6	24	14.46%	34	20.48%	24	14.46%	30	18.07%	21	12.65%	13	7.83%
0.5	16	9.64%	8	4.82%	9	5.42%	9	5.42%	17	10.24%	7	4.22%
0.4	4	2.41%	1	0.60%	1	0.60%	1	0.60%	2	1.20%	3	1.81%
0.3					1	0.60%	2	1.20%				
0.1			1	0.60%								
Total	166	100.00%	166	100.00%	166	100.00%	166	100.00%	166	100.00%	166	100.00%

Summary General Elections

Quotas	2011		2007		2002		1997		1992		1989	
> 1.0	34	20.48%	41	24.70%	35	21.08%	34	20.48%	49	29.52%	61	36.75%
0.5-0.9	128	77.11%	123	74.10%	129	77.71%	129	77.71%	115	69.28%	102	61.45%
< 0.5	4	2.41%	2	1.20%	2	1.20%	3	1.81%	2	1.20%	3	1.81%
Total	166	100.00%	166	100.00%	166	100.00%	166	100.00%	166	100.00%	166	100.00%

VOTE MANAGEMENT 2011

Fine Gael had a disastrous election in 2002 and got its poorest seats-to-votes ratio since the Dáil was increased to 166 seats in 1981. It managed to convert its 22.48% of the first-preference vote into only 18.7% of the seats and got less seats share than votes share for the first time. Its ratio of 83% was bettered by all of the main parties except Sinn Féin. It improved considerably in 2007 and increased its seats-to-votes ratio to a more normal 112.5%. It went on to beat this in 2011 with its best performance to date of 127%, or a seats bonus of 16, the highest ever achieved by a party since PR was first used in 1922. Fine Gael's best performance in 2011 was in Mayo, where Enda Kenny managed to bring home three running mates for a remarkable four out of five and a feat never achieved previously. Fine Gael won three seats from 2.4 quotas in the five seaters of Carlow-Kilkenny, Cavan-Monaghan, and Wicklow and managed three from just 2.2 quotas in Dublin South. It was also in contention for a remarkable three out of four seats in Galway East and Longford-Westmeath.

Labour may not have had a great election in 2007 but it got its best seats-to-votes ratio to date of 119%, which was well above its average of 104% since the Dáil was increased to 166 seats in 1981. It dropped below this high point in 2011 with a seats-to-votes ratio of 115%, or a seats bonus of five.

Fianna Fáil took vote management seriously for the first time in 1997 and with practically the same vote as 1992, the party managed an extra nine seats. By running the minimum number of candidates and with better distribution of its votes, it got one of its best returns of seats for votes, with a ratio of 118% compared to 105% in 1992. It repeated this performance in 2002 and again achieved a seats-to-vote ratio of 118%, which was well above its average since 1981 of 108%. It fell below this level in 2007 as it won three fewer seats than 2002 with the same vote, to give it a ratio of 113%. Fianna Fáil had last won 78 seats in 1981 but it required 45.26% of the first-preference vote. In 2007, it did it with four percentage points less. But it was all change for Fianna Fáil in 2011 with the collapse in its vote dropping it into a negative seats bonus for the first time as it got a seats-to-votes ratio of just 69%, or 10 seats less than its 17.45% first-preference vote merited.

Smaller parties do not usually get a seats bonus and Sinn Féin was no exception to that rule. It managed a seats-to-votes ratio of 85% in this latest election, its best return since this latest version of Sinn Féin won its first seat in 1997. Despite this, it was two seats less than its 9.94% of the first-preference vote warranted.

GENERAL ELECTION 26/2/2011				
Party	% First Pref	Seats	Actual	Bonus
FG	36.10%	60	76	+16
LB	19.45%	32	37	+5
FF	17.45%	29	19	-10
SF	9.94%	16	14	-2
ULA	2.68%	4	5	+1
GP	1.85%	3	0	-3
Others	12.53%	21	14	-7
Total	100.00%	165	165	0

Election 2011

* No Contest Dail	SEAT	Fine Gael % Vote	S	% Seat	% S/V	Labour % Vote	S	% Seat	% S/V	Fianna Fail % Vote	S	% Seat	% S/V
1 1918	73												
2 1921*	128												
3 1922	128	38.48%	58	45.31%	117.76%	21.33%	17	13.28%	62.27%	21.26%	36	28.13%	132.29%
4 1923	153	38.97%	63	41.18%	105.66%	10.62%	14	9.15%	86.16%	27.40%	44	28.76%	104.96%
5 1927	153	27.45%	47	30.72%	111.91%	12.55%	22	14.38%	114.57%	26.12%	44	28.76%	110.10%
6 1927	153	38.69%	62	40.52%	104.74%	9.07%	13	8.50%	93.68%	35.17%	57	37.25%	105.93%
7 1932	153	35.28%	57	37.25%	105.60%	7.71%	7	4.58%	59.34%	44.47%	72	47.06%	105.82%
8 1933	153	30.47%	48	31.37%	102.96%	5.71%	8	5.23%	91.57%	49.70%	77	50.33%	101.26%
9 1937	138	34.82%	48	34.78%	99.89%	10.25%	13	9.42%	91.91%	45.23%	69	50.00%	110.55%
10 1938	138	33.32%	45	32.61%	97.87%	10.02%	9	6.52%	65.09%	51.93%	77	55.80%	107.45%
11 1943	138	23.09%	32	23.19%	100.43%	15.68%	17	12.32%	78.56%	41.87%	67	48.55%	115.96%
12 1944	138	20.48%	30	21.74%	106.15%	8.77%	8	5.80%	66.10%	48.90%	76	55.07%	112.62%
13 1948	147	19.83%	31	21.09%	106.35%	8.69%	14	9.52%	109.60%	41.85%	68	46.26%	110.53%
14 1951	147	25.75%	40	27.21%	105.67%	11.40%	16	10.88%	95.48%	46.28%	69	46.94%	101.42%
15 1954	147	31.98%	50	34.01%	106.36%	12.06%	19	12.93%	107.17%	43.36%	65	44.22%	101.98%
16 1957	147	26.63%	40	27.21%	102.18%	9.11%	12	8.16%	89.61%	48.33%	78	53.06%	109.79%
17 1961	144	32.02%	47	32.64%	101.93%	11.65%	16	11.11%	95.37%	43.83%	70	48.61%	110.91%
18 1965	144	34.08%	47	32.64%	95.77%	15.38%	22	15.28%	99.34%	47.67%	72	50.00%	104.89%
19 1969	144	34.10%	50	34.72%	101.82%	17.02%	18	12.50%	73.44%	45.79%	75	52.08%	113.74%
20 1973	144	35.08%	54	37.50%	106.90%	13.71%	19	13.19%	96.24%	46.24%	69	47.92%	103.63%
21 1977	148	30.49%	43	29.05%	95.29%	11.63%	17	11.49%	98.77%	50.63%	84	56.76%	112.10%
22 1981	166	36.46%	65	39.16%	107.40%	9.89%	15	9.04%	91.37%	45.26%	78	46.99%	103.82%
23 1982	166	37.30%	63	37.95%	101.75%	9.12%	15	9.04%	99.08%	47.26%	81	48.80%	103.25%
24 1982	166	39.21%	70	42.17%	107.55%	9.36%	16	9.64%	102.98%	45.20%	75	45.18%	99.96%
25 1987	166	27.07%	51	30.72%	113.49%	6.45%	12	7.23%	112.08%	44.15%	81	48.80%	110.52%
26 1989	166	29.29%	55	33.13%	113.12%	9.48%	15	9.04%	95.32%	44.15%	77	46.39%	105.06%
27 1992	166	24.47%	45	27.11%	110.78%	19.31%	33	19.88%	102.95%	39.11%	68	40.96%	104.74%
28 1997	166	27.95%	54	32.53%	116.39%	10.40%	17	10.24%	98.47%	39.33%	77	46.39%	117.94%
29 2002	166	22.48%	31	18.67%	83.07%	10.77%	21	12.65%	117.46%	41.48%	81	48.80%	117.64%
30 2007	166	27.32%	51	30.72%	112.46%	10.13%	20	12.05%	118.94%	41.56%	78	46.99%	113.06%
31 2011	166	36.10%	76	45.78%	126.82%	19.40%	37	22.29%	114.89%	17.40%	20	12.05%	69.24%
1918-2011	149	30.77%	50	33.63%	109.31%	11.53%	17	11.16%	96.77%	41.86%	68	45.95%	109.77%
1981-2011	166	30.73%	56	33.80%	109.97%	11.63%	20	12.11%	104.11%	39.85%	72	43.13%	108.24%

WOMEN ELECTED 2011

Twenty five women deputies were returned to the 31st Dáil, up one on the outgoing Dáil, as Maureen O'Sullivan had been elected in a by-election in Dublin Central in 2009. This is the highest number of women elected in a general election to date, with the previous record at 23, which was achieved in 1992, 2002 and 2007. Eight (six in 2007) outgoing women TDs lost their seats – six Fianna Fáil, one Fine Gael and one Green Party, with Deirdre Clune the only non-government female deputy to lose her seat. A further six women deputies retired. Fourteen women were elected for the first time and two former deputies, Frances Fitzgerald and Catherine Murphy, regained their seats.

In all elections to date, women have won 260 out of the 4,744 seats filled, or just 5.5%. Out of 1,235 TDs in Dáil Éireann to date, only 92 (7.5%) were women. The PDs had the best female representation with 17 of their 44 (39%) seats won between 1987 and 2007 held by women. The Fianna Fáil female representation is just 4%, with Fine Gael on 6% and Labour on 8%. The Greens got their first female deputy with the election of Mary White in 2007. Mildred Fox became the first independent female deputy when she was elected at a by-election in 1995 caused by the death of her father. She was joined by Marian Harkin in 2002 but both retired in 2007. There are two female independents in the 31st Dáil – Maureen O'Sullivan and Catherine Murphy.

Mary Harney is now the longest-serving woman TD, with 30 years' unbroken service from 1981 to 2011. Mary Reynolds is in second place, having won nine general elections, the same as Mary Harney and having served for 25 years in Sligo-Leitrim – from 1932 to 1933 and from 1937 to 1961. Síle de Valera is in third place, having served for 24 years and Mary Coughlan is in fourth place with 24 years' service, from 1987 to 2011, just ahead of Mary O'Rourke on 23 years' service. Róisín Shortall is the longest-serving female in the present Dáil, with 18 years' service since 1992.

National seats & votes share Main parties 1918-2011

	Candidate	Party	Constituency	1st	%	Quotas	Seat
1	Shortall, Roisin*	LB	Dublin North West	9,359	28.52%	1.14	1
2	Burton, Joan*	LB	Dublin West	9,627	22.67%	1.13	1
3	Creighton, Lucinda*	FG	Dublin South East	6,619	18.96%	0.95	2
4	Tuffy, Joanna*	LB	Dublin Mid-West	7,495	17.54%	0.88	1
5	Fitzgerald, Frances**	FG	Dublin Mid-West	7,281	17.04%	0.85	2
6	Doherty, Regina	FG	Meath East	8,677	20.30%	0.81	2
7	Mitchell O'Connor, Mary	FG	Dun Laoghaire	9,087	16.03%	0.80	3
8	Mitchell, Olivia*	FG	Dublin South	9,635	13.26%	0.80	3
9	Collins, Joan	PBPA	Dublin South Central	6,574	13.07%	0.77	4
10	Daly, Clare	SP	Dublin North	7,513	15.22%	0.76	3
11	Lynch, Kathleen*	LB	Cork North Central	7,676	14.72%	0.74	2
12	O'Sullivan, Jan*	LB	Limerick East	6,353	14.71%	0.74	4
13	Mulherin, Michelle	FG	Mayo	8,851	11.94%	0.72	3
14	Collins, Aine	FG	Cork North West	7,884	17.24%	0.69	3
15	Humphreys, Heather	FG	Cavan-Monaghan	8,144	11.43%	0.69	5
16	Murphy, Catherine**	NP	Kildare North	6,911	13.49%	0.67	3
17	Byrne, Catherine*	FG	Dublin South Central	5,604	11.14%	0.66	2
18	Phelan, Ann	LB	Carlow-Kilkenny	8,072	10.95%	0.66	1
19	McDonald, Mary Lou	SF	Dublin Central	4,526	13.08%	0.65	4
20	O'Sullivan, Maureen*	NP	Dublin Central	4,139	11.96%	0.60	3
21	McLellan, Sandra	SF	Cork East	6,292	11.05%	0.55	4
22	McFadden, Nicky	FG	Longford-Westmeath	6,129	10.65%	0.53	3
23	Conway, Ciara	LB	Waterford	5,554	10.34%	0.52	3
24	Corcoran Kennedy, Marcella	FG	Laois Offaly	5,817	7.84%	0.47	2
25	Ferris, Anne	LB	Wicklow	5,436	7.71%	0.46	4
	*Outgoing TD	9					
	**Former TD	2					
	New TD	14					

Election 2011

Women in the Dáil 1918-2011

Dáil	Election	General	By-Elect	Total	FG	LB	FF	SF	ULA	GP	PD	Others	Total	TD's
1	1918	73		73				1					1	
2	1921	128		128				6					6	
3	1922	128		128			2						2	
4	1923	153	21	174	1		4						5	
5	1927	153	2	155	1		2	1					4	
6	1927	153	7	160	1								1	
7	1932	153		153	2		1						3	
8	1933	153	5	158	1		1						2	
9	1937	138		138	2								2	
10	1938	138	2	140	2		1						3	
11	1943	138		138	2		1						3	
12	1944	138	10	148	2		3						5	
13	1948	147	3	150	2		3						5	
14	1951	147	9	156	2		3						5	
15	1954	147	7	154	1	1	3					1	6	
16	1957	147	8	155	2		3						5	
17	1961	144	6	150	2	1	3						6	
18	1965	144	7	151	2	1	2						5	
19	1969	144	6	150	2		1						3	
20	1973	144	7	151	2	1	2						5	
21	1977	148	3	151	2	1	4						7	
22	1981	166		166	6	1	4						11	
23	1982	166	2	168	5	1	2						8	
24	1982	166	3	169	9	1	4						14	
25	1987	166		166	5		5				4		14	
26	1989	166		166	6		5				2		13	
27	1992	166	7	173	5	5	6				4	3	23	
28	1997	166	6	172	6	4	8				2	2	22	
29	2002	166	2	168	2	7	7				4	3	23	
30	2007	166	3	169	5	7	7			1	1	2	23	
31	2011	166		166	11	8		2	2			2	25	
Women*					91	39	87	10	2	1	17	13	260	92
Total*		4,618	126	4,744	1,503	490	2,037	233	5	16	44	416	4,744	1,235
% Women					6.05%	7.96%	4.27%	4.29%	40.00%	6.25%	38.64%	3.13%	5.48%	7.45%

*Includes 14 By-Elections
**Includes 126 By-Elections

Election Facts

"Fine Gael's Deirdre Clune was the only outgoing non-government female deputy to lose her seat"
Sean Donnelly

Lost Expenses 2011

Party	2011			2007	2002	1997	1992
	Candidates	Lost Expenses	%	Lost Expenses	Lost Expenses	Lost Deposit	Lost Deposit
FG	104		0.00%	4	9	8	7
LB	68		0.00%	12	8	10	14
FF	75	3	4.00%	0	0	1	6
SF	41	4	9.76%	17	12	3	39
ULA	20	11	55.00%	2	3	2	
GP	43	39	90.70%	26	17	15	15
WP	6	6	100.00%	6	8	6	16
CS	8	8	100.00%	7	23	8	
PD				21	6	9	2
Others	201	167	83.08%	71	77	117	92
Total	566	238	42.05%	166	163	179	191
Candidates		566		470	463	484	482
Lost Expenses %		42.05%		35.32%	35.21%	36.98%	39.63%

A candidate loses the right to reclaim their election expenses if they fail to reach at least 25% of the quota by the time they are eliminated

Lowest vote-getters 2011

	Candidate	Party	Constituency	1st Prefs	%
1	O Ceallaigh, Peadar	FN	Dublin South East	18	0.05%
2	Cooney, Benny	NP	Dublin Central	25	0.07%
3	Keigher, John	NP	Dublin South East	27	0.08%
4	Forkin, Sean	NP	Mayo	29	0.04%
5	Johnston, Liam	FN	Dublin Central	48	0.14%
6	Larkin, Matt	NP	Limerick City	59	0.14%
7	Cox, Michael	NP	Laois-Offaly	60	0.08%
8	Glynn, Robert	NP	Louth	61	0.09%
9	Hollywood, Thomas	NP	Dublin Central	65	0.19%
10	King, Thomas	NP	Galway West	65	0.11%
11	Dalton, John	NP	Carlow-Kilkenny	70	0.09%
12	Zaidan, Eamonn	NP	Dublin South	71	0.10%
13	Kiersey, Gerard	NP	Waterford	73	0.14%
14	Carroll, Kevin	NP	Wicklow	74	0.10%
15	Hyland, John Pluto	NP	Dublin Central	77	0.22%
16	Watson, Noel	NP	Dublin South East	89	0.25%
17	Linehan, Gerard	NP	Cork South Central	90	0.14%
18	Kearns, Sean	NP	Roscommon-South Leit	91	0.19%
19	O'Driscoll, Finbar	NP	Cork South Central	92	0.14%
20	O'Rourke, Fergus	NP	Cork North Central	95	0.18%

Close finishes 2011

	Constituency	Quota	Winner	Party	Final Votes	Loser	Party	Final Votes	Margin
1	Galway West	10,105	Sean Kyne	FG	9,112	Catherine Connolly	NP	9,095	17
2	Wicklow	11,751	Stephen Donnelly	NP	9,966	John Brady	SF	9,854	112
3	Cork North Central	10,428	Dara Murphy	FG	9,515	Pat Burton	FG	9,233	282
4	Cavan-Monaghan	11,880	Heather Humphreys	FG	10,861	Kathryn Reilly	SF	10,340	521
5	Dublin Mid West	8,545	Derek Keating	FG	7,703	Eoin O Broin	SF	7,151	552
6	Sligo-North Leitrim	11,108	Michael Colreavy	SF	9,711	Eamon Scanlon	FF	9,125	586
7	Cork South West	11,415	Michael McCarthy	LB	10,754	Denis O'Donovan	FF	10,155	599
8	Cork East	11,387	Sandra McLellan	SF	9,785	Kevin O'Keeffe	FF	9,136	649
9	Limerick	11,261	Niall Collins	FF	10,809	James Heffernan	LB	10,104	705
10	Waterford	10,745	John Halligan	NP	9,818	Brendan Kenneally	FF	8,945	873
11	Kerry South	11,096	Michael Healy-Rae	NP	10,326	Tom Sheahan	FG	9,409	917
12	Louth	13,864	Peter Fitzpatrick	FG	12,323	James Carroll	FF	11,388	935
13	Kildare South	9,568	Sean O Fearghail	FF	8,707	Paddy Kennedy	NP	7,710	997
14	Dublin North	9,870	Alan Farrell	FG	9,159	Darragh O'Brien	FF	8,067	1,092

Election 2011

	Candidate	Party	Constituency	1st Prefs	%	Quota	M/F	Count
1	Noonan, Michael*	FG	Limerick City	13,291	30.77%	1.54	M	1
2	Kenny, Enda*	FG	Mayo	17,472	23.56%	1.41	M	1
3	Ross, Shane	NP	Dublin South	17,075	23.50%	1.41	M	1
4	Rabbitte, Pat*	LB	Dublin South West	12,867	27.40%	1.37	M	1
5	Heydon, Martin	FG	Kildare South	12,755	33.33%	1.33	M	1
6	Doherty, Pearse*	SF	Donegal South West	14,262	32.97%	1.32	M	1
7	Flanagan, Terence*	FG	Dublin North East	12,332	29.47%	1.18	M	1
8	Lowry, Michael*	NP	Tipperary North	14,104	29.22%	1.17	M	1
9	Shortall, Roisin*	LB	Dublin North West	9,359	28.52%	1.14	F	1
10	Burton, Joan*	LB	Dublin West	9,627	22.67%	1.13	F	1
11	Wall, Jack*	LB	Kildare South	10,645	27.82%	1.11	M	1
12	Adams, Gerry	SF	Louth	15,072	21.74%	1.09	M	1
13	Deenihan, Jimmy*	FG	Kerry North-West Limer	12,304	26.97%	1.08	M	1
14	Ring, Michael*	FG	Mayo	13,180	17.77%	1.07	M	1
15	Wallace, Mick	NP	Wexford	13,329	17.65%	1.06	M	1
16	Sherlock, Sean*	LB	Cork East	11,862	20.84%	1.04	M	1
17	Reilly, Dr. James*	FG	Dublin North	10,178	20.63%	1.03	M	1
18	Gilmore, Eamon*	LB	Dun Laoghaire	11,468	20.23%	1.01	M	1
19	O'Dowd, Fergus*	FG	Louth	13,980	20.17%	1.01	M	1
20	Martin, Micheal*	FF	Cork South Central	10,715	16.73%	1.00	M	1
21	O Caolain, Caoimhghin*	SF	Cavan-Monaghan	11,913	16.71%	1.00	M	1
22	Bruton, Richard*	FG	Dublin North Central	9,685	24.98%	1.00	M	2
23	Deasy, John*	FG	Waterford	10,718	19.95%	1.00	M	3
24	Donohoe, Paschal	FG	Dublin Central	6,903	19.94%	1.00	M	2
25	Hayes, Brian*	FG	Dublin South West	9,366	19.94%	1.00	M	2

	Surname	First Name	Party	Constituency	First Elected	Elections Won
1	Kenny	Enda	FG	Mayo	24/11/1975	12
2	Quinn	Ruairi	LB	Dublin South East	16/06/1977	10
3	Noonan	Michael	FG	Limerick East	11/06/1981	10
4	Bruton	Richard	FG	Dublin North Central	18/02/1982	9
5	McGinley	Dinny	FG	Donegal South West	18/02/1982	9
6	O'Dea	Willie	FF	Limerick East	18/02/1982	9
7	Durkan	Bernard	FG	Kildare North	11/06/1981	9
8	Browne	John	FF	Wexford	24/11/1982	8
9	Kirk	Seamus	FF	Louth	24/11/1982	8
10	Kitt	Michael	FF	Galway East	04/03/1975	10
11	Barrett	Sean	FG	Dun Laoghaire	11/06/1981	9
12	Shatter	Alan	FG	Dublin South	11/06/1981	9
13	Deenihan	Jimmy	FG	Kerry North	17/02/1987	7
14	Howlin	Brendan	LB	Wexford	17/02/1987	7
15	Lowry	Michael	NP	Tipperary North	17/02/1987	7
16	Stagg	Emmet	LB	Kildare North	17/02/1987	7
17	Gilmore	Eamon	LB	Dun Laoghaire	15/06/1989	6
18	Hogan	Phil	FG	Carlow-Kilkenny	15/06/1989	6
19	Martin	Micheal	FF	Cork South Central	15/06/1989	6
20	Rabbitte	Pat	LB	Dublin South West	15/06/1989	6
			First elected at by-election		Interrupted Service	

ELECTIONS 1918-2011

The 1918 general election was the last all-Ireland general election to the United Kingdom parliament at Westminster. The Sinn Féin members of the House of Commons became members of the first Dáil Éireann, which met in Dublin on 21 January 1919. The new assembly elected a cabinet. The second Dáil met for the first time on 26 August 1921 and again elected a cabinet. The cabinet was superseded by the Provisional Government in January 1922, which was in turn superseded by the Executive Council in December 1922.

The first and second Dála lacked official status, being private meetings of Sinn Féin MPs returned at general elections held under the authority of the British government in 1918 and 1921, though the second Dáil subsequently received effective official recognition as the legitimate parliament of southern Ireland under the terms of the Anglo Irish Treaty of 1921. The general election to the third Dáil was initiated by the Irish Free State (Agreement) Act, passed by the British parliament in March 1922 and was sanctioned by the second Dáil in May. Elections to subsequent Dála were held under the authority of a sovereign Irish government.

Elections were operated under a system of proportional representation using the single transferable vote from 1921 onwards – however, as all the seats in the general election of 1921 were uncontested, the system was not brought into use until 1922.

Elections 1918-2011

	Dail	Seats	Electorate	Valid	%	Candidates
1	1918	73				73
2	1921*	128				128
3	1922	128	1,031,342	621,587	60.27%	176
4	1923	153	1,784,918	1,053,955	59.05%	376
5	1927	153	1,730,177	1,146,460	66.26%	377
6	1927	153	1,728,093	1,170,869	67.75%	265
7	1932	153	1,691,993	1,274,026	75.30%	279
8	1933	153	1,724,420	1,386,558	80.41%	246
9	1937	138	1,775,055	1,324,449	74.61%	255
10	1938	138	1,697,323	1,286,259	75.78%	214
11	1943	138	1,816,142	1,331,709	73.33%	354
12	1944	138	1,776,950	1,217,349	68.51%	252
13	1948	147	1,800,210	1,323,443	73.52%	407
14	1951	147	1,785,144	1,331,573	74.59%	297
15	1954	147	1,763,209	1,335,202	75.73%	303
16	1957	147	1,738,278	1,227,019	70.59%	289
17	1961	144	1,670,860	1,168,404	69.93%	301
18	1965	144	1,683,019	1,253,122	74.46%	281
19	1969	144	1,735,388	1,318,953	76.00%	373
20	1973	144	1,783,604	1,350,537	75.72%	335
21	1977	148	2,118,606	1,603,027	75.66%	376
22	1981	166	2,275,450	1,718,211	75.51%	404
23	1982	166	2,275,450	1,665,133	73.18%	366
24	1982	166	2,335,153	1,688,720	72.32%	365
25	1987	166	2,445,515	1,777,165	72.67%	466
26	1989	166	2,448,810	1,656,813	67.66%	371
27	1992	166	2,557,036	1,724,853	67.46%	482
28	1997	166	2,741,262	1,788,985	65.26%	484
29	2002	166	3,002,173	1,857,902	61.89%	463
30	2007	166	3,110,914	2,065,810	66.41%	471
31	2011	166	3,209,249	2,220,359	69.19%	567
Average		149	2,042,612	1,444,429	70.71%	335

*No contest **Note:** Total electorate in 1922 was 1,430,024 as eight constituencies were uncontested.

Newly elected independent TD for Wexford Mick Wallace talks to the media as he arrives for the first sitting of the 31st Dail.

GOVERNMENTS

The government elected in 2011 is the fourth Fine Gael/Labour coalition. The 1994-1997 'Rainbow Coalition' was the first between Fine Gael, Labour and Democratic Left and the only one to be formed without a general election. The Fianna Fáil/Green/Progressive Democrat government elected in 2007 was the fifth coalition government involving Fianna Fáil. There have been three Fianna Fáil/PD and one Fianna Fáil/Labour coalition. There have also been two inter-party governments, in 1948 and 1954. Fianna Fáil has been part of 19 of the 29 governments since the foundation of the state and in power on its own on 14 occasions.

The 2011 Fine Gael/Labour coalition has by far the largest majority (60) in the history of the state. Only four previous governments had majorities in double figures: 1938 (16), 1944 (14) and 1977 (20) – all Fianna Fáil governments along with the 36-seat majority of the Fianna Fáil/Labour Party government in the 27th Dáil in 1992. The Fianna Fáil/Green/PD coalition elected in 2007 had a combined total of 86 seats and also had the support of four of the five independents to give it a comfortable majority. Minority governments are not unusual, as of the 29 governments to date, 15 had no majority with three having a majority of just one.

Enda Kenny is the 12th Taoiseach and the fifth from Fine Gael. Éamon de Valera is by far the longest-serving Taoiseach, having served eight terms. WT Cosgrave and CJ Haughey each served four terms and Seán Lemass, Jack Lynch and Bertie Ahern served three terms. JA Costello, Garrett FitzGerald and Albert Reynolds each served on two occasions. Liam Cosgrave served only one term as Taoiseach (1973-1977) and Brian Cowen also did just one term and served for the second shortest period behind Albert Reynolds. John Bruton had the shortest period in office – December 1994 to June 1997.

Micheál Martin became the eighth leader of Fianna Fáil when he won the leadership election on 26 January 2011. Brian Cowen had been elected leader designate of Fianna Fáil on 8 April 2008 but did not officially take over the leadership until 8 May, when he was elected Taoiseach. He thus became the seventh leader of Fianna Fáil, all of whom went on to serve as Taoiseach. Éamon de Valera was by far the longest-serving leader of the party, having served 33 years from 1926 until he was elected President of Ireland in 1959. Bertie Ahern was the next longest-serving leader, having served for 14 years from 1994 until 6 May 2008. Jack Lynch and Charles Haughey served as leaders for 13 years with Seán Lemass serving for seven and Albert Reynolds leader for just two years – from 1992 to 1994. Bertie Ahern was unique in that he did not inherit the position of Taoiseach as he was in opposition for the first two years of his leadership of Fianna Fáil, unlike the rest of de Valera's successors, who became Taoiseach following their elevation to party leader, as did their recent leader Brian Cowen.

There have been 10 leaders of Fine Gael/Cumann na nGaedheal and, unlike Fianna Fáil, only five of them have gone on to become Taoiseach with one of them, John Bruton, doing so without a general election.

There have been 10 leaders of the Labour Party with none of them reaching the office of Taoiseach.

Elections 1918-2011

Dail	Election Date	Seats	Government	Taoiseach (from 1937)	Ceann Comhairle
1	14th Dec 1918	73	Sinn Fein	C. Brugha 22/1/19-1/4/19	Sean T. O'Kelly
			Sinn Fein	E. de Valera 1/4/19-26/8/21	
2	24th May 1921	128	Sinn Fein	E. de Valera 26/8/21-9/1/22	Eoin MacNeill
			Sinn Fein	A. Griffith 10/1/22-12/8/22*	
			Sinn Fein	W.T. Cosgrave 12/8/22-9/9/22	
			Provisional Government	M. Collins 16/1/22-22/8/22	
			Provisional Government	W.T. Cosgrave 25/8/22-6/12/22	
3	16th June 1922	128	Pro Treaty	W.T. Cosgrave	Michael Hayes
4	27th Aug 1923	153	Cumann na nGael	W.T. Cosgrave	Michael Hayes
5	9th June 1927	153	Cumann na nGael	W.T. Cosgrave	Michael Hayes
6	15th Sept 1927	153	Cumann na nGael	W.T. Cosgrave	Michael Hayes
7	16th Feb 1932	153	Fianna Fail	E. de Valera	Frank Fahy
8	24th Jan 1933	153	Fianna Fail	E. de Valera	Frank Fahy
9	1st July 1937	138	Fianna Fail	E. de Valera	Frank Fahy
10	17th June 1938	138	Fianna Fail	E. de Valera	Frank Fahy
11	23rd June 1943	138	Fianna Fail	E. de Valera	Frank Fahy
12	30th May 1944	138	Fianna Fail	E. de Valera	Frank Fahy
13	4th Feb 1948	147	Inter Party	J.A. Costello	Frank Fahy
14	30th May 1951	147	Fianna Fail	E. de Valera	Frank Fahy
15	18th May 1954	147	Inter Party	J.A. Costello	Patrick Hogan
16	5th Mar 1957	147	Fianna Fail	E. de Valera to 23/6/1959	Patrick Hogan
				S. Lemass from 23/6/1959	Patrick Hogan
17	4th Oct 1961	144	Fianna Fail	S. Lemass	Patrick Hogan
18	7th Apr 1965	144	Fianna Fail	S. Lemass to 10/11/1966	Patrick Hogan to 1968
				J. Lynch from 10/11/1966	Cormac Breslin from 1968
19	18th June 1969	144	Fianna Fail	J. Lynch	Cormac Breslin
20	28th Feb 1973	144	Fine Gael/Labour	L. Cosgrave	Sean Treacy
21	16th June 1977	148	Fianna Fail	J. Lynch to 11/12/1979	Joe Brennan died 13/7/1980
				C.J. Haughey from 11/12/1979	Padraig Faulkner from 16/10/80
22	11th June 1981	166	Fine Gael/Labour	G. Fitzgerald	John O'Connell
23	18th Feb 1982	166	Fianna Fail	C.J. Haughey	John O'Connell
24	24th Nov 1982	166	Fine Gael/Labour	G. Fitzgerald	Thomas J. Fitzpatrick
25	17th Feb 1987	166	Fianna Fail	C.J. Haughey	Sean Treacy
26	15th June 1989	166	Fianna Fail/PD	C.J. Haughey to 11/2/1992	Sean Treacy
				A. Reynolds from 11/2/1992	Sean Treacy
27	25th Nov 1992	166	Fianna Fail /Labour	A. Reynolds to 15th Dec 1994	Sean Treacy
			FG/Lab/DL	J. Bruton from 5th Dec 1994	Sean Treacy
28	6th June 1997	166	Fianna Fail/PD	B. Ahern	Seamus Pattison
29	17th May 2002	166	Fianna Fail/PD	B. Ahern	Dr. Rory O'Hanlon
30	24th May 2007	166	Fianna Fail/GP/PD	B. Ahern to 7/5/08	John O'Donoghue to 14/10/09
				B. Cowen from 7/5/08	Seamus Kirk from 14/10/09
31	25th Feb 2011	166	Fine Gael/Labour	Enda Kenny	Sean Barrett
Total	31	4,618	29	16	16

1. Cathal Brugha was acting President of the First Dáil, 22 January-1 April 1919.

2. Upon his release from prison, Éamon de Valera became President of the first Dáil, 1 April 1919-26 August 1921, and President of the second Dáil from 26 August 1921 to 9 January 1922. De Valera and others who opposed the Anglo-Irish Treaty withdrew from the Dáil in January 1922.

3. Michael Collins was Chairman of the Provisional Government which came into being after the Dail ratified the Anglo-Irish Treaty in January 1922.

4. WT Cosgrave became Chairman of the Provisional Government following the assassination of Michael Collins on 22 August 1922.

5. From December 1922 until December 1937, the office of Prime Minister was known as President of the Executive Council. Following the adoption of the 1937 Constitution the title was changed to 'An Taoiseach'.

Election Facts

"Before 2011, Fianna Fáil's lowest ever vote was 26.1% in June 1927, and its lowest vote since 1932 was 39.1% in 1992. Before 2011, its lowest number of seats was 44 in June 1927 and its lowest after 1932 was 65 in 1954"
Professor Michael Gallagher, TCD

President of the Executive Council/Taoiseach: Days In Office

	Head of Government	Terms	From	To	Days
1	Eamon de Valera	10	01/04/1919	23/06/1959	8748
2	Bertie Ahern	3	26/06/1997	07/05/2008	3968
3	W.T. Cosgrave	5	12/08/1922	16/02/1932	3512
4	Jack Lynch	3	10/11/1966	11/12/1979	3205
5	Sean Lemass	3	23/06/1959	10/11/1966	2697
6	Charles Haughey	4	11/12/1979	11/02/1992	2646
7	John A. Costello	2	04/02/1948	05/03/1957	2233
8	Garret Fitzgerald	2	30/06/1981	10/03/1987	1799
9	Liam Cosgrave	1	14/03/1973	05/07/1977	1574
10	Albert Reynolds	2	11/02/1992	15/12/1994	1038
11	Brian Cowen	1	07/05/2008	09/03/2011	1036
12	John Bruton	1	15/12/1994	26/06/1997	924
13	Michael Collins	1	16/01/1922	22/08/1922	218
14	Arthur Griffith	1	10/01/1922	12/08/1922	214
15	Cathal Brugha	1	22/01/1919	01/04/1919	69
16	Enda Kenny		09/03/2011		

Broken Service

Main Party leaders – Fianna Fáil

	Leader	From	To	Years
1	Eamon de Valera	1926	1959	33
2	Sean Lemass	1959	1966	7
3	Jack Lynch	1966	1979	13
4	Charles Haughey	1979	1992	13
5	Albert Reynolds	1992	1994	2
6	Bertie Ahern	1994	2008	14
7	Brian Cowen	2008	2010	2
8	Michael Martin	26/01/2011		

Main Party leaders – Fine Gael*

	Leader	From	To	Years
1	General Eoin O'Duffy	1933	1934	1
2	W.T. Cosgrave	1934	1944	10
3	General Richard Mulcahy	1944	1959	15
4	James Dillon	1959	1965	6
5	Liam Cosgrave	1965	1977	12
6	Garret Fitzgerald	1977	1987	10
7	Alan Dukes	1987	1990	3
8	John Bruton	1990	2001	11
9	Michael Noonan	2001	2002	1
10	Enda Kenny	Jun-02		
	*Cumann na nGaedheal merged with the Blueshirts and the			
	Centre Party to form Fine Gael in September 1933			

Main Party leaders – Labour

	Leader	From	To	Years
1	Tom Johnson	1922	1927	5
2	T.J. O'Connell	1927	1932	5
3	William Norton	1932	1960	28
4	Brendan Corish	1960	1977	17
5	Frank Cluskey	1977	1981	4
6	Michael O'Leary	1981	1982	1
7	Dick Spring	1982	1997	15
8	Ruairi Quinn	1997	2002	5
9	Pat Rabbitte	2002	2007	5
10	Eamon Gilmore	Sep-07		

Election Facts

"Dublin Mid-West was the constituency where Fine Gael increased its vote most – the party's support increased from 12% to 30.93%"
Sean Donnelly

OVERALL RESULTS 1918-2011

Turnout

The valid poll has averaged 70.71% from 1922 to 2011. The turnout in 2011 was up three percentage points on 2007 but still below the average. The turnout has shown a steady decline since 1969 and the 2007 election was the first occasion on which this decline was arrested. There was further improvement in 2011. The present figures are well below the largest turnout in 1933 (80.41%). Question marks remain over the state of the electoral register and so these figures come with a serious health warning and until an electoral commission is set up and the register of electors is reformed, it is extremely difficult to assess an accurate level of turnout.

Fine Gael

Fine Gael has averaged 50 seats per election contested from 30.77% of the first-preference vote. It has done better since 1981 with an average of 56 seats from an average first-preference vote of 30.73%. Fine Gael achieved its highest share of the vote in the second election of 1982 when it got 39.21%, but it has failed to reach those heights since and was down to just 31 seats and 22.48% in 2002, its lowest since 1948. It recovered most of its losses in 2007 with its vote up to 27.32% and it won 51 seats. It improved considerably on that performance in 2011, winning 36.10% of the vote and a record 76 seats.

Fine Gael got its largest share of seats (45.78%) in 2011. Its previous best performance was in 1922 when it won 45.31% of the seats. It has now won 40% or more of the seats at five elections.

Fine Gael has an average seats-to-votes ratio of 109% since 1922. It has managed to win a larger share of seats than votes on all but four occasions, with its poorest performance in 2002 when it got just 83%. It improved its ratio considerably in 2007, winning 112% and improved it considerably more in 2011, managing 127%, the best ratio to date by any party.

Labour

Labour has averaged 11.53% of the vote since 1922, winning on average 17 seats per election. It has done slightly better since 1981 with an average of 20 seats from an average first-preference vote of 11.63%. It achieved its highest share of the vote in 1922 when it got 21.33%, with its next best coming in 1992 when Dick Spring won 19.31% and 33 seats. But it failed to reach those heights subsequently and dropped to just 17 seats and 10.40% at the next election in 1997 and won 10.13% and 20 seats in 2007. But like its government partners Fine Gael, it had a very good result in 2011 and beat the 'Spring Tide' election result of 1992, winning 19.45% and a record 37 seats.

Labour got its largest share of seats (22.29%) in 2011, beating its previous best of 19.88% in 1992. Its next best performance was in 1965 when it won 15.28% of the seats. It took a more modest 12.05% of the seats in 2007. Labour has an average seats-to-votes ratio of just 97% since 1922. It has done better since 1981 with its average up to 104%. But overall Labour has performed poorly in its conversion of votes into seats and has only got over 100% on nine occasions. It improved its ratio considerably at the last three elections, winning 115% in 2011, 117% in 2002 and gaining its best to date (119%) in 2007.

Fianna Fáil

Fianna Fáil has averaged 68 seats and 41.86% of the first-preference vote since 1922. It has not done so well since the Dáil was increased to its present level of 166 seats in 1981, with an average of 72 seats from an average first-preference vote of 39.85%. Fianna Fáil achieved its highest share of the vote in 1938 when it got 51.93%. It is the only party to achieve more than 50% of the vote in any one election and it repeated this in 1977 with 50.63%. Fianna Fáil dropped below 40% for the first time since 1927 when it got just 39.11% in 1992, with little improvement in 1997 when it won 39.33%. It got back above the 40% level in 2002, winning 41.48% and got practically the same in 2007 (41.56%). But it was all change in 2011 with the party vote collapsing to just 17.45% and a mere 20 seats.

Fianna Fáil got its largest share of seats in 1977 when it won an overall majority with 84 of the 148 seats on offer, or 56.76% of the seats. Its next best performance was in 1938 when it won 55.80% of the seats. The nation's largest party prior to this latest election has won 50% or more of the seats at seven elections to date, the last being in 1977.

Fianna Fáil has an average seats-to-votes ratio of 110% since 1922. It has managed to win a larger share of seats than votes on all but two occasions, the second election of 1982 and the latest election in 2011 when it managed only a 69% seats-to-votes ratio. It had considerably improved its ratio in the previous three elections, managing 118% in both 1997 and 2002 and 113% in 2007 to offset the drop in its first-preference vote.

Distribution of seats and share of the first-preference vote 1918-2011

* No Contest

Dáil	Year	Seats	FG S	FG %	LB S	LB %	FF S	FF %	SF S	SF %	SP S	SP %	PBPA S	PBPA %	GP S	GP %	WP S	WP %	CS S	CS %	PD S	PD %	Others S	Others %
1	1918	73							73														4	
2	1921*	128							124															
3	1922	128	58	38.48%	17	21.33%	36	21.26%															17	18.93%
4	1923	153	63	38.97%	14	10.62%	44	27.40%															32	23.01%
5	1927	153	47	27.45%	22	12.55%	44	26.12%	5	3.61%													35	30.26%
6	1927	153	62	38.69%	13	9.07%	57	35.17%															21	17.07%
7	1932	153	57	35.28%	7	7.71%	72	44.47%															17	12.53%
8	1933	153	48	30.47%	8	5.71%	77	49.70%															20	14.12%
9	1937	138	48	34.82%	13	10.25%	69	45.23%															8	9.70%
10	1938	138	45	33.32%	9	10.02%	77	51.93%															7	4.72%
11	1943	138	32	23.09%	17	15.68%	67	41.87%															22	19.37%
12	1944	138	30	20.48%	8	8.77%	76	48.90%															24	21.85%
13	1948	147	31	19.83%	14	8.69%	68	41.85%															34	29.63%
14	1951	147	40	25.75%	16	11.40%	69	46.28%															22	16.57%
15	1954	147	50	31.98%	19	12.06%	65	43.36%		0.15%													13	12.44%
16	1957	147	40	26.63%	12	9.11%	78	48.33%	4	5.35%													13	10.59%
17	1961	144	47	32.02%	16	11.65%	70	43.83%		3.12%													11	9.39%
18	1965	144	47	34.08%	22	15.38%	72	47.67%															3	2.86%
19	1969	144	50	34.10%	18	17.02%	75	45.79%															1	3.09%
20	1973	144	54	35.08%	19	13.71%	69	46.24%	2	2.41%								1.14%					2	3.83%
21	1977	148	43	30.49%	17	11.63%	84	50.63%		1.01%								1.70%					4	5.55%
22	1981	166	65	36.46%	15	9.89%	78	45.26%			1	0.70%					1	1.72%					5	4.26%
23	1982	166	63	37.30%	15	9.12%	81	47.26%			1	0.80%					3	2.29%					4	3.02%
24	1982	166	70	39.21%	16	9.36%	75	45.20%				0.64%			1	0.40%	2	3.25%					3	2.97%
25	1987	166	51	27.07%	12	6.45%	81	44.15%		1.85%						1.54%	4	3.79%			14	11.85%	4	4.44%
26	1989	166	55	29.29%	15	9.48%	77	44.15%		1.21%					1	1.40%	7	4.97%			6	5.49%	5	3.88%
27	1992	166	45	24.47%	33	19.31%	68	39.11%		1.61%					1	2.76%	1	0.67%			10	4.68%	9	8.75%
28	1997	166	54	27.95%	17	10.40%	77	39.33%	1	2.55%	1	0.70%			2	3.85%		0.44%		0.47%	4	4.68%	10	10.73%
29	2002	166	31	22.48%	21	10.77%	81	41.48%	5	6.51%	1	0.80%			6	4.69%		0.22%		0.26%	8	3.96%	13	9.67%
30	2007	166	51	27.32%	20	10.13%	78	41.56%	4	6.94%		0.64%			6	1.85%		0.15%		0.08%	2	2.73%	5	5.76%
31	2011	166	76	36.10%	37	19.45%	20	17.45%	14	9.94%	2	1.21%	2	0.97%		0.75%		0.14%		0.09%			15	12.81%
	1918-2011	149	50	30.77%	17	11.53%	68	41.86%	15	1.95%	1	0.16%	2	0.06%	2	0.75%	1	0.82%		0.04%	7	1.42%	13	10.63%
	1981-2011	166	56	30.73%	20	11.63%	72	39.85%	3	3.69%	1	0.37%	2	0.15%	2	1.73%	2	1.66%		0.09%	7	3.28%	7	6.81%

Election Facts

"The highest vote-getter in any constituency between 1918 and 2011 was Cumann na nGaedheal leader General Richard Mulcahy, who secured 22,005 votes in Dublin in 1923"
Sean Donnelly

Elections 1918-2011

National seats and votes share main parties 1918-2011

Dail	Year	SEAT	Fine Gael % Vote	S	% Seat	% S/V	Labour % Vote	S	% Seat	% S/V	Fianna Fail % Vote	S	% Seat	% S/V
1	1918	73												
2	1921*	128												
3	1922	128	38.48%	58	45.31%	117.76%	21.33%	17	13.28%	62.27%	21.26%	36	28.13%	132.29%
4	1923	153	38.97%	63	41.18%	105.66%	10.62%	14	9.15%	86.16%	27.40%	44	28.76%	104.96%
5	1927	153	27.45%	47	30.72%	111.91%	12.55%	22	14.38%	114.57%	26.12%	44	28.76%	110.10%
6	1927	153	38.69%	62	40.52%	104.74%	9.07%	13	8.50%	93.68%	35.17%	57	37.25%	105.93%
7	1932	153	35.28%	57	37.25%	105.60%	7.71%	7	4.58%	59.34%	44.47%	72	47.06%	105.82%
8	1933	153	30.47%	48	31.37%	102.96%	5.71%	8	5.23%	91.57%	49.70%	77	50.33%	101.26%
9	1937	138	34.82%	48	34.78%	99.89%	10.25%	13	9.42%	91.91%	45.23%	69	50.00%	110.55%
10	1938	138	33.32%	45	32.61%	97.87%	10.02%	9	6.52%	65.09%	51.93%	77	55.80%	107.45%
11	1943	138	23.09%	32	23.19%	100.43%	15.68%	17	12.32%	78.56%	41.87%	67	48.55%	115.96%
12	1944	138	20.48%	30	21.74%	106.15%	8.77%	8	5.80%	66.10%	48.90%	76	55.07%	112.62%
13	1948	147	19.83%	31	21.09%	106.35%	8.69%	14	9.52%	109.60%	41.85%	68	46.26%	110.53%
14	1951	147	25.75%	40	27.21%	105.67%	11.40%	16	10.88%	95.48%	46.28%	69	46.94%	101.42%
15	1954	147	31.98%	50	34.01%	106.36%	12.06%	19	12.93%	107.17%	43.36%	65	44.22%	101.98%
16	1957	147	26.63%	40	27.21%	102.18%	9.11%	12	8.16%	89.61%	48.33%	78	53.06%	109.79%
17	1961	144	32.02%	47	32.64%	101.93%	11.65%	16	11.11%	95.37%	43.83%	70	48.61%	110.91%
18	1965	144	34.08%	47	32.64%	95.77%	15.38%	22	15.28%	99.34%	47.67%	72	50.00%	104.89%
19	1969	144	34.10%	50	34.72%	101.82%	17.02%	18	12.50%	73.44%	45.79%	75	52.08%	113.74%
20	1973	144	35.08%	54	37.50%	106.90%	13.71%	19	13.19%	96.24%	46.24%	69	47.92%	103.63%
21	1977	148	30.49%	43	29.05%	95.29%	11.63%	17	11.49%	98.77%	50.63%	84	56.76%	112.10%
22	1981	166	36.46%	65	39.16%	107.40%	9.89%	15	9.04%	91.37%	45.26%	78	46.99%	103.82%
23	1982	166	37.30%	63	37.95%	101.75%	9.12%	15	9.04%	99.08%	47.26%	81	48.80%	103.25%
24	1982	166	39.21%	70	42.17%	107.55%	9.36%	16	9.64%	102.98%	45.20%	75	45.18%	99.96%
25	1987	166	27.07%	51	30.72%	113.49%	6.45%	12	7.23%	112.08%	44.15%	81	48.80%	110.52%
26	1989	166	29.29%	55	33.13%	113.12%	9.48%	15	9.04%	95.32%	44.15%	77	46.39%	105.06%
27	1992	166	24.47%	45	27.11%	110.78%	19.31%	33	19.88%	102.95%	39.11%	68	40.96%	104.74%
28	1997	166	27.95%	54	32.53%	116.39%	10.40%	17	10.24%	98.47%	39.33%	77	46.39%	117.94%
29	2002	166	22.48%	31	18.67%	83.07%	10.77%	21	12.65%	117.46%	41.48%	81	48.80%	117.64%
30	2007	166	27.32%	51	30.72%	112.46%	10.13%	20	12.05%	118.94%	41.56%	78	46.99%	113.06%
31	2011	166	36.10%	76	45.78%	126.82%	19.40%	37	22.29%	114.89%	17.40%	20	12.05%	69.24%
	1918-2011	149	30.77%	50	33.63%	109.31%	11.53%	17	11.16%	96.77%	41.86%	68	45.95%	109.77%
	1981-2011	166	30.73%	56	33.80%	109.97%	11.63%	20	12.11%	104.11%	39.85%	72	43.13%	108.24%

* No Contest

Election Facts

"The economy was the chief influence on how people chose to vote but it is remarkable that the emotional side of voting was so prominent with more than one in three voters claiming to feel angry or let down" Millward Brown Lansdowne/RTÉ General Election 2011 Exit Poll

SEATS WON BY INDEPENDENTS AND FORMER PARTIES

Nuns vote at Drumcondra
National School, Dublin

The largest of the former parties were the Farmers and Clann na Talmhan, which won a total of 42 and 43 seats respectively. The Farmers Party, also known as the Farmer's Union, was an organisation of the larger farmers and won 15 seats at its peak in 1923. Clann na Talmhan was founded by John Donnellan in 1938 to represent small farmers and it won 11 seats in 1943 but had declined to two by 1961.

The Centre Party was founded in 1932 by three independent TDs who were later joined by James Dillon. It won 11 seats in 1933 and merged with Blueshirts and Cumann na nGaedheal in September 1933 to form Fine Gael.

Clann na Poblachta was founded in July 1946 by Seán MacBride and other former members of the IRA. It won 10 seats in 1948 and was part of the inter-party government. It declined after this and was reduced to a single seat by 1965, when it was dissolved.

National League was founded by Captain William Redmond, son of John Redmond, former Home Rule Party MP, in September 1926. It won eight seats in June 1927 but declined after that and was dissolved in 1931.

National Labour Party was formed when the ITGWU disaffiliated from the Labour Party, with five of its eight TDs forming the new party. It was part of the first Inter-Party Government in 1948 and it rejoined the mother party in 1950.

Neil Blaney split from Fianna Fáil following the 1970 'Arms Crisis' and set up Independent Fianna Fáil in Donegal. The seat stayed within the Blaney family with the exception of a short period between April 1996 (when the by-election caused by Neil Blaney's death was lost to Cecilia Keaveney of Fianna Fáil) and the general election in June 1997. The party rejoined Fianna Fáil in 2006 and Niall Blaney, nephew of Neil, won a seat for Fianna Fáil in Donegal North-East in 2007. He retired prior to the 2011 election to bring to an end the Blaney dynasty in Dáil Éireann.

Democratic Left split from the Workers' Party in 1992 with all of its TDs moving to the new party, leaving former TD Tomás MacGiolla as the main personality within the Workers' Party. Democratic Left amalgamated with the Labour Party in 1999 with two of its members going on to lead the new party – Pat Rabbitte and present Tánaiste Eamon Gilmore.

The Progressive Democrats were formed in 1985 and won 14 seats at their first general election in 1987. They experienced a major reversal at their next election in 1989 and were reduced to just six seats but the Dáil arithmetic was in their favour to allow Des O'Malley form a coalition government with his former cabinet colleague Charles Haughey. The party increased its seats to 10 in 1992, dropped to just four in 1997, but was back in government and remained there until it was dissolved in 2009.

Independent and defunct parties' seats and share of the first preference vote 1918-2011

Dail		Seats	PD S	PD %	DL S	DL %	CnaP S	CnaP %	Nat Lab S	Nat Lab %	CnaT S	CnaT %	Centre P S	Centre P %	Nat Lge S	Nat Lge %	Farmers S	Farmers %	Others S	Others %
1	1918	73																		
2	1921*	128																	4	
3	1922	128															7	7.84%	10	11.09%
4	1923	153															15	12.07%	17	10.94%
5	1927	153													8	7.29%	11	8.89%	16	14.08%
6	1927	153													2	1.62%	6	6.37%	13	9.08%
7	1932	153													3	2.07%			14	10.46%
8	1933	153											11	9.15%					9	4.97%
9	1937	138																	8	9.70%
10	1938	138																	7	4.72%
11	1943	138									11	9.80%							11	9.57%
12	1944	138							4	2.69%	9	10.08%							11	9.08%
13	1948	147					10	13.21%	5	2.55%	7	5.58%							12	8.26%
14	1951	147					2	4.07%			6	3.58%							14	8.92%
15	1954	147					3	3.82%			5	3.83%							5	4.79%
16	1957	147					1	1.68%			3	2.36%							9	6.55%
17	1961	144					1	1.13%			2	1.51%							8	6.75%
18	1965	144					1	0.75%											2	2.11%
19	1969	144																	1	3.09%
20	1973	144																	2	3.77%
21	1977	148																	4	5.55%
22	1981	166																	5	4.26%
23	1982	166																	4	3.02%
24	1982	166																	3	2.97%
25	1987	166	14	11.85%															4	4.44%
26	1989	166	6	5.49%															5	3.88%
27	1992	166	10	4.68%	4	2.78%													5	5.97%
28	1997	166	4	4.68%	4	2.51%													6	8.11%
29	2002	166	8	3.96%															13	9.49%
30	2007	166	2	2.73%															5	5.76%
31	2011	166																	14	12.81%

Independent candidate for Dublin Central Maureen O'Sullivan celebrates her election at the RDS count centre

Top vote-getters 1918-2011

	Name	Party	Votes	Constituency	Election
1	Richard Mulcahy	CG	22,005	Dublin North	1923
2	Kevin O'Higgins	CG	20,821	Dublin County	1923
3	James Walsh	SF	20,801	Cork City	1918
4	Liam de Roiste	SF	20,506	Cork City	1918
5	Jack Lynch	FF	20,079	Cork City	1977
6	Brian Cowen	FF	19,102	Laois-Offaly	2007
7	Willie O'Dea	FF	19,082	Limerick East	2007
8	Eamon de Valera	FF	18,574	Clare	1933
9	Alfie Byrne	NP	18,170	Dublin North	1932
10	Wiliam T. Cosgrave	CG	18,125	Cork Borough	1932
11	Alfie Byrne	NP	17,780	Dublin North	1927(J)
12	Eamon de Valera	R	17,762	Clare	1923
13	James Dolan	SF	17,711	Leitrim	1918
14	Wiliam T. Cosgrave	CG	17,709	Carlow-Kilkenny	1923
15	Charles J. Haughey	FF	17,637	Dublin North Central	1981
16	Enda Kenny	FG	17,472	Mayo	2011
17	Wiliam T. Cosgrave	CG	17,395	Cork Borough	1927(S)
18	Eithne Fitzgerald	LB	17,256	Dublin South	1992
19	James Walsh	CG	17,151	Cork Borough	1923
20	Michael Collins	CT	17,106	Cork Mid-North	1922
21	Shane Ross	NP	17,075	Dublin South	2011
22	Sean T. O'Kelly	FF	17,053	Dublin North	1933
23	Sean Lemass	FF	16,399	Dublin South	1943
24	Stephen Barrett	FG	16,393	Cork Borough	1954
25	Eamon de Valera	FF	16,159	Clare	1957

Red: Current TD

Top vote-getters per constituency 1918-2011

Constituency	Top Votegetter	Party	Votes	Election
Carlow-Kilkenny	William T.Cosgrave	CG	17,709	1923
Cavan-Monaghan	Brendan Smith	FF	15,548	2007
Clare	Eamon de Valera	FF	18,574	1933
Cork	James Walsh	SF	20,801	1918
Donegal	Pearse Doherty	SF	14,262	2011
Dublin	Richard Mulcahy	CG	22,005	1923
Universities	Eoin MacNeill	SF	1,644	1918
Galway	Padraic O Maille	SF	11,754	1918
Kerry	Jimmy Deenihan	FG	12,697	2007
Kildare	Martin Heydon	FG	12,755	2011
Laoighis-Offaly	Brian Cowen	FF	19,102	2007
Limerick	Willie O'Dea	FF	19,082	2007
Longford-Westmeath	Laurence Ginnell	SF	12,433	1918
Louth	Gerry Adams	SF	15,072	2011
Mayo	Enda Kenny	FG	17,472	2011
Meath	John Bruton	FG	13,037	1997
Roscommon	Gerard Boland	FF	10,719	1938
Sligo-Leitrim	James Dolan	SF	17,711	1918
Tipperary	Michael Lowry	NP	14,104	2011
Waterford	Cathal Brugha	SF	12,890	1918
Wexford	Mick Wallace	NP	13,329	2011
Wicklow	Liam Kavanagh	LB	11,843	1992

Red: 2011 Election

Elections 1918-2011

	Surname	Forename	Constituency	Party	Terms	From	To	Service	Born	Died
1	Smith	Patrick	Cavan	FF	17	27/08/1923	16/06/1977	53.81	17/07/1901	18/03/1982
2	Aiken	Frank	Louth	FF	16	27/08/1923	28/02/1973	49.51	13/02/1898	18/05/1983
3	Blaney	Neil T.	Donegal North East	IFF	15	07/12/1948	08/11/1995	46.92	30/10/1922	08/11/1995
4	McEllistrim	Thomas	Kerry North	FF	15	27/08/1923	18/06/1969	45.81	14/10/1894	04/12/1973
5	Pattison	Seamus	Carlow-Kilkenny	LB	13	04/10/1961	24/05/2007	45.64	19/04/1936	
6	Everett	James	Wicklow	LB	16	16/06/1922	18/12/1967	45.51	1/5/1894	18/12/1967
7	MacEntee	Sean*	Monaghan/Dublin SE	FF	16	21/01/1919	18/06/1969	45.43	1889	10/01/1984
8	Ryan	James	Wexford	FF	16	21/01/1919	07/04/1965	45.01	6/12/1891	25/09/1970
9	Lemass	Sean F.	Dublin South Central	FF	15	18/11/1924	18/06/1969	44.58	15/7/1899	11/05/1971
10	Flanagan	Oliver J.	Laoighis-Offaly	FG	14	23/06/1943	17/02/1987	43.66	22/05/1920	26/04/1987
11	De Valera	Eamon*	Mayo East/Clare	FF	17	21/01/1919	04/10/1961	42.70	14/10/1882	29/08/1975
12	Corry	Martin J.	Cork North East	FF	14	09/06/1927	18/06/1969	42.03	12/12/1890	14/02/1979
13	McGilligan	Patrick*	N.U.I. / Dublin N.C.	FG	14	03/11/1923	07/04/1965	41.43	12/4/1889	15/11/1979
14	Mulcahy	Gen. Richard	Dublin / Tipperary S	FG	14	21/01/1919	04/10/1961	40.80	10/5/1886	16/12/1971
15	Breslin	Cormac	Donegal-Leitrim	FF	12	01/07/1937	16/06/1977	39.96	25/04/1902	23/01/1978
16	Boland	Gerald	Roscommon	FF	13	27/08/1923	04/10/1961	38.11	25/05/1885	05/01/1973
17	MacEoin	Gen. Sean*	Longford-Westmeath/S	FG	14	24/05/1921	07/04/1965	38.09	1893	07/07/1973
18	Cosgrave	Liam	Dun Laoghaire	FG	11	23/06/1943	11/06/1981	37.97	13/04/1920	
19	Spring	Dan	Kerry North	LB	11	23/06/1943	11/06/1981	37.97	01/07/1910	01/01/1998
20	Kennedy	Michael*	Lngfrd-Westmeath/Me	FF	13	09/06/1927	14/02/1965	37.69		14/02/1965
21	Brady	Sean	Dun Laoghaire	FF	12	15/09/1927	07/04/1965	37.56	28/5/1890	24/02/1969
22	Briscoe	Robert	Dublin South West	FF	12	15/09/1927	07/04/1965	37.56	25/9/1894	30/05/1969
23	Dillon	James*	Donegal/Monaghan	FG	12	16/02/1932	18/06/1969	37.34	26/09/1902	10/02/1986
24	Andrews	David	Dun Laoghaire	FF	11	07/04/1965	17/05/2002	37.11	15/03/1935	
25	Briscoe	Ben	Dublin South Central	FF	11	07/04/1965	17/05/2002	37.11	11/03/1934	
26	Molloy	Bobby	Galway West	PD	11	07/04/1965	17/05/2002	37.11	06/07/1936	
27	Breen	Dan	Tipperary South	FF	12	27/08/1923	07/04/1965	36.92	11/8/1894	27/12/1969
28	Hogan	Patrick	Clare	LB	13	27/08/1923	24/01/1969	36.71	1886	24/01/1969
29	O Briain	Donnchadh	Limerick West	FF	11	24/01/1933	18/06/1969	36.40	17/11/1897	22/09/1981
30	Corish	Brendan	Wexford	LB	11	04/12/1945	18/02/1982	36.21	19/11/1918	17/02/1990
31	Haughey	Charles J.	Dublin North Central	FF	11	05/03/1957	25/11/1992	35.73	16/09/1925	13/06/2006
32	Harte	Paddy	Donegal North East	FG	11	04/10/1961	06/06/1997	35.67	26/07/1931	
33	Treacy	Sean	Tipperary South	NP	11	04/10/1961	06/06/1997	35.67	23/09/1923	
34	De Valera	Vivion	Dublin Central	FF	10	04/12/1945	11/06/1981	35.52	13/12/1910	16/02/1982
35	Costello	John A.	Dublin South East	FG	10	24/01/1933	18/06/1969	35.46	20/6/1891	05/01/1976
36	Bruton	John	Meath	FG	11	18/06/1969	01/11/2004	35.37	18/05/1947	
37	Kenny	Enda	Mayo	FG	12	12/11/1975		35.49	24/04/1951	
38	Childers	Erskine*	Lgford-Wmeath/Monag	FF	11	17/06/1938	01/06/1973	34.96	11/12/1905	17/11/1974
39	Morrissey	Daniel	Tipperary North	FG	13	16/06/1922	05/03/1957	34.72		1981
40	Moran	Michael	Mayo West	FF	10	17/06/1938	28/02/1973	34.70	25/12/1912	06/05/1983
41	Fahy	Frank	Galway South	FF	14	21/01/1919	14/07/1953	34.48	12/11/1880	14/07/1953
42	O'Malley	Desmond	Limerick East	PD	11	22/05/1968	17/05/2002	33.99	01/02/1939	
43	Dockrell	Maurice E.	Dublin Central	FG	10	23/06/1943	16/06/1977	33.98	06/10/1908	09/12/1986
44	Davin	William	Laoighis-Offaly	LB	13	16/06/1922	01/03/1956	33.71	1890	01/03/1956
45	Ahern	Bertie	Dublin Central	FF	10	16/06/1977	25/02/2011	33.70	12/09/1951	
46	O'Hanlon	Rory	Cavan-Monaghan	FF	10	16/06/1977	25/02/2011	33.70	07/02/1934	
47	O'Keeffe	Jim	Cork South West	FG	10	16/06/1977	25/02/2011	33.70	31/03/1941	
48	Woods	Michael	Dublin North East	FF	10	16/06/1977	25/02/2011	33.70	08/12/1935	
49	Killilea(sen)	Mark	Galway North	FF	11	09/06/1927	04/10/1961	33.38	1896	29/09/1970
50	Lynch	Jack	Cork Borough	FF	9	04/02/1948	11/06/1981	33.35	15/08/1917	20/10/1999
51	Bartley	Gerald	Galway West	FF	11	16/02/1932	07/04/1965	33.14	12/06/1898	10/05/1974
52	Norton	William*	Dublin Co. / Kildare	LB	12	18/02/1926	04/12/1963	33.10	1900	04/12/1963
53	Quinn	Ruairi	Dublin South East	LB	10	16/06/1977		33.21	22/04/1946	
54	Doyle	Peadar	Dublin South West	FG	12	27/08/1923	04/08/1956	32.94		04/08/1956
55	Davern	Noel	Tipperary South	FF	8	18/06/1969	24/05/2007	32.25	24/12/1945	
56	Traynor	Oscar	Dublin North East	FF	12	11/03/1925	04/10/1961	32.15	21/3/1886	21/12/1963
57	Derrig	Thomas*	Mayo/Carlow-Kilkenny	FF	13	24/05/1921	19/11/1956	31.71		19/11/1956
58	Ruttledge	Patrick	Mayo North	FF	13	24/05/1921	08/05/1952	30.96	1892	08/05/1952
59	Byrne	Alfred	Dublin North East	NP	13	16/06/1922	13/03/1956	30.75	17/3/1882	13/03/1956
60	O'Leary	John	Kerry South	FF	10	07/12/1966	06/06/1997	30.50	03/05/1933	
61	Murphy	Michael Pat	Cork South West	LB	8	30/05/1951	11/06/1981	30.03	12/03/1919	28/10/2000
62	Noonan	Michael	Limerick East	FG	10	11/06/1981		29.91	21/05/1943	
63	Bruton	Richard	Dublin North Central	FG	9	18/02/1982		29.22	15/03/1953	
64	McGinley	Dinny	Donegal South West	FG	9	18/02/1982		29.22	27/04/1945	
65	O'Dea	Willie	Limerick East	FF	9	18/02/1982		29.22	01/11/1952	

Red: **Current TD** Green: **Broken service** *Elected in more than one constituency
Note: **Service of members of the 31st Dáil is calculated up to 10/6/2011**

Shortest Serving TDs 1918-2011

	Surname	Forename	Constituency	Party	Terms	From	To	Years Service
1	McCann	Pierce	Tipperary East	SF	1	21/01/1919	06/03/1919	0.12
2	Doherty	Kieran	Cavan-Monaghan	HBlk	1	11/06/1981	02/08/1981	0.14
3	Carter	Michael	Leitrim-Sligo	F	1	09/06/1927	15/09/1927	0.27
4	Clery	Prof. Arthur	N.U.I.	NP	1	09/06/1927	15/09/1927	0.27
5	Cullen	Denis	Dublin North	LB	1	09/06/1927	15/09/1927	0.27
6	Duffy	William	Galway	NL	1	09/06/1927	15/09/1927	0.27
7	Falvey	Thomas	Clare	R	1	09/06/1927	15/09/1927	0.27
8	Garahan	Hugh	Longford-Westmeath	F	1	09/06/1927	15/09/1927	0.27
9	Gill	John	Laoighis-Offaly	LB	1	09/06/1927	15/09/1927	0.27
10	Hewson	Gilbert	Limerick	NP	1	09/06/1927	15/09/1927	0.27
11	Horgan	John	Cork Borough	NL	1	09/06/1927	15/09/1927	0.27
12	Jinks	John	Leitrim-Sligo	NL	1	09/06/1927	15/09/1927	0.27
13	Lynch	Gilbert	Galway	LB	1	09/06/1927	15/09/1927	0.27
14	Mullen	Eugene	Mayo South	FF	1	09/06/1927	15/09/1927	0.27
15	O'Gorman	David	Cork East	F	1	09/06/1927	15/09/1927	0.27
16	Quill	Timothy	Cork North	LB	1	09/06/1927	15/09/1927	0.27
17	Shannon	James	Wexford	LB	1	09/06/1927	15/09/1927	0.27
18	Tynan	Thomas	Laoighis-Offaly	FF	1	09/06/1927	15/09/1927	0.27
19	Kennedy	Hugh	Dublin South	CG	1	25/10/1923	05/06/1924	0.61
20	Drohan	Frank	Waterford	SF	1	24/05/1921	05/01/1922	0.62
21	Lee	George	Dublin South	FG	1	05/06/2009	08/02/2010	0.68
22	Acheson	Carrie	Tipperary South	FF	1	11/06/1981	18/02/1982	0.69
23	Agnew	Paddy	Louth	Hblk	1	11/06/1981	18/02/1982	0.69
24	Joyce	Carey	Cork East	FF	1	11/06/1981	18/02/1982	0.69
25	Loftus	Sean D.	Dublin North East	NP	1	11/06/1981	18/02/1982	0.69

Lowest vote-getters 1918-2011

	Candidate	Party	Constituency	1st Prefs	Election
1	Maria McCool	NP	Dublin North West	13	1997
2	Peadar O Ceallaigh	NP	Dublin South East	18	2011
3	Aidan Ryan	NP	Limerick East	19	2002
4	Hugh O'Brien	NP	Clare	21	1981
5	David Henry	NP	Dublin South Central	23	1997
6	Jim Tallon	NP	Meath	24	1997
7	Seamus Cunningham	NP	Longford-Westmeath	24	2007
8	John Olahan	NP	Dublin North West	25	1992
9	Benny Cooney	NP	Dublin Central	25	2011
10	Noel O'Gara	NP	Dublin South East	27	2007
11	John Keigher	NP	Dublin South East	27	2011
12	Patrick Moore	NP	Limerick East	28	2007
13	John Harpur	NP	Dublin South East	29	1997
14	Sean Forkin	NP	Mayo	29	2011
15	Patrick Clarke	NP	Dublin South East	29	1987
16	Maurice Fitzgerald	NP	Cork South Central	30	2007
17	Michael Murphy	NP	Cork South Central	31	1987
18	Barbara Hyland	NP	Dublin North West	33	1987
19	James Tallon	NP	Wexford	33	1987
20	Peter O'Sullivan	NP	Dublin South East	34	2007
21	Ciara Malone	NP	Dublin West	36	1997
22	Norman Hunt	NP	Dublin North Central	36	1997
23	Sean Gormley	NP	Meath	36	1987
24	Patrick Shelley	NP	Dublin Central	39	1997
25	Lar Fraser	NP	Dublin North East	39	1997

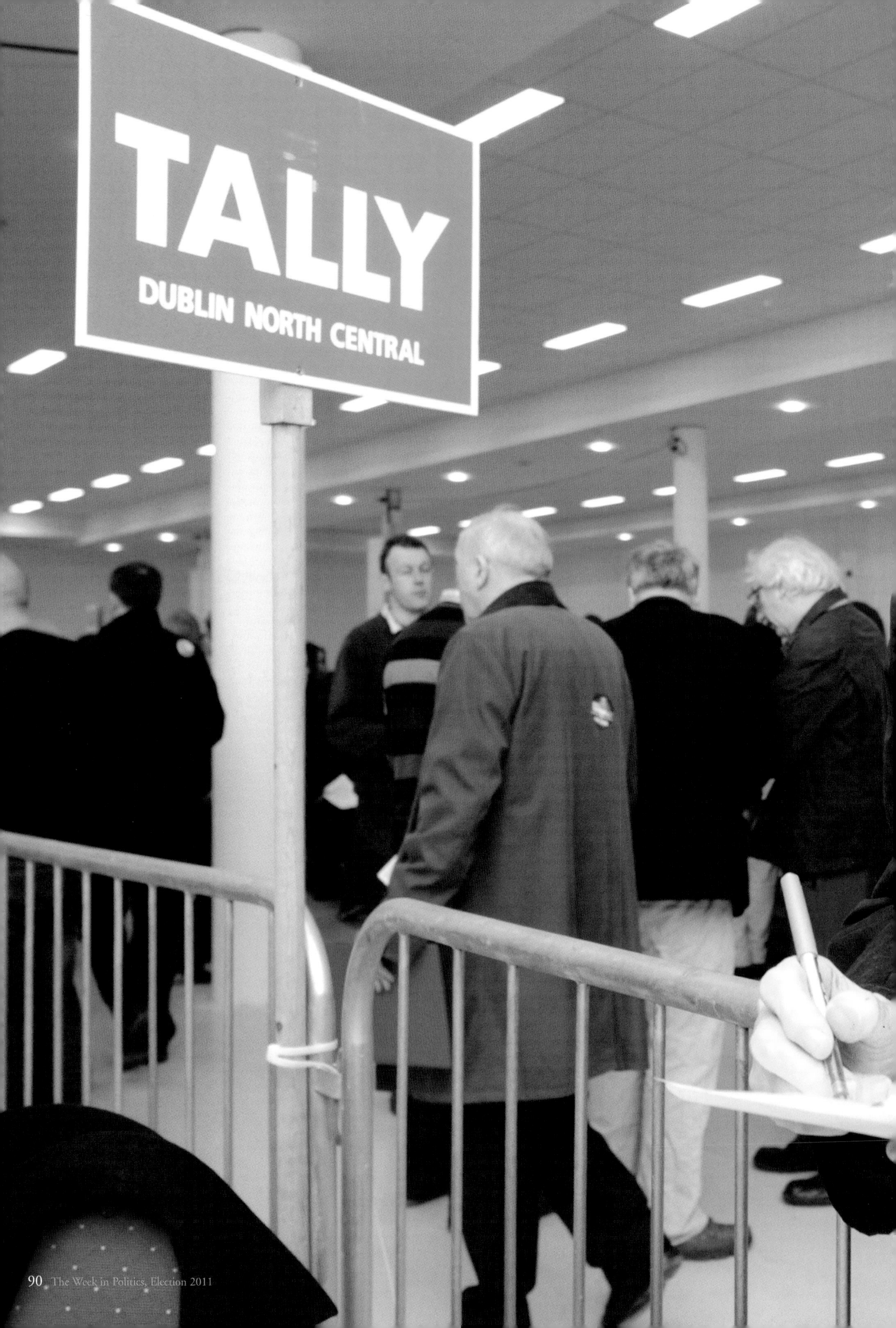
TALLY
DUBLIN NORTH CENTRAL

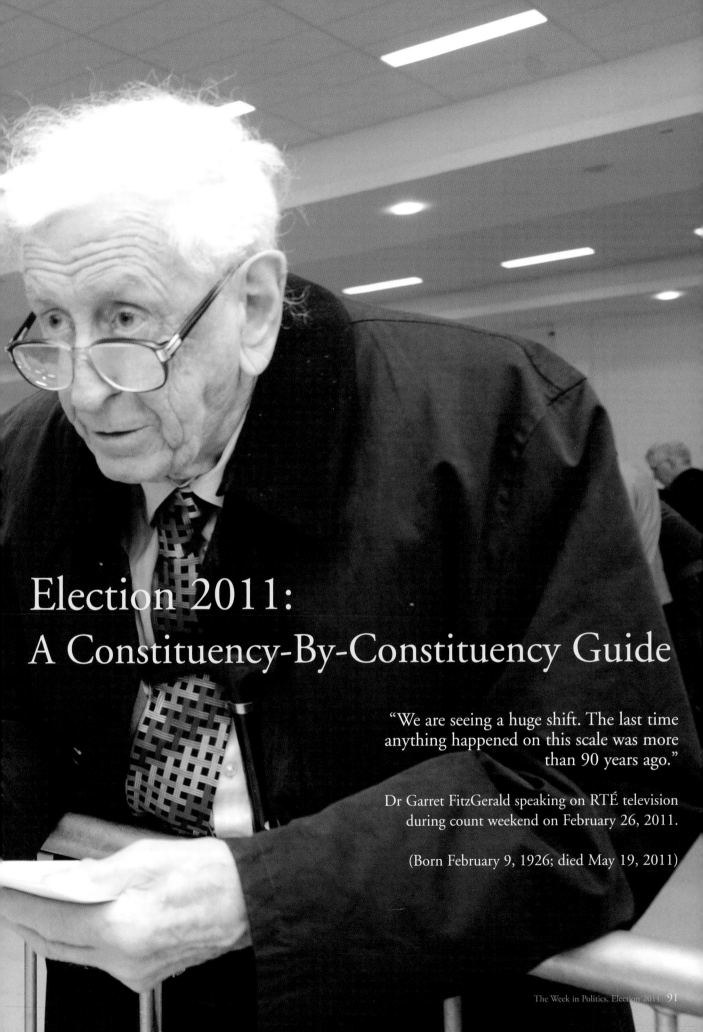

Election 2011:
A Constituency-By-Constituency Guide

"We are seeing a huge shift. The last time anything happened on this scale was more than 90 years ago."

Dr Garret FitzGerald speaking on RTÉ television during count weekend on February 26, 2011.

(Born February 9, 1926; died May 19, 2011)

ConorMcMorrow introduces you to the 166 TDs in the 31st Dáil – their heroes, the heartbreak they witnessed on the doorsteps and what they do in their spare time

Know your TDs: From canoeing down the Zambezi to the Pamplona Bull Run

Jubilant cheers rang out in count centres in the 'wee' hours of 27 February as successful candidates were hoisted up on their supporters' shoulders. And 76 of the current crop of TDs will forever recall 9 March. The day they walked into the Dáil chamber for the first time. Those are the happy memories. But this was also a gloomy election.

In our TD biographies, you will see how the 24-day campaign brought each deputy into the homes of the voters of Ireland. They met with families struggling to cope under the dark cloud of the economic crisis.

"I know a normal couple, who have four children under the age of eight, who both lost their jobs and they had their home repossessed. I will never forget the mother in the High Court begging the judge to take the house off them as she could no longer cope with the pressure from the banks to pay back money they did not have. People like them are the collateral damage of the Celtic Tiger," explains one newly elected Fine Gael TD.

One of his party colleagues says he realised how serious the economic crisis was "when 10 young people from a village in my area emigrated to Australia in one group".

A new rural TD believes "the future looks bleak for GAA clubs. There used to be 18th and 21st birthday parties. Now emigration parties have taken over".

A veteran TD was shocked "when a young constituent told me she had more friends in Sydney and London than she had in Dublin".

A new opposition TD turns to a sporting occasion as he recounts a day when the severity of the recession really struck him: "The rugby match between South Africa and Ireland in November 2010. The world champions were here and the Aviva stadium was half empty."

Despite the common perception that our politicians live in ivory towers, they have not been immune to the recession. One Sinn Féin TD tells us she entered public life after she lost the job she had held for 16 years.

Another new TD recounts the heartbreak of "the day I closed the door on the retail business I ran for 20 years, and my family had run for generations, for the last time".

Most TDs recall the day Ajai Chopra and his IMF colleagues arrived in Dublin as the moment that crystallised how serious the economic crisis had become.

However, the tales of how the TDs arrived in the 31st Dáil are not all miserable.

Take the story of the Labour TD who had a stroke in 2008 and made a remarkable recovery through rehabilitation.

Or her party colleague who explains: "I have suffered from cerebral palsy and I believe that any disability should not inhibit people from achieving in life."

A Cabinet minister also reveals: "I had a severe stutter until the age of 16 before I overcame the speech impediment."

As well as the personal histories of the 166 Dáil deputies, election experts Trinity College Professor Michael Gallagher and expert pollster Sean Donnelly have analysed how each vote was cast.

Donnelly has crunched every number and compiled tables displaying a constituency-by-constituency breakdown of first-preference votes, each party's share of the vote and detailed transfer analysis.

Within our TD biographies, each deputy was asked which politician, living or deceased, they most admired. While one Cabinet minister reveals that he admires former French president François Mitterand, another takes inspiration from his predecessor, Charles deGaulle.

Barack Obama, Michael Collins, Jim Kemmy, Seán Lemass and Nelson Mandela are among the figures revered by our TDs.

A Fine Gael TD tells how he is one of the founding members of Dubai's first GAA club, while a party colleague likes nothing better than taking to the roads on his motorbike.

One of the 14 Sinn Féin TDs is a karate enthusiast while a Labour TD was an extra in several Irish films.

And then there's the TD who paddled a canoe down Africa's Zambezi River while another recounts how he participated in the annual Pamplona Bull Run in Spain. Perfect preparation for going into government in this climate, one might say.

So here they are – the 31st Dáil.

A Cabinet Mminister also reveals: "I had a severe stutter until the age of 16 before I overcame the speech impediment"

Paschal Donohoe, Fine Gael candidate for Dublin Central, waits anxiously to hear if he has won his seat at the count centre at the RDS in Dublin

Carlow-Kilkenny (5 seats)

A reversal of fortune as Fine Gael wins three out of five for the first time and Fianna Fáil is reduced to just a single seat

Elected

Ann Phelan (Lab) Count 12, John McGuinness* (FF) Count 12, John Paul Phelan (FG) Final count, Phil Hogan* (FG) Final count, Pat Deering (FG) Final count.

Analysis by Sean Donnelly

There were no Constituency Commission boundary changes here since 2007 and it remained a five-seat constituency. This was another example of Fine Gael's good vote management in this election as it managed to convert 2.4 quotas into three seats. Its vote was up 10 percentage points on 2007 and John Paul Phelan topped the poll, just ahead of outgoing deputy Phil Hogan. This constituency, like many others, came down to a battle for the final seat, this time between Carlow-based Pat Deering of Fine Gael and Bobby Aylward of Fianna Fáil. Deering was in the frame in fifth place on the first count and about 700 votes ahead of Aylward. He maintained his advantage throughout the count and went on to take the final seat by a comfortable margin.

Former Ceann Comhairle Seamus Pattison represented Labour here from 1961 until his retirement in 2007 when the party failed to retain his seat. It increased its vote in this election by seven percentage points on the party's 2007 performance and with one quota between the party's two candidates it was well-placed to regain its seat. Kilkenny-based Ann Phelan was well ahead of running mate, Carlow-based Des Hurley, on the first count and she went on to take the first seat on the 12th count.

This was another very poor result for Fianna Fáil as the party went from three seats in 2007 to just one in 2011, despite getting its best first-preference vote of this election – 28.10% in this five-seater. MJ Nolan retired and Jennifer Murnane O'Connor replaced him on the ticket. The Fianna Fáil vote was down by 20 percentage points but with 1.7 quotas it should have been in contention for a second seat. But its vote was spread over three candidates and Fianna Fáil ended up with just a single seat as Aylward lost the battle for the final seat.

Sinn Féin increased its vote by six percentage points but with just 0.6 quotas spread over two candidates, the party's leading candidate Kathleen Funchion was too far off the pace and was outside the frame on the first count with less than half a quota. She thus had little chance of a seat and so it proved.

Outgoing Green Party TD and Minister of State Mary White lost her seat when she got just 2.8% of the first-preference vote and she, like many of her party colleagues, lost the right to reclaim her expenses.

Conor MacLiam of the Socialist Party, the widower of the late Susie Long, did poorly and got just 2% of the vote. He lost his right to reclaim his expenses, as did the seven independent candidates, who all polled poorly.

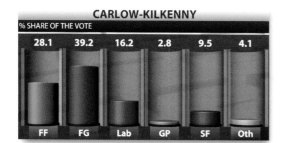

CARLOW-KILKENNY

% SHARE OF THE VOTE

FF	FG	Lab	GP	SF	Oth
28.1	39.2	16.2	2.8	9.5	4.1

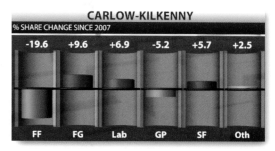

CARLOW-KILKENNY

% SHARE CHANGE SINCE 2007

FF	FG	Lab	GP	SF	Oth
-19.6	+9.6	+6.9	-5.2	+5.7	+2.5

*outgoing TDs

ANN PHELAN (Lab)

Home Address: Brandondale, Graiguenamanagh, Co Kilkenny.
Phone: 086 3294420 (M) 059 9724310 (H) 01 6183216 (LH)
Email: ann.phelan@oireachtas.ie
Website: www.labour.ie/annphelan/
Twitter: twitter.com/annphelan1
Facebook: Yes.
Birth Place/Date: Graiguenamanagh, September 1961.
Marital Status/Family: Married to Kieran Phelan; 2 daughters, 1 son.
Education: Brigidin College Goresbridge; Waterford IT.
Occupation: Public representative. Formerly accounts secretary.
Biography: She secured 8,072 first-preference votes to get elected on the 12th count in her first Dáil election. Elected to Kilkenny County Council 2004 and 2009.
Hobbies: Swimming, walking and horse riding.
Did you know? Ann suffered a stroke in April 2008 while out horse riding. She has made a remarkable recovery through rehabilitation.
Politician (living or deceased) you most admire: Mary Robinson.
Priority as a TD? I come from a disadvantaged area and I want to create jobs in the area.
Why did you stand for election? I have been asked to stand a number of times but this is the first time that I have been in a position to devote all my energy to the election.
Is there any particular event that brought home to you just how serious the economic crisis had become? Seeing GAA and soccer clubs getting decimated by the emigration of our young people. It is like the 1980s all over again.

JOHN McGUINNESS (FF)

Constituency Address: 11 O'Loughlin Road, Kilkenny.
Phone: 087 2855 834 (M) 056 7770672 (O) 01 6183137 (LH)
Email: john@johnmcguinness.ie or john.mcguinness@oireachtas.ie
Website: www.johnmcguinness.ie
Facebook: facebook/johnmcguinness
Birth Place/Date: Kilkenny, 1955.
Marital Status/Family: Married to Margaret; 3 sons, 1 daughter.
Education: CBS Kilkenny.
Occupation: Full-time public representative.
Biography: Party spokesperson on Small Business Regulatory Framework. First elected to Dáil in 1997 and re-elected at each subsequent election. Minister of State for Trade and Commerce 2007-2009. Member, Kilkenny Corporation 1979-2003. Mayor of Kilkenny 1996-1997 (third generation of family to serve as Mayor of Kilkenny Borough). Member, Kilkenny County Council 1991-2003.
Hobbies: Reading, walking and following Kilkenny hurling.
Did you know? John served for many years on Kilkenny Borough Council with his late father Mick McGuinness and they made history by being the only father and son team to be elected to a council in Ireland.
Politician (living or deceased) you most admire: Seán Lemass and Bill Clinton.
Priority as a TD? To influence legislation in the best interest of the country and the people I serve.
Why did you stand for election? To take a stand on national and local issues.
Is there any particular event that brought home to you just how serious the economic crisis had become? The closure of small business, the loss of jobs and the debt crisis.

JOHN PAUL PHELAN (FG)

Home Address: Smithstown, Tullogher, Mullinavat, Co Kilkenny.
Phone: 056 7793210l (O) 01 6184202 (LH)
Email: : johnpaul.phelan@oireachtas.ie
Website: johnpaul.phelan@oireachtas.ie
Twitter: twitter.com/jpphelan
Facebook: Yes.
Birth Place/Date: Waterford, September 1978.
Marital Status/Family: Single.
Education: Good Counsel College, New Ross; Waterford IT (BBS economics and finance). Holds a diploma in law and currently studying legal studies at the King's Inns.
Occupation: Full-time public representative.
Biography: Topped the poll in Election 2011 to become a first-time deputy. Elected to the Seanad in 2002. Elected to Kilkenny County Council in 1999. Narrowly lost out on a Dáil seat in 2007 general election.
Hobbies: GAA player and supporter, plays rugby, avid reader.
Did you know? The youngest outgoing member of the Seanad, John Paul was also the youngest ever councillor elected to Kilkenny County Council at 20 years old.
Politician (living or deceased) you most admire: Michael Noonan.
Priority as a TD? Create jobs, boost confidence and ensure nobody else has to leave our country to find work.
Why did you stand for election? I believe I have the mix of youth, experience, drive and commitment to get Ireland back to work.
Is there any particular event that brought home to you just how serious the economic crisis had become? Before the election I went through the phonebook on my mobile to see how many friends and supporters I could mobilise to help with canvassing, postering etc. As I thumbed down through the numbers, I was stunned by the number of people my own age who had emigrated all over the world.

Carlow-Kilkenny

PHIL HOGAN (FG)

Home Address: Grovine, Co Kilkenny.
Phone: 056 771490 (CO) 01 6183000 (LH)
Email: phil.hogan@oireachtas.ie
Website: www.philhogan.ie
Facebook: Yes.
Birth Place/Date: Kilkenny, July 1950.
Marital Status/Family: Separated; 1 son.
Education: Mill Hill College, Freshford, Co Kilkenny; St Kieran's College, Kilkenny and University College, Cork.
Occupation: Full-time public representative. Auctioneer and qualified teacher.
Biography: Phil was first elected to the Dáil in 1989 and has been returned in all subsequent elections. Currently Minister for the Environment, Community and Local Government. In December 1994 he was appointed Minister of State at the Department of Finance, with responsibility for Public Expenditure and the Office of Public Works. He resigned in February 1995. Senator 1987-1989. Member Kilkenny County Council 1982-2003. In Fine Gael, he has held a number of positions including Parliamentary Party chairman, director of Organisation, Enterprise spokesman as well as Consumer Affairs, Regional Affairs and Food Industry positions.
Hobbies: Member of GAA, Kilkenny Archaeological Society and Castlecomer Golf Club.
Did you know? Phil resigned as Minister of State in 1995 – an unusual political event.
Politician (living or deceased) you most admire: My late father, Councillor Tom Hogan.
Priority as a TD? Help create a better Ireland.
Why did you stand for election? To help my community and my country.
Is there any particular event that brought home to you just how serious the economic crisis had become? When we were forced to invite in the IMF.

PAT DEERING (FG)

Home Address: Ballyoliver, Rathvilly, Co Carlow.
Phone: 087 6674024 (M) 01 6184235 (LH)
Email: Patdeering@eircom.net
Website: www.patdeering.ie
Birth Place/Date: St Brigids, Carlow, February 1967.
Marital Status/Family: Married to Paula Byrne; 1 son, 1 daughter.
Education: Ballyfin College, Co Laois; Tullow Community School, Co Carlow; Piltown Agricultural College, Co Kilkenny.
Occupation: Public representative and farmer.
Biography: Secured 7,470 first-preference votes to get elected in first general election. Elected to Carlow County Council in 2009 and took the place of his father Michael Deering, who had served for 42 years before him.
Hobbies: GAA activist and a member of Rathvilly GAA club.
Did you know? Pat served as chairman to Carlow County Board GAA and resigned in early 2010 to follow his political career.
Politician (living or deceased) you most admire: Michael Collins.
Priority as a TD? To represent the people of Carlow and help secure jobs for them. It is a priority that I help maintain services such as hospitals etc for the people of Carlow.
Why did you stand for election? I wanted to represent the people of Carlow as I felt they had lacked real representation for the last few years.
Is there any particular event that brought home to you just how serious the economic crisis had become? The number of people who have had their houses repossessed in my own area after the property bubble burst.

First preference votes

	Candidate	Party	1st	%	Quota	Count	Status
	Seats	**5**			**12,291**		
1	Phelan, Ann	LB	8,072	10.95%	0.66	12	Made Quota
2	McGuinness, John*	FF	9,531	12.92%	0.78	12	Made Quota
3	Phelan, John Paul	FG	10,929	14.82%	0.89	12	Made Quota
4	Hogan, Phil*	FG	10,525	14.27%	0.86	13	Elected
5	Deering, Pat	FG	7,470	10.13%	0.61	13	Elected
6	Aylward, Bobby*	FF	6,762	9.17%	0.55	13	Not Elected
7	Funchion, Kathleen	SF	4,075	5.53%	0.33	11	Eliminated
8	Murnane O'Connor, Jennifer	FF	4,428	6.00%	0.36	10	Eliminated
9	Hurley, Des	LB	3,908	5.30%	0.32	9	Eliminated
10	Cassin, John	SF	2,958	4.01%	0.24	8	Eliminated
11	White, Mary*	GP	2,072	2.81%	0.17	7	No Expenses
12	MacLiam, Conor	SP	1,135	1.54%	0.09	6	No Expenses
13	Kelly, Stephen	NP	601	0.81%	0.05	6	No Expenses
14	Couchman, Johnny	NP	384	0.52%	0.03	5	No Expenses
15	O'Hara, John	NP	253	0.34%	0.02	4	No Expenses
16	Leahy, Ramie	NP	256	0.35%	0.02	3	No Expenses
17	Murphy, David	NP	195	0.26%	0.02	2	No Expenses
18	Walsh, Noel G.	NP	119	0.16%	0.01	1	No Expenses
19	Dalton, John	NP	70	0.09%	0.01	1	No Expenses

*Outgoing TD Valid Poll: 73,743 Quota: 12,291 No Expenses limit: 3,073

Party votes

Party	2011					2007					Change	
	Cand	1st	%	Quota	Seats	Cand	1st	%	Quota	Seats	%	Seats
FG	3	28,924	39.22%	2.35	3	3	20,031	29.61%	1.78	1	+9.61%	+2
LB	2	11,980	16.25%	0.97	1	2	6,324	9.35%	0.56		+6.90%	+1
FF	3	20,721	28.10%	1.69	1	3	32,272	47.70%	2.86	3	-19.60%	-2
SF	2	7,033	9.54%	0.57		1	2,568	3.80%	0.23		+5.74%	
SP	1	1,135	1.54%	0.09							+1.54%	
GP	1	2,072	2.81%	0.17		1	5,386	7.96%	0.48	1	-5.15%	-1
PD						1	1,073	1.59%	0.10		-1.59%	
Others	7	1,878	2.55%	0.15							+2.55%	
Total	19	73,743	100.0%	12,291	5	11	67,654	100.0%	11,276	5	0.00%	0
Electorate	105,449	69.93%					102,016	66.32%			+3.62%	
Spoiled	821	1.10%					705	1.03%			+0.07%	
Turnout	74,564	70.71%					68,359	67.01%			+3.70%	

Transfer analysis

From	To	FG	LB	FF	SF	SP	GP	Others	Non Trans
LB	6,552	1,669	2,447	865	301				1,270
		25.47%	37.35%	13.20%	4.59%				19.38%
FF	5,636	1278	433	2,760	332				833
		22.68%	7.68%	48.97%	5.89%				14.78%
SF	10,405	1,796	2,603	1,626	1,885				2,495
		17.26%	25.02%	15.63%	18.12%				23.98%
SP	1,217	244	280	158	288		85		162
		20.05%	23.01%	12.98%	23.66%		6.98%		13.31%
GP	2,278	705	743	458	209				163
		30.95%	32.62%	20.11%	9.17%				7.16%
NP	2,309	441	357	288	357	82	121	431	232
		19.10%	15.46%	12.47%	15.46%	3.55%	5.24%	18.67%	10.05%
Total	28,397	6,133	6,863	6,155	3,372	82	206	431	5,155
		21.60%	24.17%	21.67%	11.87%	0.29%	0.73%	1.52%	18.15%

Carlow-Kilkenny

Count details

Candidate	Party	1st	2nd Walsh Dalton	3rd Murphy Votes	4th Leahy Votes	5th O'Hara Votes	6th Couchman Votes	7th MacLiam Kelly	8th White Votes	9th Cassin Votes	10th Hurley Votes	11th Murnane Votes	12th Funchion Votes	13th Phelan A Surplus
			Seats 5										**Quota 12,291**	
Phelan, Ann	LB		+13	+13	+27	+28	+18	+355	+536	+124	+2,447	+433	+2,094	-1,869
		8,072	8,085	8,098	8,125	8,153	8,171	8,526	9,062	9,186	11,633	12,066	**14,160**	12,291
McGuinness, John*	FF		+12	+5	+35	+12	+17	+155	+172	+60	+109	+1,697	+825	
		9,531	9,543	9,548	9,583	9,595	9,612	9,767	9,939	9,999	10,108	11,805	**12,630**	12,630
Phelan, John Paul	FG		+10	+10	+26	+18	+24	+166	+233	+51	+112	+132	+506	+357
		10,929	10,939	10,949	10,975	10,993	11,017	11,183	11,416	11,467	11,579	11,711	12,217	**12,574**
Hogan, Phil*	FG		+12	+3	+18	+7	+22	+185	+162	+34	+152	+87	+563	+227
		10,525	10,537	10,540	10,558	10,565	10,587	10,772	10,934	10,968	11,120	11,207	11,770	**11,997**
Deering, Pat	FG		+4	+9	+8	+11	+95	+57	+310	+274	+670	+1,059	+368	+151
		7,470	7,474	7,483	7,491	7,502	7,597	7,654	7,964	8,238	8,908	9,967	10,335	**10,486**
Aylward, Bobby	FF		+10	+3	+11	+10	+1	+70	+61	+33	+44	+1,063	+401	+141
		6,762	6,772	6,775	6,786	6,796	6,797	6,867	6,928	6,961	7,005	8,068	8,469	8,610
Funchion, Kathleen	SF		+14	+12	+20	+23	+18	+300	+111	+1,885	+301	+332	-7,091	
		4,075	4,089	4,101	4,121	4,144	4,162	4,462	4,573	6,458	6,759	7,091	Eliminated	
Murnane O'Connor, J.	FF		+3	+3	+1	+18	+40	+40	+225	+307	+571	-5,636		
		4,428	4,431	4,434	4,435	4,453	4,493	4,533	4,758	5,065	5,636	Eliminated		
Hurley, Des	LB		+2	+9	+9	+24	+26	+113	+207	+385	-4,683			
		3,908	3,910	3,919	3,928	3,952	3,978	4,091	4,298	4,683	Eliminated			
Cassin, John	SF		+1	+7	+4	+33	+31	+182	+98	-3,314				
		2,958	2,959	2,966	2,970	3,003	3,034	3,216	3,314	Eliminated				
White, Mary	GP		+5	+5	+16	+8	+29	+143	-2,278					
		2,072	2,077	2,082	2,098	2,106	2,135	2,278	Eliminated					
MacLiam, Conor	SP		+9	+13	+22	+21	+17	-1,217						
		1,135	1,144	1,157	1,179	1,200	1,217	Eliminated						
Kelly, Stephen	NP		+24	+21	+35	+53	+86	-820						
		601	625	646	681	734	820	Eliminated						
Couchman, Johnny	NP		+6	+20	+13	+48	-471							
		384	390	410	423	471	Eliminated							
O'Hara, John	NP		+17	+57	+18	-345								
		253	270	327	345	Eliminated								
Leahy, Ramie	NP		+16	+5	-277									
		256	272	277	Eliminated									
Murphy, David	NP		+12	-207										
		195	207	Eliminated										
Walsh, Noel G	NP		-119											
		119	Eliminated											
Dalton, John	NP		-70											
		70	Eliminated											
Non-transferable			+19	+12	+14	+31	+47	+271	+163	+161	+277	+833	+2,334	+993
Cumulative			19	31	45	76	123	394	557	718	995	1,828	4,162	5,155
Total		73,743	73,743	73,743	73,743	73,743	73,743	73,743	73,743	73,743	73,743	73,743	73,743	73,743

Election Facts

"Carlow-Kilkenny was Fianna Fáil's top constituency as the party secured 28.1% of the vote but still only won one seat"

Sean Donnelly

Cavan-Monaghan (5 seats)

Another big Fine Gael performance as it takes three out of five seats for the first time

Elected

Caoimhghín Ó Caoláin* (SF) Count 1, Brendan Smith* (FF) Count 8, Joe O'Reilly (FG) Final count, Seán Conlan (FG) Final count, Heather Humphreys (FG) Final count.

Analysis by Sean Donnelly

There were no boundary changes here since 2007 and it remained a five-seat constituency. This was another big performance in a five-seater from Fine Gael as it managed to convert 2.4 quotas into three seats. Its three leading candidates were grouped closely together on the first count with its fourth candidate, Peter McVitty, well off the pace in ninth place. Outgoing senator Joe O'Reilly was the party's leading vote getter and he was just ahead of newcomers Heather Humphreys and Seán Conlan. They went on to take the final three seats with Humphreys holding off Kathryn Reilly of Sinn Féin for the final seat. Its performance was enhanced by the fact that Fine Gael ran three new Dáil candidates, two of whom got elected, as long-serving deputy Seymour Crawford had retired ahead of the election.

The Sinn Féin vote was up six percentage points and with 1.6 quotas it was in contention for a second seat. Caoimhghín Ó Caoláin topped the poll and was just over the quota on the first count. His running mate Kathryn Reilly was outside the frame in sixth place on the first count and was eventually beaten by Fine Gael for the final seat by a margin of just 521 votes.

This was another poor performance by Fianna Fáil with its vote down 18 percentage points on 2007 to just 20.15%, and it lost two seats, leaving outgoing

minister Brendan Smith as its sole representative after this election. Margaret Conlon was outside the frame in seventh place on the first count with just 0.4 of a quota and was virtually out of contention. Veteran Fianna Fáil TD and former Cabinet minister and Ceann Comhairle Rory O'Hanlon retired ahead of the election.

Labour failed to perform here as it got just 6% and newcomer Liam Hogan was never in contention. Four non-party candidates contested, including New Vision's John McGuirk but all (along with the Green's Darcy Lonergan) failed to get enough votes to allow them reclaim their expenses.

CAVAN-MONAGHAN

% SHARE OF THE VOTE

FF	FG	Lab	GP	SF	Oth
20.1	39.6	5.6	0.7	25.9	8.0

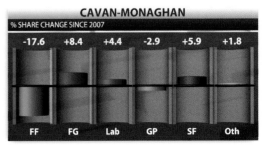

CAVAN-MONAGHAN

% SHARE CHANGE SINCE 2007

FF	FG	Lab	GP	SF	Oth
-17.6	+8.4	+4.4	-2.9	+5.9	+1.8

*outgoing TDs

Cavan-Monaghan

CAOIMHGHÍN Ó CAOLÁIN (SF)

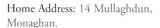

Home Address: 14 Mullaghdun, Monaghan.
Phone: 047 82917 (O) 01 6183005 (LH)
Email: caoimhghin.ocaolain@oireachtas.ie
Website: www.sinnfein.ie
Birth Place/Date: Monaghan, September 1953.
Marital Status/Family: Married to Briege McGinn; 4 daughters, 1 son.
Education: St Mary's CBS, Monaghan.
Occupation: Full-time public representative. Former bank official.
Biography: Party spokesperson on Health and Children. Secured 11,913 first-preference votes to get elected on the first count. Caoimhghín was first elected a Dáil deputy in 1997 and he was the first Sinn Féin TD to be elected after the party abandoned the policy of abstentionism. He was the party's leader in the Dáil from 2002 to 2011. He unsuccessfully contested the 1987, 1989 and 1992 general elections.
Did you know? Caoimhghín was director of elections for Kieran Doherty who was elected TD for Cavan-Monaghan in 1981 and died on hunger strike in Long Kesh.
Priority as a TD? The reunification of Ireland and its people; an equitable, fair and prosperous future with justice and peace for all.
Why did you stand for election? To aid the achievement of all of the above.
Is there any particular event that brought home to you just how serious the economic crisis had become? By far the greatest tragedies in this economic crisis are the tragedies of people taking their own lives. That is an appalling reality that I have encountered directly. We can never fully answer the question of why individuals choose suicide but I know of cases where financial pressure pushed vulnerable people over the brink.

BRENDAN SMITH (FF)

Home Address: 3 Carrickfern, Cavan.
Phone: 049 4362366 (O) 01 6183376 (LH)
Email: brendan.smith@oireachtas.ie
Birth Place/Date: Cavan, June 1956.
Marital Status/Family: Married to Anne McGarry.
Education: Bawnboy National School; St Camillus College Killucan, Co Westmeath; UCD (BA in politics and economics).
Occupation: Full-time public representative.
Biography: Party spokesperson on Education and Skills. First elected in 1992 and re-elected at each subsequent general election. He was appointed Minister for Agriculture, Fisheries and Food on 7 May, 2008. He was Minister of State at the Department of Health and Children with special responsibility for Children June 2007-May 2008 and attended Cabinet meetings. Minister of State at the Department of Agriculture and Food with special responsibility for Food and Horticulture 2004-2007.
Hobbies: Member of the GAA, enjoys watching most sports, does some walking.
Did you know? Brendan served as political adviser to former Tánaiste John Wilson for 15 years prior to his own election in 1992.
Politician (living or deceased) you most admire: Sean Lemass and his Fianna Fáil ministerial colleagues whose policies dramatically improved access to education.
Priority as a TD? To continue to work effectively on behalf of all constituents, contribute to my party's work nationally and to support vigorously the creation of much-needed employment.
Why did you stand for election? I want to continue my work which fortunately for me the electorate of Cavan/Monaghan have endorsed at successive elections.
Is there any particular event that brought home to you just how serious the economic crisis had become? The loss of jobs and the impact on individuals and families. Creation of employment is of the utmost importance.

JOE O'REILLY (FG)

Home Address: 2 The Willows, Chapel Road, Bailieborough, Co Cavan.
Phone: 042 9666580 (H) 086 2444321 (M) 01 6183721 (LH)
Email: joe.oreilly@oireachtas.ie
Website: www.joeoreilly.ie
Twitter: Yes.
Facebook: Yes.
Birth Place/Date: Cavan, April 1955.
Marital Status/Family: Married to Mary Tully; 3 sons.
Education: St Aidan's Comprehensive, Cootehill; UCD; DIT; TCD; and St Patrick's College, Drumcondra.
Occupation: Public representative, former publican and retired primary school teacher.
Biography: He secured 8,333 first-preference votes to get elected on the ninth and final count at his second attempt. He narrowly lost out on a seat in the 2007 general election when Fianna Fáil's Margaret Conlon pipped him for the last seat. He was elected to the Seanad after the general election in 2007, his second term in the Seanad, as he was previously a senator from 1989 to 1992. He was a member of Cavan County Council from 1985 to 2007. Former chair of Cavan County Council 2004-2005.
Hobbies: Reading, travel and socialising.
Did you know? Joe was a champion Irish debater in secondary school.
Politician (living or deceased) you most admire: Charles Stewart Parnell.
Priority as a TD? To do anything I can do to get people working.
Why did you stand for election? To bring about change for the better and rectify our public finances and create jobs.
Is there any particular event that brought home to you just how serious the economic crisis had become? The most interesting event at a macro level was watching Mr Ajai Chopra and his colleagues from the IMF walk through Dublin and at a micro level it has been seeing the amount of young people who are out of work.

SEÁN CONLAN (FG)

Home Address: Ballybay, Co Monaghan.
Phone: O87 6679306 (M) 01 6183154 (LH)
Website: sean.conlan@oireachtas.ie
Facebook: facebook/seanconlan
Birth Place/Date: Dublin, 1975.
Marital Status/Family: Single.
Education: Ballybay NS; St Macartan's College, Monaghan; UCD (BA honours degree in economics); The Law Society.
Occupation: Public representative. Solicitor and bar owner.
Biography: He garnered 7,864 first preference votes to get elected on the ninth and final count at his first attempt. He has been a member of Ballybay Town Council since 2009 and he is a son of John F Conlon, who was a TD from 1969 to 1987. John Francis Conlan was an adviser to James Dillon during his leadership of Fine Gael.
Hobbies: Kayaking, surfing, listening to music and reading.
Did you know? Seán was chairperson of Young Fine Gael while at UCD.
Politician (living or deceased) you most admire: Michael Collins.
Priority as a TD? Locally, my priorities are job creation, attracting investment and promoting industry, business, agriculture, education, and development of services at Monaghan and Cavan General Hospitals. Nationally, to promote economic policies which will create jobs, and help the emigration and personal debt crises. In the long run, I want to help bring about the change necessary to create a united Ireland.
Why did you stand for election? To achieve the above.
Is there any particular event that brought home to you just how serious the economic crisis had become? The September 2008 blanket banks guarantee was a huge mistake and the government continued to make a series of mistakes, such as the nationalisation of Anglo Irish Bank in the six months that followed the guarantee. Most of our current problems stem from that period.

HEATHER HUMPHREYS (FG)

Home Address: Dernaroy, Newbliss, Co Monaghan.
Phone: 086 2380765 (M) 01 6183408 (LH)
Email: heather.humphreys@oireachtas.ie
Facebook: Yes.
Birth Place/Date: Monaghan.
Marital Status/Family: Married to Eric Humphreys; 2 daughters.
Education: St Aidan's Comprehensive in Cootehill, Co Cavan.
Occupation: Public representative. Formerly manager of Cootehill Credit Union, Co Cavan.
Biography: Heather was elected on the back of 8,144 first preferences on the ninth and final count at her first attempt. She was co-opted onto Monaghan County Council in 2003, when she replaced former TD Seymour Crawford. She was elected to the council in 2004 with 18.1% of the vote and in 2009 with 23.9%. Mayor of County Monaghan in 2009-2010.
Hobbies: Reading and playing the piano.
Did you know? Humphreys is only the second woman to be elected in the area since the Cavan-Monaghan constituency was formed.
Politician (living or deceased) you most admire: Franklin D Roosevelt.
Priority as a TD? Jobs for young people so they are not forced to emigrate.
Why did you stand for election? I live in the real world, I know the issues and I want to try and make a difference.
Is there any particular event that brought home to you just how serious the economic crisis had become? In my work as a credit union manager I saw the huge financial difficulties that people are facing and the way people are despairing about not being able to meet their commitments. There are so many people worried about losing their homes.

Election Facts
Just over half of voters believe that a Fine Gael and Labour coalition is very or fairly likely to run its full five-year term, rising to nearly two thirds of Fine Gael or Labour voters" Millward Brown Lansdowne/RTÉ General Election 2011 Exit Poll

Cavan-Monaghan

	Seats	5			11,880		
Candidate		Party	1st	%	Quota	Count	Status
1 O Caolain, Caoimhghin*		SF	11,913	16.71%	1.00	1	Made Quota
2 Smith, Brendan*		FF	9,702	13.61%	0.82	8	Made Quota
3 O'Reilly, Joe		FG	8,333	11.69%	0.70	9	Elected
4 Conlan, Sean		FG	7,864	11.03%	0.66	9	Elected
5 Humphreys, Heather		FG	8,144	11.43%	0.69	9	Elected
6 Reilly, Kathryn		SF	6,539	9.17%	0.55	9	Not Elected
7 Conlon, Margaret*		FF	4,658	6.54%	0.39	7	Eliminated
8 Hogan, Liam		LB	4,011	5.63%	0.34	6	Eliminated
9 McVitty, Peter		FG	3,858	5.41%	0.32	5	Eliminated
10 Treanor, Seamus		NP	1,974	2.77%	0.17	4	No Expenses
11 Forde, Caroline		NP	1,912	2.68%	0.16	3	No Expenses
12 McGuirk, John		NV	1,708	2.40%	0.14	2	No Expenses
13 Lonergan, Darcy		GP	530	0.74%	0.04	1	No Expenses
14 Duffy, Joseph		NP	129	0.18%	0.01	1	No Expenses

*Outgoing TD Valid poll: 71,275 Quota: 11,880 No expenses limit: 2,971

Party votes

		2011					2007				Change	
Party	Cand	1st	%	Quota	Seats	Cand	1st	%	Quota	Seats	%	Seats
FG	4	28,199	39.56%	2.37	3	2	20,528	31.20%	1.56	1	+8.36%	+2
LB	1	4,011	5.63%	0.34		1	796	1.21%	0.06		+4.42%	
FF	2	14,360	20.15%	1.21	1	3	24,851	37.77%	1.89	3	-17.63%	-2
SF	2	18,452	25.89%	1.55	1	1	13,162	20.01%	1.00	1	+5.88%	
GP	1	530	0.74%	0.04		1	2,382	3.62%	0.18		-2.88%	
Others	4	5,723	8.03%	0.48		2	4,068	6.18%	0.31		+1.85%	
Total	14	71,275	100.0%	11,880	5	10	65,787	100.0%	13,158	5	0.00%	0
Electorate	99,178	71.87%					92,248	71.32%			+0.55%	
Spoiled	867	1.20%					760	1.14%			+0.06%	
Turnout	72,142	72.74%					66,547	72.14%			+0.60%	

Transfer analysis

From	To	FG	LB	FF	SF	Others	Non Trans
FG	4,246	2,926	205	539	438		138
		68.91%	4.83%	12.69%	10.32%		3.25%
LB	4,998	2,054		676	1,303		965
		41.10%		13.53%	26.07%		19.31%
FF	8,066	2,200		3,430	713		1,723
		27.27%		42.52%	8.84%		21.36%
GP	530	135	107	62	68	134	24
		25.47%	20.19%	11.70%	12.83%	25.28%	4.53%
NP	6,714	2,205	675	879	1,279	857	819
		32.84%	10.05%	13.09%	19.05%	12.76%	12.20%
Total	24,554	9,520	987	5,586	3,801	991	3,669
		38.77%	4.02%	22.75%	15.48%	4.04%	14.94%

Election Facts
"Since 1918, the longest serving TD in the Dáil was Fianna Fáil's Patrick Smith from the old Cavan constituency. He served as a TD for almost 54 years and a total of 17 Dáil terms"
Sean Donnelly

Count details

Candidate	Party	1st	2nd Lonergan Duffy	3rd McGuirk Votes	4th Forde Votes	5th Treanor Votes	6th McVitty Votes	7th Hogan Votes	8th Conlon Votes	9th Smith Surplus
Seats	**5**								**Quota**	**11,880**
O Caolain, Caoimhghin*	SF	11,913	11,913	11,913	11,913	11,913	11,913	11,913	11,913	11,913
			+32	+83	+275	+157	+521	+467	+3,430	-2,787
Smith, Brendan*	FF	9,702	9,734	9,817	10,092	10,249	10,770	11,237	14,667	11,880
			+28	+51	+187	+80	+1,813	+709	+104	+129
O'Reilly, Joe	FG	8,333	8,361	8,412	8,599	8,679	10,492	11,201	11,305	11,434
			+60	+301	+94	+409	+434	+733	+728	+555
Conlan, Sean	FG	7,864	7,924	8,225	8,319	8,728	9,162	9,895	10,623	11,178
			+57	+173	+147	+365	+679	+612	+348	+336
Humphreys, Heather	FG	8,144	8,201	8,374	8,521	8,886	9,565	10,177	10,525	10,861
			+85	+234	+431	+597	+438	+1,303	+257	+456
Reilly, Kathryn	SF	6,539	6,624	6,858	7,289	7,886	8,324	9,627	9,884	10,340
			+45	+114	+62	+173	+18	+209	-5,279	
Conlon, Margaret*	FF	4,658	4,703	4,817	4,879	5,052	5,070	5,279	Eliminated	
			+133	+129	+254	+266	+205	-4,998		
Hogan, Liam	LB	4,011	4,144	4,273	4,527	4,793	4,998	Eliminated		
			+23	+31	+295	+39	-4,246			
McVitty, Peter	FG	3,858	3,881	3,912	4,207	4,246	Eliminated			
			+33	+372	+279	-2,658				
Treanor, Seamus	NP	1,974	2,007	2,379	2,658	Eliminated				
			+81	+174	-2,167					
Forde, Caroline	NP	1,912	1,993	2,167	Eliminated					
			+52	-1,760						
McGuirk, John	NV	1,708	1,760	Eliminated						
			-530							
Lonergan, Darcy	GP	530	Eliminated							
			-129							
Duffy, Joseph	NP	129	Eliminated							
Non-transferable			+30	+98	+143	+572	+138	+965	+412	+1,311
Cumulative			30	128	271	843	981	1,946	2,358	3,669
Total		71,275	71,275	71,275	71,275	71,275	71,275	71,275	71,275	71,275

Sinn Féin leader Gerry Adams with Caoimhghín Ó Caoláin at the launch of the party's election manifesto in February

Clare (4 seats)

Fine Gael becomes the biggest party in Clare for the first time

Elected

Pat Breen* (FG) Count 11, Michael McNamara (Lab) Count 11, Joe Carey* (FG) Final count, Timmy Dooley* (FF) Final count.

Analysis by Michael Gallagher

There were no changes to the boundaries here since 2007. With nearly twice as many votes as anyone else, Fine Gael became the biggest party in Clare. Its incumbents, Pat Breen and Joe Carey, were re-elected without a bother, though Carey may be a little concerned by the strong vote of the third Fine Gael candidate, Tony Mulcahy.

Since the foundation of the State this had been a Fianna Fáil stronghold, represented by Éamon de Valera for over 40 years. With the retirement of former minister Tony Killeen, Timmy Dooley seemed to have a clear run, but when Dr John Hillery, son of former president (and Clare TD) Patrick Hillery, emerged as the second Fianna Fáil candidate, it became apparent that while Fianna Fáil seemed certain of one seat, it might not be Dooley. The battle between the two of them was intense, but Dooley had a 600-vote lead on the ninth count, after which Hillery was eliminated.

Favourite for the remaining seat was independent James Breen, who had been a TD here between 2002 and 2007. While he increased his vote slightly over 2007, it was obvious from the first count that he would not be returning to Leinster House.

Instead, this seat was taken by new Labour candidate, farmer and barrister, Michael McNamara. Since Patrick Hogan, who subsequently became Ceann Comhairle, won a seat here in 1951, Labour had only once taken a seat, through Dr Moosajee Bhamjee in 1992, and having won 1.6% of the votes in 2007 it could hardly have had Clare high on its target list. However, McNamara had gained valuable exposure through his 2009 European Parliament campaign, when he had won over 12,000 votes, many in Clare, as an independent, and he increased the Labour vote share more than nine-fold to sail into the second seat.

*outgoing TDs

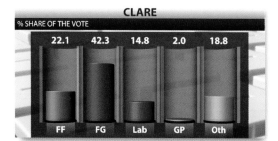

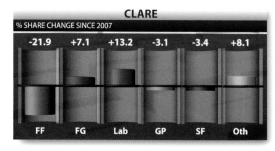

PAT BREEN (FG)

Home Address: Lisduff, Ballynacally, Co Clare.
Constituency Offices: Parkview House, Lower Market Street Car Park, Ennis, and the Square, Kilrush.
Phone: 087 2422136 (M) 065 6868466 (O) 065 6868486 (Fax) 01 6184224 (LH)
Email: pat.breen@oireachtas.ie
Website: www.patbreen.ie
Twitter: www.twitter.com/PatBreen1
Facebook: www.facebook.com/PatBreenTD
Birth Place/Date: March 1957.
Marital Status/Family: Married; 2 sons.
Education: St Flannan's College, Ennis and Limerick Institute of Technology.
Occupation: Full-time public representative and farmer.
Biography: Topped the poll with 9,855 first-preference votes in 2011. First elected in 2002 and re-elected in 2007. Fine Gael's spokesperson on Overseas Aid and Human Rights in the 30th Dáil and chairman of the Dáil's Sub-Committee on Overseas Aid. Previously Fine Gael's deputy spokesperson on Transport and Enterprise, Trade and Employment with special responsibility for small business. Has served on a number of Dáil Committees: the European Affairs Committee; the Oireachtas Transport Committee; the Privileges and Procedures; the House Services Committee and the Committee on Enterprise and Small Business. Member, Clare County Council 1999-2003.
Hobbies: Walking, golfing and travelling when I get the time.
Politician (living or deceased) you most admire: Senator Michael Howard.
Priority as a TD? Job creation to stop young people emigrating.
Why did you stand for election? To ensure Clare's problems are given the priority they deserve in every government department and to see Shannon Airport restored as a catalyst for economic revival in our region.

MICHAEL McNAMARA (Lab)

Home Address: Scariff, Co Clare.
Phone: 01 6183879 (LH)
Website: www.labour.ie/michaelmcnamara
Facebook: Yes.
Birth Place/Date: Clare, March 1974.
Marital Status/Family: Single.
Education: St Flannan's College, Ennis; UCC; the University of Louvain and the King's Inns.
Occupation: Farmer and barrister.
Biography: Michael won 8,572 first-preference votes and got elected on the 11th count on his first attempt. He is the first Labour TD to be elected in the Clare constituency since Dr Moosajee Bhamjee's surprise election in the 1992 'Spring Tide'. In 2009 he stood as an independent candidate in the European elections in the Ireland North-West constituency and he secured 12,744 first-preference votes, 2.9% share of the vote. Provided legal support for RTE's *Prime Time* programme from November 1997 to September 2000.
Hobbies: Tennis, outdoor pursuits, member of Scariff GAA Club and the IFA.
Did you know? Michael has worked as a human rights lawyer with the Organisation for Security and Co-operation in Europe in Eastern Europe and with the United Nations in Afghanistan, before returning to Ireland in 2005 to run his family farm and practise at the Bar. Also worked in Yemen, Pakistan, Iraq and Sudan as an independent electoral observer.
Politician (living or deceased) you most admire: Daniel O'Connell.
Priority as a TD? To reform our economic priorities and system of governance.
Why did you stand for election? As above. Is there any particular event that brought home to you just how serious the economic crisis had become? I don't think that people actually realise where we are economically as a state yet and the events that will bring that home for people have yet to occur.

JOE CAREY (FG)

Address: Francis St, Ennis, Co Clare.
Phone: 086 4032019 (M) 065 6891199 (O) 01 6183337 (LH)
Email: joe.carey@oireachtas.ie
Website: www.joecarey.ie
Twitter: @joecareytd
Facebook: Yes.
Birth Place/Date: June 1975.
Marital Status/family: Married to Grace; 1 daughter.
Education: St Flannan's College, Ennis; Athlone Institute of Technology.
Occupation: Full-time public representative. Formerly accountant.
Biography: Secured 7,840 first-preference votes to get elected on the 12th count. He was first elected to Dáil Éireann in 2007, winning a second seat for Fine Gael in Clare for the first time since 1989. Elected to Clare County Council 1999 and re-elected in 2004. Son of former Clare TD and Minister of State, Donal Carey.
Hobbies: Member Clarecastle GAA, fondly known as the Magpies. Avid follower of horse and greyhound racing.
Did you know? Joe won an All-Ireland juvenile handball gold medal in Mosney.
Politician (living or deceased) you most admire: Enda Kenny.
Priority as a TD? To create a more favourable environment for employment, to ensure that fairness is applied in how politics works. To help realise the potential of Shannon International Airport as a driver for the mid-west region.
Why did you stand for election? I want to be part of a political movement that transforms our economy and provides opportunity for our young people.
Is there any particular event that brought home to you just how serious the economic crisis had become? The scale and initial rate of unemployment is the single issue that has had the greatest economic impact. The issue is becoming embedded and is the root of many other problems.

Clare

TIMMY DOOLEY (FF)

Home Address: 8 The Old Forge, Tulla, Co Clare.
Phone: 065 6891115 (O)
01 6183514 (LH)
Email: timmy.dooley@oireachtas.ie
Website: www.timmydooley.ie
Twitter: Yes.
Facebook: Yes.
Birth Place/Date: Clare, February 1969.
Marital Status/Family: Married; 2 children.
Education: Scariff Community College.
Occupation: Full-time public representative.
Biography: Party spokesperson on Transport, Tourism and Sport. Elected with 6,789 first-preference votes in 2011. Topped the poll with 10,791 at first attempt in 2007. Elected to Seanad Éireann at first attempt in 2002.
Hobbies: Attending GAA and rugby matches.
Politician (living or deceased) you most admire: Seán Lemass.
Priority as a TD? Job creation in Clare, mortgage debt relief and access to credit for SMEs and farmers.
Why did you stand for election? From an early age I was interested in current affairs and politics generally. Having had strong opinions as to how things should be done, I felt the best way for me to influence the management of the country was to offer myself to the electorate.
Is there any particular event that brought home to you just how serious the economic crisis had become? The increase in suicide rates.

Michael McNamara (left) with fellow election candidate Ivana Bacik, who ran in Dún Laoghaire, and Labour leader Eamon Gilmore

Election Facts

"Support for Fine Gael rises with age but it is the most chosen party in each age group and farmers are most drawn to the party"
Millward Brown Lansdowne/RTÉ General Election 2011 Exit Poll

First preference votes

	Candidate	Party	1st	%	Quota	Count	Status
	Seats	4			11,584		
1	Breen, Pat*	FG	9,855	17.02%	0.85	11	Made Quota
2	McNamara, Michael	LB	8,572	14.80%	0.74	11	Made Quota
3	Carey, Joe*	FG	7,840	13.54%	0.68	12	Made Quota
4	Dooley, Timmy*	FF	6,789	11.72%	0.59	12	Elected
5	Breen, James #	NP	6,491	11.21%	0.56	12	Not Elected
6	Mulcahy, Tony	FG	6,829	11.79%	0.59	10	Eliminated
7	Hillery, Dr. John	FF	6,015	10.39%	0.52	9	Eliminated
8	Markham, Brian	NP	1,543	2.66%	0.13	8	No Expenses
9	Meaney, Brian	GP	1,154	1.99%	0.10	7	No Expenses
10	Connolly, Jim	NP	978	1.69%	0.08	6	No Expenses
11	McAleer, Madeline	NP	428	0.74%	0.04	5	No Expenses
12	Cronin, Ann	NP	419	0.72%	0.04	5	No Expenses
13	Walshe, Gerry	NP	328	0.57%	0.03	4	No Expenses
14	Ferrigan, Sarah	NP	252	0.44%	0.02	3	No Expenses
15	McCabe, J.J.	NP	248	0.43%	0.02	2	No Expenses
16	Brassil, Patrick	NP	175	0.30%	0.02	1	No Expenses

* Outgoing TD #Former TD Valid poll: 57,916 Quota: 11,584 No expenses limit: 2,897

Party votes

Party	Cand	1st	%	Quota	Seats	Cand	1st	%	Quota	Seats	%	Seats
			2011					2007			Change	
FG	3	24,524	42.34%	2.12	2	4	19,854	35.21%	1.76	2	+7.13%	
LB	1	8,572	14.80%	0.74	1	1	892	1.58%	0.08		+13.22%	+1
FF	2	12,804	22.11%	1.11	1	3	24,824	44.03%	2.20	2	-21.92%	-1
SF						1	1,929	3.42%	0.17		-3.42%	
GP	1	1,154	1.99%	0.10		1	2,858	5.07%	0.25		-3.08%	
PD						1	810	1.44%	0.07		-1.44%	
Others	9	10,862	18.75%	0.94		1	5,218	9.25%	0.46		+9.50%	
Total	16	57,916	100.0%	11,584	4	12	56,385	100.0%	11,278	4	0.00%	0
Electorate		82,745	69.99%				79,555	70.88%			-0.88%	
Spoiled		579	0.99%				385	0.68%			+0.31%	
Turnout		58,495	70.69%				56,770	71.36%			-0.67%	

Transfer analysis

From	To	FG	LB	FF	GP	Others	Non Trans
FG	9,188	6,218	1,331	424		788	427
		67.68%	14.49%	4.61%		8.58%	4.65%
FF	6,468	1,002	567	3,526		1,054	319
		15.49%	8.77%	54.51%		16.30%	4.93%
GP	1,339	381	513	138		200	107
		28.45%	38.31%	10.31%		14.94%	7.99%
NP	5,447	1,136	900	597	185	2,063	566
		20.86%	16.52%	10.96%	3.40%	37.87%	10.39%
Total	22,442	8,737	3,311	4,685	185	4,105	1,419
		38.93%	14.75%	20.88%	0.82%	18.29%	6.32%

Clare

Seats	4												Quota	11,584
Candidate	Party	1st	2nd Brassil Votes	3rd McCabe Votes	4th Ferrigan Votes	5th Walshe Votes	6th McAleer Cronin	7th Connolly Kelly	8th Meaney Votes	9th Markham Votes	10th Hillery Votes	11th Mulcahy Votes	12th Breen Surplus
			+10	+14	+17	+21	+32	+135	+123	+272	+509	+2,346	-1,750
Breen, Pat*	FG	9,855	9,865	9,879	9,896	9,917	9,949	10,084	10,207	10,479	10,988	13,334	11,584
			+9	+34	+44	+38	+174	+200	+513	+401	+567	+1,331	
McNamara, Michael	LB	8,572	8,581	8,615	8,659	8,697	8,871	9,071	9,584	9,985	10,552	11,883	11,883
			+19	+17	+12	+18	+47	+75	+132	+174	+283	+2,344	+1,528
Carey, Joe*	FG	7,840	7,859	7,876	7,888	7,906	7,953	8,028	8,160	8,334	8,617	10,961	12,489
			+6	+11	+7	+10	+35	+48	+57	+108	+3,526	+368	+56
Dooley, Timmy*	FF	6,789	6,795	6,806	6,813	6,823	6,858	6,906	6,963	7,071	10,597	10,965	11,021
			+55	+37	+16	+63	+133	+234	+107	+542	+1,054	+622	+166
Breen, James #	NP	6,491	6,546	6,583	6,599	6,662	6,795	7,029	7,136	7,678	8,732	9,354	9,520
			+3	+29	+5	+15	+51	+48	+126	+122	+210	-7,438	
Mulcahy, Tony	FG	6,829	6,832	6,861	6,866	6,881	6,932	6,980	7,106	7,228	7,438	Eliminated	
			+5	+24	+9	+13	+27	+68	+81	+226	-6,468		
Hillery, Dr. John	FF	6,015	6,020	6,044	6,053	6,066	6,093	6,161	6,242	6,468	Eliminated		
			+4	+18	+20	+52	+188	+239	+93	-2,157			
Markham, Brian	NP	1,543	1,547	1,565	1,585	1,637	1,825	2,064	2,157	Eliminated			
			+4	+5	+9	+15	+79	+73	-1,339				
Meaney, Brian	GP	1,154	1,158	1,163	1,172	1,187	1,266	1,339	Eliminated				
			+24	+13	+16	+44	+141	-1,216					
Connolly, Jim	NP	978	1,002	1,015	1,031	1,075	1,216	Eliminated					
			+1	+21	+37	+22	-509						
McAleer, Madeline	NP	428	429	450	487	509	Eliminated						
			+10	+11	+57	+24	-521						
Cronin, Ann	NP	419	429	440	497	521	Eliminated						
			+4	+8	+12	-352							
Walshe, Gerry	NP	328	332	340	352	Eliminated							
			+8	+5	-265								
Ferrigan, Sarah	NP	252	260	265	Eliminated								
			+4	-252									
McCabe, J.J.	NP	248	252	Eliminated									
			-175										
Brassil, Patrick	NP	175	Eliminated										
Non-transferable			+9	+5	+4	+17	+123	+96	+107	+312	+319	+427	
Cumulative			9	14	18	35	158	254	361	673	992	1,419	1,419
Total		57,916	57,916	57,916	57,916	57,916	57,916	57,916	57,916	57,916	57,916	57,916	57,916

Labour leader Eamon Gilmore on the campaign trail in Dublin

Cork East (4 seats)

Historic win for Sinn Féin as Fianna Fáil fails to take a seat

Elected

Seán Sherlock* (Lab) Count 1, David Stanton* (FG) Count 5, Tom Barry (FG) Final count, Sandra McLellan (SF) Final count.

Analysis by Michael Gallagher

There was a significant boundary change in this constituency since the last election. It lost the areas of Ballynaglogh, Glenville, Carrig, Watergrasshill, Kildinan, Ballynamona and Rahan. This meant that a population of 4,255 was transferred to Cork North Central.

Since Ned O'Keeffe joined the Fianna Fáil ticket here in November 1982 this had been a bastion for the party, with O'Keeffe and Michael Ahern taking two of the four seats at every election up to 2007, albeit with just the occasional hint of a certain creative tension between the two of them. In 2011, this was yet another of the constituencies where Fianna Fáil plunged from two seats to none. O'Keeffe senior retired and was succeeded on the ticket by his son Kevin, but many observers felt that Fianna Fáil's only hope of retaining one seat would have been to run just one candidate, and so it proved; Ahern was eliminated on the fourth count, and O'Keeffe finished 600 votes short of a seat.

Fine Gael was always going to win two seats; the only question was which of David Stanton's two running mates would accompany him to Leinster House. This race was won by Mallow-based councillor Tom Barry, who had a lead of almost 1,000 votes over Pa O'Driscoll at the decisive stage.

That left two seats for the taking for Labour, if the party managed its votes properly. However, it spectacularly failed to do this, Seán Sherlock running over 6,000 ahead of his running mate, former TD John Mulvihill. If just 700 of Sherlock's voters had switched to Cobh-based Mulvihill, Labour would have taken two seats here. Instead, Mulvihill was eliminated on the seventh count, and his transfers enabled Sinn Féin's Sandra McLellan from Youghal to overhaul Kevin O'Keeffe and win Sinn Féin's first seat in this constituency, becoming the only opposition TD from Cork East in the 31st Dáil.

*outgoing TDs

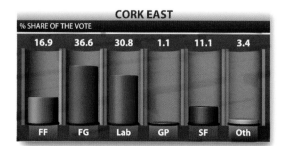

CORK EAST					
% SHARE OF THE VOTE					
16.9	36.6	30.8	1.1	11.1	3.4
FF	FG	Lab	GP	SF	Oth

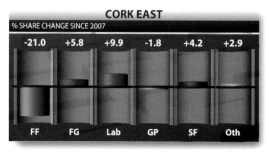

CORK EAST					
% SHARE CHANGE SINCE 2007					
-21.0	+5.8	+9.9	-1.8	+4.2	+2.9
FF	FG	Lab	GP	SF	Oth

Cork East

SEÁN SHERLOCK (Lab)

Home Address: Davis Lane, Main Street, Mallow, Co Cork.
Phone: 022 53523 (O) 087 7402057 (M) 01 6184049 (LH)
Email: sean.sherlock@oir.ie
Website: www.seansherlock.ie
Twitter: twitter.com/seansherlocktd
Birth Place/Date: Cork, December 1972.
Marital Status/Family: Single.
Education: Patrician Academy, Mallow; College of Commerce, Cork; University College Galway (BA economics and politics).
Occupation: Full-time public representative.
Biography: Secured 11,862 votes to top the poll in Election 2011. Minister of State for Research and Innovation. First elected to the Dáil in 2007. Labour's spokesman on agriculture in the 30th Dáil. Co-opted onto Mallow Town Council and Cork County Council in 2003 and elected to both in 2004.
Hobbies: Member Blackwater Kayaking Club, Mallow Rugby Club, and Mountaineering Club of Ireland.
Did you know? Seán is a son of the late Joe Sherlock, Sinn Féin the Workers' Party TD for Cork East (1981-1982), Workers' Party TD (1987-1992), Labour TD (2002-2007) and senator (1993-1997).
Politician (living or deceased) you most admire: My late father Joe Sherlock.
Priority as a TD? Job creation – we have to restore jobs and economic growth so we can stem the tide of emigration.
Why did you stand for election? I felt strongly that the dominant political parties did not best serve the interests of the Irish citizen. To try to effect positive change. It may sound like a cliché but I love our republic and I want to be part of creating a country we can all be proud of.
Is there any particular event that brought home to you just how serious the economic crisis had become? There was a series of chain events that led to the economic crisis but the banking crisis above any other issue is the single event that has negatively impacted on people's lives.

DAVID STANTON (FG)

Home Address: B29 St Mary's Road, Midleton, Co Cork.
Phone: 1890 337889 (Dáil) 021 4632867 (CO) 01 6183181 (LH)
Email: david.stanton@oir.ie
Twitter: twitter.com/davidstantontd
Facebook: facebook/davidstanton
Birth Place/Date: Cork, February 1957.
Marital Status/Family: Married to Mary Lehane; 4 sons.
Education: St Colman's Community College, Midleton, UCC.
Occupation: Full-time public representative.
Biography: First elected to Dáil in 1997, on his first attempt. Re-elected in 2002, 2007 and 2011.
Hobbies: Walking, reading.
Did you know? David was a member and a commissioned officer in the FCA for 19 years prior to his election.
Politician (living or deceased) you most admire: Nelson Mandela.
Priority as a TD? Improve conditions for job creation and retention.
Why did you stand for election? I want to make a positive difference to my local area and the country.
Is there any particular event that brought home to you just how serious the economic crisis had become? When 10 young people from a village in my area emigrated to Australia in one group.

TOM BARRY (FG)

Home Address: Monanimy, Upper Killavullen, Mallow, Co Cork.
Phone: 086 2506572 (M) 022 26816 (CO) 016183328 (LH)
Email: tom.barry@oireachtas.ie
Website: www.tombarry.ie
Twitter: twitter.com/tbarry
Facebook: Yes.
Birth Place/Date: Cork, October 1968
Marital Status/Family: Married to Dr Kathy Quane; 3 children.
Education: De La Salle College, Waterford; UCC.
Occupation: Public representative. Agri-businessman who owns and runs a company called BWarehousing.
Biography: Tom garnered 5,798 first-preference votes to get elected on the seventh and final count in his first general election attempt. Member Cork County Council since 2009.
Hobbies: Time off with my family, all sports and gardening.
Did you know? Tom has been highly involved in trying to restore the Irish sugar industry.
Politician (living or deceased) you most admire: Edmund Burke.
Priority as a TD? To re-establish indigenous industries and create jobs.
Why did you stand for election? I run a business and I have three young children. If we don't get industries back up and running, all we will do is rear our kids to send them abroad so I have a civic duty and a responsibility to them.
Is there any particular event that brought home to you just how serious the economic crisis had become? I know a normal couple who have four children under the age of eight who both lost their jobs and they had their home repossessed. I will never forget seeing the mother in the High Court begging the judge to take the house off them as she could no longer cope with the pressure from the banks to pay back money they did not have. People like them are the collateral damage of the Celtic Tiger.

SANDRA McLELLAN (SF)

Home Address: Ardrath, Youghal, Co Cork.
Phone: 086 3752944 (M) 01 6183122 (LH)
Email: sandramclellan@eircom.net or Sandra.mclellan@oireachtas.ie
Birth Place/Date: Youghal, May 1961.
Marital Status/family: Married to Liam; 3 children.
Education: Loreto Convent Youghal.
Occupation: Full-time public representative. Formerly SIPTU shop steward in an electronics factory, where she worked for 16 years before losing her job in 2004.
Biography: Party spokesperson on Arts, Heritage, Tourism and Sport. Secured 6,292 first-preference votes to get elected in the seventh and final count in her first general election. She was first elected to Youghal Town Council in 2004 and topped the poll on her re-election in 2009. She was the first Sinn Féin Mayor of Youghal in 2009-2010.
Hobbies: Sports. But I am now just a spectator.
Did you know? Sandra is the first woman TD in the East Cork constituency since Fine Gael's Myra Barry in 1979.
Politician (living or deceased) you most admire: Mary Robinson. She campaigned tirelessly for womens' rights and human rights and succeeded in becoming the first female president of Ireland.
Priority as a TD? Job creation in Cork East.
Why did you stand for election? When you enter public life it is a natural ambition to want to progress to a higher level and I want to make a difference.
Is there any particular event that brought home to you just how serious the economic crisis had become? The large volume of people that took to the streets in Dublin last November for their own reasons and marched united as one to protest against the introduction of spending cuts and tax increases introduced by the government.

Fine Gael's Richard Bruton (left) chats to election candidates David Stanton (centre, Cork East) and Frank Feighan (right, Roscommon-South Leitrim) before Enda Kenny's address to the party's election candidates in January; Willie Broderick, David Stanton's campaign manager, is in the background

Cork East

	Seats	4			11,387		
	Candidate	Party	1st	%	Quota	Count	Status
1	Sherlock, Sean*	LB	11,862	20.84%	1.04	1	Made Quota
2	Stanton, David*	FG	10,019	17.60%	0.88	5	Made Quota
3	Barry, Tom	FG	5,798	10.18%	0.51	7	Made Quota
4	McLellan, Sandra	SF	6,292	11.05%	0.55	7	Elected
5	O'Keeffe, Kevin	FF	5,024	8.82%	0.44	7	Not Elected
6	Mulvihill, John #	LB	5,701	10.01%	0.50	6	Eliminated
7	O'Driscoll, Pa	FG	5,030	8.83%	0.44	4	Eliminated
8	Ahern, Michael*	FF	4,618	8.11%	0.41	3	Eliminated
9	O'Neill, Paul	NV	1,056	1.85%	0.09	2	No Expenses
10	Harty, Malachy	GP	635	1.12%	0.06	2	No Expenses
11	Cullinane, Claire	CPPC	510	0.90%	0.04	2	No Expenses
12	Bulman, Patrick	CPPC	212	0.37%	0.02	2	No Expenses
13	Burke, Paul	NP	176	0.31%	0.02	2	No Expenses
13	*Outgoing # Former TD		56,933	100.00%	11,387	2,847	No Expenses

* Outgoing TD #Former TD Valid poll: 56,933 Quota: 11,387 No expenses limit: 2,847

		2011					2007				Change	
Party	Cand	1st	%	Quota	Seats	Cand	1st	%	Quota	Seats	%	Seats
FG	3	20,847	36.62%	1.83	2	2	16,602	30.85%	1.54	1	+5.76%	+1
LB	2	17,563	30.85%	1.54	1	2	11,249	20.91%	1.05	1	+9.94%	
FF	2	9,642	16.94%	0.85		2	20,431	37.97%	1.90	2	-21.03%	-2
SF	1	6,292	11.05%	0.55	1	1	3,672	6.82%	0.34		+4.23%	+1
GP	1	635	1.12%	0.06		1	1,572	2.92%	0.15		-1.81%	
Others	4	1,954	3.43%	0.17		2	282	0.52%	0.03		+2.91%	
Total	13	56,933	100.0%	11,387	4	10	53,808	100.0%	10,762	4	0.00%	0
Electorate		83,658	68.05%				84,354	63.79%			+4.27%	
Spoiled		526	0.92%				477	0.88%			+0.04%	
Turnout		57,459	68.68%				54,285	64.35%			+4.33%	

From	To	FG	LB	FF	SF	GP	Others	Non Trans
FG	6,528	4,719	307	667	383			452
		72.29%	4.70%	10.22%	5.87%			6.92%
LB	7,572	1,898	172	716	2,252	5	13	2,516
		25.07%	2.27%	9.46%	29.74%	0.07%	0.17%	33.23%
FF	4,798	971	402	2,666	326			433
		20.24%	8.38%	55.56%	6.79%			9.02%
GP	640	228	126	60	131			95
		35.63%	19.69%	9.38%	20.47%			14.84%
NP	1,967	702	389	183	401			292
		35.69%	19.78%	9.30%	20.39%			14.84%
Total	21,505	8,518	1,396	4,292	3,493	5	13	3,788
		39.61%	6.49%	19.96%	16.24%	0.02%	0.06%	17.61%

Count details

Candidate	Party	1st	2nd	3rd	4th	5th	6th	7th
			Sherlock Surplus	O'Neill Harty Cullinane Bulman Burke Lonergan Duffy	Ahern Votes	O'Driscoll Votes	Stanton Surplus	Mulvihill Votes
			−475					
Sherlock, Sean*	LB	11,862	11,387	11,387	11,387	11,387	11,387	11,387
			+28	+571	+463	+1,390	−1,084	
Stanton, David*	FG	10,019	10,047	10,618	11,081	12,471	11,387	11,387
			+90	+209	+300	+2,501	+828	+1,724
Barry, Tom	FG	5,798	5,888	6,097	6,397	8,898	9,726	11,450
			+53	+532	+326	+325	+58	+2,199
McLellan, Sandra	SF	6,292	6,345	6,877	7,203	7,528	7,586	9,785
			+42	+79	+2,666	+590	+77	+658
O'Keeffe, Kevin	FF	5,024	5,066	5,145	7,811	8,401	8,478	9,136
			+172	+515	+402	+186	+121	−7,097
Mulvihill, John #	LB	5,701	5,873	6,388	6,790	6,976	7,097	Eliminated
			+56	+150	+208	−5,444		
O'Driscoll, Pa	FG	5,030	5,086	5,236	5,444	Eliminated		
			+16	+164	−4,798			
Ahern, Michael*	FF	4,618	4,634	4,798	Eliminated			
			+8	−1,064				
O'Neill, Paul	NV	1,056	1,064	Eliminated				
			+5	−640				
Harty, Malachy	GP	635	640	Eliminated				
			+3	−513				
Cullinane, Claire	CPPC	510	513	Eliminated				
			+1	−213				
Bulman, Patrick	CPPC	212	213	Eliminated				
			+1	−177				
Burke, Paul	NP	176	177	Eliminated				
Non-transferable				+387	+433	+452		+2,516
Cumulative			0	387	820	1,272	1,272	3,788
Total		56,933	56,933	56,933	56,933	56,933	56,933	56,933

Seats: 4 Quota: 11,387

Election Facts
"The reason for the upsurge in candidates, to a record of 566, was a huge increase in the number of independents, from 85 in 2007 to around 200 (depending on how an independent is defined) in 2011"
Professor Michael Gallagher, TCD

Cork North-Central (4 seats)

Massive swing to the left in Cork North-Central

Elected

Jonathan O'Brien (SF) Count 8, Kathleen Lynch* (Lab) Count 10, Billy Kelleher* (FF) Final count, Dara Murphy (FG) Final count.

Analysis by Michael Gallagher

The redrawing of the boundaries here saw a population of 8,559 transferred from Cork East and Cork North-West into this constituency. It meant that Cork North-Central was extended further northwards and westwards into the rural areas and the commuter towns north of Cork city.

Another success for Sinn Féin, as Jonathan O'Brien headed the poll and reached the quota seven counts later. He received 2,500 transfers when the Socialist Party's Mick Barry was eliminated on the eighth count. Barry significantly improved his own vote over 2007, though without coming close to taking the seat that one opinion poll had seemed to promise.

Fianna Fáil was very satisfied with its performance. Noel O'Flynn had stood down at the behest of party leader Micheál Martin, to maximise the chances that Billy Kelleher, as Fianna Fáil's sole candidate, would be re-elected. Given how well this strategy worked here, Martin may wish he had been firmer with some other recalcitrant incumbents. The Fianna Fáil vote dropped from 36% to 15%, but Kelleher just managed to keep his nose ahead of the two Fine Gael candidates to take the third seat.

Kelleher was aided by the expansion of the constituency to include some rural areas from Cork

East and Cork North-West into this predominantly urban constituency.

Both government parties had entertained hopes of taking two seats but had to settle for one. Labour became the strongest party, with 26% of the votes. Its votes were shared fairly evenly between incumbent Kathleen Lynch and running mate John Gilroy. Given that Gilroy was only 63 votes behind Fine Gael's Dara Murphy when he was eliminated, it is possible that a more even distribution would have enabled Gilroy to reap sufficient Fine Gael transfers to take him above Billy Kelleher and into a seat.

The major increase in support for the left (Labour, Sinn Féin and the Socialist Party all making significant advances) meant that this was one of the very few constituencies in the country where Fine Gael's support actually fell compared with 2007. No doubt the retirement of 30-year veteran Bernard Allen was a factor in this. There was a major battle between the two first-time Fine Gael candidates for the seat. Dara Murphy trailed Glanmire-based Pat Burton throughout the count, until the elimination of Labour's Gilroy on the 10th count took him ahead of his running mate, and in the end he had a margin of nearly 300 votes to spare over Burton.

CORK NORTH CENTRAL

% SHARE OF THE VOTE

FF	FG	Lab	GP	SF	Oth
15.1	26.2	26.5	1.0	15.2	16.0

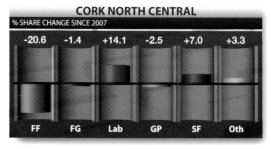

CORK NORTH CENTRAL

% SHARE CHANGE SINCE 2007

FF	FG	Lab	GP	SF	Oth
-20.6	-1.4	+14.1	-2.5	+7.0	+3.3

JONATHAN O'BRIEN (SF)

Home Address: 11 Fairfield Green, Cork City.
Phone: 01 6184040 (LH)
Website: www.sinnfein.ie
Twitter: twitter.com/jobrien_sf
Facebook: facebook/jonathanOBrienTD
Birth Place/Date: Cork City, 1971.
Marital Status/Family: Married to Gillian; 2 sons, 2 daughters.
Education: North Monastery Secondary School, Cork.
Occupation: Full-time public representative.
Biography: Party spokesperson on Justice, Equality and Defence. Secured 7,923 first-preference votes to top the poll and get elected on the eighth count. He unsuccessfully contested the 2002 and 2007 general elections. He failed to win a seat in the 1999 local elections but he was co-opted to Cork City Council in 2001 and retained his seat in 2004 and 2009. He served as Mayor of Cork in 2010.
Hobbies: No time for hobbies!
Did you know? ? Jonathan is a director of Cork City Football Club.
Politician (living or deceased) you most admire: Nelson Mandela.
Priority as a TD? Secure greater investment for Cork North-Central to improve infrastructure, increase rehab services for drug addicts.
Why did you stand for election? I felt I could do a better job representing my community than what was already there and to advance the Republican struggle.
Is there any particular event that brought home to you just how serious the economic crisis had become? Seeing people lose their homes and jobs and watching friends leave the country.

KATHLEEN LYNCH (Lab)

Home Address: Farrancleary, Assumption Road, Blackpool, Cork.
Phone: 01 6183000 (LH) 021 4399930/021 4212463 (CO)
Website: www.labour.ie/kathleenlynch
Twitter: twitter.com/kathleenlynch
Facebook: facebook/kathleenlynch
Birth Place/Date: Cork, July 1953.
Marital Status/Family: Married to Bernard; 1 son, 3 daughters.
Education: Blackpool school.
Occupation: Full-time public representative.
Biography: First elected to Cork City Council as a Workers' Party representative in 1985. A founder member of Democratic Left, she was elected to the Dáil in a by-election in 1994 but subsequently lost her seat in the 1997 general election. She was re-elected in 2002, 2007 and 2011. Minister of State for Disability, Equality and Mental Health in the current government. Sister in law of Ciaran Lynch, TD for Cork South Central.
Politician (living or deceased) you most admire: Nelson Mandela.
Priority as a TD? To address the current economic crisis and create jobs.
Why did you stand for election? I first stood for election in 1985 to extend my role as a community activist.
Is there any particular event that brought home to you just how serious the economic crisis had become? Friends and relatives losing jobs and the financial effect negative equity and spiralling debt is having on family life.

BILLY KELLEHER (FF)

Home Address: 28A Ballyhooley Road, Dillon's Cross, Cork.
Phone: 021 4502289 (CO) 01 6183219 (LH)
Email: billykelleher@eircom.net or billy.kelleher@oireachtas.ie
Website: www.billykelleher.com
Birth Place/Date: Cork, January 1968.
Marital Status/Family: Married to Liza Davis; 3 children.
Education: Upper Glanmire NS; Sacred Heart College, Carrignavar, Co Cork.
Occupation: Public representative.
Biography: Party spokesperson on Health. Secured 7,896 first-preference votes to get re-elected on the 11th and final count. He was first elected in 1997 and he has been returned in each subsequent general election. In 2007 he was appointed Minister of State for Labour Affairs and in April 2009 he was appointed Minister of State for Trade and Commerce. He unsuccessfully contested the 1992 general election and he was appointed to the Seanad in 1993 by then Taoiseach Albert Reynolds. He was elected to Cork City Council in 1999.
Hobbies: Walking, GAA and rugby.
Politician (living or deceased) you most admire: Seán Lemass and Mikhail Gorbachev.
Priority as a TD? As an opposition TD to hold the government to account for their Programme for Government.
Why did you stand for election? To get a mandate from the people of Cork North-Central to continue the work that I have been doing since becoming a public representative.
Is there any particular event that brought home to you just how serious the economic crisis had become? Witnessing the growing queues at the social and community welfare offices.

Cork North-Central

DARA MURPHY (FG)

Address: Gardener's Hill, St Lukes' Cross, Cork.
Phone: 086 2533729 (M) 01 6183862 (LH)
Email: dara_Murphy@oireachtas.ie
Twitter: Yes.
Facebook: Yes.
Birth Place/Date: Cork, December 1969.
Marital Status/Family: Married to Tanya; 3 children.
Education: Christian Brothers College, Cork; UCC.
Occupation: Public representative. Formerly self-employed in catering industry.
Biography: He secured 6,597 first-preference votes to get elected on 11th count in his first general election. He was first elected as a councillor in 2004 when he garnered 1,011 first preferences. From Mayfield, he was the Lord Mayor of Cork in 2009-2010.
Hobbies: Cooking, reading non-fiction historical books, cycling, walking and spending time with his family.
Did you know? Last year Dara was the youngest Lord Mayor of Cork since Micheál Martin.
Politician (living or deceased) you most admire: John Bruton.
Priority as a TD? To change politics and how it is delivered.
Why did you stand for election? I believe we need a new generation of politicians and I believe I have something to contribute to that.
Is there any particular event that brought home to you just how serious the economic crisis had become? I was canvassing in a middle-class part of my constituency when I met a man in his 40s who told me he was on suicide watch. He was in a state of despair as he had been self-employed for his entire working life and he is in a position that he never thought he would be in. It is sobering to meet a man like that.

Cllr Mick Barry, Socialist Party candidate for Cork North-Central, calls for a general strike in protest at government cutbacks

First preference votes

	Seats	4			10,428		
	Candidate	Party	1st	%	Quota	Count	Status
1	O'Brien, Jonathan	SF	7,923	15.20%	0.76	8	Made Quota
2	Lynch, Kathleen*	LB	7,676	14.72%	0.74	10	Made Quota
3	Kelleher, Billy*	FF	7,896	15.14%	0.76	11	Elected
4	Murphy, Dara	FG	6,597	12.65%	0.63	11	Elected
5	Burton, Pat	FG	7,072	13.56%	0.68	11	Not Elected
6	Gilroy, John	LB	6,125	11.75%	0.59	9	Eliminated
7	Barry, Mick	SP	4,803	9.21%	0.46	8	Eliminated
8	O'Sullivan, Padraig	NV	1,020	1.96%	0.10	7	No Expenses
9	Conway, Kevin	NP	958	1.84%	0.09	6	No Expenses
10	Tynan, Ted	WP	681	1.31%	0.07	5	No Expenses
11	Walsh, Ken	GP	524	1.01%	0.05	4	No Expenses
12	Rea, Harry	CS	324	0.62%	0.03	3	No Expenses
13	Adams, John	CPPC	282	0.54%	0.03	2	No Expenses
14	Ashu-Arrah, Benjamin	NP	161	0.31%	0.02	1	No Expenses
15	O'Rourke, Fergus	NP	95	0.18%	0.01	1	No Expenses

*Outgoing TD Valid poll: 52,137 Quota: 10,428 No expenses limit: 2,608

Party votes

		2011					2007				Change	
Party	Cand	1st	%	Quota	Seats	Cand	1st	%	Quota	Seats	%	Seats
FG	2	13,669	26.22%	1.31	1	2	11,674	27.57%	1.38	1	-1.35%	
LB	2	13,801	26.47%	1.32	1	1	5,221	12.33%	0.62	1	+14.14%	
FF	1	7,896	15.14%	0.76	1	2	15,136	35.74%	1.79	2	-20.60%	-1
SF	1	7,923	15.20%	0.76	1	1	3,456	8.16%	0.41		+7.04%	+1
SP	1	4,803	9.21%	0.46		1	1,700	4.01%	0.20		+5.20%	
GP	1	524	1.01%	0.05		1	1,503	3.55%	0.18		-2.54%	
WP	1	681	1.31%	0.07		1	263	0.62%	0.03		+0.69%	
CS	1	324	0.62%	0.03							+0.62%	
Others	5	2,516	4.83%	0.24		4	3,394	8.01%	0.40		-3.19%	
Total	15	52,137	100.0%	10,428	4	13	42,347	100.0%	8,470	4	0.00%	
Electorate		75,302	69.24%				67,777	62.48%			+6.76%	
Spoiled		572	1.09%				471	1.10%			-0.01%	
Turnout		52,709	70.00%				42,818	63.17%			+6.82%	

Transfer analysis

From	To	FG	LB	FF	SF	SP	GP	WP	Others	Non Trans
LB	10,953	3,576	4,173	1,021						2,183
		32.65%	38.10%	9.32%						19.93%
SF	703	123	548	32						
		17.50%	77.95%	4.55%						
SP	5,319	426	1,765	158	2,564					406
		8.01%	33.18%	2.97%	48.20%					7.63%
GP	558	171	185	42	31	37		17	56	19
		30.65%	33.15%	7.53%	5.56%	6.63%		3.05%	10.04%	3.41%
WP	741	64	164	34	201	191			51	36
		8.64%	22.13%	4.59%	27.13%	25.78%			6.88%	4.86%
NP	3,163	719	745	412	412	288	34	43	216	294
		22.73%	23.55%	13.03%	13.03%	9.11%	1.07%	1.36%	6.83%	9.29%
Total	21,437	5,079	7,580	1,699	3,208	516	34	60	323	2,938
		23.69%	35.36%	7.93%	14.96%	2.41%	0.16%	0.28%	1.51%	13.71%

Cork North-Central

Count details

Seats	4										Quota	10,428
Candidate	Party	1st	2nd Ashu O'Rourke	3rd Adams Votes	4th Rea Votes	5th Walsh Votes	6th Tynan Votes	7th O'Sullivan Conway	8th Barry Votes	9th O'Brien Surplus	10th Gilroy Votes	11th Lynch Surplus
O'Brien, Jonathan	SF		*+19*	*+36*	*+44*	*+31*	*+201*	*+313*	*+2,564*	*-703*		
		7,923	7,942	7,978	8,022	8,053	8,254	8,567	11,131	10,428	10,428	10,428
Lynch, Kathleen*	LB		*+20*	*+38*	*+15*	*+98*	*+106*	*+283*	*+1,268*	*+411*	*+4,173*	*-3,660*
		7,676	7,696	7,734	7,749	7,847	7,953	8,236	9,504	9,915	14,088	10,428
Kelleher, Billy*	FF		*+37*	*+8*	*+40*	*+42*	*+34*	*+327*	*+158*	*+32*	*+609*	*+412*
		7,896	7,933	7,941	7,981	8,023	8,057	8,384	8,542	8,574	9,183	9,595
Murphy, Dara	FG		*+18*	*+27*	*+40*	*+86*	*+41*	*+229*	*+233*	*+85*	*+1,011*	*+1,148*
		6,597	6,615	6,642	6,682	6,768	6,809	7,038	7,271	7,356	8,367	9,515
Burton, Pat	FG		*+32*	*+13*	*+38*	*+85*	*+23*	*+322*	*+193*	*+38*	*+637*	*+780*
		7,072	7,104	7,117	7,155	7,240	7,263	7,585	7,778	7,816	8,453	9,233
Gilroy, John	LB		*+9*	*+20*	*+4*	*+87*	*+58*	*+356*	*+497*	*+137*	*-7,293*	
		6,125	6,134	6,154	6,158	6,245	6,303	6,659	7,156	7,293	Eliminated	
Barry, Mick	SP		*+23*	*+50*	*+27*	*+37*	*+191*	*+188*	*-5,319*			
		4,803	4,826	4,876	4,903	4,940	5,131	5,319	Eliminated			
O'Sullivan, Padraig	NV		*+30*	*+35*	*+51*	*+47*	*+47*	*-1,230*				
		1,020	1,050	1,085	1,136	1,183	1,230	Eliminated				
Conway, Kevin	NP		*+11*	*+27*	*+24*	*+9*	*+4*	*-1,033*				
		958	969	996	1,020	1,029	1,033	Eliminated				
Tynan, Ted	WP		*+7*	*+19*	*+17*	*+17*	*-741*					
		681	688	707	724	741	Eliminated					
Walsh, Ken	GP		*+6*	*+19*	*+9*	*-558*						
		524	530	549	558	Eliminated						
Rea, Harry	CS		*+2*	*+5*	*-331*							
		324	326	331	Eliminated							
Adams, John	CPPC		*+31*	*-313*								
		282	313	Eliminated								
Ashu-Arrah, Benjamin	NP		*-161*									
		161	Eliminated									
O'Rourke, Fergus	NP		*-95*									
		95	Eliminated									
Non-transferable			*+11*	*+16*	*+22*	*+19*	*+36*	*+245*	*+406*		*+863*	*+1,320*
Cumulative			11	27	49	68	104	349	755	755	1,618	2,938
Total		52,137	52,137	52,137	52,137	52,137	52,137	52,137	52,137	52,137	52,137	52,137

Fianna Fáil TD Billy Kelleher and his wife Liza at the election count in Cork City Hall

Cork North-West (3 seats)

First woman candidate elected in Cork North-West

Elected

Michael Creed* (FG) Count 5, Michael Moynihan* (FF) Final count, Áine Collins (FG) Final count.

Analysis by Michael Gallagher

A population of 4,334 from the areas of Kilcullen, Dromore, Mountrivers and Kilshannig was moved to Cork North-Central in a change to this constituency's boundaries since 2007.

This used to be solid Fine Gael territory, with the party taking two of the three seats at each of the six elections of the 1981-1992 period. In 1997, Fianna Fáil moved into the majority position and remained there, but the nationwide swing away from Fianna Fáil and towards Fine Gael made it a virtual certainty that Fine Gael would pick up a second seat, and so it did.

Michael Creed was sure to head the poll – though his decision to oppose Enda Kenny in the failed heave of June last year may have cost him a junior ministerial position – and the main interest within Fine Gael lay in the race between the other two candidates. In the event, Áine Collins won almost twice as many votes as Derry Canty, whose base in the south of the constituency meant that the odds were always against him. Collins, centrally located near Millstreet, became the first woman ever elected for the constituency.

Labour's Martin Coughlan performed creditably but he needed to do a little better than this to pick up a seat in an area where Labour has had no representation since Paddy McAuliffe lost his seat in 1969.

Fianna Fáil's performance was disastrous by the standards of previous elections but not bad in the context of 2011. Batt O'Keeffe's arrival in 2007, following a redrawing of the constituencies, had caused some upheaval, and he departed in even more turbulent circumstances. During the fateful 18 hours that spelled the end of the government on 19-20 January, he both resigned from government and stated that he would not be contesting the election, leaving the party's fortunes in Cork North-West in the hands of Michael Moynihan, a TD since 1997. With the aid of nearly 1,700 transfers from his running mate Daithí Ó Donnabháin, Moynihan, well ensconced locally though with no national profile, took the second seat fairly comfortably.

*outgoing TDs

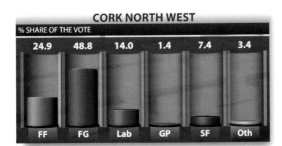

CORK NORTH WEST

% SHARE OF THE VOTE

FF	FG	Lab	GP	SF	Oth
24.9	48.8	14.0	1.4	7.4	3.4

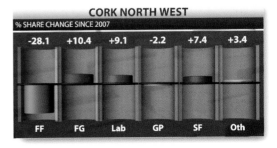

CORK NORTH WEST

% SHARE CHANGE SINCE 2007

FF	FG	Lab	GP	SF	Oth
-28.1	+10.4	+9.1	-2.2	+7.4	+3.4

Cork North-West

MICHAEL CREED (FG)

Home Address: 1 Sullane Weirs, Macroom, Co Cork.
Phone: 087 2424631 (M) 026 41835 (CO) 01 6183525 (LH)
Email: michael.creed@oireachtas.ie
Website: www.michaelcreed.ie
Birth Place/Date: Cork, June 1963.
Marital Status/Family: Married to Sinead; 3 children.
Education: Inchigeela NS; St Colman's College, Fermoy; De La Salle College, Macroom; UCC.
Occupation: Full-time public representative.
Biography: Member of Cork County Council 1985-2007. County Mayor 2005/2006. First elected to Dáil Éireann in 1989 and served until 2002. Re-elected in 2007. Has served on the Fine Gael front-bench as spokesperson on Education and most recently on Agriculture.
Hobbies: Golf, Gaelic games, soccer, rugby and reading.
Did you know? Michael once ran the Dublin city marathon.
Politician (living or deceased) you most admire: Nelson Mandela.
Priority as a TD? Contribute to the government's programme for national recovery.
Why did you stand for election? Job creation as unemployment has trebled in the area since 2007 and emigration is at epidemic levels. One of my personal goals is to see agriculture and the agri-food sector being given the status it deserves as a key economic driver. At a local level, Cork North-West has been deprived of important infrastructure such as the N22 Macroom by-pass, a proper broadband network and a safe secondary roads network.
Is there any particular event that brought home to you just how serious the economic crisis had become? The constant stream of people calling into my constituency office who are having difficulty paying mortgages and paying for the most basic of necessities, really brings home how difficult the economic climate has become.

MICHAEL MOYNIHAN (FF)

Home Address: Meens, Kiskeam, Mallow, Co Cork.
Phone: 087 2745810 (M) 029 51299 (CO) 01 6183595 (LH)
Email: michael@michaelmoynihantd.ie
Website: www.michaelmoynihantd.ie
Birth Place/Date: January 1968.
Marital Status/Family: Married; 1 daughter.
Education: Boherbue NS; Boherbue Comprehensive.
Occupation: Public representative. Farmer.
Biography: Party spokesperson on Agriculture and Food. First elected to Dáil Éireann in 1997. Re-elected in 2002, 2007 and 2011.
Hobbies: Member of Kiskeam GAA Club and an avid reader.
Politician (living or deceased) you most admire: Seán Moylan, Seán Lemass.
Priority as a TD? To enact the changes needed to return the country to a sound economic and financial footing, job creation so young qualified people can stay in Ireland and ensure the most vulnerable are supported and protected.
Why did you stand for election? Since I was first elected I have had the opportunity to assist and help a huge amount of people in various ways, all for the betterment of them and their families. I am committed to continuing that work and to conveying the concerns and views of the people of Cork North-West to the government and in Dáil Éireann.
Is there any particular event that brought home to you just how serious the economic crisis had become? The huge amount of young people out of work and in difficulty with mortgages, along with massive levels of personal debt.

ÁINE COLLINS (FG)

Home Address: Laught, Rathcoole, Mallow, Co Cork.
Phone: 087 232 6945 (M) 01 6183873 (LH)
Email: aine.collins@oireachtas.ie
Birth Place/Date: Knock Brack, Banteer, Co Cork.
Marital Status/Family: Married; 3 children.
Education: Rathcoole National School; Millstreet Secondary School; North East London Polytechnic (certified public accountant).
Occupation: Public representative. Accountant, business consultant.
Biography: Secured 7,884 first-preference votes to get elected on the sixth and final count in her first general election. She served on the Fine Gael national executive from 2007-2010 but had never contested an election before 2011.
Hobbies: Reading, cooking, walking, mountain-climbing.
Did you know? Áine is the only female TD in Munster following the defeat of Deirdre Clune in Cork South-Central.
Politician (living or deceased) you most admire: Michael Collins.
Priority as a TD? Jobs creation and streamlining services to achieve greater efficiencies.
Why did you stand for election? We need to reform the way we manage the country.
Is there any particular event that brought home to you just how serious the economic crisis had become? Seeing young people leaving their airports in their droves like the 1980s and watching people get crippled after losing their jobs and struggling to pay their mortgages.

First preference votes

	Seats	3			11,436		
Candidate	Party	1st	%	Quota	Count	Status
1 Creed, Michael*	FG	10,112	22.11%	0.88	5	Made Quota
2 Moynihan, Michael*	FF	8,845	19.34%	0.77	6	Elected
3 Collins, Aine	FG	7,884	17.24%	0.69	6	Elected
4 Coughlan, Martin	LB	6,421	14.04%	0.56	6	Not Elected
5 Canty, Derry	FG	4,325	9.46%	0.38	4	Eliminated
6 O'Grady, Des	SF	3,405	7.44%	0.30	3	Eliminated
7 O Donnabhain, Daithi	FF	2,545	5.56%	0.22	2	No Expenses
8 Foley, Anne	PBPA	1,552	3.39%	0.14	1	No Expenses
9 Collins, Mark	GP	651	1.42%	0.06	1	No Expenses

*Outgoing TD Valid poll: 45,740 Quota: 11,436 No expenses limit: 2,860

Party votes

		2007					2007				Change	
Party	Cand	1st	%	Quota	Seats	Cand	1st	%	Quota	Seats	%	Seats
FG	3	22,321	48.80%	1.95	2	2	17,913	38.42%	1.54	1	+10.38%	+1
LB	1	6,421	14.04%	0.56		1	2,288	4.91%	0.20		+9.13%	
FF	2	11,390	24.90%	1.00	1	3	24,732	53.05%	2.12	2	-28.15%	-1
SF	1	3,405	7.44%	0.30							+7.44%	
PBPA	1	1,552	3.39%	0.14							+3.39%	
GP	1	651	1.42%	0.06		1	1,687	3.62%	0.14		-2.20%	
Total	9	45,740	100.0%	11,436	3	7	46,620	100.0%	11,656	3	0.00%	0
Electorate		62,870	72.75%				64,085	72.75%			+0.01%	
Spoiled		454	0.98%				401	0.85%			+0.13%	
Turnout		46,194	73.48%				47,021	73.37%			+0.10%	

Transfer analysis

From	To	FG	LB	FF	SF	Non Trans
FG	6,071	4,122	1,176	315		458
		67.90%	19.37%	5.19%		7.54%
FF	2,633	518	189	1,690	136	100
		19.67%	7.18%	64.19%	5.17%	3.80%
SF	4,052	1,152	1,697	409		794
		28.43%	41.88%	10.09%		19.60%
PBPA	1,552	448	454	178	360	112
		28.87%	29.25%	11.47%	23.20%	7.22%
GP	651	188	191	74	151	47
		28.88%	29.34%	11.37%	23.20%	7.22%
Total	14,959	6,428	3,707	2,666	647	1,511
		42.97%	24.78%	17.82%	4.33%	10.10%

Cork North-West

Count details

Candidate	Party	1st	2nd Foley Collins	3rd O Donnabhain Votes	4th O'Grady Votes	5th Canty Votes	6th Creed Surplus
			+152	+162	+371	+1,618	-979
Creed, Michael*	FG	10,112	10,264	10,426	10,797	12,415	11,436
			+164	+1,690	+409	+254	+61
Moynihan, Michael*	FF	8,845	9,009	10,699	11,108	11,362	11,423
			+339	+122	+393	+1,796	+708
Collins, Aine	FG	7,884	8,223	8,345	8,738	10,534	11,242
			+645	+189	+1,697	+966	+210
Coughlan, Martin	LB	6,421	7,066	7,255	8,952	9,918	10,128
			+145	+234	+388	-5,092	
Canty, Derry	FG	4,325	4,470	4,704	5,092	Eliminated	
			+511	+136	-4,052		
O'Grady, Des	SF	3,405	3,916	4,052	Eliminated		
			+88	-2,633			
O Donnabhain, Daithi	FF	2,545	2,633	Eliminated			
			-1,552				
Foley, Ann	PBPA	1,552	Eliminated				
			-651				
Collins, Mark	GP	651	Eliminated				
Non-transferable			+159	+100	+794	+458	
Cumulative			159	259	1,053	1,511	1,511
Total		45,740	45,740	45,740	45,740	45,740	45,740

Seats 3   Quota 11,436

Moments after she is deemed elected, Fine Gael's Áine Collins is in a jubilant at Macroom count centre

Cork South-Central (5 seats)

Fianna Fáil holds two seats in party leader's constituency

Elected

Micheál Martin* (FF) Count 1, Ciarán Lynch* (Lab) Count 9, Simon Coveney* (FG) Count 10, Jerry Buttimer (FG) Count 11, Michael McGrath* (FF) Final count.

Analysis by Michael Gallagher

There were no changes to this urban constituency's boundaries since 2007. In an election of such upheaval, the big story here was 'hardly any change'. Four of the five incumbents were re-elected, and there was no change of seats between parties. Moreover, it was possibly Fianna Fáil's best result in the entire country, showing that Micheál Martin's accession to the party leadership certainly had some impact. The party's vote dropped by a mere 16% on 2007 – the second smallest in the country – and it managed to hold both of the seats it won in 2007, one of only two constituencies where it did not lose a seat. Martin himself headed the poll – one of only two Fianna Fáil candidates nationwide to do this – but the real test was whether the other Fianna Fáil incumbent Michael McGrath, sometimes tipped as a future party leader himself, would join him in the Dáil. He did so with surprising ease, finishing over 2,000 votes ahead of the runner-up.

This runner-up was Sinn Féin's Chris O'Leary, who had switched both party and constituency since 2007, when he won a mere 1,503 votes as a Green candidate in Cork North-Central. Now he won more than three times as many votes as Green senator Dan Boyle, whose defeat in 2007 had been one of the shocks of that election but whose support now plunged to a meagre 1,640 votes, only 500 more than he had

received when he first stood way back in 1992.

The two parties of the incoming government had unspectacular results. The third seat that Fine Gael had targeted never came into view. Jerry Buttimer increased his own vote impressively and took the fourth seat, but his victim was Fine Gael incumbent Deirdre Clune, who has now been elected twice (1997 and 2007) but has never been re-elected. The Fine Gael vote management here was poor, in contrast to the machine-like efficacy achieved in most other constituencies, but even perfect vote management probably would not have delivered three seats on this occasion.

Labour doubled its vote, but the effect was only to turn a rather marginal seat into a safe one. Ciarán Lynch added over 3,000 votes to his 2007 tally, but it was to be his sister-in-law from Cork North-Central who got the call when the junior ministries were allocated.

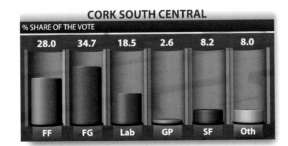

CORK SOUTH CENTRAL

% SHARE OF THE VOTE

FF	FG	Lab	GP	SF	Oth
28.0	34.7	18.5	2.6	8.2	8.0

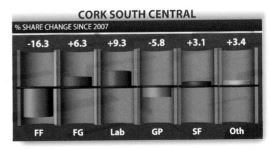

CORK SOUTH CENTRAL

% SHARE CHANGE SINCE 2007

FF	FG	Lab	GP	SF	Oth
-16.3	+6.3	+9.3	-5.8	+3.1	+3.4

*outgoing TDs

Cork South-Central

MICHEÁL MARTIN (FF)

Constituency Address: 137 Evergreen Road, Turner's Cross, Cork.
Home Address: Lios Laoi, 16 Silver Manor, Ballinlough, Co Cork.
Phone: 01 6184350 (LH) 021 4320088 (CO)
Email: michealmartintd@eircom.net
Website: www.michealmartin.ie
Birth Place/Date: Cork, August 1960.
Marital Status/Family: Married with young family.
Education: Coláiste Chriost Rí, Cork; UCC (BA, HDipED, MA).
Occupation: Public representative.
Biography: First elected a TD in 1989 and re-elected at each subsequent general election. Elected Uachtarán Fhianna Fáil January 2011. Current party spokesperson on Northern Ireland. Minister for Foreign Affairs (2008-2011), Minister for Enterprise, Trade and Employment (2004-2008), Minister for Health and Children (2000-2004), Minister for Education (1997-2000). Fianna Fáil frontbench spokesperson on Education and the Gaeltacht (1995-1997). First elected to Cork Corporation in 1985 and served as Lord Mayor of Cork from 1992 to 1993.
Hobbies: Sport, walking, swimming, history, reading.
Did you know? Micheál Martin is the author of *Freedom to Choose: Cork and Party Politics in Ireland 1918-1932*.
Politician (living or deceased) you most admire: Seán Lemass and Jack Lynch
Priority as a TD? Reform of and improvements to our education system.
Why did you stand for election? I stood for election to continue to serve the people of Cork South-Central whom I have served since 1989 but also to offer a new kind of political leadership in Ireland.

CIARÁN LYNCH (Lab)

Constituency Address: 29 St Patrick's Mills, Douglas, Cork.
Phone: 086 6033923 (M) 021 4366200 (O)
Email: ciaran.lynch@oir.ie
Website: www.ciaranlynch.ie
Facebook: Yes.
Twitter: twitter.com/CiaranLynchTD
Birth Place/Date: Cork, June 1964.
Marital Status/Family: Father of 2 children.
Education: WIT (education management); UCC (social studies).
Occupation: Full-time public representative. Formerly Cork City VEC Adult Literacy Organiser.
Biography: First elected to Dáil in 2007. Elected to Cork City Council in 2004. Labour's spokesperson on housing and local government in 31st Dáil.
Hobbies: Fishing, movies and reading.
Did you know? Ciarán is a good cook and irons his own shirts.
Politician (living or deceased) you most admire: Nelson Mandela.
Priority as a TD? To work tirelessly on behalf of families and their communities. Support growth and prosperity that leads to job creation. Ensure necessary reforms to get Ireland back on its feet are implemented in a fair manner.
Why did you stand for election? To make people's quality of life better. My role as a government TD over the next five years is to get Ireland back to work, so we can restore the quality of people's lives. But there is no magic wand solution to our economic troubles. There are tough decisions ahead and the days of instant gratification are over and the process of delivering meaningful improvement will take time.
Is there any particular event that brought home to you just how serious the economic crisis had become? The growing level of personal and mortgage debt, and the real fear that people have of losing their homes, along with the way the awful spectre of emigration now hangs over a new generation of young people in Ireland.

SIMON COVENEY (FG)

Home Address: Main Street, Carrigaline, Co Cork.
Phone: 087 8321755 (M) 021 4374200 (CO) 01 6183666 (LH)
Email: simon.coveney@oir.ie
Website: www.simoncoveney.ie
Twitter: @simoncoveney
Facebook: /SimonCoveneyTD
Birth Place/Date: Cork, June 1972.
Marital Status/Family: Married to Ruth; 2 daughters.
Education: Clongowes Wood College, Co Kildare; University College Cork; Gurteen Agricultural College, Co Tipperary; The Royal Agriculture College, Gloucestershire (BSc agriculture and land management).
Occupation: Full-time public representative.
Biography: Current Minister for Agriculture, Food and Marine. First elected to the Dáil in 1998. Has been Fine Gael spokesperson on Drugs and Youth Affairs; Communications, Marine and Natural Resources; Transport and the Marine. Chaired Fine Gael Policy Development Committee. Elected to the European Parliament in 2004. Member of Cork County Council from 1999 to 2003.
Hobbies: All competitive sport. Played rugby for Garryowen, Cork Constitution and Crosshaven Rugby Club. Led the 'Sail Chernobyl' project in 1997/1998.
Did you know? Simon had a severe stutter until the age of 16 before he overcame the speech impediment.
Politician (living or deceased) you most admire: Aung San Suu Kyi.
Priority as a TD? To rebuild the Irish economy and to restore confidence and pride into the Irish psyche.
Why did you stand for election? I genuinely believe I've something positive to contribute to public life. I've been privileged to have a broad education and see politics as a noble and rewarding profession.
Is there any particular event that brought home to you just how serious the economic crisis had become? Ireland losing its economic sovereignty the day the IMF arrived.

JERRY BUTTIMER (FG)

Home Address: 25 Benvoirlich Estate, Bishopstown, Cork.
Phone: 021 4541923 (H) 086 2356892 (M) 01 6183380 (LH)
Email: gerry.buttimer@oireachtas.ie
Website: www.jerrybuttimer.ie
Twitter: jerrybuttimer @jerrybuttimer
Facebook: Yes.
Birth Place/Date: Cork, March 1967.
Marital Status/Family: Single.
Education: Scoil an Spioraid Naoimh (Boys) Curraheen Road; St Finbarr's College Farranferris; St Patrick's College Maynooth; UCC.
Occupation: Public representative. Secondary school teacher and director of adult education.
Biography: Secured 7,128 first-preference votes to get elected on the 11th count. He garnered 5,180 first-preference votes in his unsuccessful 2007 general election attempt and went on to become a senator. Member Cork City Council 2004-2007.
Hobbies: Sport, cooking, reading.
Did you know? Jerry chronicled his experience as an unsuccessful candidate in the 2007 general election in a book, *Candidate: The Diary of an Election Candidate.*
Politician (living or deceased) you most admire: John Bruton, Bill Clinton.
Priority as a TD? Promote and protect employment opportunities, reform of the HSE and political reform.
Why did you stand for election? To bring about and effect political peformance and change, to promote and protect employment opportunities.
Is there any particular event that brought home to you just how serious the economic crisis had become? Locally it would be the number of businesses that are in trouble, job losses and the amount of people in negative equity and struggling to pay their mortgages. Nationally it is the arrival of the IMF.

MICHAEL McGRATH (FF)

Address: 4 North Lawn, Carrig na Curra, Carrigaline, Co Cork.
Phone: 021 4376699 (CO) 01 6183801 (LH)
Website: www.michaelmcgrath.ie
Email: michael.mcgrath@oir.ie
Facebook: Yes.
Birth Place/Date: Cork, August 1976.
Marital Status/Family: Married to Sarah; 5 children.
Education: St Peter's Community College, Passage West, Co Cork; UCC (BComm).
Occupation: Public-representative. Chartered accountant.
Biography: Party spokesperson on Public Expenditure and Public Sector Reform. First elected in 2007. Unsuccessfully contested 2002 Seanad election. Member Passage West Town Council 1999 to 2007. Member Cork County Council 2004-2007.
Hobbies: Cinema, walking, golf.
Did you know? Michael contested his first election at age 22 when he was elected to Passage West Town Council.
Politician (living or deceased) you most admire: Seán Lemass.
Priority as a TD? Support the work of securing our economic renewal.
Why did you stand for election? I genuinely believe in the value of public service. I believe I can make a real difference at a local and national level.
Is there any particular event that brought home to you just how serious the economic crisis had become? I have come across so many examples of families whose lives have been turned upside down by the economic crisis. We all need to work collectively and ensure job creation is the number one priority.

Election Facts
"Twenty five women deputies were returned to the 31st Dáil, up one on the outgoing Dáil, as Maureen O'Sullivan had been elected in a by-election in Dublin Central in 2009"
Sean Donnelly

Cork South-Central

First preference votes

	Candidate	Party	1st	%	Quota	Count	Status
	Seats	5			10,674		
1	Martin, Micheal*	FF	10,715	16.73%	1.00	1	Made Quota
2	Lynch, Ciaran*	LB	8,481	13.24%	0.79	9	Made Quota
3	Coveney, Simon*	FG	9,447	14.75%	0.89	10	Made Quota
4	Buttimer, Jerry	FG	7,128	11.13%	0.67	11	Made Quota
5	McGrath, Michael*	FF	7,221	11.28%	0.68	12	Elected
7	Clune, Deirdre*	FG	5,650	8.82%	0.53	10	Eliminated
8	Desmond, Paula	LB	3,388	5.29%	0.32	8	Eliminated
9	Finn, Mick	NP	2,386	3.73%	0.22	7	Eliminated
10	Boyle, Dan #	GP	1,640	2.56%	0.15	6	No Expenses
11	McCarthy, David	NV	880	1.37%	0.08	5	No Expenses
12	Neville, Ted	NP	523	0.82%	0.05	5	No Expenses
13	O Cadhla, Diarmaid	CPPC	508	0.79%	0.05	4	No Expenses
14	Dunphy, Sean	NP	448	0.70%	0.04	3	No Expenses
15	Isherwood, Eric	NP	193	0.30%	0.02	2	No Expenses
16	O'Driscoll, Finbar	NP	92	0.14%	0.01	2	No Expenses
17	Linehan, Gerard	NP	90	0.14%	0.01	2	No Expenses

* Outgoing #Former TD Valid Poll: 64,040 Quota: 10,674 No expenses limit: 2,670

Party votes

Party	Cand	2011 1st	%	Quota	Seats	Cand	2007 1st	%	Quota	Seats	Change %	Seats
FG	3	22,225	34.70%	2.08	2	3	16,782	28.41%	1.70	2	+6.29%	
LB	2	11,869	18.53%	1.11	1	1	5,466	9.25%	0.56	1	+9.28%	
FF	2	17,936	28.01%	1.68	2	3	26,154	44.28%	2.66	2	-16.27%	
SF	1	5,250	8.20%	0.49		1	3,020	5.11%	0.31		+3.09%	
GP	1	1,640	2.56%	0.15		1	4,945	8.37%	0.50		-5.81%	
PD						1	1,596	2.70%	0.16		-2.70%	
Others	8	5,120	8.00%	0.48		4	1,105	1.87%	0.11		+6.12%	
Total	17	64,040	100.0%	10,674	5	14	59,068	100.0%	9,845	5	0.00%	0
Electorate	91,619	69.90%					91,090	64.85%			+5.05%	
Spoiled	624	0.96%					592	0.99%			-0.03%	
Turnout	64,664	70.58%					59,660	65.50%			+5.08%	

Transfer analysis

From	To	FG	LB	FF	SF	GP	Others	Non Trans
FG	9,112	4,686		1,630	919			1,877
		51.43%		17.89%	10.09%			20.60%
LB	6,018	1,857	2,644	482	805			230
		30.86%	43.93%	8.01%	13.38%			3.82%
FF	41	7	4	27	1	1	1	
		17.07%	9.76%	65.85%	2.44%	2.44%	2.44%	0.00%
GP	1,800	669	676	151	108		78	118
		37.17%	37.56%	8.39%	6.00%		4.33%	6.56%
Others	6,055	1,214	1,499	512	1,104	159	856	711
		20.05%	24.76%	8.46%	18.23%	2.63%	14.14%	11.74%
Total	23,026	8,433	4,823	2,802	2,937	160	935	2,936
		36.62%	20.95%	12.17%	12.76%	0.69%	4.06%	12.75%

Count details

Seats: 5   Quota: 10,674

Candidate	Party	1st	2nd Martin Surplus	3rd Isherwood O'Driscoll Linehan	4th Dunphy Votes	5th O Cadhla Votes	6th McCarthy Neville Votes	7th Boyle Votes	8th Finn Votes	9th Desmond Votes	10th Lynch Surplus	11th Clune Votes	12th Buttimer Surplus
			−41										
Martin, Micheál*	FF	**10,715**	10,674	10,674	10,674	10,674	10,674	10,674	10,674	10,674	10,674	10,674	10,674
			+3	+32	+27	+50	+217	+408	+703	+2,644	−1,891		
Lynch, Ciarán*	LB	8,481	8,484	8,516	8,543	8,593	8,810	9,218	9,921	12,565	10,674	10,674	10,674
			+3	+21	+50	+37	+154	+264	+193	+362	+341		
Coveney, Simon*	FG	9,447	9,450	9,471	9,521	9,558	9,712	9,976	10,169	10,531	10,872	10,872	10,872
			+2	+20	+23	+21	+133	+226	+269	+210	+378	+4,686	−2,422
Buttimer, Jerry	FG	7,128	7,130	7,150	7,173	7,194	7,327	7,553	7,822	8,032	8,410	13,096	10,674
			+27	+26	+53	+23	+134	+151	+276	+209	+273	+632	+998
McGrath, Michael*	FF	7,221	7,248	7,274	7,327	7,350	7,484	7,635	7,911	8,120	8,393	9,025	10,023
			+1	+40	+28	+95	+274	+108	+667	+256	+549	+372	+547
O'Leary, Chris	SF	5,250	5,251	5,291	5,319	5,414	5,688	5,796	6,463	6,719	7,268	7,640	8,187
			+2	+20	+17	+20	+94	+179	+142	+240	+326	−6,690	
Clune, Deirdre*	FG	5,650	5,652	5,672	5,689	5,709	5,803	5,982	6,124	6,364	6,690	Eliminated	
			+1	+23	+43	+44	+110	+268	+250	−4,127			
Desmond, Paula	LB	3,388	3,389	3,412	3,455	3,499	3,609	3,877	4,127	Eliminated			
			+1	+53	+100	+57	+285	+78	−2,960				
Finn, Mick	NP	2,386	2,387	2,440	2,540	2,597	2,882	2,960	Eliminated				
			+1	+9	+22	+36	+92	−1,800					
Boyle, Dan #	GP	1,640	1,641	1,650	1,672	1,708	1,800	Eliminated					
				+37	+35	+85	−1,037						
McCarthy, David	NV	880	880	917	952	1,037	Eliminated						
				+24	+34	+58	−639						
Neville, Ted	NP	523	523	547	581	639	Eliminated						
				+23	+32	−563							
Ó Cadhla, Diarmaid	CPPC	508	508	531	563	Eliminated							
				+33	−481								
Dunphy, Sean	NP	448	448	481	Eliminated								
				−193									
Isherwood, Eric	NP	193	193	Eliminated									
				−92									
O'Driscoll, Finbar	NP	92	92	Eliminated									
				−90									
Linehan, Gerard	NP	90	90	Eliminated									
Non-transferable				+14	+17	+37	+183	+118	+460	+206	+24	+1,000	+877
Cumulative			0	14	31	68	251	369	829	1,035	1,059	2,059	2,936
Total			64,040	64,040	64,040	64,040	64,040	64,040	64,040	64,040	64,040	64,040	64,040

Fianna Fáil's Michael McGrath celebrates with his family and supporters in the count centre in Cork City Hall

Cork South-West (3 seats)

Three new TDs for the country's most south-westerly constituency

Elected

Jim Daly (FG) Count 5, Noel Harrington (FG) Final count, Michael McCarthy (Lab) Final count.

Analysis by Michael Gallagher

There were no changes to the boundaries of this constituency since 2007. A constituency ever since 1923, Cork South-West was represented by a Labour TD from then until 1981. Timothy J Murphy carried the torch for over 25 years, was succeeded in 1949 by his son William (at 21 years and 29 days on polling day still the youngest TD ever), and in 1951 Michael Pat Murphy (no relation) won the seat that he held comfortably until he retired in 1981. Since then, there had been a consistent pattern of two Fine Gael seats and one for Fianna Fáil, broken only when Fianna Fáil gained a seat in 2002.

With both Fine Gael veterans Jim O'Keeffe (first elected 1977) and P J Sheehan (first elected 1981) standing down, and Labour having its best opportunity for 30 years to put some red back on the map of the country's most south-westerly constituency, there was a good chance that Cork South-West would return three brand new TDs. Labour candidate Senator Michael McCarthy duly ensured this. Despite a fairly modest increase in his first-preference vote, he did well on transfers (nearly 2,200 from the elimination of the bottom seven

candidates) and held off the Fianna Fáil challenge by 600 votes.

Fine Gael was certain to hold its two seats, and nominated three candidates, who all polled well. Jim Daly from Skibbereen, more or less in the centre of the constituency, comfortably headed the poll, and it was Noel Harrington from Castletownbere who took the other seat, with 456 votes to spare over the third Fine Gael candidate, Kevin Murphy, when it mattered.

Fianna Fáil was left to contemplate the wreckage of its campaign. Its two candidates won nearly 10,800 votes between them – over 4,000 more than Labour – yet neither was elected. When incumbent Christy O'Sullivan – a surprise winner in 2007, and still regarded by some in Fianna Fáil as a blow-in as he had previously stood as an independent – was eliminated on the fourth count, only 57% of his transfers went to his running mate Denis O'Donovan, who has contested every election since 1987 but was elected only once, in 2002.

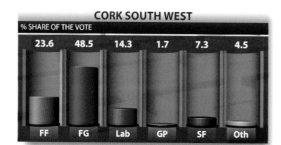

CORK SOUTH WEST
% SHARE OF THE VOTE

FF	FG	Lab	GP	SF	Oth
23.6	48.5	14.3	1.7	7.3	4.5

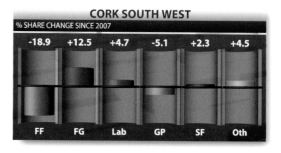

CORK SOUTH WEST
% SHARE CHANGE SINCE 2007

FF	FG	Lab	GP	SF	Oth
-18.9	+12.5	+4.7	-5.1	+2.3	+4.5

*outgoing TDs

JIM DALY (FG)

Home Address: 5 Millgrove, Clonakilty, Co Cork.
Phone: 087 7465397 (M) 01 6183886 (LH)
Email: jim.daly@oireachtas.ie
Website: www.jimdaly.ie
Twitter: @jimdalytd
Facebook: www.facebook.com/jimdaly
Birth Place/Date: Cork, December 1972.
Marital Status/Family: Married to Virge; 4 sons.
Education: Coláiste Mhuire Cobh; NUI Maynooth; Mary Immaculate College, Limerick.
Occupation: Full-time public representative. Formerly primary school teacher.
Biography: Jim secured 8,878 first-preference votes to top the poll and get elected on the fifth count. He has been a councillor since 2004 and he was Mayor of County Cork in 2010. Contested 2007 Seanad election.
Hobbies: Reading and swimming
Did you know? Jim reads every available book relating to Irish politics and history.
Politician (living or deceased) you most admire: John Hume.
Priority as a TD? Honest and effective communication with constituents.
Why did you stand for election? To enhance the quality of living for constituents.
Is there any particular event that brought home to you just how serious the economic crisis had become?
The day we saw the EU/IMF officials walking into the Central Bank on Dame Street.

NOEL HARRINGTON (FG)

Home Address: Bank Place, Castletownbere, Co Cork.
Phone: 086 8567178 (M) 027 56222 (H) 01 6183956 (LH)
Email: info@noelharrington.com or noel.harrington@oireachtas.ie
Website: www.noelharrington.com
Twitter: twitter.com/nharrington2
Facebook: facebook.com/noelharrington
Birth Place/Date: Castletownbere, December 1970.
Marital Status/Family: Married to Catherine; 2 sons 1 daughter.
Education: Beara Community School, Castletownbere, Co Cork.
Occupation: Public representative. Postmaster in Castletownbere since 1992.
Biography: Secured 6,898 first-preference votes to get elected on the sixth and final count in his first general election. Elected to Cork County Council on his first attempt in June 1999 and re-elected in 2004 and 2009. Mayor of County Cork in 2008. Unsuccessfully contested the 2007 Seanad election. Son of the late Cork county councillor Donie Harrington.
Hobbies: GAA, soccer, golf, reading, darts. Noel won a Cork County senior football championship medal with Beara in 1997.
Did you know? Noel is the first Beara person and the first Harrington to be elected to Dáil Éireann since its inception.
Priority as a TD? Help create jobs and regenerate rural communities. To get our natural resources such as fishing, farming and tourism working for the people of Ireland. Make Beara, West Cork and Ireland a better place to work, live or visit.
Why did you stand for election? To give the people of Cork South-West a strong, energetic and young voice.
Is there any particular event that brought home to you just how serious the economic crisis had become? Locally, unemployment has doubled and it is one of the highest increases of anywhere in the country. The future looks bleak for some local GAA clubs. There used to be 18th and 21st birthday parties, now emigration parties have taken over.

MICHAEL McCARTHY (Lab)

Home Address: Milleenananig, Clonakilty Road, Dunmanway, Co Cork.
Phone: 087 6481004 (M) 01 6183844 (LH)
Email: Michael.mccarthy@oireachtas.ie
Website: www.labour.ie/michaelmccarthy
Twitter: twitter.com/senmmcarthy
Facebook: www.facebook.com/pages/michael-mccarthy-TD
Birth Place/Date: Bantry, November 1976.
Marital Status/Family: Married to Nollagh Patterson; 2 sons.
Education: Colaiste Chairbre, Dunmanway, Co Cork.
Occupation: Full-time public representative.
Biography: Secured 6,533 first-preference votes to get elected on the sixth count in Cork South-West in his third general election attempt. Elected to Cork County Council in 1999 in the Skibereen electoral area. He was elected to the Seanad in 2002 and re-elected in 2007.
Hobbies: Reading, table quizzes, card drives.
Did you know? Michael is the fourth Labour Party TD to be elected from the town of Dunmanway.
Politician (living or deceased) you most admire: Dr. Noel Browne.
Priority as a TD? To ensure that West Cork is properly represented in Dáil Éireann
Why did you stand for election? I feel that I have the ability to represent the needs and views of the people of West Cork and that I have something to offer national politics.
Is there any particular event that brought home to you just how serious the economic crisis had become? We all know the unemployment statistics but driving past the dole queues is a sight to behold. I went past the dole queue in Bandon the other day and it was an unpleasant reminder to see the physical manifestation of the statistics.

Cork South-West

	Candidate	Party	1st	%	Quota	Count	Status
1	Daly, Jim	FG	8,878	19.44%	0.78	5	Made Quota
2	Harrington, Noel	FG	6,898	15.11%	0.60	6	Elected
3	McCarthy, Michael	LB	6,533	14.31%	0.57	6	Elected
4	O'Donovan, Denis #	FF	5,984	13.11%	0.52	6	Not Elected
5	Murphy, Kevin	FG	6,386	13.99%	0.56	4	Eliminated
6	O'Sullivan, Christy*	FF	4,803	10.52%	0.42	3	Eliminated
7	Hayes, Paul	SF	3,346	7.33%	0.29	2	Eliminated
8	Kearney, John	NP	772	1.69%	0.07	1	No Expenses
9	McCaughey, Kevin	GP	765	1.68%	0.07	1	No Expenses
10	McInerney, Dave	NV	493	1.08%	0.04	1	No Expenses
11	Butler, Edmund	NP	330	0.72%	0.03	1	No Expenses
12	Doonan, Paul	NV	239	0.52%	0.02	1	No Expenses
13	O'Sullivan, Michael	NP	231	0.51%	0.02	1	No Expenses

*Outgoing TD #Former TD Valid poll: 45,658 Quota: 11,415 No expenses limit: 2,854

Party votes

Party	Cand	2011 1st	%	Quota	Seats	Cand	2007 1st	%	Quota	Seats	Change %	Seats
FG	3	22,162	48.54%	1.94	2	2	15,299	36.00%	1.44	2	+12.54%	
LB	1	6,533	14.31%	0.57	1	1	4,095	9.64%	0.39		+4.67%	+1
FF	2	10,787	23.63%	0.95		2	18,093	42.57%	1.70	1	-18.95%	-1
SF	1	3,346	7.33%	0.29		1	2,150	5.06%	0.20		+2.27%	
GP	1	765	1.68%	0.07		1	2,860	6.73%	0.27		-5.05%	
Others	5	2,065	4.52%	0.18				0.00%	0.00		+4.52%	
Total	13	45,658	100.0%	11,415	3	7	42,497	100.0%	10,625	3	0.00%	0
Electorate		62,967	72.51%				61,577	69.01%			+3.50%	
Spoiled		390	0.85%				410	0.96%			-0.11%	
Turnout		46,048	73.13%				42,907	69.68%			+3.45%	

Transfer analysis

From	To	FG	LB	FF	SF	Non Trans
FG	9,039	6,170	1,542	702		625
		68.26%	17.06%	7.77%		6.91%
FF	5,215	1,296	503	2,972		444
		24.85%	9.65%	56.99%		8.51%
SF	3,743	960	1,452	530		801
		25.65%	38.79%	14.16%		21.40%
GP	765	262	196	103	107	97
		34.25%	25.62%	13.46%	13.99%	12.68%
Others	2,065	708	528	276	290	263
		34.29%	25.57%	13.37%	14.04%	12.74%
Total	20,827	9,396	4,221	4,583	397	2,230
		45.11%	20.27%	22.01%	1.91%	10.71%

Count details

Candidate	Party	1st	2nd	3rd	4th	5th	6th
			Kearney McCaughey McInerney Butler Doonan O'Sullivan	Hayes Votes	O'Sullivan Votes	Murphy Votes	Daly Surplus
			+377	+441	+812	+2,734	-1,827
Daly, Jim	FG	8,878	9,255	9,696	10,508	13,242	11,415
			+314	+267	+189	+1,900	+1,536
Harrington, Noel	FG	6,898	7,212	7,479	7,668	9,568	11,104
			+724	+1,452	+503	+1,327	+215
McCarthy, Michael	LB	6,533	7,257	8,709	9,212	10,539	10,754
			+224	+273	+2,972	+626	+76
O'Donovan, Denis #	FF	5,984	6,208	6,481	9,453	10,079	10,155
			+279	+252	+295	-7,212	
Murphy, Kevin	FG	6,386	6,665	6,917	7,212	Eliminated	
			+155	+257	-5,215		
O'Sullivan, Christy*	FF	4,803	4,958	5,215	Eliminated		
			+397	-3,743			
Hayes, Paul	SF	3,346	3,743	Eliminated			
			-772				
Kearney, John	NP	772	Eliminated				
			-765				
McCaughey, Kevin	GP	765	Eliminated				
			-493				
McInerney, Dave	NV	493	Eliminated				
			-330				
Butler, Edmund	NP	330	Eliminated				
			-239				
Doonan, Paul	NV	239	Eliminated				
			-231				
O'Sullivan, Michael	NP	231	Eliminated				
Non-transferable			+360	+801	+444	+625	
Cumulative			360	1,161	1,605	2,230	2,230
Total		45,658	45,658	45,658	45,658	45,658	45,658

Seats 3   Quota 11,415

Newly elected Fine Gael TDs Jim Daly and Noel Harrington at the Clonakilty count centre

Donegal North-East (3 seats)

Sinn Féin makes breakthrough as Fianna Fáil holds onto a single seat

Elected

Pádraig MacLochlainn (SF) Count 3, Joe McHugh* (FG) Count 8, Charlie McConalogue (FF) Final count.

Analysis by Sean Donnell

There was a boundary revision here since 2007, with a transfer of a population of 2,351 out of this constituency into Donegal South-West. All electoral divisions of the old Stranorlar Rural District are now within this constituency. However, the constituency did retain its three seats.

This contest was as good as over after the first count as the three leading candidates were well clear of the rest of the field. Fine Gael surprisingly added a second candidate, John Ryan from Inishowen, and its vote was up nine points on 2007 but with just 1.3 quotas the party was never in contention for a second seat. Joe McHugh was in second place on the first count and went on to take the second seat with the help of 65% of his running mate's transfers.

Former Fine Gael candidate Jimmy Harte, whose father Paddy was a long-time Fine Gael TD, joined the Labour Party in 2010. He managed to increase the party's vote by nine points on its poor 2007 result, but with just 4,090 first preferences, he was outside the frame on the first count with just 0.4 of a quota.

It was all change in Fianna Fáil as Dr Jim McDaid resigned his seat in November 2010 and outgoing deputy Niall Blaney announced his retirement just prior to the party's selection convention. This left Fianna Fáil with just a single candidate, newcomer Charlie McConalogue from Inishowen. There was pressure from former deputy McDaid's supporters to add a Letterkenny-based candidate but the party refused and this proved a prudent decision. The

Fianna Fáil vote was down a massive 33 points, its fourth largest loss of support in this election and McConalogue was in third place on the first count with 0.7 of a quota and nearly 2,000 votes ahead of his nearest rival John Ryan. He was unlikely to be overtaken and so it proved as the single-candidate strategy delivered for Fianna Fáil. This was in sharp contrast to the neighbouring constituency of Donegal South-West, where the party ran two candidates and ended up without a seat for the first time.

Sinn Féin went close to winning a seat here at the last election in 2007 and Pádraig MacLochlainn made no mistake in 2011 as he topped the poll and was just short of the quota on the first count. In an impressive performance, he was the first elected on the third count.

Letterkenny-based Dessie Shiels failed to take advantage of McDaid's absence, winning just 5%. Dara Blaney, son of former long-serving deputy Neil Blaney, contested his father's old constituency as a 'New Vision' candidate but did poorly and lost the right to reclaim his expenses as did three other non-party candidates and the Green representative.

*outgoing TDs

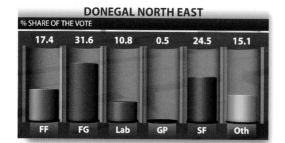

DONEGAL NORTH EAST
% SHARE OF THE VOTE

FF	FG	Lab	GP	SF	Oth
17.4	31.6	10.8	0.5	24.5	15.1

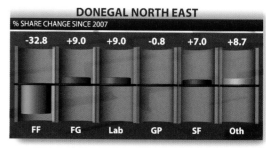

DONEGAL NORTH EAST
% SHARE CHANGE SINCE 2007

FF	FG	Lab	GP	SF	Oth
-32.8	+9.0	+9.0	-0.8	+7.0	+8.7

PÁDRAIG MacLOCHLAINN (SF)

Home Address: 13 The Meadows, Buncrana, Co Donegal
Phone: 01 6184061 (LH)
Email: pmaclsf@eircom.net or padraig.maclochlainn@oireachtas.ie
Website: www.sinnfein.ie
Birth Place/Date: Leeds, England, June 1973.
Marital Status/Family: Partner Sinéad; 1 son, 1 stepson.
Education: Early school leaver who returned to part-time education while working. Gained various certificates and a diploma in social studies.
Occupation: Public representative.
Biography: Party spokesperson on Foreign Affairs and Trade. Secured 9,278 first-preference seats to get elected on the third count in his third general election attempt. Unsuccessfully contested 2002 and 2007 general elections. He was co-opted onto Buncrana Town Council in 2002 and he was elected to Donegal County Council two years later in the 2004 local elections. He ran in the European elections in 2009 and he was the national director of Sinn Féin's campaign against the Lisbon Treaty referendum in 2008.
Hobbies: Reading, walking, and watching movies.
Did you know? Pádraig's father was a republican prisoner jailed for nine years across prisons in England.
Politician (living or deceased) you most admire: Nelson Mandela and William Wilberforce.
Priority as a TD? The separation of banking debt from sovereign debt and using the people's money for stimulating growth through investment in job retention, creation and public infrastructure.
Why did you stand for election? To effect real change for the people of Donegal North-East and Ireland.
Is there any particular event that brought home to you just how serious the economic crisis had become?
The ceding of Irish economic sovereignty to the EU/IMF.

JOE McHUGH (FG)

Home address: Claggan, Carrigart, Letterkenny, Co Donegal
Phone: 074 9164787 (CO) 01 6184242 (LH)
Email: joe.mchugh@oireachtas.ie
Website: www.DonegalMatters.com
Facebook: /joemchughtd
Birth place/Date: Letterkenny, July 1971.
Marital status/Family: Married to Olwyn Enright; 1 son, 1 daughter.
Education: Umlagh NS, Carrigart; Loreto Convent, Milford; St Patrick's College Maynooth; NUI Maynooth (BA in economics and social science; HDipEd).
Occupation: Full-time public representative. Previously a teacher and a community worker.
Biography: Secured 7,330 first-preference votes and was re-elected on the eighth count for Donegal North-East. He was first elected to Dáil Éireann in 2007. Joe McHugh served in Seanad Éireann (2002-2007) and on Donegal County Council (1999-2004).
Hobbies: Hill walking and cutting the grass.
Did you know?: Joe was a founder member of the first GAA club in Dubai.
Politician (living or deseased) you most admire: Seamus Mallon.
Priority as a TD?: To enable and empower people in my own constituency and to introduce legislation that is common-sensical and fit for purpose.
Why did you stand for election?: I stood for election to implement the policies I helped develop during 12 years as an opposition politician. I was instrumental in getting some of these policies into the Programme for Government.
Is there any particular event that brought home to you just how serious the economic crisis had become?
The arrival of the IMF.

CHARLIE McCONALOGUE (FF)

Home Address: Carrowmore, Gleneely, Carndonagh, Co Donegal.
Phone: 086 8161078 (M) 01 6183199 (LH)
Email: Charlie.mcconalogue@oireachtas.ie
Website: www.fiannafail.ie/people/charlie-mcconalogue/
Facebook: /CharlieMcConalogue
Birth Place/Date: Letterkenny, October 1977.
Marital Status/Family: Single.
Education: UCD (economics, politics and history).
Occupation: Public representative and farmer.
Biography: Party spokesperson on Children. Secured 6,613 first-preference votes to get elected on the ninth and final count in his first general election attempt. Elected to Donegal County Council in June 2009 and served as Deputy Mayor of Donegal 2009-2010.
Hobbies: All sports involving a ball!
Did you know? At 6ft5in, Charlie is a contender for the tallest TD of the 31st Dáil.
Politician (living or deceased) you most admire: Seán Lemass.
Priority as a TD? To create the right environment to promote employment; to maximise our natural resources by promoting agriculture, fisheries and tourism; to maintain and increase investment in our health services.
Why did you stand for election? I have been proud to serve my local community on Donegal County Council and I want to continue this work on a national level. I am committed to bring new energy and fresh ideas to national politics.
Is there any particular event that brought home to you just how serious the economic crisis had become? I spent February to June 2009 canvassing every day for the local elections and the number of people, particularly men, who were around home during the day, really brought home the gravity of the economic downturn and how it had really hit. Donegal particularly had a high proportion of people working in constuction so the effect in the area has been particularly severe.

Donegal North-East

First preference votes

	Candidate	Party	1st	%	Quota	Count	Status
	Seats	**3**			**9,480**		
1	MacLochlainn, Padraig	SF	9,278	24.47%	0.98	3	Made Quota
2	McHugh, Joe*	FG	7,330	19.33%	0.77	8	Made Quota
3	McConalogue, Charlie	FF	6,613	17.44%	0.70	9	Elected
4	Harte, Jimmy	LB	4,090	10.79%	0.43	9	Not Elected
5	Ryan, John	FG	4,657	12.28%	0.49	7	Eliminated
6	Shiels, Dessie	NP	1,876	4.95%	0.20	6	Eliminated
7	McGarvey, Ian	NP	1,287	3.39%	0.14	5	No Expenses
8	Blaney, Dara	NV	1,228	3.24%	0.13	4	No Expenses
9	Holmes, Betty	NP	1,150	3.03%	0.12	2	No Expenses
10	Murphy, Humphrey	GP	206	0.54%	0.02	1	No Expenses
11	Stewart, Ryan	NV	203	0.54%	0.02	1	No Expenses

*Outgoing TD Valid Poll: 37,918 Quota: 9,480 No expenses limit: 2,370

Party votes

Party	Cand	2011 1st	%	Quota	Seats	Cand	2007 1st	%	Quota	Seats	Change %	Seats
FG	2	11,987	31.61%	1.26	1	1	8,711	22.60%	0.90	1	+9.01%	
LB	1	4,090	10.79%	0.43		1	703	1.82%	0.07		+8.96%	
FF	1	6,613	17.44%	0.70	1	3	19,374	50.26%	2.01	2	-32.82%	-1
SF	1	9,278	24.47%	0.98	1	1	6,733	17.47%	0.70		+7.00%	+1
GP	1	206	0.54%	0.02		1	520	1.35%	0.05		-0.81%	
Others	5	5,744	15.15%	0.61		4	2,504	6.50%	0.26		+8.65%	
Total	11	37,918	100.0%	9,480	3	11	38,545	100.0%	9,637	3	0.00%	0
Electorate		59,084	64.18%				57,244	67.33%			-3.16%	
Spoiled		406	1.06%				386	0.99%			+0.07%	
Turnout		38,324	64.86%				38,931	68.01%			-3.15%	

Transfer analysis

From	To	FG	LB	FF	SF	Others	Non Trans
FG	7,650	3,318	1,573	1,465			1,294
		43.37%	20.56%	19.15%			16.92%
SF	105	24	18	21		42	
		22.86%	17.14%	20.00%		40.00%	
GP	206	46	36	24	36	53	11
		22.33%	17.48%	11.65%	17.48%	25.73%	5.34%
Others	6,985	1,755	1,502	853	271	1,146	1,458
		25.13%	21.50%	12.21%	3.88%	16.41%	20.87%
Total	14,946	5,143	3,129	2,363	307	1,241	2,763
		34.41%	20.94%	15.81%	2.05%	8.30%	18.49%

Count details

Seats	3									Quota	9,480
Candidate	Party	1st	2nd Murphy Stewart	3rd Holmes Votes	4th MacLochlai Surplus	5th Blaney Votes	6th McGarvey Votes	7th Shiels Votes	8th Ryan Votes	9th McHugh Surplus	
			+72	*+235*	*-105*						
MacLochlainn, Padraig	SF	9,278	9,350	9,585	9,480	9,480	9,480	9,480	9,480	9,480	
			+38	*+145*	*+11*	*+138*	*+485*	*+584*	*+3,318*	*-2,569*	
McHugh, Joe*	FG	7,330	7,368	7,513	7,524	7,662	8,147	8,731	12,049	9,480	
			+48	*+134*	*+21*	*+248*	*+191*	*+256*	*+734*	*+731*	
McConalogue, Charlie	FF	6,613	6,661	6,795	6,816	7,064	7,255	7,511	8,245	8,976	
			+72	*+139*	*+18*	*+216*	*+266*	*+845*	*+485*	*+1,088*	
Harte, Jimmy	LB	4,090	4,162	4,301	4,319	4,535	4,801	5,646	6,131	7,219	
			+53	*+161*	*+13*	*+66*	*+26*	*+105*	*-5,081*		
Ryan, John	FG	4,657	4,710	4,871	4,884	4,950	4,976	5,081	Eliminated		
			+27	*+160*	*+22*	*+214*	*+306*	*-2,605*			
Shiels, Dessie	NP	1,876	1,903	2,063	2,085	2,299	2,605	Eliminated			
			+9	*+103*	*+10*	*+244*	*-1,653*				
McGarvey, Ian	NP	1,287	1,296	1,399	1,409	1,653	Eliminated				
			+21	*+68*	*+10*	*-1,327*					
Blaney, Dara	NV	1,228	1,249	1,317	1,327	Eliminated					
			+47	*-1,197*							
Holmes, Betty	NP	1,150	1,197	Eliminated							
			-206								
Murphy, Humphrey	GP	206	Eliminated								
			-203								
Stewart, Ryan	NV	203	Eliminated								
Non-transferable			+22	+52		+201	+379	+815	+544	+750	
Cumulative			22	74	74	275	654	1,469	2,013	2,763	
Total		37,918	37,918	37,918	37,918	37,918	37,918	37,918	37,918	37,918	

The 14 Sinn Féin TDs of the current Dáil walk across the plinth at Leinster House. From left: Pádraig MacLochlainn, Michael Colreavy, Aengus Ó Snodaigh, Pearse Doherty, Peadar Tóibín, Sandra McLellan, Gerry Adams, Seán Crowe, Dessie Ellis, Caoimhghín Ó Caoláin, Martin Ferris, Brian Stanley, and Jonathan O'Brien. Mary Lou McDonald is in the background

Donegal South-West (3 seats)

Tánaiste Mary Coughlan loses her seat

Elected

Pearse Doherty* (SF) Count 1, Dinny McGinley* (FG) Final count, Thomas Pringle (Ind) Final count.

Analysis by Sean Donnelly

There was a boundary revision here since 2007, with a transfer of a population of 2,351 into this constituency from Donegal North-East. This means that all of the divisions in the old Stranorlar Rural District are now within this constituency. However, the constituency did retain its three seats.

This was one of the few constituencies where Fine Gael experienced a drop in support in this election as its vote was down three percentage points on 2007. Dinny McGinley was in second place on the first count with 0.8 of a quota and he went on to retain his seat comfortably.

The Fianna Fáil performance in this constituency was in sharp contrast to its showing in the neighbouring constituency of Donegal North-East where its single-candidate strategy delivered a seat. It was all so different in Donegal South-West as the party went from two seats in 2007 to drawing a blank for the first time since this constituency was set up in 1937. The Fianna Fáil vote was down 28 percentage points but with 0.9 of a quota it should have been in contention for a single seat.

However, its vote was spread fairly evenly between its two candidates, Tánaiste Mary Coughlan and Senator Brían Ó Domhnaill. Both candidates were outside the frame on the first count and has less than half a quota each. Ó Domhnaill's run-out in the November 2010 by-election gave him a good platform for the general election contest and he overtook Coughlan on the fourth count. But he was still too far off the pace and a relatively poor 55%

share of Coughlan's transfers sealed his and his party's fate.

Fianna Fáil's poor candidate strategy presented independent candidate Thomas Pringle with an opportunity for a surprise seat gain. The former Sinn Féin and now independent councillor was in third place on the first count, 889 votes ahead of Coughlan. He did well on transfers and went on to comfortably take the final seat ahead of Ó Domhnaill and extend his winning margin to 1,341. Pringle had performed well in November's by-election and like many a losing by-election candidate before him, went on to win a seat at the following Dáil election.

Pat 'The Cope' Gallagher resigned his Dáil seat on his election to the European Parliament in 2009. Sinn Féin's Pearse Doherty comfortably won the subsequent by-election in November 2010. He made the most of his by-election win and his Dáil performances as Sinn Féin's Finance spokesman enhanced his reputation. Doherty repeated his by-election winning performance in the general election and topped the poll. He was well over the quota on the first count and took the first seat with another impressive performance.

This was a poor performance by the Labour Party with Frank McBrearty winning just 5% of the first-preference vote to leave him out of contention. He had done poorly in the by-election and it was all downhill after that.

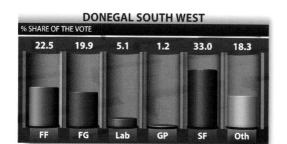

DONEGAL SOUTH WEST

% SHARE OF THE VOTE

FF	FG	Lab	GP	SF	Oth
22.5	19.9	5.1	1.2	33.0	18.3

DONEGAL SOUTH WEST

% SHARE CHANGE SINCE 2007

FF	FG	Lab	GP	SF	Oth
-28.0	-3.1	+2.3	-0.3	+11.7	+17.4

*outgoing TDs

PEARSE DOHERTY (SF)

Home Address: Machaire Chlochair, Na Doirí Beaga, Leitir Ceanainn, Co Dún na nGall.
Phone: 074 9532832 (CO) 01 6183960 (LH)
Email: pearse.doherty@oireachtas.ie
Website: www.pearsedoherty.ie
Twitter: www.twitter.com/pearsedoherty
Facebook: /Pearse.Doherty
Birth Place/Date: Glasgow, July 1977.
Marital Status/Family: Married to Róisín; 3 sons.
Education: Scoil Chonaill An Bun Beag; Pobal Scoil Gaoth Dobhair; DIT Bolton Street.
Occupation: Full time public representative.
Biography: Party spokesperson on Finance. Elected a TD in November 2010 by-election. Unsuccessfully contested general elections in 2002 and 2007, and the 2004 European elections. Became Sinn Féin's first senator when elected to Seanad agricultural panel in 2007. Member, Donegal County Council 2004-2007.
Hobbies: Reading, films.
Did you know? Pearse won a successful High Court challenge in 2010 which forced the then government to hold a by-election in Donegal South-West.
Politician (living or deceased) you most admire: Pádraig Pearse.
Priority as a TD? Job creation, the development of the north-west region and to ensure that there is fairness in budgetary decisions.
Why did you stand for election? I believe that Sinn Féin has a credible alternative vision for our country that is based on core republican values of fairness, equality and liberty and I wanted to play my part in bringing that vision to fruition.
Is there any particular event that brought home to you just how serious the economic crisis had become? Witnessing an elderly woman in her 80s in a flood of tears as she told me she was praying that someone would help her with her financial difficulties.

DINNY McGINLEY (FG)

Home Address: Magheralosk, Bunbeg, Co Donegal.
Phone: 087 414809 (M) 074 9531025 (CO) 01 6183452 (LH)
Website: www.finegael.ie
Email: dinny.mcginley@oir.ie or dinnymcginley@gmail.com
Facebook: Yes.
Birth Place/Date: Donegal, April 1945.
Marital Status/Family: Single.
Education: Bunbeg NS; Colaiste Iosagain, Ballyvourney, Co Cork; St Patrick's Teachers Training College, Drumcondra, Dublin; UCD (BA history and economics; HDipEd).
Occupation: Full-time public representative. Former principal teacher.
Biography: First elected to Dáil Eireann in February 1982 and re-elected in every subsequent general election. Current Minister of State for Gaeltacht Affairs at the Department of Arts, Heritage and Gaeltacht Affairs. Served on many Fine Gael front benches with responsibilities for Gaeltacht and Island Affairs, Youth and Sport, Defence, Emigrants' Welfare and Arts and Culture, former chairman of the Language and Culture Committee and Energy and Climate Change Committee.
Hobbies: Reading, walking, theatre and sport.
Politician (living or deceased) you most admire: Nelson Mandela.
Priority as a TD? To regain our financial and economic independence.
Why did you stand for election? To do everything possible to improve the lives of the people of Donegal South-West.
Is there any particular event that brought home to you just how serious the economic crisis had become? The arrival of the IMF as our financial masters.

THOMAS PRINGLE (Ind)

Home Address: 151 Church Road, Killybegs, Co Donegal.
Phone: 074 9741880 01 6183038 (LH)
Email: thomas.pringle@oireachtas.ie
Website: www.thomaspringle.ie
Twitter: thomaspringleTD
Facebook: votethomaspringle
Birth Place/Date: Dublin, August 1967.
Marital Status/Family: Married; 3 children.
Education: St Catherine's Vocational School, Killybegs; Letterkenny Institute of Technology.
Occupation: Public representative. Previously worked for Donegal County Council in the Killybegs Water Treatment Plant for 16 years.
Biography: Secured 5,845 first-preference votes to get elected on the fourth count. First elected to Donegal County Council in 1999 as an independent. Joined Sinn Féin in 2004 and re-elected that year on a Sinn Féin ticket. In November 2007, he left Sinn Féin and continued on the council as an independent. Re-elected in 2009. He unsuccessfully contested the 2002 general election and the 2010 by-election as an independent.
Hobbies: Reading, walking and photography.
Did you know? Thomas more than doubled his first-preference vote from 2,630 votes in the 2002 general election to 5,845 in 2011.
Politician (living or deceased) you most admire: Nelson Mandela.
Priority as a TD? To provide effective representation and put forward an alternative vision for Ireland.
Why did you stand for election? Having been a public representative since 1999 I felt I could bring something to the national stage and I feel that the party political system has not served us well.
Is there any particular event that brought home to you just how serious the economic crisis had become? The 300 staff made redundant from Donegal County Council and the impact that had on the confidence of other staff. The huge numbers of young people emigrating daily from each parish throughout Donegal.

Donegal South-West

	Candidate	Party	1st	%	Quota	Count	Status
	Seats	**3**			**10,816**		
1	Doherty, Pearse*	SF	14,262	32.97%	1.32	1	Made Quota
2	McGinley, Dinny*	FG	8,589	19.85%	0.79	5	Made Quota
3	Pringle, Thomas	NP	5,845	13.51%	0.54	5	Elected
4	Ó'Domhnaill, Brían	FF	4,789	11.07%	0.44	5	Not Elected
5	Coughlan, Mary*	FF	4,956	11.46%	0.46	4	Eliminated
6	McBrearty, Frank	LB	2,209	5.11%	0.20	3	Eliminated
7	McCahill, Stephen	NP	1,831	4.23%	0.17	3	No Expenses
8	Duffy, John	GP	527	1.22%	0.05	2	No Expenses
9	Sweeney, Ann	NV	255	0.59%	0.02	2	No Expenses

*Outgoing TD Valid poll: 43,263 Quota: 10,816 No expenses limit: 2,705

Party votes

Party	Cand	2011 1st	%	Quota	Seats	Cand	2007 1st	%	Quota	Seats	Change %	Seats
FG	1	8,589	19.85%	0.79	1	1	9,167	23.00%	0.92	1	-3.15%	
LB	1	2,209	5.11%	0.20		1	1,111	2.79%	0.11		+2.32%	
FF	2	9,745	22.53%	0.90		2	20,136	50.53%	2.02	2	-28.00%	-2
SF	1	14,262	32.97%	1.32	1	1	8,462	21.23%	0.85		+11.73%	+1
GP	1	527	1.22%	0.05		1	589	1.48%	0.06		-0.26%	
Others	3	7,931	18.33%	0.73	1	1	388	0.97%	0.04		+17.36%	+1
Total	9	43,263	100.0%	10,816	3	7	39,853	100.0%	9,964	3	0.00%	0
Electorate		64,568	67.00%				60,829	65.52%			+1.49%	
Spoiled		332	0.76%				421	1.05%			-0.28%	
Turnout		43,595	67.52%				40,274	66.21%			+1.31%	

Transfer analysis

From	To	FG	LB	FF	GP	Others	Non Trans
LB	3,003	759		516		1,036	692
		25.27%		17.18%		34.50%	23.04%
FF	5,655	782		3,110		1,036	727
		13.83%		55.00%		18.32%	12.86%
SF	3,446	539	673	574	141	1,519	
		15.64%	19.53%	16.66%	4.09%	44.08%	
GP	668	101	77	112		278	100
		15.12%	11.53%	16.77%		41.62%	14.97%
Others	2,523	599	44	432		898	550
		23.74%	1.74%	17.12%		35.59%	21.80%
Total	15,295	2,780	794	4,744	141	4,767	2,069
		18.18%	5.19%	31.02%	0.92%	31.17%	13.53%

Count details

Candidate	Party	1st	2nd Doherty Surplus	3rd Duffy Sweeney	4th McBrearty McCahill	5th Coughlan Votes
Seats	**3**				**Quota**	**10,816**
			-3,446			
Doherty, Pearse*	SF	14,262	10,816	10,816	10,816	10,816
			+539	*+159*	*+1,300*	*+782*
McGinley, Dinny*	FG	8,589	9,128	9,287	10,587	11,369
			+1,186	*+333*	*+1,775*	*+1,036*
Pringle, Thomas	NP	5,845	7,031	7,364	9,139	10,175
			+358	*+89*	*+488*	*+3,110*
Ó'Domhnaill, Brían	FF	4,789	5,147	5,236	5,724	8,834
			+216	*+87*	*+396*	*-5,655*
Coughlan, Mary*	FF	4,956	5,172	5,259	5,655	Eliminated
			+673	*+121*	*-3,003*	
McBrearty, Frank	LB	2,209	2,882	3,003	Eliminated	
			+206	*+104*	*-2,141*	
McCahill, Stephen	NP	1,831	2,037	2,141	Eliminated	
			+141	*-668*		
Duffy, John	GP	527	668	Eliminated		
			+127	*-382*		
Sweeney, Ann	NV	255	382	Eliminated		
Non-transferable				*+157*	*+1,185*	*+727*
Cumulative			0	157	1,342	2,069
Total		**43,263**	**43,263**	**43,263**	**43,263**	**43,263**

Fianna Fáil leader Micheál Martin and former education minister Mary Coughlan launch the party's education policy in February

Dublin Central (4 seats)

Fianna Fáil doesn't fare well without Bertie

Elected

Paschal Donohoe (FG) Count 2, Joe Costello* (Lab) Count 5, Maureen O'Sullivan* (Ind) Count 7, Mary Lou McDonald (SF) Final count.

Analysis by Michael Gallagher

There were no boundary changes to this four-seat constituency since 2007. From the death of George Colley in 1983 until he announced on 30 December 2010 that he would not be contesting the 2011 election, Bertie Ahern was the undisputed kingpin here. Running mates came and went, some successful and some not, all left in little doubt that their allotted role was that of subordinate hoping to pick up the crumbs from Bertie's surplus, and that they should not develop any notions of equality. Vote management elsewhere usually means trying to divide a party's votes equally among its candidates, but in Dublin Central it meant trying to direct every available first preference to Bertie and taking it from there.

How would Fianna Fáil fare without Bertie? Not well, everyone assumed, and they were right. Mary Fitzpatrick probably benefitted from the continued open antagonism of the 'Drumcondra Mafia' and from her appointment to Micheál Martin's front bench, and did well to finish as runner-up. Her time may yet come. The remaining incumbent, Cyprian Brady, may wish he had accompanied his patron into retirement. He increased his 2007 first-preference

tally by 74%, quite an achievement for a Fianna Fáil TD in 2011 – but since he had received only 939 first preferences in 2007, he still ended up amongst the also-rans in 2011. Whether Bertie Ahern himself would have been re-elected had he stood in 2011 will remain forever unknown.

The four seats sorted themselves out without much complication. Paschal Donohue of Fine Gael seemed a certainty based on his performances in 2007 and at the 2009 by-election, and he headed the poll. Labour's Joe Costello, now the veteran of the constituency, took the second seat. The third went to Maureen O'Sullivan, a former member of Tony Gregory's organisation who had won the 2009 by-election brought about by Gregory's death. Mary Lou McDonald's 13% of the vote made some wonder whether she might fall short yet again, but decent transfers, especially from former Sinn Féin councillor Christy Burke, ensured that she and Sandra McLellan in Cork East became Sinn Féin's first female TDs since Caitlín Brugha in 1927.

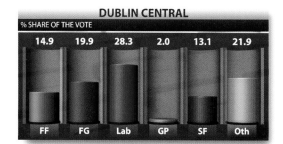

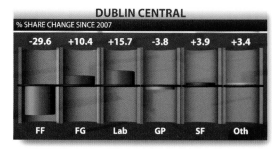

*outgoing TDs

PASCHAL DONOHOE (FG)

Home Address: Shandon Park, Phibsborough, Dublin 7.
Phone: 01 6183689 (LH)
Email: paschal.donohoe@oireachtas.ie
Website: www.paschaldonohoe.ie
Twitter: twitter.com/paschald
Facebook: facebook.com/PaschalDonohoe
Birth Place/Date: Dublin, September 1974.
Marital Status/Family: Married to Justine; 2 children.
Education: St Declan's, Cabra; Trinity College, Dublin (economics and politics).
Occupation: Full-time public representative. Formerly Irish commercial director for the consumer goods company, Procter & Gamble.
Biography: Paschal secured 6,903 first-preference votes, topping the poll and getting elected on the second count in Dublin Central. He was elected to Dublin City Council in 2004 for the Cabra-Glasnevin electoral area and was a senator since 2007.
Hobbies: Music (favourite group is Elbow) and reading (favourite author is James Lee Burke).
Did you know? Paschal is a prolific tweeter.
Politician (living or deceased) you most admire: John Bruton.
Priority as a TD? To support a government that delivers broad and prompt political reform.
Why did you stand for election? Because I am proud of my country and I want to contribute to our national recovery.
Is there any particular event that brought home to you just how serious the economic crisis had become? Whole families leaving our country looking for jobs as opposed to just sons and daughters. It marks a huge change from the 1980s and a tragic statement of their lack of faith in our national future.

JOE COSTELLO (Lab)

Home Address: 66 Aughrim Street, Dublin 7.
Phone: 087 2450777 (M) 01 6183896 (LH)
Email: joe.costello@oir.ie or joecostellotd@blogspot.com
Website: www.labour.ie/joecostello
Twitter: twitter.com/joecostellotd
Facebook: facebook.com/joecostellotd
Birth Place/Date: Sligo, July 1945.
Marital Status/Family: Married.
Education: Summerhill College Sligo; Maynooth; UCD.
Occupation: Full-time public representative.
Biography: First elected a TD in 1992. Lost seat in 1997. Member, Seanad Éireann and leader of the Labour Senate Group (1997-2002 and 1989-1992). Re-elected in 2007. Labour spokesperson on Education (2002-2003); Justice (2003-2006); Defence (2006-2007); European Affairs and Human Rights (2007-June 2010); Transport (June 2010). Appointed to Dáil Committee on Transport (June 2010). Chairperson of Labour's Policy Development Commission (1995-2002). Member, Dublin City Council (1991-2003). Deputy Lord Mayor of Dublin (1991-1992).
Hobbies: Football, reading.
Politician (living or deceased) you most admire: James Connolly.
Priority as a TD? To represent the people of my constituency.
Why did you stand for election? To help put a strong, stable government in place at this time of national crisis.
Is there any particular event that brought home to you just how serious the economic crisis had become? I served as Labour Party spokesperson on European Affairs during the last Dáil. I was appalled at the failure of the Irish government to engage with the EU as the economic crisis worsened. The blanket guarantee was the critical decision. After that, we were totally exposed as a sovereign economy.

MAUREEN O'SULLIVAN (Ind)

Home Address: 39 Fairfield Avenue, East Wall, Dublin 3.
Phone: 087 0550223 (M) 016183488 (LH)
Website: www.maureenosullivan.ie
Email: maureen.osullivan@oireachtas.ie
Birth Place/Date: Dublin, March 1951.
Marital Status/Family: Single.
Education: Mount Carmel Secondary, King's Inn Street, Dublin 1; UCD.
Occupation: Full-time public representative. Formerly secondary teacher and guidance counsellor.
Biography: Was a friend and supporter of the late independent TD Tony Gregory and was chosen by his group – his brother, canvassers, friends and supporters to contest the by-election (June 2009) caused by his death, securing the seat on that occasion. In the 2011 election she won the third seat of four in Dublin Central.
Hobbies: Reading, walking, music, history, islands (particularly Oileán Chléire).
Did you know? In 2007, Maureen received the Lord Mayor (of Dublin) award for her lifetime commitment to voluntary work with young people.
Politician (living or deceased) you most admire: Tony Gregory.
Priority as a TD? To continue his work based on principles of social justice, fairness and equality. To represent the people of Dublin Central and to continue to support issues like mental health, overseas aid, animal welfare; go háirithe bheith ann as son daoine ar an imeall.
Why did you stand for election? Because of the lifetime commitment of the late Tony Gregory to maintain his independent, community seat in the Dáil.
Is there any particular event that brought home to you just how serious the economic crisis had become? The increase in the numbers of suicides.

Dublin Central

MARY LOU McDONALD (SF)

Address: Leinster House, Kildare Street, Dublin 2.
Phone: 01 6183230 (LH)
email: marylou.mcdonald@oireachtas.ie
Website: www.maryloumcdonald.ie
Twitter: twitter.com/maryloumcdonald
Facebook: Yes.
Birth Place/Date: Dublin, May 1969.
Marital Status/Family: Married to Martin; 1 son, 1 daughter.
Education: Trinity College, Dublin; University of Limerick; Dublin City University (DCU). She studied English literature, European integration studies and human resource management.
Occupation: Full-time public representative. Formerly a consultant for the Irish Productivity Centre.
Biography: Vice-president of Sinn Féin and party spokesperson on Public Expenditure and Reform. Secured 4,526 first-preference votes to get elected on the eighth and final count in her third general election attempt. She unsuccessfully contested the Dublin West constituency in the 2002 general election and Dublin Central in 2007. She was elected an MEP for Dublin in the 2004 European elections but failed to retain her seat in 2009. She led Sinn Féin's No campaign against the Lisbon Treaty.
Priority as a TD: To take on the powerful vested interests who almost destroyed this country.
Why did you stand for election? I am involved in politics because I believe that it is possible for each and every one of us to make a difference, to bring about change, to make our country a great place to live, work and grow old.

Labour Party leader Eamon Gilmore and Dublin Central candidate Joe Costello canvass on Moore Street in Dublin

First preference votes

	Candidate	Party	1st	%	Quota	Count	Status
Seats			**4**		**6,923**		
1	Donohoe, Paschal	FG	6,903	19.94%	1.00	2	Made Quota
2	Costello, Joe*	LB	6,273	18.12%	0.91	5	Made Quota
3	O'Sullivan, Maureen*	NP	4,139	11.96%	0.60	7	Made Quota
4	McDonald, Mary Lou	SF	4,526	13.08%	0.65	8	Elected
5	Fitzpatrick, Mary	FF	3,504	10.12%	0.51	8	Not Elected
6	Clancy, Áine	LB	3,514	10.15%	0.51	6	Eliminated
7	Brady, Cyprian*	FF	1,637	4.73%	0.24	5	Eliminated
8	Perry, Cieran	NP	1,394	4.03%	0.20	4	No Expenses
9	Burke, Christy	NP	1,315	3.80%	0.19	3	No Expenses
10	Kearney, Phil	GP	683	1.97%	0.10	2	No Expenses
11	Steenson, Malachy	WP	274	0.79%	0.04	2	No Expenses
12	O'Loughlin, Paul	CS	235	0.68%	0.03	2	No Expenses
13	Hyland, John Pluto	NP	77	0.22%	0.01	1	No Expenses
14	Hollywood, Thomas	NP	65	0.19%	0.01	1	No Expenses
15	Johnston, Liam	FN	48	0.14%	0.01	1	No Expenses
16	Cooney, Benny	NP	25	0.07%	0.00	1	No Expenses

*Outgoing TD Valid Poll: 34,612 Quota: 6,923 No expenses limit: 1,731

Party votes

Party	2011					2007					Change	
	Cand	1st	%	Quota	Seats	Cand	1st	%	Quota	Seats	%	Seats
FG	1	6,903	19.94%	1.00	1	1	3,302	9.53%	0.48		+10.41%	+1
LB	2	9,787	28.28%	1.41	1	1	4,353	12.57%	0.63	1	+15.71%	
FF	2	5,141	14.85%	0.74		3	15,398	44.45%	2.22	2	-29.60%	-2
SF	1	4,526	13.08%	0.65	1	1	3,182	9.19%	0.46		+3.89%	+1
GP	1	683	1.97%	0.10		1	1,995	5.76%	0.29		-3.79%	
WP	1	274	0.79%	0.04							+0.79%	
CS	1	235	0.68%	0.03							+0.68%	
PD						1	193	0.56%	0.03		-0.56%	
Others	7	7,063	20.41%	1.02	1	5	6,216	17.95%	0.90	1	+2.46%	
Total	16	34,612	100.0%	6,923	4	13	34,639	100.0%	6,928	4	0.00%	0
Electorate		56,892	60.84%				63,423	54.62%			+6.22%	
Spoiled		457	1.30%				510	1.45%			-0.15%	
Turnout		35,069	61.64%				35,149	55.42%			+6.22%	

Transfer analysis

From	To	FG	LB	FF	SF	GP	WP	Others	Non Trans
LB	4,135			582	656			2,055	842
				14.07%	15.86%			49.70%	20.36%
FF	1,753		157	1,105	131			202	158
			8.96%	63.03%	7.47%			11.52%	9.01%
GP	703		229	73	67			290	44
			32.57%	10.38%	9.53%			41.25%	6.26%
WP	285		93	29	27			118	18
			32.63%	10.18%	9.47%			41.40%	6.32%
Others	4,192	30	984	566	1,180	20	11	1,152	249
		0.72%	23.47%	13.50%	28.15%	0.48%	0.26%	27.48%	5.94%
Total	11,068	30	1,463	2,355	2,061	20	11	3,817	1,311
		0.27%	13.22%	21.28%	18.62%	0.18%	0.10%	34.49%	11.84%

Dublin Central

Seats	4								Quota	6,923
Candidate	**Party**	**1st**	**2nd**	**3rd**	**4th**	**5th**	**6th**	**7th**	**8th**	
			Hyland Hollywood Johnston Cooney	Kearney Steenson O'Loughlin Votes	Burke Votes	Perry Votes	Brady Votes	Clancy Votes	O'Sullivan Surplus	
			+30							
Donohoe, Paschal	FG	6,903	6,933	6,933	6,933	6,933	6,933	6,933	6,933	
			+16	+139	+377	+310				
Costello, Joe*	LB	6,273	6,289	6,428	6,805	7,115	7,115	7,115	7,115	
			+32	+336	+323	+554	+202	+2,055	−718	
O'Sullivan, Maureen*	NP	4,139	4,171	4,507	4,830	5,384	5,586	7,641	6,923	
			+10	+118	+411	+357	+131	+656	+378	
McDonald, Mary Lou	SF	4,526	4,536	4,654	5,065	5,422	5,553	6,209	6,587	
			+10	+92	+22	+88	+1,105	+582	+340	
Fitzpatrick, Mary	FF	3,504	3,514	3,606	3,628	3,716	4,821	5,403	5,743	
			+18	+264	+57	+125	+157	−4,135		
Clancy, Áine	LB	3,514	3,532	3,796	3,853	3,978	4,135	Eliminated		
			+2	+36	+50	+28	−1,753			
Brady, Cyprian*	FF	1,637	1,639	1,675	1,725	1,753	Eliminated			
			+32	+106	+83	−1,615				
Perry, Cieran	NP	1,394	1,426	1,532	1,615	Eliminated				
			+8	+70	−1,393					
Burke, Christy	NP	1,315	1,323	1,393	Eliminated					
			+20	−703						
Kearney, Phil	GP	683	703	Eliminated						
			+11	−285						
Steenson, Malachy	WP	274	285	Eliminated						
			+16	−251						
O'Loughlin, Paul	CS	235	251	Eliminated						
			−77							
Hyland, John Pluto	NP	77	Eliminated							
			−65							
Hollywood, Thomas	NP	65	Eliminated							
			−48							
Johnston, Liam	FN	48	Eliminated							
			−25							
Cooney, Benny	NP	25	Eliminated							
Non-transferable			+10	+78	+70	+153	+158	+842		
Cumulative			10	88	158	311	469	1,311	1,311	
Total			34,612	34,612	34,612	34,612	34,612	34,612	34,612	34,612

Election Facts

"Fianna Fáil's candidate pattern was remarkable, in that the party ran fewer candidates that it won seats in 2007, when it won 78"
Professor Michael Gallagher, TCD

Dublin Mid-West (4 seats)

Four in every 10 voters switch from government candidates to Fine Gael/Labour

Elected

Joanna Tuffy* (Lab) Count 7, Frances Fitzgerald (FG) Count 8, Robert Dowds (Lab) Final count, Derek Keating (FG) Final count.

Analysis by Michael Gallagher

There were no boundary changes in this four-seat constituency since 2007. Here we saw the biggest swing in the entire country, with Fine Gael and Labour increasing their combined vote by a massive 39% while Fianna Fáil and the Greens dropped by 29%. The retirement of former PD leader Mary Harney, who had taken 12% of the votes in 2007, meant that four in every 10 voters switched from the Fianna Fáil/PD/Green government to the Fine Gael/Labour alternative. John Curran of Fianna Fáil, government chief whip and seen as a rising star in 2007, lost his seat, while outgoing Green TD Paul Gogarty did not even reach a quarter of the quota, the figure needed to qualify for reimbursement of campaign expenses. Gogarty did at least leave on an individual note, becoming the first TD to concede defeat via Twitter.

Fine Gael and Labour vied for supremacy here, with Fine Gael outpolling its future partner by just 76 votes. The 62% of the votes won by the two parties proved enough to take all four seats, making this just one of five constituencies in the country left without an opposition TD. Labour's Joanna Tuffy and Fine Gael Seanad leader Frances Fitzgerald, who had respectively taken the last seat and been the runner-up

in 2007, now took the first two seats comfortably. Their fates on 9 March were rather different, Fitzgerald entering Cabinet while Tuffy was left on the backbenches.

The second Labour candidate, Clondalkin-based Robert Dowds, attracted transfers from other candidates of the broad left and took the third seat. The fourth seat lay between Fine Gael's Lucan-based Derek Keating, and Eoin Ó Broin of Sinn Féin, who had finished bottom of the poll in Dún Laoghaire in 2007. After the seventh count, Ó Broin moved into third position, and the decisive elimination was that of Fianna Fáil's John Curran. SF's continued inability to attract large-scale transfers was a big factor here: Curran's transfers went heavily to the three candidates of Fine Gael and Labour still in the count, with Ó Broin receiving fewer than 10% of them, so Keating was elected with over 500 votes to spare.

*outgoing TDs

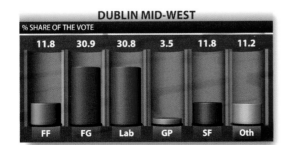

DUBLIN MID-WEST

% SHARE OF THE VOTE

FF	FG	Lab	GP	SF	Oth
11.8	30.9	30.8	3.5	11.8	11.2

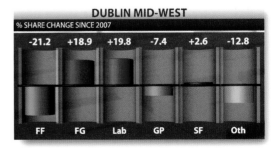

DUBLIN MID-WEST

% SHARE CHANGE SINCE 2007

FF	FG	Lab	GP	SF	Oth
-21.2	+18.9	+19.8	-7.4	+2.6	-12.8

Dublin Mid-West

JOANNA TUFFY (Lab)

Home Address: 46A Esker Lawns, Lucan.
Phone: 01 6183822 (LH)
Email: joanna.tuffy@oireachtas.ie
Website: www.joannatuffy.ie
Twitter: www.twitter.com/joannatuffytd
Facebook: Joanna Tuffy TD
Marital Status/Family: Partner Philip Long, 1 daughter.
Education: Scoil Mhuire Girls NS, Lucan; St Joseph's College, Lucan; Trinity College, Dublin; DIT Aungier Street; Law Society, Blackhall Place, Dublin.
Occupation: Public representative.
Biography: First elected a TD in 2007. Unsuccessfully contested the 2002 general election. Member of Seanad Éireann, on administrative panel, (2002-2007). Member, South Dublin County Council (1999-2003).
Hobbies: Reading books about history, films, current affairs.
Did you know? Joanna used to be a film extra, and played small parts in the films *Da*, and *Summer Lightning* and the TV series *The Irish RM*.
Politician (living or deceased) you most admire: My father Cllr Eamon Tuffy who unsuccessfully ran for the Dáil for Labour when I was a child and whose commitment to the Labour Party both as a public representative and as an activist has been a huge influence on me.
Priority as a TD? That Labour will implement measures that will reduce the gap between rich and poor. Investment in education and life-long learning.
Why did you stand for election? Because I believed that I could win a seat for Labour as a candidate and I am very committed to Labour and what the party stands for.
Is there any particular event that brought home to you just how serious the economic crisis had become? There is no particular event. What has brought it home to me most is the way it has impacted on the lives of my constituents who speak to me about the changes the economic downturn has made to their lives.

FRANCES FITZGERALD (FG)

Address: Laurel House, New Road, Clondalkin, Dublin 22.
Phone: 087 2579026 (M) 01 4577712 (CO) 01 6183771 (LH)
Email: frances.fitzgerald@oireachtas.ie
Website: www.francesfitzgerald.ie
Twitter: www.twitter.com/joinfrances
Facebook: www.facebook.com/joinfrances
Birth Place/Date: Limerick, August 1950.
Marital Status/Family: Married; 3 sons.
Education: UCD(BSoc Science); London School of Economics (Cert in social work and MSc in social administration and social work).
Occupation: Former social worker.
Biography: Current Minister for Children. Dublin South East TD (1992-2002). Unsuccessfully contested Dublin Mid-West in 2007. Member of Seanad Éireann and leader of Seanad opposition (2007-2011). Served on Oireachtas committees including: Justice; Health; the Constitution; and Social Affairs. Former Chair of the National Women's Council of Ireland (1988-1992) and Vice-President of the European Women's Lobby.
Hobbies: Theatre, reading, travel and music.
Did you know? Frances was one of two female TDs elected in the four-seat Dublin Mid-West constituency. Dublin Central is the only other Dublin constituency to have a 50% female representation rate.
Politician (living or deceased) you most admire: Nelson Mandela, Hillary Clinton, Mary Robinson and John Hume.
Priority as a TD? Getting Ireland back working and offering opportunities to our young people here in Ireland.
Why did you stand for election? As a campaigner for equality, health and social issues for years, politics seemed a logical next step to further those agendas. I have always considered the lack of critical numbers of women in Irish politics a major gap in our democracy.
Is there any particular event that brought home to you just how serious the economic crisis had become? Rising unemployment rates and the downturn in the property market gave rise to the phenomenon of negative equity, which is placing huge financial pressures on young couples.

ROBERT DOWDS (Lab)

Home Address: 43 Castle Park, Clondalkin, Dublin 22.
Phone: 087 6520360 (M) 01 6183446 (LH)
Email: robert.dowds@oireachtas.ie
Website: www.robertdowds.ie
Birth Place/Date: Dublin, May, 1953.
Marital Status/Family: Married; 2 children.
Education: Finglas Parochial NS; Trinity College; St Patrick's College, Drumcondra.
Occupation: Public representative. Formerly special education teacher and school principal.
Biography: Secured 5,643 first-preference votes to get elected on the ninth and final count in his first general election. He was a member of South Dublin County Council since 1999.
Hobbies: Reading, walking and spending time with friends.
Did you know? Robert has suffered from cerebral palsy and believes that any disability should not inhibit people from achieving in life.
Politician (living or deceased) you most admire: Michael Davitt.
Priority as a TD? To represent my constituency as effectively as possible and work for people who are under pressure in the current economic climate.
Why did you stand for election? I have had an interest in politics since I was 15 and it goes back to a desire to change the world for the better. I hope I can even change a few things and help people get treated more equally and fairly.
Is there any particular event that brought home to you just how serious the economic crisis had become? Canvassing in the recent election I had never seen people so engaged in the issues before.

DEREK KEATING (FG)

Home Address: 66 Beech Park, Lucan, Co Dublin
Contact: 087 2857435 (M) 01 6184014 (LH)
Email: Derek.keating@oireachtas.ie or info@derekkeating.net
Website: www.derekkeating.net
Twitter: twitter.com/derekkeating
Birth Place/Date: Ballyfermot, Dublin, May 1955.
Marital Status/Family: Married to Anne; 2 daughters.
Education: De La Salle Primary and Secondary Ballyfermot.
Occupation: Full-time public representative.
Biography: Secured 5,933 first-preference votes to get elected on the ninth and final count in his second general election attempt. He unsuccessfully contested the 2007 general election as an independent. He was first elected to South Dublin County Council in 1999 and remained an independent until he joined Fine Gael in August 2008.
Hobbies: Music, guitar and piano, walking, sports (varied).
Did you know? Derek used to be an independent councillor. Before that he was a member of the Progressive Democrats and he was a member of Fianna Fáil before that again.
Priority as a TD? To raise awareness of suicide and the growing threat of suicide among the population.
Is there any particular event that brought home to you just how serious the economic crisis had become? As a director of the Pieta House project I have seen a huge rise in suicide during the recession and we have had over 1,000 people who were affected by suicide visit Pieta House in the last 12 months.

Counting the votes at the RDS, Dublin

Dublin Mid-West

	Seats	4			8,545		
Candidate	**Party**	**1st**	**%**	**Quota**	**Count**	**Status**	
1 Tuffy, Joanna*	LB	7,495	17.54%	0.88	7	Made Quota	
2 Fitzgerald, Frances #	FG	7,281	17.04%	0.85	8	Made Quota	
3 Dowds, Robert	LB	5,643	13.21%	0.66	9	Elected	
4 Keating, Derek	FG	5,933	13.89%	0.69	9	Elected	
5 O Broin Eoin	SF	5,060	11.84%	0.59	9	Not Elected	
6 Curran, John*	FF	5,043	11.80%	0.59	7	Eliminated	
7 Kenny, Gino	PBPA	2,471	5.78%	0.29	6	Eliminated	
8 Gogarty, Paul*	GP	1,484	3.47%	0.17	6	No Expenses	
9 Finnegan, Mick	WP	694	1.62%	0.08	5	No Expenses	
10 Connolly, Rob	SP	622	1.46%	0.07	5	No Expenses	
11 Ryan, Michael	NP	375	0.88%	0.04	4	No Expenses	
12 McGrath, Colm	NP	253	0.59%	0.03	3	No Expenses	
13 McHale, Jim	NP	255	0.60%	0.03	2	No Expenses	
14 Smith, Niall	NP	113	0.26%	0.01	1	No Expenses	

*Outgoing TD #Former TD Valid poll: 42,722 Quota: 8,545 No expenses limit: 2,137

Party votes

		2011					2007				Change	
Party	**Cand**	**1st**	**%**	**Quota**	**Seats**	**Cand**	**1st**	**%**	**Quota**	**Seats**	**%**	**Seats**
FG	2	13,214	30.93%	1.55	2	1	4,480	12.00%	0.60		+18.93%	+2
LB	2	13,138	30.75%	1.54	2	1	4,075	10.91%	0.55	1	+19.84%	+1
FF	1	5,043	11.80%	0.59		2	12,321	33.00%	1.65	1	-21.19%	-1
SF	1	5,060	11.84%	0.59		1	3,462	9.27%	0.46		+2.57%	
SP	1	622	1.46%	0.07							+1.46%	
PBPA	1	2,471	5.78%	0.29							+5.78%	
GP	1	1,484	3.47%	0.17		1	4,043	10.83%	0.54	1	-7.35%	-1
WP	1	694	1.62%	0.08		1	366	0.98%	0.05		+0.64%	
PD						1	4,663	12.49%	0.62	1	-12.49%	-1
Others	4	996	2.33%	0.12		3	3,929	10.52%	0.53		-8.19%	
Total	**14**	**42,722**	**100.0%**	**8,545**	**4**	**11**	**37,339**	**100.0%**	**7,468**	**4**	**0.00%**	**0**
Electorate		**64,880**	**65.85%**				**61,347**	**60.87%**			**+4.98%**	
Spoiled		**471**	**1.09%**				**319**	**0.85%**			**+0.24%**	
Turnout		**43,193**	**66.57%**				**37,658**	**61.39%**			**+5.19%**	

Transfer analysis

From	To	FG	LB	FF	SF	SP	PBPA	GP	WP	Others	Non Trans
FG	668	459	178		31						
		68.71%	26.65%		4.64%						0.00%
FF	5,513	2,051	1,415		492						1,555
		37.20%	25.67%		8.92%						28.21%
SP	649	70	155	29	110		217	33			35
		10.79%	23.88%	4.47%	16.95%		33.44%	5.08%			5.39%
PBPA	3,059	552	1,161	210	806						330
		18.05%	37.95%	6.86%	26.35%						10.79%
GP	1,605	289	609	110	423						174
		18.01%	37.94%	6.85%	26.36%						10.84%
WP	735	79	175	34	125		245	38			39
		10.75%	23.81%	4.63%	17.01%	0.00%	33.33%	5.17%			5.31%
Others	1,210	202	229	87	104	27	126	50	41	214	130
		16.69%	18.93%	7.19%	8.60%	2.23%	10.41%	4.13%	3.39%	17.69%	10.74%
Total	**13,439**	**3,702**	**3,922**	**470**	**2,091**	**27**	**588**	**121**	**41**	**214**	**2,263**
		27.55%	**29.18%**	**3.50%**	**15.56%**	**0.20%**	**4.38%**	**0.90%**	**0.31%**	**1.59%**	**16.84%**

Count details

Seats	4									Quota	8,545
Candidate	Party	1st	2nd Smith Votes	3rd McHale Votes	4th McGrath Votes	5th Ryan Votes	6th Finnegan Connolly Votes	7th Kenny Gogarty Votes	8th Curran Votes	9th Fitzgerald Surplus	
Tuffy, Joanna* (LB)		7,495	+18 / 7,513	+20 / 7,533	+20 / 7,553	+80 / 7,633	+194 / 7,827	+1,121 / 8,948	8,948	8,948	
Fitzgerald, Frances# (FG)		7,281	+4 / 7,285	+18 / 7,303	+20 / 7,323	+101 / 7,424	+69 / 7,493	+410 / 7,903	+1,310 / 9,213	-668 / 8,545	
Dowds, Robert (LB)		5,643	+2 / 5,645	+16 / 5,661	+34 / 5,695	+39 / 5,734	+136 / 5,870	+649 / 6,519	+1,415 / 7,934	+178 / 8,112	
Keating, Derek (FG)		5,933	+5 / 5,938	+7 / 5,945	+19 / 5,964	+28 / 5,992	+80 / 6,072	+431 / 6,503	+741 / 7,244	+459 / 7,703	
O Broin Eoin (SF)		5,060	+6 / 5,066	+22 / 5,088	+29 / 5,117	+47 / 5,164	+235 / 5,399	+1,229 / 6,628	+492 / 7,120	+31 / 7,151	
Curran, John* (FF)		5,043	+4 / 5,047	+21 / 5,068	+27 / 5,095	+35 / 5,130	+63 / 5,193	+320 / 5,513	-5,513 / Eliminated		
Kenny, Gino (PBPA)		2,471	+10 / 2,481	+32 / 2,513	+23 / 2,536	+61 / 2,597	+462 / 3,059	-3,059 / Eliminated			
Gogarty, Paul* (GP)		1,484	+6 / 1,490	+8 / 1,498	+11 / 1,509	+25 / 1,534	+71 / 1,605	-1,605 / Eliminated			
Finnegan, Mick (WP)		694	+6 / 700	+12 / 712	+10 / 722	+13 / 735	-735 / Eliminated				
Connolly, Rob (SP)		622	+2 / 624	+10 / 634	+3 / 637	+12 / 649	-649 / Eliminated				
Ryan, Michael (NP)		375	+22 / 397	+32 / 429	+85 / 514	-514 / Eliminated					
McGrath, Colm (NP)		253	+16 / 269	+50 / 319	-319 / Eliminated						
McHale, Jim (NP)		255	+9 / 264	-264 / Eliminated							
Smith, Niall (NP)		113	-113 / Eliminated								
Non-transferable			+3	+16	+38	+73	+74	+504	+1,555		
Cumulative			3	19	57	130	204	708	2,263	2,263	
Total		42,722	42,722	42,722	42,722	42,722	42,722	42,722	42,722	42,722	

Fine Gael Dublin Mid-West TD Frances Fitzgerald arrives at Leinster House in early March

Dublin North (4 seats)

Big changes as only one outgoing deputy returned

Elected

James Reilly* (FG) Count 1, Brendan Ryan (Lab) Count 3, Clare Daly (SP) Count 6, Alan Farrell (FG) Final count.

Analysis by Sean Donnelly

There were major Constituency Commission changes here since 2007. A population of 12,768 in the Swords-Forrest/Airport area was transferred to Dublin West, and a population of 9,021 in the Portmarnock and Balgriffin areas was transferred to Dublin North-East. However, the constituency did retain its four seats.

This was another good performance by Fine Gael. With its vote up 17 percentage points and with 1.6 quotas spread between the party's two candidates it was in contention for two seats. Dr James Reilly topped the poll and was over the quota on the first count for an impressive performance by the party's deputy leader and health spokesperson. His running mate Alan Farrell failed to live up to his senior colleague's performance but his 5,310 first preferences put him in the frame and over 1,100 votes ahead of his nearest rivals. Farrell's first-count lead proved to be sufficient as he went on to beat Darragh O'Brien of Fianna Fáil for the final seat by 1,092 votes.

The Labour Party's vote was up 17 percentage points on 2007 and with 1.3 quotas for the party's two candidates it was well placed to take back the seat it had lost in 2007. Outgoing senator Brendan Ryan, whose brother Sean had previously held a Labour seat in this constituency, was just short of the quota on the first count and went on to take the second seat on the third count. Cllr Tom Kelleher polled just 6.5% and was never in contention.

This was another disastrous performance by Fianna Fáil, with its vote down 27 percentage points. However, with 0.8 quotas it should still have been in contention for a seat. But the party failed to recognise its precarious position which demanded a single-candidate strategy and with both outgoing deputies contesting, its reduced vote was split between them and both lost out. Darragh O'Brien got 4,115 first preferences to leave him outside the frame with just 0.4 of a quota on the first count. Michael Kennedy had a similar performance, winning just 3,519 first preferences. This left both of them too far behind resulting in another double loss and another blank constituency for Fianna Fáil.

Clare Daly of the Socialist Party has been knocking on the door here for the last few elections. She was tipped to win a seat in 2007 but came up short. She made no mistake at this election as she was in third place on the first count and she went on to take the third seat comfortably to become one of five TDs returned for the new United Left Alliance.

This was another poor performance by the Green Party, with former leader Trevor Sargent losing his seat. Sargent was in fifth place on the first count and could not catch up. He was eliminated on the fifth count with Farrell and Daly the main beneficiaries of his transfers.

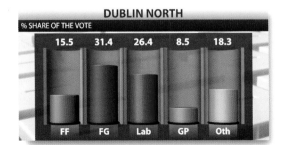

DUBLIN NORTH
% SHARE OF THE VOTE

FF	FG	Lab	GP	Oth
15.5	31.4	26.4	8.5	18.3

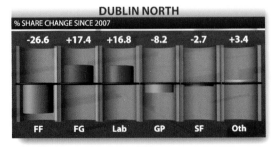

DUBLIN NORTH
% SHARE CHANGE SINCE 2007

FF	FG	Lab	GP	SF	Oth
-26.6	+17.4	+16.8	-8.2	-2.7	+3.4

*outgoing TDs

JAMES REILLY (FG)

Home Address: Seafoam, South Shore Road, Rush, Co Dublin.
Constituency Office: 19 Bridge Street, Balbriggan, Co Dublin.
Phone: 01 6183749 (LH)
Email: james.reilly@oireachtas.ie
Website: www.reilly.ie
Twitter: twitter.com/drjamesreilly
Birth Place/Date: Dublin, August 1955.
Marital Status/Family: Married to Dorothy McEvoy; 1 daughter, 4 sons.
Education: St Conleth's and CUS, Dublin; Ring, Co Waterford; Gormanstown, Co Meath; Royal College of Surgeons; Royal College of General Practitioners; Irish College of General Practitioners; Master of Medical Science at University College, Dublin.
Occupation: Full-time public representative. General practitioner.
Biography: Current Minister for Health. Secured 10,178 first preference votes to top the poll and get elected on the first count. First elected in 2007. Fine Gael frontbench spokesperson on Health and Children (2007-2011). Fine Gael deputy leader (June 2010-present). He was one of party leader Enda Kenny's staunchest allies during Richard Bruton's failed Fine Gael leadership challenge in June 2010.
A former president of the Irish Medical Organisation (IMO), he has also served as chairman of the GP Committee, president of the IMO and as chairman of the GP Development Team. He was the IMO's representative at the World Medical Association. Former member, Eastern Health Board; Council of the Society for Autistic Children. Dr Reilly has been to the fore in the development of Fine Gael's 'Fair Care' universal healthcare policy.

BRENDAN RYAN (Lab)

Home Address: Baltrasna, Skerries, Co Dublin.
Phone: 01 8490265 (H) 01 6183421 (LH)
Email: Brendan.ryan@oireachtas.ie or bren@brendan-ryan.ie
Website: www.brendan-ryan.ie
Birth Place/Date: February 1953.
Marital Status/Family: Married to Margie Monks; 3 daughters.
Education: DIT, UCD and DCU. Degree in chemistry and masters' degrees in food science and business administration.
Occupation: Full-time public representative. Previously worked as an operations manager in the food and chemicals industry sectors.
Biography: Secured 9,809 first-preference votes to get elected on the third count. Member Seanad Éireann (2007-2011). Unsuccessful Dáil candidate in 2007.
Hobbies: A keen sportsman, he played table tennis, hockey, Gaelic football and soccer. Managed soccer teams at youth and senior level in Skerries.
Did you know? Brendan is the younger brother of Sean Ryan, Labour TD for Dublin North (1989-1997 and 1998-2002) and senator (1997-1998).
Politician (living or deceased) you most admire: Nelson Mandela.
Priority as a TD? To bring about a better Ireland with Labour in government and to improve the lives of the ordinary people of Dublin North.
Why did you stand for election? To get people back to work and give some hope to the people of Ireland, especially our young people.
Is there any particular event that brought home to you just how serious the economic crisis had become? The massive increase in unemployment since 2007 with blackspots close to Dublin such as Balbriggan, with a 262% increase, and Swords, with a 226% increase.

CLARE DALY (SP)

Home Address: 21 Elmood Drive, Swords, Co Dublin.
Phone: 087 2415576 (M) 01 6183886 (LH)
Email: clare.daly@oireachtas.ie
Website: www.claredaly.ie
Facebook: Yes.
Birth Place/Date: April 1968.
Marital Status/Family: Married.
Education: Dublin City University, accounting and finance graduate.
Occupation: Airport worker.
Biography: Secured 7,513 first-preference votes to get elected on the sixth count in her fourth general election attempt. She was first elected to Fingal County Council in 1999, and subsequently topped the poll in the Swords ward in 2004 and 2009.
Hobbies: Reading, playing piano and violin (badly).
Did you know? Clare was president of the Students' Union at NIHE Dublin and later at DCU.
Politician (living or deceased) you most admire: Jim Larkin.
Priority as a TD? Defending the living standards of ordinary people and public services.
Why did you stand for election? To use the position as a platform to organise from, to champion the issues that affect ordinary people and to encourage people in the communities and workplaces to take action themselves to defend their living standards and demand investment in jobs.
Is there any particular event that brought home to you just how serious the economic crisis had become? There is no one event but rather the never-ending proportion of taxpayers' money that is being used to bail out the banks and cover the private debt of those who speculated on the Irish property market, while the jobless figures and emigration statistics rise relentlessly.

Dublin North

ALAN FARRELL (FG)

Home Address: 4 Drynam Drive, Drynam Hall, Kinsealy, Co Dublin.
Phone: 01 6184008 (LH)
Email: alan.farrell@oir.ie
Website: www.alanfarrell.ie
Twitter: twitter.com/alanfarrell
Birth Place/Date: Dublin, December 1977.
Marital Status/Family: Married.
Education: Chanel College, Coolock; Waterford IT.
Occupation: Full-time public representative.
Biography: Elected to Fingal County Council in 2004 and 2009.
Hobbies: Spectator sports, League of Ireland football, walking, golf.
Politician (living or deceased) you most admire: John Hume and JFK.
Priority as a TD? Delivery of social infrastructure.
Why did you stand for election? To deliver change.
Is there any particular event that brought home to you just how serious the economic crisis had become? The constant denial by the former government that the IMF were to arrive and their eventual arrival in the country.

Socialist Party MEP and United Left Alliance (ULA) candidate in Dublin West, Joe Higgins with Cllr Clare Daly, Socialist Party ULA candidate for Dublin North, at a United Left Alliance press conference in January

First preference votes

	Candidate	Party	1st	%	Quota	Count	Status
	Seats	**4**			**9,870**		
1	Reilly, Dr. James*	FG	10,178	20.63%	1.03	1	Made Quota
2	Ryan, Brendan	LB	9,809	19.88%	0.99	3	Made Quota
3	Daly, Clare	SP	7,513	15.22%	0.76	6	Made Quota
4	Farrell, Alan	FG	5,310	10.76%	0.54	7	Elected
5	O'Brien, Darragh*	FF	4,115	8.34%	0.42	7	Not Elected
6	Sargent, Trevor*	GP	4,186	8.48%	0.42	5	Eliminated
7	Kennedy, Michael*	FF	3,519	7.13%	0.36	4	Eliminated
8	Kelleher, Tom	LB	3,205	6.49%	0.32	3	Eliminated
9	Harrold, Mark	NP	1,512	3.06%	0.15	2	No Expenses

*Outgoing TD   Valid Poll: 49,347   Quota: 9,870   No expenses limit: 2,468

Party votes

Party	Cand	1st	%	Quota	Seats	Cand	1st	%	Quota	Seats	%	Seats
		2011					**2007**				**Change**	
FG	2	15,488	31.39%	1.57	2	1	7,667	14.03%	0.70	1	+17.35%	+1
LB	2	13,014	26.37%	1.32	1	1	5,256	9.62%	0.48		+16.75%	+1
FF	2	7,634	15.47%	0.77		3	22,998	42.09%	2.10	2	-26.62%	-2
SF						1	1,454	2.66%	0.13		-2.66%	
SP	1	7,513	15.22%	0.76	1	1	4,872	8.92%	0.45		+6.31%	+1
GP	1	4,186	8.48%	0.42		2	9,107	16.67%	0.83	1	-8.18%	-1
PD						1	1,395	2.55%	0.13		-2.55%	
Others	1	1,512	3.06%	0.15		3	1,892	3.46%	0.17		-0.40%	
Total	9	49,347	100.0%	9,870	4	13	54,641	100.0%	10,929	4	0.00%	0
Electorate		70,413	70.08%				80,221	68.11%			+1.97%	
Spoiled		452	0.91%				411	0.75%			+0.16%	
Turnout		49,799	70.72%				55,052	68.63%			+2.10%	

Transfer analysis

From	To	FG	LB	FF	SP	GP	Others	Non Trans
FG	308	165	69	21	20	27	6	
		53.57%	22.40%	6.82%	6.49%	8.77%	1.95%	
LB	3,367	683		359	1,221	686		418
		20.29%		10.66%	36.26%	20.37%		12.41%
FF	3,805	263		2,479	369	441		253
		6.91%		65.15%	9.70%	11.59%		6.65%
SP	1,302	709		246				347
		54.45%		18.89%				26.65%
GP	5,610	1,781		935	1,707			1,187
		31.75%		16.67%	30.43%			21.16%
Others	1,518	248	342	198	342	270		118
		16.34%	22.53%	13.04%	22.53%	17.79%		7.77%
Total	15,910	3,849	411	4,238	3,659	1,424	6	2,323
		24.19%	2.58%	26.64%	23.00%	8.95%	0.04%	14.60%

Dublin North

Count details

Seats	4						Quota	9,870
Candidate	Party	1st	2nd Reilly Surplus	3rd Harrold Votes	4th Kelleher Votes	5th Kennedy Votes	6th Sargent Votes	7th Daly Surplus
			-308					
Reilly, Dr. James*	FG	10,178	9,870	9,870	9,870	9,870	9,870	9,870
			+59	*+190*				
Ryan, Brendan	LB	9,809	9,868	10,058	10,058	10,058	10,058	10,058
			+20	*+342*	*+1,221*	*+369*	*+1,707*	*-1,302*
Daly, Clare	SP	7,513	7,533	7,875	9,096	9,465	11,172	9,870
			+165	*+248*	*+683*	*+263*	*+1,781*	*+709*
Farrell, Alan	FG	5,310	5,475	5,723	6,406	6,669	8,450	9,159
			+9	*+125*	*+158*	*+2,479*	*+935*	*+246*
O'Brien, Darragh*	FF	4,115	4,124	4,249	4,407	6,886	7,821	8,067
			+27	*+270*	*+686*	*+441*	*-5,610*	
Sargent, Trevor*	GP	4,186	4,213	4,483	5,169	5,610	Eliminated	
			+12	*+73*	*+201*	*-3,805*		
Kennedy, Michael*	FF	3,519	3,531	3,604	3,805	Eliminated		
			+10	*+152*	*-3,367*			
Kelleher, Tom	LB	3,205	3,215	3,367	Eliminated			
			+6	*-1,518*				
Harrold, Mark	NP	1,512	1,518	Eliminated				
Non-transferable				*+118*	*+418*	*+253*	*+1,187*	*+347*
Cumulative			0	118	536	789	1,976	2,323
Total		49,347	49,347	49,347	49,347	49,347	49,347	49,347

Fianna Fáil leader Micheál Martin, accompanied by party colleagues Darragh O'Brien (far left) and Michael Kennedy, is presented with a book by managing director of Keelings Fruit, David Keeling, during a visit to the factory in north Dublin

Dublin North-Central (3 seats)

The end of the Haughey dynasty as Fianna Fáil draws another blank in a Dublin constituency

Elected

Richard Bruton* (FG) Count 2, Aodhán Ó Ríordáin (Lab) Count 4, Finian McGrath* (Ind) Final count.

Analysis by Sean Donnelly

The boundaries were revised here since 2007 with a population of 2,758 in the Edenmore electoral division transferring in from Dublin North-East. However, the constituency did retain its three seats.

The Fine Gael vote was up 12 percentage points since 2007 and with 1.5 quotas. It was in contention for two seats. Richard Bruton topped the poll and was just nine votes short of the quota on the first count. His running mate, Naoise Ó Muirí, was in fourth place with half a quota but failed to make up his first-count deficit of over 1,000 votes on outgoing independent TD, Finian McGrath.

Labour had won a seat here in 1992 and 1997 but lost it in 2002 and failed again in 2007. The party made no mistake in this election with Aodhán Ó Ríordáin taking second place with 0.9 of a quota on the first count as he increased the Labour vote by 15 percentage points for an impressive performance.

This was another disastrous performance by Fianna Fáil with its vote down 31 percentage points. Seán Haughey did poorly and with just 0.5 quotas was in fourth place on the first count, just ahead of Ó Muirí. He failed to make any headway during the count and was overtaken by the Fine Gael man and finally eliminated on the sixth count with his transfers ensuring McGrath's election. So this election marked the end of an era in Irish politics with the Haughey name missing from Dáil Éireann for the first time since 1957.

Outgoing independent deputy Finian McGrath was in third place on the first count and went on to hold off Ó Muirí for the final seat by the very comfortable margin of 4,626 votes.

The turnout was up five percentage points in this constituency and at 73.17% was five percentage points above the average Dublin turnout of 68.20%.

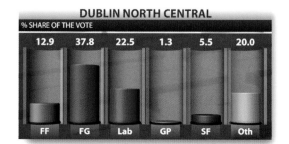

DUBLIN NORTH CENTRAL

% SHARE OF THE VOTE

FF	FG	Lab	GP	SF	Oth
12.9	37.8	22.5	1.3	5.5	20.0

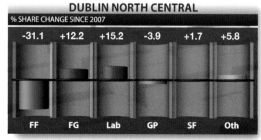

DUBLIN NORTH CENTRAL

% SHARE CHANGE SINCE 2007

FF	FG	Lab	GP	SF	Oth
-31.1	+12.2	+15.2	-3.9	+1.7	+5.8

*outgoing TDs

Dublin North-Central

RICHARD BRUTON (FG)

Home Address: 210 Griffith Avenue, Drumcondra, Dublin 9.
Phone: 01 6183103 (LH)
Email: richard.bruton@oireachtas.ie
Website: www.richardbruton.net
Birth Place/Date: Dublin, March 1953.
Marital Status/Family: Susan Meehan; 2 sons, 2 daughters.
Education: Belvedere College, Dublin; Clongowes Wood College, Co Kildare; University College Dublin; Nuffield College, Oxford (BA, MA, MPhil [Oxon] economics).
Occupation: Full-time public representative. Formerly economist.
Biography: First elected a TD in 1982. Current Minister for Enterprise, Jobs and Innovation. Minister for Enterprise and Employment (1994-1997), Minister of State at the Department of Industry and Commerce (1986-1987). Has been Fine Gael frontbench spokesperson on: Education and Science (1997-2002), Enterprise and Employment (1993-1994), Employment (1992-1993), Health (1990-1992); Energy and Communications (1987-1989), Finance (2007-2010), Enterprise, Jobs and Economic Planning (2010-2011). Senator, Agricultural panel, August 1981-1982. Richard led a failed leadership challenge against Enda Kenny in June 2010. Member, Dublin City Council (1991-1994 and 1999-2003). Member, Meath County Council 1979-1982. Brother of John Bruton, Taoiseach 1994-1997.
Priority as a TD? My priority is to get our people back to work. I will do all I can to promote innovation, cut the cost of doing business and get business the access to finance they desperately need.
Why did you stand for election? I am passionate about the need for reform – to renew politics, to reinvent the economy, to transform the public services, to create a new social contract.

AODHÁN Ó RÍORDÁIN (Lab)

Home Address: 76a Clontarf Park, Dublin 3.
Contact: O86 8190336 (M) 01 6183209 (LH)
Email: aodhan.oriordain@oireachtas.ie
Website: www.aodhanoriordain.blogspot.com
Twitter: twitter.com/aodhanoriordain
Facebook: facebook/aodhanoriordain
Birth Place/Date: Dublin, July 1976.
Marital Status/Family: Married.
Education: Malahide Community School; University College Dublin; Marino Institute of Education.
Occupation: Full-time public representative and former school principal of St Laurence O'Toole's GNS, Sheriff Street, Dublin.
Biography: First elected to Dublin City Council 2004 for the North Inner City and for Clontarf 2009. Deputy Lord Mayor of Dublin 2006-2007, Elected to Dáil Éireann at first attempt in February 2011.
Hobbies: Dublin GAA fan, Bohemians fan, Ireland soccer fan, drama nut, politics nut, coffee nut, I run and I tweet.
Did you know? Aodhán has had two of his plays staged by the National Irish Language Theatre, An Taibhdhearc, in Galway. His school football GAA team have won five county championships since 2001 and were featured in an RTÉ Radio *Documentary on One*.
Politician (living or deceased) you most admire: Noel Browne, Martin Luther King.
Priority as a TD? Employment, education and most especially educational disadvantage.
Why did you stand for election? The children that I teach in Sheriff Street have inspired me to get involved in politics to build a fairer Ireland, to allow every child the chance to succeed and to fulfil their potential, no matter who they are or where they come from.
Is there any particular event that brought home to you just how serious the economic crisis had become? For me as an Irish person, the physical arrival of the IMF team left me completely dispirited and that day I started to wonder if I would run for election or not.

FINIAN McGRATH (Ind)

Home Address: 342 Charlemont, Griffith Avenue, Marino, Dublin 9.
Constituency office: Le Cheile Community Central, Collins Avenue East, Donnycarney, Dublin 5.
Phone: 087 6738041 (M) 01 6183031 (LH)
Website: www.finianmcgrath.ie
Birth Place/Date: Tuam, Co Galway, April 1953.
Marital Status/Family: Widower; 2 daughters.
Education: CBS, Tuam, Co Galway; St Patrick's College of Education, Drumcondra.
Occupation: Former teacher and now full-time public representative.
Biography: First elected to the Dáil in 2002 and re-elected in 2007 and 2011. Elected to Dublin City Council in 1999.
Hobbies: Football and music.
Did you know? Finian was a former full-time voluntary worker and soup runner with Simon Ireland. He also came second in RTÉ'S *Charity You're A Star* TV show and raised over €86,000 for Down Syndrome Ireland.
Politician (living or deceased) you most admire: James Connolly, Tony Gregory and Nelson Mandela.
Priority as a TD: To build a fairer and better Ireland.
Why did you stand for election? To change the Irish political system and to protect the weaker sections of society.
Is there any particular event that brought home to you just how serious the economic crisis had become? A lot of my friends and neighbours have lost their jobs. The problem of emigration has returned as well. So my priority now is to end that cycle and make Ireland a better place.

First preference votes

	Seats	3			9,694		
Candidate	Party	1st	%	Quota	Count	Status
1 Bruton, Richard*	FG	9,685	24.98%	1.00	2	Made Quota
2 Ó Ríordáin, Aodhán	LB	8,731	22.52%	0.90	4	Made Quota
3 McGrath, Finian*	NP	5,986	15.44%	0.62	7	Made Quota
4 Ó Muirí, Naoise	FG	4,959	12.79%	0.51	7	Not Elected
5 Haughey, Sean*	FF	5,017	12.94%	0.52	6	Eliminated
6 McCormack, Helen	SF	2,140	5.52%	0.22	3	Eliminated
7 Lyons, John	PBPA	1,424	3.67%	0.15	2	No Expenses
8 Cooney, Donna	GP	501	1.29%	0.05	1	No Expenses
9 Clarke, Paul	NP	331	0.85%	0.03	1	No Expenses

*Outgoing TD Total poll: 38,774 Quota: 9,694 No expenses limit: 2,423

Party votes

Party	2011					2007					Change	
	Cand	1st	%	Quota	Seats	Cand	1st	%	Quota	Seats	%	Seats
FG	2	14,644	37.77%	1.51	1	1	9,303	25.55%	1.02	1	+12.22%	
LB	1	8,731	22.52%	0.90	1	1	2,649	7.27%	0.29		+15.24%	+1
FF	1	5,017	12.94%	0.52		2	16,029	44.02%	1.76	1	-31.08%	-1
SF	1	2,140	5.52%	0.22		1	1,375	3.78%	0.15		+1.74%	
PBPA	1	1,424	3.67%	0.15							+3.67%	
GP	1	501	1.29%	0.05		1	1,891	5.19%	0.21		-3.90%	
Others	2	6,317	16.29%	0.65	1	1	5,169	14.19%	0.57	1	+2.10%	
Total	9	38,774	100.0%	9,694	3	7	36,416	100.0%	9,105	3	0.00%	0
Electorate		52,992	73.17%				53,443	68.14%			+5.03%	
Spoiled		413	1.05%				342	0.93%			+0.12%	
Turnout		39,187	73.95%				36,758	68.78%			+5.17%	

Transfer analysis

From	To	FG	LB	FF	SF	PBPA	Others	Non Trans
FG	96	50		10			31	5
		52.08%		10.42%			32.29%	5.21%
LB	498	113		43			342	
		22.69%		8.63%			68.67%	
FF	5,348	996					2,875	1,477
		18.62%					53.76%	27.62%
SF	2,602	142	863	167			1,076	354
		5.46%	33.17%	6.42%			41.35%	13.60%
PBPA	1,587	65	418	51	415		545	93
		4.10%	26.34%	3.21%	26.15%		34.34%	5.86%
GP	501	108	108	36	28	98	103	20
		21.56%	21.56%	7.19%	5.59%	19.56%	20.56%	3.99%
Others	331	71	72	24	19	65	67	13
		21.45%	21.75%	7.25%	5.74%	19.64%	20.24%	3.93%
Total	10,963	1,545	1,461	331	462	163	5,039	1,962
		14.09%	13.33%	3.02%	4.21%	1.49%	45.96%	17.90%

Dublin North-Central

Candidate	Party	1st	2nd Cooney Clarke	3rd Lyons Votes	4th McCormack Votes	5th Ó Riordáin Surplus	6th Bruton Surplus	7th Haughey Votes
Seats	**3**						**Quota**	**9,694**
			+105				-96	
Bruton, Richard*	FG	9,685	9,790	9,790	9,790	9,790	9,694	9,694
			+180	+418	+863	-498		
Ó Riordáin, Aodhán	LB	8,731	8,911	9,329	10,192	9,694	9,694	9,694
			+170	+545	+1,076	+342	+31	2,875
McGrath, Finian*	NP	5,986	6,156	6,701	7,777	8,119	8,150	11,025
			+74	+65	+142	+113	+50	+996
Ó Muirí, Naoise	FG	4,959	5,033	5,098	5,240	5,353	5,403	6,399
			+60	+51	+167	+43	+10	-5,348
Haughey, Sean*	FF	5,017	5,077	5,128	5,295	5,338	5,348	Eliminated
			+47	+415	-2,602			
McCormack, Helen	SF	2,140	2,187	2,602	Eliminated			
			+163	-1,587				
Lyons, John	PBPA	1,424	1,587	Eliminated				
			-501					
Cooney, Donna	GP	501	Eliminated					
			-331					
Clarke, Paul	NP	331	Eliminated					
Non-transferable			+33	+93	+354		+5	+1,477
Cumulative			33	126	480	480	485	1,962
Total		**38,774**	**38,774**	**38,774**	**38,774**	**38,774**	**38,774**	**38,774**

The Dáil's Technical Group of independent TDs on the plinth at Leinster House: (back row, left to right) Stephen Donnelly, John Halligan, Shane Ross, Thomas Pringle and Finian McGrath; (middle, left to right) Mick Wallace, Luke 'Ming' Flanagan, Richard Boyd Barrett and Maureen O'Sullivan; (front) Catherine Murphy, Mattie McGrath and Icelandic MP Lilja Mosesdottir

Dublin North-East (3 seats)

Another Dublin three-seater, another blank for Fianna Fáil

Elected

Terence Flanagan* (FG) Count 1, Tommy Broughan* (Lab) Count 2, Seán Kenny (Lab) Final count.

Analysis by Sean Donnelly

There were major Constituency Commission changes here since 2007. A population of 9,021 in the Portmarnock and Balgriffin areas was transferred into Dublin North-East from Dublin North, and a population of 2,758 in the Edenmore electoral division was transferred to Dublin North-Central. However, the constituency did retain its three seats.

Fine Gael's single candidate, outgoing deputy Terence Flanagan, put in an impressive performance and topped the poll and was well over the quota on the first count with the Fine Gael vote up seven percentage points on 2007.

Tommy Broughan was just short of the quota on the first count and went on take the second seat on the second count. This was one of only two constituencies in the 'Spring Tide' election of 1992 to deliver two seats for Labour. Remarkably the two candidates who won in 1992 pulled off the same feat in 2011. With the party vote up 19 percentage points in this election, Labour was well-placed to repeat the 1992 performance. Seán Kenny trailed both Larry O'Toole and Averil Power on the first count but managed to do better on transfers and passed out the Sinn Féin and Fianna Fáil candidates. He comfortably took the final seat ahead of Sinn Féin in an impressive performance. Labour did well to convert 1.4 quotas

into two seats with Kenny coming from well down on the first count with just 0.4 of a quota. This was another example of Labour's strong transfer performance in this election.

This result was a disappointment for Sinn Féin and for veteran candidate Larry O'Toole. He looked well placed on the first count but the party's old failing of not gaining transfers once again came into play and O'Toole was well beaten in the battle for the final seat.

This was another disastrous performance for Fianna Fáil with its vote down 28 percentage points and with just under half a quota it was struggling. Newcomer Averil Power had been selected to replace the long-serving TD and former Cabinet minister Michael Woods, who had retired. Power was never really in contention and her first-count vote of 4,794 left her in fourth place. She was just too far off the pace and was the final candidate eliminated. Her transfers went nearly 4:1 to Kenny over O'Toole to decide the battle for the final seat.

Eamonn Blaney, son of the former long-serving Donegal deputy Neil Blaney, contested this constituency for 'New Vision' but got just 4% and was never in contention. Five candidates lost the right to reclaim their expenses, including Jimmy Guerin, brother of the late Veronica Guerin.

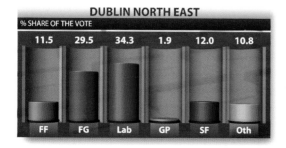

DUBLIN NORTH EAST

% SHARE OF THE VOTE

FF	FG	Lab	GP	SF	Oth
11.5	29.5	34.3	1.9	12.0	10.8

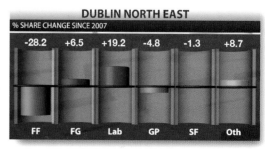

DUBLIN NORTH EAST

% SHARE CHANGE SINCE 2007

FF	FG	Lab	GP	SF	Oth
-28.2	+6.5	+19.2	-4.8	-1.3	+8.7

*outgoing TDs

Dublin North-East

TERENCE FLANAGAN (FG)

Address: Leinster House, Kildare Street, Dublin 2.
Phone: 01 6183634 (LH)
Email: terence.flanagan@oireachtas.ie
Website: www.finegael.ie
Twitter: twitter.com/tflanaganTD
Facebook: Yes.
Birth Place/Date: Dublin, January 1975.
Marital Status/Family: Single.
Education: St David's Boys NS; Chanel College, Malahide Road, Dublin; Dublin Business School, Aungier Street, Dublin.
Occupation: Full-time public representative.
Biography: Terence was elected to the 30th Dáil in 2007 and was appointed Fine Gael spokesperson on Housing. He was co-opted to Dublin City Council in October 2003 to replace Richard Bruton and elected to the council in 2004.
Hobbies: He plays percussion and is part of the Artane Senior Band, having started in the Artane Boys Band.
Did you know? Terence's favourite film is *The Shawshank Redemption*.
Politician (living or deceased) you most admire: Barack Obama.
Priority as a TD? To support local enterprise and to help ensure that all barriers to job creation are removed. To fight for the rights of special needs children. To ensure that housing standards improve in this country.
Why did you stand for election? I stood for election because I am passionate about meeting and helping people. I want to be part of a government that will make this a better country.
Is there any particular event that brought home to you just how serious the economic crisis had become? The amount of unfinished and empty houses that blot the landscape.

THOMAS P BROUGHAN (Lab)

Home Address: 18 Thormanby Lawns, Howth, Dublin 13.
Phone: 01 8477634 (CO) 01 618 3557 (LH)
Email: Thomas_p_broughan@oireachtas.ie
Website: www.tommybroughan.com
Twitter: @TommyBroughanTD
Birth Place/Date: Dublin.
Marital Status/Family: Married to Carmel.
Education: Moyle Park College, Clondalkin; UCD (BA, HDip Ed); London University (BSc (Econ); MSc (Econ).
Occupation: Full-time public representative.
Biography: First elected in the 1992 'Spring Tide' and re-elected in each subsequent general election. Member, Dublin City Council 1991-2003. Since 1992 he has been Labour's spokesperson in a number of areas: Enterprise, Trade and Employment; Social Protection; Communications; Marine and Natural Resources (Energy); and Transport. Member of Dáil Public Accounts Committee in 30th Dáil.
Hobbies: Music, walking and reading especially economics, history and literature.
Did you know? Along with a few friends, Thomas founded a small business/enterprise centre in 1987 which became the Coolock Development Council.
Politician (living or deceased) you most admire: Seán Dunne TD.
Priority as a TD? To end the banking morass and help restore our economy.
Why did you stand for election? To reverse the cuts and achieve a Labour or Labour-led government.
Is there any particular event that brought home to you just how serious the economic crisis had become? Two things stand out – the number of young constituents in mortgage difficulties and negative equity as I meet a lot of these people at my weekend constituency clinics. And the ongoing closure of shops and businesses in Dublin North-East.

SEÁN KENNY (Lab)

Home Address: 44 Woodbine Road, Raheny, Dublin 5.
Phone: 086 8126340 (M) 01 8481806 (H)
Email: info@seankenny.ie or sean.kenny@oireachtas.ie
Website: www.seankenny.ie
Birth Place/Date: Ballinasloe, October 1942.
Marital Status/Family: Married to Mairead Armstrong; 1 son, 1 daughter.
Education: Garbally College, Ballinasloe.
Occupation: Full-time public representative.
Biography: Secured 4,365 first-preference votes to get elected on the ninth count. Previously a TD from 1992 to 1997 when he was chairperson of the Social Affairs Committee and a member of the Forum for Peace and Reconciliation. First elected to Dublin City Council in 1979. Also elected at the 1999, 2004 and 2009 local elections. Lord Mayor of Dublin 1991/1992 and played a leading role in Dublin's year as European City of Culture; the launch of Temple Bar as a tourist centre and the celebration of Trinity College Dublin Quatercentenary, when he received an honorary degree from the college. Unsuccessfully contested general elections in 1981, February 1982, November 1982, 1987, 1989, and 1997.
Hobbies: Walking, cycling, gardening.
Politician (living or deceased) you most admire: Alexander Dubcek.
Priority as a TD? Job creation.
Why did you stand for election? To help the Labour Party win two seats out of three in constituency.
Is there any particular event that brought home to you just how serious the economic crisis had become? The growing number of fuel poverty cases.

First preference votes

	Seats	3			10,460		
Candidate		Party	1st	%	Quota	Count	Status
1 Flanagan, Terence*		FG	12,332	29.47%	1.18	1	Made Quota
2 Broughan, Tommy*		LB	10,006	23.92%	0.96	2	Made Quota
3 Kenny, Seán #		LB	4,365	10.43%	0.42	9	Elected
4 O'Toole, Larry		SF	5,032	12.03%	0.48	9	Not Elected
5 Power, Averil		FF	4,794	11.46%	0.46	8	Eliminated
6 Blaney, Eamonn		NV	1,773	4.24%	0.17	7	Eliminated
7 Guerin, Jimmy		NP	1,283	3.07%	0.12	6	No Expenses
8 Healy, David		GP	792	1.89%	0.08	5	No Expenses
9 Greene, Brian		SP	869	2.08%	0.08	4	No Expenses
10 Sexton, Raymond		NP	351	0.84%	0.03	3	No Expenses
11 Eastwood, Robert		NP	242	0.58%	0.02	3	No Expenses

*Outgoing TD #Former TD Valid poll: 41,839 Quota: 10,460 No expenses limit: 2,616

Party votes

Party	Cand	2011				2007				Change	
		1st	%	Quota	Seats	Cand	1st	%	Quota	Seats	%	Seats
FG	1	12,332	29.47%	1.18	1	2	8,012	22.94%	0.92	1	+6.54%	
LB	2	14,371	34.35%	1.37	2	1	5,294	15.16%	0.61	1	+19.19%	+1
FF	1	4,794	11.46%	0.46		2	13,864	39.69%	1.59	1	-28.23%	-1
SF	1	5,032	12.03%	0.48		1	4,661	13.34%	0.53		-1.32%	
SP	1	869	2.08%	0.08							+2.08%	
GP	1	792	1.89%	0.08		1	2,349	6.73%	0.27		-4.83%	
PD						1	749	2.14%	0.09		-2.14%	
Others	4	3,649	8.72%	0.35							+8.72%	
Total	11	41,839	100.0%	10,460	3	8	34,929	100.0%	8,733	3	0.00%	0
Electorate		58,542	71.47%				53,778	64.95%			+6.52%	
Spoiled		448	1.06%				323	0.92%			+0.14%	
Turnout		42,287	72.23%				35,252	65.55%			+6.68%	

Transfer analysis

From	To	LB	FF	SF	SP	GP	Others	Non Trans
FG	1,872	1,095	219	88	24	127	319	
		58.49%	11.70%	4.70%	1.28%	6.78%	17.04%	
LB	278	157	23	23	4	15	56	
		56.47%	8.27%	8.27%	1.44%	5.40%	20.14%	
FF	6,041	2,356		661				3,024
		39.00%		10.94%				50.06%
SP	935	231	25	298		62	247	72
		24.71%	2.67%	31.87%		6.63%	26.42%	7.70%
GP	1,049	364	180	77			282	146
		34.70%	17.16%	7.34%			26.88%	13.92%
Others	5,418	1,533	800	744	38	53	865	1,385
		28.29%	14.77%	13.73%	0.70%	0.98%	15.97%	25.56%
Total	15,593	5,736	1,247	1,891	66	257	1,769	4,627
		36.79%	8.00%	12.13%	0.42%	1.65%	11.34%	29.67%

Dublin North-East

Candidate	Party	1st	2nd Flanagan Surplus	3rd Broughan Surplus	4th Sexton Eastwood	5th Greene Votes	6th Healy Votes	7th Guerin Votes	8th Blaney Votes	9th Power Votes
Seats 3								Quota		**10,460**
			-1,872							
Flanagan, Terence*	FG	12,332	10,460	10,460	10,460	10,460	10,460	10,460	10,460	10,460
			+732	-278						
Broughan, Tommy*	LB	10,006	10,738	10,460	10,460	10,460	10,460	10,460	10,460	10,460
			+363	+157	+100	+231	+364	+420	+1,013	+2,356
Kenny, Seán	LB	4,365	4,728	4,885	4,985	5,216	5,580	6,000	7,013	9,369
			+88	+23	+36	+298	+77	+200	+508	+661
O'Toole, Larry	SF	5,032	5,120	5,143	5,179	5,477	5,554	5,754	6,262	6,923
			+219	+23	+73	+25	+180	+265	+462	-6,041
Power, Averil	FF	4,794	5,013	5,036	5,109	5,134	5,314	5,579	6,041	Eliminated
			+121	+19	+186	+134	+168	+554	-2,955	
Blaney, Eamonn	NV	1,773	1,894	1,913	2,099	2,233	2,401	2,955	Eliminated	
			+136	+28	+125	+113	+114	-1,799		
Guerin, Jimmy	NP	1,283	1,419	1,447	1,572	1,685	1,799	Eliminated		
			+127	+15	+53	+62	-1,049			
Healy, David	GP	792	919	934	987	1,049	Eliminated			
			+24	+4	+38	-935				
Greene, Brian	SP	869	893	897	935	Eliminated				
			+40	+6	-397					
Sexton, Raymond	NP	351	391	397	Eliminated					
			+22	+3	-267					
Eastwood, Robert	NP	242	264	267	Eliminated					
Non-transferable					+53	+72	+146	+360	+972	+3,024
Cumulative			0	0	53	125	271	631	1,603	4,627
Total		41,839	41,839	41,839	41,839	41,839	41,839	41,839	41,839	41,839

Tommy Broughan, Labour Candidate for Dublin North-East celebrates the winning of his seat at the count centre at the RDS in Dublin

Dublin North-West (3 seats)

The first constituency ever not to return either a Fine Gael or a Fianna Fáil TD

Elected

Roisin Shortall* (Lab) Count 1, Dessie Ellis (SF) Final count, John Lyons (Lab) Final count.

Analysis by Sean Donnelly

There were no boundary changes since 2007 and it remained a three-seat constituency. This was one of Labour's best performances in this election with the party's vote up 23 percentage points, its largest increase in support in this election and it managed to convert 1.7 quotas into two seats. Roisin Shortall put in one of the best performances of this election as she topped the poll with 1.1 quotas to take the first seat and she also managed to bring in a running mate. John Lyons was in third place on the first count with 0.6 quotas, over 1,000 votes ahead of outgoing minister Pat Carey. He increased his lead throughout the count and comfortably held off Fine Gael for the final seat.

Sinn Féin finally made a breakthrough in this constituency with Dessie Ellis delivering a seat. He had gone close in the past and was particularly disappointed in 2007 but he made no mistake in this election. In second place with 0.9 of a quota on the first count, he comfortably took the second seat.

Fine Gael decided to run two candidates and with

just 0.7 of a quota between them, Gerry Breen and Dr Bill Tormey were both outside the frame on the first count. Both had less than half a quota and they duly failed to win a seat. Fine Gael has now failed to win a seat here since Mary Flaherty in 1992 and this constituency was the only one in the country not to return a Fine Gael deputy in 2011.

Noel Ahern retired at this election and fellow outgoing Fianna Fáil TD Pat Carey did poorly with the Fianna Fáil vote down a massive 37 percentage points, the largest drop in support for Fianna Fáil in the country and the largest drop in the party's history. Carey was outside the frame on the first count with just 3,869 votes. He was the final candidate eliminated and his transfers favoured Lyons and ensured his election.

The turnout was up seven percentage points, one of the largest increases in this election.

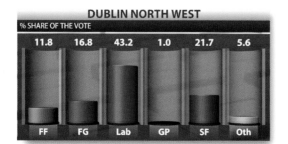

DUBLIN NORTH WEST

% SHARE OF THE VOTE

FF	FG	Lab	GP	SF	Oth
11.8	16.8	43.2	1.0	21.7	5.6

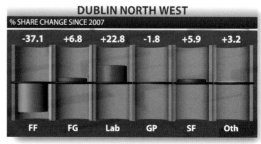

DUBLIN NORTH WEST

% SHARE CHANGE SINCE 2007

FF	FG	Lab	GP	SF	Oth
-37.1	+6.8	+22.8	-1.8	+5.9	+3.2

*outgoing TDs

Dublin North-West

RÓISÍN SHORTALL (Lab)

Home Address: 12 Iveragh Road, Gaeltacht Park, Whitehall, Dublin 9.
Phone: 01 6183593 (LH)
Email: roisin.shortall@oir.ie
Website: www.labour.ie/roisinshortall/
Birth Place/Date: Dublin, April 1954.
Marital Status/Family: Married; 3 daughters.
Education: Dominican College, Eccles Street; UCD (BA economics and politics); St Mary's College of Education, Marino.
Occupation: Full-time public representative.
Biography: Current Minister of State at the Department of Health with special responsibility for Primary Care. Topped the poll with over 9,000 first preferences in Election 2011. First elected a TD in 1992 and returned in 1997, 2002 and 2007. Labour spokesperson on Social and Family Affairs. Formerly member of Public Accounts Committee; Joint Committee on Social and Family Affairs. Member Dublin City Council 1991-2003. Chairperson Eastern Health Board 1996-1998.
Hobbies: Cinema, theatre, walking.
Did you know? In the general election, Róisín achieved the highest vote share of any Labour candidate.
Politician (living or deceased) you most admire: Noel Browne.
Priority as a TD? To seek to bring about prosperity and social justice.
Why did you stand for election? To change the government and play a part in achieving recovery for the country.
Is there any particular event that brought home to you just how serious the economic crisis had become? Last year when my daughter and most of her friends had to emigrate to find work.

DESSIE ELLIS (SF)

Home Address: 19 Dunsink Road, Finglas, Dublin 11.
Phone: 086 8541941 (M) 01 8343390 (H) 01 6183006 (LH)
Email: dessiejohn.ellis@dublincity.ie
Website: www.sinnfein.ie
Twitter: twitter.com/cllrdessieellis
Birth Place/Date: Dublin, October 1952.
Marital Status/Family: Married to Ann.
Education: St Brigid's, Finglas; St Fergal's NS, Finglas; Coláiste Eoin, Finglas; Kevin Street College of Technology.
Occupation: Technician.
Biography: Party spokesperson on Transport and Housing. Secured 7,115 first-preference votes to get elected on the seventh and final count in his third general election. He unsuccessfully contested the 2002 and 2007 general elections. He was elected to Dublin City Council in 1999 and he was re-elected in 2004 and 2009.
Hobbies: Karate, football.
Did you know? Dessie has been a keen karate fan for years and he still does it.
Politician (living or deceased) you most admire: James Connolly.
Priority as a TD? To work for the people, strive for equality in society and work towards a United Ireland.
Why did you stand for election? To represent the people of Dublin North-West as I feel I can do a good job after 12 years as a councillor and I want to bring my work at that level to the national stage.

JOHN LYONS (Lab)

Home Address: Ballymun, Dublin 11.
Phone: 01 6183280 (LH)
email: john.lyons@oireachtas.ie
Website: Labour.ie/johnlyons
Twitter: twitter.com/johnlyonsTD
Facebook: Yes.
Birth Place/Date: Dublin, June 1977.
Marital Status/Family: Single.
Education: Trinity Comprehensive, Ballymun; NUI Maynooth (BA and HDip); Trinity College (special education).
Occupation: Public representative. Formerly secondary teacher.
Biography: Secured 4,799 first-preference votes to get elected on the seventh and final count in his first general election. Co-opted onto Dublin City Council in February 2008 to replace Mary Murphy and re-elected in 2009.
Hobbies: Working out, cinema, DVDs, reading books and getting away when I can.
Did you know? John is the first in his family of seven children to stay on in secondary school.
Politician (living or deceased) you most admire: Mahatma Gandhi and Eamon Gilmore.
Priority as a TD? Social justice issues given the area that I come from.
Why did you stand for election? I genuinely believe that I could be part of a team of people that can make a real difference to the future of Irish society.
Is there any particular event that brought home to you just how serious the economic crisis had become? The fact that it is impossible to meet any family that has not been affected by the unemployment crisis.

First preference votes

	Seats	3			8,203		
Candidate	Party	1st	%	Quota	Count	Status
1 Shortall, Roisin*	LB	9,359	28.52%	1.14	1	Made Quota
2 Ellis, Dessie	SF	7,115	21.68%	0.87	7	Made Quota
3 Lyons, John	LB	4,799	14.63%	0.59	7	Elected
4 Breen, Gerry	FG	2,988	9.11%	0.36	7	Not Elected
5 Carey, Pat*	FF	3,869	11.79%	0.47	6	Eliminated
6 Tormey, Dr. Bill	FG	2,508	7.64%	0.31	5	Eliminated
7 Keegan, Andrew	PBPA	677	2.06%	0.08	4	No Expenses
8 Mooney, Sean	NP	433	1.32%	0.05	4	No Expenses
9 Dunne, John	WP	345	1.05%	0.04	4	No Expenses
10 Holohan, Ruairí	GP	328	1.00%	0.04	4	No Expenses
11 Loftus, Michael J.	NV	217	0.66%	0.03	3	No Expenses
12 Larkin, Michael	CS	173	0.53%	0.02	2	No Expenses

*Outgoing TD Valid Poll: 32,811 Quota: 8,203 No expenses limit: 2,051

Party votes

Party	Cand	1st	%	Quota	Seats	Cand	1st	%	Quota	Seats	%	Seats
FG	2	5,496	16.75%	0.67		1	3,083	9.96%	0.40		+6.79%	
LB	2	14,158	43.15%	1.73	2	1	6,286	20.30%	0.81	1	+22.85%	+1
FF	1	3,869	11.79%	0.47		2	15,124	48.84%	1.95	2	-37.05%	-2
SF	1	7,115	21.68%	0.87	1	1	4,873	15.74%	0.63		+5.95%	+1
PBPA	1	677	2.06%	0.08							+2.06%	
GP	1	328	1.00%	0.04		1	853	2.75%	0.11		-1.76%	
WP	1	345	1.05%	0.04		1	240	0.78%	0.03		+0.28%	
CS	1	173	0.53%	0.02							+0.53%	
Others	2	650	1.98%	0.08		1	505	1.63%	0.07		+0.35%	
Total	12	32,811	100.0%	8,203	3	8	30,964	100.0%	7,742	3	0.00%	0
Electorate		49,269	66.60%				51,951	59.60%			+6.99%	
Spoiled		451	1.36%				423	1.35%			+0.01%	
Turnout		33,262	67.51%				31,387	60.42%			+7.09%	

Transfer analysis

From	To	FG	LB	FF	SF	PBPA	GP	WP	Others	Non Trans
FG	2,780	1,663	474	226	248					169
		59.82%	17.05%	8.13%	8.92%					6.08%
LB	1,156	210	715	65	101	20	14	10	21	
		18.17%	61.85%	5.62%	8.74%	1.73%	1.21%	0.87%	1.82%	
FF	4,350	892	1,169		854					1,435
		20.51%	26.87%		19.63%					32.99%
PBPA	749	92	235	59	233					130
		12.28%	31.38%	7.88%	31.11%					17.36%
GP	358	44	112	28	111					63
		12.29%	31.28%	7.82%	31.01%					17.60%
WP	371	45	116	29	116					65
		12.13%	31.27%	7.82%	31.27%					17.52%
Others	959	140	217	74	195	52	16	16	115	134
		14.60%	22.63%	7.72%	20.33%	5.42%	1.67%	1.67%	11.99%	13.97%
Total	10,723	3,086	3,038	481	1,858	72	30	26	136	1,996
		28.78%	28.33%	4.49%	17.33%	0.67%	0.28%	0.24%	1.27%	18.61%

Dublin North-West

Candidate	Party	1st	2nd Shortall Surplus -1,156	3rd Larkin Votes	4th Loftus Votes	5th Keegan Mooney Dunne Holohan	6th Tormey Votes	7th Carey Votes
Shortall, Roisin*	**LB**	**9,359**	**8,203**	**8,203**	**8,203**	**8,203**	**8,203**	**8,203**
			+101	+13	+14	+628	+248	+854
Ellis, Dessie	**SF**	**7,115**	**7,216**	**7,229**	**7,243**	**7,871**	**8,119**	**8,973**
			+715	+11	+37	+632	+474	+1,169
Lyons, John	**LB**	**4,799**	**5,514**	**5,525**	**5,562**	**6,194**	**6,668**	**7,837**
			+95	+35	+14	+115	+1,663	+892
Breen, Gerry	FG	2,988	3,083	3,118	3,132	3,247	4,910	5,802
			+65	+21	+11	+158	+226	-4,350
Carey, Pat*	FF	3,869	3,934	3,955	3,966	4,124	4,350	Eliminated
			+115	+13	+12	+132	-2,780	
Tormey, Dr. Bill	FG	2,508	2,623	2,636	2,648	2,780	Eliminated	
			+20	+19	+33	-749		
Keegan, Andrew	PBPA	677	697	716	749	Eliminated		
			+11	+11	+84	-539		
Mooney, Sean	NP	433	444	455	539	Eliminated		
			+10	+7	+9	-371		
Dunne, John	WP	345	355	362	371	Eliminated		
			+14	+6	+10	-358		
Holohan, Ruairí	GP	328	342	348	358	Eliminated		
			+8	+20	-245			
Loftus, Michael J.	NV	217	225	245	Eliminated			
			+2	-175				
Larkin, Michael	CS	173	175	Eliminated				
Non-transferable				+19	+21	+352	+169	+1,435
Cumulative			0	19	40	392	561	1,996
Total		32,811	32,811	32,811	32,811	32,811	32,811	32,811

Seats 3 — Quota 8,203

Labour candidate for Dublin North-West John Lyons celebrates his election at the RDS count centre

Dublin South (5 seats)

Fine Gael takes three out of five as independent Shane Ross tops the poll with one of the biggest votes in this election

Elected
Shane Ross (Ind) Count 1, Alex White (Lab) Count 6, Olivia Mitchell* (FG) Final count, Peter Mathews (FG) Final count, Alan Shatter* (FG) Final count.

Analysis by Sean Donnelly

There were major Constituency Commission changes here since 2007. A population of 11,673 in the Cabinteely-Loughlinstown, Foxrock-Carrickmines, Foxrock-Torquay and Stillorgan-Leopardstown areas was transferred into this constituency from Dún Laoghaire. The constituency retained its five seats.

Seamus Brennan was elected here in 2007 but died in July 2008. Fine Gael's George Lee won the subsequent by-election in June 2009 but resigned his seat in February 2010. Outgoing Fianna Fáil TD Tom Kitt retired ahead of this election.

Fine Gael increased its vote by nine percentage points on 2007 and managed to convert 2.2 quotas into three seats with an excellent vote management performance. Olivia Mitchell was the party's leading vote-getter and took the third seat with 9,635 first preferences and was followed home by newcomer Peter Mathews, who took the fourth seat with 9,053. Alan Shatter had a tougher fight on his hands, winning just 7,716 first preferences to leave him in fifth place, 872 ahead of Maria Corrigan of Fianna Fáil. Shatter got the better of the transfer battle and extended his advantage to 1,448 by the final count.

The Labour vote was up eight percentage points and Alex White delivered on his strong June 2009 by-election performance, which he had been favoured to win prior to the arrival of George Lee. White got 8,524 on the first count and went on to take the second seat. His running mate Aidan Culhane got just 4,535 to leave him in eighth place and out of contention.

The big winner in this constituency was independent candidate and long-serving senator Shane Ross, who topped the poll with an impressive 17,075 first preferences or 1.41 quotas. He had the second best first-preference vote in the country behind Enda Kenny.

It was all change for Fianna Fáil as it contested this election without the names of Brennan or Kitt which had been on the ballot paper since 1981. The party selected outgoing senator Maria Corrigan but its vote collapsed and was down 32 percentage points to just 9.42%, its lowest in this election. Corrigan failed to make any inroads into her first count deficit of nearly 900 votes on Alan Shatter and was well beaten in the end.

The Green vote was down four percentage points and with just 7% Eamonn Ryan was in seventh place on the first count and virtually out of contention. Eight candidates failed to get enough votes to reclaim their expenses. This was a recurring feature of this historic election.

*outgoing TDs

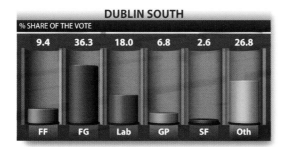

DUBLIN SOUTH

% SHARE OF THE VOTE

FF	FG	Lab	GP	SF	Oth
9.4	36.3	18.0	6.8	2.6	26.8

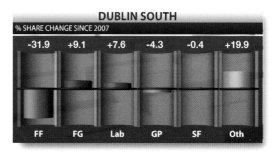

DUBLIN SOUTH

% SHARE CHANGE SINCE 2007

FF	FG	Lab	GP	SF	Oth
-31.9	+9.1	+7.6	-4.3	-0.4	+19.9

Dublin South

SHANE ROSS (Ind)

Home Address: Glenbrook, Enniskerry, Co Wicklow.
Phone: 01 2116692 (H) 01 6183014 (LH)
Email: shane.ross@oireachtas.ie
Website: www.shane-ross.ie
Twitter: @Shane_RossTD
Facebook: www.facebook.com/voteshaneross
Birth Place/Date: Dublin, July 1949.
Marital Status/Family: Married to Ruth Buchanan, broadcaster and journalist; 1 son, 1 daughter.
Education: St Stephen's School, Dundrum; Rugby School; Trinity College Dublin.
Occupation: Public representative. Author. Business editor, *Sunday Independent*.
Biography: Senator 1981-2011. Member Joint Committee on Transport and Member Joint Committee on Economic and Regulatory Affairs 2007-2011. Member Joint Committee on Enterprise and Small Business 2002-2007. Member British-Irish Parliamentary Body. Contested 1984 European election in Dublin. Member Wicklow County Council 1991-1999. Member board of Royal City of Dublin Hospital since 1982. Director of Barings New Russia Fund 1997. Director Banque Worms Haussmann International Fund Plc 1997. Honorary president of the Irish Institute of Industrial Engineers 1994-1996. Executive chairman ABMS Stockbrokers 1988-1990. He was the longest serving member of Seanad Éireann before winning the Dáil seat.
Hobbies: Tennis, walking, reading, food. Author of two best sellers *The Bankers* (jointly with journalist Nick Webb) and *Wasters*.
Did you know? Beware! He could be around for longer than most. Both his parents are alive and kicking.

ALEX WHITE (Lab)

Home Address: 1 Main Street, Rathfarnham, Dublin 14.
Contact: 01 6183972 (LH)
Email: alex.white@oireachtas.ie
Website: www.alexwhite.ie
Twitter: twitter.com/alexwhiteTD
Facebook: Yes.
Birth Place/Date: Dublin, December 1958.
Marital Status/Family: Married to Mary Corcoran; 1 daughter, 1 son.
Education: Chanel College, Coolock; Trinity College, Dublin (economics and social studies); King's Inns.
Occupation: Public representative and lawyer.
Biography: Secured 8,524 first-preference votes to get elected on the sixth count in his second general election. He unsuccessfully contested the 2007 general election and he has been a member of Seanad Éireann since then. He finished second to Fine Gael candidate George Lee in the 2009 Dublin South by-election. He was elected to South Dublin County Council in June 2004 and served as deputy mayor in 2006-2007.
He has been a practising barrister since 1994, and became a senior counsel in October 2010.
Hobbies: Music, cycling.
Did you know? Alex was a current affairs producer with RTÉ for 10 years and was producer of *The Gay Byrne Show* from 1990 until 1994.
Politician (living or deceased) you most admire: I'm not a man for heroes!
Priority as a TD? Job creation and economic recovery.
Why did you stand for election? To build a real republic through politics and active engagement, and put Ireland on a new course of recovery and reform.

OLIVIA MITCHELL (FG)

Home Address: 18 Ballawley Court, Dundrum, Dublin 16.
Phone: 01 6183088 (LH)
Email: olivia.mithcell@oireachtas.ie
Website: www.olivia.mitchell.finegael.ie
Twitter: @omitchellTD
Facebook: Yes.
Birth Place/Date: Birr, Co Offaly, July 1947.
Marital Status/family: Married to Jimmy; 2 sons, 1 daughter.
Education: Trinity College Dublin (BA, HDip Ed).
Occupation: Full-time public representative.
Biography: Olivia was elected for the fourth consecutive general election with 9,635 first-preference votes. She has been a TD for Dublin South since 1997 and has in that time been frontbench spokesperson for Arts, Sport and Tourism; Transport; Health; and Local Government. She was a county councillor from 1985 to 2003 representing both the Stillorgan and Glencullen areas on Dublin County Council and then Dún Laoghaire Rathdown County Council.
Hobbies: Reading, walking, gardening.
Did you know? Olivia got the country's highest female vote in Election 2011.
Politician (living or deceased) you most admire: WT Cosgrave.
Priority as a TD? Stop forced emigration by creating the conditions for growing jobs here in Ireland.
Why did you stand for election? The economic meltdown provides a huge opportunity to transform our governance and to improve the way we do almost everything.
Is there any particular event that brought home to you just how serious the economic crisis had become? When a young constituent told me she had more friends in Sydney and London than she had in Dublin.

PETER MATHEWS (FG)

Home Address: 64 The Rise, Mount Merrion, Co Dublin.
Phone: 086 1091500 (M) 01 6184443 (LH)
Email: peter.mathews@finegael.ie or peter.mathews@oireachtas.ie
Website: www.petermathewsfg.ie
Twitter: Yes.
Facebook: Yes.
Birth Place/Date: Dublin, August 1951.
Marital Status/Family: Married; 4 children.
Education: Gonzaga College, Dublin; UCD.
Occupation: Chartered accountant and consultant (banking and finance).
Biography: He secured 9,053 first-preference votes to get elected on the eighth and final count in his first attempt.
Hobbies: Tennis, golf, swimming, walking, bridge and reading.
Did you know? Peter ran two marathons and three mara-cycles to Belfast and back in the 1980s.
Politician (living or deceased) you most admire: Mahatma Gandhi.
Priority as a TD? To serve my constituency and my country.
Why did you stand for election? To offer my professional and business skills to the Dáil.
Is there any particular event that brought home to you just how serious the economic crisis had become? What really alarmed me was the government's approach from the first mooting of NAMA in April 2009 to the passing of the NAMA bill in the Dáil in early November 2009 and the fact that there was such a lack of proper measurement of the estimated loan loses on the banks' books, notably Anglo Irish Bank, Irish Nationwide, AIB, Bank of Ireland and EBS. There was also a failure to measure the banks' recapitalisation requirements.

ALAN SHATTER (FG)

Home Address: 57 Delbrook Manor, Ballinteer, Dublin 16.
Contact: 01 6183911 (LH) 01 6184135
Email: alan@alanshatter.com or alan.shatter@oireachtas.ie
Website: www.alanshatter.ie
Twitter: twitter.com/alanshatterTD
Facebook: Yes.
Birth Place/Date: Dublin, February 1951.
Marital Status/Family: Married to Carol Danker; 1 son, 1 daughter.
Education: High School, Dublin; Trinity College, Dublin; University of Amsterdam; Law School of the Incorporated Law Society.
Occupation: Public representative. Solicitor. Author.
Biography: Current Minister for Justice and Law Reform. First elected a TD in 1981, Alan was returned at every election up to 2002, when he lost his seat. He was re-elected in 2007. He was Fine Gael spokesperson on: Justice (June 2010-February 2011); Children (2007-2010); Justice, Law Reform and Defence (2000-2002); Health and Children (1997-2000); Equality and Law Reform (1993-1994); Justice (1992-1993); Labour (1991); Environment (1989-1991); Law Reform (1982, 1987-1988). Alan has served on a number of Dáil Committees including: the Joint Oireachtas Committee on Foreign Affairs, the Joint Oireachtas Committee on the Constitutional Amendment on Children and other committees on Women's Rights; Marital Breakdown; Building Land; Childcare; Bankruptcy and Crime.
Member, Dublin County Council 1979-1993, South Dublin County Council 1994-1999. Former chairman of Free Legal Advice Centres (FLAC).
Hobbies: Soccer, athletics, table tennis.
Did you know? In 1977, Alan published his book *Family Law in the Republic of Ireland* which was the first major academic and social commentary on Irish family law. In 1979 he published a satirical booklet, *Family Planning Irish Style,* which poked fun at contraception laws. In 1989 he published a novel called *Laura.*

Election Facts
"The independents and others (such as the United Left Alliance) have collectively scored more first preference votes than Fianna Fáil"
Millward Brown Lansdowne/RTÉ General Election 2011 Exit Poll

Dublin South

		Seats	5			12,108		
	Candidate	Party	1st	%	Quota	Count	Status
1	Ross, Shane	NP	17,075	23.50%	1.41	1	Made Quota
2	White, Alex	LB	8,524	11.73%	0.70	6	Made Quota
3	Mitchell, Olivia*	FG	9,635	13.26%	0.80	8	Made Quota
4	Mathews, Peter	FG	9,053	12.46%	0.75	8	Elected
5	Shatter, Alan*	FG	7,716	10.62%	0.64	8	Elected
6	Corrigan, Maria	FF	6,844	9.42%	0.57	8	Not Elected
7	Ryan, Eamonn*	GP	4,929	6.78%	0.41	7	Eliminated
8	Culhane, Aidan	LB	4,535	6.24%	0.37	5	Eliminated
9	Nic Cormaic, Sorcha	SF	1,915	2.64%	0.16	4	No Expenses
10	Curry, Nicola	PBPA	1,277	1.76%	0.11	3	No Expenses
11	Murphy, Jane	CS	277	0.38%	0.02	2	No Expenses
12	Hussein Hamed, Buhidma	NP	273	0.38%	0.02	2	No Expenses
13	Doyle, John	NP	246	0.34%	0.02	2	No Expenses
14	Dolan, Gerard	NP	156	0.21%	0.01	2	No Expenses
15	Whitehead, Raymond	NP	120	0.17%	0.01	2	No Expenses
16	Zaidan, Eamonn	NP	71	0.10%	0.01	2	No Expenses

*Outgoing TD Valid poll: 72,646 Quota: 12,108 No expenses limit: 3,027

Party votes

		2011					2007				Change	
Party	Cand	1st	%	Quota	Seats	Cand	1st	%	Quota	Seats	%	Seats
FG	3	26,404	36.35%	2.18	3	3	16,686	27.26%	1.64	2	+9.08%	+1
LB	2	13,059	17.98%	1.08	1	2	6,384	10.43%	0.63		+7.55%	+1
FF	1	6,844	9.42%	0.57		3	25,298	41.33%	2.48	2	-31.91%	-2
SF	1	1,915	2.64%	0.16		2	1,843	3.01%	0.18		-0.38%	
PBPA	1	1,277	1.76%	0.11							+1.76%	
GP	1	4,929	6.78%	0.41		1	6,768	11.06%	0.66	1	-4.27%	-1
CS	1	277	0.38%	0.02							+0.38%	
PD						1	4,045	6.61%	0.40		-6.61%	
Others	6	17,941	24.70%	1.48	1	1	180	0.29%	0.02		+24.40%	+1
Total	16	72,646	100.0%	12,108	5	13	61,204	100.0%	10,201	5	0.00%	0
Electorate	102,387	70.95%				89,464	68.41%				+2.54%	
Spoiled	459	0.63%				418	0.68%				-0.05%	
Turnout	73,105	71.40%				61,622	68.88%				+2.52%	

Transfer analysis

From	To	FG	LB	FF	SF	PBPA	GP	Others	Non Trans
LB	7,786	2,074	3,796	368			1,212		336
		26.64%	48.75%	4.73%			15.57%		4.32%
SF	2,617	340	1,119	164			322		672
		12.99%	42.76%	6.27%			12.30%		25.68%
PBPA	1,664	190	572	68	431		172		231
		11.42%	34.38%	4.09%	25.90%		10.34%		13.88%
GP	7,332	4,312		1,231					1,789
		58.81%		16.79%			0.00%		24.40%
Others	6,412	2,740	1,348	488	271	387	697	302	179
		42.73%	21.02%	7.61%	4.23%	6.04%	10.87%	4.71%	2.79%
Total	25,811	9,656	6,835	2,319	702	387	2,403	302	3,207
		37.41%	26.48%	8.98%	2.72%	1.50%	9.31%	1.17%	12.42%

Count details

Candidate	Party	1st	2nd Ross Surplus	3rd Murphy Hussein Doyle Dolan Whitehed Zaidan	4th Curry Votes	5th Nic Cormaic Votes	6th Culhane Votes	7th White Surplus	8th Ryan Votes
								Quota	12,108
			-4,967						
Ross, Shane	NP	17,075	12,108	12,108	12,108	12,108	12,108	12,108	12,108
			+795	*+148*	*+280*	*+660*	*+3,796*	*-2,095*	
White, Alex	LB	8,524	9,319	9,467	9,747	10,407	14,203	12,108	12,108
			+819	*+123*	*+84*	*+102*	*+396*	*+468*	*1,752*
Mitchell, Olivia*	FG	9,635	10,454	10,577	10,661	10,763	11,159	11,627	13,379
									+1,250
Mathews, Peter	FG	9,053	9,805	9,987	10,047	10,173	10,494	10,820	12,070
			+783	*+81*	*+46*	*+112*	*+228*	*+335*	*+1,310*
Shatter, Alan*	FG	7,716	8,499	8,580	8,626	8,738	8,966	9,301	10,611
			+324	*+164*	*+68*	*+164*	*+198*	*+170*	*+1,231*
Corrigan, Maria	FF	6,844	7,168	7,332	7,400	7,564	7,762	7,932	9,163
			+560	*+137*	*+172*	*+322*	*+416*	*+796*	*-7,332*
Ryan, Eamonn*	GP	4,929	5,489	5,626	5,798	6,120	6,536	7,332	*Eliminated*
			+304	*+101*	*+292*	*+459*	*-5,691*		
Culhane, Aidan	LB	4,535	4,839	4,940	5,232	5,691	*Eliminated*		
			+150	*+121*	*+431*	*-2,617*			
Nic Cormaic, Sorcha	SF	1,915	2,065	2,186	2,617	*Eliminated*			
			+178	*+209*	*-1,664*				
Curry, Nicola	PBPA	1,277	1,455	1,664	*Eliminated*				
			+19	*-296*					
Murphy, Jane	CS	277	296	*Eliminated*					
			+45	*-318*					
Hussein Hamed, Buhidma	NP	273	318	*Eliminated*					
			+97	*-343*					
Doyle, John	NP	246	343	*Eliminated*					
			+36	*-192*					
Dolan, Gerard	NP	156	192	*Eliminated*					
			+91	*-211*					
Whitehead, Raymond	NP	120	211	*Eliminated*					
			+14	*-85*					
Zaidan, Eamonn	NP	71	85	*Eliminated*					
Non-transferable				+179	+231	+672	+336		+1,789
Cumulative			0	179	410	1,082	1,418	1,418	3,207
Total		72,646	72,646	72,646	72,646	72,646	72,646	72,646	72,646

Seats 5

Dublin South TDs (from left) Alan Shatter, Peter Mathews and Olivia Mitchell address the media on the plinth in Leinster House

Dublin South-Central (5 seats)

The left sweeps the board to take four out of five seats

Elected

Eric Byrne (Lab) Count 8, Catherine Byrne* (FG) Count 12, Michael Conaghan (Lab) Final count, Joan Collins (PBP) Final count, Aengus Ó Snodaigh (SF) Final count.

Analysis by Michael Gallagher

There were no constituency boundary changes here since 2007. In the People's Republic of Dublin South-Central the left virtually swept the board, taking four of the five seats. Labour took pole position with 35% of the votes, its third best performance in the country, and two of its three candidates were elected. The main surprise was that Henry Upton, nephew and son of the two previous Labour incumbents, was the one to lose out, being outpolled by former TD Eric Byrne and by the new TD, though veteran councillor, Michael Conaghan. Byrne, who had missed out on a seat by five votes in 1992 and by 69 votes in 2007, headed the poll this time.

Sinn Féin's Aengus Ó Snodaigh was comfortably re-elected to a third term, and the other left-wing seat was taken by Joan Collins of People before Profit, part of the United Left Alliance. She virtually trebled her 2007 vote, and while her TV cameo berating Bertie Ahern outside Leinster House no doubt helped her profile, she was probably on course for a seat anyway.

The Fine Gael vote rose by 9%, but this was enough only to retain the seat it already held through Catherine Byrne (the only former professional footballer in the Dáil), with neither of her running mates coming close.

Most striking, perhaps, was the failure of Fianna Fáil, represented by Michael Mulcahy following the retirement of Seán Ardagh, to win a seat in this former stronghold. With Seán Lemass leading its team, the party won 55% of the votes here in 1951; now, it could not win even 10%.

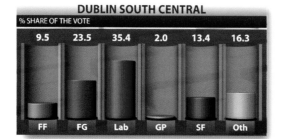

DUBLIN SOUTH CENTRAL
% SHARE OF THE VOTE

FF	FG	Lab	GP	SF	Oth
9.5	23.5	35.4	2.0	13.4	16.3

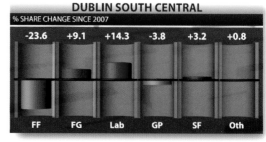

DUBLIN SOUTH CENTRAL
% SHARE CHANGE SINCE 2007

FF	FG	Lab	GP	SF	Oth
-23.6	+9.1	+14.3	-3.8	+3.2	+0.8

*outgoing TDs

ERIC BYRNE (Lab)

Address: Dáil Éireann, Leinster House, Dublin 2.
Phone: 01 6183223 (LH)
Website: www.ericbyrne.ie
Email: eric.byrne@oireachtas.ie
Twitter: @EricByrneTD
Facebook: Yes.
Birth Place/Date: Dublin, April 1947.
Marital Status/Family: Married; 2 children.
Education: Synge Street School, Dublin; Bolton Street College of Technology.
Occupation: Public representative.
Biography: I am known as an activist politician and have always believed, that as a public representative, people matter most. I have campaigned on several wide-ranging issues such as the preservation of the swimming pool in Pearse Park, the development of proper childcare facilities across Dublin South-Central, and the right to a living wage.
Hobbies: Hill-walking.
Did you know? Eric was known as 'The Marathon Man' – in relation to the 10-day count and subsequent recounts in the 1992 general election.
Politician (living or deceased) you most admire: Nelson Mandela.
Priority as a TD? Job creation. I believe that jobs are the cornerstone of our country's economic recovery.
Why did you stand for election? Since my youth I have believed politics is about standing with those who bear the impact of social, political and economic justice. Today I believe that more than ever.
Is there any particular event that brought home to you just how serious the economic crisis had become? The arrival of the IMF.

CATHERINE BYRNE (FG)

Home Address: 30 Bulfin Road, Inchicore, Dublin 8.
Phone: 086 8543276 (M) 01 6183083 (LH)
Website: www.catherinebyrne.finegael.ie
Email: catherine.byrne@oir.ie
Twitter: No.
Facebook: Yes.
Birth Place/Date: Dublin, February 1956.
Marital Status/Family: Married to Joseph Byrne; 5 children, 1 grand-daughter.
Education: Our Lady of the Wayside NS, Bluebell; Holy Faith The Coombe; Holy Faith Clarendon Street.
Occupation: Housewife and public representative.
Biography: First elected to Dublin City Council (South-West Inner City) in 1999; Lord Mayor of Dublin 2005-2006; First elected to the Dáil in 2007, and re-elected in 2011.
Hobbies: Singing, cooking.
Did you know? Catherine played League of Ireland women's soccer, and sang in a band in the 1970s.
Politician (living or deceased) you most admire: Mary Banotti.
Priority as a TD? Ensuring there is more equality in our society; giving a voice to the voiceless.
Why did you stand for election? It was a natural progression from working as a volunteer in my community.
Is there any particular event that brought home to you just how serious the economic crisis had become? Seeing people losing their jobs, the closure of small businesses in the community, and seeing young people trapped with huge mortgages.

MICHAEL CONAGHAN (Lab)

Home Address: 33 Lally Road, Ballyfermot, Dublin 10.
Phone: 01 6269892 (H) 086 1753747 (M) 01 6184033 (LH)
Website: www.labour.ie/michaelconaghan/
Birth Place/Date: Donegal, September 1944.
Marital Status/Family: Married; 2 daughters.
Education: Ard Scoil na gCeithre Maistir, Donegal Town; Manchester University; UCD.
Occupation: Public representative. Formerly a teacher for 33 years at Inchicore College of Further Education.
Biography: Secured 5,492 first-preference votes to get elected on the 13th and final count. Conaghan ran as an independent in November 1982, 1987, 1989 and 1997. Contested the February 1982 election for the Democratic Social Party led by the Limerick socialist Jim Kemmy. He joined the Labour Party in 1991 and he was elected to Dublin City Council in the 1991, 1999, 2004 and 2009 local elections.
Hobbies: Local history and heritage.
Did you know? Michael emigrated to England and worked in construction for years to save money to go to college and become a teacher.
Politician (living or deceased) you most admire: Jim Kemmy.
Priority as a TD? To make sure Labour's employment policies can impact locally in areas such as Ballyfermot. Community, arts and education development. To make sure that the industrial heritage part of our culture is not abandoned.
Why did you stand for election? Labour has concrete and practical solutions that are capable of being translated into local action.
Is there any particular event that brought home to you just how serious the economic crisis had become? The growth of unemployment figures in working-class areas and the knock-on effects that brings about in terms of the pressure people are put under.

Dublin South-Central

JOAN COLLINS (PBPA)

Home Address: 30 Ring Street, Inchicore, Dublin 8.
Phone: 086 3888151 (M) 01 6183215 (LH)
Website: www.joan-collins.org
Twitter: CllrJoanCollins
Facebook: Cllr Joan Collins
Birth Place/Date: Dublin, June 1961.
Marital Status/Family: Partner Dermot Connolly; Dermot's 2 children.
Education: St John of God Secondary School, Coolock.
Occupation: Post office clerk with An Post.
Biography: Secured 6,574 first-preference votes to get elected on the 13th count in her second general election attempt. Elected as independent councillor in the Crumlin/Kimmage ward in the 2004 local elections and re-elected as a People Before Profit Alliance councillor in the 2009 local elections. Involved in numerous campaigns such as the anti-water tax and anti-bin charge campaigns.
Hobbies: Sports, reading and time out with family.
Did you know? Joan became a YouTube hit and featured on BBC's *Panorama* when she confronted former Taoiseach Bertie Ahern outside the Dáil and asked him if he had any shame over his role in the economic collapse.
Politician (living or deceased) you most admire: Emily Pankhurst.
Priority as a TD? Job creation and to protect community resources and people.
Why did you stand for election? To offer a clear 'left' radical alternative. Our country has been brought to its knees by the recklessness of a wealthy elite aided and abetted by corrupt and incompetent politicians. We need real change; fighters for ordinary people in Dáil Éireann. Fine Gael and Labour will not deliver that change.
Is there any particular event that brought home to you just how serious the economic crisis had become? Probably the most visual event was the picture of the IMF team walking past a guy begging on the streets of Dublin. It had an air of the big bullies are in town and we are on our knees.

AENGUS Ó SNODAIGH (SF)

Constituency Address: 347 Ballyfermot Road, Dublin.
Phone: 01 6259320 (H) 01 6184084 (LH)
Website: www.aengusosnodaigh.ie
Twitter: twitter.com/aosnodaigh
Facebook: facebook/aengus o snodaigh TD
Birth Place/Date: Baile Átha Cliath, July 1964.
Marital Status/Family: Married to Aisling; 3 children.
Education: Coláiste Eoin, Dublin; University College Dublin. Fluent Irish speaker.
Occupation: Full-time public representative.
Biography: Aengus was first elected in 2002 and re-elected in 2007 and is currently Sinn Féin's spokesperson on Social Protection. He is also party whip. Bhí Aengus gafa le athchóiriú Teach na bPiarsaigh maraon le bheith ar coiste Áth Cliath '98 agus Emmet 200 agus is ball é den Coiste Uile-pháirtí Comóradh 1916. A member of the Ballyfermot Drugs Taskforce, Aengus is also treasurer of Bluebell Community Development Project (CDP) and a board member of Liberties Recycling.
Did you know? Similar to all other Sinn Féin Oireachtas members, Aengus only draws the average industrial wage. The surplus of his Leinster House income is used to fund a full-time constituency advice service and to keep constituents informed of local and national developments.
Politician (living or deceased) you most admire: Bobby Sands.
Priority as a TD? To create an equal society in a united Ireland.
Why did you stand for election? To pursue the above goal.

First preference votes

	Candidate	Seats	5			8,488	
	Candidate	Party	1st	%	Quota	Count
1	Byrne, Eric	LB	8,357	16.41%	0.98	8
2	Byrne, Catherine*	FG	5,604	11.00%	0.66	12
3	Conaghan, Michael	LB	5,492	10.78%	0.65	13
4	Collins, Joan	PBPA	6,574	12.91%	0.77	13
5	Ó Snodaigh, Aengus*	SF	6,804	13.36%	0.80	13
6	Mulcahy, Michael*	FF	4,837	9.50%	0.57	13
7	Brophy, Colm	FG	3,376	6.63%	0.40	11
8	Upton, Henry	LB	4,183	8.21%	0.49	10
9	McGinley, Ruairí	FG	2,976	5.84%	0.35	8
10	Ó hAlmhain, Oisín	GP	1,015	1.99%	0.12	7
11	O'Neill, Peter	NP	456	0.90%	0.05	7
12	Bradley, Neville	NP	323	0.63%	0.04	7
13	Callanan, Colm	CS	239	0.47%	0.03	6
14	Connolly Farrell, Seán	NP	178	0.35%	0.02	5
15	King, Paul	NP	146	0.29%	0.02	4
16	Kelly, Gerry	NP	137	0.27%	0.02	3
17	Bennett, Noel	NP	128	0.25%	0.02	2
18	Mooney, Dominic	NP	102	0.20%	0.01	1

*Outgoing TD #Former TD Valid poll: 50,927 Quota: 8,488 No expenses limit: 2,122

Party votes

Party	Cand	2011 1st	%	Quota	Seats	Cand	2007 1st	%	Quota	Seats	Change %	Seats
FG	3	11,956	23.48%	1.41	1	2	6,838	14.39%	0.86	1	+9.09%	
LB	3	18,032	35.41%	2.12	2	2	10,041	21.13%	1.27	1	+14.28%	+1
FF	1	4,837	9.50%	0.57		2	15,725	33.08%	1.99	2	-23.59%	-2
SF	1	6,804	13.36%	0.80	1	1	4,825	10.15%	0.61	1	+3.21%	
PBPA	1	6,574	12.91%	0.77	1						+12.91%	+1
GP	1	1,015	1.99%	0.12		1	2,756	5.80%	0.35		-3.81%	
WP						1	256	0.54%	0.03		-0.54%	
CS	1	239	0.47%	0.03							+0.47%	
PD						2	912	1.92%	0.12		-1.92%	
Others	7	1,470	2.89%	0.17		5	6,178	13.00%	0.78		-10.11%	
Total	18	50,927	100.0%	8,488	5	16	47,531	100.0%	7,922	5	0.00%	0
Electorate		80,268	63.45%				86,710	54.82%			+8.63%	
Spoiled		817	1.58%				789	1.63%			-0.05%	
Turnout		51,744	64.46%				48,320	55.73%			+8.74%	

Transfer analysis

From	To	FG	LB	FF	SF	PBPA	GP	Others	Non Trans
FG	11,706	6,597	1,973	823	334	780			1,199
		56.36%	16.85%	7.03%	2.85%	6.66%			10.24%
LB	4,980	1,017	2,447	279	344	607			286
		20.42%	49.14%	5.60%	6.91%	12.19%			5.74%
GP	1,051	254	371	66	81	178			101
		24.17%	35.30%	6.28%	7.71%	16.94%			9.61%
Others	1,991	370	503	156	156	320	36	282	168
		18.58%	25.26%	7.84%	7.84%	16.07%	1.81%	14.16%	8.44%
Total	19,728	8,238	5,294	1,324	915	1,885	36	282	1,754
		41.76%	26.83%	6.71%	4.64%	9.55%	0.18%	1.43%	8.89%

Dublin South-Central

Count details

Seats: 5 **Quota:** 8,488

Candidate	Party	1st	2nd (Mooney Votes)	3rd (Bennett Votes)	4th (Kelly Votes)	5th (King Votes)	6th (Connolly Votes)	7th (Callanana Votes)	8th (Ó hAlmhain O'Neill Bradley)	9th (McGinley Votes)	10th (Byrne, E Surplus)	11th (Upton Votes)	12th (Brophy Votes)	13th (Byrne, C. Surplus)
Byrne, Eric	LB	8,357	+10 8,367	+13 8,380	+11 8,391	+10 8,401	+10 8,411	+5 8,416	+305 8,721	8,721	−233 8,488	8,488	8,488	8,488
Byrne, Catherine*	FG	5,604	+6 5,610	+4 5,614	+4 5,618	+8 5,626	+4 5,630	+33 5,663	+252 5,915	+1,205 7,120	+22 7,142	+638 7,780	+4,087 11,867	−3,379 8,488
Conaghan, Michael	LB	5,492	+5 5,497	+4 5,501	+4 5,505	+4 5,509	+28 5,537	+7 5,544	+182 5,726	+93 5,819	+85 5,904	+2,290 8,194	+269 8,463	+1,395 9,858
Collins, Joan	PBPA	6,574	+11 6,585	+21 6,606	+24 6,630	+23 6,653	+38 6,691	+37 6,728	+344 7,072	+94 7,166	+28 7,194	+579 7,773	+205 7,978	+481 8,459
Ó Snodaigh, Aengus*	SF	6,804	+15 6,819	+6 6,825	+13 6,838	+11 6,849	+25 6,874	+11 6,885	+156 7,041	+70 7,111	+12 7,123	+332 7,455	+114 7,569	+150 7,719
Mulcahy, Michael*	FF	4,837	+7 4,844	+1 4,845	+5 4,850	+15 4,865	+4 4,869	+63 4,932	+127 5,059	+127 5,186	+9 5,195	+270 5,465	+233 5,698	+463 6,161
Brophy, Colm	FG	3,376	+1 3,377	+7 3,384	+3 3,387	+6 3,393	+3 3,396	+22 3,418	+119 3,537	+1,305 4,842	+5 4,847	+352 5,199	−5,199 Eliminated	
Upton, Henry	LB	4,183	+4 4,187	+5 4,192	+16 4,208	+10 4,218	+8 4,226	+5 4,231	+228 4,459	+216 4,675	+72 4,747	−4,747 Eliminated		
McGinley, Ruairí	FG	2,976	+4 2,980	+3 2,983	2,983	+8 2,991	+5 2,996	+14 3,010	+118 3,128	−3,128 Eliminated				
Ó hAlmhain, Oisín	GP	1,015	1,015	+4 1,019	+12 1,031	+7 1,038	+4 1,042	+9 1,051	−1,051 Eliminated					
O'Neill, Peter	NP	456	+9 465	+4 469	+10 479	+22 501	+38 539	+10 549	−549 Eliminated					
Bradley, Neville	NP	323	+5 328	+36 364	+4 368	+23 391	+19 410	+15 425	−425 Eliminated					
Callanan, Colm	CS	239	239	+2 241	+5 246	+1 247	+4 251	−251 Eliminated						
Connolly Farrell, Seán	NP	178	+4 182	+8 190	+8 198	+19 217	−217 Eliminated							
King, Paul	NP	146	+10 156	+2 158	+18 176	−176 Eliminated								
Kelly, Gerry	NP	137	+2 139	+4 143	−143 Eliminated									
Bennett, Noel	NP	128	128	−128 Eliminated										
Mooney, Dominic	NP	102	−102 Eliminated											
Non-transferable			+9	+4	+6	+9	+27	+20	+194	+18		+286	+291	+890
Cumulative			9	13	19	28	55	75	269	287	287	573	864	1,754
Total		50,927	50,927	50,927	50,927	50,927	50,927	50,927	50,927	50,927	50,927	50,927	50,927	50,927

Election Facts

"With 2.1 quotas, Dublin South-Central was Labour's top constituency per quota in Election 2011" Sean Donnelly

Dublin South-East (4 seats)

Fine Gael and Labour share the four seats

Elected

Ruairí Quinn* (Lab) Count 6, Lucinda Creighton* (FG) Count 6, Eoghan Murphy (FG) Count 9, Kevin Humphreys (Lab) Final count.

Analysis by Sean Donnelly

There were no boundary changes here since 2007 and it remained a four-seat constituency. This was another good performance by Fine Gael as its vote was up 17 percentage points and with 1.8 quotas the party comfortably took two seats. Outgoing deputy Lucinda Creighton topped the poll with 6,619 first preferences and was close to the quota on the first count. She went on to take the second seat on the sixth count. She was followed home by Eoghan Murphy who was in second place with 5,783 on the first count and he went on to take the third seat.

The Labour vote was up nine percentage points and the party managed to convert just 1.3 quotas into two seats at the expense of Fianna Fáil. Ruairí Quinn took the first seat with 5,407 first preferences. Kevin Humphreys had a much tougher battle as he had only half a quota on the first count and trailed Chris Andrews by 472 votes. But he won the transfer battle, in particular from independent Paul Sommerville, and went on to extend his lead over the Fianna Fáil candidate, taking the final seat by over 1,200 votes.

This constituency was another disappointment for Fianna Fáil with its vote down 17.5 percentage points to just 11%, one of the party's lowest in this election. Outgoing deputy Chris Andrews was in fourth place

on the first count, ahead of Humphreys, but was beaten by the Labour man on every count except one and Andrews duly lost his seat on the 10th and final count.

This was another poor performance by the Greens with John Gormley's vote halved to just 7%. He was in seventh place on the first count and never in contention.

Eight independents contested this area with Paul Sommerville and Dylan Haskins the only ones to get enough votes to reclaim their expenses. The business candidate Sommerville had a good media profile going into this election but it was not enough to put him in contention for a seat. One of the independents, Peadar Ó Ceallaigh, got just 18 first preferences, the lowest by any of the 566 candidates that contested this election and the second lowest on record, behind Maria McCool who got 13 first preferences in Dublin North-West in 1997.

The turnout was up seven percentage points to 60.54% in this constituency but it still had the lowest turnout of any constituency in this election, as it had in 2007.

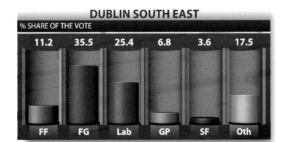

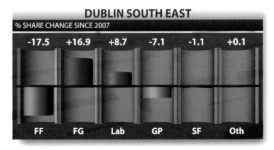

*outgoing TDs

Dublin South-East

RUAIRÍ QUINN (Lab)

Home Address: 23 Strand Road, Sandymount, Dublin 4.
Phone: 01 8896400 (Office)
Email: ruairi_quinn@education.gov.ie
Website: http://www.labour.ie/ruairiquinn/ or http://www.education.ie/
Birth Place/Date: April 1946.
Marital Status/Family: Married.
Education: Bachelor of Architecture; Higher Diploma in Ekistics.
Occupation: Architect.
Biography: Secured 5,407 first-preference votes to get elected to the seat he first won in 1977. Minister for Education and Skills. Unsuccessfully contested 1973 and 1981 general elections. Member of Seanad Éireann 1973-1977 and 1981-1982. Re-elected to the Dáil in 1982 and eight subsequent general elections. Labour spokesperson for: Education and Science 2007-2011; Enterprise Trade and Employment 2004-2007; European Affairs: 2002-2004. Labour Party leader (November 1997-October 2002); Minister for Finance (1994-1997); Minister for Enterprise and Employment (1993-1994); Minister for Public Service (1986-1987); Minister for Labour (1984-1987); Minister of State for the Environment (1982-1983). Member, Dublin City Council (1974-1977).
Hobbies: Hill walking, reading and gardening.
Politician (living or deceased) you most admire: François Mitterrand.
Priority as a TD? To transform Irish education.
Why did you stand for election? To bring about social and political change.
Is there any particular event that brought home to you just how serious the economic crisis had become? The disastrous management of the Irish economy by the Fianna Fáil/Green government has effectively put this country into economic receivership. We have lost a part of our economic sovereignty. We now have to make painful corrections to our public finances so we can pay our own way again.

LUCINDA CREIGHTON (FG)

Home Address: 75 Wilfield Road, Sandymount, Dublin 4.
Phone: 01 6194399 (O)
Email: Lucinda.creighton@taoiseach.gov.ie
Website: www.lucindacreighton.ie
Birth Place/Date: Mayo, January 1980.
Marital Status/Family: Married to Senator Paul Bradford.
Education: TCD (LLB 2002); New York Bar (2003); King's Inns (BL 2005); DCU (MA international relations 2011).
Occupation: Full-time public representative. Barrister.
Biography: Secured 6,619 first-preference votes to top the poll and regain the Dáil seat she first won in 2007. Currently Minister of State for European Affairs. Was Fine Gael spokesperson on European Affairs in 30th Dáil. Member of Dublin City Council 2004-2007.
Hobbies: Horse riding, running, reading, cooking and most sports.
Politician (living or deceased) you most admire: Chris Patten, John Bruton, Des O'Malley.
Priority as a TD? Restoring public confidence in politics.
Why did you stand for election? To practise what I preach.
Is there any particular event that brought home to you just how serious the economic crisis had become? Meeting a couple in my clinic who could not afford a uniform and shoes for their child to go to school.

EOGHAN MURPHY (FG)

Home Address: Apt 15, Block 2, Gallery Quay, Dublin 2.
Phone: 086 0863832 (M) 01 6183324 (LH)
Website: www.eoghanmurphy.ie
Email: eoghan.murphy@oireachtas.ie
Twitter: twitter.com/MurphyEoghan
Facebook: Eoghan Murphy
Birth Place/Date: April 1982.
Marital Status/Family: Single.
Education: St Mary's Star of the Sea boys' NS; St Michael's College; UCD (English and philosophy BA); King's College London (MA international relations).
Occupation: Full-time public representative.
Biography: Eoghan secured over 5,800 first-preference votes in Election 2011. He was first elected to Dublin City Council in 2009.
Before entering politics, Eoghan worked in international arms control, mostly in the area of nuclear weapon disarmament.
Hobbies: Reading biographies, adventure racing and eating burritos.
Did you know? Eoghan is one of six siblings.
Politician (living or deceased) you most admire: President John F Kennedy.
Priority as a TD? To reform our political system and its structures and to help improve Ireland's reputation abroad.
Why did you stand for election? I didn't believe that we had been served well by our politicians, nor did I believe they represented the majority of people. I bring international experience to national politics having spent four years working for organisations such as the United Nations and with the European Union on some of the most serious international issues, such as nuclear weapon disarmament.
Is there any particular event that brought home to you just how serious the economic crisis had become? In September 2010, I started putting my campaign team together for the election. By 2011, more than 10 had left the country through forced emigration. It quickly brought home to me the reality of our economic situation.

KEVIN HUMPHREYS (Lab)

Home Address: 14 O'Connell Gardens, Dublin 4.
Phone: 01 6686854 (H) 087 2989103 (M) 01 6183224 (LH)
Website: www.kevinhumphreys.ie
Twitter: twitter.com/khumphreysTD
Facebook: Yes.
Birth Place/Date: Dublin, 4 February 1958.
Marital Status/Family: Married to Catherine; 2 children.
Education: Star of the Sea primary school; Ringsend Technical Institute secondary school.
Occupation: Full-time public representative.
Biography: Secured 3,450 first-preference votes to get elected on the final count in his first general election attempt. He was first elected to Dublin City Council in 1999. He was re-elected to the council in the 2004 and 2009 local election. He was elected Deputy Mayor of Dublin in June 2009.
Hobbies: Reading and cycling.
Priority as a TD? Create jobs.
Politician (living or deceased) you most admire: President Franklin D Roosevelt.
Is there any particular event that brought home to you just how serious the economic crisis had become? The number of people losing their jobs.

Green Party Leader John Gormley canvasses in Donnybrook

Dublin South-East

First preference votes

	Candidate	Seats	4			6,984		
	Candidate	Party	1st	%	Quota	Count	Status
1	Quinn, Rauirí*	LB	5,407	15.48%	0.77	6	Made Quota
2	Creighton, Lucinda*	FG	6,619	18.96%	0.95	6	Made Quota
3	Murphy, Eoghan	FG	5,783	16.56%	0.83	9	Made Quota
4	Humphreys, Kevin	LB	3,450	9.88%	0.49	10	Elected
5	Andrews, Chris*	FF	3,922	11.23%	0.56	10	Not Elected
6	Sommerville, Paul	NP	2,343	6.71%	0.34	8	Eliminated
7	Gormley, John*	GP	2,370	6.79%	0.34	5	Eliminated
8	Haskins, Dylan	NP	1,383	3.96%	0.20	4	Eliminated
9	MacAodháin, Ruadhán	SF	1,272	3.64%	0.18	3	No Expenses
10	Flynn, Mannix	NP	1,248	3.57%	0.18	2	No Expenses
11	Mooney, Annette	PBPA	629	1.80%	0.09	1	No Expenses
12	Sheehy, Hugh	NP	195	0.56%	0.03	1	No Expenses
13	Coyle, James	NP	164	0.47%	0.02	1	No Expenses
14	Watson, Noel	NP	89	0.25%	0.01	1	No Expenses
15	Keigher, John	NP	27	0.08%	0.00	1	No Expenses
16	Ó Ceallaigh, Peadar	FN	18	0.05%	0.00	1	No Expenses

*Outgoing TD Valid poll: 34,919 Quota: 6,984 No expenses limit: 1,747

Party votes

Party	2011					2007				Change	
	Cand	1st	%	Quota	Seats	Cand	1st	%	Quota	Seats	%	Seats
FG	2	12,402	35.52%	1.78	2	1	6,311	18.65%	0.93	1	+16.87%	+1
LB	2	8,857	25.36%	1.27	2	1	5,636	16.65%	0.83	1	+8.71%	+1
FF	1	3,922	11.23%	0.56		2	9,720	28.72%	1.44	1	-17.49%	-1
SF	1	1,272	3.64%	0.18		1	1,599	4.72%	0.24		-1.08%	
PBPA	1	629	1.80%	0.09							+1.80%	
GP	1	2,370	6.79%	0.34		1	4,685	13.84%	0.69	1	-7.06%	-1
PD						1	4,450	13.15%	0.66		-13.15%	
Others	8	5,467	15.66%	0.78		6	1,441	4.26%	0.21		+11.40%	
Total	16	34,919	100.0%	6,984	4	13	33,842	100.0%	6,769	4	0.00%	0
Electorate		58,217	59.98%				63,468	53.32%			+6.66%	
Spoiled		327	0.93%				292	0.86%			+0.07%	
Turnout		35,246	60.54%				34,134	53.78%			+6.76%	

Transfer analysis

From	To	FG	LB	FF	SF	GP	Others	Non Trans
FG	1,816	279	565	292			32	648
		15.36%	31.11%	16.08%			1.76%	35.68%
LB	571	102	345	47			77	
		17.86%	60.42%	8.23%			13.49%	
SF	1,549	101	642	101		112	368	225
		6.52%	41.45%	6.52%		7.23%	23.76%	14.53%
PBPA	629	76	153	33	75	36	232	24
		12.08%	24.32%	5.25%	11.92%	5.72%	36.88%	3.82%
GP	2,908	857	1,335	250			261	205
		29.47%	45.91%	8.60%			8.98%	7.05%
Others	7,390	1,967	2,079	548	202	390	953	1,251
		26.62%	28.13%	7.42%	2.73%	5.28%	12.90%	16.93%
Total	14,863	3,382	5,119	1,271	277	538	1,923	2,353
		22.75%	34.44%	8.55%	1.86%	3.62%	12.94%	15.83%

Count details

Candidate	Party	1st	2nd Mooney Sheehy Coyle Watson Keigher O Ceallaigh	3rd Flynn Votes	4th MacAodhá Votes	5th Haskins Votes	6th Gormley Votes	7th Quinn Surplus	8th Creighton Surplus	9th Sommervill Votes	10th Murphy Surplus
			Seats 4							Quota	6,984
Quinn, Ruairí*			+155	+238	+347	+453	+955	-571			
Quinn, Ruairí*	LB	5,407	5,562	5,800	6,147	6,600	7,555	6,984	6,984	6,984	6,984
			+75	+107	+54	+114	+459		-444		
Creighton, Lucinda*	FG	6,619	6,694	6,801	6,855	6,969	7,428	7,428	6,984	6,984	6,984
			+60	+48	+47	+198	+398	+102	+279	+1,441	-1,372
Murphy, Eoghan	FG	5,783	5,843	5,891	5,938	6,136	6,534	6,636	6,915	8,356	6,984
			+118	+196	+295	+235	+380	+345	+38	+837	+527
Humphreys, Kevin	LB	3,450	3,568	3,764	4,059	4,294	4,674	5,019	5,057	5,894	6,421
			+59	+78	+101	+88	+250	+47	+49	+356	+243
Andrews, Chris*	FF	3,922	3,981	4,059	4,160	4,248	4,498	4,545	4,594	4,950	5,193
			+150	+128	+194	+381	+261	+77	+32	-3,566	
Sommerville, Paul	NP	2,343	2,493	2,621	2,815	3,196	3,457	3,534	3,566	Eliminated	
			+65	+112	+112	+249	-2,908				
Gormley, John*	GP	2,370	2,435	2,547	2,659	2,908	Eliminated				
			+109	+262	+174	-1,928					
Haskins, Dylan	NP	1,383	1,492	1,754	1,928	Eliminated					
			+133	+144	-1,549						
MacAodháin, Ruadhán	SF	1,272	1,405	1,549	Eliminated						
			+155	-1,403							
Flynn, Mannix	NP	1,248	1,403	Eliminated							
			-629								
Mooney, Annette	PBPA	629	Eliminated								
			-195								
Sheehy, Hugh	NP	195	Eliminated								
			-164								
Coyle, James	NP	164	Eliminated								
			-89								
Watson, Noel	NP	89	Eliminated								
			-27								
Keigher, John	NP	27	Eliminated								
			-18								
Ó Ceallaigh, Peadar	FN	18	Eliminated								
Non-transferable			+43	+90	+225	+210	+205		+46	+932	+602
Cumulative			43	133	358	568	773	773	819	1,751	2,353
Total		34,919	34,919	34,919	34,919	34,919	34,919	34,919	34,919	34,919	34,919

Dublin South-East candidates, (from left) Fine Gael's Lucinda Creighton, Sinn Féin's Ruadrán Mac Aodháin, independent Dylan Haskins, Green Party leader John Gormley and independent Mannix Flynn at Dublin's Unitarian Church in February, where they took part in a public discussion on the proposed incinerator in Ringsend

Dublin South-West (4 seats)

Labour takes two seats with its second best vote share of Election 2011

Elected

Pat Rabbitte* (Lab) Count 1, Brian Hayes* (FG) Count 2, Seán Crowe (SF) Count 6, Eamonn Maloney (Lab) Final count.

Analysis by Michael Gallagher

There were no boundary changes to this four-seat constituency since 2007. With Fianna Fáil on the ropes nationally, this always looked like a constituency in which the party could lose both its seats, and so it proved. Even so, the scale of the slump was astonishing. Its two TDs had each won about 8,000 first preferences in 2007; now, neither even won as many as 3,000. The rivalry between them was intense. Conor Lenihan ended up nearly 400 votes behind Charlie O'Connor, whose 2,718 first preferences was probably less than the number of times he managed to work the word 'Tallaght' into media interviews.

Three of the four seats here were nailed down from the start. Former Labour leader Pat Rabbitte received nearly 13,000 first preferences, more than any other Labour candidate in the country. For Fine Gael, Brian Hayes easily retained the seat he had regained in 2007. In 2007, the defeat of Seán Crowe of Sinn Féin had been one of the most surprising results; he had lost his seat despite having been 1/20 with the bookies on polling day to retain it. In 2011, he comfortably took the third seat.

The only uncertainty was whether the fourth and final seat would go to Fine Gael or Labour. The first-preference distribution answered this: Labour took 4,000 votes more than Fine Gael, with Dublin South-West becoming its second strongest constituency in the country. Labour took 36% of the votes. Its second candidate, Eamonn Maloney, finished over 3,000 votes ahead of the Fine Gael runner-up Cáit Keane. Labour may not have won a seat in Donegal since 1927 but, in Maloney and Michael Conaghan (Dublin SC), it does have two Donegal men in the Dáil.

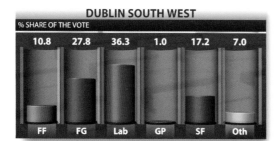

DUBLIN SOUTH WEST

% SHARE OF THE VOTE

FF	FG	Lab	GP	SF	Oth
10.8	27.8	36.3	1.0	17.2	7.0

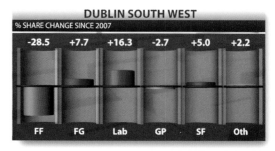

DUBLIN SOUTH WEST

% SHARE CHANGE SINCE 2007

FF	FG	Lab	GP	SF	Oth
-28.5	+7.7	+16.3	-2.7	+5.0	+2.2

*outgoing TDs

PAT RABBITTE (Lab)

Home Address: 56 Monastery Drive, Clondalkin, Dublin 22.
Phone: 01 6782004 (O) 01 6183772 (LH)
Email: minister.rabbitte@dcenr.gov.ie
Website: www.patrabbitte.ie
Facebook: Yes.
Birth Place/Date: Claremorris, Co Mayo, May 1949.
Marital Status/Family: Married; 3 daughters.
Education: St Colman's College, Claremorris, Co Mayo; University College, Galway (BA, HDipEd, LLB).
Occupation: Minister for Communications, Energy and Natural Resources.
Biography: Full-time public representative in Dublin South-West since 1989. Labour Party spokesperson on Justice. Leader of the Labour Party, October 2002-August 2007. Minister of State to the government and at the Department of Enterprise and Employment, with special responsibility for Commerce, Science and Technology and Consumer Affairs, 1994-1997. Member, Dublin County Council 1985-1995. Elected to South Dublin County Council 1999. National Secretary ITGWU (now SIPTU). President, Union of Students in Ireland 1972-1974. President, UCG Students' Union 1970-1971.
Hobbies: Reading a book, going to a match, drinking a pint.
Did you know? That Davitt's GAA Club in Ballindine, Co Mayo (home village) was opened in 1996 by Minister Rabbitte.
Politician (living or deceased) you most admire: Nye Bevan.
Priority as a TD? To help tackle inequality in Irish society.
Why did you stand for election? To offer people the choice of an alternative government in desperate economic circumstances and to be part of the struggle to turn around the economy.
Is there any particular event that brought home to you just how serious the economic crisis had become? A long queue for food by a charity in the inner city; senior citizens seeking to know: "is my few bob in the bank safe?"

BRIAN HAYES (FG)

Home Address: 48 Dunmore Park, Kingswood Heights, Dublin 24.
Phone: 01 6183567 (LH)
Website: www.brianhayes.ie
Twitter: twitter.com/brianhayestd
Facebook: facebook/Brian Hayes TD
Birth Place/Date: Dublin, August 1969.
Marital Status/Family: Married to Genevieve Deering; 3 children.
Education: Garbally College, Ballinasloe, Co Galway; St Patrick's College, Maynooth; Trinity College, Dublin.
Occupation: Full-time public representative.
Biography: Brian secured 9,366 first-preference votes and got elected on the second count in Dublin South-West. He was appointed Minister of State at the Department of Public Expenditure and Reform and at the Department of Finance with responsibility for Public Service Reform and OPW. Member South Dublin County Council (1995-2003). Taoiseach's nominee to the Seanad 1995. First elected a TD in 1997. Fine Gael spokesperson on Housing, House Prices and Urban Renewal (1997-2000); on Northern Ireland (2000-2001); Social and Community Affairs (2001-2002). He lost his seat at the 2002 general election but was elected to Seanad Éireann, where he served as Fine Gael party leader and spokesperson on Defence and Northern Ireland. Re-elected in 2007. Spokesperson for Education and Science (2007-2010) and spokesperson on Finance (October 2010-February 2011).
Hobbies: Golf and tennis.
Politican (living or deceased) you most admire: Robert Kennedy.
Priority as a TD? My priority as a TD is to help create jobs. Job creation is the number one issue in my own constituency in Dublin South-West as we have over 10,000 people unemployed. Fine Gael has serious and practical plans to get people back to work and I want to play my part in this.

SEÁN CROWE (SF)

Home Address: 16 Raithein Na Faiche, Tamhlacht, BAC 24.
Phone: 086 3864303 (M) 01 6183719 (LH)
Email: sean.crowe@oireachtas.ie
Website: www.seancrowe.ie
Facebook: Yes.
Birth Place/Date: Dublin, March 1957.
Marital Status/Family: Married.
Education: Junior School, Harolds' Cross; De La Salle National School, Nutgrove; Dundrum Technical School, Dundrum.
Occupation: Full-time public representative.
Biography: Party spokesperson on Education and Skills. First elected a TD in 2002. Lost seat in 2007 and regained seat in Election 2011. Unsuccessfully contested the 1989, 1992, 1997 general elections and 1999 Euro election. Previously spokesperson on Transport, Housing, Social and Family Affairs.
Member South Dublin County Council 1999-2003. Co-opted back onto council to replace Councillor Mark Daly in 2008 and re-elected in 2009.
Hobbies: Reading, sports, allotment holder.
Did you know? That Seán can trace his family history back to Dublin for generations.
Politician (living or deceased) you most admire: James Connolly.
Priority as a TD? Bringing greater equality and a republic based on the ideals and aspirations of the 1916 Proclamation "to pursue the happiness and prosperity of the nation and all its parts, cherishing all the children of the nation equally".
Why did you stand for election? To try and bring about a fairer and more inclusive society, giving a voice and representation to vast areas of my constituency that have largely been ignored.
Is there any particular event that brought home to you just how serious the economic crisis had become? I suppose seeing first-hand poverty and despair creeping back into areas of Dublin. Listening to the personal stories of scores of individuals and families that have no real hope of a decent job, that are struggling with bills, frightened of losing their home, seeing their children emigrating or abandoned to longer and longer dole queues.

Dublin South-West

EAMONN MALONEY (Lab)

Home Address: 84 St Maelruans Park, Tallaght, Dublin 24.
Phone: 01 6183588 (LH)
Email: eamonn.maloney@oir.ie
Facebook: Yes.
Birth Place/Date: Donegal, May 1952.
Marital Status/family: Married; 2 daughters, 1 son.
Education: Christian Brothers, Letterkenny; Letterkenny VEC.
Occupation: Full-time public representative. Worked with a recycling company until 2009 when he was made redundant after 23 years.
Biography: Secured 4,165 first-preference votes to get elected on the eighth and final count. He was first elected to South Dublin County Council in 1999 and re-elected at the 2004 and 2009 local elections.
Hobbies: Reading.
Did you know? Eamonn has a passionate interest in the heritage of Tallaght and is a regular contributor to the *Tallaght Echo* on Tallaght history. He is the author of *Tallaght A Place with History*, which was published in 2010.
Politician (living or deceased) you most admire: Jim Kemmy, 'The Limerick Socialist'.
Priority as a TD? Job creation.
Why did you stand for election? I have been a member of the Labour party since I was 14 years old. I came from a Labour family and my older brother was involved in the Labour Party before he went to Australia and joined the Australian Labour Party. We have always swapped political books and as I believe in socialist ideology I wanted to stand and try to implement it in the Dáil.
Is there any particular event that brought home to you just how serious the economic crisis had become? On a personal level, losing my own job but I have seen recessions before as I was in Ireland during the 1980s. The thing that slaps you in the face is the volume of young people leaving Ireland due to forced emigration.

Fianna Fáil leader Micheál Martin with election candidates Charlie O'Connor and Conor Lenihan at the launch of the party's Dublin South-West election campaign at Fettercairn Community Centre, Tallaght

Election Facts

"Prior to Election 2011, when Labour won 37 seats, the party's seat maximum was the 33 seats it won in 1992"
Professor Michael Gallagher, TCD

First preference votes

	Seats	4			9,393		
	Candidate	Party	1st	%	Quota	Count	Status
1	Rabbitte, Pat*	LB	12,867	27.40%	1.37	1	Made Quota
2	Hayes, Brian*	FG	9,366	19.94%	1.00	2	Made Quota
3	Crowe, Sean #	SF	8,064	17.17%	0.86	6	Made Quota
4	Maloney, Eamonn	LB	4,165	8.87%	0.44	8	Made Quota
5	Keane, Cait	FG	3,678	7.83%	0.39	8	Not Elected
6	O'Connor, Charlie*	FF	2,718	5.79%	0.29	7	Eliminated
7	Murphy, Mick	SP	2,462	5.24%	0.26	5	Eliminated
8	Lenihan, Conor*	FF	2,341	4.98%	0.25	4	Eliminated
9	Kelly, Ray	NP	823	1.75%	0.09	3	No Expenses
10	Duffy, Francis	GP	480	1.02%	0.05	3	No Expenses

*Outgoing TD #Former TD Valid poll: 46,964 Quota: 9,393 No expenses limit: 2,349

Party votes

		2011				2007				Change	
Party	Cand	1st	%	Quota	Seats	Cand	1st	%	Quota	Seats	%	Seats
FG	2	13,044	27.77%	1.39	1	1	8,346	20.04%	1.00	1	+7.74%	
LB	2	17,032	36.27%	1.81	2	1	8,325	19.99%	1.00	1	+16.28%	+1
FF	2	5,059	10.77%	0.54		2	16,355	39.27%	1.96	2	-28.49%	-2
SF	1	8,064	17.17%	0.86	1	1	5,066	12.16%	0.61		+5.01%	+1
SP	1	2,462	5.24%	0.26		1	1,580	3.79%	0.19		+1.45%	
GP	1	480	1.02%	0.05		1	1,546	3.71%	0.19		-2.69%	
Others	1	823	1.75%	0.09		1	434	1.04%	0.05		+0.71%	
Total	10	46,964	100.0%	9,393	4	8	41,652	100.0%	8,331	4	0.00%	0
Electorate		70,613	66.51%				67,148	62.03%			+4.48%	
Spoiled		511	1.08%				370	0.88%			+0.20%	
Turnout		47,475	67.23%				42,022	62.58%			+4.65%	

Transfer analysis

From	To	FG	LB	FF	SF	SP	GP	Others	Non Trans
FG	487	122	155	52	86	38	10	13	11
		25.05%	31.83%	10.68%	17.66%	7.80%	2.05%	2.67%	2.26%
LB	3,474	659	2,043	167	365	162	31	47	
		18.97%	58.81%	4.81%	10.51%	4.66%	0.89%	1.35%	
FF	7,088	1,642	1,497	1,415	139	55			2,340
		23.17%	21.12%	19.96%	1.96%	0.78%			33.01%
SF	796	149	543	77					27
		18.72%	68.22%	9.67%					3.39%
SP	2,975	187	914	160	1,278				436
		6.29%	30.72%	5.38%	42.96%				14.66%
GP	521	78	126	59	95	96			67
		14.97%	24.18%	11.32%	18.23%	18.43%			12.86%
Others	883	132	214	99	162	162			114
		14.95%	24.24%	11.21%	18.35%	18.35%			12.91%
Total	16,224	2,969	5,492	2,029	2,125	513	41	60	2,995
		18.30%	33.85%	12.51%	13.10%	3.16%	0.25%	0.37%	18.46%

Dublin South-West

Count details

Candidate	Party	1st	2nd Rabbitte Surplus	3rd Hayes Surplus	4th Kelly Duffy	5th Lenihan Votes	6th Murphy Votes	7th Crowe Surplus	8th O'Connor Votes
Seats 4								**Quota**	**9,393**
			-3,474						
Rabbitte, Pat*	**LB**	**12,867**	9,393	9,393	9,393	9,393	9,393	9,393	9,393
			+514	*-487*					
Hayes, Brian*	**FG**	**9,366**	9,880	9,393	9,393	9,393	9,393	9,393	9,393
			+365	*+86*	*+257*	*+139*	*+1,278*	*-796*	
Crowe, Sean #	**SF**	**8,064**	8,429	8,515	8,772	8,911	10,189	9,393	9,393
			+2,043	*+155*	*+340*	*+166*	*+914*	*+543*	*+1,331*
Maloney, Eamonn	**LB**	**4,165**	6,208	6,363	6,703	6,869	7,783	8,326	9,657
			+145	*+122*	*+210*	*+560*	*+187*	*+149*	*+1,082*
Keane, Cait	FG	3,678	3,823	3,945	4,155	4,715	4,902	5,051	6,133
			+115	*+31*	*+84*	*+1,415*	*+160*	*+77*	*-4,600*
O'Connor, Charlie*	FF	2,718	2,833	2,864	2,948	4,363	4,523	4,600	Eliminated
			+162	*+38*	*+258*	*+55*	*-2,975*		
Murphy, Mick	SP	2,462	2,624	2,662	2,920	2,975	Eliminated		
			+52	*+21*	*+74*	*-2,488*			
Lenihan, Conor*	FF	2,341	2,393	2,414	2,488	Eliminated			
			+47	*+13*	*-883*				
Kelly, Ray	NP	823	870	883	Eliminated				
			+31	*+10*	*-521*				
Duffy, Francis	GP	480	511	521	Eliminated				
Non-transferable				*+11*	*+181*	*+153*	*+436*	*+27*	*+2,187*
Cumulative			0	11	192	345	781	808	2,995
Total		46,964	46,964	46,964	46,964	46,964	46,964	46,964	46,964

Minister for Communications Pat Rabbitte receives his seal of office from President Mary McAleese at Áras an Uachtaráin. Taoiseach Enda Kenny looks on

Dublin West (4 seats)

Three outgoing TDs and Joe Higgins win seats in the most predictable constituency of this most volatile election

Elected

Joan Burton* (Lab) Count 1, Leo Varadkar* (FG) Count 2, Joe Higgins (SP) Count 3, Brian Lenihan* (FF) Final count.

Analysis by Sean Donnelly

There were Constituency Commission boundary changes here and the constituency increased from three to four seats for the 2011 election. The seat was gained because of a large population of 12,768 in the Swords-Forrest areas transferred in from Dublin North.

This was the most predictable constituency in this election with the three outgoing deputies joined by Joe Higgins. It was practically all over after the announcement of the first count with the four leading candidates well clear of the rest of the field.

The Fine Gael vote was up 12 percentage points and with 1.4 quotas the party could have been in contention for two seats but its vote was badly divided with Leo Varadkar just short of the quota and Kieran Dennison in fifth place with a mere 0.4 quotas. Varadkar duly took the second seat on the second count and Dennison ended up in sixth place.

The Labour vote was up 12 percentage points and with 1.5 quotas it also could have been in contention for two seats. Joan Burton topped the poll and was well over the quota on the first count and was the first deputy declared elected in the 2011 general election. Her running mate Patrick Nulty did poorly and with just 2,686 first preferences, was too far behind to feature.

Socialist Party leader Joe Higgins lost his seat here in 2007. He went on to win a European Parliament

seat in 2009 and continued his winning ways in 2011. Higgins was just short of the quota on the first count and went on to comfortably take the third seat on the third count.

This was another poor Dublin performance by Fianna Fáil as its vote was down 21 percentage points but at least the party held its seat here unlike the rest of the Dublin constituencies. Brian Lenihan was in fourth place after the first count on 6,421 first - preference votes. But he was well clear of the rest of the field and there was never any doubt that he would hold his seat. He thus become Fianna Fáil's only Dublin-based deputy. His running mate David McGuinness got just 623 first preferences and lost his expenses, as did two others.

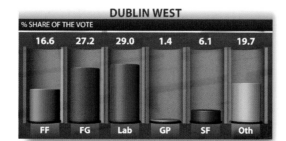

DUBLIN WEST
% SHARE OF THE VOTE

FF	FG	Lab	GP	SF	Oth
16.6	27.2	29.0	1.4	6.1	19.7

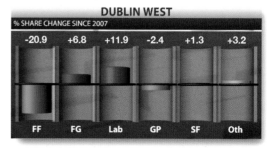

DUBLIN WEST
% SHARE CHANGE SINCE 2007

FF	FG	Lab	GP	SF	Oth
-20.9	+6.8	+11.9	-2.4	+1.3	+3.2

*outgoing TDs

JOAN BURTON (Lab)

Address: Leinster House, Kildare Street, Dublin 2.
Phone: 01 6184006 (LH)
Website: www.joanburton.ie
Email: joan.burton@oir.ie
Twitter: twitter.com/joan_burton
Facebook: Yes.
Birth Place/Date: February 1949.
Marital Status/Family: Married to Pat Carroll; 1 daughter.
Education: Stanhope Street; UCD.
Occupation: Public representative.
Biography: First elected to the Dáil in 1992 and again in 2002, re-elected in 2007. In the 2011 election Joan became the first TD to be elected. Minister for Social Protection and deputy leader of the Labour Party. Minister of State for Development Cooperation and Overseas Aid 1994-1997. As Minister of State in Foreign Affairs, she initiated a dramatic expansion of Ireland's Aid Programme in Africa. As Minister of State in Social Welfare (1992 to 1995) she initiated a series of welfare to work and education initiatives for lone parents and families on social welfare.
Hobbies: Gardening, walking, listening to music (favourite musician is Leonard Cohen), reading (favourite author is Jane Austen).
Did you know? Joan's first job was in Dunnes Stores. She was secretary of the Irish anti-apartheid movement in the 1980s. Joan was among the first women to become a qualified chartered accountant in Ireland.
Politician (living or deceased) you most admire: Julius Nyerere.
Priority as a TD? Rebuilding the economy, getting people back to work.
Why did you stand for election? To change Ireland and improve life, working and living conditions.
Is there any particular event that brought home to you just how serious the economic crisis had become? My realisation that the tax system was building a large bubble, and then a dawning sense of catastrophe from the Northern Rock collapse in September 2007.

LEO VARADKAR (FG)

Address: Leinster House, Kildare Street, Dublin 2.
Email: leo.varadkar@oireachtas.ie
Website: www.leovaradkar.ie
Birth Place/Date: Dublin, January 1979.
Marital Status/Family: Single.
Education: St Francis Xavier NS, Roselawn, Dublin 15; The King's Hospital, Palmerstown, Dublin 20; Trinity College, Dublin.
Occupation: Government minister and medical doctor (not currently practising).
Biography: Minister for Transport, Tourism and Sport. First elected a TD in 2007. Fine Gael spokesperson on Enterprise, Trade and Employment (2007-2010); Communications, Energy and Natural Resources (June 2010-February 2011). Member, Fingal County Council (2003-2007).
Hobbies: Fitness (running and training), travel, good food and wine and good company.
Did you know? Leo got the highest vote recorded in the local elections of 2004, winning nearly 5,000 votes.
Politician (living or deceased) you most admire: Michael Collins.
Priorities as a TD: Create jobs, keep taxes low, restore respect to politics, reform the public service and improve schools, hospitals, transport and sporting facilities in Dublin West.
Why did you stand for election? Initially I wanted to save the world, but now I would be happy if I could just make Ireland a better place to live.
Is there any particular event that brought home to you just how serious the economic crisis had become? What really hit me was the way people's expectations have changed. People who had hoped to move to a better house or buy a holiday home are now stuck in negative equity and debt, and see no way out. Canvassing during the election I was struck by the large number of parents in their 50s and 60s who should have been looking forward to retirement but are now in a position where they have to look after their adult children financially or have adult children who have emigrated.

JOE HIGGINS (SP)

Address: Dáil Eireann, Leinster House, Kildare Street, Dublin 2.
Phone: 01 6183370 (LH)
Email: joe.higgins@oir.ie
Website: www.joehiggins.eu
Twitter: @joehigginsTD
Facebook: www.facebook.com/joehiggins.sp
Birth Place/Date: Kerry, May 1949.
Education: Lispole National School, Co Kerry; Dingle CBS; University College Dublin.
Occupation: Full-time public representative.
Biography: A political activist since the 1970s, Joe was elected a Socialist Party TD in 1997 and retained his seat in 2002. He narrowly lost his seat in 2007 and was elected an MEP in the June 2009 European Elections. In April 1996, Joe came within 250 votes of winning the Dublin West by-election as a militant Labour/anti-water charges candidate. Elected as independent Labour councillor for Mulhuddart in Dublin West in 1991.
Did you know? Joe was expelled from the Labour Party in 1989 due to sharp disagreements over Labour going into coalition with Fine Gael.
Why did you stand for election? To fight for the interests of working-class people – workers, the unemployed and youth. To resist EU/IMF/ECB programme of savage austerity designed to rescue European and Irish banks from its consequence of reckless speculation by making ordinary people pay for their debts. To assist working people to mobilise and fight cuts in living standards and public service; to create a new mass party of the Left and fight for socialist policies as the alternative to the disastrous policies of the capitalist market.
Is there any particular event that brought home to you just how serious the economic crisis had become? When the IMF came here, it was clear that Irish capitalists and the political system had failed. They were begging other capitalists to clean up their mess by financially crucifying ordinary people.

BRIAN LENIHAN (FF)

Home Address: Longwood, Somerton Road, Strawberry Beds, Dublin 20.
Phone: 01 8220970 (O) 01 6183894 (LH)
Email: brian.lenihan@oireachtas.ie
Website: www.brianlenihan.ie
Birth Place/Date: Dublin, May 1959.
Marital Status/Family: Married to Patricia Ryan; 1 son, 1 daughter.
Education: Belvedere College, Dublin; Trinity College Dublin (BA [Mod]); Cambridge University (LLB); King's Inns.
Occupation: Public representative. Senior Counsel.
Biography: Fianna Fáil deputy leader and party spokesperson on Finance. Minister for Finance from May 2008 and served in that role until March 2011. Minister for Justice, Equality and Law Reform from June 2007 to May 2008. Prior to that was Minister of State with responsibility for Children. He was first elected to the Dáil in April 1996 in the by-election caused by the death of his father, Brian, who had been a deputy for Dublin West since 1977. During the 28th Dáil Brian Lenihan was chairperson of the All-Party Oireachtas Committee on the Constitution.
Hobbies: Reading, on a wide variety of subjects, hill walking.
Priority as a TD? Taking all steps necessary to stabilise and increase employment.
Why did you stand for election? I was put forward by the local Fianna Fáil organisation to defend the record of the outgoing government in circumstances of extraordinary difficulty and to advance the national objectives of the party.
Is there any particular event that brought home to you just how serious the economic crisis had become? Yes, a whole series of briefings at the Department of Finance and events which took place after my appointment as Minister for Finance.

Leo Varadkar, Fine Gael leader Enda Kenny and Richard Bruton on the campaign trail in Dublin, where they outlined the party's plan to rationalise state agencies

Election Facts
"I met a Fianna Fáil minister the other day. He looked terrible, tired and drawn. I asked him how it was going. 'You have no idea how bad it is,' he replied, looking for all the world like a First World War veteran explaining the facts of life in the trenches to a new recruit. 'It's awful out there' David McCullagh, RTÉ

Dublin West

	Seats	4			8,495		
	Candidate	Party	1st	%	Quota	Count	Status
1	Burton, Joan*	LB	9,627	22.67%	1.13	1	Made Quota
2	Varadkar, Leo*	FG	8,359	19.68%	0.98	2	Made Quota
3	Higgins, Joe #	SP	8,084	19.03%	0.95	3	Made Quota
4	Lenihan, Brian*	FF	6,421	15.12%	0.76	5	Elected
5	Nulty, Patrick	LB	2,686	6.32%	0.32	5	Not Elected
6	Dennison, Kieran	FG	3,190	7.51%	0.38	4	Eliminated
7	Donnelly, Paul	SF	2,597	6.11%	0.31	3	Eliminated
8	McGuinness, David	FF	623	1.47%	0.07	2	No Expenses
9	O'Gorman, Roderic	GP	605	1.42%	0.07	2	No Expenses
10	Esebamen, Clement	NP	280	0.66%	0.03	2	No Expenses

*Outgoing TD #Former TD Valid poll: 42,472 Quota: 8,495 No expenses limit: 2,124

Party votes

Party	Cand	2011				Cand	2007				Change	
		1st	%	Quota	Seats		1st	%	Quota	Seats	%	Seats
FG	2	11,549	27.19%	1.36	1	1	6,928	20.39%	0.82	1	+6.80%	
LB	2	12,313	28.99%	1.45	1	1	5,799	17.06%	0.68	1	+11.93%	
FF	2	7,044	16.59%	0.83	1	2	12,726	37.45%	1.50	1	-20.86%	
SF	1	2,597	6.11%	0.31		1	1,624	4.78%	0.19		+1.34%	
SP	1	8,084	19.03%	0.95	1	1	5,066	14.91%	0.60		+4.13%	+1
GP	1	605	1.42%	0.07		1	1,286	3.78%	0.15		-2.36%	
PD						1	553	1.63%	0.07		-1.63%	
Others	1	280	0.66%	0.03							+0.66%	
Total	10	42,472	100.0%	8,495	4	8	33,982	100.0%	8,496	3	0.00%	+1
Electorate		62,348	68.12%				52,193	65.11%			+3.01%	
Spoiled		327	0.76%				206	0.60%			+0.16%	
Turnout		42,799	68.65%				34,188	65.50%			+3.14%	

Transfer analysis

From	To	FG	LB	FF	SF	SP	GP	Others	Non Trans
FG	3,693		1,628	966					1,099
			44.08%	26.16%					29.76%
LB	1,132	254	500	81	49	220	20	8	
		22.44%	44.17%	7.16%	4.33%	19.43%	1.77%	0.71%	
FF	631	79	108	227	42	122			53
		12.52%	17.12%	35.97%	6.66%	19.33%			8.40%
SF	2,749	253	1,251	273					972
		9.20%	45.51%	9.93%					35.36%
GP	625	77	107	225	42	121			53
		12.32%	17.12%	36.00%	6.72%	19.36%			8.48%
Others	288	36	49	104	19	56			24
		12.50%	17.01%	36.11%	6.60%	19.44%			8.33%
Total	9,118	699	3,643	1,876	152	519	20	8	2,201
		7.67%	39.95%	20.57%	1.67%	5.69%	0.22%	0.09%	24.14%

Count details

Candidate	Party	1st	2nd Burton Surplus	3rd McGuinness O'Gorman Esebamen	4th Donnelly Votes	5th Dennison Votes
Seats	**4**				**Quota**	**8,495**
Burton, Joan*	LB	9,627	-1,132 8,495	8,495	8,495	8,495
Varadkar, Leo*	FG	8,359	+196 8,555	8,555	8,555	8,555
Higgins, Joe #	SP	8,084	+220 8,304	+299 8,603	8,603	8,603
Lenihan, Brian*	FF	6,421	+73 6,494	+556 7,050	+273 7,323	+966 8,289
Nulty, Patrick	LB	2,686	+500 3,186	+264 3,450	+1,251 4,701	+1,628 6,329
Dennison, Kieran	FG	3,190	+58 3,248	+192 3,440	+253 3,693	-3,693 Eliminated
Donnelly, Paul	SF	2,597	+49 2,646	+103 2,749	-2,749 Eliminated	
McGuinness, David	FF	623	+8 631	-631 Eliminated		
O'Gorman, Roderic	GP	605	+20 625	-625 Eliminated		
Esebamen, Clement	NP	280	+8 288	-288 Eliminated		
Non-transferable Cumulative			0	+130 130	+972 1,102	+1,099 2,201
Total			42,472	42,472	42,472	42,472

Socialist Party MEP and United Left Alliance (ULA) candidate in Dublin West Joe Higgins canvasses in Ongar, west Dublin

Dún Laoghaire (4 seats)

Good vote-management wins Fine Gael two seats

Elected
Eamon Gilmore* (Lab) Count 1, Sean Barrett* (FG) Count 8, Mary Mitchell O'Connor (FG) Count 10, Richard Boyd Barrett (PBP) Final count.

Analysis by Michael Gallagher

Dún Laoghaire lost territory containing about 12,000 people, mainly in Cabinteely and Foxrock, to Dublin South, and was reduced from a five-seater to a four-seater, making it more competitive than ever, especially as all five incumbents stood for re-election.

Only two of them made it back to Leinster House. The smiles were on the faces of Fine Gael and the ULA, while Fianna Fáil and, surprisingly, Labour were not so happy.

For Fine Gael, Dún Laoghaire was traditionally a happy hunting ground. The party took three seats out of five here in November 1982, but by 2002 it had lost them all. The rebuilding was spectacularly successful; Seán Barrett returned to the Dáil in 2007, and in 2011 he was joined by new TD Mary Mitchell O'Connor. The party won a less than overwhelming 35% of the votes, but good vote management turned this comfortably into two seats.

Labour was also hoping for two seats, and party leader Eamon Gilmore was joined on the ticket by Senator Ivana Bacik, who had done well in two previous electoral outings without being successful in either. With good vote-management Labour would have been sure of two seats. Instead, Gilmore got

almost twice as many first preferences as Bacik; the margin between the two, over 5,000 votes, proved costly when Bacik was eliminated on the 10th count, because if just 250 of Gilmore's first preferences had been switched to Bacik, she would have taken a seat.

Instead, her elimination carried Richard Boyd Barrett of People before Profit into a seat. Boyd Barrett had come close in 2007 when Dún Laoghaire had been a five-seater, and now overcame the tougher challenge of getting elected in a four-seater.

The game of chicken played in the months before the election by the two Fianna Fáil candidates, Barry Andrews and Mary Hanafin, both of them ministers, had fascinated the nation and appalled party headquarters. Despite hints and entreaties, neither would move to the emptier territory of Dublin South, and, inevitably, both lost their seats. To complete the rout of the outgoing government, Green TD and junior minister Ciarán Cuffe barely reached 2,000 votes and did not even qualify for reimbursement of his expenses.

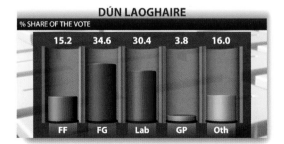

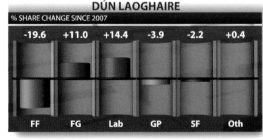

*outgoing TDs

EAMON GILMORE (Lab)

Home Address: Shankill, Co Dublin.
Phone: 01 6182112 (LH) 01 4082138 (Iveagh House)
Website: www.labour.ie/eamongilmore/
Facebook: www.facebook.com/EamonGilmore
Birth Place/Date: Caltra, Co Galway, April 1955.
Marital Status/Family: Married to Carol Hanney; 2 sons,1 daughter.
Education: Caltra NS, Co Galway; St Joseph's College, Garbally, Ballinasloe; UCG (Degree in psychology).
Occupation: Tánaiste and Minister for Foreign Affairs and Trade.
Biography: Appointed as Tánaiste and Minister for Foreign Affairs and Trade in March 2011. Became leader of the Labour Party in September 2007. Labour spokesperson on Environment, Housing and Local Government from 2002 to 2007. Minister of State at the Department of the Marine 1994-1997. First elected to Dáil in 1989 and re-elected at each subsequent election.
Hobbies: Sport, cooking and reading.
Did you know? Eamon grew up on a small family farm in east Galway.
Politician (living or deceased) you most admire: Martin Luther King.
Priority as a TD? Getting people back to work and the economy growing again.
Why did you stand for election? I believe in democracy. There is no greater honour or privilege than being freely chosen by fellow citizens to represent them in the national parliament. I enjoy challenges and solving problems for people and being a TD allows me to do that.
Is there any particular event that brought home to you just how serious the economic crisis had become? The IMF's arrival.

SEÁN BARRETT (FG)

Home Address: Avondale, Ballinclea Road, Killiney, Co Dublin.
Phone: 01 6183343 (LH)
Email: ceann.comhairle@oireachtas.ie
Website: www.ceanncomhairle.oireachtas.ie/
Birth Place/Date: Dublin, August 1944.
Marital Status/Family: Married to Sheila Hyde; 5 children.
Education: CBS Dún Laoghaire; CBC, Monkstown; Presentation College, Glasthule, Co Dublin.
Occupation: Full time public representative. Formerly company director and insurance broker.
Biography: Elected Ceann Comhairle of the 31st Dáil on 9 March 2011. First elected a TD for Dún Laoghaire in June 1981 and re-elected at each subsequent election until the 2002 general election, when he did not contest the election. Re-elected a TD for Dún Laoghaire in May 2007. Fine Gael spokesman on Foreign Affairs in 30th Dáil. Minister for Sport (1982-1987), Minister for Defence and the Marine (1994-1997). President of the EU Council of Ministers during Ireland's presidency in 1996. Member, of Dublin County Council (1974-1982) and chairman (1981-1982).
Hobbies: Golf, reading history and biography books.
Did you know? Seán played GAA and rugby at club level.

MARY MITCHELL O'CONNOR (FG)

Home Address: 31 Maple Manor, Cabinteely, Co Dublin.
Phone: 086 8186725 (M) 01 6183302 (LH)
Website: www.marymitchelloconnor.com
Twitter: Yes.
Facebook: Yes.
Birth Place/Date: Galway.
Marital Status/Family: Divorced; 2 sons.
Education: Presentation Convent, Tuam, Co Galway; Carysfort College, Blackrock, Co Dublin; NUI Maynooth.
Occupation: Former school principal.
Biography: Secured 9,087 first-preference votes to get elected on the 10th count in her first general election. Elected to Dún Laoghaire Rathdown Council in 2004 for the Progressive Democrats. Joined Fine Gael in December 2007 and re-elected to the council on the Fine Gael ticket in 2009.
Hobbies: Reading.
Did you know? Mary used to be a Progressive Democrat councillor.
Politician (living or deceased) you most admire: John F Kennedy
Priority as a TD? To increase women's representation in the Dáil and make improvements in the education sector.
Why did you stand for election? I stood for election to improve the lives of people, and our country.
Is there any particular event that brought home to you just how serious the economic crisis had become? When I realised that there were 7,492 unemployed people in Dún Laoghaire in January 2011 compared to 2,622 in June 2007.

Dún Laoghaire

RICHARD BOYD BARRETT
(PBPA)

Home Address: Brigadoon, Station Road, Glenageary, Co Dublin.
Phone: 01 6183449 (LH)
Email Richard.BoydBarrett@oireachtas.ie
Website: www.richardboydbarrett.ie
Twitter: twitter.com/RBoydBarrett
Facebook: facebook/ Richard Boyd Barrett
Birth Place/Date: London, November 1967.
Marital Status/Family: Single; 2 boys (son and step son).
Education: Johnstown NS; St Michael's College; UCD (BA and MA in English Lit).
Occupation: Full-time public representative
Biography: Unsuccessfully contested the 2002 and 2007 general elections. Member, Dun Laoghaire-Rathdown County Council (2009-2011). Founding member of People Before Profit Alliance and United Left Alliance. Chairperson of Irish Anti-War Movement.
Hobbies: Reading, writing, music, theatre, film, walking, soccer.
Did you know? As a teenager, Richard attended fundraising gigs for UK miners' strike, anti-racist and anti-war campaigns, which first led to an interest in politics.
Politician (living or deceased) you most admire: The anonymous heroes of every people's struggle against injustice, oppression and exploitation from the first slave revolts, to the recent Irish pensioner's medical-card protests, to the current revolutions in Egypt and the Arab world.
Priority as a TD? To campaign for jobs, the protection of public services, social and international solidarity and a more thorough-going participatory democracy.
Why did you stand for election? To use the Dáil position as a platform to promote movements of people power to achieve all of the above.
Is there any particular event that brought home to you just how serious the economic crisis had become? Seeing people queuing up for the dole in Dún Laoghaire with the queue stretching up another street and people hiding their faces when buses and traffic passed because of the humiliation they felt.

Former Fianna Fáil minister and election candidate for Dún Laoghaire Mary Hanafin concedes defeat

First preference votes

	Candidate	Party	1st	%	Quota	Count	Status
	Seats	4			11,336		
1	Gilmore, Eamon*	LB	11,468	20.23%	1.01	1	Made Quota
2	Barrett, Sean*	FG	10,504	18.53%	0.93	8	Made Quota
3	Mitchell O'Connor, Mary	FG	9,087	16.03%	0.80	10	Made Quota
4	Boyd Barrett, Richard	PBPA	6,206	10.95%	0.55	11	Elected
5	Hanafin, Mary*	FF	5,090	8.98%	0.45	11	Not Elected
6	Bacik, Ivana	LB	5,749	10.14%	0.51	9	Eliminated
7	Andrews, Barry*	FF	3,542	6.25%	0.31	7	Eliminated
8	Cuffe, Ciaran*	GP	2,156	3.80%	0.19	6	No Expenses
9	Boyhan, Victor	NP	834	1.47%	0.07	5	No Expenses
10	Haughton, Carl	NP	456	0.80%	0.04	5	No Expenses
11	Patton, Trevor	NP	445	0.79%	0.04	5	No Expenses
12	Fitzgerald, Daire	CS	434	0.77%	0.04	4	No Expenses
13	Crawford, Nick	NV	394	0.70%	0.03	3	No Expenses
14	Deegan, Mick	NP	311	0.55%	0.03	2	No Expenses

*Outgoing TD Valid poll: 56,676 Quota: 11,336 No expenses limit: 2,835

Party votes

Party	Cand	1st	%	Quota	Seats	Cand	1st	%	Quota	Seats	%	Seats
		2011					2007				Change	
FG	2	19,591	34.57%	1.73	2	3	13,832	23.56%	1.41	1	+11.01%	+1
LB	2	17,217	30.38%	1.52	1	2	9,392	16.00%	0.96	1	+14.38%	
FF	2	8,632	15.23%	0.76		2	20,471	34.87%	2.09	2	-19.64%	-2
SF						1	1,292	2.20%	0.13		-2.20%	
PBPA	1	6,206	10.95%	0.55	1	1	5,233	8.91%	0.53		+2.04%	+1
GP	1	2,156	3.80%	0.19		1	4,534	7.72%	0.46	1	-3.92%	
CS	1	434	0.77%	0.04							+0.77%	
PD						1	3,959	6.74%	0.40		-6.74%	
Others	5	2,440	4.31%	0.22							+4.31%	
Total	14	56,676	100.0%	11,336	4	11	58,713	100.0%	9,786	5	0.00%	0
Electorate	80,115	70.74%					89,035	65.94%			+4.80%	
Spoiled	481	0.84%					397	0.67%			+0.17%	
Turnout	57,157	71.34%					59,110	66.39%			+4.95%	

Transfer analysis

From	To	FG	LB	FF	PBPA	GP	Others	Non Trans
FG	2,056	142	46	670	920			278
		6.91%	2.24%	32.59%	44.75%			13.52%
LB	7,438	2,573	77	885	2,483	2	3	1,415
		34.59%	1.04%	11.90%	33.38%	0.03%	0.04%	19.02%
FF	3,886	760	307	2,268	281			270
		19.56%	7.90%	58.36%	7.23%			6.95%
GP	2,429	791	753	387	337			161
		32.56%	31.00%	15.93%	13.87%			6.63%
Others	3,249	871	374	464	567	271	372	330
		26.81%	11.51%	14.28%	17.45%	8.34%	11.45%	10.16%
Total	19,058	5,137	1,557	4,674	4,588	273	375	2,454
		26.95%	8.17%	24.53%	24.07%	1.43%	1.97%	12.88%

Dún Laoghaire

Count details

Candidate	Party	1st	2nd Gilmore Surplus	3rd Deegan Votes	4th Crawford Votes	5th Fitzgerald Votes	6th Boyhan Haughton Patton	7th Cuffe Votes	8th Andrews Votes	9th Barrett Surplus	10th Bacik Votes	11th Mitchell Surplus
			−132									
Gilmore, Eamon*	LB	11,468	11,336	11,336	11,336	11,336	11,336	11,336	11,336	11,336	11,336	11,336
			+12	+22	+35	+93	+247	+361	+449	−387		
Barrett, Sean*	FG	10,504	10,516	10,538	10,573	10,666	10,913	11,274	11,723	11,336	11,336	11,336
			+7	+26	+43	+76	+329	+430	+311	+142	+2,554	−1,669
Mitchell O'Connor, Mary	FG	9,087	9,094	9,120	9,163	9,239	9,568	9,998	10,309	10,451	13,005	11,336
			+22	+43	+61	+52	+411	+337	+281	+40	+2,461	+880
Boyd Barrett, Richard	PBPA	6,206	6,228	6,271	6,332	6,384	6,795	7,132	7,413	7,453	9,914	10,794
			+6	+11	+23	+87	+175	+214	+2,268	+139	+876	+531
Hanafin, Mary*	FF	5,090	5,096	5,107	5,130	5,217	5,392	5,606	7,874	8,013	8,889	9,420
			+77	+31	+47	+12	+284	+753	+307	+46	−7,306	
Bacik, Ivana	LB	5,749	5,826	5,857	5,904	5,916	6,200	6,953	7,260	7,306	Eliminated	
			+3	+9	+15	+25	+119	+173	−3,886			
Andrews, Barry*	FF	3,542	3,545	3,554	3,569	3,594	3,713	3,886	Eliminated			
			+2	+29	+35	+12	+195	−2,429				
Cuffe, Ciaran*	GP	2,156	2,158	2,187	2,222	2,234	2,429	Eliminated				
			+1	+16	+61	+29	−941					
Boyhan, Victor	NP	834	835	851	912	941	Eliminated					
			+1	+43	+63	+31	−594					
Haughton, Carl	NP	456	457	500	563	594	Eliminated					
			+1	+21	+33	+15	−515					
Patton, Trevor	NP	445	446	467	500	515	Eliminated					
				+7	+9	−450						
Fitzgerald, Daire	CS	434	434	441	450	Eliminated						
				+44	−438							
Crawford, Nick	NV	394	394	438	Eliminated							
				−311								
Deegan, Mick	NP	311	311	Eliminated								
Non-transferable				+9	+13	+18	+290	+161	+270	+20	+1,415	+258
Cumulative			0	9	22	40	330	491	761	781	2,196	2,454
Total		56,676	56,676	56,676	56,676	56,676	56,676	56,676	56,676	56,676	56,676	56,676

Seats 4 — Quota 11,336

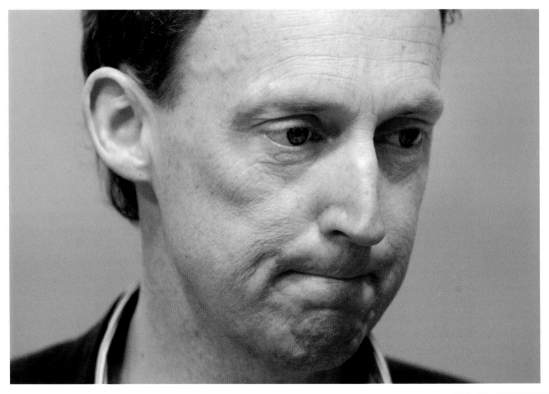

Former Fianna Fáil Minister for Children Barry Andrews concedes defeat in Dún Laoghaire

Galway East (4 seats)

Labour wins its first seat in this constituency as Fine Gael is in contention for three out of four seats

Elected
Michael Kitt* (FF) Count 8, Paul Connaughton (FG) Count 8, Ciaran Cannon (FG) Count 8, Colm Keaveney (Lab) Final count.

Analysis by Sean Donnelly

There were no boundary changes here since 2007 and it remained a four-seat constituency. The long-serving outgoing Fine Gael deputies Paul Connaughton and Ulick Burke retired, so Fine Gael had to field a new team. It managed to convert its 2.1 quotas into two seats and was even in contention for a remarkable three out of four. Paul Connaughton, son of the former deputy, topped the poll with 7,255 first preferences. He was just ahead of former Progressive Democrats' leader and outgoing senator Ciaran Cannon and they were both elected on the penultimate count. Tom McHugh was in the frame in fourth place on the first count with half a quota and in contention for the final seat. Fine Gael's fourth candidate, Jimmy McClearn, was in sixth place on the first count.

The big battle in this constituency was for the final seat, with five candidates in contention. The Labour vote was up 10 percentage points and with 0.7 quotas it was well placed for a seat, but its vote was spread over two candidates which made the task more difficult. Though he was only in eighth place after the first count, Colm Keavney did well on transfers and went on to beat McHugh for the final seat. This was the biggest move up through a count achieved in this election and Keaveney was helped in no small way by a 53% transfer from his running mate Lorraine Higgins, which resulted in him leap-frogging McHugh and he retained his advantage with a final winning margin of 1,278 votes.

Fianna Fáil had another poor performance in this constituency with its vote down by 22 percentage points and the party lost one of its seats. Long-serving TD Noel Treacy retired ahead of the election. Fianna Fáil's other outgoing deputy, Michael P Kitt, was in third place on the first count. He was helped by 64% of Dolan's transfers and this moved him up to first place and he retained this lead and was elected on the eighth count. His running mate Micheal Dolan was well off the pace with just 4,109 first preferences and was never in contention.

The independents did well in this constituency, winning nearly a quota between the three of them. Sean Canney was in fifth place on the first count with 5,567 and Tim Broderick was in seventh with 5,137 first preferences. Broderick moved into fourth place with the help of 28% of fellow Ballinasloe based Dermot Connolly's (Sinn Féin) transfers on the third count and he maintained this position until the seventh count. The Tuam factor then came into play with Canney's transfers favouring McHugh and Keaveney. Broderick was eliminated by a mere five votes.

*outgoing TDs

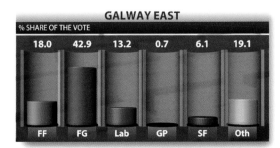

GALWAY EAST

% SHARE OF THE VOTE

FF	FG	Lab	GP	SF	Oth
18.0	42.9	13.2	0.7	6.1	19.1

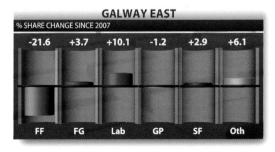

GALWAY EAST

% SHARE CHANGE SINCE 2007

FF	FG	Lab	GP	SF	Oth
-21.6	+3.7	+10.1	-1.2	+2.9	+6.1

Galway East

MICHAEL P KITT (FF)

Home Address: Castleblakeney, Ballinasloe, Co Galway.
Phone: 087 2544345 (M) 01 6183473 (LH) 093 70139 (CO)
Website: www.michaelkitt.com
Email: michael.kitt@oireachtas.ie
Birth Place/Date: Tuam, Co Galway, 1950.
Marital Status/family: Married to Catherine; 3 sons, 1 daughter.
Education: St Jarlath's College, Tuam; St Patrick's College, Drumcondra, Dublin; NUI Galway; UCD.
Occupation: Full-time public representative. Formerly primary school teacher.
Biography: Current Leas Ceann-Comhairle and party spokesperson on Housing, Planning and Gaeltacht Affairs. First elected a TD in 1975 at a by-election. Lost seat in 1977. Re-elected in 1981. Lost seat in 2002 but regained it in 2007. Member of Seanad Éireann (1977-1981 and 2002-2007). Minister of State at the Department of the Environment, Heritage and Local Government, (Local Services) (May 2008-April 2009); Minister of State at the Department of Foreign Affairs, (Overseas Development) (June 2007-May 2008); Minister of State at the Department of the Taoiseach (1991-1992). Chairman of Dáil Education and Science committee (1997-2002). Member, Galway County Council 1975-1991 (chairman, 1985-1986). Son of Michael F Kitt TD (1948-1951, 1957-1975) and brother of Tom Kitt (Dublin South TD 1987-2011) and Áine Brady (Kildare North TD 2007-2011).
Hobbies: Gaelic football (member of Caltra GAA club), golf, walking and reading.
Did you know? Michael was a member of the Students' Union at St Patrick's College, Drumcondra in 1969-1970 and Taoiseach Enda Kenny was in the same year.
Politician (living or deceased) you most admire: Nelson Mandela.
Priority as a TD? To provide employment opportunities.
Why did you stand for election? To continue to represent the people of Galway East.
Is there any particular event that brought home to you just how serious the economic crisis had become? The emigration of so many graduates and young people.

PAUL CONNAUGHTON (FG)

Home Address: Mountbellew, Ballinasloe, Co Galway.
Phone: 087 2354682 (M) 01 6184373 (LH)
Email: paul.connaughton@oireachtas.ie
Website: www.finegael.ie
Twitter: ww.twitter.com/connaughtonpaul
Facebook: Yes.
Birth Place/Date: Galway, January 1982.
Marital Status/Family: Engaged and getting married in July.
Education: Holy Rosary College, Mountbellew; Mountbellew Agricultural College; GMIT (business degree); NUI Galway (HDip in Marketing).
Occupation: Public representative. Youth worker with Foróige for the last four years.
Biography: Secured 7,255 first-preference votes to get elected on the eighth count in his first general election. He was elected to Galway County Council at his first attempt in the local elections in 2009. Son of Paul Connaughton, Fine Gael TD for Galway East 1981-2011.
Hobbies: GAA and soccer.
Politician (living or deceased) you most admire: Michael Collins.
Priority as a TD? To help fix this country and create jobs.
Why did you stand for election? As I am 29 years old I am part of the generation that is most affected by the actions of the last government. I have friends who have been crippled with mortgages and who are losing their jobs.
Is there any particular event that brought home to you just how serious the economic crisis had become? Like people all over the country, when I saw the IMF delegation arriving in Dublin it really brought home how serious the situation was.

CIARAN CANNON (FG)

Home Address: Carrabane, Athenry, Co Galway.
Phone: 087 2283377 (M) 01 6183185 (LH)
Email: ciaran.cannon@oireachtas.ie
Website: www.ciarancannon.ie
Twitter: www.twitter.com/ciarancannon
Facebook: Yes
Birth Place/Date: Galway, September 1965.
Marital Status/Family: Married to Niamh Lawless; 1 son.
Education: Presentation College, Athenry, Co Galway; Trinity College Dublin (computer science); also studied public administration.
Occupation: Public representative. Runs a small business with his wife Niamh.
Biography: Minister of State with special responsibility for Training and Skills. Secured 6,927 first-preference votes to get elected in his second general election. He unsuccessfully contested the 2007 general election for the Progressive Democrats and he was nominated by the Taoiseach to become a senator. He was leader of the PDs for a short period and he joined Fine Gael in 2009.
Ciaran was elected to Galway County Council in 2004.
Hobbies: Music, cycling, reading, travel.
Did you know? Ciaran has won a number of song-writing awards and has completed a 500-mile charity cycle on six occasions.
Politician (living or deceased) you most admire: Nelson Mandela.
Priority as a TD? To ensure that our people receive the very best in education, training and skills so that they are empowered to reach the very pinnacle of their potential.
Why did you stand for election? To play my part in shaping the Ireland that my son and his peers will inherit.
Is there any particular event that brought home to you just how serious the economic crisis had become? The very fact that we are forced into considering the scaling back of resources for children and adults with special needs indicates how serious our crisis has become.

Newspaper headlines call on Taoiseach Brian Cowen to announce a general election

COLM KEAVENEY (Lab)

Home Address: Kilcreevanty, Tuam, Co Galway.
Phone: 087 6776812 (M) 01 6183821 (LH)
Email: colm.keaveney@oireachtas.ie
Website: www.colmkeaveney.ie
Twitter: twitter.com/colm_keaveney
Facebook: Yes.
Birth Place/Date: Galway, January 1971.
Marital Status/Family: Married; 3 sons.
Education: St Jarlath's College Tuam; Letterkenny IT; Smurfit Business School UCD.
Occupation: Public representative and SIPTU trade union organiser.
Biography: Secured 4,254 first-preference votes to get elected on the ninth count in his third general election. He was elected to Galway County Council in 2004 and 2009.
Hobbies: Current affairs, gardening and spending time with his family.
Did you know? Colm was president of Union of Students' in Ireland in 1995-1996 when Niamh Breathnach introduced free fees.
Politician (living or deceased) you most admire: Noel Browne.
Priority as a TD? To protect the little public services that we have left in rural Ireland, reform politics, deliver jobs and stop emigration.
Why did you stand for election? To fight for the notion of a civilised society.
Is there any particular event that brought home to you just how serious the economic crisis had become? Meeting parents who cannot afford to put food in their children's lunchboxes. Meeting people who had their electricity cut off and others who have taken down doors and fixtures and fittings to feed a fire to keep warm.

Galway East

	Candidate	Party	1st	%	Quota	Count	Status
	Seats	**4**			**11,856**		
1	Kitt, Michael P.*	FF	6,585	11.11%	0.56	8	Made Quota
2	Connaughton, Paul	FG	7,255	12.24%	0.61	8	Made Quota
3	Cannon, Ciaran	FG	6,927	11.69%	0.58	8	Made Quota
4	Keaveney, Colm	LB	4,254	7.18%	0.36	9	Elected
5	McHugh, Tom	FG	5,832	9.84%	0.49	9	Not Elected
6	Broderick, Tim	NP	5,137	8.67%	0.43	7	Eliminated
7	Canney, Seán	NP	5,567	9.39%	0.47	6	Eliminated
8	McClearn, Jimmy	FG	5,395	9.10%	0.46	5	Eliminated
9	Higgins, Lorrainne	LB	3,577	6.03%	0.30	4	Eliminated
10	Dolan, Michael F.	FF	4,109	6.93%	0.35	3	Eliminated
11	Connolly, Dermot	SF	3,635	6.13%	0.31	2	Eliminated
12	O'Donnell, Emer	NP	601	1.01%	0.05	1	No Expenses
13	Kennedy, Ciaran	GP	402	0.68%	0.03	1	No Expenses

*Outgoing TD Valid poll: 59,276 Quota: 11,856 No expenses limit: 2,965

Party votes

Party	Cand	2011 1st	2011 %	2011 Quota	2011 Seats	Cand	2007 1st	2007 %	2007 Quota	2007 Seats	Change %	Change Seats
FG	4	25,409	42.87%	2.14	2	4	21,832	39.13%	1.96	2	+3.74%	+0
LB	2	7,831	13.21%	0.66	1	1	1,747	3.13%	0.16		+10.08%	+1
FF	2	10,694	18.04%	0.90	1	3	22,137	39.68%	1.98	2	-21.64%	-1
SF	1	3,635	6.13%	0.31		1	1,789	3.21%	0.16		+2.93%	
GP	1	402	0.68%	0.03		1	1,057	1.89%	0.09		-1.22%	
PD						1	3,321	5.95%	0.30		-5.95%	
Others	3	11,305	19.07%	0.95		3	3,911	7.01%	0.35		+12.06%	
Total	13	59,276	100.0%	11,856	4	14	55,794	100.0%	11,159	4	0.00%	0
Electorate		83,651	70.86%				81,684	68.30%			+2.56%	
Spoiled		560	0.94%				480	0.85%			+0.08%	
Turnout		59,836	71.53%				56,274	68.89%			+2.64%	

Transfer analysis

From	To	FG	LB	FF	SF	Others	Non Trans
FG	5,987	4,181	233	430		885	258
		69.83%	3.89%	7.18%		14.78%	4.31%
LB	4,651	1,149	2,451	267		544	240
		24.70%	52.70%	5.74%		11.70%	5.16%
FF	5,284	953	640	2,666		425	600
		18.04%	12.11%	50.45%		8.04%	11.36%
SF	3,723	730	959	363		1,331	340
		19.61%	25.76%	9.75%		35.75%	9.13%
GP	402	108	131	37	36	73	17
		26.87%	32.59%	9.20%	8.96%	18.16%	4.23%
Others	15,397	6,776	2,532	2,683	52	834	2,520
		44.01%	16.44%	17.43%	0.34%	5.42%	16.37%
Total	35,444	13,897	6,946	6,446	88	4,092	3,975
		39.21%	19.60%	18.19%	0.25%	11.54%	11.21%

Count details

Seats		4							Quota	11,856
Candidate	Party	1st	2nd O'Donnell Kennedy	3rd Connolly Votes	4th Dolan Votes	5th Higgins Votes	6th McClearn Votes	7th Canney Votes	8th Broderick Votes	9th Kitt Surplus
Kitt, Michael P.*	FF		+47	+228	+2,666	+267	+430	+892	+1,735	-994
Kitt, Michael P.*	FF	6,585	6,632	6,860	9,526	9,793	10,223	11,115	12,850	11,856
Connaughton, Paul	FG		+55	+247	+245	+289	+1,733	+1,053	+1,733	
Connaughton, Paul	FG	7,255	7,310	7,557	7,802	8,091	9,824	10,877	12,610	12,610
Cannon, Ciaran	FG		+134	+207	+297	+560	+1,837	+317	+1,582	
Cannon, Ciaran	FG	6,927	7,061	7,268	7,565	8,125	9,962	10,279	11,861	11,861
Keaveney, Colm	LB		+90	+349	+92	+2,451	+233	+1,167	+1,170	+320
Keaveney, Colm	LB	4,254	4,344	4,693	4,785	7,236	7,469	8,636	9,806	10,126
McHugh, Tom	FG		+36	+82	+84	+91	+611	+1,635	+294	+183
McHugh, Tom	FG	5,832	5,868	5,950	6,034	6,125	6,736	8,371	8,665	8,848
Broderick, Tim	NP		+105	+1,036	+238	+330	+795	+724	-8,365	
Broderick, Tim	NP	5,137	5,242	6,278	6,516	6,846	7,641	8,365	Eliminated	
Canney, Seán	NP		+78	+295	+187	+214	+90	-6,431		
Canney, Seán	NP	5,567	5,645	5,940	6,127	6,341	6,431	Eliminated		
McClearn, Jimmy	FG		+45	+194	+144	+209	-5,987			
McClearn, Jimmy	FG	5,395	5,440	5,634	5,778	5,987	Eliminated			
Higgins, Lorrainne	LB		+236	+610	+228	-4,651				
Higgins, Lorrainne	LB	3,577	3,813	4,423	4,651	Eliminated				
Dolan, Michael F.	FF		+46	+135	-4,290					
Dolan, Michael F.	FF	4,109	4,155	4,290	Eliminated					
Connolly, Dermot	SF		+88	-3,723						
Connolly, Dermot	SF	3,635	3,723	Eliminated						
O'Donnell, Emer	NP		-601							
O'Donnell, Emer	NP	601	Eliminated							
Kennedy, Ciaran	GP		-402							
Kennedy, Ciaran	GP	402	Eliminated							
Non-transferable			+43	+340	+109	+240	+258	+643	+1,851	+491
Cumulative			43	383	492	732	990	1,633	3,484	3,975
Total		59,276	59,276	59,276	59,276	59,276	59,276	59,276	59,276	59,276

Taoiseach Enda Kenny with his newly appointed ministers of state at Government Buildings.
From left: Jan O'Sullivan, Ciaran Cannon, Brian Hayes, Lucinda Creighton, Roisin Shorthall, and Michael Ring

Galway West (5 seats)

Fine Gael holds off independents for the final seat

Elected

Éamon Ó Cuív* (FF) Count 8, Derek Nolan (Lab) Count 10, Brian Walsh (FG) Count 12, Noel Grealish* (Ind) Final count, Seán Kyne (FG) Final count.

Analysis by Sean Donnelly

There were no boundary changes here since 2007 and it remained a five-seat constituency.

Veteran Fine Gael TD Pádraic McCormack retired prior to the 2007 general election but was persuaded to run again and went on to retain his seat. He had decided to run again in 2011 but was beaten at the convention and finally retired. The Fine Gael vote was up 10 percentage points and with 1.8 quotas, it should have been well placed for two seats but its vote was divided over four candidates and this led to a struggle for the final seat. Brian Walsh was in fourth place on the first count with 5,425 votes and he went on to take the third seat on the penultimate count. Its second candidate Sean Kyne had a much tougher battle. He was in seventh place on the first count behind independent candidate Catherine Connolly and running mate Fidelma Healy Eames. He battled with both of them throughout the count and was just 54 votes ahead of his running mate when she was eliminated at the end of the 11th count. He then fell behind Connolly on the 12th count and had to rely on a better share of Walsh's small surplus to finally see off Connolly by a mere 17 votes. This was the closest winning margin of this election.

The long-serving Labour TD and former minister Michael D Higgins retired at this election as he intends to seek the Labour nomination for the presidential election. In his absence, the Labour Party turned to councillor Derek Nolan and he put in an

impressive performance and topped the poll with 7,489 first preferences and went on to take the second seat on the 10th count.

The Fianna Fáil vote was down 16 percentage points and with just 1.3 quotas spread over its three candidates, one seat was as much as it could hope for. Outgoing Minister Éamon Ó Cuív was in second place on the first count with 7,441 and he went on to comfortably retain his seat on the eighth count. Long-serving TD Frank Fahey did poorly, winning just 6% and he was eliminated on the seventh count. Fianna Fáil's third candidate, Michael Crowe, got just 3% and was never in contention.

Noel Grealish was elected for the Progressive Democrats in 2007 but he became an independent on the dissolution of the party in 2009. He was in third place on the first count and went on to take the fourth seat on the final count. Former Labour councillor Catherine Connolly was in sixth place on the first count with just half a quota and she was just ahead of Kyne of Fine Gael. She battled with Fine Gael for the final seat but eventually lost out following a couple of recounts.

Sinn Féin's Trevor Ó Clochartaigh doubled the party's vote but with just 6%, he was too far off the pace in eighth place.

*outgoing TDs

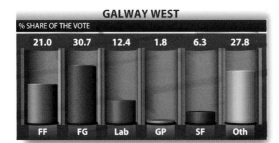

GALWAY WEST

% SHARE OF THE VOTE

FF	FG	Lab	GP	SF	Oth
21.0	30.7	12.4	1.8	6.3	27.8

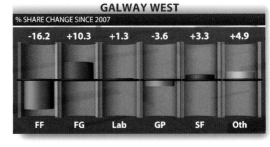

GALWAY WEST

% SHARE CHANGE SINCE 2007

FF	FG	Lab	GP	SF	Oth
-16.2	+10.3	+1.3	-3.6	+3.3	+4.9

ÉAMON Ó CUÍV (FF)

Home Address: Corr na Móna, Co na Gaillimhe.
Phone: 091 562846 (CO) 01 6184231 (LH)
Email: info@eamonocuiv.ie
Website: www.eamonocuiv.ie
Twitter: www.twitter.com/eamonocuiv
Facebook: www.facebook.com/eamonocuiv
Birth Place/Date: Dublin, June 1950.
Marital Status/Family: Married to Áine; 3 sons, 1 daughter.
Education: Oatlands College, Mount Merrion, Dublin.
Occupation: Public representative.
Biography: Party spokesperson on Communications, Energy and Natural Resources. Secured 7,476 first-preference votes to get re-elected to the seat he first won in 1992. He has held that seat in each subsequent election. Minister for Defence and Minister for the Environment, Heritage and Local Government for a short period in 2011 during the final days of 30th Dáil. Minister for Social Protection (2010-2011); Minister for Community, Rural and Gaeltacht Affairs (2002-2010); Minister for Community, Rural and Gaeltacht Affairs (2002-2007); Minister of State at the Department of Agriculture, Food and Rural Development (2001-2002); Minister of State at the Department of Arts, Heritage, Gaeltacht and Islands with special responsibility for the Gaeltacht, Irish language and island development (1997-2001). Member Galway County Council (1991-1997). Member of the Forum for Peace and Reconciliation (1994-1997). Member of Seanad Éireann (1989-1992). Grandson of Éamon de Valera.
Hobbies: Member of GAA.
Did you know? Although often associated with rural Ireland and rural development, Éamon grew up in Dublin 4.
Priority as a TD? To make Ireland a better place for us all to live in and to promote justice and freedom internationally.
Why did you stand for election? To continue to serve.
Is there any particular event that brought home to you just how serious the economic crisis had become? Yes. When the government had to cut social welfare rates.

DEREK NOLAN (Lab)

Home Address: 3 Crescent View, Riverside, Galway.
Phone: 091 561006 (H) 01 6183827 (LH)
Email: derek.nolan@oireachtas.ie
Website: www.dereknolan.com
Twitter: twitter.com/dereknolan_1
Facebook: Yes.
Birth Place/Date: Galway, October 1982.
Marital Status/Family: Single.
Education: St Mary's College, Galway; NUI Galway.
Occupation: Trainee solicitor.
Biography: Secured 7,502 first-preference votes to get elected in his first general election attempt. Elected to Galway City Council in June 2009.
Hobbies: Reading, walking, travelling.
Did you know? Derek is the youngest Labour TD in the 31st Dáil.
Politician (living or deceased) you most admire: Michael D Higgins.
Priority as a TD? Job creation.
Why did you stand for election? I believe in a different kind of politics and I want to offer people that choice.
Is there any particular event that brought home to you just how serious the economic crisis had become? I met a constituent in Galway who was the pension age. She had been single all her life, worked hard and she was heartbroken as her entire pension was wiped out. She was more than upset. She was in despair and that really brought home the absolute reality of how bad things were.

BRIAN WALSH (FG)

Home Address: Drum East, Bushy Park, Galway.
Contact: 086 8333054 (M) 01 6184236 (LH)
Website: www.brianwalshcampaign.ie
Twitter: Yes.
Facebook: Yes.
Birth Place/Date: Galway, September 1972.
Marital Status/Family: Married to Fiona; 1 daughter.
Education: St Joseph's College, Nun's Island ('The Bish'), Galway; GMIT.
Occupation: Public representative. Also runs own financial management business.
Biography: Secured 5,425 first-preference votes to get elected in his first general election. He was elected to Galway City Council in 2004 and re-elected in 2009. He was Galway City Mayor in 2002.
Hobbies: Reading, current affairs, GAA, horse-racing, soccer, gardening.
Did you know? Brian was president of the Students' Union in GMIT in 1993.
Politician (living or deceased) you most admire: Michael Collins.
Priority as a TD? Jobs and I want to prioritise investment in mental health services.
Why did you stand for election? I enjoy being a public representative locally and I believe I can do a better job at national level.
Is there any particular event that brought home to you just how serious the economic crisis had become? The loss of our sovereignty through the arrival of the IMF was the most significant statement to hammer home the seriousness of the situation for the country. Locally, it was the funding cuts for the most vulnerable people like carers' assistants and special needs assistants; and to see traditional successful family owned businesses having to close because of the lack of a modest credit flow.

Galway West

NOEL GREALISH (Ind)

Home Address: Carnmore, Oranmore, Co Galway.
Constituency Office: Briarhill Business Park, Briarhill, Galway.
Phone: 086 8509466 (M) 091 764807 (CO)
Email: noel.grealish@oireachtas.ie
Website: www.noelgrealish.com
Facebook: www.facebook.com/noelgrealishtd
Birth Place/Date: Galway, December 1965.
Marital Status/Family: Single.
Education: Carnmore NS; St Mary's College, Galway.
Occupation: Public representative. Company director.
Biography: First elected to Galway County Council in 1999, elected to Dáil Éireann in 2002 and successfully re-elected in 2007 and 2011. A former member of the Progressive Democrats.
Hobbies: Golf, reading.
Priority as a TD? Job creation.
Why did you stand for election? Job creation, economic recovery and protection of family homes for those in mortgage difficulty.

SEÁN KYNE (FG)

Home Address: Clydagh, Moycullen, Galway.
Phone: 087 6137372 (M) 01 6184426 (LH)
Email: sean.kyne@oireachtas.ie or kynesean@eircom.net
Website: www.seankyne.ie
Twitter: @seankyne
Facebook: Yes.
Birth Place/Date: Galway, May 1975.
Marital Status/Family: Single.
Education: Masters agricultural science UCD.
Occupation: Full-time public representative and agri-environmental consultant.
Biography: Secured 4,550 first-preference votes to get elected in his second general election attempt. He got elected with 17 votes more than Catherine Connolly after two recounts. He unsuccessfully contested the 2007 general election. Seán was first elected to Galway County Council in 2004 and he was re-elected in 2009.
Hobbies: Walking, reading and TV.
Did you know? Sean did a bungee jump and sky dive in Queenstown, New Zealand.
Politician (living or deceased) you most admire: Franklin D Roosevelt and Lyndon B Johnson.
Priority as a TD? Job creation and protection, reform of SAC (special area of conservation) designations to allow for easier infrastructural development in Connemara.
Why did you stand for election? As the senior councillor for Fine Gael in Connemara, I wanted to be a voice in government for Connemara and for the farming community within the constituency.
Is there any particular event that brought home to you just how serious the economic crisis had become? The difference in the mood of the people at the doors between canvassing for the local elections in 2009 and the general election in 2011 and the way that mood has changed to one of despair.

Election Facts

"Prior to Election 2011, the biggest inter-election loss for any party was the 23 seats lost by Fine Gael between the elections of 1997 and 2002. Fianna Fáil's biggest loss was nine seats between 1989 and 1992. But all records were shattered in 2011 when Fianna Fáil lost 58 seats"
Professor Michael Gallagher, TCD

First preference votes

	Seats	5			10,105		
	Candidate	Party	1st	%	Quota	Count	Status
1	Cuiv, Éamon Ó*	FF	7,441	12.27%	0.74	8	Made Quota
2	Nolan, Derek	LB	7,489	12.35%	0.74	10	Made Quota
3	Walsh, Brian	FG	5,425	8.95%	0.54	12	Made Quota
4	Grealish, Noel*	NP	6,229	10.27%	0.62	13	Elected
5	Kyne, Seán	FG	4,550	7.51%	0.45	13	Elected
6	Connolly, Catherine	NP	4,766	7.86%	0.47	13	Not Elected
7	Healy Eames, Fidelma	FG	5,046	8.32%	0.50	11	Eliminated
8	Ó Clochartaigh, Trevor	SF	3,808	6.28%	0.38	9	Eliminated
9	Fahey, Frank*	FF	3,448	5.69%	0.34	7	Eliminated
10	Naughten, Hildegarde	FG	3,606	5.95%	0.36	6	Eliminated
11	Welby, Thomas	NP	3,298	5.44%	0.33	5	Eliminated
12	Crowe, Michael	FF	1,814	2.99%	0.18	4	No Expenses
13	Walsh, Eamon	NP	1,481	2.44%	0.15	3	No Expenses
14	Brolcháin, Niall Ó	GP	1,120	1.85%	0.11	2	No Expenses
15	Cubbard, Mike	NP	853	1.41%	0.08	1	No Expenses
16	Holmes, Uinseann Eoin	NP	186	0.31%	0.02	1	No Expenses
17	King, Thomas	NP	65	0.11%	0.01	1	No Expenses

*Outgoing TD Valid poll: 60,625 Quota: 10,105 No expenses limit: 2,527

Party votes

Party	Cand	2011 1st	%	Quota	Seats	Cand	2007 1st	%	Quota	Seats	Change %	Seats
FG	4	18,627	30.72%	1.84	2	3	11,235	20.39%	1.22	1	+10.33%	+1
LB	1	7,489	12.35%	0.74	1	1	6,086	11.05%	0.66	1	+1.31%	
FF	3	12,703	20.95%	1.26	1	3	20,468	37.15%	2.23	2	-16.20%	-1
SF	1	3,808	6.28%	0.38		1	1,629	2.96%	0.18		+3.32%	
GP	1	1,120	1.85%	0.11		1	3,026	5.49%	0.33		-3.64%	
PD						3	8,868	16.10%	0.97	1	-16.10%	-1
Others	7	16,878	27.84%	1.67	1	3	3,784	6.87%	0.41		+20.97%	+1
Total	17	60,625	100.0%	10,105	5	15	55,096	100.0%	9,183	5	0.00%	0
Electorate		88,840	68.24%				86,602	63.62%			+4.62%	
Spoiled		643	1.05%				533	0.96%			+0.09%	
Turnout		61,268	68.96%				55,629	64.24%			+4.73%	

Transfer analysis

From	To	FG	LB	FF	SF	GP	Others	Non Trans
FG	11,135	7,573	416	153	40		2,281	672
		68.01%	3.74%	1.37%	0.36%		20.48%	6.04%
LB	326	104					222	
		31.90%					68.10%	
FF	6,990	1,186	493	2,959	281		1,736	335
		16.97%	7.05%	42.33%	4.02%		24.84%	4.79%
SF	4,683	661	1,016				2,026	980
		14.11%	21.70%				43.26%	20.93%
GP	1,153	274	334	91	72		354	28
		23.76%	28.97%	7.89%	6.24%		30.70%	2.43%
Others	6,232	1,927	683	1,189	482	33	1,659	259
		30.92%	10.96%	19.08%	7.73%	0.53%	26.62%	4.16%
Total	30,519	11,725	2,942	4,392	875	33	8,278	2,274
		38.42%	9.64%	14.39%	2.87%	0.11%	27.12%	7.45%

Galway West

Count details

Seats: 5 Quota: 10,105

Candidate	Party	1st	2nd Cubbard Holmes King	3rd O Brolchain Votes	4th Walsh, E Votes	5th Crowe Votes	6th Welby Votes	7th Naughton Votes	8th Fahey Votes	9th Cuiv Surplus	10th O Clochart Votes	11th Nolan Surplus	12th Healy-E Votes	13th Walsh, B Surplus
Cuiv, Éamon Ó*	FF	7,441	+45 / 7,486	+61 / 7,547	+102 / 7,649	+549 / 8,198	+729 / 8,927	+108 / 9,035	+2,103 / 11,138	-1,033 / 10,105	10,105	10,105	10,105	10,105
Nolan, Derek	LB	7,489	+183 / 7,672	+334 / 8,006	+260 / 8,266	+197 / 8,463	+240 / 8,703	+416 / 9,119	+189 / 9,308	+107 / 9,415	+1,016 / 10,431	-326 / 10,105	10,105	10,105
Walsh, Brian	FG	5,425	+48 / 5,473	+42 / 5,515	+129 / 5,644	+225 / 5,869	+95 / 5,964	+1,044 / 7,008	+234 / 7,242	+101 / 7,343	+148 / 7,491	+29 / 7,520	+2,707 / 10,227	-122 / 10,105
Grealish, Noel*	NP	6,229	+117 / 6,346	+50 / 6,396	+193 / 6,589	+221 / 6,810	+306 / 7,116	+208 / 7,324	+592 / 7,916	+396 / 8,312	+370 / 8,682	+54 / 8,736	+1,075 / 9,811	+18 / 9,829
Kyne, Seán	FG	4,550	+31 / 4,581	+49 / 4,630	+74 / 4,704	+25 / 4,729	+1,012 / 5,741	+729 / 6,470	+151 / 6,621	+84 / 6,705	+324 / 7,029	+45 / 7,074	+1,946 / 9,020	+92 / 9,112
Connolly, Catherine	NP	4,766	+207 / 4,973	+241 / 5,214	+285 / 5,499	+104 / 5,603	+285 / 5,888	+260 / 6,148	+242 / 6,390	+161 / 6,551	+1,656 / 8,207	+168 / 8,375	+708 / 9,083	+12 / 9,095
Healy Eames, Fidelma	FG	5,046	+34 / 5,080	+93 / 5,173	+117 / 5,290	+57 / 5,347	+140 / 5,487	+1,055 / 6,542	+170 / 6,712	+89 / 6,801	+189 / 6,990	+30 / 7,020	-7,020 Eliminated	
Ó Clochartaigh, Trevor	SF	3,808	+119 / 3,927	+72 / 3,999	+97 / 4,096	+45 / 4,141	+266 / 4,407	+40 / 4,447	+141 / 4,588	+95 / 4,683	-4,683 Eliminated			
Fahey, Frank*	FF	3,448	+26 / 3,474	+15 / 3,489	+37 / 3,526	+307 / 3,833	+184 / 4,017	+45 / 4,062	-4,062 Eliminated					
Naughten, Hildegarde	FG	3,606	+49 / 3,655	+90 / 3,745	+113 / 3,858	+50 / 3,908	+85 / 3,993	-3,993 Eliminated						
Welby, Thomas	NP	3,298	+27 / 3,325	+20 / 3,345	+139 / 3,484	+20 / 3,504	-3,504 Eliminated							
Crowe, Michael	FF	1,814	+41 / 1,855	+15 / 1,870	+25 / 1,895	-1,895 Eliminated								
Walsh, Eamon	NP	1,481	+100 / 1,581	+43 / 1,624	-1,624 Eliminated									
Brolcháin, Niall Ó	GP	1,120	+33 / 1,153	-1,153 Eliminated										
Cubbard, Mike	NP	853	-853 Eliminated											
Holmes, Uinseann Eoin	NP	186	-186 Eliminated											
King, Thomas	NP	65	-65 Eliminated											
Non-transferable			+44	+28	+53	+95	+162	+88	+240		+980		+584	
Cumulative			44	72	125	220	382	470	710	710	1,690	1,690	2,274	2,274
Total		60,625	60,625	60,625	60,625	60,625	60,625	60,625	60,625	60,625	60,625	60,625	60,625	60,625

Kerry North-Limerick West (3 seats)

Change of dynasties sees Spring in as McEllistrim loses out

Elected

Jimmy Deenihan* (FG) Count 1, Arthur Spring (Lab) Final count, Martin Ferris* (SF) Final count.

Analysis by Michael Gallagher

This is a significantly redrawn constituency, with about 4,000 voters around Castleisland moved into Kerry South and around 10,000 voters from west Limerick found themselves part of this constituency.

Only one of the candidates was from the Limerick part of the constituency, John Sheahan from Glin, and he was the surprise of the election, polling a very strong fourth.

In a three-seater, that's not quite good enough, though, and this was one of the most predictable constituencies in the country. The collapse of Fianna Fáil support nationally meant that Tom McEllistrim really had no chance of retaining his seat. The third of the dynasty to hold a seat here, like his father and grandfather – both also called Tom – he tended to concentrate on the grassroots rather than hold forth in the Dáil chamber or to the media.

The other two incumbents were comfortably re-elected. Jimmy Deenihan, now a cabinet minister, has firmly established himself as the dominant figure in the constituency, and has led Fine Gael to heights (41% of the vote) that it has never before reached in Kerry. Martin Ferris of Sinn Féin, having won his seat narrowly in 2002, has been reasonably secure at subsequent elections.

The newcomer was Labour's Arthur Spring who, with a little help from his uncle Dick, nearly doubled the party vote from its 2007 base, and he took Tom McEllistrim's seat. Extraordinarily, there has been both a Spring and a McEllistrim on the ballot paper at all but one (2007) of the last 21 elections. The Spring dynasty dates only to 1943, 20 years after the first Tom McEllistrim was elected, but for the moment the Springs are in and the McEllistrims are out.

*outgoing TDs

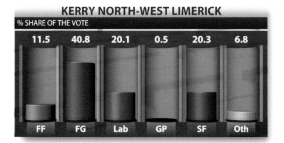

KERRY NORTH-WEST LIMERICK
% SHARE OF THE VOTE

FF	FG	Lab	GP	SF	Oth
11.5	40.8	20.1	0.5	20.3	6.8

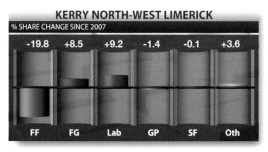

KERRY NORTH-WEST LIMERICK
% SHARE CHANGE SINCE 2007

FF	FG	Lab	GP	SF	Oth
-19.8	+8.5	+9.2	-1.4	-0.1	+3.6

Kerry North-Limerick West

JIMMY DEENIHAN (FG)

Home Address: 70 Ashfield, Listowel, Co Kerry.
Constituency office: 18A, The Square, Listowel, Co Kerry.
Phone: 01 6313806 (LH) 068 57446 (CO)
Website: www.jimmydeenihan.com
Facebook: Yes.
Birth Place/Date: Finuge, 1952.
Marital Status/Family: Married to Mary Dowling.
Education: Dromclough NS; St Michael's College, Listowel; St Mary's College, Twickenham, London; National College of Physical Education, Limerick (BEd).
Occupation: Full-time public representative. Formerly teacher.
Biography: Secured 12,304 first preferences in a poll-topping performance that saw him returned to the Dáil on the first count. He was appointed Minister for Arts, Heritage and Gaeltacht Affairs. Deenihan has been a TD since 1987. He was Minister of State at the Department of Agriculture, Food and Forestry 1994-1997. He unsuccessfully contested the November 1982 general election and he was a senator from 1982-1987.
Hobbies: Cycling, walking, GAA.
Did you know? Jimmy won five All-Ireland medals and only conceded one point as a corner back in his six All-Ireland final appearances with Kerry.
Politician (living or deceased) you most admire: Daniel O'Connell.
Priority as a TD? Job creation.
Why did you stand for election? I got involved in politics after I was approached to run in the November 1982 general election.
Is there any particular event that brought home to you just how serious the economic crisis had become? The arrival of the IMF in Ireland.

ARTHUR SPRING (Lab)

Home Address: 1 Brook Lodge, Oak View, Tralee, Co Kerry.
Phone: 087 0977260 (M) 066 7125337 (CO) 01 6183471 (LH)
Email: arthur.spring@oireachtas.ie
Website: www.labour.ie/arthurspring/
Twitter: twitter.com/springaj
Facebook: www.facebook.com/arthurjspring
Birth Place/Date: Tralee.
Marital Status/Family: Married to Fiona.
Education: CBS Tralee; Cistercian College Roscrea; Dublin Institute of Technology and Jönköping International Business School, Sweden, qualifying with a BSc in management.
Occupation: Public representative. Businessman, owns a juice bar in Tralee. Formerly worked in finance, working for companies including Anglo Irish Bank and Bank of Ireland.
Biography: Secured 9,159 first-preference votes to get elected in his first general election. He has won back the Labour seat that his uncle Dick Spring, the former Tánaiste, lost to Sinn Féin's Martin Ferris in 2002.
He topped the poll in both the Kerry County Council and Tralee Town Council elections in 2009.
Hobbies: Interested in all sports and outdoor activities. Interested in a wide variety of music, reading and socialising.
Did you know? He lived in Sweden for a year while studying.
Politician (living or deceased) you most admire: Mahatma Gandhi.
Priority as a TD? Jobs, Jobs, Jobs. To reduce the rate of unemployment both locally and nationally.
Why did you stand for election? I felt that I needed to stand up and be involved in making a change for the better.
Is there any particular event that brought home to you just how serious the economic crisis had become? The IMF bailout in November 2010.

MARTIN FERRIS (SF)

Home Address: 'Glenrowan', The Village, Ardfert, Co Kerry.
Phone: 066 7129545 (CO) 01 6184248 (LH)
Website: www.sinnfein.ie
Email: martin.ferris@oireachtas.ie
Facebook: Yes.
Birth Place/Date: Kerry, March 1952.
Marital Status/Family: Married to Marie; 3 sons, 3 daughters and 8 grandchildren.
Education: Barrow National School, Ardfert, Co Kerry; CBS (The Green), Tralee.
Occupation: Full-time elected representative, former fisherman.
Biography: Party spokesperson on Communications, Energy and Natural Resources. First elected in 2002. Unsuccessfully contested the 1997 general election. Elected to Tralee Town and Kerry County Councils in 1999. Became a member of Sinn Féin Ard Comhairle in 1983. He was arrested on board the Marita Ann in 1984, attempting to import arms for the IRA. Imprisoned in Portlaoise Prison, 1984-1994. Also served prison sentences in 1970s. A member of the party's negotiating team for the Good Friday Agreement in 1998. Daughter Toiréasa Ferris is a member of Tralee Town and Kerry County Council and former Mayor of Kerry.
Hobbies: Walking, GAA and other sports.
Did you know? Martin spent 47 days on hunger strike in Portlaoise Prison in 1976.
Politician (living or deceased) you most admire: James Connolly and Nelson Mandela.
Priority as a TD? Changing the nature of politics in Ireland for good; ending cronyism and political and financial elitism, which has ruined so many lives.
Why did you stand for election? As a republican I believe it is my duty to do all I can to promote republican politics, to stand up for ordinary people, the vulnerable and those with no voice.
Is there any particular event that brought home to you just how serious the economic crisis had become? There were a number, but the day the IMF arrived stands out particularly.

First preference votes

	Candidate	Party	1st	%	Quota	Count	Status
	Seats	3			11,404		
1	Deenihan, Jimmy*	FG	12,304	26.97%	1.08	1	Made Quota
2	Spring, Arthur	LB	9,159	20.08%	0.80	7	Made Quota
3	Ferris, Martin*	SF	9,282	20.35%	0.81	7	Made Quota
4	Sheahan, John	FG	6,295	13.80%	0.55	7	Not Elected
5	McEllistrim, Tom*	FF	5,230	11.47%	0.46	6	Eliminated
6	O'Brien, Bridget	NP	1,455	3.19%	0.13	5	No Expenses
7	Fitzgibon, Mary	NP	706	1.55%	0.06	4	No Expenses
8	Locke, Sam	NP	486	1.07%	0.04	4	No Expenses
9	Reidy, Michael	NV	357	0.78%	0.03	3	No Expenses
10	Donovan, Tom	GP	239	0.52%	0.02	2	No Expenses
11	McKenna, John	NP	101	0.22%	0.01	2	No Expenses

*Outgoing TD Valid poll: 45,614 Quota: 11,404 No expenses limit: 2,851

Party votes

| Party | Cand | 2011 | | | | Cand | 2007 | | | | Change | |
		1st	%	Quota	Seats		1st	%	Quota	Seats	%	Seats
FG	2	18,599	40.77%	1.63	1	1	12,697	32.30%	1.29	1	+8.48%	
LB	1	9,159	20.08%	0.80	1	1	4,287	10.90%	0.44		+9.17%	+1
FF	1	5,230	11.47%	0.46		2	12,304	31.30%	1.25	1	-19.83%	-1
SF	1	9,282	20.35%	0.81	1	1	8,030	20.43%	0.82	1	-0.08%	
GP	1	239	0.52%	0.02		1	747	1.90%	0.08		-1.38%	
Others	5	3,105	6.81%	0.27		4	1,248	3.17%	0.13		+3.63%	
Total	11	45,614	100.0%	11,404	3	10	39,313	100.0%	9,829	3	0.00%	0
Electorate		63,614	71.70%				56,216	69.93%			+1.77%	
Spoiled		413	0.90%				334	0.84%			+0.05%	
Turnout		46,027	72.35%				39,647	70.53%			+1.83%	

Transfer analysis

From	To	FG	LB	FF	SF	GP	Others	Non Trans
FG	900	382	256	45	158	8	51	
		42.44%	28.44%	5.00%	17.56%	0.89%	5.67%	
FF	5,678	902	1,560		1,252			1,964
		15.89%	27.47%		22.05%			34.59%
GP	247	34	70	22	35		73	13
		13.77%	28.34%	8.91%	14.17%		29.55%	5.26%
Others	3,794	431	1,200	381	689		565	528
		11.36%	31.63%	10.04%	18.16%		14.89%	13.92%
Total	10,619	1,749	3,086	448	2,134	8	689	2,505
		16.47%	29.06%	4.22%	20.10%	0.08%	6.49%	23.59%

Election Facts

"The exit poll results have identified a very angry and outraged population, with worry and fear very evident. Hope and confidence are severely lacking – so much reassurance is necessary from the new government. At a time of such national economic challenge, this could be a very tricky challenge" Millward Brown Lansdowne/RTÉ General Election 2011 Exit Poll

Kerry North-Limerick West

Count details

Candidate	Party	1st	2nd Deenihan Surplus	3rd Donovan McKenna	4th Reidy Votes	5th Fitzgibon Locke	6th O'Brien Votes	7th McEllistrim Votes
Seats 3						**Quota**	**11,404**	
			-900					
Deenihan, Jimmy*	FG	12,304	11,404	11,404	11,404	11,404	11,404	11,404
			+256	+99	+57	+376	+738	+1,560
Spring, Arthur	LB	9,159	9,415	9,514	9,571	9,947	10,685	12,245
			+158	+49	+51	+244	+380	+1,252
Ferris, Martin*	SF	9,282	9,440	9,489	9,540	9,784	10,164	11,416
			+382	+49	+55	+111	+250	+902
Sheahan, John	FG	6,295	6,677	6,726	6,781	6,892	7,142	8,044
			+45	+31	+23	+122	+227	-5,678
McEllistrim, Tom*	FF	5,230	5,275	5,306	5,329	5,451	5,678	Eliminated
			+22	+44	+56	+373	-1,950	
O'Brien, Bridget	NP	1,455	1,477	1,521	1,577	1,950	Eliminated	
			+16	+43	+84	-849		
Fitzgibon, Mary	NP	706	722	765	849	Eliminated		
			+6	+6	+21	-519		
Locke, Sam	NP	486	492	498	519	Eliminated		
			+5	+11	-373			
Reidy, Michael	NV	357	362	373	Eliminated			
			+8	-247				
Donovan, Tom	GP	239	247	Eliminated				
			+2	-103				
McKenna, John	NP	101	103	Eliminated				
Non-transferable				+18	+26	+142	+355	+1,964
Cumulative			0	18	44	186	541	2,505
Total		**45,614**	**45,614**	**45,614**	**45,614**	**45,614**	**45,614**	**45,614**

Fine Gael candidate Jimmy Deenihan, Labour candidate Arthur Spring and Sinn Féin candidate Martin Ferris at the Kerry North-Limerick West election count at the Brandon Conference Centre in Tralee

Photo: ©McMonagle.com

Kerry South (3 seats)

First constituency for 60 years to return two independents

Elected

Brendan Griffin (FG) Count 5, Tom Fleming (Ind) Final count, Michael Healy-Rae (Ind) Final count.

Analysis by Michael Gallagher

There was a major boundary change here with a population of 5,098 around Castleisland and Cordal transferred from the old Kerry North constituency. It remains a three-seat constituency.

Everything changed in Kerry South, as one incumbent retired and the other two were defeated. Jackie Healy-Rae hung up his tartan cap after 14 years and handed over the mantle to his son Michael, who proved equally adept at enunciating the well-rehearsed 'I am not a gombeen politician and it is disrespectful to the people of Kerry for the Dublin media to say so' line. It worked for his father and it worked for him – though, to establish that he is his own man, his cap of choice is usually black.

The sole Fianna Fáil candidate was John O'Donoghue, who had fought the 2007 campaign as a senior government minister. Much had changed since; he had first been shuffled off against his will to the post of Ceann Comhairle and had then become the first occupant of that office to have to stand down after the disclosure of his remarkable expenses claims. These were shaky credentials in an election where Fianna Fáil itself was on the ropes, and O'Donoghue did not last beyond the fourth count. His departure speech, claiming credit for obtaining the funding for the building in which the votes were counted, was eloquent indeed.

Fine Gael, often seatless in this constituency, won more votes than Fianna Fáil and Labour combined, but not quite enough for two seats. Tom Sheahan, who had won a seat for Fine Gael in 2007 after the party had been unrepresented here since 1987, was surprisingly unseated by his youthful running mate Brendan Griffin, who gained national publicity by promising to take only half of a TD's salary if elected, a pledge he found himself unexpectedly called upon to live up to.

In contrast, the Labour vote actually dropped, the only constituency in the country where this happened, and a marked contrast to the Labour surge in north Kerry.

With Fianna Fáil and Labour struggling, independents won 42% of the votes, and Kerry South became the first constituency for 60 years to return two independents. Joining Michael Healy-Rae in the 31st Dáil was Tom Fleming, who, as a Fianna Fáil candidate, had finished a close runner-up in both 2002 and 2007 and who was now aided by the transfer of a sizeable pocket of votes around Castleisland, close to his own base of Scartaglin, into Kerry South. Fianna Fáil may regret not selecting Fleming as its sole candidate; as it was, Kerry became yet another county left without a Fianna Fáil TD.

*outgoing TDs

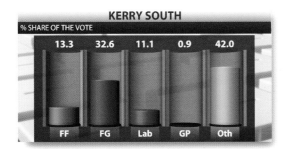

KERRY SOUTH
% SHARE OF THE VOTE

FF	FG	Lab	GP	Oth
13.3	32.6	11.1	0.9	42.0

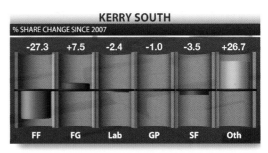

KERRY SOUTH
% SHARE CHANGE SINCE 2007

FF	FG	Lab	GP	SF	Oth
-27.3	+7.5	-2.4	-1.0	-3.5	+26.7

Kerry South

BRENDAN GRIFFIN (FG)

Home Address: Keel, Castlemaine, Co Kerry.
Phone: 087 6528841 (M) 01 6184480 (LH)
Email: brendan.griffin@oireachtas.ie
Website: www.brendangriffin.ie
Twitter: cllrbgriffin
Facebook: Brendan Griffin
Birth Place/Date: Cork, March 1982.
Marital Status/Family: Married to Róisín.
Education: Castledrum NS; Intermediate School Killorglin; NUI Galway (BA Hons history, sociology and politics).
Occupation: Full-time public representative. Formerly a publican. Also previously worked as a teacher and in the hotel industry.
Biography: Topped poll with 8,808 first preferences to win Dáil seat in his first general election attempt. Elected to Kerry County Council in 2009, topping the poll in the Dingle electoral area. Unsuccessfully contested 2004 local elections. Parliamentary assistant to Jimmy Deenihan TD (2004-2007).
Hobbies: Plays soccer with Mainebank FC and Gaelic football with Keel GAA. Big Beatles and REM fan.
Did you know? Brendan entered the Dáil on his 29th birthday on 9 March. Charles Haughey was elected Taoiseach by the Dáil the day Brendan was born.
Politician (living or deceased) you most admire: Too many to mention one.
Priority as a TD? Contribute to our economic recovery and help rebuild our republic.
Why did you stand for election? I felt that the country was calling on a new generation and new calibre of public representatives to step up to the mark.
Is there any particular event that brought home to you just how serious the economic crisis had become? The faces missing from my local soccer and GAA club training and watching groups of men standing around the post office after dropping their kids off at school as they have no work to go to.

TOM FLEMING (Ind)

Home Address: Scartaglin Village, Co Kerry.
Phone: 087 7814781 (M) 01 6183354 (CO) 01 6183354 (LH)
Email: tomflemingmcc1@gmail.com or tom.fleming@oireachtas.ie
Website: www.tomflemingelection.com
Birth Place/Date: Kerry, February 1951.
Marital Status/Family: Married to Lena; 3 daughters.
Education: Scartaglin NS; St Patrick's College, Castleisland, Co Kerry.
Occupation: Public representative and publican.
Biography: Secured 6,416 first-preference votes to get elected in his third general election attempt. He was first elected to Kerry County Council in 1985 and he was re-elected at each subsequent general election for Fianna Fáil. He left Fianna Fáil shortly before the 2011 general election and decided to run as an independent.
Hobbies: Sport and walking.
Did you know? In 2002 and 2007, he contested the general elections as the running mate of former Fianna Fáil minister John O'Donoghue, narrowly missing out on a seat on both occasions.
Politician (living or deceased) you most admire: Barack Obama for his positive outlook at a time of global recession.
Priority as a TD? To tackle national issues such as cuts to the disabled, the blind, carers, student nurses and the increase in third-level fees. To address the two-tier health system.
Why did you stand for election? I believe I have a role to play in job creation and helping to give young people a more positive future by trying to prevent forced emigration.
Is there any particular event that brought home to you just how serious the economic crisis had become? I think that giving a blanket guarantee to the banks, based on misinformation from the bank chiefs, was a regretful day for this country.

MICHAEL HEALY-RAE (Ind)

Home Address: Sandymount, Kilgarvan, Co Kerry.
Phone: 087 2461678 (M) 064 6632467 (CO) 01 6184319 (LH)
Email: michael.healyrae@oireachtas.ie or cllrmhealyrae@eircom.net
Facebook: Michael Healy-Rae
Birth Place/Date: Kilgarvan.
Marital Status/Family: Married to Eileen; 5 children.
Education: Kenmare Vocational School; Salesian Brothers Pallaskenry, Co Limerick.
Occupation: Public representative. Also shopkeeper and runs plant hire business.
Biography: Secured 6,670 first-preference votes to get elected in his first general election attempt. He was first elected to Kerry County Council in 1999 and he was re-elected in 2004 and 2009. He has been Mayor of Kerry on two occasions and he is currently a member of the HSE and the Citizens Information Board. Son of Jackie Healy-Rae, TD for Kerry South, 1997-2011.
Hobbies: Shooting, walking, hill climbing and a strong interest in all sports.
Did you know? Michael was the winner of the RTÉ reality television series *Celebrities Go Wild*, with celebrities such as the late Katy French and former Olympic swimmer Michelle de Bruin, in 2007.
Politician (living or deceased) you most admire: My father.
Priority as a TD? Job creation.
Why did you stand for election? To do my part in genuinely working to help Ireland recover and dig ourselves out of the desperate situation which we are presently in. This past election campaign has been all about jobs, jobs, jobs – that is the big issue for everyone at present and the fact that so many people are finding it so difficult to manage financially.
Is there any particular event that brought home to you just how serious the economic crisis had become? The mass of emigration from small communities in south Kerry that have lost 30 or 40 people, which is a major blow to any rural area.

First preference votes

	Candidate	Party	1st	%	Quota	Count	Status
	Seats	3			11,096		
1	Griffin, Brendan	FG	8,808	19.85%	0.79	5	Made Quota
2	Fleming, Tom	NP	6,416	14.46%	0.58	6	Elected
3	Healy-Rae, Michael	NP	6,670	15.03%	0.60	6	Elected
4	Sheahan, Tom*	FG	5,674	12.79%	0.51	6	Not Elected
5	Gleeson, Michael	SKIA	4,939	11.13%	0.45	4	Eliminated
6	O'Donoghue, John*	FF	5,917	13.33%	0.53	3	Eliminated
7	Moloney, Marie	LB	4,926	11.10%	0.44	2	Eliminated
8	Comerford, Oonagh	GP	401	0.90%	0.04	1	No Expenses
9	Behal, Richard	NP	348	0.78%	0.03	1	No Expenses
10	Finn, Dermot	NP	281	0.63%	0.03	1	No Expenses
10	*Outgoing		44,380	100.00%	11,096	2,775	No Expenses

* Outgoing TD Valid poll: 44,380 Quota: 11,096 No expenses limit: 2,775

Party votes

Party	Cand	2011 1st	%	Quota	Seats	Cand	2007 1st	%	Quota	Seats	Change %	Seats
FG	2	14,482	32.63%	1.31	1	2	9,795	25.09%	1.00	1	+7.54%	
LB	1	4,926	11.10%	0.44		1	5,263	13.48%	0.54		-2.38%	
FF	1	5,917	13.33%	0.53		2	15,868	40.65%	1.63	1	-27.32%	-1
SF						1	1,375	3.52%	0.14		-3.52%	
GP	1	401	0.90%	0.04		1	738	1.89%	0.08		-0.99%	
Others	5	18,654	42.03%	1.68	2	1	5,993	15.35%	0.61	1	+26.68%	+1
Total	10	44,380	100.0%	11,096	3	8	39,032	100.0%	9,759	3	0.00%	0
Electorate		59,629	74.43%				53,660	72.74%			+1.69%	
Spoiled		299	0.67%				293	0.75%			-0.08%	
Turnout		44,679	74.93%				39,325	73.29%			+1.64%	

Transfer analysis

From	To	FG	LB	FF	Others	Non Trans
FG	1,540	741			505	294
		48.12%			32.79%	19.09%
LB	5,132	1,912		240	2,588	392
		37.26%		4.68%	50.43%	7.64%
FF	6,200	1,600			3,782	818
		25.81%			61.00%	13.19%
GP	401	77	80	17	208	19
		19.20%	19.95%	4.24%	51.87%	4.74%
Others	7,666	3,233	126	26	2,952	1,329
		42.17%	1.64%	0.34%	38.51%	17.34%
Total	20,939	7,563	206	283	10,035	2,852
		36.12%	0.98%	1.35%	47.92%	13.62%

Election Facts
"Transfer patterns indicate that Independents/Others and Labour received the highest next vote ahead of Fine Gael"
Millward Brown
Lansdowne/RTÉ General
Election 2011 Exit Poll

Kerry South

Candidate	Party	1st	2nd Comerford Behal Finn	3rd Moloney Votes	4th O'Donoghue Votes	5th Gleeson Votes	6th Griffin Surplus
Seats 3						**Quota**	**11,096**
			+135	+1,071	+851	+1,771	-1,540
Griffin, Brendan	FG	8,808	8,943	10,014	10,865	12,636	11,096
			+132	+809	+1,389	+1,643	+308
Fleming, Tom	NP	6,416	6,548	7,357	8,746	10,389	10,697
			+119	+623	+1,734	+983	+197
Healy-Rae, Michael	NP	6,670	6,789	7,412	9,146	10,129	10,326
			+62	+841	+749	+1,342	+741
Sheahan, Tom*	FG	5,674	5,736	6,577	7,326	8,668	9,409
			+283	+1,156	+659	-7,037	
Gleeson, Michael	SKIA	4,939	5,222	6,378	7,037	Eliminated	
			+43	+240	-6,200		
O'Donoghue, John*	FF	5,917	5,960	6,200	Eliminated		
			+206	-5,132			
Moloney, Marie	LB	4,926	5,132	Eliminated			
			-401				
Comerford, Oonagh	GP	401	Eliminated				
			-348				
Behal, Richard	NP	348	Eliminated				
			-281				
Finn, Dermot	NP	281	Eliminated				
Non-transferable			+50	+392	+818	+1,298	+294
Cumulative			50	442	1,260	2,558	2,852
Total		**44,380**	**44,380**	**44,380**	**44,380**	**44,380**	**44,380**

Newly elected South Kerry TDs Michael Healy-Rae, Independent, Brendan Griffin, Fine Gael and Tom Fleming, Independent, commiserate with former Ceann Comhairle John O'Donoghue, who lost his seat in the constituency

Kildare North (4 seats)

Another gain for Fine Gael as Fianna Fáil loses both of its seats

Elected

Bernard Durkan* (FG) Count 2, Emmet Stagg* (Lab) Count 3, Catherine Murphy (Ind) Final count, Anthony Lawlor (FG) Final count.

Analysis by Sean Donnelly

There was a minor boundary revision here with a population of 1,314 in the Kilpatrick and Newtown areas transferred into this constituency from the Kildare South constituency. However, it remained a four-seat constituency.

This was another good performance by Fine Gael as its vote was up 12 percentage points and with 1.7 quotas, the party was well placed to win two seats. The long serving Bernard Durkan topped the poll and was just short of the quota on the first count. His running mate Anthony Lawlor had a more modest level of support, with 6,882 first preferences to leave him with 0.7 quotas and he went on to comfortably hold off Áine Brady for the final seat.

The Labour vote was up 12 percentage points and with 1.5 quotas, the party should have been in contention for two seats. Emmet Stagg was short of the quota on the first count and went on to comfortably take the second seat on the third count. His running mate John McGinley was in fifth place on the first count but the gap between the Labour man and Fine Gael's Lawlor was just too big and he was eventually eliminated at the end of the fourth count, with his transfers favouring Murphy (45%) and Lawlor (22%).

This was another poor Fianna Fáil performance with its vote down 25 percentage points and it lost both of its seats. Both outgoing deputies – Áine Brady and Michael Fitpatrick – decided to contest and between them they got just 0.7 quotas. The division of the party vote left both candidates too far behind after the first count. Brady was in sixth place on the first count; 63% of her running mate's transfers moved her up to fifth place but that was as good as it got and the Minister of State was well beaten in the end.

Catherine Murphy won the by-election in 2004, which was caused by the appointment of Charlie McCreevy as EU Commissioner. Murphy was a surprise loser in 2007 but made no mistake in 2011 as she was in third place on the first count with 6,911 votes and went on to take the third seat on the final count.

The Sinn Féin vote was up three percentage points but with just 6%, Martin Kelly was in seventh place and out of contention.

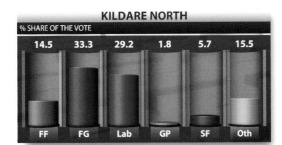

KILDARE NORTH					
% SHARE OF THE VOTE					
14.5	33.3	29.2	1.8	5.7	15.5
FF	FG	Lab	GP	SF	Oth

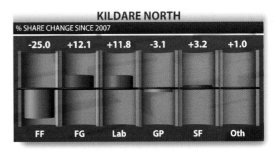

KILDARE NORTH					
% SHARE CHANGE SINCE 2007					
-25.0	+12.1	+11.8	-3.1	+3.2	+1.0
FF	FG	Lab	GP	SF	Oth

*outgoing TDs

Kildare North

BERNARD DURKAN (FG)

Home Address: Timard, Maynooth, Co Kildare.
Phone: 01 6286063/6183191 (LH)
Website: www.bernarddurkan.finegael.ie
Email: bernard.durkan@oireachtas.ie
Birth Place/Date: Swinford, Co Mayo, March 1945.
Marital Status/Family: Married to Hilary Spence, 2 sons.
Education: St John's National School, Carramore, Co Mayo.
Occupation: Full-time public representative. Formerly agricultural contractor.
Biography: First elected to the Dáil in 1981 – he lost his seat the following year. Elected in November 1982, and has been returned to the Dáil in successive general elections. Minister of State at the Department of Social Welfare (1994-1997). Chairperson of European Affairs Committee in 30th Dáil. Fine Gael frontbench spokesperson on Communications and Natural Resources in 29th Dáil. Fine Gael Chief Whip from 2002-2004. Member of Public Accounts Committee 1989 to 2002. Also served as party spokesperson on: Health, Food, Trade and Industry; Insurance; Overseas Development Aid; and Human Rights. Member of Kildare County Council 1976-1994 (chairperson 1986-87).
Hobbies: Reading. Films. Taking to the roads on a motorbike.
Did you know? Bernard has a number of vintage vehicles; including a 1967 Volkswagen Beetle, and two tractors from the 1960s.
Politician (living or deceased) you most admire: Michael Collins, Arthur Griffith, Abraham Lincoln.
Priority as a TD? To provide responsible representation.
Why did you stand for election? To try to make a positive difference both locally and nationally.
Is there any particular event that brought home to you just how serious the economic crisis had become? When I saw constituents with mortgages that stretched them to the limit – even when both people in the house were working and interest rates were low.

EMMET STAGG (Lab)

Home Address: Lodge Park, Straffan, Co Kildare.
Phone: 087 6728555 (M) 01 6183013 (LH)
Email: emmet.stagg@oireachtas.ie
Website: www.labour.ie/emmetstagg
Birth Place/Date: Mayo, October 1944.
Marital Status/Family: Married to Mary Morris; 1 daughter, 1 son.
Education: CBS, Ballinrobe; Kevin Street College of Technology (medical laboratory scientist).
Occupation: Full-time public representative.
Biography: Emmet has been a member of the Dáil since 1987 and has been re-elected on six occasions. Minister for Housing (1993-1994), Minister of State at the Department of Transport, Energy and Communications (1994-1997). Member, Kildare County Council (1978-1993 and 1999-2002), chairman in 1985.
Hobbies: Fishing, shooting, gardening and reading.
Did you know? Emmet was the first Irish minister to address a planning hearing in the UK in relation to the attempts to build an underground nuclear dump in Cumbria – Nirex. Ireland and local Cumbrian groups successfully won the case and the proposal did not proceed.
Politician (living or deceased) you most admire: Noel Browne.
Priority as a TD? To get our people back working through job creation.
Why did you stand for election? I want to play my part along with my party in bringing forward policies to get our country back working and to stabilise the economy. I also want to ensure that the poorest in society are cushioned against the cutbacks to pay for our economic ills.
Is there any particular event that brought home to you just how serious the economic crisis had become? At my advice service, the constant stream of people who have lost their jobs, whose mortgages are in arrears, and people thinking of emigrating again. It's the coalface where you hear real problems and try to assist people.

CATHERINE MURPHY (Ind)

Address: Unit 4, the Post House, Leixlip Shopping Mall, Leixlip, Co Kildare.
Phone: 087 2696450 (M) 01 6183099 (LH)
Email: catherine.murphy@oireachtas.ie
Website: www.catherinemurphy.ie
Twitter: twitter.com/murphycatherine
Facebook: Yes.
Birth Place/Date: Dublin, September 1953.
Marital Status/Family: Married.
Education: IPA/NCC higher diploma in computer studies.
Occupation: Public representative.
Biography: First elected a TD in 2005 Kildare North by-election caused by the appointment of Charlie McCreevy as EU Commissioner. Lost Dáil seat in 2007. Founding member Leixlip Town Commission 1988. Member, Kildare County Council (1991-2005 and 2009-2011). Member, the Workers' Party (mid 1980s-1992). Founding member of Democratic Left, 1992 and joined Labour after merger in 1999. Became an independent in 2003.
Hobbies: Reading, sport, history and genealogy.
Did you know? Catherine's grandparents took part in the 1916 Rising (Four Courts); one of them, her grandfather William Murnane, going so far as to be interned in the Frongoch Internment Camp in Wales for his part.
Politician (living or deceased) you most admire: Mary Robinson.
Priority as a TD? Political and public service reform. To create a fair and equitable system that works efficiently on behalf of the people of Ireland.
Why did you stand for election? I firmly believe that if you're not a part of the solution, then you're a part of the problem. The knowledge and experience I have gained over the years can help change the system at a national level.
Is there any particular event that brought home to you just how serious the economic crisis had become? I think the telltale sign of this crisis is not any one big dramatic event but the quiet day-to-day despair a wide spectrum of people are feeling.

ANTHONY LAWLOR (FG)

Home Address: 14 River Lawns, Kill, Co Kildare.
Phone: 087 2753942 (M) 01 6183007 (LH)
Email: anthony.lawlor@oireachtas.ie
Website: www.anthonylawlor.ie
Twitter: anthonylawlorfg
Facebook: anthonylawlorfg
Birth Place/Date: Dublin, June 1959.
Marital Status/Family: Married to Margaret.
Education: Naas CBS; Dominican College Newbridge; Multyfarnham Agricultural College; UCD (BAgSc); NUI Maynooth (HDipEd).
Occupation: Public representative.
Biography: Anthony secured 6,882 first-preference votes to get elected on the fifth and final count. He was co-opted onto Kildare County Council in January 1998 following the death of his mother Patsy Lawlor. He was re-elected in the 1999 local elections, topping the poll when he stood as an independent candidate. He stepped down from the council in 2004 and shortly afterwards joined Fine Gael. He was elected to Kildare County Council in 2009 for Fine Gael.
Hobbies: Rugby, GAA, golf and reading history.
Did you know? Anthony spent two years overseas with Voluntary Services Overseas (VSO) as a community worker in Vanuatu, an island nation located in the South Pacific Ocean, from 1984 to 1986.
Politician (living or deceased) you most admire: Michael Collins and John F Kennedy.
Priority as a TD? To develop an environment for the creation of sustainable jobs.
Why did you stand for election? I felt that I wanted to make a real contribution to bring about the change to our country that is needed.
Is there any particular event that brought home to you just how serious the economic crisis had become? The increase in demand for the services of the St Vincent de Paul from all sections of Irish society.

Posters in the window of a house in Dublin's south inner city, warning off Fianna Fáil and Green Party canvassers

Kildare North

	Seats	4			10,245		
	Candidate	Party	1st	%	Quota	Count	Status
1	Durkan, Bernard*	FG	10,168	19.85%	0.99	2	Made Quota
2	Stagg, Emmet*	LB	9,718	18.97%	0.95	3	Made Quota
3	Murphy, Catherine #	NP	6,911	13.49%	0.67	5	Made Quota
4	Lawlor, Anthony	FG	6,882	13.44%	0.67	5	Elected
5	Brady, Áine*	FF	4,777	9.33%	0.47	5	Not Elected
6	McGinley, John	LB	5,261	10.27%	0.51	4	Eliminated
7	Kelly, Martin	SF	2,896	5.65%	0.28	3	Eliminated
8	Fitzpatrick, Michael*	FF	2,659	5.19%	0.26	2	Eliminated
9	Fitzgerald, Shane	GP	905	1.77%	0.09	1	No Expenses
10	Doyle-Higgins, Eric	NP	423	0.83%	0.04	1	No Expenses
11	Beirne, Michael	NP	422	0.82%	0.04	1	No Expenses
12	Murphy, Bart	NP	200	0.39%	0.02	1	No Expenses

* Outgoing TD #Former TD Valid poll: 51,222 Quota: 10,245 No expenses limit: 2,562

Party votes

Party	Cand	1st	%	Quota	Seats	Cand	1st	%	Quota	Seats	%	Seats
FG	2	17,050	33.29%	1.66	2	2	9,590	21.22%	1.06	1	+12.07%	+1
LB	2	14,979	29.24%	1.46	1	1	7,882	17.44%	0.87	1	+11.80%	
FF	2	7,436	14.52%	0.73		2	17,851	39.50%	1.97	2	-24.98%	-2
SF	1	2,896	5.65%	0.28		1	1,103	2.44%	0.12		+3.21%	
GP	1	905	1.77%	0.09		1	2,215	4.90%	0.25		-3.13%	
PD						1	983	2.18%	0.11		-2.18%	
Others	4	7,956	15.53%	0.78	1	3	5,567	12.32%	0.62	1	+3.21%	+1
Total	12	51,222	100.0%	10,245	4	11	45,191	100.0%	9,039	4	0.00%	0
Electorate		77,959	65.70%				71,311	63.37%			+2.33%	
Spoiled		388	0.75%				232	0.51%			+0.24%	
Turnout		51,610	66.20%				45,423	63.70%			+2.50%	

Transfer analysis

From	To	FG	LB	FF	SF	Others	Non Trans
LB	6,449	1,421		467		2,923	1,638
		22.03%		7.24%		45.32%	25.40%
FF	2,714	209	389	1,717	68	222	109
		7.70%	14.33%	63.26%	2.51%	8.18%	4.02%
SF	3,111	384	859	194		1,020	654
		12.34%	27.61%	6.24%		32.79%	21.02%
GP	905	206	226	87	68	261	57
		22.76%	24.97%	9.61%	7.51%	28.84%	6.30%
NP	1,045	238	260	101	79	302	65
		22.78%	24.88%	9.67%	7.56%	28.90%	6.22%
Total	14,224	2,458	1,734	2,566	215	4,728	2,523
		17.28%	12.19%	18.04%	1.51%	33.24%	17.74%

Kildare North

Count details

Candidate	Party	1st	2nd Fitzgerald Doyle Beirne Murphy	3rd Fitzpatrick Votes	4th Kelly Votes	5th McGinley Votes
Seats 4					**Quota**	**10,245**
Durkan, Bernard*	FG	10,168	+252 **10,420**	10,420	10,420	10,420
Stagg, Emmet*	LB	9,718	+258 9,976	+288 **10,264**	10,264	10,264
Murphy, Catherine #	NP	6,911	+563 7,474	+222 7,696	+1,020 8,716	+2,923 11,639
Lawlor, Anthony	FG	6,882	+192 7,074	+209 7,283	+384 7,667	+1,421 9,088
Brady, Áine*	FF	4,777	+133 4,910	+1,717 6,627	+194 6,821	+467 7,288
McGinley, John	LB	5,261	+228 5,489	+101 5,590	+859 6,449	-6,449 Eliminated
Kelly, Martin	SF	2,896	+147 3,043	+68 3,111	-3,111 Eliminated	
Fitzpatrick, Michael*	FF	2,659	+55 2,714	-2,714 Eliminated		
Fitzgerald, Shane	GP	905	-905 Eliminated			
Doyle-Higgins, Eric	NP	423	-423 Eliminated			
Beirne, Michael	NP	422	-422 Eliminated			
Murphy, Bart	NP	200	-200 Eliminated			
Non-transferable			+122	+109	+654	+1,638
Cumulative			122	231	885	2,523
Total		**51,222**	**51,222**	**51,222**	**51,222**	**51,222**

Fianna Fáil leader Micheál Martin (centre) campaigns in Naas, Co Kildare, with Kildare candidates Seán Ó Fearghaíl and Áine Brady

Kildare South (3 seats)

Fine Gael reclaims seat in former leader's constituency

Elected

Martin Heydon (FG) Count 1, Jack Wall* (Lab) Count 1, Seán Ó Fearghaíl* (FF) Final count.

Analysis by Michael Gallagher

There was a minor boundary revision here with a population of 1,314 from the Kilpatrick and Newtown areas transferred to Kildare North.

It was a very predictable constituency in the context of 2011. Labour's Jack Wall would be re-elected, Martin Heydon would reclaim a seat for Fine Gael after nine years, and one of the two Fianna Fáil incumbents would survive the deluge.

So it proved. Martin Heydon took a third of the votes in the constituency, the highest share of any candidate in the country, and achieved Fine Gael's fourth largest vote gain outside Dublin. This was of course, in the constituency of the party's former leader, Alan Dukes, who lost his seat in 2002.

Jack Wall, who, unusually for a Labour TD, has a strong GAA background, was elected on the first count for the first time in his career.

Fianna Fáil duly took its one seat, the loser being Seán Power, a five-term veteran, and the victor Seán Ó Fearghaíl. Remarkably, Ó Fearghaíl had started out on the road before Power, having first stood in 1987 and losing on three further occasions before finally being elected in 2002. There was almost a sting in the tail on this occasion, as independent councillor Paddy Kennedy from Newbridge nearly deprived Fianna Fáil of any representation. Aided by over 1,000 votes from Heydon's surplus, and by nearly 1,700 votes upon the elimination of fellow Newbridge candidate Jason Turner of Sinn Féin, he finished fewer than 1,000 votes behind Ó Fearghaíl on the seventh count.

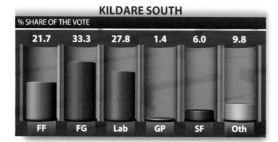

KILDARE SOUTH

% SHARE OF THE VOTE

FF	FG	Lab	GP	SF	Oth
21.7	33.3	27.8	1.4	6.0	9.8

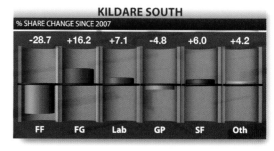

KILDARE SOUTH

% SHARE CHANGE SINCE 2007

FF	FG	Lab	GP	SF	Oth
-28.7	+16.2	+7.1	-4.8	+6.0	+4.2

*outgoing TDs

MARTIN HEYDON (FG)

Home Address: Blackrath, Colbinstown, Co Kildare.
Phone: 087 6262546 (M) 045 487624 (CO) 01 6183017 (LH)
Email: martinheydonfg@gmail.com or martin.heydon@oireachtas.ie
Website: www.martinheydon.com
Twitter: twitter.com/martinheydon
Facebook: facebook.com/martin heydon
Birth Place/Date: Dublin, August 1978.
Marital Status/family: Single.
Education: Crookstown NS, Ballitore Athy; Cross and Passion College, Kilcullen; Kildalton Agricultural College, Kilkenny.
Occupation: Public representative. Also runs family farm in Kilcullen.
Biography: Elected in his first general election attempt. Member, Kildare County Council (2009-2011).
Hobbies: GAA, horse racing and current affairs.
Did you know? Martin achieved the highest percentage vote of any candidate in the country at 33.3% to regain the seat held until 2002 by Alan Dukes.
Politician (living or deceased) you most admire: WT Cosgrave.
Priority as a TD? Political reform – as a young politician, I believe now is the time to change our system. The people have demanded it and we as a party now have an opportunity to prove that all political parties are not the same.
Why did you stand for election? I believe I have something to add and could effect change. I watched from the sidelines as the bank guarantee was introduced and felt I needed to do more than just talk about it.
Is there any particular event that brought home to you just how serious the economic crisis had become? I remember canvassing a housing estate, where the houses were worth €500,000 each, and a man came out and broke down crying at the door. He had lost his job and he was about to lose his home. That crystallised it for me and I will never assume that because somebody seems wealthy that they are not under severe financial pressure.

JACK WALL (Lab)

Home Address: Castlemitchell, Athy, Co Kildare.
Phone: 087 2570275 (M) 01 6183571 (LH) 059 8632874 (CO)
Email: jack.wall@oireachtas.ie
Website: www.kildaresouth.com
Birth Place/Date: Castledermot, Co Kildare, July 1945.
Marital Status/Family: Married to Ann Byrne; 2 sons, 2 daughters.
Education: Castledermot Vocational School; Kevin Street College of Technology, Dublin.
Occupation: Full-time public representative. Formerly electrician.
Biography: First elected a TD in 1997 and re-elected in 2002, 2007 and 2011. Previously Labour spokesperson on Arts, Sport and Tourism; Agriculture; and Defence. Member of Seanad Éireann (1993-1997). Member, Kildare County Council 1999-2003; Member, Athy Urban District Council 1994-2003.
Hobbies: I am a sports fanatic. I like all sports especially GAA and golf.
Did you know? Jack spent his younger years representing Kildare on the hurling pitch, winning junior, intermediate and senior B All-Irelands with the Lilywhites, and he also served as chairman of Kildare GAA county board from 1989 to 1999.
Politician (living or deceased) you most admire: Michael D Higgins.
Priority as a TD? Education and jobs. We have to ensure everyone gets a proper education and we have to create job opportunities for people.
Why did you stand for election? I initially went into politics as I felt that I had something to offer and I had a good knowledge of communities. Now I can see that these communities are under threat from unemployment, drugs problems and a lack of facilities, so I want to help them.
Is there any particular event that brought home to you just how serious the economic crisis had become? I see it on a daily basis in my constituency office in Athy, where people come in with concerns over issues ranging from housing to education. The amount of unemployment, personal debt and mortgage arrears is a sign of how bad things are.

SEÁN Ó FEARGHAÍL (FF)

Home Address: 4 Offaly Street, Athy, Co Kildare.
Phone: 059 8634805 (CO) 01 6183948 (LH)
Website: www.seanofearghail.ie
Twitter: twitter.com/SOFearghail
Facebook: facebook/Sean O'Fearghail
Birth Place/Date: Kildare, April, 1960.
Marital Status/family: Married to Mary Clare Meaney; 3 daughters, 1 son.
Education: De La Salle Primary School and St Joseph's Academy, Kildare.
Occupation: Full-time public representative and businessman.
Biography: Party whip and spokesperson on Foreign Affairs and Trade. First elected to Kildare County Council in 1985. Elected to Seanad Éireann in 2000. He was subsequently elected to Dáil Éireann in the 2002 general election and was re-elected in 2007 and 2011.
Hobbies: Reading, music, travelling and spending time with good friends.
Did you know? Seán is a pioneer of the voluntary housing movement in Kildare, that has housed more than 300 families to date.
Politician (living or deceased) you most admire: Hillary Clinton.
Priority as a TD? Helping to rectify the economy and returning the country to job creation and growth.
Why did you stand for election? Having been initially elected to the Oireachtas during the Celtic Tiger period, I relished the challenge of contesting another election in more adverse national circumstances, in order to be part of the drive to rebuild Ireland's economy and redefine Fianna Fáil's future as a positive political force.
Is there any particular event that brought home to you just how serious the economic crisis had become? Meeting members of hard-working families who can no longer afford to pay their mortgages or to provide for their children the support and opportunities that were previously taken for granted.

Kildare South

	Candidate	Party	1st	%	9,568 Quota	Count	Status
Seats	3						
1	Heydon, Martin	FG	12,755	33.33%	1.33	1	Made Quota
2	Wall, Jack*	LB	10,645	27.82%	1.11	1	Made Quota
3	Ó Fearghaíl, Seán*	FF	4,514	11.80%	0.47	7	Elected
4	Kennedy, Paddy	NP	2,806	7.33%	0.29	7	Not Elected
5	Power, Sean*	FF	3,793	9.91%	0.40	6	Eliminated
6	Turner, Jason	SF	2,308	6.03%	0.24	5	Eliminated
7	Reid, Clifford T.	NP	926	2.42%	0.10	4	No Expenses
8	Cummins, Vivian	GP	523	1.37%	0.05	3	No Expenses

*Outgoing TD Valid poll: 38,270 Quota: 9,568 No expenses limit: 2,392

Party votes

Party	Cand	2011 1st	2011 %	2011 Quota	2011 Seats	Cand	2007 1st	2007 %	2007 Quota	2007 Seats	Change %	Change Seats
FG	1	12,755	33.33%	1.33	1	2	5,939	17.17%	0.69		+16.16%	
LB	1	10,645	27.82%	1.11	1	1	7,154	20.68%	0.83	1	+7.13%	
FF	2	8,307	21.71%	0.87	1	2	17,425	50.37%	2.01	2	-28.67%	
SF	1	2,308	6.03%	0.24							+6.03%	
GP	1	523	1.37%	0.05		1	2,136	6.18%	0.25		-4.81%	
PD						1	1,513	4.37%	0.17		-4.37%	
Others	2	3,732	9.75%	0.39		1	424	1.23%	0.05		+8.53%	
Total	8	38,270	100.0%	9,568	3	8	34,591	100.0%	8,648	3	0.00%	0
Electorate		58,867	65.01%				56,670	61.04%			+3.97%	
Spoiled		353	0.91%				347	0.99%			-0.08%	
Turnout		38,623	65.61%				34,938	61.65%			+3.96%	

Transfer analysis

From	To	FF	SF	GP	Others	Non Trans
FG	3,187	961	302	421	1,503	
		30.15%	9.48%	13.21%	47.16%	
LB	1,077	274	212	101	490	
		25.44%	19.68%	9.38%	45.50%	
FF	4,888	3,155			869	864
		64.55%			17.78%	17.68%
SF	3,253	475			1,685	1,093
		14.60%			51.80%	33.60%
GP	1,045	177	82		535	251
		16.94%	7.85%		51.20%	24.02%
NP	1,873	246	349		769	509
		13.13%	18.63%		41.06%	27.18%
Total	15,323	5,288	945	522	5,851	2,717
		34.51%	6.17%	3.41%	38.18%	17.73%

> ### Election Facts
> "The shortest serving TD in the Dáil since 1918 was Pierce McCann. He was a Sinn Féin TD from January 21 1919 until his death on March 6 in the same year, a period of 44 days"
> Sean Donnelly

Count details

Candidate	Party	1st	2nd Heydon Surplus	3rd Wall Surplus	4th Cummins Votes	5th Reid Votes	6th Turner Votes	7th Power Votes
			Seats 3				Quota	9,568
			-3,187					
Heydon, Martin	FG	12,755	9,568	9,568	9,568	9,568	9,568	9,568
				-1,077				
Wall, Jack*	LB	10,645	10,645	9,568	9,568	9,568	9,568	9,568
			+447	*+136*	*+80*	*+138*	*+237*	*+3,155*
Ó Fearghaíl, Seán*	FF	4,514	4,961	5,097	5,177	5,315	5,552	**8,707**
			+1,019	*+256*	*+306*	*+769*	*+1,685*	*+869*
Kennedy, Paddy	NP	2,806	3,825	4,081	4,387	5,156	6,841	7,710
			+514	*+138*	*+97*	*+108*	*+238*	*-4,888*
Power, Sean*	FF	3,793	4,307	4,445	4,542	4,650	4,888	Eliminated
			+302	*+212*	*+82*	*+349*	*-3,253*	
Turner, Jason	SF	2,308	2,610	2,822	2,904	3,253	Eliminated	
			+484	*+234*	*+229*	*-1,873*		
Reid, Clifford T.	NP	926	1,410	1,644	1,873	Eliminated		
			+421	*+101*	*-1,045*			
Cummins, Vivian	GP	523	944	1,045	Eliminated			
Non-transferable					*+251*	*+509*	*+1,093*	*+864*
Cumulative			0	0	251	760	1,853	2,717
Total		38,270	38,270	38,270	38,270	38,270	38,270	38,270

Labour leader Eamon Gilmore poses for photographers at the party's final press conference of the election campaign

Laois-Offaly (5 seats)

Only one seat changed hands as FF vote fell by 30%

Elected

Charles Flanagan* (FG) Count 8, Marcella Corcoran Kennedy (FG) Final count, Barry Cowen (FF) Final count, Brian Stanley (SF) Final count, Seán Fleming* (FF) Final count.

Analysis by Michael Gallagher

A revision of the constituency boundary here saw a population of 4,276 in the former Roscrea No. 2 Rural District transferred to Tipperary North. Laois-Offaly retained its five seats.

When Brian Cowen, who took over 19,000 first preferences in 2007, announced on 31 January that he would not be contesting the 2011 election, other parties immediately fixed covetous eyes on one if not two of the three seats that Fianna Fáil had won at every election since 1977.

In the event, only one seat changed hands in Laois-Offaly. Although the Fianna Fáil vote dropped by virtually 30%, the party held two of its seats, making this the only constituency in the country, other than the leader's Cork South-Central, where it won more than one seat. The party literature here looked like it used to in better days, featuring all the candidates and asking people to 'Vote 1, 2, 3 in order of your choice', rather than the now more common format of candidate advertisements asking people to 'Vote No. 1 for Me' with the names of any running mate(s) in tiny print at the bottom. The Taoiseach was replaced on the ticket by his brother Barry, who polled more than 8,000 first preferences and retained the family seat quite comfortably. Seán Fleming had been given no advancement by either Bertie Ahern or Brian Cowen, and this may now have helped him as he stayed ahead of junior minister John Moloney, his fellow Laois Fianna Fáil TD, to return to the Dáil for a fourth term in which he finally has a front-bench position.

Fine Gael had hoped to win three seats here for the first time since 1973, but its vote rose by less than the national average and it was never in the running for the last seat. It retained its existing two seats without difficulty, the retiring Olwyn Enright being succeeded by Marcella Corcoran Kennedy, based in Birr like Enright herself. Charlie Flanagan headed the poll as his father used to do for many years, but, just as in 1994, he had made the mistake of expressing no confidence in his party leader nine months before that leader became Taoiseach, and despite his years of service on the opposition front bench, he found himself on the back benches when the party entered government.

The only seat lost by Fianna Fáil was taken by Sinn Féin's Brian Stanley, who almost trebled his 2007 vote to win the party's first seat here since independence. He owed this partly to his ability, not shared by all Sinn Féin candidates, to attract transfers, picking up over 3,700 from first count to last and thus widening his lead over the only serious challenger, John Whelan of Labour. Whelan polled respectably, given the fallout over his selection as the Labour candidate, but the dispute cannot have helped.

Other candidates polled nearly 20% of the votes between them, but this was spread among 12 candidates. Dissident Fianna Fáiler John Foley and county councillor John Leahy both topped 4,000 first preferences, but in the end most of their votes transferred back to the major party candidates.

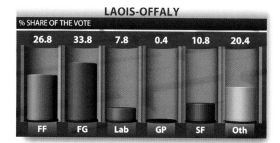

LAOIS-OFFALY

% SHARE OF THE VOTE					
26.8	33.8	7.8	0.4	10.8	20.4
FF	FG	Lab	GP	SF	Oth

LAOIS-OFFALY

% SHARE CHANGE SINCE 2007					
-29.6	+6.4	+5.4	-0.7	+5.7	+12.8
FF	FG	Lab	GP	SF	Oth

*outgoing TDs

CHARLES FLANAGAN (FG)

Home Address: Glenlahan, Portlaoise, Co Laois.
Phone: 057 8620232 (CO) 01 6183625 (LH)
Email: charlie.flanagan@oireachtas.ie
Website: www.charlesflanagan.finegael.ie
Twitter: twitter.com/charlieflanagan
Birth Place/Date: Dublin, November 1956.
Marital Status/Family: Married to Mary McCormack; 2 daughters
Education: Coláiste na Rinne, Waterford; Knockbeg College, Carlow; University College Dublin; Incorporated Law Society.
Occupation: Public representative. Solicitor.
Biography: First elected in 1987. Lost his seat in 2002 and re-elected in 2007. Has held numerous roles on Fine Gael front bench: Justice, Equality and Law Reform (2007-2011); Enterprise, Trade and Employment (2001-2002); Chief Whip (1997-2001); spokesperson on Criminal Law Reform and Northern Ireland (1997-2002); Health (1993-1994); Transport and Tourism (1992-1993); Law reform (1988-1990); Chief Whip (1990-1992). Member, Laois County Council from 1984 to 2004.
Hobbies: Hiking, swimming and reading.
Did you know? Charlie is the son of Oliver J Flanagan, TD for Laois-Offaly from 1943-1987.
Politician (living or deceased) you most admire: Daniel O'Connell.
Priority as a TD? Effective public service for the common good.
Why did you stand for election? I am committed to public service and wanted to continue my work as a representative for the people of Laois-Offaly.
Is there any particular event that brought home to you just how serious the economic crisis had become? The issues that people have come to me with have changed: mortgage arrears, businesses going under, young people emigrating – everyone is affected by the economic crisis.

MARCELLA CORCORAN KENNEDY (FG)

Home Address: Oakley Park, Clareen, Birr Co Offaly.
Phone: 057 9131208 (CO) 087 6330039 (M) 01 6184075 (LH)
Email: marcella.corcorankennedy@oireachtas.ie
Website: www.corcorankennedy.ie
Twitter: twitter.com/CorcoranKennedy
Facebook: Marcella Corcoran Kennedy
Birth Place/Date: January 1963.
Marital Status/Family: Married.
Education: High Street NS, Belmont, Co Offaly; St Josephs of Cluny and St Saran's Ferbane; Roscrea Community College, Co Tipperary; Boston College Effective Politics Programme.
Occupation: Public representative and home-maker. Worked for the ESB for 11 years.
Biography: Secured 5,817 first-preference votes to get elected in her first general election attempt. Elected to Offaly County Council in 1999 and 2004 but lost her seat in 2009. Marcella is chairperson and company director of Birr Theatre and Arts Centre, company director of Filmbase and a member of FilmOffaly.
Hobbies: Drama, walking, reading, cycling, painting and astronomy.
Did you know? Marcella is the third generation of public representative in theCorcoran family.
Politician (living or deceased) you most admire: Michael Collins.
Priority as a TD? To improve the economic, social and cultural life of our citizens.
Why did you stand for election? I believe in public service and that it is time to put service back into public service. I want to represent the constituency to the best of my ability.
Is there any particular event that brought home to you just how serious the economic crisis had become? In September 2008, the government provided a blanket guarantee for the Irish banking system and subsequently nationalised Anglo Irish Bank. These actions were a clear indication that we were in serious economic turmoil.

BARRY COWEN (FF)

Home Address: Lahinch, Clara, Co Offaly.
Office: Grand Canal House, William Street, Tullamore, Co Offaly.
Phone: 057 9321976 (CO) 01 6183662 (LH)
Email: barry.cowen@oireachtas.ie
Website: www.fiannafail.ie
Facebook: Yes.
Birth Place/Date: Dublin, August 1967.
Marital Status/Family: Married to Mary; 2 sons, 2 daughters.
Education: Cistercian College, Roscrea, Co Tipperary.
Occupation: Public representative. Auctioneer and valuer.
Biography: Party spokesperson on Social Protection. Secured 8,257 first-preference votes to get elected in his first general election attempt. He was first elected to Offaly County Council in 1999 and he was re-elected in 2004 and 2009.
Hobbies: GAA, golf and all sports.
Did you know? Barry is the younger brother of former Taoiseach Brian Cowen and son of the late Bernard ('Ber') Cowen, Fianna Fáil TD for Laois-Offaly from 1969-1973 and 1977-1984.
Politician (living or deceased) you most admire: John Hume.
Priority as a TD? To be considered by my electorate as representing them in their best interests in the best possible means and manner.
Why did you stand for election? I sought election because I believed I had garnered experience and competence with the capacity and willingness to be a good representative in Dáil Éireann for my constituency.
Is there any particular event that brought home to you just how serious the economic crisis had become? The EU/IMF bailout.

Laois-Offaly

BRIAN STANLEY (SF)

Home Address: 40 Clonroosk Abbey, Portlaoise.
Phone: 057 8662851 (H) 01 6183987 (LH)
Email: brian.stanley@oireachtas.ie
Facebook: Brian Stanley
Birth Place/Date: January 1958.
Education: Mountrath Vocational School; Waterford Institute of Technology.
Occupation: Public representative.
Biography: Party spokesperson on Environment, Community and Local Government. Secured 8,039 first-preference votes to get elected. Unsuccessfully contested 2002 and 2007 general elections. He was elected to Portlaoise Town Council in 1999 and Laois County Council in 2004. He was re-elected to the county council in 2009. Board of Management of Portlaoise College.
Hobbies: Swimming.
Did you know? Brian almost tripled his vote between the 2002 and 2011 general elections.
Politician (living or deceased) you most admire: James Connolly.
Priority as a TD? Jobs, economy, housing, health, political reform and sovereignty.
Why did you stand for election? To bring about political change.

SEÁN FLEMING (FF)

Address: Castletown, Portlaoise, Co Laois.
Phone: 057 8732922 (CO) 01 6183472 (LH)
Email: sean.fleming@oireachtas.ie
Website: www.fiannafail.ie/people/sean-fleming/
Facebook: Yes.
Birth Place/Date: Laois, February 1958.
Marital Status/Family: Married to Mary.
Education: The Swan NS; Heywood Community School; UCD (BComm). Fellow of the Institute of Chartered Accountants in Ireland.
Occupation: Full-time public representative.
Biography: Fianna Fáil front-bench spokesperson on Public Sector Reform. First elected in 1997 and re-elected in 2002, 2007 and 2011. Former chairman of the Oireachtas Environment, Heritage and Local Government Committee; former Chairman of the Oireachtas Finance and Public Service Committee. Former member of the Dáil Public Accounts Committee. Member, Laois County Council 1999-2003.
Hobbies: Attending sporting fixtures, Tidy Towns work, gardening and DIY. Member of Castletown Tidy Towns, Treasurer Castletown/Slieve Bloom GAA Club.
Did you know? Seán is the third youngest of a 10 – seven boys and three girls.
Politician (living or deceased) you most admire: Nelson Mandela.
Priority as a TD? To improve the quality of life and standard of living for people in my area.
Why did you stand for election? I stood for election as I believe I can do good for Laois and the people of Laois and that I can help improve the quality of life and services for people in the constituency.
Is there any particular event that brought home to you just how serious the economic crisis had become? I have seen a lot of people losing their jobs, who have been unable to get back into the workforce.

Election Facts

"The highest vote-getter in any constituency between 1918 and 2011 was Cumann na nGaedhael leader General Richard Mulcahy who secured 22,005 votes in Dublin in 1923"
Sean Donnelly

First preference votes

	Candidate	Seats	5		12,360		
	Candidate	Party	1st	%	Quota	Count	Status
1	Flanagan, Charles*	FG	10,427	14.06%	0.84	8	Made Quota
2	Corcoran Kennedy, Marcella	FG	5,817	7.84%	0.47	13	Made Quota
3	Cowen, Barry	FF	8,257	11.13%	0.67	13	Elected
4	Stanley, Brian	SF	8,032	10.83%	0.65	13	Elected
5	Fleming, Sean*	FF	6,024	8.12%	0.49	13	Elected
6	Whelan, John	LB	5,802	7.82%	0.47	13	Not Elected
7	Foley, John	NP	4,465	6.02%	0.36	12	Eliminated
8	Moloney, John*	FF	5,579	7.52%	0.45	11	Eliminated
9	Quinn, Liam	FG	4,482	6.04%	0.36	10	Eliminated
10	Leahy, John	NP	4,882	6.58%	0.39	9	Eliminated
11	Moran, John	FG	4,306	5.81%	0.35	7	Eliminated
12	Fitzpatrick, Eddie	NP	2,544	3.43%	0.21	6	No Expenses
13	Adebari, Rotimi	NP	628	0.85%	0.05	5	No Expenses
14	Bracken, John	NP	625	0.84%	0.05	5	No Expenses
15	Fitzpatrick, Ray	SP	561	0.76%	0.05	5	No Expenses
16	McDonnell, Fergus	NP	525	0.71%	0.04	5	No Expenses
17	Dumpleton, Liam	NP	382	0.52%	0.03	4	No Expenses
18	Fanning, James	NP	335	0.45%	0.03	3	No Expenses
19	Fettes, Christopher	GP	306	0.41%	0.02	2	No Expenses
20	Boland, John	NP	119	0.16%	0.01	1	No Expenses
21	Cox, Michael	NP	60	0.08%	0.00	1	No Expenses

* Outgoing TD Valid poll: 74,158 Quota: 12,360 No expenses limit: 3,091

Party votes

		2011					2007				Change	
Party	Cand	1st	%	Quota	Seats	Cand	1st	%	Quota	Seats	%	Seats
FG	4	25,032	33.75%	2.03	2	3	19,560	27.36%	1.64	2	+6.39%	
LB	1	5,802	7.82%	0.47		2	1,703	2.38%	0.14		+5.44%	
FF	3	19,860	26.78%	1.61	2	4	40,307	56.38%	3.38	3	-29.60%	-1
SF	1	8,032	10.83%	0.65	1	1	3,656	5.11%	0.31		+5.72%	+1
SP	1	561	0.76%	0.05							+0.76%	
GP	1	306	0.41%	0.02		1	812	1.14%	0.07		-0.72%	
PD			0.00%	0.00		1	4,233	5.92%	0.36		-5.92%	
Others	10	14,565	19.64%	1.18		4	1,220	1.71%	0.10		+17.93%	
Total	21	74,158	100.0%	12,360	5	16	71,491	100.0%	11,916	5	0.00%	0
Electorate	108,142	68.57%					103,673	68.96%			-0.38%	
Spoiled	1,055	1.40%					662	0.92%			+0.49%	
Turnout	75,213	69.55%					72,153	69.60%			-0.05%	

Transfer analysis

From	To	FG	LB	FF	SF	SP	GP	Others	Non Trans
FG	11,867	7,767	902	1,098	520			938	642
		65.45%	7.60%	9.25%	4.38%			7.90%	5.41%
FF	6,399	269	394	4,224	645			290	577
		4.20%	6.16%	66.01%	10.08%			4.53%	9.02%
SP	604	117	73	64	110			189	51
		19.37%	12.09%	10.60%	18.21%			31.29%	8.44%
GP	308	73	85	23	16	22		83	6
		23.70%	27.60%	7.47%	5.19%	7.14%		26.95%	1.95%
NP	18,644	4,097	1,770	3,841	2,452	21	2	2,579	3,882
		21.97%	9.49%	20.60%	13.15%	0.11%	0.01%	13.83%	20.82%
Total	37,822	12,323	3,224	9,250	3,743	43	2	4,079	5,158
		32.58%	8.52%	24.46%	9.90%	0.11%	0.01%	10.78%	13.64%

Laois-Offaly

Candidate	Party	1st	2nd Boland Cox Votes	3rd Fettes Votes	4th Fanning Votes	5th Dumpleto Votes	6th Adebari Bracken McDonne Fitzpatric Votes	7th Fitzpatric Votes	8th Moran Votes	9th Flanagan Surplus	10th Leahy Votes	11th Quinn Votes	12th Moloney Votes	13th Foley Votes
Seats 5													Quota 12,360	12,360
Flanagan, Charles*	FG	10,427	+5 / 10,432	+16 / 10,448	+21 / 10,469	+22 / 10,491	+169 / 10,660	+347 / 11,007	+2,508 / 13,515	-1,155 / 12,360	12,360	12,360	12,360	12,360
Corcoran Kennedy, Marcella	FG	5,817	+21 / 5,838	+33 / 5,871	+48 / 5,919	+59 / 5,978	+185 / 6,163	+126 / 6,289	+306 / 6,595	+394 / 6,989	+1,302 / 8,291	+3,546 / 11,837	+269 / 12,106	+1,022 / 13,128
Cowen, Barry	FF	8,257	+24 / 8,281	+4 / 8,285	+17 / 8,302	+30 / 8,332	+165 / 8,497	+139 / 8,636	+11 / 8,647	+4 / 8,651	+763 / 9,414	+242 / 9,656	+998 / 10,654	+1,206 / 11,860
Stanley, Brian	SF	8,032	+10 / 8,042	+16 / 8,058	+21 / 8,079	+53 / 8,132	+461 / 8,593	+326 / 8,919	+193 / 9,112	+58 / 9,170	+623 / 9,793	+269 / 10,062	+645 / 10,707	+1,068 / 11,775
Fleming, Sean*	FF	6,024	+2 / 6,026	+10 / 6,036	+7 / 6,043	+7 / 6,050	+51 / 6,101	+105 / 6,206	+363 / 6,569	+116 / 6,685	+153 / 6,838	+129 / 6,967	+3,226 / 10,193	+658 / 10,851
Whelan, John	LB	5,802	+3 / 5,805	+85 / 5,890	+22 / 5,912	+39 / 5,951	+304 / 6,255	+234 / 6,489	+275 / 6,764	+101 / 6,865	+423 / 7,288	+526 / 7,814	+394 / 8,208	+818 / 9,026
Foley, John	NP	4,465	+4 / 4,469	+9 / 4,478	+22 / 4,500	+24 / 4,524	+406 / 4,930	+560 / 5,490	+16 / 5,506	+7 / 5,513	+817 / 6,330	+901 / 7,231	+290 / 7,521	-7,521 / Eliminated
Moloney, John*	FF	5,579	+9 / 5,588	+9 / 5,597	+10 / 5,607	+9 / 5,616	+54 / 5,670	+319 / 5,989	+104 / 6,093	+23 / 6,116	+177 / 6,293	+106 / 6,399	-6,399 / Eliminated	
Quinn, Liam	FG	4,482	+4 / 4,486	+13 / 4,499	+17 / 4,516	+10 / 4,526	+93 / 4,619	+165 / 4,784	+564 / 5,348	+449 / 5,797	+478 / 6,275	-6,275 / Eliminated		
Leahy, John	NP	4,882	+17 / 4,899	+9 / 4,908	+52 / 4,960	+72 / 5,032	+227 / 5,259	+179 / 5,438	+11 / 5,449	+3 / 5,452	-5,452 / Eliminated			
Moran, John	FG	4,306	+1 / 4,307	+11 / 4,318	+8 / 4,326	+2 / 4,328	+45 / 4,373	+64 / 4,437	-4,437 / Eliminated					
Fitzpatrick, Eddie	NP	2,544	+9 / 2,553	+12 / 2,565	+21 / 2,586	+33 / 2,619	+157 / 2,776	-2,776 / Eliminated						
Adebari, Rotimi	NP	628	+6 / 634	+28 / 662	+13 / 675	+16 / 691	-691 / Eliminated							
Bracken, John	NP	625	+31 / 656	+9 / 665	+9 / 674	+21 / 695	-695 / Eliminated							
Fitzpatrick, Ray	SP	561	+1 / 562	+22 / 584	+10 / 594	+10 / 604	-604 / Eliminated							
McDonnell, Fergus	NP	525	+1 / 526	+1 / 527	+6 / 533	+9 / 542	-542 / Eliminated							
Dumpleton, Liam	NP	382	+11 / 393	+6 / 399	+37 / 436	-436 / Eliminated								
Fanning, James	NP	335	+8 / 343	+9 / 352	-352 / Eliminated									
Fettes, Christopher	GP	306	+2 / 308	-308 / Eliminated										
Boland, John	NP	119	-119 / Eliminated											
Cox, Michael	NP	60	-60 / Eliminated											
Non-transferable			+10	+6	+11	+20	+215	+212	+86		+716	+556	+577	+2,749
Cumulative			10	16	27	47	262	474	560	560	1,276	1,832	2,409	5,158
Total		74,158	74,158	74,158	74,158	74,158	74,158	74,158	74,158	74,158	74,158	74,158	74,158	74,158

Limerick (3 seats)

Fine Gael gains but the Collins dynasty survives

Elected

Dan Neville* (FG) Final count, Patrick O'Donovan (FG) Final count, Niall Collins* (FF) Final count.

Analysis by Michael Gallagher

This is more or less the old Limerick West, having gained some territory in the east from Limerick East and lost some in the west to Kerry North. It made the constituency representative of most of rural county Limerick, excluding the western parts.

Since its creation as a three-seater in 1948, it had been one of the most stable constituencies in the country, returning two Fianna Fáil TDs at every election, bar 1997.

Fianna Fáil's decision to run just one candidate, following the last-minute retirement of John Cregan, therefore showed how much things had changed. However, some things remain the same: the Collins family has won a seat here at every election since grandfather James was first elected in 1948, and incumbent Niall maintained this family tradition. Moreover, he headed the poll, the only Fianna Fáil candidate apart from party leader Micheál Martin to do this.

Fine Gael was assured of two seats. Incumbent Dan Neville was re-elected, and the party's second seat was taken by the youthful Patrick O'Donovan, a former president of Young Fine Gael, from Newcastle West,

who won more than twice as many votes as Bill O'Donnell, nephew of former minister Tom. O'Donnell and O'Donovan had publicly clashed with each other on Limerick County Council prior to the election over cuts to the minimum wage. O'Donnell had refused to back a motion calling for a reversal of the reduction to the pay rate, saying the cut could save businesses and jobs.

Labour's James Heffernan trebled the party's vote share, but despite his impressive performance he was 700 votes behind Niall Collins on the last count. There were three other constituencies where the party won a seat with less than the 17.6% that Heffernan garnered. Former IFA president John Dillon polled respectably but was never in contention for a seat.

*outgoing TDs

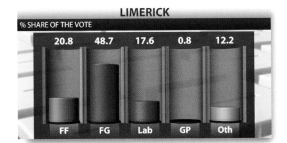

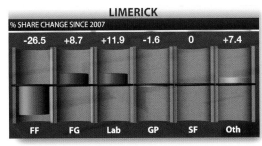

Limerick

DAN NEVILLE (FG)

Home Address: Kiltannan, Croagh, Co Limerick.
Phone: 086 2435536 (M) 069 63610 (CO) 01 6183356 (LH)
Email: dan.neville@oireachtas.ie
Website: www.danneville.ie
Twitter: twitter.com/Dan Neville TD
Facebook: facebook.com/people/Dan-Neville-Td
Birth Place/Date: Croagh, Co Limerick.
Marital Status/Family: Widowed; 2 sons, 2 daughters.
Education: Kilfinny National School; CBS Adare; University of Limerick.
Occupation: Public representative. Previously personnel manager (human resources) and industrial engineer.
Biography: Elected to Dáil Éireann 1997, 2002, 2007 and 2011. Member of Seanad Éireann 1989-997. Member of Limerick County Council 1985-2003.
Hobbies: Walking, reading and sport.
Did you know? Dan is co-founder, director and president of the Irish Association of Suicidology (www.ias.ie). He is a member of the International Association for Suicide Prevention and on the Advisory Council of the College of Psychiatry of Ireland.
Politician (living or deceased) you most admire: Michael Collins.
Priority as a TD? To support and progress the government's programme for economic recovery and its programme to reform the mental health services and prevent suicide.
Why did you stand for election? To progress the Fine Gael policies for government, and to represent the people of the constituency to the best of my ability.
Is there any particular event that brought home to you just how serious the economic crisis had become? The increases in unemployment and in emigration.

PATRICK O'DONOVAN (FG)

Home Address: Churchtown Road, Newcastle West, Co Limerick.
Phone: 069 78660 (H) 01 6183610 (LH)
Email: patrick.odonovan@oireachtas.ie
Website: www.patrickodonovan.ie
Twitter: twitter.com/podonovan
Facebook: Patrick O'Donovan
Birth Place/Date: Limerick, March 1977.
Marital Status/Family: Single.
Education: Courtenay National School, Newcastle West; Scoil Mhuire agus Íde, Newcastle West; University College Cork, BSc (Chemistry); Mary Immaculate College, Limerick, graduate diploma in primary education.
Occupation: Primary teacher, formerly industrial chemist, environmental health and safety officer.
Biography: Secured 8,597 first-preference votes to get elected to the Dáil on his first attempt. He previously served as a member of Limerick County Council. He was co-opted to the council in 2003, elected in 2004 and re-elected in 2009.
Hobbies: Walking and cycling. President of Newcastle West and District Lions Club.
Did you know? Patrick previously served as president of Young Fine Gael.
Politician (living or deceased) you most admire: Michael Collins.
Priority as a TD? To create an environment in which jobs can be created and to help restore trust in politics.
Why did you stand for election? I believe it was time for a younger generation of politicians who have fresh ideas and are committed to helping the people and I wanted to play a part in leading change in Ireland.
Is there any particular event that brought home to you just how serious the economic crisis had become? The arrival of the IMF on the streets of Dublin brought it home for people how bad things were and how the last government oversaw the collapse of the economy.

NIALL COLLINS (FF)

Home Address: Red House Hill, Patrickswell, Co Limerick.
Phone: 086 8355219 (M) 061 300149 (CO) 01 6183577 (LH)
Email: niall.collins@oireachtas.ie
Website: www.fiannafail.ie or www.niallcollinstd.ie
Facebook: Yes.
Birth Place/Date: Limerick, March 1973.
Marital Status/Family: Married to Eimear; 2 children.
Education: St Munchin's College, Limerick; Limerick Institute of Technology.
Occupation: Full-time public representative. Formerly accountant.
Biography: Party spokesperson on Environment, Community and Local Government. Elected to Dáil in 2011 for second time. First elected in 2007.
Hobbies: GAA, rugby, running and anything active.
Did you know? Niall achieved the highest Fianna Fáil percentage vote (21%) in Ireland in Election 2011.
Politician (living or deceased) you most admire: Nelson Mandela.
Priority as a TD? To continue to represent people in a fair and balanced manner.
Why did you stand for election? I like representing people and I receive positive feedback for my efforts.
Is there any particular event that brought home to you just how serious the economic crisis had become? The many unfinished ghost estates that will be returned to agricultural land use again.

First preference votes

	Seats	3			11,261		
	Candidate	Party	1st	%	Quota	Count	Status
1	Neville, Dan*	FG	9,176	20.37%	0.81	4	Made Quota
2	O'Donovan, Patrick	FG	8,597	19.09%	0.76	4	Made Quota
3	Collins, Niall*	FF	9,361	20.78%	0.83	4	Elected
4	Heffernan, James	LB	7,910	17.56%	0.70	4	Not Elected
5	Dillon, John	NP	4,395	9.76%	0.39	3	Eliminated
6	O'Donnell, William	FG	4,152	9.22%	0.37	2	Eliminated
7	Cremin, Con	NP	430	0.95%	0.04	1	No Expenses
8	Sherlock, Seamus	NP	419	0.93%	0.04	1	No Expenses
9	Wall, Stephen	GP	354	0.79%	0.03	1	No Expenses
10	O'Doherty, Patrick	NP	247	0.55%	0.02	1	No Expenses

*Outgoing TD Valid poll: 45,041 Quota: 11,261 No expenses limit: 2,816

Party votes

		2011				2007				Change	
Party	Cand	1st	%	Quota	Seats	Cand	1st	%	Quota	Seats	%	Seats
FG	3	21,925	48.68%	1.95	2	2	16,153	39.95%	1.60	1	+8.73%	+1
LB	1	7,910	17.56%	0.70		1	2,277	5.63%	0.23		+11.93%	
FF	1	9,361	20.78%	0.83	1	2	19,097	47.23%	1.89	2	-26.45%	-1
GP	1	354	0.79%	0.03		1	969	2.40%	0.10		-1.61%	
PD						1	1,935	4.79%	0.19		-4.79%	
Others	4	5,491	12.19%	0.49							+12.19%	
Total	10	45,041	100.0%	11,261	3	7	40,431	100.0%	10,108	3	0.00%	0
Electorate		65,083	69.21%				58,712	68.86%			+0.34%	
Spoiled		471	1.03%				381	0.93%			+0.10%	
Turnout		45,512	69.93%				40,812	69.51%			+0.42%	

Transfer analysis

From	To	FG	LB	FF	Others	Non Trans
FG	4,222	2,902	657	265	308	90
		68.74%	15.56%	6.28%	7.30%	2.13%
GP	354	107	79	31	91	46
		30.23%	22.32%	8.76%	25.71%	12.99%
Others	6,171	2,332	1,458	1,152	281	948
		37.79%	23.63%	18.67%	4.55%	15.36%
Total	10,747	5,341	2,194	1,448	680	1,084
		49.70%	20.41%	13.47%	6.33%	10.09%

Election Facts

"The largest number of seats commanded by a government was 101 out of 166 seats in the Fianna Fáil-Labour government elected in 1992, which lasted less than two years" Professor Michael Gallagher, TCD

Limerick

Candidate	Party	1st	2nd Cremin Sherlock Wall O'Doherty	3rd O'Donnell Votes	4th Dillon Votes
			+171	+1,344	+1,037
Neville, Dan*	FG	9,176	9,347	10,691	11,728
			+196	+1,558	+965
O'Donovan, Patrick	FG	8,597	8,793	10,351	11,316
			+127	+265	+1,056
Collins, Niall*	FF	9,361	9,488	9,753	10,809
			+326	+657	+1,211
Heffernan, James	LB	7,910	8,236	8,893	10,104
			+372	+308	-5,075
Dillon, John	NP	4,395	4,767	5,075	Eliminated
			+70	-4,222	
O'Donnell, William	FG	4,152	4,222	Eliminated	
			-430		
Cremin, Con	NP	430	Eliminated		
			-419		
Sherlock, Seamus	NP	419	Eliminated		
			-354		
Wall, Stephen	GP	354	Eliminated		
			-247		
O'Doherty, Patrick	NP	247	Eliminated		
Non-transferable			+188	+90	+806
Cumulative			188	278	1,084
Total		45,041	45,041	45,041	45,041

Seats 3 — Quota 11,261

Newly elected Fine Gael TD for Dún Laoghaire Mary Mitchell O'Connor drives her car over the plinth at Leinster House in early March

Limerick City (4 seats)

Noonan tops the poll in one of the country's least marginal constituencies

Elected

Michael Noonan* (FG) Count 1, Kieran O'Donnell* (FG) Count 5, Willie O'Dea* (FF) Count 6, Jan O'Sullivan* (Lab) Final count.

Analysis by Michael Gallagher

This constituency was affected by boundary redrawing, losing an area with over 17,000 people to the new Limerick County and consequently changing from a mainly urban five-seater to an overwhelmingly urban four-seater.

As a four-seater, it was one of the most predictable constituencies in the country. Fine Gael's Michael Noonan, restored to front-bench prominence as an unforeseen but fortuitous sideeffect of the heave against Enda Kenny the previous summer, headed the poll with his largest vote ever, and the party vote advanced by nearly 18 percentage points, its second biggest gain in the country. Nearly 3,000 votes from Noonan's surplus helped Kieran O'Donnell into the second seat.

Willie O'Dea had headed the poll here with a sizeable surplus at every election going back to 1989, but now he lost over 12,000 of his huge 2007 vote, the national swing against Fianna Fáil being compounded by the local difficulties that had seen him leave the government a year earlier. This was still enough to secure him the third seat, but his running mate Peter Power, a junior minister seemingly on the way up, found himself down among the also-rans and was eliminated on the sixth count.

The Labour vote was up, and Jan O'Sullivan was comfortably re-elected, but hopes that the party could take a second seat for her running mate Joe Leddin came nowhere near materialising. Sinn Féin's Maurice Quinlivan gained publicity through his role in the events that brought about O'Dea's downfall in 2010 and achieved runner-up status, but on this showing, Limerick City is one of the least marginal constituencies in the country.

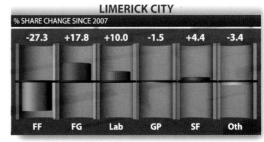

*outgoing TDs

Limerick City

MICHAEL NOONAN (FG)

Home Address: 18 Gouldavoher Estate, Fr Russell Road, Limerick.
Phone: 01 6767571 (LH), 061 229350 (H) 061 229350 (CO)
Email: michael.noonan@oireachtas.ie
Birth Place/Date: Limerick, May 1943
Marital Status/Family: Married to Florence Knightly; 3 sons, 2 daughters.
Education: St Patrick's Secondary School, Glin, Co Limerick; St Patrick's Teacher Training College, Dublin; University College Dublin (BA, HDipEd).
Occupation: Full-time public representative and Minister for Finance.
Biography: Secured 13,159 votes to top poll. Current Minister for Finance. Minister for Health (1994-1997). Spokesperson on Transport, Energy and Communications (1993-94); spokesperson on Finance (1987-1993). Minister for Industry, Commerce and Trade and Minister for Energy respectively (1986-1987); Minister for Justice (1982-1986); spokesperson on Education (1981). First elected a TD in 1981. Leader of Fine Gael and party's spokesperson on Northern Ireland (February 2001-May 2002). Fine Gael front-bench spokesperson on Finance (2010-2011 and 1997-2001). Member, Limerick County Council (1974-1981 and 1991-1994). Member, Mid-Western Health Board (1991-1994).
Hobbies: Reading and sport.
Politician living or deceased you most admire: Charles De Gaulle.
Priority as Minister for Finance: To make Ireland a prosperous country where it is good to live and rear a family.

KIERAN O'DONNELL (FG)

Address: 27 William Street, Limerick.
Phone: 086 8430202 (M) 061 204040 (O) 01 6183808 (LH)
Website: www.kieranodonnell.ie
Email: kieran.odonnell@oireachtas.ie
Twitter: Yes.
Facebook: Kieran O'Donnell
Birth Place/Date: Limerick City, May 1963.
Marital Status/Family: Married to Phil; 4 children.
Education: UL business graduate and chartered accountant.
Occupation: Full-time public representative. Previously ran his own chartered accountancy practice.
Biography: First elected a TD in 2007. Fine Gael deputy spokesperson on Finance (2007-October 2010). Served on the Finance Committee, the Economic and Regulatory Affairs Committee and the Enterprise Committee in the 30th Dáil. Member, Limerick County Council (2004-2007).
Hobbies: Reading and sport.
Did you know? In July 2008, Kieran became the first member of the 30th Dáil to bring the main banks before the Oireachtas Finance committee to discuss the credit crisis.
Politician (living or deceased) you most admire: Michael Collins.
Priority as a TD? To represent the best interests of my Limerick city constituency and work towards getting Ireland working again as quickly as possible.
Why did you stand for election? As a sitting TD, I see every day the need for people to have committed and strong representation. I understand the challenges facing Irish families and I believe I have the know-how to make life better for my constituents. With my background in finance and business, I can also contribute in a very real way to our national economic recovery.
Is there any particular event that brought home to you just how serious the economic crisis had become? The emigration of so many of our young people over the last three years.

WILLIE O'DEA (FF)

Home Address: 2 Glenview Gardens, Farranshone, Limerick.
Phone: 061 454488 (CO) 01 6184259 (LH)
Website: willieodea.ie
Twitter: twitter.com/willieodeaLIVE
Facebook: facebook/WillieO'Dea
Birth Place/Date: Kilteely, Co Limerick, November 1952.
Marital Status/Family: Married to Geraldine Kennedy.
Education: Patrician Brothers College Ballyfin, Co Laois; University College Dublin; King's Inns, Dublin; Institute of Certified Accountants.
Occupation: Full-time public representative.
Biography: Party spokesperson on Enterprise, Jobs and Innovation. First elected a TD in February 1982. Minister for Defence (September 2004-February 2010); Minister of State at the Department of Justice, Equality and Law Reform (with responsibility for Equality Issues) (2002-2004); Minister of State at the Department of Education (1997-2002); Minister of State at the Departments of Justice and Health (1993-1994); Minister of State at the Department of Justice (1992-1993)
Hobbies: Reading, rugby, horse racing, GAA and walking.
Did you know? Willie is a regular contributor to various media outlets.
Politician (living or deceased) you most admire: Seán Lemass.
Priority as a TD? To get the country back on the path to economic growth and help create jobs for all the people of the country.
Why did you stand for election? I wanted to help play a part in reviving our economy and helping create more jobs.
Is there any particular event that brought home to you just how serious the economic crisis had become? When I got a phone call late one night that there was a possibility that the banks may not be able to open for business the following day and that the ATMs would not be able to provide cash. That was the night of the bank guarantee and it really brought home to me how serious the crisis was and the impact it could have on the country.

JAN O'SULLIVAN (Lab)

Home Address: 7 Lanahrone Avenue, Corbally, Limerick.
Phone: 01 6182316 (LH)
Email: jan.osullivan@oireachtas.ie
Website: www.labour.ie/janosullivan
Twitter: @janosullivanTD
Facebook: facebook.com/ JanOSullivanTD
Birth Place/Date: Limerick, December 1950.
Marital Status/Family: Married; 2 adult children.
Education: Villiers School, Limerick; Trinity College, MA; HDipEd. UCC; Montessori diploma.
Occupation: Full-time public representative. Formerly pre-school teacher.
Biography: First elected to Dáil in 1998 in a by-election caused by the death of Jim Kemmy. Minister of State for Trade and Development at the Department of Foreign Affairs and Trade. Labour spokesperson on Health in 30th Dáil. Previously party spokesperson on Equality and Education and Science. Member of Seanad and leader of Labour Party in Seanad (1993-1997). Member, Limerick City Council (1985-2003). Mayor of Limerick (1993-1994). Member of Democratic Socialist Party until it merged with the Labour Party.
Hobbies: Hillwalking, music, reading, watching rugby.
Did you know? Jan was Limerick City's only female Alderman.
Politician (living or deceased) you most admire: Jim Kemmy.
Priority as a TD? Jobs for people in Ireland.
Why did you stand for election? To be part of the team that will bring Ireland back to prosperity and opportunity for all.
Is there any particular event that brought home to you just how serious the economic crisis had become? The arrival of Ajai Chopra and his colleagues to our shores.

The front pages of newspapers the day after the governemt announces its application for a bailout from the EU/IMF

Limerick City

		FIRST PREFERENCE VOTES						
	Seats	4			8,638			
Candidate		Party	1st	%	Quota	Count	Status	
1 Noonan, Michael*		FG	13,291	30.77%	1.54	1	Made Quota	
2 O'Donnell, Kieran*		FG	5,405	12.52%	0.63	5	Made Quota	
3 O'Dea, Willie*		FF	6,956	16.11%	0.81	6	Made Quota	
4 O'Sullivan, Jan*		LB	6,353	14.71%	0.74	7	Elected	
5 Quinlivan, Maurice		SF	3,711	8.59%	0.43	7	Not Elected	
6 Leddin, Joe		LB	2,411	5.58%	0.28	7	Not Elected	
7 Power, Peter*		FF	2,303	5.33%	0.27	5	Eliminated	
8 Kiely, Kevin		NP	1,129	2.61%	0.13	4	No Expenses	
9 Prendiville, Cian		SP	721	1.67%	0.08	4	No Expenses	
10 Cahill, Sheila		GP	490	1.13%	0.06	3	No Expenses	
11 O'Donoghue, Conor		CS	186	0.43%	0.02	2	No Expenses	
12 Riordan, Denis		NP	173	0.40%	0.02	2	No Expenses	
13 Larkin, Matt		NP	59	0.14%	0.01	2	No Expenses	

*Outgoing TD Valid poll: 43,188 Quota: 8,638 No expenses limit: 2,160

Party votes

Party	Cand	2011 1st	%	Quota	Seats	Cand	2007 1st	%	Quota	Seats	Change %	Seats
FG	2	18,696	43.29%	2.16	2	2	12,601	25.52%	1.53	2	+17.77%	
LB	2	8,764	20.29%	1.01	1	1	5,098	10.33%	0.62	1	+9.97%	
FF	2	9,259	21.44%	1.07	1	3	24,042	48.69%	2.92	2	-27.25%	-1
SF	1	3,711	8.59%	0.43		1	2,081	4.21%	0.25		+4.38%	
SP	1	721	1.67%	0.08							+1.67%	
GP	1	490	1.13%	0.06		1	1,296	2.62%	0.16		-1.49%	
CS	1	186	0.43%	0.02							+0.43%	
PD						1	3,354	6.79%	0.41		-6.79%	
Others	3	1,361	3.15%	0.16		5	903	1.83%	0.11		+1.32%	
Total	13	43,188	100.0%	8,638	4	14	49,375	100.0%	8,230	5	0.00%	-1
Electorate		64,909	66.54%				76,874	64.23%			+2.31%	
Spoiled		429	0.98%				431	0.87%			+0.12%	
Turnout		43,617	67.20%				49,806	64.79%			+2.41%	

Transfer analysis

From	To	FG	LB	FF	SF	SP	GP	Others	Non Trans
FG	4,653	2,901	986	509	118	19	30	90	
		62.35%	21.19%	10.94%	2.54%	0.41%	0.64%	1.93%	
FF	3,319		1,157	1,656	240				266
			34.86%	49.89%	7.23%				8.01%
SP	799	87	238	153	237				84
		10.89%	29.79%	19.15%	29.66%				10.51%
GP	542	131	220	66	17	30		36	42
		24.17%	40.59%	12.18%	3.14%	5.54%		6.64%	7.75%
Others	1,743	250	446	314	435	29	22	70	177
		14.34%	25.59%	18.01%	24.96%	1.66%	1.26%	4.02%	10.15%
Total	11,056	3,369	3,047	2,698	1,047	78	52	196	569
		30.47%	27.56%	24.40%	9.47%	0.71%	0.47%	1.77%	5.15%

Count details

Candidate	Party	1st	2nd Noonan Surplus	3rd O'Donoghue Riordan Larkin	4th Cahill Votes	5th Kiely Prendiville Votes	6th Power Votes	7th O'Dea Surplus
			-4,653					
Noonan, Michael*	FG	13,291	8,638	8,638	8,638	8,638	8,638	8,638
			+2,901	*+108*	*+131*	*+229*		
O'Donnell, Kieran*	FG	5,405	8,306	8,414	8,545	8,774	8,774	8,774
			+413	*+34*	*+29*	*+336*	*+1,656*	*-786*
O'Dea, Willie*	FF	6,956	7,369	7,403	7,432	7,768	9,424	8,638
			+769	*+39*	*+153*	*+414*	*+351*	*+441*
O'Sullivan, Jan*	LB	6,353	7,122	7,161	7,314	7,728	8,079	8,520
			+118	*+48*	*+17*	*+624*	*+116*	*+124*
Quinlivan, Maurice	SF	3,711	3,829	3,877	3,894	4,518	4,634	4,758
			+217	*+17*	*+67*	*+214*	*+158*	*+207*
Leddin, Joe	LB	2,411	2,628	2,645	2,712	2,926	3,084	3,291
			+96	*+30*	*+37*	*+67*	*-2,533*	
Power, Peter*	FF	2,303	2,399	2,429	2,466	2,533	Eliminated	
			+71	*+70*	*+36*	*-1,306*		
Kiely, Kevin	NP	1,129	1,200	1,270	1,306	Eliminated		
			+19	*+29*	*+30*	*-799*		
Prendiville, Cian	SP	721	740	769	799	Eliminated		
			+30	*+22*	*-542*			
Cahill, Sheila	GP	490	520	542	Eliminated			
			+11	*-197*				
O'Donoghue, Conor	CS	186	197	Eliminated				
			+5	*-178*				
Riordan, Denis	NP	173	178	Eliminated				
			+3	*-62*				
Larkin, Matt	NP	59	62	Eliminated				
Non-transferable				*+40*	*+42*	*+221*	*+252*	*+14*
Cumulative			0	40	82	303	555	569
Total			**43,188**	**43,188**	**43,188**	**43,188**	**43,188**	**43,188**

Seats 4 — Quota 8,638

Michael Noonan, then Fine Gael spokesman on finance, and his deputy Brian Hayes at the party's press conference on the banking system in February

Longford-Westmeath (4 seats)

Fine Gael goes close to winning a remarkable three out of four as Fianna Fáil hangs on to a single seat

Elected

Willie Penrose* (Lab) Count 2, James Bannon* (FG) Count 6, Nicky McFadden (FG) Final count, Robert Troy (FF) Final count.

Analysis by Sean Donnelly

There were no boundary changes here since 2007 and it remained a four-seat constituency. Fine Gael's vote was up seven percentage points and with 1.9 quotas, it was well in line for two seats and remarkably was even in contention for a third. James Bannon led the way with 9,129 first preferences and he went on to take the second seat on the sixth count. Outgoing senator Nicky McFadden and councillor Peter Burke were within 500 votes of one another on the first count and were in a battle with Robert Troy of Fianna Fáil for the final two seats. In the end, McFadden took the Athlone seat and Burke lost out to Troy.

Willie Penrose once again topped the poll as the Labour vote was up nine percentage points but with just 1.3 quotas on the first count, the party was unlikely to improve on its single seat. Former Progressive Democrat deputy Mae Sexton did poorly, winning just 3,960 first preferences to leave her too far behind in seventh place. A better division of the Labour vote would have given the party a better chance but Penrose's poll-topping performance put an end to that.

The Fianna Fáil vote was down 22 percentage points and with just one quota, one seat was as much as the party could hope for. Its vote was divided among three candidates – the two outgoing deputies

Mary O'Rourke and Peter Kelly, along with newcomer Robert Troy. They were not helped by the presence of former party colleague Kevin 'Boxer' Moran on the ticket, as he was just behind Kelly and outpolled O'Rourke with 3,707 first preferences. Troy was in sixth place ahead of his party colleagues on the first count and he retained his advantage throughout the count and went on to beat Fine Gael for the final seat. He was one of only three new deputies elected for Fianna Fáil in this disastrous election.

The Sinn Féin vote doubled in this election and Paul Hogan was in fifth place on the first count with 0.4 quotas. He survived the various counts and was the last candidate eliminated, with his transfers favouring Athlone-based McFadden.

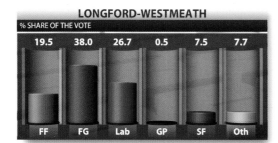

LONGFORD-WESTMEATH

% SHARE OF THE VOTE

FF	FG	Lab	GP	SF	Oth
19.5	38.0	26.7	0.5	7.5	7.7

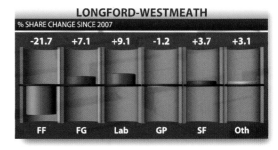

LONGFORD-WESTMEATH

% SHARE CHANGE SINCE 2007

FF	FG	Lab	GP	SF	Oth
-21.7	+7.1	+9.1	-1.2	+3.7	+3.1

*outgoing TDs

WILLIE PENROSE (Lab)

Home Address: Ballintue, Ballynacargy, Co Westmeath.
Phone: 044 9343987/8882595 (CO) 01 6183734 (LH)
Email: ministerofstate@environ.ie
Birth Place/Date: Mullingar, August 1956.
Marital Status/Family: Married to Anne; 3 daughters.
Education: Ballynacargy NS; St Mary's CBS Mullingar; Multyfarnham Agricultural College; University College Dublin; and King's Inns.
Occupation: Barrister-at-Law, public representative.
Biography: Minister for Housing and Planning in the Department of the Environment, Community and Local Government. First Elected to Dáil Éireann in 1992 and re-elected at each subsequent general election. Chairperson of Labour parliamentary party in 28th and 29th Dáil; chairperson of Joint Oireachtas Committee on Enterprise, Trade and Employment, and Labour Party spokesperson on Enterprise, Trade and Employment (2007-February 2011); chairperson of the Joint Oireachtas Committee on Social and Family Affairs and Labour Party spokesperson on Social and Family Affairs (2002-2007); Labour Party spokesperson on Agriculture and Food (1997-2002); Labour Party spokesperson on Agriculture, Food and Rural Development (1992-1997). Member of Westmeath County Council (1984-2003).
Hobbies: GAA, soccer, reading.
Politician (living or deceased) you most admire: Noel Browne.
Priority as a TD? To make a positive contribution to getting the country back on its feet, so that we can make our own decisions again, free of supervisory influences.
Is there any particular event that brought home to you just how serious the economic crisis had become? With the arrival of the IMF and the central role of the troika in our affairs, I realised that our financial independence and sovereignty was severely compromised, and that represented a very serious issue.

JAMES BANNON (FG)

Home Address: Newtown House, Legan, Co Longford.
Phone: 087 2031816 (M) 043 3336185 (CO) 01 6184226 (LH)
Email: james.bannon@oireachtas.ie
Website: www.jamesbannon.finegael.org/
Twitter: James Bannon TD
Facebook: facebook.com/jamesbannonTD
Birth Place/Date: Legan, Co Longford, March 1958.
Education: Mercy Secondary School, Ballymahon, Co Longford.
Occupation: Full-time public representative.
Biography: Member of Seanad Éireann (29th Dáil), Dáil Éireann (30th and 31st Dáil)
Hobbies: Enjoys drama (member of Legan Drama Group) and books of Longford-Westmeath interest.
Did you know? James has an extensive collection of books by Longford-Westmeath authors Maria Edgeworth and Oliver Goldsmith.
Politician (living or deceased) you most admire: Michael Collins.
Priority as a TD? Jobs and full broadband roll-out for Longford-Westmeath.
Why did you stand for election? My concern for the people of Longford-Westmeath, particularly in relation to jobs, businesses, farming and health.
Is there any particular event that brought home to you just how serious the economic crisis had become? Negative equity, particularly among young house buyers and the proliferation of 'ghost estates'.

NICKY McFADDEN (FG)

Home Address: 9 Arcadia Crescent, Athlone.
Contact: 090 6478004 (H) 087 6771267 (M) 01 6183938 (LH)
Email: nicky.mcfadden@oireachtas.ie
Website: www.nickymcfadden.ie
Twitter: twitter.com/senmcfadden
Facebook: Yes.
Birth Place/Date: Athlone, December 1962.
Marital Status/Family: Divorced; 2 children.
Education: St Joseph's College, Summerhill, Athlone; Athlone IT (diploma in legal studies).
Occupation: Full-time public representative. Formerly medical secretary and ESB employee.
Biography: Secured 6,129 first-preference votes to get elected. After unsuccessfully contesting the 2007 general election she was elected to Seanad Éireann. She was first elected to Athlone Town Council in 1999, when she topped the poll. In 2003 she was co-opted onto Westmeath County Council when her father, Brendan McFadden, retired.
Hobbies: Walking, socialising with and cooking dinner for friends and spending time with family.
Did you know? Nicky is the first female Fine Gael TD in Westmeath.
Politician (living or deceased) you most admire: John Hume.
Priority as a TD? Create a stimulus for jobs.
Why did you stand for election? I stood for election because I wanted to be a strong voice for people who are voiceless, and for small businesses. I have never seen such heartache and pain as I witnessed during the recent election campaign.
Is there any particular event that brought home to you just how serious the economic crisis had become? The fact that so many people were involved in the building industry during the boom and now 'Breakfast Roll Man' is struggling and out of work with little prospect of finding work.

Longford-Westmeath

ROBERT TROY (FF)

Home Address: Dominic Street, Mullingar, Co Westmeath.
Phone: 044 9330769 (CO) 01 6183059 (LH)
Email: robert.troy@oireachtas.ie
Website: www.roberttroy.ie
Twitter: Yes.
Facebook: Yes.
Birth Place/Date: Ballynacargy, January 1982.
Marital Status/Family: Single.
Education: Empor National School, Ballynacargy; St Finian's College Mullingar; Currently studying for a BES at Trinity College.
Occupation: Former postmaster in Ballynacargy.
Biography: Party spokesperson on Arts and Heritage. Secured 4,275 first-preference votes to get elected. Elected to Westmeath County Council in 2004 and re-elected in 2009. Involved with voluntary groups including the North Westmeath Suicide Outreach Group, the North Westmeath Hospice, the Mullingar St Patrick's Day Parade Committee, the Mullingar Arts Centre.
Hobbies: GAA, watching television when I get the time and socialising with friends.
Did you know? I was the youngest member of Westmeath County Council when I was first elected in 2004.
Politician (living or deceased) you most admire: Seán Lemass and Albert Reynolds.
Priority as a TD? To support sustainable businesses and create jobs for Longford-Westmeath and to encourage local volunteerism.
Why did you stand for election? While Ireland is undoubtedly facing difficult times, I also believe that it is a great opportunity for reform within politics. As a young person working and living locally, I had first-hand knowledge of many of the difficulties that are facing the people of the Westmeath-Longford area both financially and socially.
Is there any particular event that brought home to you just how serious the economic crisis had become? The loss of so many GAA players and clubs finding it difficult to field teams because of emigration.

Fine Gael leader Enda Kenny holds six-month old May Hennelly while canvassing at Golden Island Shopping Centre, Athlone

First preference votes

	Candidate	Seats	4			11,506		
	Candidate	Party	1st	%	Quota	Count	Status
1	Penrose, Willie*	LB	11,406	19.83%	0.99	2	Made Quota
2	Bannon, James*	FG	9,129	15.87%	0.79	6	Made Quota
3	McFadden, Nicky	FG	6,129	10.65%	0.53	8	Elected
4	Troy, Robert	FF	4,275	7.43%	0.37	8	Elected
5	Burke, Peter	FG	6,629	11.52%	0.58	8	Not Elected
6	Hogan, Paul	SF	4,339	7.54%	0.38	7	Eliminated
7	Kelly, Peter*	FF	3,876	6.74%	0.34	5	Eliminated
8	Moran, Kevin "Boxer"	NP	3,707	6.44%	0.32	4	Eliminated
9	Sexton, Mae #	LB	3,960	6.88%	0.34	3	Eliminated
10	O'Rourke, Mary*	FF	3,046	5.30%	0.26	2	Eliminated
11	Boland, John	NP	330	0.57%	0.03	1	No Expenses
12	Kinahan, Siobhán	GP	309	0.54%	0.03	1	No Expenses
13	D'Arcy, David	NV	159	0.28%	0.01	1	No Expenses
14	Cooney, Benny	NP	130	0.23%	0.01	1	No Expenses
15	Jackson, Donal	NP	101	0.18%	0.01	1	No Expenses

*Outgoing TD #Former TD Valid poll: 57,525 Quota: 11,506 No expenses limit: 2,877

Party votes

Party	2011					2007					Change	
Party	Cand	1st	%	Quota	Seats	Cand	1st	%	Quota	Seats	%	Seats
FG	3	21,887	38.05%	1.90	2	3	16,999	30.95%	1.55	1	+7.09%	+1
LB	2	15,366	26.71%	1.34	1	1	9,692	17.65%	0.88	1	+9.06%	
FF	3	11,197	19.46%	0.97	1	3	22,599	41.15%	2.06	2	-21.69%	-1
SF	1	4,339	7.54%	0.38		1	2,136	3.89%	0.19		+3.65%	
GP	1	309	0.54%	0.03		1	960	1.75%	0.09		-1.21%	
PD						1	2,298	4.18%	0.21		-4.18%	
Others	5	4,427	7.70%	0.38		3	232	0.42%	0.02		+7.27%	
Total	15	57,525	100.0%	11,506	4	13	54,916	100.0%	10,984	4	0.00%	0
Electorate		85,918	66.95%				83,980	65.39%			+1.56%	
Spoiled		661	1.14%				613	1.10%			+0.03%	
Turnout		58,186	67.72%				55,529	66.12%			+1.60%	

Transfer analysis

From	To	FG	LB	FF	SF	Others	Non Trans
FG	934	284		267	147		236
		30.41%		28.59%	15.74%		25.27%
LB	4,175	2,128		762	519	226	540
		50.97%		18.25%	12.43%	5.41%	12.93%
FF	8,262	2238	129	4148	460	434	853
		27.09%	1.56%	50.21%	5.57%	5.25%	10.32%
SF	6,487	2,199		644			3,644
		33.90%		9.93%			56.17%
GP	309	74	72	39	38	58	28
		23.95%	23.30%	12.62%	12.30%	18.77%	9.06%
NP	5,279	2,391	168	606	984	134	996
		45.29%	3.18%	11.48%	18.64%	2.54%	18.87%
Total	25,446	9,314	369	6,466	2,148	852	6,297
		36.60%	1.45%	25.41%	8.44%	3.35%	24.75%

Longford-Westmeath

Count details

Seats 4								**Quota**	**11,506**
Candidate	Party	1st	2nd Boland Kinahan D'Arcy Cooney Jackson	3rd O'Rourke Votes	4th Sexton Votes	5th Moran Votes	6th Kelly Votes	7th Bannon Surplus	8th Hogan Votes
Penrose, Willie*	LB	11,406	+154 → 11,560	11,560	11,560	11,560	11,560	11,560	11,560
Bannon, James*	FG	9,129	+49 → 9,178	+114 → 9,292	+1,596 → 10,888	+129 → 11,017	+1,423 → 12,440	-934 → 11,506	11,506
McFadden, Nicky	FG	6,129	+111 → 6,240	+386 → 6,626	+363 → 6,989	+1,917 → 8,906	+165 → 9,071	+174 → 9,245	+1,419 → 10,664
Troy, Robert	FF	4,275	+48 → 4,323	+1,130 → 5,453	+171 → 5,624	+329 → 5,953	+2,537 → 8,490	+267 → 8,757	+644 → 9,401
Burke, Peter	FG	6,629	+88 → 6,717	+90 → 6,807	+169 → 6,976	+171 → 7,147	+60 → 7,207	+110 → 7,317	+780 → 8,097
Hogan, Paul	SF	4,339	+125 → 4,464	+183 → 4,647	+519 → 5,166	+897 → 6,063	+277 → 6,340	+147 → 6,487	-6,487 Eliminated
Kelly, Peter*	FF	3,876	+28 → 3,904	+481 → 4,385	+591 → 4,976	+185 → 5,161	-5,161 Eliminated		
Moran, Kevin "Boxer"	NP	3,707	+192 → 3,899	+434 → 4,333	+226 → 4,559	-4,559 Eliminated			
Sexton, Mae #	LB	3,960	+86 → 4,046	+129 → 4,175	-4,175 Eliminated				
O'Rourke, Mary*	FF	3,046	+55 → 3,101	-3,101 Eliminated					
Boland, John	NP	330	-330 Eliminated						
Kinahan, Siobhán	GP	309	-309 Eliminated						
D'Arcy, David	NV	159	-159 Eliminated						
Cooney, Benny	NP	130	-130 Eliminated						
Jackson, Donal	NP	101	-101 Eliminated						
Non-transferable			+93	+154	+540	+931	+699	+236	+3,644
Cumulative			93	247	787	1,718	2,417	2,653	6,297
Total		**57,525**	**57,525**	**57,525**	**57,525**	**57,525**	**57,525**	**57,525**	**57,525**

Election Facts

"The 2011 General Election has redrawn the political map of Ireland, absolutely"
Millward Brown Lansdowne/RTÉ General Election 2011 Exit Poll

Louth <small>(5 seats)</small>

Gerry Adams tops the poll and Fianna Fáil draws another blank

Elected

Seamus Kirk* (FF) Automatically returned, Gerry Adams (SF) Count 1, Fergus O'Dowd* (FG) Count 1, Gerald Nash (Lab) Count 12, Peter Fitzpatrick (FG) Final count.

Analysis by Sean Donnelly

There were major Constituency Commission changes here since the 2007 election. The number of seats was increased from four to five, and the boundaries of the constituency were expanded to include a population of 17,333 transferring in from the areas of St Mary's and Julianstown, previously in Meath East.

Seamus Kirk was automatically returned as the outgoing Ceann Comhairle, meaning only four of the five seats were contested in the election.

Fine Gael came close to winning a second seat here in 2007 but Mairead McGuinness failed to deliver. The party's vote was up just two percentage points in one of its poorer performances of this election but with 1.6 quotas, it was in contention for two seats. Fergus O'Dowd was Fine Gael's leading vote-getter and was over the quota on the first count. His running mate, Louth Gaelic football manager Peter Fitzpatrick, was in fourth place on the first count with a more modest 7,845 first preferences and he battled with Fianna Fáil for the final seat. Fitzpatrick's first-count lead was sufficient to withstand the challenge of James Carroll of Fianna Fáil.

The Labour vote was up 14 percentage points and with one quota the party was well-placed to regain the seat previously held by Michael Bell. Labour surprisingly ran two candidates and Gerald Nash was in third place on the first count with 8,718 and he went on to take the fourth seat on the penultimate

count. Mary Moran was a late addition to the ticket and her 4,546 first preferences left her in seventh place on the first count and never in contention. Her transfers (57%) put Nash over the quota.

Outgoing TD Dermot Ahern was among the Fianna Fáil ministers to retire ahead of this election. The Fianna Fáil vote was down a huge 26 percentage points and with just 0.8 quotas spread over its two candidates, the party struggled to retain even one seat. Senator James Carroll was its leading candidate with 5,681 first preferences but this left him with just 0.4 of a quota. Likewise, his running mate Declan Breathnach, with 5,177 and 0.4 of a quota, was also outside the frame and out of contention. This was another case of Fianna Fáil running too many candidates, dividing its depressed vote and failing to win a seat.

There was much media attention on this constituency following the arrival of Sinn Féin president Gerry Adams. Outgoing Sinn Féin deputy Arthur Morgan retired and Adams decided to enter southern politics. Adams topped the poll with the third-largest number of first preferences (15,072) in this election, behind Enda Kenny (17,472) and Shane Ross (17,075).

*outgoing TDs

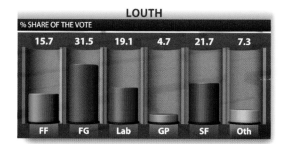

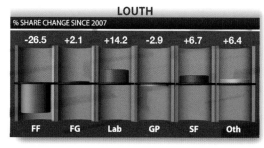

Louth

SEAMUS KIRK (FF)

Home Address: Rathiddy, Knockbridge, Co Louth.
Phone: 042 9331032 (H) 01 6183362 (LH)
Website: www.fiannafail.ie
Email: seamus.kirk@oireachtas.ie
Birth Place/Date: Drumkeith, Co Louth. April 1945.
Marital Status/family: Married to Mary McGeough; 3 sons, 1 daughter.
Education: Dundalk CBS.
Occupation: Public Representative. Farmer.
Biography: Party spokesperson on Horticulture and Rural Affairs. First elected a TD in November 1982, he has been returned as a Fianna Fáil TD on each subsequent election up to 2007. He was appointed Ceann Comhairle in October 2009 following the resignation of John O'Donoghue and as Ceann Comhairle he was automatically returned to the 31st Dáil.
Member, Louth County Council 1974-1985; East Border Region Committee 1974-1985.
Hobbies: GAA.
Did you know? Seamus played Gaelic football with St Bride's GAA club in Knockbridge near Dundalk during a playing career that also saw him play for Louth. He played for Louth from 1963 up to a national league match against Down in Drogheda in October 1972 when got a serious leg injury. He remained in a plaster for nearly two years and he has had many subsequent orthopaedic operations since then, culminating in a fused ankle in 2002.

GERRY ADAMS (SF)

Home Address: Ballymakellett, Ravensdale, Co Louth.
Phone: 01 6184442 (LH)
Website: www.sinnfein.ie
Facebook: Yes.
Blog: Leargas.blogspot.com
Birth Place/Date: Belfast, October 1948.
Marital Status/Family: Married to Colette; 1 son.
Education: St Finian's Primary School, West Belfast; St Mary's Grammar School, Barrack Street, Falls Road, Belfast.
Occupation: Full-time public representative.
Biography: Secured 15,072 first-preference votes to top poll. He won the seat held by Arthur Morgan since 2002. Sinn Féin's president since 1983, he is now the party's leader in the Dáil. He resigned as MLA and MP for West Belfast to contest Election 2011. Elected an MP for West Belfast in 1983 until 1992 when he lost to Joe Hendron. Re-elected an MP for West Belfast 1997-2011. West Belfast member of the Northern Ireland Assembly 1998-December 2010.
Hobbies: Hill-walking, reading, listening to music. Potting trees and planting them. GAA.
Politician (living or deceased) you most admire: Nelson Mandela and Bill Clinton.
Priority as a TD? To represent the people of Louth and East Meath and also to promote and advance the republican goals for Irish reunification.
Why did you stand for election? In the time leading up to my decision to stand in the South, I had spoken to a lot of people who were telling me about the huge difficulties they were facing in their lives. I met two families on flights to the United States last year who had emigrated to the US in the 1980s. They had returned to Ireland during the 1990s and, after losing everything, they said they were returning to America, never to return. That sense of despair was my primary motivation in standing for election in Louth.

FERGUS O'DOWD (FG)

Address: Unit 6, 84 West Street, Drogheda, Co Louth.
Phone: 01 6183078 (LH) 041 9842275 (CO)
Email: fergus.odowd@oireachtas.ie
Website: www.finegael.ie
Twitter: http://twitter.com/#!/Fergusodowd
Facebook: Yes.
Birth Place/Date: Thurles, Co Tipperary, September 1948.
Marital Status/family: Married to Agnes; 3 sons.
Education: Drogheda CBS; Crawford Technical Institute, Cork (qualified as a rural science teacher in 1972).
Occupation: Full-time public representative.
Biography: Minister of State based in the Departments of Environment and Local Government and also in the Department of Communications, Energy and Natural Resources. First elected to the Dáil in May, 2002. Member of Seanad Éireann (1997-2002). Previously Fine Gael spokesperson on Transport and Marine; Environment, Heritage and Local Government; Community, Rural and Gaeltacht Affairs. Member, Louth County Council 1979-2003. He served three terms as Mayor of Drogheda. Founding chairman of the Droichead Arts Centre, Drogheda.
Hobbies: Swimming, reading, in particular books about French history.
Did you know? Fergus's favourite author is Ernest Hemingway, and his favourite book is *Partners in Revolution, the United Irishmen and France* by Marianne Elliott.
Politician (living or deceased) you most admire: President Bill Clinton.
Priority as a TD? To represent my constituents to the best of my ability.
Why did you stand for election? To try to make a real difference in the lives of ordinary people.
Is there any particular event that brought home to you just how serious the economic crisis had become? When I see so many of our young people, so bright, so talented and well-educated, being unemployed and forced to emigrate.

GERALD NASH (Lab)

Home Address: 115 Newfield, Drogheda, Co Louth.
Phone: 087 2716816 (M) 01 6183576 (LH)
Website: www.geraldnash.com
Birth Place/Date: Drogheda, December 1975.
Marital Status/Family: Not married.
Education: St Joseph's CBS, Drogheda; University College, Dublin.
Occupation: Public representative.
Biography: Spent 10 years as a public relations consultant to the not-for-profit sector. He has also spent a period self-employed where he advised small and medium enterprises. Heavily involved in youth, sports and arts organisations. A member of the Drogheda United FC steering group, he is also involved with Boyne Rovers FC and has played Gaelic Football with Newtown Blues GFC.
Hobbies: Soccer, theatre, cinema and reading.
Did you know? He served as Mayor of Drogheda, Ireland's largest town, at just 28 years of age in 2004.
Politician (living or deceased) you most admire: James Connolly.
Priority as a TD? Job creation and political reform.
Why did you stand for election? I stood for election to ensure that we arrest the collapse in the economy, create jobs and usher in a new generation of political leaders, intent on reforming politics.
Is there any particular event that brought home to you just how serious the economic crisis had become? Unequivocally, the arrival of the EU/IMF to bail the country out and solve the problems that had been stored up for years previously was our worst moment, as it symbolised the loss of our sovereignty.

PETER FITZPATRICK (FG)

Home Address: 18 Belfry Gardens, Dundalk, Co Louth.
Constituency office: 2 The Courthouse Square, Dundalk, Co Louth.
Phone: 086 2512577 (M) 042 9330100 (CO) 01 6183563 (LH)
Website: www.peterfitzpatrick.finegael.ie
Facebook: Yes.
Birth Place/Date: Dundalk, May 1962.
Marital Status/Family: Married; 1 son, 2 daughters.
Education: De la Salle Dundalk; O'Fiaich College, Dundalk.
Occupation: Businessman.
Biography: Secured 7,845 first-preference votes to get elected in his first ever election.
Hobbies: GAA and golf.
Did you know? Peter is the manager of the Louth Gaelic football team that were beaten by a controversial Meath goal in the last minute of the 2010 Leinster football championship. He also played football for Louth in the mid-1980s.
Politician (living or deceased) you most admire: Dr Garret FitzGerald.
Priority as a TD? Truth and honesty.
Why did you stand for election? I feel I have something to offer the electorate.
Is there any particular event that brought home to you just how serious the economic crisis had become? Seeing a rise in poverty within my own constituency and having three players from the Louth football team emigrate to Australia in search of work.

Sinn Féin leader Gerry Adams is congratulated by eight-year-old Kaillyn Leavy from Ardee after topping the poll in Louth

Election Facts
"Between 1981 and 2011, the average number of TDs to lose their seats at each election was 26"
Professor Michael Gallagher, TCD.

Louth

	Candidate	Party	1st	%	Quota	Count	Status
	Seats	**4**			**13,864**		
1	Kirk, Seamus*	FF	Returned Automatically				Ceann Comhairle
2	Adams, Gerry	SF	15,072	21.74%	1.09	1	Made Quota
3	O'Dowd, Fergus*	FG	13,980	20.17%	1.01	1	Made Quota
4	Nash, Gerald	LB	8,718	12.58%	0.63	12	Made Quota
5	Fitzpatrick, Peter	FG	7,845	11.32%	0.57	13	Elected
6	Carroll, James	FF	5,681	8.20%	0.41	13	Not Elected
7	Moran, Mary	LB	4,546	6.56%	0.33	11	Eliminated
8	Breathnach, Declan	FF	5,177	7.47%	0.37	10	Eliminated
9	Dearey, Mark	GP	3,244	4.68%	0.23	9	Eliminated
10	Clare, Thomas	NV	2,233	3.22%	0.16	8	No Expenses
11	Matthews, Fred	NP	957	1.38%	0.07	7	No Expenses
12	Godfrey, Frank	NP	649	0.94%	0.05	7	No Expenses
13	Wilson, Robin	NP	536	0.77%	0.04	6	No Expenses
14	Martin, Luke	NP	224	0.32%	0.02	5	No Expenses
15	Crilly, Gerry	NP	222	0.32%	0.02	5	No Expenses
16	Bradley, David	NP	174	0.25%	0.01	4	No Expenses
17	Glynn, Robert	NP	61	0.09%	0.00	2	No Expenses

*Outgoing TD Valid poll: 69,319 Quota: 13,864 No expenses limit: 3,467

Party votes

Party	Cand	2011 1st	%	Quota	Seats	Cand	2007 1st	%	Quota	Seats	Chang %
FG	2	21,825	31.48%	1.57	2	3	16,159	29.37%	1.47	1	+2.11%
LB	2	13,264	19.13%	0.96	1	1	2,739	4.98%	0.25		+14.16%
FF	2	10,858	15.66%	0.78	1	3	23,181	42.14%	2.11	2	-26.47%
SF	1	15,072	21.74%	1.09	1	1	8,274	15.04%	0.75	1	+6.70%
GP	1	3,244	4.68%	0.23		1	4,172	7.58%	0.38		-2.90%
WP						1	193	0.35%	0.02		-0.35%
Others	8	5,056	7.29%	0.36		2	296	0.54%	0.03		+6.76%
Total	16	69,319	100.0%	13,864	5	12	55,014	100.0%	11,003	4	0.00%
Electorate		99,530	69.65%				86,007	63.96%			+5.68%
Spoiled		871	1.24%				592	1.06%			+0.18%
Turnout		70,190	70.52%				55,606	64.65%			+5.87%

Transfer analysis

From	To	FG	LB	FF	GP	Others	Non Trans
FG	116	50	41	10	4	11	
		43.10%	35.34%	8.62%	3.45%	9.48%	
LB	7,730	1,697	3,962	677			1,394
		21.95%	51.25%	8.76%			18.03%
FF	6,001	696	722	3942			641
		11.60%	12.03%	65.69%			10.68%
SF	1,208	153	416	136	114	389	
		12.67%	34.44%	11.26%	9.44%	32.20%	
GP	3,939	948	1,653	686			652
		24.07%	41.96%	17.42%			16.55%
NP	6,599	934	1,536	1,080	577	1,143	1,329
		14.15%	23.28%	16.37%	8.74%	17.32%	20.14%
Total	25,593	4,478	8,330	6,531	695	1,543	4,016
		17.50%	32.55%	25.52%	2.72%	6.03%	15.69%

Count details

Seats: 4 — Quota: 13,864

Candidate	Party	1st	2nd Adams Surplus	3rd Glynn Votes	4th O'Dowd Surplus	5th Bradley Votes	6th Martin / Crilly Votes	7th Wilson Votes	8th Matthews / Godfrey Votes	9th Clare Votes	10th Dearey Votes	11th Breathnach Votes	12th Moran Votes	13th Nash Surplus
Adams, Gerry	SF	15,072	−1,208 / 13,864	13,864	13,864	13,864	13,864	13,864	13,864	13,864	13,864	13,864	13,864	13,864
O'Dowd, Fergus*	FG	13,980	13,980	13,980	−116 / 13,864	13,864	13,864	13,864	13,864	13,864	13,864	13,864	13,864	13,864
Nash, Gerald	LB	8,718	+224 / 8,942	+6 / 8,948	+36 / 8,984	+14 / 8,998	+39 / 9,037	+61 / 9,098	+306 / 9,404	+417 / 9,821	+659 / 10,480	+178 / 10,658	+3,962 / 14,620	−756 / 13,864
Fitzpatrick, Peter	FG	7,845	+153 / 7,998	+4 / 8,002	+50 / 8,052	+17 / 8,069	+61 / 8,130	+47 / 8,177	+298 / 8,475	+507 / 8,982	+948 / 9,930	+696 / 10,626	+1,144 / 11,770	+553 / 12,323
Carroll, James	FF	5,681	+68 / 5,749	+2 / 5,751	+8 / 5,759	+15 / 5,774	+18 / 5,792	+11 / 5,803	+184 / 5,987	+494 / 6,481	+288 / 6,769	+3,942 / 10,711	+474 / 11,185	+203 / 11,388
Moran, Mary	LB	4,546	+192 / 4,738	+4 / 4,742	+5 / 4,747	+1 / 4,748	+60 / 4,808	+100 / 4,908	+216 / 5,124	+312 / 5,436	+994 / 6,430	+544 / 6,974	−6,974 Eliminated	
Breathnach, Declan	FF	5,177	+68 / 5,245	5,245	+2 / 5,247	+16 / 5,263	+22 / 5,285	+12 / 5,297	+76 / 5,373	+230 / 5,603	+398 / 6,001	−6,001 Eliminated		
Dearey, Mark	GP	3,244	+114 / 3,358	+4 / 3,362	+4 / 3,366	+8 / 3,374	+47 / 3,421	+85 / 3,506	+166 / 3,672	+267 / 3,939	−3,939 Eliminated			
Clare, Thomas	NV	2,233	+85 / 2,318	+6 / 2,324	+4 / 2,328	+62 / 2,390	+66 / 2,456	+113 / 2,569	+455 / 3,024	−3,024 Eliminated				
Matthews, Fred	NP	957	+47 / 1,004	+9 / 1,013	+2 / 1,015	+9 / 1,024	+65 / 1,089	+118 / 1,207	−1,207 Eliminated					
Godfrey, Frank	NP	649	+65 / 714	+13 / 727	+4 / 731	+23 / 754	+27 / 781	+48 / 829	−829 Eliminated					
Wilson, Robin	NP	536	+56 / 592	+5 / 597	+1 / 598	+12 / 610	+82 / 692	−692 Eliminated						
Martin, Luke	NP	224	+65 / 289	+4 / 293	293	+7 / 300	−300 Eliminated							
Crilly, Gerry	NP	222	+30 / 252	+2 / 254	254	+13 / 267	−267 Eliminated							
Bradley, David	NP	174	+37 / 211	+4 / 215	215	−215 Eliminated								
Glynn, Robert	NP	61	+4 / 65	−65 Eliminated										
Non-transferable			0	+2	+2	+18	+80	+97	+335	+797	+652	+641	+1,394	
Cumulative			0	2	2	20	100	197	532	1,329	1,981	2,622	4,016	4,016
Total		69,319	69,319	69,319	69,319	69,319	69,319	69,319	69,319	69,319	69,319	69,319	69,319	69,319

Mayo (5 seats)

A record-breaking four out of five for Enda Kenny and Fine Gael

Elected

Enda Kenny* (FG) Count 1, Michael Ring* (FG) Count 1, Michelle Mulherin (FG) Final count, Dara Calleary* (FF) Final count, John O'Mahony* (FG) Final count.

Analysis by Sean Donnelly

There were no Constituency Commission boundary changes here since 2007 and it remained a five-seat constituency. This constituency was over as a contest following the first count, as the leading five contenders were well clear of the rest of the field.

The Fine Gael vote was up 11 percentage points to a remarkable 65% of the first preference vote and with 3.9 quotas, it was on track to succeed in its aim of winning four seats. Enda Kenny topped the poll with 17,472 first preferences, the highest in this election and with 1.4 quotas he took the first seat on the first count. He was joined by Michael Ring, who was also elected on the first count. Michelle Mulherin, who lost out in 2007, made no mistake in this election and she was in third place on the first count and went on to take the third seat. John O'Mahony was a surprise winner in 2007 and the former Galway All-Ireland winning manager was in fourth place on the first count and went on take the final seat.

Beverley Flynn contested the 2007 election as an independent candidate and she rejoined Fianna Fáil in April 2008. She announced in December 2010 that she would not be contesting the general election. The Fianna Fáil vote was down eight percentage points and with just one quota spread over two candidates,

one seat was as much as they could hope for. Dara Calleary had won a seat here in 2007 at his first attempt and had performed well in the 30th Dáil. He was in fifth place on the first count and went on to take the fourth seat comfortably. A late addition to the ticket, Lisa Chambers got 3,343 first preferences to leave her well off the pace in eighth place and out of contention.

This was a disappointing performance by Labour with former independent deputy Dr Jerry Cowley, winning just 5% to leave him outside the frame on the first count with 0.3 quotas and out of contention.

Sinn Féin surprisingly ran two female candidates – Rose Conway-Walsh and Thérèse Ruane – and between them they got just 6.5% and both were too far off the pace to contest for a seat.

Independent local councillor Michael Kilcoyne had been fancied for a seat in the run-up to this election, but with just under 4,000 first preferences he was out of contention.

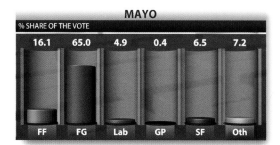

MAYO

% SHARE OF THE VOTE

FF	FG	Lab	GP	SF	Oth
16.1	65.0	4.9	0.4	6.5	7.2

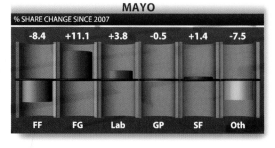

MAYO

% SHARE CHANGE SINCE 2007

FF	FG	Lab	GP	SF	Oth
-8.4	+11.1	+3.8	-0.5	+1.4	-7.5

*outgoing TDs

ENDA KENNY (FG)

Address: Tucker Street, Castlebar, Co Mayo.
Phone: 094 9025600 (O)
Website: www.gov.ie/www.merrionstreet.ie/ www.FineGael.ie
Email: taoiseach@taoiseach.ie
Birth Place/Date: April 1951.
Marital Status/Family: Married to Fionnuala; 3 children.
Education: St Patrick's Teacher Training College.
Occupation: Teacher.
Biography: Elected to the Dáil in 1975 (Longest serving TD in the Dáil); Minister for Tourism and Trade (1994-1997); elected as leader of Fine Gael in 2002; elected Taoiseach 9 March 2011.
Hobbies: Hillwalking, cycling, attending GAA matches, sporting occasions, reading (history in particular).
Did you know? Enda Kenny is president of his local GAA Club, Islandeady, climbed Kilimanjaro in 2003 and he has climbed Croagh Patrick over 100 times.
Priority as Taoiseach: To provide leadership, direction and purpose to the people of Ireland and to help harness their optimism and resilience in tackling the economic challenges facing the country. To make decisions which benefit our country and our people.
Why did you stand for election? To give a voice to the people of Mayo and to participate in politics at a national level to help make Ireland a better and fairer country to live in.
Is there any particular event that brought home to you just how serious the economic crisis had become? The arrival of the IMF/EU/ECB and the attendant loss of financial sovereignty was the final judgement on the failed banking and economic policies pursued by previous governments. This government's priority is to fix a broken economy, stimulate growth through job creation, lead by example through reform and put the citizen back at the centre of politics. In so doing we want to ensure that Ireland returns to full financial independence in as short a timeframe as possible. By 2016, I want to see that Ireland is the best small country in the world in which to do business.

MICHAEL RING (FG)

Address: Quay Street, Westport, Co Mayo
Phone: 098 25734 (CO) 01 6183838 (LH)
Email: michael.ring@oireachtas.ie
Website: www.michaelringtd.com
Twitter: Yes.
Facebook: Yes.
Birth Place/Date: Westport, December 1953.
Marital Status/Family: Married to Anne; 3 children.
Education: Westport Vocational School.
Occupation: Full-time public representative.
Biography: Current Minister of State at the Department of Transport, Tourism and Sport. First elected a TD in 1994 in the Mayo West by-election caused by Pádraig Flynn's appointment as Ireland's EU Commissioner. Has served as Fine Gael's spokesperson on Agriculture and Food; Health and Children; Social and Family Affairs; Community, Rural and Gaeltacht Affairs; Social Protection. Voted backbencher of the Year (1995), best performer in the Dáil (2001) by the *Sunday Tribune*. Previously served on British-Irish Inter-Parliamentary Body.
Hobbies: Walking and cycling.
Did you know? In 1971, Michael was part of the Mayo Vocational School team that won the All-Ireland for the first time ever.
Politician (living or deceased) you most admire: Liam Cosgrave.
Priority as a TD? To increase the number of overseas tourists to Ireland.
Why did you stand for election? To serve the people and make the necessary changes to improve the quality of life for people.
Is there any particular event that brought home to you just how serious the economic crisis had become? People approaching politicians for assistance who would never in their life have had to approach a politician before.

MICHELLE MULHERIN (FG)

Home Address: 47 Moy Heights, Ballina, Co Mayo.
Phone: 087 9317406 (M) 01 6183065 (LH)
email: michelle.mulherin@oireachtas.ie
Website: www.finegael.ie
Twitter: twitter.com/mulherinfg
Facebook: Yes.
Birth Place/Date: Castlebar, January 1972.
Marital Status/Family: Single.
Education: St Mary's Convent of Mercy, Ballina; UCD; Law Society of Ireland.
Occupation: Public representative. Solicitor.
Biography: Secured 8,851 first-preference votes to get elected in the eighth and final count at her second attempt to win a Dáil seat. Elected to Ballina Town Council in 1999, Mayo County Council in 2004 and re-elected to both in 2009 and topped the poll in each. She was Mayor of Ballina in 2008 and 2009.
Hobbies: Basketball and amateur drama.
Did you know? Michelle was the first female Fine Gael representative on Ballina Town Council and Mayo County Council and she is now the party's first female TD for Mayo.
Politician (living or deceased) you most admire: Mary Robinson.
Priority as a TD? Job creation, through the development of indigenous resources in Mayo such as wind, wave and biomass and the development of tourism and agricultural sectors.
Why did you stand for election? I really enjoy being part of our democracy. Politics may have a bad name but it allows you meet the most noble people who restore your faith in humanity every time.

Mayo

DARA CALLEARY (FF)

Home Address: 8 Quignalecka, Sligo Road, Ballina, Co Mayo.
Phone: 096 777613 (CO) 01 6183331(LH) 086 2238810 (M)
Email: dara.calleary@oireachtas.ie
Website: www.daracalleary.ie
Twitter: twitter.com/daracallearytd
Facebook: facebook.com/daracalleary
Birth Place/Date: Mayo, May 1973.
Marital Status/Family: Single.
Education: St Oliver Plunkett NS (The Quay), Ballina; St Muredach's College, Ballina; Trinity College Dublin (BA Hons in business and politics).
Occupation: Full-time public representative. Former manager Chamber Development and BMW Regional Co-Ordinator Chambers Ireland.
Biography: Party spokesperson on Justice, Equality and Defence. Secured 8,577 first-preference votes to get elected on the eighth and final count. Calleary was first elected to the Dáil in the 2007 general election. He served as Minister of State for Labour Affairs and Public Service Transformation 2009-2011.
Did you know? Dara is the son of Seán Calleary, TD for East Mayo 1973-1992 and grandson of Phelim Calleary, TD for North Mayo 1952-1969.
Politician (living or deceased) you most admire: John F Kennedy.
Priority as a TD? Employment.
Why did you stand for election? To contribute to my local community, my county and my country.
Is there any particular event that brought home to you just how serious the economic crisis had become? The failure of the banks to give credit to small businesses.

JOHN O'MAHONY (FG)

Home Address: D'Alton Street, Claremorris, Co Mayo.
Contact: 094 9373560 (CO) 01 6183706 (LH)
Email: john.omahony@oireachtas.ie
Website: www.johnomahony.ie
Twitter: www.twitter.com/omahonytd
Facebook: /john.omahonytd
Birth Place/Date: Kilmovee, Mayo, June 1953.
Marital Status/Family: Married to Gerardine; 5 daughters.
Education: NUI Maynooth; NUI Galway, (BA history, geography), HDipEd.
Occupation: Full-time public representative. Formerly secondary school teacher.
Biography: John was first elected to Dáil Éireann in 2007. He was appointed the Fine Gael spokesperson on Sport and member of the Joint Committees on Tourism, Culture, Sport, Community, Equality and Gaeltacht Affairs and on Education and Skills.
Hobbies: GAA, team management and sport in general, walking and jogging.
Did you know? John won two All-Ireland medals as player with Mayo. Managed Galway Senior Footballers to All-Ireland titles in 1998 and 2001. Managed two under-21 winning All-Ireland teams – Mayo 1983 and Galway 2002. The only manager to manage three different counties to provincial titles (Mayo, Leitrim and Galway).
Politician (living or deceased) you most admire: John Hume.
Priority as a TD? To secure investment in infrastructure, facilities, jobs and enterprise in Mayo. To contribute to and support national and local economic recovery. To secure jobs and opportunities for the people of Mayo. Investment in education and young people.
Why did you stand for election? To advocate and act in the interests of my constituents and my country.
Is there any particular event that brought home to you just how serious the economic crisis had become? The arrival of the IMF in Ireland in November 2010.

First preference votes

	Candidate	Party	1st	%	Quota	Count	Status
	Seats	**5**			**12,360**		
1	Kenny, Enda*	FG	17,472	23.56%	1.41	1	Made Quota
2	Ring, Michael*	FG	13,180	17.77%	1.07	1	Made Quota
3	Mulherin, Michelle	FG	8,851	11.94%	0.72	8	Made Quota
4	Calleary, Dara*	FF	8,577	11.57%	0.69	8	Made Quota
5	O'Mahony, John*	FG	8,667	11.69%	0.70	8	Elected
6	Kilcoyne, Michael	NP	3,996	5.39%	0.32	8	Not Elected
7	Cowley, Dr. Jerry #	LB	3,644	4.91%	0.29	7	Eliminated
8	Conway-Walsh, Rose	SF	2,660	3.59%	0.22	6	Eliminated
9	Chambers, Lisa	FF	3,343	4.51%	0.27	5	Eliminated
10	Ruane, Thérése	SF	2,142	2.89%	0.17	4	No Expenses
11	Daly, Martin	NV	893	1.20%	0.07	3	No Expenses
12	Carey, John	GP	266	0.36%	0.02	3	No Expenses
13	Clarke, Loretta	NP	218	0.29%	0.02	3	No Expenses
14	McDonnell, Dermot	NP	216	0.29%	0.02	3	No Expenses
15	Forkin, Sean	NP	29	0.04%	0.00	3	No Expenses

*Outgoing TD #Former TD Valid poll: 74,154 Quota: 12,360 No expenses limit: 3,090

Party votes

		2011				2007				Change	
Party	Cand	1st	%	Quota	Seats	Cand	1st	%	Quota	Seats	%	Seats
FG	4	48,170	64.96%	3.90	4	4	38,426	53.83%	3.23	3	+11.13%	+1
LB	1	3,644	4.91%	0.29		1	831	1.16%	0.07		+3.75%	
FF	2	11,920	16.07%	0.96	1	3	17,459	24.46%	1.47	1	-8.38%	
SF	2	4,802	6.48%	0.39		1	3,608	5.05%	0.30		+1.42%	
GP	1	266	0.36%	0.02		1	580	0.81%	0.05		-0.45%	
PD						1	296	0.41%	0.02		-0.41%	
Others	5	5,352	7.22%	0.43		2	10,186	14.27%	0.86	1	-7.05%	-1
Total	15	74,154	100.0%	12,360	5	13	71,386	100.0%	11,898	5	0.00%	0
Electorate		101,160	73.30%				98,696	72.33%			+0.97%	
Spoiled		641	0.86%				700	0.97%			-0.11%	
Turnout		74,795	73.94%				72,086	73.04%			+0.90%	

Transfer analysis

From	To	FG	LB	FF	SF	GP	Others	Non Trans
FG	5,932	4,103	393	346	288	16	786	
		69.17%	6.63%	5.83%	4.86%	0.27%	13.25%	
LB	5,899	1,912		775			1,242	1,970
		32.41%		13.14%			21.05%	33.40%
FF	3,619	235	185	2,539	160		334	166
		6.49%	5.11%	70.16%	4.42%		9.23%	4.59%
SF	6,965	1,145	1,420	781	1,428		856	1,335
		16.44%	20.39%	11.21%	20.50%		12.29%	19.17%
GP	282	83	43	42	47		38	29
		29.43%	15.25%	14.89%	16.67%		13.48%	10.28%
Others	1,423	418	214	213	240		194	144
		29.37%	15.04%	14.97%	16.87%		13.63%	10.12%
Total	24,120	7,896	2,255	4,696	2,163	16	3,450	3,644
		32.74%	9.35%	19.47%	8.97%	0.07%	14.30%	15.11%

Mayo

Count details

Candidate	Party	1st	2nd Kenny Surplus	3rd Ring Surplus	4th Daly / Carey / Clarke / McDonnell / Forkin	5th Ruane Votes	6th Chambers Votes	7th Conway Votes	8th Cowley Votes
			−5,112						
Kenny, Enda*	FG	17,472	12,360	12,360	12,360	12,360	12,360	12,360	12,360
				−820					
Ring, Michael*	FG	13,180	13,180	12,360	12,360	12,360	12,360	12,360	12,360
			+1,963	+296	+324	+143	+95	+490	1,141
Mulherin, Michelle	FG	8,851	10,814	11,110	11,434	11,577	11,672	12,162	13,303
			+168	+30	+194	+94	+2,539	+620	+775
Calleary, Dara*	FF	8,577	8,745	8,775	8,969	9,063	11,602	12,222	12,997
			+1,623	+221	+177	+176	+140	+336	+771
O'Mahony, John*	FG	8,667	10,290	10,511	10,688	10,864	11,004	11,340	12,111
			+645	+74	+232	+181	+334	+675	+1,242
Kilcoyne, Michael	NP	3,996	4,641	4,715	4,947	5,128	5,462	6,137	7,379
			+311	+82	+257	+235	+185	+1,185	*−5,899*
Cowley, Dr. Jerry #	LB	3,644	3,955	4,037	4,294	4,529	4,714	5,899	Eliminated
			+92	+61	+126	+1,428	+160	*−4,527*	
Conway-Walsh, Rose	SF	2,660	2,752	2,813	2,939	4,367	4,527	Eliminated	
			+121	+27	+61	+67	*−3,619*		
Chambers, Lisa	FF	3,343	3,464	3,491	3,552	3,619	Eliminated		
			+118	+17	+161	*−2,438*			
Ruane, Thérése	SF	2,142	2,260	2,277	2,438	Eliminated			
			+26	+7	*−926*				
Daly, Martin	NV	893	919	926	Eliminated				
			+14	+2	*−282*				
Carey, John	GP	266	280	282	Eliminated				
			+8	+2	*−228*				
Clarke, Loretta	NP	218	226	228	Eliminated				
			+21	+1	*−238*				
McDonnell, Dermot	NP	216	237	238	Eliminated				
			+2		*−31*				
Forkin, Sean	NP	29	31	31	Eliminated				
Non-transferable					+173	+114	+166	+1,221	+1,970
Cumulative			0	0	173	287	453	1,674	3,644
Total		74,154	74,154	74,154	74,154	74,154	74,154	74,154	74,154

Seats 5 — Quota 12,360

Election Facts

"Opinions are evenly divided about whether the incoming government should focus most on reducing spending on health, social services etc, or increasing taxes while maintaining these services"
Millward Brown Lansdowne/RTÉ General Election 2011 Exit Poll

Meath East (3 seats)

Another blank for Fianna Fáil as Fine Gael and Labour both gain seats

Elected
Dominic Hannigan (Lab) Final count, Regina Doherty (FG) Final count, Shane McEntee* (FG) Final count.

Analysis by Sean Donnelly

This constituency was created before the 2007 general election and it formed the eastern part of the old five-seat Meath constituency. There have been major Constituency Commission changes here since 2007. A population of 17,333 in the areas of St Mary's and Julianstown was transferred to Louth. A population of 6,776 in the Kells area was transferred in from Meath West. The number of seats remained the same with three TDs returned.

This constituency was virtually over as a contest following the first count as the leading three contenders were well clear of the rest of the field.

The Fine Gael vote was up 15 percentage points and with 1.6 quotas equally divided between its two candidates it was well-placed to take two seats. Outgoing deputy Shane McEntee was in second place on the first count, just ahead of his running mate Regina Doherty. The two Fine Gael candidates were within 117 votes of one another and they were duly elected on the fourth and final count.

The Labour vote was up nine percentage points and Dominic Hannigan who had been widely tipped for a win here duly delivered. He topped the poll with just under 9,000 first preferences and went on to take the first seat on the final count.

This was another disaster for Fianna Fáil as the party's vote was down 24 percentage points and it lost both of its seats. Mary Wallace retired but Fianna Fáil decided to replace her. Thomas Byrne was the party's leading candidate but with just 5,715 first preferences was well outside the frame on the first count and struggling. He trailed Doherty by nearly 3,000 votes. The second Fianna Fáil candidate, Nick Killian, got just 2,669 first preferences and was never in contention. He was eliminated early and 54% of his transfers went to his running mate.

The Sinn Féin vote was up five percentage points to leave Michael Gallagher in fifth place but with just 3,795 first preferences he was too far off the pace and out of contention.

*outgoing TDs

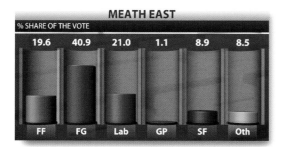

MEATH EAST % SHARE OF THE VOTE					
19.6	40.9	21.0	1.1	8.9	8.5
FF	FG	Lab	GP	SF	Oth

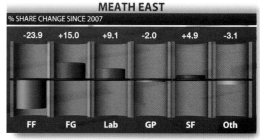

MEATH EAST % SHARE CHANGE SINCE 2007					
-23.9	+15.0	+9.1	-2.0	+4.9	-3.1
FF	FG	Lab	GP	SF	Oth

Meath East

DOMINIC HANNIGAN (Lab)

Home Address: Dunshaughlin, Co Meath.
Phone: 087 6418960 (M) 01 835 3871(CO)
01 6184007 (LH)
Email: dominic.hannigan@oireachtas.ie
Website: www.dominichannigan.com
Twitter: twitter.com/domhannigan
Facebook: Yes.
Birth Place/Date: July 1965.
Education: Cushenstown NS, Kilmoon, Co
Meath; St Mary's CBS Secondary School,
Drogheda; UCD (engineering degree); City
University, London (Masters in Transport);
University of London (Masters in Finance).
Occupation: Public representative and
businessman.
Biography: Hannigan topped the poll in
Meath East with 8,994 first-preference
votes. He stood unsuccessfully in the 2007
general election and the 2005 Meath by-
election. He has been a member of Seanad
Éireann since 2007 and he was elected to
Meath County Council in 2004.
Hobbies: Dominic supports Drogheda
United, Spurs and enjoys hill walking.
Did you know? Dominic was a member of
UCD Students Union in 1982 and he has
climbed Kilimanjaro and Machu Pichu.
Priority as a TD? Help create jobs.

REGINA DOHERTY (FG)

Home Address: 2 Glebe Park, Rathoath, Co
Meath.
Phone: 087 2680182 (M) 01 6183573
(LH)
Email: regina.doherty@oireachtas.ie
Website: www.reginadoherty.com
Twitter: twitter.com/reginado
Facebook: Yes.
Birth Place/Date: Dublin, January 1971.
Marital Status/Family: Married to Declan
Doherty; 2 sons, 2 daughters.
Education: St Mary's Holy Faith, Glasnevin;
College of Marketing and Design, Dublin.
Occupation: Public representative.
Previously worked in sales.
Biography: Secured 8,677 first-preference
votes to get elected in her second general
election attempt. She unsuccessfully
contested the 2007 general election.
Hobbies: Reading, music, singing and GAA.
Did you know? Regina paddled a canoe
down the Zambezi River in Zimbabwe.
**Politician (living or deceased) you most
admire:** Nora Owen.
Priority as a TD? Job creation.
Why did you stand for election? I am
passionate about public service.
**Is there any particular event that brought
home to you just how serious the economic
crisis had become?** The most shocking thing
for me has been people approaching me and
asking for help in getting council housing
because they have lost their homes.

SHANE McENTEE (FG)

Home Address: Mitchelstown, Castletown,
Navan, Co Meath.
Phone: 01 6072756 (Department office)
041 9882727/ 041 9882477 (CO)
01 6184447 (LH)
Website: www.shanemcentee.com
Facebook: facebook/ShaneMcEntee
Birth Place/Date: Meath, December 1956.
Marital Status/family: Married to Kathleen
Corbally, 1 son, 2 daughters.
Occupation: Full-time public representative
and publican.
Biography: A TD since winning 2005
Meath by-election. Minister of State for the
Department of Agriculture and the Marine
with special responsibilities for Food, Food
Safety and Horticulture. Fine Gael deputy
spokesperson on Road Safety (2007-
October 2010); deputy spokesperson for
Agriculture with Special Responsibility for
Food and Fisheries (October 2010-2011).
Hobbies: GAA. Shane has successfully
trained numerous football teams over the
last 20 years, including Meath minors.
Did you know? Shane was a farmer for over
15 years and an agricultural sales rep
throughout the last few of those years.
**Politician (living or deceased) you most
admire:** Michael Collins.
Priority as a TD? To work for the people
who have democratically elected me and
represent them fairly and to the best of my
ability.
Why did you stand for election? I have
been a member of Fine Gael since I was 15
years' old. My entire family have been
involved in Fine Gael at grass roots for as
long as I can remember, so it seemed like a
natural progression.
**Is there any particular event that brought
home to you just how serious the economic
crisis had become?** Families are struggling to
stay afloat due to redundancies; in many
cases both parents have lost their jobs. I have
also met many young people who have no
hope of work after college and are
contemplating emigration.

First preference votes

	Seats	3			10,689		
	Candidate	Party	1st	%	Quota	Count	Status
1	Hannigan, Dominic	LB	8,994	21.04%	0.84	4	Made Quota
2	Doherty, Regina	FG	8,677	20.30%	0.81	4	Elected
3	McEntee, Shane*	FG	8,794	20.57%	0.82	4	Elected
4	Byrne, Thomas*	FF	5,715	13.37%	0.53	4	Not Elected
5	Gallagher, Michael	SF	3,795	8.88%	0.36	3	Eliminated
6	Bonner, Joe	NP	2,479	5.80%	0.23	3	Eliminated
7	Killian, Nick	FF	2,669	6.24%	0.25	2	Eliminated
8	Keogan, Sharon	NV	1,168	2.73%	0.11	1	No Expenses
9	Ó Buachalla, Seán	GP	461	1.08%	0.04	1	No Expenses

* Outgoing TD Valid poll: 42,752 Quota: 10,689 No expenses limit: 2,673

Party votes

Party	2011					2007					Change	
	Cand	1st	%	Quota	Seats	Cand	1st	%	Quota	Seats	%	Seats
FG	2	17,471	40.87%	1.63	2	2	11,129	25.88%	1.04	1	+14.99%	+1
LB	1	8,994	21.04%	0.84	1	1	5,136	11.94%	0.48		+9.10%	+1
FF	2	8,384	19.61%	0.78		2	18,735	43.56%	1.74	2	-23.95%	-2
SF	1	3,795	8.88%	0.36		1	1,695	3.94%	0.16		+4.94%	
GP	1	461	1.08%	0.04		1	1,330	3.09%	0.12		-2.01%	
PD						1	957	2.23%	0.09		-2.23%	
Others	2	3,647	8.53%	0.34		3	4,025	9.36%	0.37		-0.83%	
Total	9	42,752	100.0%	10,689	3	11	43,007	100.0%	10,752	3	0.00%	0
Electorate		64,873	65.90%				67,443	63.77%			+2.13%	
Spoiled		346	0.80%				359	0.83%			-0.03%	
Turnout		43,098	66.43%				43,366	64.30%			+2.13%	

Transfer analysis

From	To	FG	LB	FF	SF	Others	Non Trans
FF	2,719	595	286	1,462	67	208	101
		21.88%	10.52%	53.77%	2.46%	7.65%	3.71%
GP	461	108	110	64	46	110	23
		23.43%	23.86%	13.88%	9.98%	23.86%	4.99%
NP	8,267	2,416	2,992	982	117	277	1,483
		29.22%	36.19%	11.88%	1.42%	3.35%	17.94%
Total	11,447	3,119	3,388	2,508	230	595	1,607
		27.25%	29.60%	21.91%	2.01%	5.20%	14.04%

Election Facts
"The final salutary lesson for Fianna Fáil is that only just over 1 in 3 of those who voted for them in 2011 can envisage Fianna Fáil leading a government within the next 10 years" Millward Brown Lansdowne/RTÉ General Election 2011 Exit Poll

Meath East

Candidate	Party	1st	2nd Keoghan O Buachalla Votes	3rd Killian Votes	4th Bonner Gallagher Votes
Seats 3				Quota	10,689
			+389	+286	+2,713
Hannigan, Dominic	LB	8,994	9,383	9,669	12,382
			+181	+447	+1,142
Doherty, Regina	FG	8,677	8,858	9,305	10,447
			+200	+148	+1,001
McEntee, Shane*	FG	8,794	8,994	9,142	10,143
			+177	+1,462	+819
Byrne, Thomas*	FF	5,715	5,892	7,354	8,173
			+163	+67	-4,025
Gallagher, Michael	SF	3,795	3,958	4,025	Eliminated
			+387	+208	-3,074
Bonner, Joe	NP	2,479	2,866	3,074	Eliminated
			+50	-2,719	
Killian, Nick	FF	2,669	2,719	Eliminated	
			-1,168		
Keogan, Sharon	NV	1,168	Eliminated		
			-461		
Ó Buachalla, Seán	GP	461	Eliminated		
Non-transferable			+82	+101	+1,424
Cumulative			82	183	1,607
Total		42,752	42,752	42,752	42,752

Fianna Fail Leader Micheál Martin campaigns in Kells with local candidate Thomas Byrne (centre) and Meath footballer Joe Sheridan (left)

Meath West (3 seats)

Sinn Féin makes breakthrough as Fianna Fáil ends up seatless

Elected

Damien English* (FG) Count 3, Peadar Tóibín (SF) Final count, Ray Butler (FG) Final count.

Analysis by Sean Donnelly

This constituency was created before the 2007 general election and it formed the western part of the old five-seat Meath constituency. There have also been major Constituency Commission changes here since 2007. A population of 6,776 in the Kells area has been transferred out to Meath East. The number of seats remained the same with three TDs returned.

Fine Gael's vote was up 17 percentage points and with 1.8 quotas it was on track for two seats. Outgoing deputy Damien English comfortably topped the poll, well clear of his nearest rivals and he went on to take the first seat on the third count. On the first count, newcomer Ray Butler was just 170 votes behind Labour's Jenny McHugh but he won the transfer battle, in particular with the help of 55% of running mate Yore's transfers. The third Fine Gael candidate, Catherine Yore, would be disappointed with her performance as she had been fancied for a seat and had to settle for her transfers electing her running mate.

The Labour vote was up nine percentage points and with half a quota Jenny McHugh was in the frame in third place on the first count. She was just ahead of Fine Gael's Ray Butler but Fine Gael had too much of an advantage and she was overtaken and lost the battle for the final seat by a margin of 1,128 votes.

This was another poor performance by Fianna Fáil with its vote down a massive 33 percentage points, its second largest loss of support in this election and it lost its two seats. Long-serving TD and senior minister Noel Dempsey retired and Fianna Fáil decided to replace him with 2005 by-election candidate Shane Cassells. Outgoing deputy Johnny Brady did poorly and was well off the pace on the first count and never recovered. Cassells had a similar performance and this division of a depleted Fianna Fáil vote left it with no chance of a seat. This was another example of Fianna Fáil fielding too many candidates.

This was another breakthrough in this election for Sinn Féin with its vote up six percentage points to 0.7 of a quota. Peadar Tóibín was in second place on the first count, well clear of his nearest rivals and he went on to win the second seat on the fifth and final count. Joe Reilly had done well here for Sinn Féin in 2007 when he was the last candidate standing. His strong performance was a forerunner to Tóibín's success in 2011.

*outgoing TDs

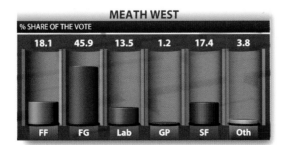

MEATH WEST
% SHARE OF THE VOTE

FF	FG	Lab	GP	SF	Oth
18.1	45.9	13.5	1.2	17.4	3.8

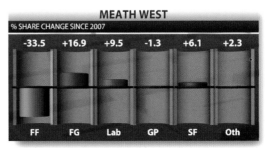

MEATH WEST
% SHARE CHANGE SINCE 2007

FF	FG	Lab	GP	SF	Oth
-33.5	+16.9	+9.5	-1.3	+6.1	+2.3

Meath West

DAMIEN ENGLISH (FG)

Home Address: Castlemartin, Navan, Co Meath
Phone: 086 8143495 (M) 046 9071667 (CO) 01 6184012 (LH)
Email: damien.english@oireachtas.ie
Website: www.damienenglish.ie
Facebook: Yes.
Birth Place/Date: Louth, February 1978.
Marital Status/Family: Married to Laura Kenny; 1 son.
Education: Bohermeen NS, Navan; Pobalscoil Chiarán, Kells; DIT Aungier Street (accountancy and business); Dublin Business School (Chartered Institute of Management Accountants (CIMA) exams).
Occupation: Full-time pubic representative.
Biography: First elected to Dáil Éireann in 2002 when he was the Dáil's youngest TD at 22 years' old. Fine Gael deputy finance spokesperson (June 2010-February 2011); spokesperson for Small Business and Labour Affairs (2007-2010); Drugs, Alcohol and Crime Prevention (2004-2007). Elected to Meath County Council in 1999.
Hobbies: Running, football and rugby.
Did you know? Damien runs marathons, has climbed Kilimanjaro and has participated in the famous bull running event in Pamplona, Spain.
Politician (living or deceased) you most admire: Michael Collins
Priority as a TD? Locally, the new regional hospital, job creation and the Dublin-Navan train service. Nationally, job creation, getting credit flowing from the banks, establishing a strategic investment bank and healthcare reform.
Why did you stand for election? Navan was a town of 30,000 people with no TD when I decided to contest the 2002 general election.
Is there any particular event that brought home to you just how serious the economic crisis had become? Accompanying Michael Noonan and other opposition TDs into the Department of Finance in November 2010 and being shown the books for the first time was when I realised just how bad things were.

PEADAR TÓIBÍN (SF)

Home Address: 123 An Coillearnach, An Uaimh, Co na Mí.
Phone: 01 6183518 (LH)
Email: peadartoibin@gmail.com or peadar.toibin@oireachtas.ie
Website: www.peadartoibin.ie
Twitter: Toibin1
Birth Place/Date: Louth, June 1974.
Marital Status/Family: Married.
Education: UCD (BA economics and politics and postgrad in enterprise studies, Michael Smurfit School of Business); NUI Maynooth (certificate in training and further education).
Occupation: Full-time public representative. Formerly self-employed management consultant.
Biography: Party spokesperson on Enterprise, Jobs, Innovation and An Gaeltacht. Secured 6,989 first-preference votes in 2011 to take second of three seats. Member, Navan Town Council (2009-2011). Deputy Mayor of Navan 2010.
Hobbies: Hill walking, the Irish language, reading (especially history), GAA and rugby.
Did you know? Peadar is the first Sinn Féin TD elected in Meath since Liam Mellows was elected in 1918.
Politician (living or deceased) you most admire: Bobby Sands – as a young boy I was awestruck by the selfless sacrifice of him and his comrades.
Priority as a TD? I want to see full Irish independence, the creation of a prosperous and fair economy and the development of properly funded and functioning health and education services. Ba mhaith liom tacaíocht le athbheochan an Gaeilge freisin.
Why did you stand for election? To help achieve the above.
Is there any particular event that brought home to you just how serious the economic crisis had become? While canvassing, I came across a mother who skipped meals to allow her children eat properly. Another family whose son needed to go to the doctor and as a result his older brother could not be sent to the dentist. An elderly couple could not afford to keep the heat on through the winter. Another family was preparing to lose their son to emigration.

RAY BUTLER (FG)

Home Address: 7 Swift Court, Trim, Co Meath.
Phone: 087 2596680 (M) 046 9486717 (CO) 01 6183378 (LH)
Email: ray.butler@oireachtas.ie
Website: www.finegael.ie
Facebook: Yes.
Birth Place/Date: Virginia, Co Cavan, December 1965.
Marital Status/family: Married to Marie; 4 children.
Education: Kells CBS.
Occupation: Full-time public representative.
Biography: Secured 5,262 first-preference votes to get elected in his first general election. Elected to Trim Town Council in 2004 and re-elected in 2009. Elected to Meath County Council in 2009.
Hobbies: Interested in all sports, mainly ball games including GAA and soccer. Also a fan of greyhound racing.
Did you know? Ray is the driving force behind Trim's annual St Patrick's Day parade.
Politician (living or deceased) you most admire: Michael Collins
Priority as a TD? Job creation, support community projects, improve public transport in Meath and Westmeath, public service and healthcare reform.
Why did you stand for election? I first got involved out of a strong desire to serve my community. I am still driven by that same principle.
Is there any particular event that brought home to you just how serious the economic crisis had become? The day I closed the door on the retail business that I ran for 20 years, and my family had run for generations, for the last time. And the realisation that I, like many more, may not be able to support my wife and four children and the fear of losing my home. Being self-employed meant that I had no way of qualifying for social welfare despite paying my taxes for decades.

First preference votes

	Candidate	Party	1st	%	Quota	Count	Status
		Seats	3		10,045		
1	English, Damien*	FG	9,290	23.12%	0.92	3	Made Quota
2	Tóibín, Peadar	SF	6,989	17.40%	0.70	5	Elected
3	Butler, Ray	FG	5,262	13.10%	0.52	5	Elected
4	McHugh, Jenny	LB	5,432	13.52%	0.54	5	Not Elected
5	Brady, Johnny*	FF	3,789	9.43%	0.38	4	Eliminated
6	Yore, Catherine	FG	3,898	9.70%	0.39	3	Eliminated
7	Cassells, Shane	FF	3,496	8.70%	0.35	2	Eliminated
8	Irwin, Fiona	GP	479	1.19%	0.05	1	No Expenses
9	Ball, Stephen	NP	475	1.18%	0.05	1	No Expenses
10	Stevens, Daithi	NP	387	0.96%	0.04	1	No Expenses
11	Carolan, Ronan	NP	258	0.64%	0.03	1	No Expenses
12	MacMeanmain, Manus	CS	234	0.58%	0.02	1	No Expenses
13	McDonagh, Seamus	WP	189	0.47%	0.02	1	No Expenses

*Outgoing TD Valid poll: 40,178 Quota: 10,045 No expenses limit: 2,512

Party votes

Party	Cand	2011 1st	2011 %	2011 Quota	2011 Seats	Cand	2007 1st	2007 %	2007 Quota	2007 Seats	Change %	Change Seats
FG	3	18,450	45.92%	1.84	2	3	11,745	29.03%	1.16	1	+16.89%	+1
LB	1	5,432	13.52%	0.54		1	1,634	4.04%	0.16		+9.48%	
FF	2	7,285	18.13%	0.73		2	20,874	51.59%	2.06	2	-33.45%	-2
SF	1	6,989	17.40%	0.70	1	1	4,567	11.29%	0.45		+6.11%	+1
GP	1	479	1.19%	0.05		1	1,011	2.50%	0.10		-1.31%	
WP	1	189	0.47%	0.02							+0.47%	
CS	1	234	0.58%	0.02							+0.58%	
Others	3	1,120	2.79%	0.11		2	633	1.56%	0.06		+1.22%	
Total	13	40,178	100.0%	10,045	3	10	40,464	100.0%	10,116	3	0.00%	0
Electorate	62,776	64.00%				56,267	71.91%				-7.91%	
Spoiled	413	1.02%				388	0.95%				+0.07%	
Turnout	40,591	64.66%				40,852	72.60%				-7.94%	

Transfer analysis

From	To	FG	LB	FF	SF	Non Trans
FG	4,208	2,305	754	372	444	333
		54.78%	17.92%	8.84%	10.55%	7.91%
FF	10,068	1,856	1,192	2,191	1,247	3,582
		18.43%	11.84%	21.76%	12.39%	35.58%
GP	479	153	100	52	102	72
		31.94%	20.88%	10.86%	21.29%	15.03%
WP	189	60	39	21	40	29
		31.75%	20.63%	11.11%	21.16%	15.34%
NP	1,354	432	281	147	290	204
		31.91%	20.75%	10.86%	21.42%	15.07%

Election Facts

"36% of voters cited feeling angry or let down as the one issue or problem that influenced their decision as to how they voted in Election 2011"
Millward Brown Lansdowne/RTÉ General Election 2011 Exit Poll

Meath West

Candidate	Party	1st	2nd Irwin Ball Stevens Carolan MacMeanmain McDonagh	3rd Cassells Votes	4th Yore Votes	5th Brady Votes
English, Damien*	FG	9,290	+319 9,609	+513 10,122	10,122	10,122
Tóibín, Peadar	SF	6,989	+432 7,421	+290 7,711	+444 8,155	+957 9,112
Butler, Ray	FG	5,262	+152 5,414	+160 5,574	+2,305 7,879	+1,047 8,926
McHugh, Jenny	LB	5,432	+420 5,852	+188 6,040	+754 6,794	+1,004 7,798
Brady, Johnny*	FF	3,789	+85 3,874	+2,191 6,065	+372 6,437	−6,437 Eliminated
Yore, Catherine	FG	3,898	+174 4,072	+136 4,208	−4,208 Eliminated	
Cassells, Shane	FF	3,496	+135 3,631	−3,631 Eliminated		
Irwin, Fiona	GP	479	−479 Eliminated			
Ball, Stephen	NP	475	−475 Eliminated			
Stevens, Daithi	NP	387	−387 Eliminated			
Carolan, Ronan	NP	258	−258 Eliminated			
MacMeanmain, Manus	CS	234	−234 Eliminated			
McDonagh, Seamus	WP	189	−189 Eliminated			
Non-transferable			+305	+153	+333	+3,429
Cumulative			305	458	791	4,220
Total		**40,178**	**40,178**	**40,178**	**40,178**	**40,178**

Seats 3 — Quota 10,045

From left: Cllr Derek Keating, Richard Bruton, Enda Kenny and Cllr Catherine Yore outside Fine Gael HQ in February

Roscommon-South Leitrim

(3 seats)

Independent Luke 'Ming' Flanagan wins a seat at Fianna Fáil's expense

Elected
Luke 'Ming' Flanagan (Ind) Count 4, Frank Feighan* (FG) Final count, Denis Naughten* (FG) Final count.

Analysis by Sean Donnelly

This constituency was created before the 2007 general election from the Roscommon part of the old Longford-Roscommon constituency and the southern portion of Co Leitrim. There were also significant changes here since 2007. A population of 3,376 in the area north of Carrick-on-Shannon was transferred from this constituency to Sligo-North Leitrim. The number of seats remained the same with three TDs returned.

The three leading candidates were well clear of the rest of the field and this constituency was virtually over as a contest following the declaration of the first count.

This was one of the few constituencies in which the Fine Gael vote was down on 2007, albeit by less than 1%. But with 1.5 quotas, the party was well-placed to retain its two seats. Denis Naughten topped the poll with 9,320 first preferences and went on to take the third seat on the final count. His fellow outgoing deputy Frank Feighan was in second place on the first count and also went on to retain his seat on the final count.

The big surprise here was the performance of independent candidate Luke 'Ming' Flanagan, who ran on a New Vision ticket. Flanagan was in third place on the first count, just behind the two outgoing Fine Gael deputies and he went on to take the first seat on the fourth count.

The Fianna Fáil vote was down 24 percentage points and the party lost its single outgoing seat. Outgoing Minister of State Michael Finneran retired and was replaced by Ivan Connaughton and Gerry Kilrane. Between them, they garnered just 0.6 quotas, or just 0.3 of a quota each, to leave the two of them well outside the frame on the first count and out of contention.

Former independent councillor John Kelly joined the Labour Party for this election and increased the party vote by eight percentage points but with just 0.4 of a quota, he was in fifth place on the first count and out of contention.

Sinn Féin will be disappointed with its performance here as its vote was up just one percentage point on 2007 and with just 4,637 first preferences, Martin Kenny was out of contention.

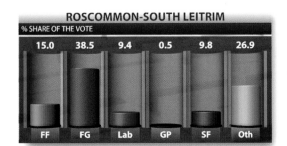

ROSCOMMON-SOUTH LEITRIM
% SHARE OF THE VOTE

FF	FG	Lab	GP	SF	Oth
15.0	38.5	9.4	0.5	9.8	26.9

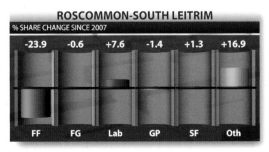

ROSCOMMON-SOUTH LEITRIM
% SHARE CHANGE SINCE 2007

FF	FG	Lab	GP	SF	Oth
-23.9	-0.6	+7.6	-1.4	+1.3	+16.9

Roscommon-South Leitrim

LUKE 'MING' FLANAGAN (Ind)

Home Address: Priory House, Barrack Street, Castlerea, Co Roscommon.
Contact: 01 6183058 (LH)
Website: www.lukemingflanagan.ie
Twitter: twitter.com/lukeming
Facebook: Yes.
Birth Place/Date: Roscommon, January 1972.
Education: "I see life as an education. I learned more in the two times that I was in Castlerea Prison than I ever learned in any other educational institution."
Occupation: Full-time public representative.
Biography: Secured 8,925 first-preference votes to get elected on the fourth count in his third general election. Flanagan unsuccessfully contested the 2007 election in this constituency and the 1997 general election in Galway West. He was an independent candidate in the Connacht-Ulster constituency for the 1999 European elections. He was elected to Roscommon County Council in 2004 and re-elected at the 2009 local elections. In June 2010 he was elected Mayor of Roscommon.
Hobbies: Running, snooker, kayaking.
Did you know? Luke is a direct descendant of the first person ever to speak in the Dáil – Fr Michael O'Flanagan.
Politician (living or deceased) you most admire: I have never thought about that.
Priority as a TD? Improve the lot of my constituents and people generally over the next five years.
Why did you stand for election? I felt the previous representation was not good enough.
Is there any particular event that brought home to you just how serious the economic crisis had become? The rugby match between South Africa and Ireland in November 2010. The world champions were here and the Aviva stadium was half empty.

FRANK FEIGHAN (FG)

Home Address: Bridge Street, Boyle, Co Roscommon.
Phone: 086 8331234 (M) 071 9662608/62115 (CO) 01 6183289 (LH)
Website: www.frankfeighan.finegael.ie
Twitter: twitter.com/frankfeighan
Facebook: Yes.
Birth Place/Date: Roscommon, July 1962.
Marital Status/Family: Married.
Education: St Joseph's NS, Boyle; St Mary's College, Boyle.
Occupation: Full-time public representative.
Biography: Secured 8,983 first-preference votes to get re-elected. First elected to the Dáil in 2007. Appointed Fine Gael front-bench spokesperson on Community, Equality and Gaeltacht Affairs in July 2010. Member of the Seanad 2002-2007. Member, Roscommon County Council 1999-2003.
Hobbies: Member of both Boyle GAA Club and Boyle Celtic soccer club. Member of Boyle Musical Society and his local choir.
Did you know? Frank took part in RTÉ's *You're A Star* TV talent show.
Priority as a TD? To work with my government colleagues to implement the party's five-point plan to help create the environment to stimulate the economy, create jobs and get credit flowing to the small business sector.
Why did you stand for election? Since my early 20s, I have been a community activist, helping to bring improvements to my town, county and constituency. Standing for election for the first time in 2007 was a natural progression.
Is there any particular event that brought home to you just how serious the economic crisis had become? The scourge of emigration has unfortunately returned, with the brightest and best leaving our shores. I have seen the evidence at first hand, with the decimation of some rural GAA clubs because of emigration.

DENIS NAUGHTEN (FG)

Address: Abbey Street, Roscommon.
Phone: 086 1708800 (M) 090 6627557 (CO) 01 6183545 (LH)
Email: denis.naughten@oireachtas.ie
Website: www.denisnaughten.ie
Twitter: twitter.com/DenisNaughten
Facebook: facebook/DenisNaughten
Birth Place/Date: Roscommon, June 1973.
Marital Status/Family: Married to Mary Tiernan; 2 sons, 1 daughter.
Education: Ardkeenan NS; St Aloysius College, Athlone; UCD (BSc) and UCC (Researcher in Food Microbiology).
Occupation: Full-time public representative. Formerly research scientist.
Biography: First elected in 1997 and re-elected in 2002, 2007 and 2011. Fine Gael front-bench spokesperson on Immigration and Integration (2007-2010); Agriculture and Food (2004-2007); Transport (2002-2004); Enterprise; Trade and Employment (2000-2001). Elected to Seanad Éireann in a by-election on the agricultural panel in January 1997. Member, Roscommon County Council (1997-2003). Son of the late Liam Naughten, TD (1982-1989) and senator (1981-1982 and 1989-1996).
Hobbies: All sports. Played Gaelic football with Clann na nGael GAA club and won county and provincial athletic titles with Moore AC.
Did you know? Denis was the youngest ever member of Seanad Éireann.
Politician (living or deceased) you most admire: John Bruton.
Priority as a TD? Focusing on our economic strengths by supporting and creating jobs in the agri-food, tourism and small businesses sectors.
Why did you stand for election? Dáil Éireann needs positive and constructive voices in these difficult times.
Is there any particular event that brought home to you just how serious the economic crisis had become? Watching a local business close and lay off staff because of the failure to access credit.

First preference votes

	Seats	3			11,877		
	Candidate	Party	1st	%	Quota	Count	Status
1	Flanagan, Luke "Ming"	NV	8,925	18.79%	0.75	4	Made Quota
2	Feighan, Frank*	FG	8,983	18.91%	0.76	6	Made Quota
3	Naughten, Denis*	FG	9,320	19.62%	0.78	6	Made Quota
4	Connaughton, Ivan	FF	4,070	8.57%	0.34	6	Not Elected
5	Kenny, Martin	SF	4,637	9.76%	0.39	5	Eliminated
6	Kelly, John	LB	4,455	9.38%	0.38	3	Eliminated
7	McDermott, John	NP	3,770	7.94%	0.32	2	Eliminated
8	Kilrane, Gerry	FF	3,033	6.38%	0.26	1	Eliminated
9	McDaid, Garreth	GP	220	0.46%	0.02	1	No Expenses
10	Kearns, Sean	NP	91	0.19%	0.01	1	No Expenses

*Outgoing TD Valid poll: 47,504 Quota: 11,877 No expenses limit: 2,970

Party votes

		2011					2007				Change	
Party	Cand	1st	%	Quota	Seats	Cand	1st	%	Quota	Seats	%	Seats
FG	2	18,303	38.53%	1.54	2	2	18,031	39.13%	1.57	2	-0.60%	
LB	1	4,455	9.38%	0.38		1	832	1.81%	0.07		+7.57%	
FF	2	7,103	14.95%	0.60		2	17,897	38.84%	1.55	1	-23.89%	-1
SF	1	4,637	9.76%	0.39		1	3,876	8.41%	0.34		+1.35%	
GP	1	220	0.46%	0.02		1	836	1.81%	0.07		-1.35%	
Others	3	12,786	26.92%	1.08	1	2	4,605	9.99%	0.40		+16.92%	+1
Total	10	47,504	100.0%	11,877	3	9	46,077	100.0%	11,520	3	0.00%	0
Electorate		60,998	77.88%				62,437	73.80%			+4.08%	
Spoiled		531	1.11%				393	0.85%			+0.26%	
Turnout		48,035	78.75%				46,470	74.43%			+4.32%	

Transfer analysis

From	To	FG	LB	FF	SF	Others	Non Trans
LB	4,894	1,959		398	516	1,701	320
		40.03%		8.13%	10.54%	34.76%	6.54%
FF	3,033	529	147	1,187	664	397	109
		17.44%	4.85%	39.14%	21.89%	13.09%	3.59%
SF	6,108	2,734		749			2,625
		44.76%		12.26%			42.98%
GP	220	38	11	86	48	29	8
		17.27%	5.00%	39.09%	21.82%	13.18%	3.64%
Others	4,245	1,825	281	544	243	1,209	143
		42.99%	6.62%	12.82%	5.72%	28.48%	3.37%
Total	18,500	7,085	439	2,964	1,471	3,336	3,205
		38.30%	2.37%	16.02%	7.95%	18.03%	17.32%

Election Facts

"Just over 7 in 10 voters saw at least one of the televised leader debates in their various guises. There seems to have been no clear winner across the whole series, with Micheál Martin edging ahead of Enda Kenny and Eamon Gilmore in a distant third place. Just as many people said that no one came out best, though"Millward Brown Lansdowne/RTÉ General Election 2011 Exit Poll

Roscommon-South Leitrim

Count details

Candidate	Party	1st	2nd Kilrane McDaid Kearns	3rd McDermott Votes	4th Kelly Votes	5th Flanagan Surplus	6th Kenny Votes
Seats 3						Quota	11,877
Flanagan, Luke "Ming"	NV	8,925	+326 / 9,251	+1,197 / 10,448	+1,701 / 12,149	-272 / 11,877	11,877
Feighan, Frank*	FG	8,983	+474 / 9,457	+445 / 9,902	+1,228 / 11,130	+109 / 11,239	+2,027 / 13,266
Naughten, Denis*	FG	9,320	+109 / 9,429	+1,189 / 10,618	+731 / 11,349	+66 / 11,415	+707 / 12,122
Connaughton, Ivan	FF	4,070	+1,309 / 5,379	+477 / 5,856	+398 / 6,254	+31 / 6,285	+749 / 7,034
Kenny, Martin	SF	4,637	+732 / 5,369	+157 / 5,526	+516 / 6,042	+66 / 6,108	-6,108 / Eliminated
Kelly, John	LB	4,455	+162 / 4,617	+277 / 4,894	-4,894 / Eliminated		
McDermott, John	NP	3,770	+112 / 3,882	-3,882 / Eliminated			
Kilrane, Gerry	FF	3,033	-3,033 / Eliminated				
McDaid, Garreth	GP	220	-220 / Eliminated				
Kearns, Sean	NP	91	-91 / Eliminated				
Non-transferable			+120	+140	+320		+2,625
Cumulative			120	260	580	580	3,205
Total		**47,504**	**47,504**	**47,504**	**47,504**	**47,504**	**47,504**

Luke 'Ming' Flanagan outside Leinster House

Sligo-North Leitrim (3 seats)

Gains for Fine Gael and Sinn Féin at Fianna Fáil's expense

Elected

John Perry* (FG) Count 8, Tony McLoughlin (FG) Final count, Michael Colreavy (SF) Final count.

Analysis by Sean Donnelly

Just before the 2007 general election, this constituency was formed from the old Sligo-Leitrim constituency which lost part of Co Leitrim south of Lough Allen. Since 2007, there have been significant further changes. A population of 3,376 in the area north of Carrick-on-Shannon was transferred into the Roscommon-South Leitrim constituency. The number of seats remained the same, with three TDs returned.

Fine Gael gained a seat in this constituency despite a two percentage point drop in its vote as it managed to convert 1.5 quotas into two seats. Outgoing deputy John Perry topped the poll with 8,663 first preferences and he went on to take the first seat. His running mate Tony McLoughlin was in second place in the first count and comfortably took the second seat on the final count.

The big battle here was for the final seat, between Sinn Féin, Fianna Fáil and to a lesser extent Labour.

Michael Colreavy narrowly increased the Sinn Féin vote but it was enough to put him in the frame on the first count with 5,911 votes. Colreavy was just under 900 votes ahead of his nearest rival Eamon Scanlon and that was sufficient, as he held off the Fianna Fáil challenge and took the final seat by a margin of 646 votes.

The Fianna Fáil vote was down 19 percentage points and with just 0.9 of a quota evenly spread over its two candidates, the party fell short of a seat. Outgoing deputy Jimmy Devins decided to retire and Eamon Scanlon was the party's leading vote getter with 5,075 first preferences. This left him in fourth place on the first count, just ahead of his running mate Marc MacSharry. Scanlon failed to bridge the first-count gap between himself and Sinn Féin's Colreavy, despite a 48% vote transfer from his running mate MacSharry.

Labour had high hopes of a seat gain here with former journalist Susan O'Keeffe on the ticket. She joined the party prior to the European elections in 2009 and she contested that election in the Ireland North-West constituency. She disappointed once again in this election and with just 4,553 on the first count, was in sixth place and well beaten in the end. Her transfers divided evenly among the three winning candidates.

Former Labour members Veronica Cawley and Declan Bree both unsuccessfully contested as independents and their presence did not help the Labour cause.

*outgoing TDs

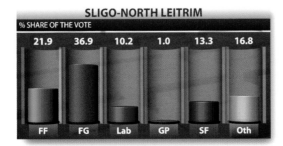

SLIGO-NORTH LEITRIM
% SHARE OF THE VOTE

FF	FG	Lab	GP	SF	Oth
21.9	36.9	10.2	1.0	13.3	16.8

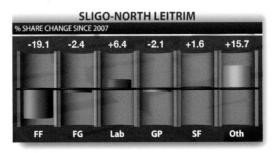

SLIGO-NORTH LEITRIM
% SHARE CHANGE SINCE 2007

FF	FG	Lab	GP	SF	Oth
-19.1	-2.4	+6.4	-2.1	+1.6	+15.7

Sligo-North Leitrim

JOHN PERRY (FG)

Home Address: Carrownanty, Ballymote, Co Sligo.
Phone: 087 2459407 (M) 01 6312243 (O) 01 6183765 (LH)
Website: www.sligomatters.ie
Email: john.perry@deti.ie
Birth Place/Date: Ballymote, August 1956.
Marital Status/Family: Married to Marie; 1 son.
Education: Ballymote NS; Corran College Ballymote.
Occupation: Public representative. Retail business.
Biography: First elected in 1997 and re-elected in 2002, 2007 and 2011. Minister of State at the Department of Enterprise with Special Responsibility for Small Business. Previously Fine Gael spokesperson on Science, Technology, Small Business and Enterprise and the Border Counties (1997-2000); the Marine (October 2004-2007); Small Business (July 2010-February 2011). Former chair of the Joint Dáil Committee on EU Scrutiny.
Hobbies: Horses, walking and reading.
Did you know? John was awarded Gael of the Year by the Queens County Parade Committee in 2008 for work developing links between New York and Ireland.
Politician (living or deceased) you most admire: Enda Kenny.
Priority as a TD? To serve the people of the Sligo-North Leitrim constituency in an honest, direct and results-focused way and to help kick-start a revolution in the small business sector.
Why did you stand for election? I saw the need for somebody with a long involvement in family-run business and community activism.
Is there any particular event that brought home to you just how serious the economic crisis had become? The closure of many viable businesses locally because of a lack of access to credit from banks.

TONY McLOUGHLIN (FG)

Home Address: Beechlawn, Barnasragh, Sligo.
Phone: 087 6633587 (M) 01 6183537 (LH)
Email: tony.mcloughlin@oireachtas.ie
Website: www.finegael.ie
Birth Place/Date: Sligo, January 1949.
Marital Status/Family: Married to Paula; 2 sons, 1 daughter.
Education: Mount St Joseph's College, Roscrea, Co Tipperary.
Occupation: Public representative. Sales executive.
Biography: Secured 7,715 first-preference votes to get elected on the ninth and final count. The last time he contested a general election was 30 years ago in 1981. He was elected to Sligo County Council in 1985 and he was re-elected at every subsequent local election, including the most recent local elections in 2009.
Hobbies: Swimming, football and walking.
Did you know? Tony's late uncle Joe McLoughlin served as a TD for Sligo-Leitrim from 1961-1977.
Politician (living or deceased) you most admire: Garrett FitzGerald.
Priority as a TD? Job creation and increased investment for Sligo-North Leitrim.
Why did you stand for election? It has always been my ambition to represent the people of Sligo-North Leitrim at national level, having served as a local representative for many years.

MICHAEL COLREAVY (SF)

Address: Sinn Féin office, Main Street, Manorhamilton, Co Leitrim.
Phone: 01 6183745 (LH)
Email: michael@colreavy.net or michael.colreavy@oireachtas.ie
Website: www.sinnfein.ie
Birth Place/Date: Leitrim, September 1948.
Marital Status/family: Married to Alice; 4 sons, 4 daughters.
Education: Summerhill College, Sligo; National Computing Centre, England (diploma in systems analysis); Institute of Public Administration (diploma in healthcare management).
Occupation: Public representative. Formerly an IT projects manager with the HSE.
Biography: Party spokesperson on Agriculture, Food and Marine. Secured 5,911 first-preference votes to get elected in his first general election attempt. He was first elected to Leitrim County Council in 1999 and he was re-elected at the two subsequent local elections in 2004 and 2009. He was chairman of the county council in 2000/2001.
Hobbies: Sports and Irish music.
Did you know? Colreavy is the first Sinn Féin TD in this constituency since John Joe McGirl topped the poll with over 7,000 votes in 1957. McGirl was in prison at the time and his party's campaign slogan was "get him in to get him out".
Politician (living or deceased) you most admire: Michael Collins.
Priority as a TD? To raise the living standards of people in Sligo/Leitrim and protect/promote quality public services.
Why did you stand for election? To help bring about change for the better.
Is there any particular event that brought home to you just how serious the economic crisis had become? The levels of emigration and desperation among people that were perceived to have been middle class, as they are now the 'new poor'.

First preference votes

	Seats	3			11,108		
	Candidate	Party	1st	%	Quota	Count	Status
1	Perry, John*	FG	8,663	19.50%	0.78	8	Made Quota
2	McLoughlin, Tony	FG	7,715	17.37%	0.69	9	Made Quota
3	Colreavy, Michael	SF	5,911	13.30%	0.53	9	Elected
4	Scanlon, Eamon*	FF	5,075	11.42%	0.46	9	Not Elected
5	O'Keeffe, Susan	LB	4,553	10.25%	0.41	7	Eliminated
6	MacSharry, Marc	FF	4,633	10.43%	0.42	6	Eliminated
7	Bree, Declan #	ULA	2,284	5.14%	0.21	5	Eliminated
8	Clarke, Michael	NP	2,415	5.44%	0.22	4	No Expenses
9	Cawley, Veronica	NP	1,119	2.52%	0.10	3	No Expenses
10	Love, Alwyn Robert	NV	779	1.75%	0.07	3	No Expenses
11	McSharry, Gabriel	NP	747	1.68%	0.07	2	No Expenses
12	Gogan, Johnny	GP	432	0.97%	0.04	1	No Expenses
13	Cahill, Dick	NP	102	0.23%	0.01	1	No Expenses

*Outgoing TD #Former TD Valid poll: 44,428 Quota: 11,108 No expenses limit: 2,777

Party votes

		2011					2007				Change	
Party	Cand	1st	%	Quota	Seats	Cand	1st	%	Quota	Seats	%	Seats
FG	2	16,378	36.86%	1.47	2	3	15,684	39.27%	1.57	1	-2.41%	+1
LB	1	4,553	10.25%	0.41		1	1,555	3.89%	0.16		+6.35%	
FF	2	9,708	21.85%	0.87		2	16,360	40.97%	1.64	2	-19.12%	-2
SF	1	5,911	13.30%	0.53	1	1	4,684	11.73%	0.47		+1.58%	+1
GP	1	432	0.97%	0.04		1	1,209	3.03%	0.12		-2.06%	
Others	6	7,446	16.76%	0.67		2	442	1.11%	0.04		+15.65%	
Total	13	44,428	100.0%	11,108	3	10	39,934	100.0%	9,985	3	0.00%	0
Electorate	63,432	70.04%					57,517	69.43%			+0.61%	
Spoiled	409	0.91%					396	0.98%			-0.07%	
Turnout	44,837	70.69%					40,330	70.12%			+0.57%	

Transfer analysis

From	To	FG	LB	FF	SF	Others	Non Trans
FG	865	527		183	155		
		60.92%		21.16%	17.92%		
LB	6,646	3,042		553	1,477		1,574
		45.77%		8.32%	22.22%		23.68%
FF	5,586	1,445	550	2,690	364		537
		25.87%	9.85%	48.16%	6.52%		9.61%
GP	432	84	126	29	49	135	9
		19.44%	29.17%	6.71%	11.34%	31.25%	2.08%
Others	8,477	2,005	1,417	1,548	1,815	896	796
		23.65%	16.72%	18.26%	21.41%	10.57%	9.39%
Total	22,006	7,103	2,093	5,003	3,860	1,031	2,916
		32.28%	9.51%	22.73%	17.54%	4.69%	13.25%

Election Facts

"Prior to Election 2011, when Fine Gael won 76 seats, the party's seat maximum was the 70 seats it won in November 1982"
Professor Michael Gallagher, TCD

Sligo-North Leitrim

Candidate	Party	1st	2nd Gogan Cahill	3rd McSharry Votes	4th Cawley Love Alywn	5th Clarke Votes	6th Bree Votes	7th MacSharry Votes	8th O'Keeffe Votes	9th Perry Surplus
Seats 3									Quota	11,108
			+40	+38	+227	+580	+220	+651	+1,554	-865
Perry, John*	FG	8,663	8,703	8,741	8,968	9,548	9,768	10,419	**11,973**	11,108
			+63	+113	+236	+193	+379	+794	+1,488	+527
McLoughlin, Tony	FG	7,715	7,778	7,891	8,127	8,320	8,699	9,493	10,981	**11,508**
			+61	+260	+233	+381	+929	+364	+1,477	+155
Colreavy, Michael	SF	5,911	5,972	6,232	6,465	6,846	7,775	8,139	9,616	**9,771**
			+22	+68	+70	+390	+74	+2,690	+553	+183
Scanlon, Eamon*	FF	5,075	5,097	5,165	5,235	5,625	5,699	8,389	8,942	9,125
			+156	+60	+444	+217	+666	+550	-6,646	
O'Keeffe, Susan	LB	4,553	4,709	4,769	5,213	5,430	6,096	6,646	Eliminated	
			+14	+39	+179	+437	+284	-5,586		
MacSharry, Marc	FF	4,633	4,647	4,686	4,865	5,302	5,586	Eliminated		
			+50	+46	+383	+183	-2,946			
Bree, Declan #	ULA	2,284	2,334	2,380	2,763	2,946	Eliminated			
			+16	+32	+144	-2,607				
Clarke, Michael	NP	2,415	2,431	2,463	2,607	Eliminated				
			+21	+31	-1,171					
Cawley, Veronica	NP	1,119	1,140	1,171	Eliminated					
			+57	+45	-881					
Love, Alwyn Robert	NV	779	836	881	Eliminated					
			+23	-770						
McSharry, Gabriel	NP	747	770	Eliminated						
			-432							
Gogan, Johnny	GP	432	Eliminated							
			-102							
Cahill, Dick	NP	102	Eliminated							
Non-transferable			+11	+38	+136	+226	+394	+537	+1,574	
Cumulative			11	49	185	411	805	1,342	2,916	2,916
Total		44,428	44,428	44,428	44,428	44,428	44,428	44,428	44,428	44,428

Sligo-North Leitrim United
Left Alliance candidate
Declan Bree canvassing in
Sligo Town

Tipperary North (3 seats)

Lowry's vote hits record high

Elected

Michael Lowry* (Ind) Count 1, Noel Coonan* (FG) Count 2, Alan Kelly (Lab) Final count.

Analysis by Michael Gallagher

Parts of southwest Offaly, with a population of 4,276, were transferred to this three-seat constituency since 2007. It included Moneygall, the ancestral Offaly home of the US president Barack Obama.

There was a familiar pattern to the headline result here though. Michael Lowry may not bask in the approval of the Moriarty Tribunal or the national media, but if anything, that seems to increase the loyalty of his supporters in Tipperary North. Lowry headed the poll, as he has done at every election since he became an independent in 1997, and pushed his vote total to a new record high. He won 14,104, or 29% of the first-preference votes. Just to rub it in, it was his surplus that took incumbent Fine Gael TD Noel Coonan into the second seat.

FF had taken two of the three seats here as recently as 2002, but the odds were against it holding even one in 2011. Máire Hoctor, seen as a dissident after Brian Cowen dropped her from her junior ministerial post in April 2009, had the advantage of being the party's sole candidate, and she did not do badly; she increased her personal vote, and at a mere 17.8%, the swing away from Fianna Fáil was one of the smallest in the country.

However, that was not enough. For Labour, Kathleen O'Meara had stepped aside after mounting strong challenges in 1997, 2002 and 2007, and the party standard-bearer was former senator Alan Kelly. He had left the Seanad to run in the European Parliament elections in 2009 and was elected as MEP for the South constituency. Although he vowed in that campaign not to contest the next general election, a request from the party leader was enough to lure him home. He nearly doubled the party's vote share and took the final seat over 2,000 votes ahead of Hoctor. His European Parliament seat remained within Tipperary, passing on to Clonmel-based Phil Prendergast.

*outgoing TDs

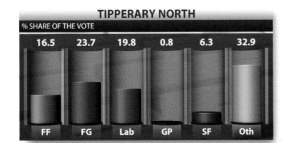

TIPPERARY NORTH

% SHARE OF THE VOTE

FF	FG	Lab	GP	SF	Oth
16.5	23.7	19.8	0.8	6.3	32.9

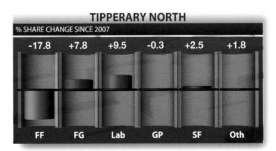

TIPPERARY NORTH

% SHARE CHANGE SINCE 2007

FF	FG	Lab	GP	SF	Oth
-17.8	+7.8	+9.5	-0.3	+2.5	+1.8

Tipperary North

MICHAEL LOWRY (Ind)

Home Address: Holycross, Thurles, Co Tipperary.
Phone: 0504 22022 (CO) 0504 23349 (Fax) 01 6183000 (LH)
Email: michael.lowry@oireachtas.ie
Website: www.michaellowry.ie
Twitter: www.twitter.com/michael_lowry
Facebook: /michaellowrytd
Birth Place/Date: Tipperary, March 1954.
Marital Status/Family: 2 sons, 1 daughter.
Education: Thurles CBS.
Occupation: Public representative. Business owner.
Biography: Elected a TD in February 1987 and re-elected at each of the six subsequent general elections. Initially a Fine Gael TD, he stood as an independent in the 1997 general elections and has remained an independent TD since then. He was Minister for Transport, Energy and Communications from 1994 until November 1996 when he resigned. He resigned from Fine Gael's parliamentary party in 1997. He has topped the poll in each subsequent election. He supported the Fianna Fáil/Greens government in the 30th Dáil in return for investment in his constituency. Prominent administrator in the GAA in the early 1980s as chairman of the Tipperary County Committee and chairman of the Semple Stadium Development Committee. First elected to Tipperary North Riding County Council in 1979.
Hobbies: Avid interest in all sports, particularly GAA and horse racing.
Did you know? He increased his vote in Election 2011 despite supporting the government in the 30th Dáil.
Politician (living or deceased) you most admire: Liam Cosgrave.
Priority as a TD? The creation of an economic climate that provides job opportunities.
Why did you stand for election? Because I am committed to politics and to public service.
Is there any particular event that brought home to you just how serious the economic crisis had become? The collapse of Allied Irish Bank, which was once a bastion of Irish banking.

NOEL COONAN (FG)

Address: Gortnagoona, Roscrea, Co Tipperary.
Phone: 086 2427733 (M) 0504 32544 (O)
Email: noel.coonan@oireachtas.ie
Website: www.noelcoonan.com
Twitter: http://twitter.com/#!/NoelCoonanTD
Birth Place/Date: Roscrea, January 1951.
Marital Status/Family: Married.
Education: Shanakill NS, Roscrea; CBS Templemore.
Occupation: Public representative.
Biography: Elected to the Dáil in 2007 and re-elected in 2011. Fine Gael's deputy spokesperson on Agriculture with Special Responsibility for Common Agricultural Policy (CAP) Reform (October 2010-February 2011). Unsuccessfully contested 2002 general election. Member of Seanad Éireann (Cultural and Educational Panel) 2002-2007. Elected to Tipperary North County Council (1991), Templemore UDC (1994). Re-elected Tipperary North County Council (1999) and Templemore UDC (1999).
Hobbies: Gaelic games, rugby, horse racing, card playing and rural rambling.
Did you know? Noel is a founding member and President of the Collins22 Society and deeply involved in creating an awareness of the life and times of Michael Collins.
Politician (living or deceased) you most admire: Michael Collins.
Priority as a TD? To enhance the lives of my constituents by protecting existing employment. To stem the heartbreak of emigration. To protect and promote rural Irish customs and pastimes.
Why did you stand for election? To achieve priorities as outlined above through a Fine Gael-led government and to bring political stability to the country.
Is there any particular event that brought home to you just how serious the economic crisis had become? The bank bailout, the collapse of the banking and construction industries and the failure of the regulatory process indicated just how serious the Irish economic crisis had become.

ALAN KELLY (Lab)

Home Address: Loughtea, Ballina, Nenagh, Co Tipperary.
Constituency Offices: 1 Summerhill, Nenagh, Co Tipperary and Rosemary Square, Roscrea, Co Tipperary.
Dáil Office: Department of Transport, Tourism and Sport, Kildare Street, Dublin 2.
Phone: 067 34190 (CO) 086 6061101 (M)
Email: alan.kelly@oireachtas.ie or office@alankelly.ie
Website: www.alankelly.ie
Twitter: @alankellylabour
Facebook: /AlanKellylabour
Birth Place/Date: Limerick, July 1975.
Marital Status/Family: Married to Regina O'Connor; 1 daughter.
Education: Nenagh CBS; UCC (BA Hons English and history, MPhil in political history); Boston College (cert in leadership); UCD/Smurfit Business School.
Occupation: Minister of State. Formerly MEP, senator, ebusiness manager with Fáilte Ireland.
Biography: Secured 9,559 first-preference votes to get elected in his first general election attempt. He was elected to the Seanad's agricultural panel in 2007 and to the European parliament in 2009.
Hobbies: Tipperary and Portroe Hurling, Munster rugby, Manchester United, swimming, reading non-fiction.
Did you know? Alan comes from the same small village, Portroe, as 2010 All-Ireland winning Tipperary hurling manager Liam Sheedy, Tipperary Rose of Tralee Aoife Kelly and US Economic Envoy to Northern Ireland, Declan Kelly (brother).
Politician (living or deceased) you most admire: Jim Kemmy, Thomas Johnson.
Priority as a TD? Export-led jobs, jobs, jobs... and fairness in society.
Why did you stand for election? Money should not be the medium by which our education or health services are delivered.
Is there any particular event that brought home to you just how serious the economic crisis had become? Meeting the volume of young people who are emigrating and the number of young couples who, unlike previous generations, haven't even got that option because they are in so much personal debt.

First preference votes

	Seats	3			12,069		
	Candidate	Party	1st	%	Quota	Count	Status
1	Lowry, Michael*	NP	14,104	29.22%	1.17	1	Made Quota
2	Coonan, Noel*	FG	11,425	23.67%	0.95	2	Made Quota
3	Kelly, Alan	LB	9,559	19.80%	0.79	3	Elected
4	Hoctor, Máire*	FF	7,978	16.53%	0.66	3	Not Elected
5	Morris, Séamus	SF	3,034	6.29%	0.25	2	Eliminated
6	Clancy, Billy	NV	1,442	2.99%	0.12	2	No Expenses
7	O'Malley, Olwyn	GP	409	0.85%	0.03	2	No Expenses
8	Bopp, Kate	NP	322	0.67%	0.03	2	No Expenses
8	*Outgoing		48,273	100.00%	12,069	3,018	No Expenses

*Outgoing TD Valid poll: 48,273 Quota: 12,069 No expenses limit: 3,018

Party votes

		2011					2007				Change	
Party	Cand	1st	%	Quota	Seats	Cand	1st	%	Quota	Seats	%	Seats
FG	1	11,425	23.67%	0.95	1	1	7,061	15.89%	0.64	1	+7.78%	
LB	1	9,559	19.80%	0.79	1	1	4,561	10.27%	0.41		+9.54%	+1
FF	1	7,978	16.53%	0.66		2	15,245	34.31%	1.37	1	-17.78%	-1
SF	1	3,034	6.29%	0.25		1	1,672	3.76%	0.15		+2.52%	
GP	1	409	0.85%	0.03		1	495	1.11%	0.04		-0.27%	
PD						1	634	1.43%	0.06		-1.43%	
Others	3	15,868	32.87%	1.31	1	2	14,763	33.23%	1.33	1	-0.36%	
Total	8	48,273	100.0%	12,069	3	9	44,431	100.0%	11,108	3	0.00%	0
Electorate		63,235	76.34%				57,084	77.83%			-1.50%	
Spoiled		516	1.06%				352	0.79%			+0.27%	
Turnout		48,789	77.16%				44,783	78.45%			-1.30%	

Transfer analysis

From	To	FG	LB	FF	SF	GP	Others	Non Trans
SF	3,180		1,111	614				1,455
			34.94%	19.31%				45.75%
GP	429		150	83				196
			34.97%	19.35%				45.69%
Others	4,040	705	1,245	766	146	20	241	917
		17.45%	30.82%	18.96%	3.61%	0.50%	5.97%	22.70%
Total	7,649	705	2,506	1,463	146	20	241	2,568
		9.22%	32.76%	19.13%	1.91%	0.26%	3.15%	33.57%

Election Facts

"Roughly 1 in 3 Labour or Fine Gael voters go to each other, while the Green voters move in the main to Labour and Fine Gael"
Millward Brown
Lansdowne/RTÉ General Election 2011 Exit Poll

Tipperary North

Candidate	Party	1st	2nd Lowry Surplus -2,035	3rd Morris Clancy O'Malley Bopp
Seats 3			**Quota**	**12,069**
Lowry, Michael*	NP	**14,104**	12,069	12,069
			+705	
Coonan, Noel*	FG	**11,425**	12,130	12,130
			+545	+1,961
Kelly, Alan	LB	**9,559**	10,104	**12,065**
			+378	+1,085
Hoctor, Máire*	FF	7,978	8,356	9,441
			+146	-3,180
Morris, Séamus	SF	3,034	3,180	Eliminated
			+211	-1,653
Clancy, Billy	NV	1,442	1,653	Eliminated
			+20	-429
O'Malley, Olwyn	GP	409	429	Eliminated
			+30	-352
Bopp, Kate	NP	322	352	Eliminated
Non-transferable				+2,568
Cumulative			0	2,568
Total		**48,273**	**48,273**	**48,273**

Ruairí Quinn, Alan Kelly, Liz McManus and Eamon Gilmore at the launch of Labour's 'Development of broadband infrastructure key to jobs and recovery plan' initiative

Tipperary South (3 seats)

Former Fianna Fáil TD wins seat after shedding party colours

Elected

Séamus Healy (Ind) Count 3, Tom Hayes* (FG) Count 4, Mattie McGrath* (Ind) Final count.

Analysis by Michael Gallagher

There were no boundary changes to this three-seat constituency since 2007. Indeed Fianna Fáil's achievement that year, when it took two of the three seats, ousting left-wing independent Séamus Healy, was one of the surprises of that election. In 2011, Healy, now part of the United Left Alliance, was certain to regain his seat, and Fine Gael incumbent Tom Hayes was equally sure to retain his.

That left just one seat between four credible contenders: Fianna Fáil junior minister Martin Mansergh, Labour senator Phil Prendergast, Fine Gael's second candidate Michael Murphy, and Mattie McGrath. McGrath had been elected for Fianna Fáil in 2007, but had rapidly acquired maverick status, and in June 2010 he lost the party whip, becoming an independent TD, for voting against the government bill banning stag hunting. At the end of January 2011 he left Fianna Fáil itself and announced that he would be standing as an independent.

Martin Mansergh, whose PhD thesis was on the history of 18th-Century France on the eve of the Revolution, may have sensed the upheaval that was about to happen. Indeed, his assertion on RTÉ radio on election count day that this was 'not a wipe-out' for Fianna Fáil had a ring of Marie Antoinette about it. Sure enough, as the tumbrils left the counting centre and rolled through the streets of Clonmel, it was Dr Mansergh's Dáil career that they bore away.

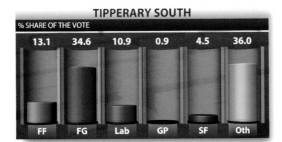

TIPPERARY SOUTH
% SHARE OF THE VOTE

FF	FG	Lab	GP	SF	Oth
13.1	34.6	10.9	0.9	4.5	36.0

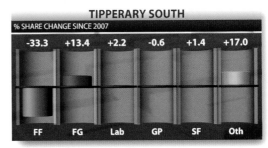

TIPPERARY SOUTH
% SHARE CHANGE SINCE 2007

FF	FG	Lab	GP	SF	Oth
-33.3	+13.4	+2.2	-0.6	+1.4	+17.0

*outgoing TDs

Tipperary South

SÉAMUS HEALY (Ind)

Address: 56 Queen Street, Clonmel,
Co Tipperary
Phone: 087 2802199 (M) 052 6121883
(CO)
Email: seamus.healy@oireachtas.ie
Facebook: Yes.
Birth Place/Date: Clonmel, August 1950.
Marital Status/Family: Married.
Education: CBS High School, Clonmel.
Occupation: Public representative. Former
hospital administrator at South Tipperary
General Hospital.
Biography: Elected to Dáil in 2011 as a
United Left Alliance candidate. First
elected a TD in June 2000 at a by-election
caused by the death of Labour TD Michael
Ferris. Re-elected in 2002 and lost his seat
in 2007. Unsuccessfully contested general
elections in 1987, 1989, 1992 and 1997.
Member, Clonmel Borough Council
(1985-2004). Member, South Tipperary
County Council (1991-2004) and co-opted
back onto council in July 2007. Mayor of
Clonmel 1994-1995. Member of the
IMPACT National Executive. Treasurer of
the Old Bridge Community Association;
Director of Cuan Saor Women's Refuge
and director of the Elm Park Childcare
Committee; chairperson of the Save Our
Hospital committee.
Hobbies: Scouting, walking.
Did you know? Séamus supports Leeds Utd
Football Club.
**Politician (living or deceased) you most
admire:** James Connolly.
Priority as a TD? Employment/tackling
unemployment.
Why did you stand for election? As a
general election candidate, I campaigned
for the retention and expansion of acute
hospital services at South Tipperary
General Hospital; an end to the bank
bailouts and obscene salaries; a fairer
taxation system; an emergency job creation
programme and an end to junkets.
**Is there any particular event that brought
home to you just how serious the economic
crisis had become?** Dole queues spilling out
onto the streets.

TOM HAYES (FG)

Home Address: Cahervillahow, Golden,
Co Tipperary.
Phone: 087 8105016 (M) 062 62892/052
6180731 (O) 01 6183168 (LH)
Email: tom.hayes@oireachtas.ie
Website: www.tomhayes.ie
Twitter: twitter.com/tomhayestd
Facebook: Yes.
Birth Place/Date: Cahervillahow, Golden,
February 1952.
Marital Status/family: Married to Marian
Hayes; 3 sons.
Education: Mount Melleray College,
Waterford; Tipperary Vocational School;
and UCC (diploma in public
administration).
Occupation: Full-time public
representative.
Biography: First elected a TD in July 2001
at a by-election caused by the death of Fine
Gael TD Theresa Ahearn. Fine Gael deputy
spokesperson on Agriculture and Food
(2001-2002); spokesperson on Heritage
and Rural Affairs (2002-2007); chairperson
of party since 2002; spokesperson on Road
Safety (2010-2011). Member of Seanad
(1997-2001). Member, Tipperary South
Riding County Council (1991-2003).
Hobbies: GAA, horse and greyhound
racing, rugby and traditional music.
**Politician (living or deceased) you most
admire:** WT Cosgrave.
Priority as a TD? Job retention and
creation in South Tipperary to prevent the
emigration of young people.
Why did you stand for election? I first
entered politics to help people in my area.
Improving people's lives, assisting the local
community, supporting our local economy,
are all rewarding and important parts of a
TD's role.
**Is there any particular event that brought
home to you just how serious the economic
crisis had become?** The emigration of so
many young people is the sorriest sight. I
am also greatly concerned at the number of
people I am meeting who cannot make
ends meet and are facing losing their
homes. The effect on people's mental
health is also very worrying.

MATTIE McGRATH (Ind)

Address: 2 Joyce's Lane, The Quay,
Clonmel, Co Tipperary.
Phone: 086 8184307 (M) 052 6129155
(CO)
Website: www.mattiemcgrath.ie
Email: mattie.mcgrath@oireachtas.ie
Facebook:
facebook.com/MattieMcGrathTD
Birth Place/Date: September 1958.
Marital Status/family: Married to Margaret;
8 children.
Education: St Joseph's College, Cahir;
Kildalton Agricultural College,
Co Kilkenny.
Occupation: Public representative and self-
employed businessman.
Biography: First elected a TD in 2007 for
Fianna Fáil, he lost the party whip after he
voted against the government on the
wildlife bill to ban stag hunting in June
2010 and successfully contested the 2011
election as an independent. Member South
Tipperary County Council (1999-2007).
Chairperson South Tipperary County
Council (2004-2005).
Hobbies: Irish culture, GAA.
**Politician (living or deceased) you most
admire:** Seán Lemass.
Priority as a TD? To bring about real
political reform as demanded by the
electorate in the recent election.
Why did you stand for election? To work
to improve the living standards of all
families in my constituency.
**Is there any particular event that brought
home to you just how serious the economic
crisis had become?** The arrival of the IMF
in our country and effectively taking over
our powers of decision-making in relation
to financial matters.

First preference votes

	Seats	3			10,341		
	Candidate	Party	1st	%	Quota	Count	Status
1	Healy, Séamus #	ULA	8,818	21.32%	0.85	3	Made Quota
2	Hayes, Tom*	FG	8,896	21.51%	0.86	4	Made Quota
3	McGrath, Mattie*	NP	6,074	14.69%	0.59	5	Elected
4	Murphy, Michael	FG	5,402	13.06%	0.52	5	Not Elected
5	Mansergh, Martin*	FF	5,419	13.10%	0.52	4	Eliminated
6	Prendergast, Phil	LB	4,525	10.94%	0.44	2	Eliminated
7	Browne, Michael	SF	1,860	4.50%	0.18	1	No Expenses
8	McNally, Paul	GP	367	0.89%	0.04	1	No Expenses

*Outgoing TD #Former TD Valid poll: 41,361 Quota: 10,341 No expenses limit: 2,586

Party votes

		2011					2007				Change	
Party	Cand	1st	%	Quota	Seats	Cand	1st	%	Quota	Seats	%	Seats
FG	2	14,298	34.57%	1.38	1	1	8,200	21.14%	0.85	1	+13.42%	
LB	1	4,525	10.94%	0.44		1	3,400	8.77%	0.35		+2.17%	
FF	1	5,419	13.10%	0.52		3	18,004	46.42%	1.86	2	-33.32%	-2
SF	1	1,860	4.50%	0.18		1	1,198	3.09%	0.12		+1.41%	
ULA	1	8,818	21.32%	0.85	1						+21.32%	+1
GP	1	367	0.89%	0.04		1	591	1.52%	0.06		-0.64%	
PD						2	541	1.39%	0.06		-1.39%	
Others	1	6,074	14.69%	0.59	1	2	6,848	17.66%	0.71		-2.97%	+1
Total	8	41,361	100.0%	10,341	3	11	38,782	100.0%	9,696	3	0.00%	0
Electorate	57,420	72.03%					54,637	70.98%			+1.05%	
Spoiled	432	1.03%					330	0.84%			+0.19%	
Turnout	41,793	72.78%					39,112	71.59%			+1.20%	

Transfer analysis

From	To	FG	LB	FF	Others	Non Trans
LB	4,966	1,813		277	2,452	424
		36.51%		5.58%	49.38%	8.54%
FF	5,948	1,315			2,565	2,068
		22.11%			43.12%	34.77%
SF	1,860	400	368	141	835	116
		21.51%	19.78%	7.58%	44.89%	6.24%
GP	367	79	73	28	164	23
		21.53%	19.89%	7.63%	44.69%	6.27%
Others	924	506		83	335	
		54.76%		8.98%	36.26%	
Total	14,065	4,113	441	529	6,351	2,631
		29.24%	3.14%	3.76%	45.15%	18.71%

Election Facts
"William Norton was the longest serving leader of the Labour party. He was leader for 28 years from 1932 to 1960"
Sean Donnelly

Tipperary South

Candidate	Party	1st	2nd Browne McNally	3rd Prendergast Votes	4th Healy Surplus	5th Mansergh Votes
Seats 3					**Quota**	**10,341**
			+724	+1,723	-924	
Healy, Séamus #	ULA	8,818	9,542	11,265	10,341	10,341
			+318	+972	+277	
Hayes, Tom*	FG	8,896	9,214	10,186	10,463	10,463
			+275	+729	+335	+2,565
McGrath, Mattie*	NP	6,074	6,349	7,078	7,413	9,978
			+161	+841	+229	+1,315
Murphy, Michael	FG	5,402	5,563	6,404	6,633	7,948
			+169	+277	+83	-5,948
Mansergh, Martin*	FF	5,419	5,588	5,865	5,948	Eliminated
			+441	-4,966		
Prendergast, Phil	LB	4,525	4,966	Eliminated		
			-1,860			
Browne, Michael	SF	1,860	Eliminated			
			-367			
McNally, Paul	GP	367	Eliminated			
Non-transferable			+139	+424		+2,068
Cumulative			139	563	563	2,631
Total			**41,361**	**41,361**	**41,361**	**41,361**	**41,361**

Séamus Healy, newly elected independent TD for Tipperary South, gives his victory speech, watched by Martin Mansergh (Fianna Fáil), Tom Hayes (Fine Gael) and Mattie McGrath (Independent)

Waterford (4 seats)

First woman in 59 years elected in Waterford

Elected
John Deasy* (FG) Count 3, Paudie Coffey (FG) Count 9, Ciara Conway (Lab) Count 10, John Halligan (Ind) Final count.

Analysis by Michael Gallagher

There were no changes to the boundaries of this four-seat constituency that comprises almost the entire county of Waterford, excluding only a population of 1,500 north of the Comeragh Mountains.

After Martin Cullen moved from the PDs to Fianna Fáil in 1994, this became one of the most predictable constituencies in the country, consistently returning two Fianna Fáil TDs and one each from Fine Gael and Labour.

In 2011 it was clear that Fine Gael would advance to two seats, and it duly did. John Deasy headed the poll, and an even divide of the Fine Gael vote ensured that running mate Paudie Coffey was not far behind.

Waterford, despite its urban centres, has never been a Labour stronghold. When Tom Kyne won a seat here in 1948 he became the first Labour TD for 25 years, and when he retired in 1977 it took the party 12 years to regain the seat through Brian O'Shea. With O'Shea now retiring himself, there was some concern that the seat could be lost, but the national swing to the party ensured that it was not. Waterford city councillor Séamus Ryan was favourite to take the seat, but he was outpolled by Ciara Conway, who took a seat despite the competition in her Dungarvan

base from poll-topper Deasy, being aided by strong Tramore connections. She became the first woman to represent the constituency since the death of Bridget Mary Redmond in 1952.

The main excitement lay in the race for the final seat. With Cullen's retirement due to ill-health in March 2010, Waterford-based Brendan Kenneally – son and grandson of TDs, and not to be confused with the poet of similar name – was the sole Fianna Fáil candidate. Even though the party vote share dropped by a massive 32 percentage points, the fifth largest in the country, it seemed that he had a chance, as on first preferences he was over 2,000 votes ahead of his two rivals. However, the main challenger turned out not to be Sinn Féin's David Cullinane, who might have lacked the transfer-friendliness to overhaul Kenneally, but John Halligan, a Waterford city councillor who had run twice with little success for the Workers' Party. Now running as an independent, Halligan trebled his first-preference vote, and with the aid of over 2,000 transfers on Cullinane's elimination, he sailed past Kenneally to take the last seat with nearly 1,000 votes to spare.

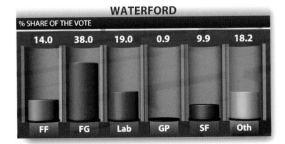

WATERFORD

% SHARE OF THE VOTE

FF	FG	Lab	GP	SF	Oth
14.0	38.0	19.0	0.9	9.9	18.2

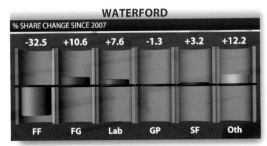

WATERFORD

% SHARE CHANGE SINCE 2007

FF	FG	Lab	GP	SF	Oth
-32.5	+10.6	+7.6	-1.3	+3.2	+12.2

*outgoing TDs

Waterford

JOHN DEASY (FG)

Home Address: Kilrush, Dungarvan, Co Waterford.
Constituency Office: 20 Grattan Square, Dungarvan.
Phone: 058 43003 (CO) 01 6183596 (LH)
Email: john.deasy@oireacahtas.ie
Website: www.johndeasy.finegael.ie
Birth Place/Date: Dungarvan, October 1967.
Marital Status/Family: Married to Maura Derrane.
Education: Coláiste na Rinne, Ring, Dungarvan; St Augustine's College, Dungarvan; Mercyhurst College, Erie, Pennsylvania, USA (BA history and communications); University College, Cork (BCL).
Occupation: Public Representative. Formerly US Congressional aide.
Biography: First elected to the Dáil in 2002. Fine Gael's frontbench spokesperson on Justice, Equality and Law Reform (2002-2004); chairman of Dáil's European Affairs Committee (2004-2007). Member Waterford County Council (1999-2003), Member, Dungarvan Town Council (1999-2003). Formerly legislative assistant for Senator John Heinz in US Senate (1990-1991) and Representative Ronald K Machtley in US House of Representatives (1993-1995). Son of Austin Deasy (TD 1977-2002 and senator 1973-1977)

PAUDIE COFFEY (FG)

Home Address: Mount Bolton, Portlaw, Co Waterford.
Phone: 051 835867 (O) 01 6183902 (LH)
Email: paudie.coffey@oireachtas.ie
Website: www.paudiecoffey.finegael.ie
Twitter: http://twitter.com/#!/PaudieCoffey
Facebook: facebook/Paudie Coffey
Birth Place/Date: Waterford, May 1969.
Marital Status/Family: Married to Suzanne Coffey, 2 daughters, 1 son.
Education: St Declan's Community College, Kilmacthomas; Waterford; Regional Technical College (WIT); UCD.
Occupation: Full-time public representative and businessman. Formerly ESB employee for 20 years.
Biography: Member of Seanad Éireann (2007-2011). Elected to Waterford County Council in 1999 and re-elected in 2004. Former Mayor of Waterford.
Hobbies: All sports. Member of Portlaw GAA Club. Also enjoys reading, and watching films.
Did you know? Paudie has played at every level of hurling from minor to senior inter-county. He also coached the Waterford under-21 Hurling Team.
Politician (living or deceased) you most admire: Michael Collins.
Priority as a TD? Getting the people of Waterford back to work, ensuring university status is achieved for WIT and developing a strong agri-food sector and fisheries sector.
Why did you stand for election? I stood on a platform of job creation, reform and on regional issues.
Is there any particular event that brought home to you just how serious the economic crisis had become? Personal indebtedness, retail and factory closures, house repossessions and emigration are the obvious indicators of the depth of this crisis. Unemployment has more than doubled in Waterford so it is essential to restore stability, confidence and growth in our economy.

CIARA CONWAY (Lab)

Home Address: 34 Cluain Garbhan, Abbeyside, Dungarvan, Co Waterford.
Phone: 086 1022958 (M) 01 6184011 (LH)
Email: ciara.conway@oireachtas.ie
Website: www.labour.ie/ciaraconway
Twitter: @ciaramconway
Facebook: www.facebook.com/ciaraconway
Birth Place/Date: Waterford.
Marital Status/family: Single; 1 daughter.
Education: Holy Cross NS, Tramore; Our Lady of Mercy Secondary School, Waterford; NUI Galway (BA Hons public and social policy), UCC (masters in social work), Waterford IT (masters in business administration).
Occupation: Public representative. Social worker with Barnardos.
Biography: Elected on the 10th count in her first general election. Elected to Dungarvan Town Council in 2009.
Hobbies: Swimming, mentor with Abbeyside Ladies Football Club, member of Abbeyside /Ballinacourty GAA Club, music enthusiast (never misses the Electric Picnic).
Did you know? Ciara is the youngest female TD in the 31st Dáil.
Politician (living or deceased) you most admire: Nelson Mandela.
Priority as a TD? To be a voice for fairness and equality. As a young, single mum and a former frontline health worker, I'm not a typical politician. Having worked in child protection services, I have a keen interest in the areas of health and children.
Why did you stand for election? It has been over 50 years since a woman was elected in this constituency. The people of Waterford were crying out for change and as a young, educated woman I represent that change. I will endeavour to put Waterford on the map as a tourist destination, a great place for industry and for third-level education to develop and flourish.
Is there any particular event that brought home to you just how serious the economic crisis had become? A huge number of families have been affected by job losses. Waterford had the devastating loss of the Waterford Crystal factory and the loss of pensions for many workers.

JOHN HALLIGAN (Ind)

Home Address: 47 Johns Hill, Waterford.
Phone: 086 2678622 (M) 01 6183498 (LH)
Email: john.halligan@oireachtas.ie
Website: www.johnhalligan.net
Facebook: Yes.
Birth Place/Date: Waterford, January, 1955.
Marital Status/family: Living with partner; 3 daughters.
Education: St John's Manor School; Mount Sion Christian Brothers Secondary School; Waterford Technical College.
Occupation: Public representative. Formerly radio operator for Bell Lines and previously a supervisor for Performance Sail Craft.
Biography: Secured 5,546 first-preference votes to get elected on the 11th and final count and become Waterford's first independent TD in over 70 years. Unsuccessfully contested 2002 and 2007 general elections for the Workers' Party. Elected to Waterford City Council for the Workers' Party in 1999 and re-elected in 2004. Independent candidate in the 2009 local elections and topped the poll. Mayor of Waterford 2009/2010.
Hobbies: Mountain climbing, walking, swimming and sailing.
Did you know? John sailed in the famous Christian Radich tall ship for 10 days in 2010 from Norway across the North Sea to England.
Politician (living or deceased) you most admire: James Connolly, because of his mantra that "every social issue is a political issue".
Priority as a TD? People have lost belief in politics and politicians so, like a lot of the new TDs, I want to try to restore confidence in politics so that people realise that not all politicians are bad.
Why did you stand for election? I want to fight injustice and help people out.
Is there any particular event that brought home to you just how serious the economic crisis had become? When I was Mayor of Waterford, I used to meet small business owners who were despairing and almost suicidal because of their financial worries and the way the banks wrecked this country.

John Halligan calls for a referendum on the IMF bailout deal

Waterford

	Candidate	Party	1st	%	Quota	Count	Status
		Seats	4		10,745		
1	Deasy, John*	FG	10,718	19.95%	1.00	3	Made Quota
2	Coffey, Paudie	FG	9,698	18.05%	0.90	9	Made Quota
3	Conway, Ciara	LB	5,554	10.34%	0.52	10	Made Quota
4	Halligan, John	NP	5,546	10.32%	0.52	11	Elected
5	Kenneally, Brendan*	FF	7,515	13.99%	0.70	11	Not Elected
6	Cullinane, David	SF	5,342	9.94%	0.50	9	Eliminated
7	Ryan, Seamus	LB	4,638	8.63%	0.43	8	Eliminated
8	Higgins, Tom	NP	1,130	2.10%	0.11	7	No Expenses
9	Collery, Justin	NP	967	1.80%	0.09	7	No Expenses
10	Tobin, Joe	WP	873	1.63%	0.08	6	No Expenses
11	Conway, Joe	NP	725	1.35%	0.07	5	No Expenses
12	Power, Jody	GP	462	0.86%	0.04	4	No Expenses
13	Nutty, Ben	FN	257	0.48%	0.02	3	No Expenses
14	Waters, Declan	NP	222	0.41%	0.02	2	No Expenses
15	Kiersey, Gerard	NP	73	0.14%	0.01	1	No Expenses
15	*Outgoing		53,720	100.00%	10,745	2,687	No Expenses

*Outgoing TD Valid poll: 53,720 Quota: 10,745 No expenses limit: 2,687

Party votes

Party	Cand	1st	%	Quota	Seats	Cand	1st	%	Quota	Seats	%	Seats
		2011					2007				Change	
FG	2	20,416	38.00%	1.90	2	3	13,552	27.36%	1.37	1	+10.64%	+1
LB	2	10,192	18.97%	0.95	1	1	5,610	11.33%	0.57	1	+7.65%	
FF	1	7,515	13.99%	0.70		3	23,025	46.49%	2.32	2	-32.50%	-2
SF	1	5,342	9.94%	0.50		1	3,327	6.72%	0.34		+3.23%	
GP	1	462	0.86%	0.04		1	1,049	2.12%	0.11		-1.26%	
WP	1	873	1.63%	0.08		1	1,708	3.45%	0.17		-1.82%	
Others	7	8,920	16.60%	0.83	1	3	1,257	2.54%	0.13		+14.07%	+1
Total	15	53,720	100.0%	10,745	4	13	49,528	100.0%	9,906	4	0.00%	0
Electorate		78,435	68.49%				73,434	67.45%			+1.04%	
Spoiled		578	1.06%				430	0.86%			+0.20%	
Turnout		54,298	69.23%				49,958	68.03%			+1.20%	

Transfer analysis

From	To	FG	LB	FF	SF	GP	WP	Others	Non Trans
FG	491			63				216	212
				12.83%				43.99%	43.18%
LB	5,113	533	2,792	239	430			925	194
		10.42%	54.61%	4.67%	8.41%			18.09%	3.79%
SF	6,298		1,966	575				2,229	1,528
			31.22%	9.13%				35.39%	24.26%
GP	501	78	177	33	27		19	143	24
		15.57%	35.33%	6.59%	5.39%		3.79%	28.54%	4.79%
WP	937	56	250	64	178			331	58
		5.98%	26.68%	6.83%	19.00%			35.33%	6.19%
Others	3,746	904	918	356	321	39	45	800	363
		24.13%	24.51%	9.50%	8.57%	1.04%	1.20%	21.36%	9.69%
Total	17,086	1,571	6,103	1,330	956	39	64	4,644	2,379
		9.19%	35.72%	7.78%	5.60%	0.23%	0.37%	27.18%	13.92%

Count details

Candidate	Party	1st	2nd Kiersey Votes	3rd Waters Votes	4th Nutty Votes	5th Power Votes	6th Conway Votes	7th Tobin Votes	8th Higgins Collery	9th Ryan Votes	10th Cullinane Votes	11th Coffey Surplus
			+13	+20								
Deasy, John*	FG	10,718	10,731	10,751	10,751	10,751	10,751	10,751	10,751	10,751	10,751	10,751
			+7	+32	+37	+78	+147	+56	+648	+533		-491
Coffey, Paudie	FG	9,698	9,705	9,737	9,774	9,852	9,999	10,055	10,703	11,236	11,236	10,745
			+6	+5	+32	+111	+159	+70	+487	+2,792	+1,966	
Conway, Ciara	LB	5,554	5,560	5,565	5,597	5,708	5,867	5,937	6,424	9,216	11,182	11,182
			+6	+17	+25	+45	+137	+275	+397	+925	+2,229	+216
Halligan, John	NP	5,546	5,552	5,569	5,594	5,639	5,776	6,051	6,448	7,373	9,602	9,818
			+6	+34	+12	+33	+72	+64	+232	+239	+575	+63
Kenneally, Brendan*	FF	7,515	7,521	7,555	7,567	7,600	7,672	7,736	7,968	8,207	8,782	8,845
			+5	+14	+26	+27	+44	+178	+232	+430	-6,298	
Cullinane, David	SF	5,342	5,347	5,361	5,387	5,414	5,458	5,636	5,868	6,298	Eliminated	
			+6	+8	+12	+66	+61	+180	+142	-5,113		
Ryan, Seamus	LB	4,638	4,644	4,652	4,664	4,730	4,791	4,971	5,113	Eliminated		
			+3	+17	+14	+37	+26	+19	-1,246			
Higgins, Tom	NP	1,130	1,133	1,150	1,164	1,201	1,227	1,246	Eliminated			
			+4	+12	+42	+50	+54	+37	-1,166			
Collery, Justin	NP	967	971	983	1,025	1,075	1,129	1,166	Eliminated			
			+5	+11	+17	+19	+12	-937				
Tobin, Joe	WP	873	878	889	906	925	937	Eliminated				
			+4	+9	+13	+11	-762					
Conway, Joe	NP	725	729	738	751	762	Eliminated					
				+3	+36	-501						
Power, Jody	GP	462	462	465	501	Eliminated						
			+4	+15	-276							
Nutty, Ben	FN	257	261	276	Eliminated							
			+1	-223								
Waters, Declan	NP	222	223	Eliminated								
			-73									
Kiersey, Gerard	NP	73	Eliminated									
			+3	+26	+10	+24	+50	+58	+274	+194	+1,528	+212
Cumulative			3	29	39	63	113	171	445	639	2,167	2,379
Total			53,720	53,720	53,720	53,720	53,720	53,720	53,720	53,720	53,720	53,720

Seats 4 — Quota 10,745

Election Facts

"49% of voters cited the economy as the one issue or problem that influenced their decision as to how they voted in Election 2011"
Millward Brown Lansdowne/RTÉ General Election 2011 Exit Poll

Wexford (5 seats)

Independent Mick Wallace wins a seat at his first attempt as Fianna Fáil loses out

Elected

Mick Wallace (Ind) Count 1, Brendan Howlin* (Lab) Count 4, John Browne* (FF) Final count, Liam Twomey (FG) Final count, Paul Kehoe* (FG) Final count.

Analysis by Sean Donnelly

There were no boundary changes here since 2007 and it remained a five-seat constituency. Property developer and independent candidate Mick Wallace caused a major surprise in this constituency with his poll-topping performance. He got a remarkable 13,329 first preferences and was well over the quota on the first count. The rest of the results paled into insignificance behind the scale of Wallace's performance.

Fine Gael had targeted three seats in this five-seater but the arrival of Wallace put paid to that ambition. The party vote was up three percentage points and with just 2.1 quotas it was unlikely to take more than two seats. Outgoing deputy Michael D'Arcy was the big loser as former deputy Liam Twomey took his seat. Twomey was first elected as an independent TD in 2002. He later joined Fine Gael and was made its health spokesperson but he lost his seat in 2007 to D'Arcy. The final seat was always going to be between himself and D'Arcy and so it proved with Twomey overturning the 2007 result. Chief Whip Paul Kehoe, despite coming third of the three Fine Gael candidates, went on to take the party's first seat when he took the fourth seat on the final count. D'Arcy lost the transfer battle to Twomey. The Gorey man had taken a prominent anti-Kenny position in Fine Gael's attempted leadership coup in June 2010, and ended up on the losing side again in 2011.

The Labour vote was up seven percentage points but with just 1.2 quotas it was unlikely to improve on its single seat. Brendan Howlin was in second place on the first count with 11,005 first preferences and went on to retain his seat on the fourth count. His running mate, Pat Cody, had a much more modest performance, winning just 4,457 first preferences to leave him well out of contention.

The Fianna Fáil vote was down 24 percentage points and with just 1.1 quotas spread over the party's two outgoing deputies, one seat was as much as it could hope for. John Browne was outside the frame in sixth place on the first count and was ahead of running mate Sean Connick. Browne won the transfer battle and stayed ahead and went on to take the third seat on the final count with the help of 58% of Connick's transfers.

The Sinn Féin vote was down two percentage points on 2007. Anthony Kelly got just 4,353 on the first count and his vote may have been affected by the presence of former party councillor John Dwyer, who ran as an independent.

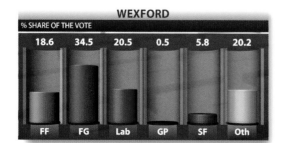

WEXFORD — % SHARE OF THE VOTE					
18.6	34.5	20.5	0.5	5.8	20.2
FF	FG	Lab	GP	SF	Oth

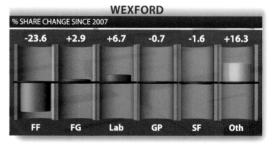

WEXFORD — % SHARE CHANGE SINCE 2007					
-23.6	+2.9	+6.7	-0.7	-1.6	+16.3
FF	FG	Lab	GP	SF	Oth

*outgoing TDs

MICK WALLACE (Ind)

Home Address: Wellingtonbridge, Co Wexford.
Contact: 01 6183287 (LH)
Website: www.mickwallace.net
Birth Place/Date: Wexford, November 1955.
Marital Status/Family: Divorced; 3 sons, 1 daughter.
Education: Ballymitty NS; St Augustine's College, Dungarvan, Co Waterford; Good Counsel College, New Ross, Co Wexford.
Occupation: Builder.
Biography: Secured 13,329 first-preference votes to top the poll and get elected in the first count in his first ever foray into politics. Wallace became one of the stories of Election 2011 as he only decided to run for election in early February and polling day was on 25 February.
Hobbies: Football, reading, food, wine and good company (in no particular order!).
Did you know? Mick managed five under-18 Wexford Youths football teams to All-Ireland titles.
Politician (living or deceased) you most admire: Charles Stewart Parnell.
Priority as a TD? To change the political system.
Why did you stand for election? I feel a responsibility to try and the change the system and work towards a fairer society.
Is there any particular event that brought home to you just how serious the economic crisis had become? The government's handling of the banking crisis because it has been the biggest disaster in the history of the State.

BRENDAN HOWLIN (Lab)

Address: Whiterock Hill, Wexford.
Phone: 01 6318021
Email: brendan.howlin@oir.ie
Website: www.per.ie
Birth Place/Date: Wexford, May 1956.
Marital Status/Family: Single.
Education: Wexford CBS; St Patrick's College of Education.
Occupation: Government minister. Formerly national school teacher.
Biography: First elected a TD in 1987. Current Minister for Public Expenditure and Reform; Leas-Cheann Comhairle of Dáil Éireann (June 2007-February 2011); Minister for the Environment (December 1994-1997); Minister for Health (January 1993-November 1994). Member of Seanad Éireann (1982–1987). Former deputy leader of the Labour Party.
Hobbies: Relaxing with friends, watching sport.
Politician (living or deceased) you most admire: Brendan Corish.
Priority as a TD? Restore confidence in public administration and politics.
Why did you stand for election? Original motivation to serve my local community and follow in footsteps of Brendan Corish.
Is there any particular event that brought home to you just how serious the economic crisis had become? Members of the public attending my constituency office outlining the direct impact of the crisis on their lives.

JOHN BROWNE (FF)

Address: 34 Beech Park, Enniscorthy, Co. Wexford.
Constituency Office: Lower Church Street, Enniscorthy.
Phone: 087 2469234 (M) 053 9235046 (CO) 01 6183094 (LH)
Email: john.browne@oireachtas.ie
Website: JohnBrowneTD.ie
Facebook: John Browne
Birth Place/Date: Enniscorthy, August 1948.
Marital Status/family: Married to Judy; 4 children.
Education: Marshalstown Primary School, Enniscorthy; CBS Secondary School.
Occupation: Public representative. Salesman.
Biography: Party spokesperson on Marine and Fisheries. Elected to Dáil Éireann for the eighth time in 2011. Current chairman of Fianna Fáil. Minister of State at the Department of Communications, the Marine and Natural Resources (2002-2004 and 2006-2007); Minister of State at the Department of Agriculture and Food (2004-2006).
Hobbies: Hurling, football, soccer.
Did you know? John played hurling with Wexford.
Politician (living or deceased) you most admire: Bill Clinton.
Priority as a TD? To serve the people of Wexford.
Why did you stand for election? To win a seat for Fianna Fáil.
Is there any particular event that brought home to you just how serious the economic crisis had become? The collapse of the building industry with the consequent loss of jobs, especially for young people.

Wexford

DR LIAM TWOMEY (FG)

Address: Anne Street, Wexford town.
Phone: 087 8267940 (M) 053 9146682
(CO) 01 6184299
Email: liam.twomey@oireachtas.ie
Website: www.liamtwomey.org
Twitter: twitter.com/LiamTwomey
Facebook: Yes.
Birthplace/Date: Cork, April 1967.
Marital Status/Family: Married to Dr Liz
O'Sullivan; 2 sons, 1 daughter.
Education: Farranferris, Cork; Trinity
College, Dublin.
Occupation: Public representative and
doctor.
Biography: First elected a TD in 2002 as
an independent. Joined Fine Gael in
September 2004 and appointed
spokesperson on Health and Children. Lost
Dáil seat in 2007. Fine Gael Finance
spokesperson and deputy leader in Seanad
(2007-2011).
Hobbies: Spending as much time as possible
with my children before they grow up.
Did you know? Liam grew up in West
Cork only two miles from the birthplace of
Michael Collins and the first Christmas
present his wife gave him was a book on
the life of Collins.
**Politician (living or deceased) that you
most admire:** Michael Collins.
Priority as a TD? To be an effective
national politician in the Dáil and to never
forget the words of Tip O'Neill, former
speaker of the US Congress: "All politics
are local"!
Why did you stand for election? In 2002,
the threat to our health services in Wexford
got me involved in politics. Now, every
single issue that affects an individual, group
or community in Wexford that requires
political input is my priority.
**Is there any particular event that brought
home to you just how serious the economic
crisis had become?** The day that Olli Rehn,
EU Commissioner of Economic and
Monetary Affairs, was interviewed on the
front page of the *Irish Times*, a month
before the IMF came in, before Brian
Lenihan admitted that the budget
adjustment was going to be €15bn, not
€7bn.

PAUL KEHOE (FG)

Address: 7 Weafer Street, Enniscorthy, Co
Wexford.
Phone: 053 9243558 (CO) 01 6184473 (LH)
Email: paul.kehoe@taoiseach.gov.ie
Website: www.paulkehoe.com
Facebook: Yes.
Birth Place/Date: Wexford, January 1973.
Marital Status/Family: Married to Brigid
O'Connor.
Education: St Mary's CBS, Enniscorthy;
Kildalton Agricultural College.
Occupation: Full-time public
representative. Sales/marketing and
farming.
Biography: First elected in 2002
representing the Wexford constituency and
was Fine Gael Chief Whip from 2004. He
was reappointed as Chief Whip on his re-
election in September 2007. Re-elected to
Dáil Eireann in 2011 and was appointed
Government Chief Whip and Minister of
State at the Departments of the Taoiseach
and Defence on 9 March 2011.
Hobbies: Sports, walking, member of
Ballyhogue GAA Club.
Did you know? Paul won a Mácra na
Feirme National Leadership award.
**Politician (living or deceased) you most
admire:** Ivan Yates.
Priority as a TD? To stop emigration.
Why did you stand for election? To make a
difference.
**Is there any particular event that brought
home to you just how serious the economic
crisis had become?** The amount of young
people emigrating.

First preference votes

	Seats	5			12,590		
	Candidate	Party	1st	%	Quota	Count	Status
1	Wallace, Mick	NP	13,329	17.65%	1.06	1	Made Quota
2	Howlin, Brendan*	LB	11,005	14.57%	0.87	4	Made Quota
3	Browne, John*	FF	7,352	9.73%	0.58	7	Made Quota
4	Twomey, Liam #	FG	9,230	12.22%	0.73	7	Elected
5	Kehoe, Paul*	FG	8,386	11.10%	0.67	7	Elected
6	D'Arcy, Michael*	FG	8,418	11.14%	0.67	7	Not Elected
7	Connick, Sean*	FF	6,675	8.84%	0.53	6	Eliminated
8	Kelly, Anthony	SF	4,353	5.76%	0.35	4	Eliminated
9	Cody, Pat	LB	4,457	5.90%	0.35	3	Eliminated
10	Dwyer, John	NP	908	1.20%	0.07	2	No Expenses
11	O'Brien, Séamus	PBPA	741	0.98%	0.06	2	No Expenses
12	Forde, Danny	GP	391	0.52%	0.03	2	No Expenses
13	Roseingrave, Siobhán	NP	175	0.23%	0.01	2	No Expenses
14	De Valera, Ruairí	NP	119	0.16%	0.01	2	No Expenses

*Outgoing TD #Former TD Valid poll: 75,539 Quota: 12,590 No expenses limit: 3,147

Party votes

		2011					2007				Change	
Party	Cand	1st	%	Quota	Seats	Cand	1st	%	Quota	Seats	%	Seats
FG	3	26,034	34.46%	2.07	2	3	21,658	31.56%	1.89	2	+2.90%	
LB	2	15,462	20.47%	1.23	1	1	9,445	13.77%	0.83	1	+6.70%	
FF	2	14,027	18.57%	1.11	1	3	28,949	42.19%	2.53	2	-23.62%	-1
SF	1	4,353	5.76%	0.35		1	5,068	7.39%	0.44		-1.62%	
PBPA	1	741	0.98%	0.06							+0.98%	
GP	1	391	0.52%	0.03		1	802	1.17%	0.07		-0.65%	
PD						1	2,162	3.15%	0.19		-3.15%	
Others	4	14,531	19.24%	1.15	1	1	532	0.78%	0.05		+18.46%	+1
Total	14	75,539	100.0%	12,590	5	11	68,616	100.0%	11,437	5	0.00%	0
Electorate	111,063	68.01%				103,562	66.26%				+1.76%	
Spoiled	812	1.06%				827	1.19%				-0.13%	
Turnout	76,351	68.75%				69,443	67.05%				+1.69%	

Transfer analysis

From	To	FG	LB	FF	SF	PBPA	GP	Others	Non Trans
LB	6,676	2,528	2,852	753	280				263
		37.87%	42.72%	11.28%	4.19%				3.94%
FF	7,515	1,936		4,357					1,222
		25.76%		57.98%					16.26%
SF	5,181	1,841		678					2,662
		35.53%		13.09%					51.38%
PBPA	778	151	237	110	152				128
		19.41%	30.46%	14.14%	19.54%				16.45%
GP	399	77	121	57	78				66
		19.30%	30.33%	14.29%	19.55%				16.54%
NP	2,006	485	594	290	318	37	8	65	209
		24.18%	29.61%	14.46%	15.85%	1.84%	0.40%	3.24%	10.42%

Election Facts
"Roisin Shortall is the longest-serving female in the present Dáil with over 18 years of service since 1992"
Sean Donnelly

Wexford

Count details

Candidate	Party	1st	2nd Wallace Surplus	3rd Dwyer / O'Brien / Forde / Roseingrave / De Valera	4th Cody Votes	5th Kelly Votes	6th Howlin Surplus	7th Connick Votes
Seats 5							**Quota**	**12,590**
			−739					
Wallace, Mick	NP	13,329	12,590	12,590	12,590	12,590	12,590	12,590
			+161	+496	+2,852		−1,924	
Howlin, Brendan*	LB	11,005	11,166	11,662	14,514	14,514	12,590	12,590
			+42	+76	+279	+426	+225	+4,357
Browne, John*	FF	7,352	7,394	7,470	7,749	8,175	8,400	12,757
			+73	+168	+498	+549	+582	+790
Twomey, Liam #	FG	9,230	9,349	9,526	9,693	10,453	10,874	11,596
			+119	+176	+168	+760	+421	+722
Kehoe, Paul*	FG	8,386	8,459	8,627	9,125	9,674	10,256	11,046
			+48	+129	+365	+532	+494	+424
D'Arcy, Michael*	FG	8,418	8,466	8,595	8,960	9,492	9,986	10,410
			+69	+270	+130	+252	+119	−7,515
Connick, Sean*	FF	6,675	6,744	7,014	7,144	7,396	7,515	Eliminated
			+69	+479	+280	−5,181		
Kelly, Anthony	SF	4,353	4,422	4,901	5,181	Eliminated		
			+48	+247	−4,752			
Cody, Pat	LB	4,457	4,505	4,752	Eliminated			
			+35	−943				
Dwyer, John	NP	908	943	Eliminated				
			+37	−778				
O'Brien, Séamus	PBPA	741	778	Eliminated				
			+8	−399				
Forde, Danny	GP	391	399	Eliminated				
			+20	−195				
Roseingrave, Siobhán	NP	175	195	Eliminated				
			+10	−129				
De Valera, Ruairí	NP	119	129	Eliminated				
Non-transferable				+403	+180	+2,662	+83	+1,222
Cumulative			0	403	583	3,245	3,328	4,550
Total		75,539	75,539	75,540	75,539	75,539	75,539	75,539

Brendan Howlin on the campaign trail in Enniscorthy accompanied by Labour leader Eamon Gilmore

Wicklow (5 seats)

Fine Gael emerges as the dominant party to take three seats

Elected

Andrew Doyle* (FG) Count 16, Billy Timmins* (FG) Count 17, Simon Harris (FG) Final count, Anne Ferris (Lab) Final count, Stephen Donnelly (Ind) Final count.

Analysis by Michael Gallagher

There were no boundary change here since 2007 but with 24 candidates, the most in the country, this was always likely to be a long count. So it proved with demands for recounts protracting matters further. As well as the five candidates elected, the constituency can claim a sixth TD, as Pat Deering, the Fine Gael TD for Carlow-Kilkenny, lives in the area of east Carlow that, to the resentment of its inhabitants, makes up part of the Wicklow constituency.

Fine Gael emerged as the dominant party, winning close to 40% of the votes and three of the five seats. In 2002 it had been down to 16% and one seat, so this represented very impressive growth. Andrew Doyle, first elected in 2007, headed the poll, Billy Timmins was second home, and yet another case of good Fine Gael vote management meant that the youthful newcomer Simon Harris came in third.

Labour suffered from the retirement of former deputy leader Liz McManus. The party's vote scarcely rose compared with 2007, and its three candidates made heavy weather of holding the seat in a constituency where in 2002, when the national conditions were much less favourable, it had come within 20 votes of taking two seats. Despite receiving fewer than half of running mate Tom Fortune's transfers on the 16th count, Anne Ferris took the fourth seat quite securely.

Fianna Fáil had won two seats in 2007, but one of these disappeared quite quickly when Joe Behan left the party in October 2008. He stood now as an independent but was never in the race. Fianna Fáil ran two candidates, outgoing TD and junior minister Dick Roche being joined on the ticket by Councillor Pat Fitzgerald from Arklow. Although Roche led on first preferences, Fitzgerald overhauled him. The elimination on the 14th count of Roche, whose combative style as a politician was not to everyone's liking, provoked wild applause among supporters of other parties in the counting centre.

With only 11% of the votes, Fianna Fáil was well short of a seat, and the fifth seat lay between Sinn Féin's John Brady and independent Stephen Donnelly. Brady led on first preferences, but Donnelly, who used his media appearances impressively during the campaign, fared better on transfers and took the last seat by just over 100 votes.

*outgoing TDs

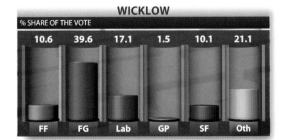

WICKLOW

% SHARE OF THE VOTE

FF	FG	Lab	GP	SF	Oth
10.6	39.6	17.1	1.5	10.1	21.1

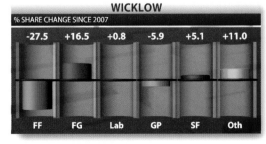

WICKLOW

% SHARE CHANGE SINCE 2007

FF	FG	Lab	GP	SF	Oth
-27.5	+16.5	+0.8	-5.9	+5.1	+11.0

Wicklow

ANDREW DOYLE (FG)

Address: 2A Lower Mall, Wicklow Town
Phone: 086 837009 (M) 0404 66622 (O)
Email: Andrew.doyle@oireachtas.ie
Website: www.andrewdoyle.ie
Facebook: facebook.com/andrewdoyle
Birth Place/Date: Wicklow, July 1960.
Marital Status/Family: Married to Ann; 3 sons, 1 daughter.
Education: Trooperstown and Rathdrum National Schools; De La Salle secondary School, Wicklow; Rockwell Agricultural College.
Occupation: Public representative. Farmer.
Biography: First elected a TD in 2007. Fine Gael's Food and Horticulture spokesperson (June 2010-February 2011). Member, Wicklow County Council (1999-2007). Chairman of Wicklow County Council (2005-2006). Member of Oireachtas Committee on Agriculture, Food and Fisheries and Committee on Climate Change and Energy Security in 30th Dáil.
Hobbies: Hill-walking, watching my children play various sports, and enjoying the company of friends. I also enjoy working on my farm.
Did you know? Andrew spent a year in New Zealand (1981-1982) as the recipient of a Stephen Cullinane scholarship for young farmers.
Politician (living or deceased) you most admire: John Hume, Nelson Mandela, and the late Jim Mitchell.
Priority as a TD? To restore confidence in the political system. To help our nation's economic recovery.
Why did you stand for election? I believe it's better to get involved rather than criticise from the outside and, with four children, I have a personal interest in seeing this county's fortune restored to and maintained at a sensible level.
Is there any particular event that brought home to you just how serious the economic crisis had become? The day the IMF and ECB were seen walking in to meet our former government ministers, in effect to take over our national fiscal affairs, as it was the point when the political 'spin' and denial of the last government was finally exposed.

BILLY TIMMINS (FG)

Home Address: Baltinglass, Co Wicklow.
Phone: 087 8159090 (M) 01 6183384 (LH)
Website: www.billytimmins.finegael.ie
Twitter: www.twitter.com/Billy_Timmins
Facebook: Yes.
Birth Place/Date: October 1959.
Marital Status/family: Married to Madeline; 2 sons, 3 daughters.
Education: Ballyfin College; NUI Galway.
Occupation: Full time public representative. Formerly officer who served with the UN in Lebanon and Cyprus.
Biography: First elected in 1997 and at each subsequent general election. Member, Wicklow County Council (1999-2004). Previously Fine Gael frontbench spokesperson on Agriculture and Food (2002-2004); Defence (2004-2007); and Foreign Affairs (2007-2010). His father Godfrey was a Fine Gael TD for Wicklow.
Hobbies: GAA, history and genealogy.
Did you know? Billy was a member of the Baltinglass GAA team that won the club football All-Ireland in 1990.
Politician (living or deceased) you most admire: Liam Cosgrave, my father Godfrey and George Jones MCC Wicklow, all honest and selfless people.
Priority as a TD? To make Ireland a better place for all.
Why did you stand for election? To make Ireland a better place for all.
Is there any particular event that brought home to you just how serious the economic crisis had become? Unfortunately the events are like leaves falling from the autumn trees but hopefully things will improve but it will take hard work and hard decisions on all our behalf.

SIMON HARRIS (FG)

Home Address: 79 Redford Park, Greystones, Co Wicklow.
Phone: 01 2764619 (O) 01 6183805 (LH)
Website: www.simonharris.ie
Twitter: www.twitter.com/SimonHarrisTD
Facebook: /CllrSimonHarris
Birth Place/Date: Dublin, October 1986.
Marital Status/Family: Single.
Education: St David's Secondary School, Greystones; DIT Aungier Street.
Occupation: Full-time public representative. Formerly parliamentary assistant to Frances Fitzgerald.
Biography: Secured 8,726 first-preference votes in his first general election attempt. Elected to Wicklow County Council and Greystones Town Council in June 2009, topping the poll in both. In 2002, Simon established an Autism support and lobby group, the Wicklow Triple A Alliance, to provide support to families living with autism.
Hobbies: Socialising with friends and family, reading, cinema.
Did you know? Simon was awarded a Greystones Person of the Year award in 2002 in recognition of his work as a disability advocate.
Politician (living or deceased) you most admire: Liam Cosgrave Snr.
Priority as a TD? Providing a voice to special educational needs and mental health issues in the Dáil.
Why did you stand for election? I believe we need a diversity of voice in the Dáil and my generation has a right and an obligation to be heard in the political process. I also wanted to ensure issues such as disability matters are championed in the Dáil. I have watched friends emigrate due to the economic crisis and I wanted to play my part in creating a stable, alternative government.
Is there any particular event that brought home to you just how serious the economic crisis had become? To be told by a management consultant that her most frequent advice to clients is to go to the St Vincent de Paul and MABS [Money Advice and Budgeting Service].

ANNE FERRIS (Lab)

Home Address: 10 Seapoint Court, Bray, Co Wicklow.
Phone: 01 2865144 (H) 01 2764699 (Bray office) 01 6183539 (LH)
Website: www.labour.ie/anneferris
Birth Place/Date: Dublin.
Marital Status/Family: 3 daughters.
Education: St Agnes' Primary School, Crumlin; Goldenbridge Secondary School, Inchicore; Maynooth College (diploma in women's studies).
Occupation: Full-time public representative.
Biography: Anne is a new deputy. She worked for Liz McManus's Bray constituency office for 18 years. Co-opted onto Bray Town Council in January 1995 and re-elected in 1999 and 2004. Chairperson of Bray Town Council (2000-2001 and 2004-2005). Co-opted to fill Liz McManus's seat on Wicklow County Council in 2003 and re-elected in 2004. Former member, Wicklow VEC. Director of the Mermaid Arts Centre and Bray Tourism. Formerly Director of Bray Chamber of Commerce. SIPTU member.
Hobbies: Walking, reading (especially political biographies), theatre and cinema.
Did you know? Anne became the second ever female chairperson of Wicklow County Council in 2007.
Politician (living or deceased) you most admire: Hillary Clinton.
Priority as a TD? To represent the people I met on the campaign that lost their jobs, are worried about losing their homes and the self-employed people who have lost their jobs and are not entitled to social welfare payments.
Why did you stand for election? To keep a Labour seat and keep Liz McManus' seat, as women are grossly under-represented in the Dáil.
Is there any particular event that brought home to you just how serious the economic crisis had become? The number of families I've met where a son or a daughter has been forced to go abroad to look for work. It is frustrating that so many bright and educated people are being forced to emigrate.

STEPHEN DONNELLY (Ind)

Home Address: Greystones, Co Wicklow.
Phone: 01 6184293 (LH)
Email: stephen.donnelly@oireachtas.ie
Website: www.stephendonnelly.ie
Twitter: www.twitter.com/donnellystephen
Facebook: /DonnellyforWicklow
Birth Place/Date: Dublin.
Marital Status/Family: Married to Susan Leavy; 2 sons.
Education: St. David's Greystones; University College Dublin (mechanical engineering); MIT in Boston (engineering); Harvard (master in public administration in international development).
Occupation: Public representative. Formerly management consultant with McKinsey & Company and the London-based consulting firm Eden McCallum.
Biography: Secured 6,530 first-preference votes in his first electoral outing.
Hobbies: Spending time with family, hill walking, swimming, movies and live music of all kinds.
Politician (living or deceased) you most admire: Nelson Mandela and Mahatma Gandhi.
Priority as a TD? Stimulate job creation; get the debt under control; access our full pool of talent. Radically improve our secondary school standards. Push teaching standards in our third-level institutions; reform healthcare (including equal access); make the Dáil more effective and inclusive.
Why did you stand for election? I believe that Ireland can have a bright future as a leading small country in Europe if we begin to make the right economic and social decisions, and if we radically reform the political system.
Is there any particular event that brought home to you just how serious the economic crisis had become? For the past number of years the political system has put the interests of the rich and powerful over the interests of the people. This culminated in the IMF coming to Ireland. The day the IMF team arrived in Dublin is the day I decided to stand for election.

Election Facts
"Mildred Fox (Wicklow TD 1995-2007) became the first independent female deputy when she was elected at a by-election in 1995 which was caused by the death of her father, Johnny Fox"
Sean Donnelly

Wicklow

	Seats	5				11,751		
	Candidate	Party	1st	%	Quota	Count	Status
1	Doyle, Andrew*	FG	10,035	14.23%	0.85	16	Made Quota
2	Timmins, Billy*	FG	9,165	13.00%	0.78	17	Made Quota
3	Harris, Simon	FG	8,726	12.38%	0.74	19	Elected
4	Ferris, Anne	LB	5,436	7.71%	0.46	19	Elected
5	Donnelly, Stephen	NP	6,530	9.26%	0.56	19	Elected
6	Brady, John	SF	7,089	10.06%	0.60	19	Not Elected
7	Fitzgerald, Pat	FF	3,576	5.07%	0.30	16	Eliminated
8	Fortune, Tom	LB	3,420	4.85%	0.29	15	Eliminated
9	Behan, Joe*	NP	4,197	5.95%	0.36	14	Eliminated
10	Roche, Dick*	FF	3,891	5.52%	0.33	13	Eliminated
11	Kavanagh, Conal	LB	3,231	4.58%	0.27	12	Eliminated
12	Dempsey, Peter	NP	1,409	2.00%	0.12	11	No Expenses
13	Byrne, Niall	GP	1,026	1.46%	0.09	11	No Expenses
14	Kelly, Nicky	NP	518	0.73%	0.04	10	No Expenses
15	Kiernan, Donal	NP	403	0.57%	0.03	10	No Expenses
16	Kinsella, Gerry	FN	324	0.46%	0.03	9	No Expenses
17	Kavanagh, Pat	FN	291	0.41%	0.02	8	No Expenses
18	Finnegan, Eugene	NP	286	0.41%	0.02	7	No Expenses
19	Keddy, Charlie	NP	233	0.33%	0.02	6	No Expenses
20	Mulvihill, Michael	NP	187	0.27%	0.02	5	No Expenses
21	Fitzgerald, Anthony	NP	184	0.26%	0.02	4	No Expenses
22	Tallon, Jim	NP	166	0.24%	0.01	3	No Expenses
23	Clarke, Thomas	NP	103	0.15%	0.01	2	No Expenses
24	Carroll, Kevin	NP	74	0.10%	0.01	1	No Expenses

*Outgoing TD Valid poll: 70,500 Quota: 11,751 No expenses limit: 2,938

Party votes

Party	Cand	2011 1st	%	Quota	Seats	Cand	2007 1st	%	Quota	Seats	Change %	Seats
FG	3	27,926	39.61%	2.38	3	2	15,033	23.15%	1.39	2	+16.46%	+1
LB	3	12,087	17.14%	1.03	1	2	10,608	16.34%	0.98	1	+0.81%	
FF	2	7,467	10.59%	0.64		3	24,706	38.05%	2.28	2	-27.46%	-2
SF	1	7,089	10.06%	0.60		1	3,234	4.98%	0.30		+5.07%	
GP	1	1,026	1.46%	0.09		1	4,790	7.38%	0.44		-5.92%	
PD						1	903	1.39%	0.08		-1.39%	
Others	14	14,905	21.14%	1.27	1	5	5,651	8.70%	0.52		+12.44%	+1
Total	24	70,500	100.0%	11,751	5	15	64,925	100.0%	10,821	5	0.00%	0
Electorate		95,339	73.95%				91,492	70.96%			+2.98%	
Spoiled		811	1.14%				554	0.85%			+0.29%	
Turnout		71,311	74.80%				65,479	71.57%			+3.23%	

Transfer analysis

From	To	FG	LB	FF	SF	GP	Others	Non Trans
FG	356	120	122		57		57	
		33.71%	34.27%		16.01%		16.01%	
LB	8,785	2,140	4,606	258	622		603	556
		24.36%	52.43%	2.94%	7.08%		6.86%	6.33%
FF	11,133	2,453	940	2,296	900		1,377	3,167
		22.03%	8.44%	20.62%	8.08%		12.37%	28.45%
GP	1,113	257	233	174	109		245	95
		23.09%	20.93%	15.63%	9.79%		22.01%	8.54%
NP	9,693	2,474	1,867	938	1,077	87	2,472	778
		25.52%	19.26%	9.68%	11.11%	0.90%	25.50%	8.03%
Total	31,080	7,444	7,768	3,666	2,765	87	4,754	4,596
		23.95%	24.99%	11.80%	8.90%	0.28%	15.30%	14.79%

Wicklow

Count details

Seats: 6 Quota: 11,761

Candidate	Party	1st	2nd Carroll	3rd Clarke	4th Tallon	5th Fitzgerald	6th Mulvihill	7th Keddy	8th Finnegan	9th Kavanagh	10th Kinsella	11th Kelly/Kiernan	12th Dempsey/Byrne	13th Kavanagh	14th Roche	15th Behan	16th Fortune	17th Fitzgerald	18th Doyle Surplus	19th Timmins Surplus
Doyle, Andrew*	FG	10,035	+3 10,038	+2 10,040	+16 10,056	+14 10,070	+36 10,106	+11 10,117	+16 10,133	+18 10,151	+56 10,207	+57 10,264	+302 10,566	+316 10,882	+205 11,087	+535 11,622	+369 11,991	11,991	−240 11,751	11,751
Timmins, Billy*	FG	9,165	+2 9,167	+4 9,171	+10 9,181	+13 9,194	+8 9,202	+11 9,213	+11 9,224	+17 9,241	+12 9,253	+67 9,320	+147 9,467	+289 9,756	+428 10,184	+266 10,450	+279 10,729	+1,138 11,867	11,867	−116 11,751
Harris, Simon	FG	8,726	+3 8,729	+6 8,735	+6 8,741	+11 8,752	+3 8,755	+37 8,792	+46 8,838	+9 8,847	+25 8,872	+66 8,938	+195 9,133	+120 9,253	+191 9,444	+690 10,134	+767 10,901	+491 11,392	+67 11,459	+53 11,512
Ferris, Anne	LB	5,436	+3 5,439	+13 5,452	+4 5,456	+13 5,469	+7 5,476	+5 5,481	+33 5,514	+45 5,559	+18 5,577	+80 5,657	+340 5,997	+928 6,925	+111 7,036	+677 7,713	+2,530 10,243	+705 10,948	+94 11,042	+28 11,070
Donnelly, Stephen	NP	6,530	+6 6,536	+21 6,557	+14 6,571	+33 6,604	+20 6,624	+23 6,647	+45 6,692	+40 6,732	+60 6,792	+127 6,919	+470 7,389	+119 7,508	+162 7,670	+906 8,576	+404 8,980	+929 9,909	+37 9,946	+20 9,966
Brady, John	SF	7,089	+1 7,090	+9 7,099	+16 7,115	+5 7,120	+24 7,144	+19 7,163	+24 7,187	+33 7,220	+49 7,269	+135 7,404	+272 7,676	+211 7,887	+140 8,027	+599 8,626	+411 9,037	+760 9,797	+42 9,839	+15 9,854
Fitzgerald, Pat	FF	3,576	3,576	3,576	+16 3,592	+6 3,598	+6 3,604	+7 3,611	+2 3,613	+3 3,616	+2 3,618	+54 3,672	+388 4,060	+80 4,140	+2,296 6,436	+462 6,898	+106 7,004	−7,004 Eliminated		
Fortune, Tom	LB	3,420	+1 3,421	+2 3,423	3,423	+4 3,427	+8 3,435	+33 3,468	+14 3,482	+13 3,495	+12 3,507	+44 3,551	+108 3,659	+1,148 4,807	+124 4,931	+351 5,282	−5,282 Eliminated			
Behan, Joe*	NP	4,197	+3 4,200	+7 4,207	+3 4,210	+13 4,223	+8 4,231	+14 4,245	+32 4,277	+13 4,290	+22 4,312	+95 4,407	+144 4,551	+80 4,631	+286 4,917	−4,917 Eliminated				
Roche, Dick*	FF	3,891	3,891	+4 3,895	+3 3,898	+23 3,921	+5 3,926	+18 3,944	+20 3,964	+3 3,967	+10 3,977	+33 4,010	+47 4,057	+72 4,129	−4,129 Eliminated					
Kavanagh, Conal	LB	3,231	+3 3,234	+3 3,237	+6 3,243	+6 3,249	+11 3,260	+12 3,272	+8 3,280	+16 3,296	+21 3,317	+52 3,369	+134 3,503	−3,503 Eliminated						
Dempsey, Peter	NP	1,409	+6 1,415	+19 1,434	+20 1,454	+6 1,460	+8 1,468	+10 1,478	+8 1,486	+11 1,497	+19 1,516	+157 1,673	−1,673 Eliminated							
Byrne, Niall	GP	1,026	+1 1,027	+4 1,031	+2 1,033	+5 1,038	+4 1,042	+3 1,045	+9 1,054	+19 1,073	+19 1,092	+21 1,113	−1,113 Eliminated							
Kelly, Nicky	NP	518	+4 522	+1 523	+11 534	+2 536	+6 542	+7 549	+7 556	+15 571	+14 585	−585 Eliminated								
Kiernan, Donal	NP	403	+2 405	405	+1 406	+9 415	+4 419	+14 433	+11 444	+12 456	+16 472	−472 Eliminated								
Kinsella, Gerry	FN	324	+1 325	+2 327	+4 331	+4 335	+11 346	+13 359	+3 362	+32 394	−394 Eliminated									
Kavanagh, Pat	FN	291	+2 293	+5 298	+2 300	+2 302	+11 313	+9 322	+5 327	−327 Eliminated										
Finnegan, Eugene	NP	286	+2 288	+5 293	+2 295	+8 303	+2 305	+4 309	−309 Eliminated											
Keddy, Charlie	NP	233	+3 236	+5 241	+20 261	+1 262	+4 266	−266 Eliminated												
Mulvihill, Michael	NP	187	+1 188	+3 191	+4 195	+1 196	−196 Eliminated													
Fitzgerald, Anthony	NP	184	184	+1 185	+1 186	−186 Eliminated														
Tallon, Jim	NP	166	166	+3 169	−169 Eliminated															
Clarke, Thomas	NP	103	+22 125	−125 Eliminated																
Carroll, Kevin	NP	74	−74 Eliminated																	
Non-transferable / Cumulative			+5 5	+6 11	+8 19	+7 26	+10 36	+16 52	+15 67	+28 95	+39 134	+69 203	+239 442	+140 582	+186 768	+431 1,199	+416 1,615	+2,981 4,596	4,596	4,596
Total		70,500	70,500	70,500	70,500	70,500	70,500	70,500	70,500	70,500	70,500	70,500	70,500	70,500	70,500	70,500	70,500	70,500	70,500	70,500

Did you know that Ronnie Drew's father-in-law was a presidential candidate? Pollster **Sean Donnelly** reveals some quirky facts and figures from elections past and present

Did you know?

The 2011 election had the highest number of retirements to date (39), which was well above the previous highest (29) in June 1927. This number included the three deputies who had retired earlier but for whom the by-elections had not been held – George Lee, Fine Gael, Dublin South; Martin Cullen, Fianna Fáil, Waterford; and Dr James McDaid, Fianna Fáil, Donegal North-East.

There was a high rate of attrition in Election 2011 with 45 outgoing deputies losing their seats, up 15 on 2007. There are 84 new TDs (49 in 2007) in the 31st Dáil, eight of whom were former deputies.

It was all change in Cork South-West and Kerry South, as all three TDs returned in both three-seaters were new members. There were also three new deputies in 12 other constituencies, which contrasts sharply with 2007 when only two constituencies, Cork South-Central and Dublin North, elected three new deputies. With all this change it came as no surprise that not a single constituency returned the same deputies as 2007.

A record 566 candidates contested the 2011 general election, which was well ahead of the previous high of 484 in 1997.

Two constituencies – Laois-Offaly and Mayo – had the same quota (12,360 in 2011). They also happen to be the home constituencies of the previous and present Taoiseach.

The Fianna Fáil vote dropped 29.6 percentage points in two constituencies – Dublin Central and Laois-Offaly. They also happen to be the home constituencies of the previous two Taoisígh.

The People Before Profit Alliance won its first two Dáil seats in Election 2011 and was joined by two Socialist Party deputies and the Workers' and Unemployed Action Group (WUAG) leader Seamus Healy to give the United Left Alliance (ULA) five TDs in the 31st Dáil.

The most surprising constituency: take your pick.

The most predictable constituency: Dublin West.

Election 2011 promised to be the election of the new parties but some of them never even got to the starting line. In the end, New Vision fielded 20 candidates and its only success was Luke 'Ming' Flanagan in Roscommon-South Leitrim, with most of the others failing to save their expenses. Another New Vision called 'Fís Nua' ran five candidates but all did poorly as did the four who ran for

CPPC (An Chaothdhail Phobail/ The People's Convention) in the Cork area.

Highest first preference vote per party:
Fine Gael: Mayo 64.96%
Labour: Dublin North West 43.15%
Fianna Fáil: Carlow-Kilkenny 28.10%
Sinn Féin: Donegal South-West 32.97%

Fine Gael got the largest increase in its vote in Dublin Mid-West where its vote was up 19 percentage points. Labour got its best increase of 23 percentage points in Dublin North-West. In contrast, Fianna Fáil suffered its greatest loss in support in Dublin North-West where it was down by 37 percentage points.

Fine Gael won a record four out of five seats in Mayo and won three seats in four constituencies. Labour won two seats in six constituencies, all in Dublin. Fianna Fáil won two seats in only two constituencies, – Cork South-Central, the home of its present leader, and Laois-Offaly, the home constituency of its previous leader.

Fine Gael won a record 76 seats in Election 2011, beating its previous best of 70 in November 1982. It gained two seats in three constituencies – Carlow-Kilkenny, Cavan-Monaghan and Dublin Mid-West.

Michael Noonan was the leading vote-getter in Election 2011 with 1.54 quotas (13,291 first preferences) in Limerick City and was followed by Enda Kenny with 1.41 (17,472) in Mayo, and Shane Ross with 1.41 (17,075) in Dublin South. Kenny's and Ross's first-preference votes moved them up to 16th and 21st place on the top vote-getters list to date, which is headed by Richard Mulcahy, who got 22,005 votes in 1923.

Fine Gael got the best ever seats bonus in Election 2011 as it managed to win 45.78% of the seats from just 36.10% of the first-preference vote and gained a seat bonus of 16. Labour managed a seat bonus of five but Fianna Fáil was again the big loser as it won 10 seats less than its first-preference vote warranted.

A record 25 women were elected in 2011, up two on the previous best which was achieved in 1992, 2002 and 2007. Six women deputies retired at this election and eight lost their seats. Fourteen women were elected for the first time, with two former deputies regaining their seats. Roisin Shortall is the longest-serving woman in the 31st Dáil with over 18 years' service since 1992. Mary Harney, who retired ahead of Election 2011, is the longest-serving

woman deputy with 30 years' continuous service, having won nine elections between 1981 and 2007. Fourteen of the 92 women elected to Dáil Éireann were called Mary.

The government formed in 2011 is the fourth Fine Gael/Labour coalition. The 1994-1997 'Rainbow Coalition' was the first between Fine Gael, Labour and Democratic Left, and the only one to be formed without a general election. Fianna Fáil has been part of 19 of the 29 governments since the foundation of the State and in power on its own on 14 occasions.

Enda Kenny is the 12th Taoiseach and the fifth from Fine Gael. John Bruton was the shortest-serving Taoiseach – he served from December 1994 to June 1997.

The turnout has been in decline since 1969 but the 2007 election reversed that trend with the turnout up 4.5 points on the previous election in 2002. The 2011 election showed further improvement with the turnout up another three percentage points.

Fianna Fáil has won a total of 17,536,438 first-preference votes, or 41.86%, since the first PR election in 1922. Fine Gael has aggregated 12,890,666 (30.77%), and Labour's total is 4,828,562 (11.53%).

The 4,618 general election and 126 by-election seats have been held by 1,235 individual TDs with each deputy serving an average four terms.

On average, the Dáil is made up of 72% outgoing TDs, 22% new TDs and 6% former deputies. Limerick West has never returned a former member.

Patrick Smith is the longest-serving member of Dáil Éireann, having won 17 elections between 1923 and 1973. Enda Kenny is the longest-serving member in the 31st Dáil, having been first elected at a by-election in 1975 which was caused by the death of his father, Henry. His 12 election victories and over 35 years of continuous service to date leaves him in 37th place on the list of longest-serving members in Dáil Éireann. The longest-serving members in the present Dáil are all members of the government – Enda Kenny, Ruairí Quinn (33 years' service), Michael Noonan (30), Richard Bruton (29) and Dinny McGinley (29).

Fine Gael got the largest share, 29%, of all transfers in 2011, down from 31% in 2007. Labour got 18%, with Fianna Fáil down from 26% in 2007 to 17%, and Sinn Féin doubling its 2007 share to 7%.

Patrick McCartan, TD for Leix-Offaly 1918-1923, contested the presidential election in 1945. His daughter, the late Deirdre Drew, was married to Ronnie Drew of the Dubliners. The comedian Brendan O'Carroll's mother, Maureen O'Carroll, was a Labour Party TD for Dublin North-Central from 1954 to 1957. The actor Don Wycherley's father, Florence Wycherley, was an Independent Farmers' TD for Cork West from 1957 to 1961.

Politicians and political journalists bookmark their lives with general elections. Veteran former RTÉ political journalist **Sean Duignan** recounts the elections he shared with his old friend and colleague, the late Gerald Barry

The Last Word:
Elections with Gerry

E lections have been part of my life for as long as I can remember. Take 1951 for example – that was the year my father Peadar Duignan won a seat for Fianna Fáil in Galway West.

Then in the 1960s as I started out as a journalist, I initially covered elections in a peripheral way. I became a political correspondent in the 1970s and elections have bookmarked my life since then.

Election 2011 is one that will always stay with me, marked as it was by my visits to see my good friend and former colleague Gerry Barry in hospital.

As Gerry Barry's life ebbed away, the Election 2011 count was showing on a television set in his hospital ward. Standing by his bedside, other counts he had masterfully covered came to mind. Only this time, the inimitable Barry touch was sadly missing.

Gerry's first general election for RTÉ was in 1973, when Fianna Fáil had been in power for 16 years, and Jack Lynch's popularity was widely expected to ensure he would continue in office. Fianna Fáil actually increased its share of the vote, and the combined Fine Gael/Labour share was reduced, but Gerry was among the first to spot that a more effective use of transfers would shade victory for the coalition partners. It was my first experience of Gerry's shrewd political sense.

During Election '77, political correspondents, including myself, airily ignored opinion polls indicating that the Liam Cosgrave-led "government of all the talents" was likely to be defeated. Indeed, I ventured over the airwaves that, if, by some freak, Fianna Fáil did win, it would amount to the greatest comeback since Lazarus.

Gerry had been warning me not to dismiss the polls and, as the first results came in, he also famously predicted the 84-seat Fianna Fáil landslide, much to even Jack Lynch's mystification. And as Gerry predicted, Lazarus-like, Lynch and 83 of his party colleagues did make that comeback in 1977. But Lynch's grip on power slipped and he was retired

from politics two years later.

By the time of the three 1981-'82 elections, Gerry, by now the main presenter of RTÉ's *This Week* programme, was recognised as among the country's most reliable political pundits. A series of interviews he conducted with bitter rivals Charles Haughey and Garret FitzGerald were considered classics of their kind. FitzGerald chose *This Week* to launch his constitutional crusade for a more liberal Republic, and Haughey, in the course of a probing Barry interview, memorably rounded on his critics within Fianna Fáil: "Go dance on someone else's grave."

Gerry was fascinated by the rise of the Progressive Democrats, anticipating the party's early success in Election '87 when it won 14 seats. By that time, he was working as Political Editor of the *Sunday Tribune* alongside his lifetime friend Vincent Browne. Interestingly, he was less positive about the PDs' long-term prospects, reminding me that the party emerged from what was essentially an internal Fianna Fáil feud, and that the Irish political landscape was littered with the remains of such offshoots.

Again, Gerry was among the first to spot the logical conclusion to the Election '89 stalemate. The outcome was a hung Dáil and a month of political turmoil amid a gathering consensus that another election was unavoidable. Labour's Barry Desmond did suggest that a Fianna Fáil/Progressive Democrat coalition was the answer to the impasse, an opinion that was widely dismissed on the basis of the poisonous relationship between Haughey and Des O'Malley, as well as Fianna Fáil's "core principle" anti-coalitionism. When I suggested to Gerry that, apart from all the other arguments in favour of another election, the Haughey/O'Malley vendetta made a Fianna Fáil/PD government almost unthinkable, he quoted Benjamin Disraeli: "In politics, a majority is the best repartee". He and Barry Desmond were proven right.

The run-up to Election '92 included the famous

> "If Fianna Fáil wins this election it will be the greatest comeback since Lazarus"
> *Sean Duignan,*
> *1977*

The late Gerald Barry

to O'Malley outside cabinet meetings as "crap, pure crap", a phrase he later repeated in the course of an RTÉ News interview. It cost Reynolds dearly as it perfectly fitted the grotesque caricature being drawn of him by the opposition. In the event, the election resulted in Fianna Fáil losing nine seats to wind up with 68, a performance which was then widely regarded within the party as little short of disgraceful.

Amazingly, Reynolds survived to put together a coalition of 101 seats with the Labour Party. It was a majority of over 30 seats. Yet less than two years later, the whole thing came tumbling down.

After the collapse of that Reynolds-Spring administration and the relatively short-lived John Bruton-led Rainbow government, Election '97 was the first of three successive Bertie Ahern electoral triumphs.

Gerry, by now back to his beloved *This Week* at RTÉ, closely monitored the apparently irresistible Ahern progress over the next decade, and his series of interviews with Ahern during that period, particularly those conducted on the eve of each of the three elections, were once again models of polite rigour. Throughout that period, he kept telling me it was no coincidence that Ahern's phenomenal popularity ran in direct parallel to the Celtic Tiger delirium.

The fates ordained that Gerry did not cover Election 2011, but just before he was admitted to hospital, we discussed the unavoidable drubbing Fianna Fáil would endure at the hands of the electorate.

"I figure they could go as low as 32, maybe even 31 seats, Gerry."

"More like 21, Diggy."

And so, of course, it came to pass.

Haughey observation about Bertie Ahern just months before the Boss was finally ousted. Ahern was sitting in the Sycamore Room of Government Buildings with Gerry, Stephen Collins and Sam Smyth. Haughey put his head around the door, pointed at Ahern, and declared: "He's the man. He's the best, the most skilful, the most devious and the most cunning of them all." Gerry noted that Ahern, as if sensing the description would haunt him for the rest of his career, simply muttered: "That's all I need."

Soon afterwards, Albert Reynolds became Taoiseach – I took on the job of government press secretary against Gerry's advice – and within months Reynolds' prophecy that the Fianna Fáil/PD coalition would prove "a temporary little arrangement" was dismally fulfilled. His Beef Tribunal description of O'Malley as "dishonest" brought about the collapse of the government and a general election campaign which proved a veritable nightmare for Reynolds, not to mention his hapless press secretary.

A low point of that Fianna Fáil campaign came during a *Sunday Tribune* interview with Gerry when Reynolds described a suggestion that he never spoke

Leabharlanna Fhine Gall

Abbreviations of Political Parties

Main Parties

FF	Fianna Fáil
FG	Fine Gael (Cumann na nGaedheal to 1937)
LB	Labour (founded 1912)
SF	Sinn Féin
GP	Green Party
SP	Socialist Party (founded 1997)
PBPA	People Before Profit Alliance (replaced SW 2007)
ULA	United Left Alliance (founded 2010)
WP	Workers' Party (SFWP : Sinn Féin The Workers Party to 1982)
CS	Christian Solidarity Party (founded 1995)
SKIA	South Kerry Independent Alliance
WUAG	Workers Unemployed Action Group (Tipperary South)
NP	Non Party / Independent / Others

Former Parties

BP	Businessmens Party 1923
CnaP	Clann na Poblachta 1946-1965
CP	Centre Party 1932-1933; later merged with Fine Gael
CnaT	Clann na Talmhan 1938-1965
DL	Democratic Left (split from WP in 1992, merged with Labour 1999)
DSP	Democratic Socialist Party 1982-1991 (merged with Labour)
F	Farmers' Party 1922-1932
FRR	Fathers Rights-Responsibility Party (2006-2007)
IFF	Independent Fianna Fáil (Donegal 1970-2006)
Ind F	Independent Farmer
Ind LB	Independent Labour
Ind R	Independent Republican 1957
Ind UW	Independent Unemployed Worker 1957
IWL	Irish Workers League 1927
MR	Monetary Reform 1943-1944
NLB	National Labour 1943-1950
NL	National League 1926-1931
NL/Nlaw	Natural Law Party 1996-2000
NPD	National Progressive Democrat 1958-1963
NT	National Party 1996-1998
PA	Progressive Association 1923
PD	Progressive Democrats (21/12/85-8/11/08)
SLP	Socialist Labour Party 1981
SW	Socialist Workers Party (1997-2007)

Abbreviations in TD Biographies (Pages 94-291)

(CO) Constituency Office, (LH) Leinster House, (M) Mobile.

Index